105—

D0772574

NOVELS
for Students

Advisors

Susan Allison: Head Librarian, Lewiston High School, Lewiston, Maine. Standards Committee Chairperson for Maine School Library (MASL) Programs. Board member, Julia Adams Morse Memorial Library, Greene, Maine. Advisor to Lewiston Public Library Planning Process.

Jennifer Hood: Young Adult/Reference Librarian, Cumberland Public Library, Cumberland, Rhode Island. Certified teacher, Rhode Island. Member of the New England Library Association, Rhode Island Library Association, and the Rhode Island Educational Media Association.

Ann Kearney: Head Librarian and Media Specialist, Christopher Columbus High School, Miami, Florida, 1982–2002. Thirty-two years as Librarian in various educational institutions ranging from grade schools through graduate programs. Library positions at Miami-Dade Community College, the University of Miami's Medical School Library, and Carrollton School in Coconut Grove, Florida. B.A. from University of Detroit, 1967 (magna cum laude); M.L.S., University of Missouri–Columbia, 1974. Volunteer Project Leader for a school in rural Jamaica; volunteer with Adult Literacy programs.

Laurie St. Laurent: Head of Adult and Children's Services, East Lansing Public Library, East Lansing, Michigan, 1994–. M.L.S. from Western Michigan University. Chair of Michigan Library Association's 1998 Michigan Summer Reading Program; Chair of the Children's Services Division in 2000–2001; and Vice-President of the Association in 2002–2003. Board member of several regional early childhood literacy organizations and member of the Library of Michigan Youth Services Advisory Committee.

Heidi Stohs: Instructor in Language Arts, grades 10–12, Solomon High School, Solomon, Kansas. Received B.S. from Kansas State University; M.A. from Fort Hays State University.

NOVELS
for Students

Presenting Analysis, Context, and Criticism
on Commonly Studied Novels

VOLUME 28

GALE
CENGAGE Learning™

Detroit • New York • San Francisco • New Haven, Conn • Waterville, Maine • London

GALE
CENGAGE Learning™

Novels for Students, Volume 28

Project Editor: Ira Mark Milne

Rights Acquisition and Management: Jermaine Bobbitt, Vernon English, Leitha Etheridge-Sims, Sara Teller

Composition: Evi Abou-El-Seoud

Manufacturing: Drew Kalasky

Imaging: Lezlie Light

Product Design: Pamela A. E. Galbreath, Jennifer Wahi

Content Conversion: Civie Green, Katrina Coach

Product Manager: Meggin Condino

31143007840128
809.3 Nov
Novels for students.

© 2009 Gale, Cengage Learning

ALL RIGHTS RESERVED. No part of this work covered by the copyright herein may be reproduced, transmitted, stored, or used in any form or by any means graphic, electronic, or mechanical, including but not limited to photocopying, recording, scanning, digitizing, taping, Web distribution, information networks, or information storage and retrieval systems, except as permitted under Section 107 or 108 of the 1976 United States Copyright Act, without the prior written permission of the publisher.

Since this page cannot legibly accommodate all copyright notices, the acknowledgments constitute an extension of the copyright notice.

For product information and technology assistance, contact us at **Gale Customer Support, 1-800-877-4253.**
For permission to use material from this text or product, submit all requests online at **www.cengage.com/permissions.**
Further permissions questions can be emailed to **permissionrequest@cengage.com**

While every effort has been made to ensure the reliability of the information presented in this publication, Gale, a part of Cengage Learning, does not guarantee the accuracy of the data contained herein. Gale accepts no payment for listing; and inclusion in the publication of any organization, agency, institution, publication, service, or individual does not imply endorsement of the editors or publisher. Errors brought to the attention of the publisher and verified to the satisfaction of the publisher will be corrected in future editions.

Gale
27500 Drake Rd.
Farmington Hills, MI, 48331-3535

ISBN-13: 978-0-7876-8685-7
ISBN-10: 0-7876-8685-9

ISSN 1094-3552

This title is also available as an e-book.
ISBN-13: 978-1-4144-3832-0
ISBN-10: 1-4144-3832-X
Contact your Gale, a part of Cengage Learning sales representative for ordering information.

Printed in the United States of America
1 2 3 4 5 6 7 13 12 11 10 09

Table of Contents

The Informed Dialogue: Interacting with Literature

When we pick up a book, we usually do so with the anticipation of pleasure. We hope that by entering the time and place of the novel and sharing the thoughts and actions of the characters, we will find enjoyment. Unfortunately, this is often not the case; we are disappointed. But we should ask, has the author failed us, or have we failed the author?

We establish a dialogue with the author, the book, and with ourselves when we read. Consciously and unconsciously, we ask questions: "Why did the author write this book?" "Why did the author choose that time, place, or character?" "How did the author achieve that effect?" "Why did the character act that way?" "Would I act in the same way?" The answers we receive depend upon how much information about literature in general and about that book specifically we ourselves bring to our reading.

Young children have limited life and literary experiences. Being young, children frequently do not know how to go about exploring a book, nor sometimes, even know the questions to ask of a book. The books they read help them answer questions, the author often coming right out and *telling* young readers the things they are learning or are expected to learn. The perennial classic, *The Little Engine That Could,* tells its readers that, among other things, it is good to help others and brings happiness:

"Hurray, hurray," cried the funny little clown and all the dolls and toys. "The good little boys and girls in the city will be happy because you helped us, kind, Little Blue Engine."

In picture books, messages are often blatant and simple, the dialogue between the author and reader one-sided. Young children are concerned with the end result of a book—the enjoyment gained, the lesson learned—rather than with how that result was obtained. As we grow older and read further, however, we question more. We come to expect that the world within the book will closely mirror the concerns of our world, and that the author will *show* these through the events, descriptions, and conversations within the story, rather than *telling* of them. We are now expected to do the interpreting, carry on our share of the dialogue with the book and author, and glean not only the author's message, but comprehend how that message and the overall affect of the book were achieved. Sometimes, however, we need help to do these things. *Novels for Students* provides that help.

A novel is made up of many parts interacting to create a coherent whole. In reading a novel, the more obvious features can be easily spotted—theme, characters, plot—but we may overlook the more subtle elements that greatly influence how the novel is perceived by the reader: viewpoint, mood and tone, symbolism, or the use of humor. By focusing on both the obvious and more subtle literary elements within a novel, *Novels for Students* aids readers in both analyzing for message and in determining how and why that message is communicated. In the discussion on Harper Lee's *To Kill a Mockingbird* (Vol. 2), for example, the mockingbird as a symbol of innocence is dealt with, among other things, as is the importance of Lee's use of humor which "enlivens a serious plot, adds depth to the characterization, and creates a sense of familiarity and universality." The reader comes to understand the internal elements of each novel discussed—as well as the external influences that help shape it.

"The desire to write greatly," Harold Bloom of Yale University says, "is the desire to be elsewhere, in a time and place of one's own, in an originality that must compound with inheritance, with an anxiety of influence." A writer seeks to create a unique world within a story, but although it is unique, it is not disconnected from our own world. It speaks to us *because* of what the writer brings to the writing from our world: how he or she was raised and educated; his or her likes and dislikes; the events occurring in the real world at the time of the writing, and while the author was growing up. When we know what an author has brought to his or her work, we gain a greater insight into both the "originality" (the world of the book), and the things that "compound" it. This insight enables us to question that created world and find answers more readily. By informing ourselves, we are able to establish a more effective dialogue with both book and author.

Novels for Students, in addition to providing a plot summary and descriptive list of characters—to remind readers of what they have read—also explores the external influences that shaped each book. Each entry includes a discussion of the author's background, and the historical context in which the novel was written. It is vital to know, for instance, that when Ray Bradbury was writing *Fahrenheit 451* (Vol. 1), the threat of Nazi domination had recently ended in Europe, and the McCarthy hearings were taking place in Washington, D.C. This information goes far in answering the question, "Why did he write a story of oppressive government control and book burning?" Similarly, it is important to know that Harper Lee, author of *To Kill a Mockingbird,*was born and

raised in Monroeville, Alabama, and that her father was a lawyer. Readers can now see why she chose the south as a setting for her novel—it is the place with which she was most familiar—and start to comprehend her characters and their actions.

Novels for Students helps readers find the answers they seek when they establish a dialogue with a particular novel. It also aids in the posing of questions by providing the opinions and interpretations of various critics and reviewers, broadening that dialogue. Some reviewers of *To Kill A Mockingbird,* for example, "faulted the novel's climax as melodramatic." This statement leads readers to ask, "Is it, indeed, melodramatic?" "If not, why did some reviewers see it as such?" "If it is, why did Lee choose to make it melodramatic?" "Is melodrama ever justified?" By being spurred to ask these questions, readers not only learn more about the book and its writer, but about the nature of writing itself.

The literature included for discussion in *Novels for Students* has been chosen because it has something vital to say to us. *Of Mice and Men, Catch-22, The Joy Luck Club, My Antonia, A Separate Peace* and the other novels here speak of life and modern sensibility. In addition to their individual, specific messages of prejudice, power, love or hate, living and dying, however, they and all great literature also share a common intent. They force us to *think*—about life, literature, and about others, not just about ourselves. They pry us from the narrow confines of our minds and thrust us outward to confront the world of books and the larger, real world we all share. *Novels for Students* helps us in this confrontation by providing the means of enriching our conversation with literature and the world, by creating an *informed* dialogue, one that brings true pleasure to the personal act of reading.

Sources

Harold Bloom, *The Western Canon, The Books and School of the Ages,* Riverhead Books, 1994.

Watty Piper, *The Little Engine That Could,* Platt & Munk, 1930.

Anne Devereaux Jordan
Senior Editor, TALL (Teaching and Learning Literature)

Introduction

Purpose of the Book

The purpose of *Novels for Students* (*NfS*) is to provide readers with a guide to understanding, enjoying, and studying novels by giving them easy access to information about the work. Part of Gale's "For Students" Literature line, *NfS* is specifically designed to meet the curricular needs of high school and undergraduate college students and their teachers, as well as the interests of general readers and researchers considering specific novels. While each volume contains entries on "classic" novels frequently studied in classrooms, there are also entries containing hard-to-find information on contemporary novels, including works by multicultural, international, and women novelists.

The information covered in each entry includes an introduction to the novel and the novel's author; a plot summary, to help readers unravel and understand the events in a novel; descriptions of important characters, including explanation of a given character's role in the novel as well as discussion about that character's relationship to other characters in the novel; analysis of important themes in the novel; and an explanation of important literary techniques and movements as they are demonstrated in the novel.

In addition to this material, which helps the readers analyze the novel itself, students are also provided with important information on the lit-

erary and historical background informing each work. This includes a historical context essay, a box comparing the time or place the novel was written to modern Western culture, a critical essay, and excerpts from critical essays on the novel. A unique feature of *NfS* is a specially commissioned critical essay on each novel, targeted toward the student reader.

To further aid the student in studying and enjoying each novel, information on media adaptations is provided (if available), as well as reading suggestions for works of fiction and nonfiction on similar themes and topics. Classroom aids include ideas for research papers and lists of critical sources that provide additional material on the novel.

Selection Criteria

The titles for each volume of *NfS* were selected by surveying numerous sources on teaching literature and analyzing course curricula for various school districts. Some of the sources surveyed included: literature anthologies; *Reading Lists for College-Bound Students: The Books Most Recommended by America's Top Colleges*; textbooks on teaching the novel; a College Board survey of novels commonly studied in high schools; a National Council of Teachers of English (NCTE) survey of novels commonly studied in high schools; the NCTE's *Teaching Literature in High School: The Novel*; and the Young Adult Library Services Association (YALSA) list of best books for young adults of the past twenty-five years.

Input was also solicited from our advisory board, as well as from educators from various areas. From these discussions, it was determined that each volume should have a mix of "classic" novels (those works commonly taught in literature classes) and contemporary novels for which information is often hard to find. Because of the interest in expanding the canon of literature, an emphasis was also placed on including works by international, multicultural, and women novelists. Our advisory board members—educational professionals—helped pare down the list for each volume. If a work was not selected for the present volume, it was often noted as a possibility for a future volume. As always, the editor welcomes suggestions for titles to be included in future volumes.

How Each Entry Is Organized

Each entry, or chapter, in *NfS* focuses on one novel. Each entry heading lists the full name of the novel, the author's name, and the date of the novel's publication. The following elements are contained in each entry:

Introduction: a brief overview of the novel which provides information about its first appearance, its literary standing, any controversies surrounding the work, and major conflicts or themes within the work.

Author Biography: this section includes basic facts about the author's life, and focuses on events and times in the author's life that inspired the novel in question.

Plot Summary: a factual description of the major events in the novel. Lengthy summaries are broken down with subheads.

Characters: an alphabetical listing of major characters in the novel. Each character name is followed by a brief to an extensive description of the character's role in the novel, as well as discussion of the character's actions, relationships, and possible motivation.

Characters are listed alphabetically by last name. If a character is unnamed—for instance, the narrator in *Invisible Man*—the character is listed as "The Narrator" and alphabetized as "Narrator." If a character's first name is the only one given, the name will appear alphabetically by that name.

Variant names are also included for each character. Thus, the full name "Jean Louise Finch" would head the listing for the narrator of *To Kill a Mockingbird*, but listed in a separate cross-reference would be the nickname "Scout Finch."

Themes: a thorough overview of how the major topics, themes, and issues are addressed within the novel. Each theme discussed appears in a separate subhead and is easily accessed through the boldface entries in the Subject/Theme Index.

Style: this section addresses important style elements of the novel, such as setting, point of view, and narration; important literary devices used, such as imagery, foreshadowing, symbolism; and, if applicable, genres to which the work might have belonged, such as Gothicism or Romanticism. Literary terms are explained within the entry but can also be found in the Glossary.

Historical Context: this section outlines the social, political, and cultural climate *in which the author lived and the novel was created*. This section may include descriptions of related historical events, pertinent aspects of daily life in the culture, and the artistic and literary sensibilities of the time in which the work was written. If the novel is a historical work, information regarding the time in which the novel is set is also included. Each section is broken down with helpful subheads.

Critical Overview: this section provides background on the critical reputation of the novel, including bannings or any other public controversies surrounding the work. For older works, this section includes a history of how the novel was first received and how perceptions of it may have changed over the years; for more recent novels, direct quotes from early reviews may also be included.

Criticism: an essay commissioned by *NfS* which specifically deals with the novel and is written specifically for the student audience, as well as excerpts from previously published criticism on the work (if available).

Sources: an alphabetical list of critical material used in compiling the entry, with full bibliographical information.

Further Reading: an alphabetical list of other critical sources which may prove useful for the student. It includes full bibliographical information and a brief annotation.

In addition, each entry contains the following highlighted sections, set apart from the main text as sidebars:

Media Adaptations: if available, a list of important film and television adaptations of the novel, including source information. The list also includes stage adaptations, audio recordings, musical adaptations, etc.

Topics for Further Study: a list of potential study questions or research topics dealing with the novel. This section includes questions related to other disciplines the student may be studying, such as American history, world history, science, math, government, business, geography, economics, psychology, etc.

Compare and Contrast: an "at-a-glance" comparison of the cultural and historical differences between the author's time and culture and late twentieth century or early twenty-first century Western culture. This box includes pertinent parallels between the major scientific, political, and cultural movements of the time or place the novel was written, the time or place the novel was set (if a historical work), and modern Western culture. Works written after the mid-1970s may not have this box.

What Do I Read Next?: a list of works that might complement the featured novel or serve as a contrast to it. This includes works by the same author and others, works of fiction and nonfiction, and works from various genres, cultures, and eras.

Other Features

NfS includes "The Informed Dialogue: Interacting with Literature," a foreword by Anne Devereaux Jordan, Senior Editor for *Teaching and Learning Literature* (*TALL*), and a founder of the Children's Literature Association. This essay provides an enlightening look at how readers interact with literature and how *Novels for Students* can help teachers show students how to enrich their own reading experiences.

A Cumulative Author/Title Index lists the authors and titles covered in each volume of the *NfS* series.

A Cumulative Nationality/Ethnicity Index breaks down the authors and titles covered in each volume of the *NfS* series by nationality and ethnicity

A Subject/Theme Index, specific to each volume, provides easy reference for users who may be studying a particular subject or theme rather than a single work. Significant subjects from events to broad themes are included, and the entries pointing to the specific theme discussions in each entry are indicated in **boldface**.

Each entry may include illustrations, including photo of the author, stills from film adaptations, maps, and/or photos of key historical events, if available.

Citing Novels for Students

When writing papers, students who quote directly from any volume of *Novels for Students* may use the following general forms. These examples are based on MLA style; teachers may request that students adhere to a different style, so the following examples may be adapted as needed.

When citing text from *NfS* that is not attributed to a particular author (i.e., the Themes, Style, Historical Context sections, etc.), the following format should be used in the bibliography section:

> "*Night*." *Novels for Students*. Ed. Marie Rose Napierkowski. Vol. 4. Detroit: Gale, 1998. 234–35.

When quoting the specially commissioned essay from *NfS* (usually the first piece under the "Criticism" subhead), the following format should be used:

> Miller, Tyrus. Critical Essay on "*Winesburg, Ohio*." *Novels for Students*. Ed. Marie Rose Napierkowski. Vol. 4. Detroit: Gale, 1998. 335–39.

When quoting a journal or newspaper essay that is reprinted in a volume of *NfS*, the following form may be used:

> Malak, Amin. "Margaret Atwood's *The Handmaid's Tale* and the Dystopian Tradition." *Canadian Literature* No. 112 (Spring 1987), 9–16; excerpted and reprinted in *Novels for Students*, Vol. 4, ed. Marie Rose Napierkowski (Detroit: Gale, 1998), pp. 133–36.

When quoting material reprinted from a book that appears in a volume of *NfS*, the following form may be used:

> Adams, Timothy Dow. "Richard Wright: 'Wearing the Mask.'" In *Telling Lies in Modern American Autobiography*. University of North Carolina Press, 1990. 69–83; excerpted and reprinted in *Novels for Students*, Vol. 1, ed. Diane Telgen (Detroit: Gale, 1997), pp. 59–61.

We Welcome Your Suggestions

The editorial staff of *Novels for Students* welcomes your comments and ideas. Readers who wish to suggest novels to appear in future volumes, or who have other suggestions, are cordially invited to contact the editor. You may contact the editor via e-mail at: **ForStudentsEditors @cengage.com.** Or write to the editor at:

Editor, *Novels for Students*
Gale
27500 Drake Road
Farmington Hills, MI 48331-3535

Literary Chronology

1755: Jane Austen is born on December 16 in the village of Steventon in Hampshire, England.

1817: Jane Austen dies of complications from an unknown illness on July 18 in Winchester, England.

1818: Jane Austen's *Northanger Abbey* is posthumously published.

1821: Fyodor Dostoevsky is born on November 11 in Moscow, Russia.

1828: Leo Tolstoy is born as Lev Nikolayevich Tolstoy on September 9 on his wealthy family's estate in Tula province, Russia.

1859: Arthur Conan Doyle is born on May 22 in Edinburgh, Scotland.

1864: Fyodor Dostoevsky's *Notes from Underground* is published in Russian as *Zapiski iz podpol'ia*.

1873: Ford Madox Ford is born Ford Madox Hueffer on December 17 in Merton, Surrey, England.

1873–1877: Leo Tolstoy's *Anna Karenina* is first serialized in the Russian periodical *Ruskii Vestnik*.

1881: Fyodor Dostoevsky dies of a lung hemorrhage associated with emphysema and an epileptic seizure on February 9 in Staraya Russa, Russia.

1882: Virginia Woolf is born as Adeline Virginia Stephen on January 25 in London.

1901–1902: Sir Arthur Conan Doyle's *The Hound of the Baskervilles* is published in serialized form from August 1901 to April 1902 in the British magazine the *Strand*.

1902: John Steinbeck is born on February 27 in Salinas, California.

1910: Leo Tolstoy dies in Astapovo, Russia on November 20 and is buried in a peasant-style grave in a wood near his once noble family estate.

1915: Ford Madox Ford's *The Good Soldier* is published.

1922: Kurt Vonnegut Jr. is born on November 11 in Indianapolis, Indiana.

1930: Sir Arthur Conan Doyle dies of a heart attack on July 7 in Sussex, England.

1931: Virginia Woolf's *The Waves* is published.

1933: Yoko Kawashima Watkins is born in Harbin, Manchuria (though she is a Japanese citizen).

1936: Don DeLillo is born on November 20 in the Bronx, New York.

1939: Ford Madox Ford dies of heart failure on June 26 in Deauville, France.

1939: John Steinbeck is awarded the Pulitzer Prize for *The Grapes of Wrath*.

1941: Virginia Woolf dies from suicide by drowning on March 28 in the River Ouse, Sussex, England.

1945: John Steinbeck's novel *Cannery Row* is published.

1954: Jan (Janis) Mary Hudson is born on April 27 in Calgary, Alberta, Canada.

1959: Tsitsi Dangarembga is born in Mukoto, Southern Rhodesia (now Zimbabwe).

1962: John Steinbeck is awarded the Nobel Prize for Literature.

1963: Kurt Vonnegut Jr.'s *Cat's Cradle* is published.

1968: John Steinbeck dies of a heart attack on December 20 in New York City.

1969: Edwidge Danticat is born on January 19 in Port-au-Prince, Haiti.

1971: Kiran Desai is born on September 3 in New Delhi, India.

1984: Jan Hudson's *Sweetgrass* is published.

1985: Don De Lillo's novel *White Noise* is published.

1986: Yoko Kawashima Watkins's *So Far from the Bamboo Grove* is published.

1988: Tsitsi Dangarembga's *Nervous Conditions* is published.

1989: Tsitsi Dangarembga's *Nervous Conditions* wins the African division of the Commonwealth Writers Prize.

1990: Jan Hudson dies from sudden respiratory failure associated with viral pneumonia on April 22 in Edmonton, Alberta, Canada.

1998: Kiran Desai's *Hullabaloo in the Guava Orchard* is published.

2004: Edwidge Danticat's *The Dew Breaker* is published.

2006: Kiran Desai is awarded the Man Booker Prize for fiction for *The Inheritance of Loss*.

2007: Kurt Vonnegut Jr. dies in a Manhattan hospital on April 11 from brain injuries suffered several weeks earlier from a fall in his New York City apartment.

Acknowledgments

The editors wish to thank the copyright holders of the excerpted criticism included in this volume and the permissions managers of many book and magazine publishing companies for assisting us in securing reproduction rights. We are also grateful to the staffs of the Detroit Public Library, the Library of Congress, the University of Detroit Mercy Library, Wayne State University Purdy/ Kresge Library Complex, and the University of Michigan Libraries for making their resources available to us. Following is a list of the copyright holders who have granted us permission to reproduce material in this volume of *NFS*. Every effort has been made to trace copyright, but if omissions have been made, please let us know.

COPYRIGHTED EXCERPTS IN *NFS*, VOLUME 28, WERE REPRODUCED FROM THE FOLLOWING PERIODICALS:

American Notes & Queries, v. 13, 1974. Copyright © 1974 by Helen Dwight Reid Educational Foundation. Reproduced with permission of the Helen Dwight Reid Educational Foundation, published by Heldref Publications, 1319 18th Street, NW, Washington, DC 20036-1802.—*English Language Notes*, v. XXV, September, 1997. Copyright © 1997 Regents of the University of Colorado. Reproduced by permission.—*English Literature in Transition 1880-1920*, v. 48, spring 2005. Copyright © 2005 *English Literature in Transition: 1880-1920*. Reproduced by permission.—*Explicator*, v. 37, summer, 1979; v. 53, fall, 1994; v. 56, winter,

1998. Copyright © 1979, 1994, 1998 by Helen Dwight Reid Educational Foundation. All reproduced with permission of the Helen Dwight Reid Educational Foundation, published by Heldref Publications, 1319 18th Street, NW, Washington, DC 20036-1802.—*Globe and Mail*, June 10, 1998. Copyright © 1998 Globe Interactive, a division of Bell Globemedia Publishing, Inc. Reprinted with permission from Globe and Mail.—*Journal of Evolutionary Psychology*, v. 25, 2004. Copyright © 2004 Institute for Evolutionary Psychology. Reproduced by permission.—*Morning News*, April 20, 2004 for "Birnbaum v. Edwidge Danticat," by Robert Birnbaum. Reproduced by permission of the publisher and the author.—*New York Times Book Review*, March 21, 2004. Copyright © 2004 by The New York Times Company. Reprinted with permission.—*Notes on Contemporary Literature*, v. 24, 1994. Copyright © 1994 by William S. Doxey. Reproduced by permission.—*Novel: A Forum on Fiction*, v. 24, autumn, 1990. Copyright © 1990 NOVEL Corp. Reproduced with permission.—*Reading Teacher*, v. 42, May, 1989. Copyright © 1989 International Reading Association. Reproduced by permission of the International Reading Association.—*Research in African Literatures*, v. 26, summer, 1995; v. 38, winter, 2007. Copyright © 1995, 1997 Indiana University Press. Both reproduced by permission.—*The Slavic and East European Journal*, v. 25, summer 1981. Copyright © 1981 by AATSEEL of the U.S., Inc. Reproduced by permission.—*Telegram &*

Gazette, November 29, 2002; January 29, 2003. Copyright © 2002, 2003 Telegram & Gazette Corporation. Both reproduced by permission.—*Toronto Star*, June 10, 1998. Copyright © 1998 Toronto Star Newspapers, Ltd. Reprinted with permission of Torstar Syndication Services.—*Transition*, v. 79, 1999. For "Louder than Bombs," by Amitava Kumar. Reproduced by permission of the author. —*Women's Review of Books*, v. 21, May, 2004. Copyright © 2004 Women's Review of Books. Reproduced by permission.—*Wordsworth Circle*, v. 33, winter, 2002. Copyright © 2002 Marilyn Gaull. Reproduced by permission of the editor.—*World Literature Today*, v. 79, January-April, 2005. Copyright © 2005 by *World Literature Today*. Reproduced by permission of the publisher.

COPYRIGHTED EXCERPTS IN *NFS*, VOLUME 28, WERE REPRODUCED FROM THE FOLLOWING BOOKS:

Dangarembga, Tsitsi. From *Nervous Conditions*. Seal Press, 2004. Copyright © 1988 by Tsitsi Dangarembga. All rights reserved. Used with permission of Ayebia Clarke Publishing Ltd and Lynne Rienner Publishers, Inc.—Benson, Jackson J. From "*Cannery Row* and Steinbeck as Spokesman for the 'Folk Tradition,'" in *The Short Novels of John Steinbeck: Critical Essays with a Checklist to Steinbeck Criticism*. Edited by Jackson J. Benson. Duke University Press, 1990. Copyright © 1990 Duke University Press. All rights reserved. Used by permission of the publisher.—Brewster, Dorothy. From *Virginia Woolf*. New York University Press, 1962. Copyright © 1962 by New York University. Copyright renewed © 1990 by Fred Lawrence Giles. All rights reserved. Reproduced by permission.—Hughes Jr., Robert S. From "'Some Philosophers in the Sun': Steinbeck's *Cannery Row*," in *The Short Novels of John Steinbeck: Critical Essays with a Checklist to Steinbeck Criticism*. Edited by Jackson J. Benson. Duke University Press, 1990. Copyright © 1990 Duke University Press. All rights reserved. Used by permission of the publisher.—Lisca, Peter. From "*Cannery Row*: Escape into the Counterculture," in *The Short Novels of John Steinbeck: Critical Essays with a Checklist to Steinbeck Criticism*. Edited by Jackson J. Benson. Duke University Press, 1990. Copyright © 1990 Duke University Press. All rights reserved. Used by permission of the publisher.—Marder, Herbert. From *The Measure of Life: Virginia Woolf's Last Years*. Cornell University Press, 2000. Copyright © 2000 by Cornell University. Used by permission of the publisher, Cornell University Press.—Pribic, Rado. From "*Notes from Underground*: One Hundred Years After the Author's Death," in *Dostoevski and the Human Condition After a Century*. Edited by Alexej Ugrinsky, Frank S. Lambasa, and Valija K. Ozolins. Greenwood Press, 1986. Copyright © 1986 by Hofstra University. All rights reserved. Reproduced by permission of Greenwood Publishing Group, Inc., Westport, CT.

Contributors

Susan Andersen: Andersen holds a Ph.D. in English and teaches literature and writing. Entry on *Hullabaloo in the Guava Orchard*. Original essay on *Hullabaloo in the Guava Orchard*.

Bryan Aubrey: Aubrey holds a Ph.D. in English. Entries on *The Dew Breaker* and *Nervous Conditions*. Original essays on *The Dew Breaker* and *Nervous Conditions*

Catherine Dominic: Dominic is a novelist and freelance editor and writer. Entries on *Northanger Abbey* and *Notes from Underground*. Original essays on *Northanger Abbey* and *Notes from Underground*.

Klay Dyer: Dyer holds a Ph.D. in English literature and has published extensively on fiction, poetry, film, and television. He is also a freelance university teacher, writer, and educational consultant. Entries on *Anna Karenina* and *Sweetgrass*. Original essays on *Anna Karenina* and *Sweetgrass*.

Joyce Hart: Hart is a published author of more than twenty books. Entry on *So Far from the Bamboo Grove*. Original essay on *So Far from the Bamboo Grove*.

Neil Heims: Heims is a writer and teacher living in Paris. Entries on *Cannery Row* and *White Noise*. Original essays on *Cannery Row* and *White Noise*.

Diane Andrews Henningfeld: Henningfeld is a professor of English who writes widely for educational publishers. Entry on *The Waves*. Original essay on *The Waves*.

Sheri Metzger Karmiol: Karmiol has a doctorate in English Renaissance literature. She teaches literature and drama at the University of New Mexico, where she is a lecturer in the university's honors program. Karmiol is also a professional writer and the author of several reference texts on poetry and drama. Entry on *Cat's Cradle*. Original essay on *Cat's Cradle*.

David Kelly: Kelly teaches literature and creative writing at two colleges in Illinois. Entry on *The Good Soldier*. Original essay on *The Good Soldier*.

Kathleen Wilson: Wilson is a freelance writer and editor. Entry on *The Hound of the Baskervilles*. Original essay on *The Hound of the Baskervilles*.

Anna Karenina

LEO TOLSTOY

1873–1877

When it was first serialized in the Russian periodical *Ruskii Vestnik* from 1873 to 1877, *Anna Karenina* was a powerful and controversial novel. Indeed, to many readers, including Tolstoy himself, it signaled a radical shift in the already impressive history of the novel as a literary form. With its sweeping and complex plot lines, subtle characterizations, and blend of romance and social commentary, *Anna Karenina* is often mentioned in the same breath as Cervantes's *Don Quixote* (1605) and Laurence Sterne's *The Life and Opinions of Tristram Shandy* (1759–1767), both of which have permanently altered and defined the novel. Indeed, these books reset the standard for novel writing.

Although *Anna Karenina* is often considered a novel about love, lust, and adultery, it is interesting to realize that one of the most crucial plot elements (the scene during which Anna and Vrónsky consummate their affair) is strategically underdeveloped. It is marked only by a series of ellipses linking chapters ten and eleven in the second part of the novel. Sex is ostensibly erased from a novel about passion and adultery, and thus the book emphasizes ideas rather than actions. Moreover, as Tolstoy underscores, it is the ripple of repercussions stemming from the characters' actions that lead ultimately to disappointment. In the final and tragic act of Anna's suicide, readers recognize the theme that Tolstoy has been building towards: Anna's love, like that of Shakespeare's Desdemona or Thomas

Leo Tolstoy (*The Library of Congress*)

Hardy's Tess, is energized by the inevitability of tragedy rather than the joys of romance.

A recent edition of *Anna Karenina*, translated by Richard Pevear and Larissa Volokhonsky, was published by Viking in 2000.

AUTHOR BIOGRAPHY

Lev Nikolayevich Tolstoy (known most commonly in English as Leo Tolstoy) was born into a wealthy Russian family on September 9, 1828. He was born on his family's estate in Tula province, and he had three brothers and one sister. His childhood was remarkable in the sense that it was spent enjoying the luxuries of the family estate and the opportunities available to him in Moscow. However, Tolstoy's childhood was also tragic given that his mother died when he was two. When he was nine, his father was murdered while traveling.

Tolstoy was left in the care of his aunt, Madame Ergolsky, who took on the responsibility of his upbringing and education. The latter proved quite the challenge; her nephew was an intelligent young man with very little interest or aptitude for formal academics. Persuaded to

attend Kazan University when he turned sixteen, he studied law and Oriental languages, with a particular interest in what he considered the great heroic cultures of the past. In 1847, unpopular and disenchanted with university life, he left Kazan in the middle of a school term without completing his degree. Many critics suggest that Tolstoy's depictions of socially awkward and disenfranchised characters (Konstantin Lévin in *Anna Karenina*, for instance) are drawn from his experiences at the university.

In 1851, Tolstoy visited one of his brothers, who had enlisted in the Russian Army. Inspired by the experience, Tolstoy himself enlisted, serving in the Crimean War (1854–1856). Many of his experiences during this period were recounted in his collection of battlefield observations, *Sebastopol Sketches* (1855). It was a period of his life that figured prominently, too, in his trilogy of autobiographical novels: *Childhood* (1852), *Boyhood* (1854), and *Youth* (1857).

With his writing career underway and his military career completed, Tolstoy continued to develop as a thinker and writer. He gathered experience through further travels across Europe, worked to establish a school for peasant children, and began to focus his writing on expressing his liberal views on education and innovative educational theories and practices. Education as an ideal to which all people should aspire remained central to Tolstoy's quest to achieve moral stability in a rapidly changing world.

In 1862, Tolstoy married Sofya Andreyevna Behrs (1844–1919). The couple had a large family, and Sofya supported her husband as he wrote his two greatest novels: *War and Peace* (first serialized from 1865–1869) and *Anna Karenina* (1873–1877). While writing the latter novel, Tolstoy underwent a spiritual conversion. Imagining himself more as a sage than as an artist, Tolstoy, in opposition to his family's desires, rid himself of material possessions and began to live according to a radically new moral compass. His actions brought him into sharp disagreement not only with his wife and children but also with the Russian Orthodox Church, which excommunicated him in 1901.

Tolstoy died in Astapovo, Russia on November 20, 1910. He was buried in a peasant-style grave in a wood near his once noble family estate.

MEDIA ADAPTATIONS

- The first major film adaptation of *Anna Karenina* appeared under the same title in 1935, when director Clarence Brown cast Greta Garbo in the title role along with Frederic March (Vrónsky), Basil Rathbone (Karénin), and Maureen O'Sullivan (Kitty).

- The story was once again adapted as a film of the same title in 1948, when Julien Duvivier cast Vivien Leigh as Anna and Kieron Moore as her lover. This is an almost melodramatic and very loosely based adaptation.

- Yet another notable film adaptation made with the same title is the 1997 adaptation (directed by Bernard Rose), starring Sophie Marceau and Sean Bean. This was the first Western production of the novel to be filmed in Russia.

- Television adaptations have also made regular appearances on small screens across the world, beginning in 1961 with a production under the same title with Claire Bloom as Anna and Sean Connery as Vrónsky.

- The 1977 British miniseries produced under the same title was directed by Basil Coleman, and was nominated for two Emmy awards. The cast includes Nicola Pagett as Anna, and Stuart Wilson as Vrónsky.

- More recently, a 2000 British miniseries based on the novel, and produced under the book's original title, won numerous production awards. More importantly, it provides an excellent sense of the parallel stories of the major couples in the novel. Directed by David Blair, this version stars Helen McCrory as Anna and Kevin McKidd as Vrónsky.

- A 1985 American production of a made-for-television-film, directed by Simon Langton and starring Jacqueline Bisset (Anna) and Christopher Reeve (Vrónsky), was also released under the same title.

- The novel was adapted under the same title into a ballet, performed by the Bolshoi Ballet (1974), with Maya Plisetskaya and Alexander Godunov dancing in the title roles.

PLOT SUMMARY

Part One, Chapters 1–34

Anna Karenina is a long, intricately patterned novel divided into eight parts, each consisting of a series of short chapters. It begins with one of the most famous lines in literature: "All happy families are alike; each unhappy family is unhappy in its own way." This statement sets the tone for the complex plot that follows.

The novel opens in the home of Prince Stepán Arkádyich Oblónsky, known more commonly as Stiva. His is a household in chaos due, in part, to the discovery that Stiva has been unfaithful to his wife Dárya Alexandrovna (Dolly). Dolly is devastated by her discovery of a note that proves without doubt that her husband is an adulterer. Deeply troubled by the situation, Stiva remains oddly unremorseful, a man with a passion for amorous adventure that he cannot control. To his mind, his behavior is perfectly natural, so he finds the family pressure to apologize to his wife unusual and, in the end, ineffective. When he does finally visit Dolly in her room, Stiva is rejected openly despite his admonitions to remember the good times in their marriage. Hopeful that another woman might influence his wife more positively, Stiva asks his married sister, Anna Karenina, to come from her home in St. Petersburg and convince Dolly not to leave Stiva.

Heading off to his office, Stiva is met by an old friend, Konstantin Lévin, who has just resigned his position within the *zemstvo* (village administrative committee) and has come to the city to discuss an important matter with his friend. Stiva surmises that the discussion will focus on Lévin's love for Ekaterína Shcherbátsky (Kitty).

During his stay in Moscow, Lévin stays with his half-brother Sergéi Kóznyshev, whose philosophic view of the world has often put him at odds with his family. The brothers discuss Lévin's intentions to reconnect with their estranged, and now sickly, brother Nikolái, despite Sergéi's admonition that Nikolái wishes to be left alone.

Going to the skating rink at Moscow's Zoological Gardens, Lévin searches for Kitty, who often ventures there for exercise. After finding her, the two spend time together skating until Kitty's mood suddenly changes, and she sends the now confused Lévin away. Unsure of what has happened, Lévin heads off to dinner with Stiva hoping to find the cause of Kitty's dramatic change in mood. Lévin finds out from Stiva that a military officer named Count Alexéi Vrónsky is also competing for Kitty's affections. The two men then turn to a discussion of Stiva's situation with Dolly. Lévin voices his displeasure with his old friend, which Stiva dismisses almost nonchalantly as the expected response of a moralist.

Meanwhile, Kitty's mother, Princess Shcherbátsky (known only as the Old Princess), considers the benefits and detriments of Lévin or Vrónsky as potential matches for her daughter. Relieved that no choice has been made, she is also keenly aware that the new generation of aristocratic women are turning away from the long-held tradition of having their marriages arranged by their parents. Lévin steps boldly forward, visiting Kitty one evening with a marriage proposal. Acknowledging her affection for him, Kitty declines his offer, telling him that it is Vrónsky that she loves. Lévin is devastated, a feeling that is exacerbated when he later meets his rival and finds that he is impressed by Vrónsky.

Vrónsky and Stiva cross paths at the train station. The former is there to meet his mother who is arriving from St. Petersburg, and the latter is there to meet Anna. When the train arrives, Vrónsky greets his mother, who introduces him to Anna. The connection between Anna and Vrónsky is immediate, based as much on personality and intellect as sexual energy. When the group leaves the train station, a worker is run over by a train and killed. A debate follows about whether the incident was accidental or a

suicide. To Anna the point is moot because the death is "a bad omen" of things to come.

Upon meeting with Dolly, Anna convinces her sister-in-law that Stiva is suffering intense regret because of his betrayal. She also convinces Dolly that Stiva is capable of moving beyond what she calls his infatuation. People like Stiva "may be unfaithful," she explains, "but their hearth and wife are sacred to them."

With Dolly and Stiva reconciled, the household's focus turns to an upcoming ball. At the ball, Vrónsky sees Anna for the second time. She is dressed beautifully in a black gown. Although Vrónsky waltzes often with Kitty, she is stunned when, for the final mazurka (a Polish folk dance) of the evening, he instead chooses Anna as his partner.

Although the status of the relationship between Kitty and Vrónsky is the focus of much discussion within the Oblónsky home, it is Anna who struggles most profoundly with the presence of the young army officer in her life. Torn between her growing attraction to Vrónsky, her concern with Kitty's opinion of her, and her own sense of loyalty to her family in St. Petersburg, Anna decides to return home. On her way there, she is immediately relieved to leave the soldier behind, but at the same time she is tormented by doubt and anxiousness. Later, when Anna realizes that Vrónsky has followed her to St. Petersburg, she is overwhelmed by a combination of excitement and pride. Although Anna is unable to sleep after she discovers Vrónsky's intentions, there is "nothing unpleasant or gloomy" in the "reveries that filled her imagination." Thus, Anna is forced to acknowledge that there is "something joyful, burning, and exciting" about her feelings for Vrónsky.

Upon arriving in St. Petersburg, Vrónsky is introduced to Anna's husband, Alexéi Karénin. Watching the couple together, and noticing the absence of passion between Anna and her husband, the officer is certain that Karénin does not love his wife. Based on this belief, Vrónsky makes arrangements to attend the various social and cultural events that Anna attends.

Part Two, Chapters 1–35
Part Two of the novel opens with concern on the part of family and friends for Kitty's health, which declines dramatically following Vrónsky's public slight of her at the ball in Moscow. Doctors are consulted, but Dolly realizes that

Kitty has been brought to near collapse by her rejection of Lévin followed by Vrónsky's rejection of her.

In St. Petersburg, Anna finds her life defined more and more by Vrónsky and his socialite cousin, Princess Elizavéta Tverskóy (Betsy). Anna becomes increasingly distant from her former family friend, the morally righteous Countess Lydia Ivánovna. As the breach between the two grows, rumors about Anna's scandalous relationship with Vrónsky begin to spread.

Despite the pending scandal, Anna and Vrónsky continue to meet regularly at Betsy's. They meet even though Anna pleads with Vrónsky to end their relationship and to ask Kitty for her forgiveness. Somewhat unaware of what is unfolding around him, Karénin reflects on his sense that his relationship with Anna is being undermined. Acknowledging his jealousy, he is at the same time aware that his jealousy is illogical, a response based in an unfounded emotion rather than a response based in logic and even open-mindedness. After confronting his wife one evening about the possible consequences of what he assumes to be her less-than-respectful behavior, Karénin is confused by Anna's indignation and her argument that she has a right to have some entertainment in her life. Karénin counters with the argument that such desires should be kept hidden. When Karénin reasserts his love for her, Anna responds by wondering what love really means.

Leaping forward in time by almost a year, the novel refocuses on Anna and Vrónsky in the moments following the sexual consummation of their relationship. Distraught, and fearing that she has lost everything, Anna sobs and says that all she has in her life now is Vrónsky. After falling into a fitful sleep, Anna dreams that both Karénin and Vrónsky are her husbands.

Unable to overcome his sadness over Kitty's rejection, Lévin keeps himself busy with the frustrating business of estate farming. He also cares for his half-brother Nikolái, who suffers from tuberculosis. Lévin's spirits are revived during a surprise visit from Stiva, who provides Lévin with details of Kitty's failing health. Lévin believes her illness is caused in part by her treatment of him, which he interprets as a sign of her feelings for him. Their discussion then turns to business, and more specifically to Stiva's plans to sell part of his family estate to a merchant who Lévin later slights. Stiva concludes the sale

against his friend's best advice, and then he accuses Lévin of snobbery.

Vrónsky and Anna continue to deepen their relationship in full view of St. Petersburg high society. Upon learning that Anna is pregnant (and that he is likely the father of her unborn child), Vrónsky urges her to leave Karénin and to live openly and honestly with him. He does not realize that her devotion to her son, Sergéi, holds her in her marriage, which remains, on the surface at least, as it always has. Simmering below the surface, though, is Karénin's growing hostility towards his wife. He reminds her repeatedly that her worry when Vrónsky is injured during a horse race, for instance, is wholly improper. Pushed by her husband to quit her relationship with the officer, Anna confesses openly that she loves Vrónsky. Karénin is shocked, and demands that she continue to appear committed to their marriage until they agree upon a solution to the situation. As is so often his reaction to situations both personal and professional, Karénin shows himself to be a man almost obsessed with appearances and with how his actions might look to people of high standing within society.

While Anna's story continues to unfold in St. Petersburg, Kitty visits a German spa in the hopes of recovering her health. While she is there, Kitty meets and befriends a young woman named Varvára (Várenka) who has devoted her life to charity and good deeds. Kitty also meets a woman named Madame Stahl, a seemingly religious invalid who also presents Kitty with an influential model of piety and righteousness. However, Madame Stahl is also a vain woman whose piety is not necessarily sincere.

Part Three, Chapters 1–32

Lévin visits with his half-brother, Sergéi. The two men converse at length about the conditions of the rural peasantry, local politics, and the responsibility of the landowners to tend to the local affairs of their tenants. After working in his fields the next day, Lévin receives a letter from Dolly. Having moved to the country in order to reduce household expenses, Dolly is struggling to adapt to rural hardships. Lévin begins to visit Dolly again, which only serves to reawaken his feelings for Kitty. His love for Kitty is further renewed when he catches a glimpse of her in a passing carriage.

Back in St. Petersburg, Karénin struggles with his feelings for Anna following her admission of adultery. Growing increasingly distant from his family, he decides, nonetheless, that the best punishment for Anna is to deny her the divorce she so deeply desires. Anna is stunned by Karénin's decision, and she contemplates leaving him and taking their son with her. But in the end, Anna decides to agree to Karénin's plan, maintaining the appearances dictated by her social standing.

In light of Anna's pregnancy, Vrónsky is torn between continuing his military career (his primary source of income) and following a self-imposed code of conduct that would force him to resign his position (should he decide to make public his affair with a married woman). Setting off for Anna's country home, where she has arranged a meeting, Vrónsky tries to convince Anna to abandon her marriage and to apply for a divorce. Anna admits that her pride, as well as her love for her son, will keep her from ever doing so.

Meanwhile, Karénin's standing in society rises, bolstered only momentarily by a brilliant political speech that he delivers on the relocation of the Russian native tribes. Despite his wife's affair, he remains steadfast as he maintains the illusion of a happy marriage. His demands of Anna are simple: there will be no divorce and Vrónsky will never set foot in his home.

Back in the country, Lévin struggles with his renewed feelings for Kitty, and the matter is exacerbated by Dolly's persistent attempts to bring the two together for a meeting. Heading away from his farm (and from Kitty) to visit a friend, Lévin is drawn into deep philosophical discussions about farming and the conditions of the peasantry. He continues his journey, visiting his dying half-brother Nikolái. Their conversations bring him to contemplate death, and he resolves to live his life to the fullest.

Part Four, Chapters 1–13

Anna and Karénin continue to uphold the illusion of their marriage, sharing a house despite the fact that they are almost totally estranged from one another. Both wish for an end to the situation, but neither can see a workable solution. Breaking her husband's rule, Anna invites Vrónsky to her home when Karénin is out attending a meeting. Karénin returns earlier than expected, and he confronts his wife and her lover. A heated argument follows, during which Vrónsky recognizes a mean spiritedness and pettiness in Anna that leave him saddened. For her part, Anna erupts in anger against her husband, attacking his character. When her anger subsides, Anna tells Vrónsky that she has had a dream of her pending death during childbirth. Karénin tells Anna that he plans to initiate divorce proceedings, and he threatens to take their son away from her.

After visiting a lawyer in St. Petersburg in order to set the divorce in motion, Karénin goes off to work in the rural provinces, having been in a professional slide since his speech. He then encounters Stiva and Dolly, who, despite Karénin's obvious coldness, invite him to dinner. Lévin, Kitty, and a number of locals, will also be attending. Karénin accepts the invitation. At the dinner, he witnesses Lévin and Kitty's reconciliation, and he spends the evening listening to discussions on numerous topics, including education and women's rights.

The dinner brings numerous threads of the narrative together. Karénin confides to Dolly that he is divorcing Anna, despite the fact that it will ruin her. Lévin and Kitty reunite; they apologize for their past mistakes and decide to marry in the near future. Lévin believes that he should be totally honest with his affianced, so allows her to read his private journals, which reveal him to be an agnostic. The journals also reveal that he slept with a number of women prior to meeting Kitty. Upset at both of these discoveries, Kitty forgives him and the couple move forward with their plans.

Karénin, however, has been passed over in his bid for a coveted government post. To make matters worse, he receives news that Anna has delivered a baby girl, and that Anna is suffering what appears to be a fatal fever in the aftermath. Rushing home, he finds Anna being tended by Vrónsky. Certain that she is dying, Anna begs Karénin to forgive both her and her lover, which he does. Leaving the house, and tormented by thoughts of Anna's death, Vrónsky attempts suicide, but survives.

Karénin reflects upon his forgiveness, and on the affection he feels for the newborn child, also named Anna. Karénin overhears a conversation during which Betsy pleads with Anna to see the depressed and suicidal Vrónsky once more before he is stationed, and he informs his wife that he will tolerate the affair on the condition that the family is not disgraced. Stiva arrives and negotiates a solution to the situation: Karénin will claim to be the adulterer because a divorce on these grounds will protect Anna's reputation. Informed of the plan, Vrónsky visits Anna, affirming his love for her. Anna, however, argues that Karénin is being overly generous, and she rejects his plan for a divorce. Instead, Vrónsky resigns his commission with the army, and the two lovers go abroad.

Part Five, Chapters 1–33

Following his engagement to Kitty, Lévin attends a legally mandated meeting with a priest, and he also attends a bachelor party in his honor. After facing his last minute insecurities about the wedding, Lévin and Kitty are finally married amidst many tears and much celebration. Returning to their country estate, the couple settle somewhat uncomfortably into married life, with Lévin chafing at times under his sudden lack of freedom and his wife's jealousy. Nevertheless, the marriage is a happy one.

Less happy in his decision is Vrónsky, who finds life in Italy (where he and Anna are now staying), less than satisfying. Anna, on the other hand, feels her spirits lift once the taint of disgrace that had dogged her in Russia is no longer a factor. While Anna recovers from the emotional havoc caused by the rumors that have dogged her for so long, Vrónsky takes up painting as a means of fending off his growing frustration with his life. The attempt is unsuccessful. Anna and Vrónsky expand their circle of acquaintances to include a Russian painter who agrees to paint a portrait of Anna.

While Lévin and Kitty go to tend to Nikolái on his deathbed, Karénin struggles to understand why his life has become defined by failure and misery. At this point in the novel, the narrator steps forward for a brief period in order to fill readers in on Karénin's personal history.

Returning to St. Petersburg, Anna and Vrónsky settle into a hotel and attempt to revitalize their social life, but to no avail. High society shuns them, and Anna meanwhile struggles with her own waning sense of love for her daughter and with the knowledge that she has abandoned her son. In a futile effort to reenter society, Anna agrees to attend the opera with one of her old, unmarried aunts, much to Vrónsky's displeasure. Fearing the response that Anna might have to endure, Vrónsky follows his lover to the opera and spies on her. He watches in dismay as she is insulted repeatedly by the other patrons; for her part, Anna returns home angry, and with a sense of desperation. Anna and Vrónsky depart soon thereafter for the countryside, where they stay for a brief period before returning again to the city.

Part Six, Chapters 1–32

Unhappy with her place in the country, and unable to adjust to the conditions and culture of rural life, Dolly moves in with Lévin and Kitty for the summer. Kitty's friend Várenka and Lévin's half-brother Sergéi also join the group. The latter two are immediately attracted to each other, but nothing will ever come of it because Sergéi remains forever loyal to the memory of a deceased lover. Stiva joins the group with a friend, Veslóvsky, who irritates Lévin immensely. A clumsy man who consumes copious amounts of food and flirts openly with Kitty, Veslóvsky engages in conversations about love and social conventions in a tone that makes Kitty uncomfortable and leads Lévin to expel him from the house.

Dolly decides to visit Anna, and as she heads for the city, she reflects on her ideas about life, love, and living according to a set of rules that acknowledges the power of emotion and spirit. On the way, Dolly encounters Anna and some friends on horseback, an activity that Russian society considers inappropriate for a lady of Anna's standing. Dolly is simultaneously envious of her friend's freedom and anxious for her friend's future, and she promises Vrónsky that she will speak with Anna about accepting Karénin's offer for a respectable divorce.

During an elaborate and costly dinner, Anna and her group of friends discuss an eclectic range of issues, from Western architecture to the current state of local government. Following dinner, Dolly fulfills her promise to Vrónsky, approaching Anna about accepting Karénin's offer of divorce. Believing that to ask for her freedom is to acknowledge both privately and publicly that she has acted improperly, Anna refuses to humiliate herself by asking him again for that freedom, so Dolly decides to return to the country, suddenly thankful for the family and friends that she has.

Vrónsky announces that he is traveling to an outlying province on business, and his path crosses with Lévin. A series of political discussions between the two follow. When the former officer returns home, Anna is frustrated and irritable. She refuses to be separated from

Vrónsky again, even on minor business trips, and she finally agrees to write Karénin to ask for the divorce that he had once offered her.

Part Seven, Chapters 1–31

Having returned to Moscow, Lévin and Kitty are anxious about the impending birth of their first child. Lévin is also anxious about life in the city, which he finds expensive, crowded, and driven only by profit and loss. After attending an evening concert, Lévin meets Stiva, Vrónsky, and others for an evening of drinking, gambling, and crude conversation. Stiva proposes a surprise visit to see Anna, whom Lévin has heard about but has never met. When Lévin and Anna finally do meet later that evening, they immediately feel comfortable in conversation. Anna tells Lévin that she does not believe that Kitty can ever truly forgive her without personally living the nightmare Anna's life has now become. Lévin agrees, and promises to relay this message to his wife.

Returning home, Lévin is acutely aware of his growing fascination with Anna, and a jealous Kitty, sensing this, provokes an argument. In the meantime, Anna rebukes Vrónsky for his growing coldness towards her and for spending time away from her with his friends.

Soon after Lévin begins to grow accustomed to city life, Kitty awakens him in the middle of the night and announces that she is in labor. Fearful for Kitty's life, he is shocked by the birth of his son. Rather than being joyous or pensive, Lévin feels an odd mixture of pity and revulsion when he first sees his newborn son.

As the financial situation worsens in the Oblónsky household, Dolly demands full control over her portion of the family fortune. Her demand prompts Stiva to secure a government position, and this brings him into contact with Karénin. Karénin treats Stiva respectfully but tells him that he no longer has any interest in Anna or her life. Nevertheless, he promises to give Stiva a decision regarding the divorce. Soon after, following a conversation with Landau, a noted French psychic, Karénin refuses Anna's request for a respectable divorce.

Both Anna and Vrónsky are unhappy; they are being driven apart by Anna's almost paranoid jealousy. The lovers also argue about such issues as fidelity, women's rights, and education. When Stiva announces Karénin's decision, Anna demands that they leave for the country

immediately. Vrónsky tries to explain that this is not possible because he has business to settle and has also planned to visit his mother. The couple argues all day, until Vrónsky leaves for the train station on his way to see his mother. Anna falls into despair, believing that the relationship is over. Desperate, she sends Vrónsky a telegram, begging him to return immediately. He replies with a curt telegram, saying that he cannot return right away, and she misinterprets this as a cold dismissal of her.

Anna is resolved to be at the station when Vrónsky returns, and she sets out across the city to get there in time to meet him. While she waits at the station, Anna is at times disoriented and without focus, and she comes to the conclusion that Vrónsky's passion for her has long faded, and that he is now staying with her out of a sense of duty rather than on account of his love for her. Anna's disgust with what she sees as the artificiality of the world and the shallowness of the people around her is coupled with a desire to punish Vrónsky, and she throws herself under the wheels of an approaching train. Her last moments are a powerful blend of confusion and regret.

Part Eight, Chapters 1–19

The closing section of the novel opens two months after Anna's suicide. Vrónsky has reenlisted in the army and speaks of Anna with animosity. Karénin has taken custody of the baby girl born to his late wife. The final pages of the novel are mostly devoted to Lévin, who undergoes a deep spiritual transformation that demonstrates Tolstoy's belief that life can be lived for a higher ideal. Lévin's transformation also underscores an alternative to the example set by Anna's life and death.

CHARACTERS

Varvára Andréevna
See Várenka

Betsy
Betsy (Princess Elizavéta Fyódorovna Tverskóy) is Vrónsky's first cousin. She becomes a wealthy and influential friend of the disgraced Anna. Much like Anna herself, Betsy has a propensity for living life to the fullest, which often brings her into conflict with social conventions.

Dolly

Dolly (Princess Dárya Alexándrovna Oblónsky) is Stiva's wife and Kitty's older sister. Her discovery of her husband's adultery opens the novel, and effectively introduces the moral and emotional issues that begin to further unfold with Anna's arrival. Dolly understands the subtleties of social and personal relationships, so when Anna is ostracized by society for her affair with Vrónsky, Dolly is very understanding and supportive. Appreciative of Anna's pursuit of happiness, she is at the same time increasingly aware of the happiness in her own life when confronted with Anna's sorrows.

Countess Lydia Ivánovna

Countess Lydia Ivánovna was originally a friend of Anna's. However, after learning about Anna's affair, the deeply religious woman becomes Anna's harshest critic. Ivánovna will not forgive Anna or speak with her, and she is secretly in love with Anna's husband. Ivánovna represents high society in Russia, which views adultery and infidelity with an unfounded moral righteousness.

Alexéi Alexándrovich Karénin

Alexéi Alexándrovich Karénin is an image-conscious, conservative, and duty-bound man. Holding various posts as a government official, Karénin is a passionless man trapped in a loveless marriage with the beautiful Anna. Distant from his wife and son, his primary concern is for his reputation and status. When he is made aware of his wife's affair with Vrónsky, for instance, Karénin briefly considers the idea of challenging Vrónsky to a duel, but opts instead to punish his wife by denying her the divorce that she desires. Later, when he does extend an offer of divorce, he does so only under the condition that their son remain in his custody. Throughout the novel, Karénin's motivations are, in fact, quite complex. At times, he worries about Anna's reputation should he grant her a divorce (she would lose all social standing given the scandal). At other times, he is concerned primarily about his own reputation (that of a man who lost his wife to a lover). And at other times still, the overwhelming sense is that he is simply trying to punish Anna for cuckolding him.

Standing as a marked contrast to Anna's emotional openness, and even to Kitty's gradual attainment of emotional maturity, Karénin locks his emotions away, hiding them. He suggests that Anna should do the same with her desires. Considered more broadly, Karénin represents what Tolstoy viewed as the rational inhumanity of an increasingly bureaucratic culture, which transforms the human condition into easily understood and manageable equations, rules, and measurable quotas. To leave Karénin, as Anna does, is to reject both literally and symbolically the superficial conventionality that he comes to represent.

Sergéi Alexéich Karénin

Also known as Seryózha, Sergéi Alexéich Karénin is Anna and Karénin's son. Although he is a boy with a good disposition, his father's treatment of him is cold and dismissive. When his mother deserts her family in order to be with her lover, she does so at the expense of her relationship with her son, though she never gives up in her attempts to visit him.

Anna Arkádyevna Karénina

Anna Arkádyevna Karénina is the protagonist of the novel that bears her name. Intelligent, well-read, and beautiful, she is aristocratic in birth and in spirit. Married to Alexéi Alexándrovich Karénin, a cold, unloving man, Anna wishes to live by her deeply held belief that love is stronger than anything, including responsibility, duty, or oppressive social conventions. Following a chance meeting with an army officer named Count Alexéei Kiríllovich Vrónsky, Anna begins her journey down a path that most of her peers see as adulterous but that she views as an honest expression of her desires for happiness and fulfillment. Her relationship with Vrónsky is, she believes, an authentic counterpoint to the stagnant, superficial marriage in which she is trapped. Remaining deeply devoted to her son, Anna confronts the double standards that shape the culture of St. Petersburg—she is held almost solely responsibly for her affair.

Pregnant with what is likely Vrónsky's child, Anna confesses her affair to her husband. He reacts with hostility tempered by practical resolve. Rather than granting her a divorce, he forces Anna to live a lie, pretending the marriage is sound in order to protect the family name and his own reputation. For a woman to whom artificiality is abhorrent, the arrangement wears heavily on Anna, and she finally flees with her lover to Italy before returning to Russia to live as an outcast within high society. Increasingly at odds with both Vrónsky and the world around her, Anna is isolated from her friends, out of touch with her children, and fearful of losing Vrónsky (whom she pushes away with her jealousy and paranoia). In a final and tragic statement of her desperation, Anna throws herself under a train.

Despite the tragic ending of her life, readers inevitably have mixed feelings and sympathy for Anna as a woman who harbors an intensely passionate spirit and determination to live her life fully and on her own terms. Forced to endure what she comes to see as the nightmare of her life, Anna remains a complex and troubling symbol of the quest for autonomy within an alienating and oppressive world.

Kitty

Princess Ekaterína Alexándrovna Shcherbátsky is a vibrant and beautiful woman who is pursued early in the novel by both Lévin and Vrónsky. Initially, she rejects Lévin and chooses Vrónsky, only to be slighted when Vrónsky falls in love with Anna. Debilitated by this turn of events, Kitty falls into ill health, planning to visit a German spa as part of her recovery. She later reconnects with Lévin at a dinner party at the Oblónsky country house, where the two rekindle their affection for each other and eventually settle into a relatively harmonious marriage filled with mutual support and caring.

At first, Kitty is an evasive woman who is unable or unwilling to communicate her deepest emotions to those around her. Kitty is written by Tolstoy as the most obvious counterpoint to the way Anna expresses her feelings regardless of the consequences to herself or to those around her. Over a period of years, though, Kitty moves towards a more balanced understanding of her feelings for Lévin. This maturation allows her to settle into a life that is more peaceful and dramatically less tragic than Anna's life.

Kóstya

See Konstantín Dmítrich Lévin

Sergéi Ivánovich Kóznyshev

Sergéi Ivánovich Kóznyshev is the half-brother of Konstantín and Nikolái Lévin. A well-known but often ignored intellectual and writer, he represents the modern intellectuals who are unable to embrace life other than as an intellectual exercise. His intellectualism prevents him from feeling the passion and emotion that is essential in love and in political commitment.

Landau

Landau is the French psychic who consults with Karénin, and influences his decision not to give Anna a respectable divorce.

Konstantín Dmítrich Lévin

Also known as Kóstya, Konstantín Dmítrich Lévin develops across the course of the novel as a minor protagonist, a character as important to the development of the novel as its title figure. An idealistic landowner, Lévin is not as socially polished as many of the other characters in the novel. Nevertheless, his pursuit and long courtship of Kitty does finally settle into a stable, loving marriage. Moreover, his spiritual regeneration, not Anna's suicide, concludes the novel on a powerful note of personal and social redemption. Importantly, Lévin's final discovery is learned from a peasant. This underscores Tolstoy's belief in simplicity as essential to the future of modern society.

Lévin is arguably the most independent thinker in Tolstoy's novel, and he does not fit into any of the obvious categories that come to define Russian society. In contrast to most of the other characters, he is a balanced and analytical thinker, willing to acknowledge the benefits of theories on agricultural production, for instance, but at the same time he is critical of many of the practical limitations that render these self-same theories problematic in the real world. Preferring the isolation of his farm over the trendy intellectualism of the city, and the pleasures of hard labor over the social scene of Moscow or St. Petersburg, Lévin is a vital counterpoint to Anna's search for self-defined (or, perhaps, self-contained) happiness.

Nikolái Dmítrich Lévin

Nikolái Dmítrich Lévin is the Lévin's sickly half-brother. Tolstoy's depiction of Nikolái represents both the strengths and weaknesses of the radical democratic movement emerging in Russia near the end of the nineteenth century. At once intensely intellectual, idealistic, and deeply committed to his ideas, he is at the same time detached from the practical world. His ideas remain simply ideas, and are never put into action in such a way as to have a wide reaching impact on the culture around him.

Masha

Masha (Márya Nikoláevna) is a reformed prostitute who becomes Nikolái's final companion.

Márya Nikoláevna
See Masha

Princess Dárya Alexándrovna Oblónsky
See Dolly

Prince Stepán Arkádyich Oblónsky
See Stiva

Old Princess
Old Princess (Princess Shcherbátsky) is the mother of Dolly, Kitty, and Natalie. Unlike her practical husband, she initially advises Kitty to favor Vrónsky as a suitor over Lévin.

Seryózha
See Sergéi Alexéich Karénin

Prince Alexander Dmítrievich Shcherbátsky
Prince Alexander Dmítrievich Shcherbátsky is the aristocratic father of Dolly, Kitty, and Natalie. He is a very practical man in the sense that he sees Vrónsky's true nature, and would thus rather that his daughter Kitty chose Lévin as her husband instead.

Princess Ekaterína Alexándrovna Shcherbátsky
See Kitty

Princess Shcherbátsky
See Old Princess

Madame Stahl
Madame Stahl is a seemingly religious invalid who Kitty meets during her visit to a German health spa. An influential model of piety and righteousness, and a key figure in Kitty's spiritual education, Madame Stahl is a controversial figure. As Kitty's father points out, Madame Stahl is also a vain woman whose piety is actually a veneer for her faults, not a meaningful component of her being.

Stiva
Stiva (Prince Stepán Arkádyich Oblónsky) is Anna's aristocratic brother and a government official cursed with what he calls an amorous nature; that is, he is a serial adulterer. His wife, Dolly, finds out about one of his affairs, which threatens to destroy their marriage. This discovery spurs Stiva to invite his sister, Anna, to visit, which in turn leads to her first meeting with Vrónsky.

Believing that life is meant to be lived fully without hesitation or regret, Stiva is drawn by Tolstoy as an amicable and likeable character. Despite his lack of self control, he is not a cruel man, but is, as he claims often, trapped by the contradictions between his nature and the conservatism of Russian culture. Although he regrets that his adultery is discovered, for instance, he does not regret engaging in adultery itself. At the same time, his selfish and shortsighted behavior serves as a commentary on the vacuous and even corrupt nature of the culture in which he lives.

Princess Elizavéta Fyódorovna Tverskóy
See Betsy

Várenka
Várenka (Varvára Andréevna) is a virtuous young woman befriended by Kitty during her stay at a German spa. She becomes an inspiration to Kitty and spurs Kitty's recovery from ill health following the rejection by Vrónsky.

Later, in part six of the novel, while visiting Lévin at his country estate, Várenka meets his half-brother Sergéi. The two are immediately attracted to each other and their relationship flourishes. Out picking mushrooms together one day, both of them realize that Sergéi is on the cusp of proposing marriage. At the last moment, however, he finds himself unable to make the offer, choosing instead to remain loyal to the memory of a deceased lover to whom he has dedicated himself. The opportunity for the two to be together is lost forever, an example in the novel of allowing nostalgia or empty devotion to get in the way of a rejuvenating love.

Váska
Known commonly as Váska (Vásenka Veslóvsky) is a close friend of Stiva's. During a visit with the Lévins, Veslóvsky lavishes attention on Kitty to the point that her husband becomes jealous and throws him out of the house.

Vásenka Veslóvsky
See Váska

Count Alexéi Kiríllovich Vrónsky
Alexéi Kiríllovich Vrónsky is a handsome military officer who was, in Tolstoy's original drafts, a poetic hero of great passion committed to the ideals of independence and unrestrained living. As the novel took shape, however, Vrónsky became

more of a common figure, conforming in many ways to the social ideals of his day. Indeed, Vrónsky is occupied with the practicalities of making a living, and, unlike Anna, he keeps a low profile in the face of social disgrace. He is imagined by Anna to be the polar opposite of her husband (with whom he shares a common first name), and Vrónsky is indeed capable of a great, accommodating love for Anna (unlike her husband). However, Vrónsky's preoccupation with the practical is a trait that is also held by Karénin.

Countess Vrónsky

Never given a first name, the Countess is the opinionated mother of Count Alexéi Kiríllovich Vrónsky.

THEMES

Conflict between Personal Emotions and Social Conventions

One of the central concerns of *Anna Karenina* is the often tragic conflict between the energies of private passion and inner emotions and the social conventions that are put in place to contain or control them. In such characters as Anna and Stiva, readers recognize lives being guided wholly by emotional responses and desires. Anna feels unloved by Karénin, so she responds openly to her feelings for Vrónsky. When she finally confesses her feelings to her husband, nothing really changes. Social conventions dictate that Anna and her husband should maintain the status quo, which means that they must continue to appear together as a married couple.

Anna, the adulterous wife, is aligned neatly with a life lived honestly, while her wronged husband is guilty of both a public and private duplicity. Willing to live a false life and to repress the truth of his own emotions as well as those of his wife, Karénin becomes both a not so subtle representation of a culture that values an outward image of propriety over any real integrity. In the end, too, Karénin's approach to life, not Anna's, can be seen as one of the primary sources of the tragedy of the human condition.

Sadly, as Tolstoy indicates throughout the novel, the Karénins' duplicitous arrangement is more commonplace than one might imagine among aristocratic Russians. In part four, for instance, there is mention made of Stiva's new mistress (a ballerina) while he visits his wife

TOPICS FOR FURTHER STUDY

- Given that Tolstoy very carefully marks the idea of vengeance as crucial to his novel (see the epigraph that he has chosen), the idea of avenging oneself is often overlooked in discussions of the novel. Write an essay discussing how various actions and reactions in the novel are grounded in a belief in vengeance rather than in the Christian values of selflessness and charity.

- Select some film or television adaptations of the novel and view them with your class. Afterwards, conduct a discussion contrasting and comparing these adaptations to the original novel. How are the themes presented in each version? What has been changed? How do these changes make the adaptation more, or less, effective?

- Construct a journal of works of nineteenth or early twentieth-century art (paintings and photographs, most obviously) that you feel would effectively reflect the various backdrops against which this novel is set: Moscow, St. Petersburg, and the Russian countryside.

- Rewrite one or more parts of *Anna Karenina* in terms of the culture of your day. Whereas Tolstoy's characters spend a great deal of time discussing agricultural methods and the influence of Western Europe, what would a more contemporary version of Lévin, for instance, spend his time contemplating?

- Construct a timeline of the important social, cultural, and scientific events that occurred during the original serialization of *Anna Karenina* (1873–1877). Include clear references to the points in the novel that draw on these events, ideas, or creations, either in a primary role or as a part of the backdrop against which the story unfolds.

Dolly in the country. The implications are clear: either he has learned to hide the evidence of his amorous nature more carefully or his wife has decided to turn a blind eye to his philandering. The upper levels of Russian culture are, Tolstoy seems to suggest, defined in large part by a commitment to illusion and deception.

Few characters in the novel go unscathed. Regarding Anna, Tolstoy points out through a series of parallel relationships that a life ruled by emotion and passion can be equally as dangerous as a life ruled by social convention. Anna suffers greatly for conducting her affair with Vrónsky so publicly. Vrónsky also grows colder towards Anna over time. When Kitty becomes deeply enamored with the devoted and apparently virtuous Madame Stahl, she commits herself very quickly to a life of piety, devotion, and charity. Her father points out to Kitty, however, that Madame Stahl is not so much an angel of virtue as she is a vain woman, bedridden by choice in order to conceal her stubby and unsightly legs.

Thus, if Karénin is painfully closed off, hiding behind appearance and surface, then Anna and Kitty live openly in their interaction with things as they appear at the surface. This causes unnecessary disappointment and pain for those around Anna and Kitty. In other words, readers are invited to see what either woman might choose not to see: that Madame Stahl is a hypocrite and that Vrónsky is simply another, ordinary man with his own foibles and limitations.

Forgiveness

There are a number of key moments in *Anna Karenina* during which the Christian doctrine of forgiveness figures prominently, most notably Karénin's forgiveness of Anna and Vrónsky, and Lévin and Kitty's mutual forgiveness as they set the stage for their reconciliation. But as is often the case in Tolstoy's masterpiece, such generalized solutions rarely solve problems directly, if at all. Although Lévin and Kitty do manage to move through forgiveness towards a harmonious and mutually beneficial marriage, Anna turns away from Karénin's selfless gesture. Rejecting his plans for a respectable divorce, she instead flees from St. Petersburg with her lover. Tolstoy seems determined to remind readers through these characterizations, as well as through his epigraph to the novel ("Vengeance is mine; I will repay"), that the modern world is one in which the ideals of Christian doctrine can no longer function as a universal balm for the ills of the individual.

Adultery

Tolstoy is very careful in his depiction of the two adulterers in *Anna Karenina*, resisting traditional representations of the adulterous woman, in particular, as being driven by an unrestrained and morally degenerative passion. While Anna and Vrónsky are clearly attracted to each other as sexual beings, they are drawn together more powerfully by an attraction grounded in the abstractions of spirit, personality, and intellect. Appearing at the ball in a tasteful but elegant black dress, Anna rejects the familiar stereotype of the dangerous woman dressed in such flamboyant colors as lilac (as Kitty suggests) or, more conventionally, red. In fact, Anna herself is often startled by her reactions to Vrónsky, finding herself torn between her passions and her devotion to her own maternal, familial loyalties.

Although she is most obviously compared with her brother Stiva, Anna is also very closely aligned with Lévin. Both are confronted with obstacles to their happiness and, as they see it, to the truthful expression of their personal desires. Whereas Lévin withdraws from society following his rejection by Kitty, Anna slowly realizes that she would rather suffer within her adulterous relationship (which to her is a true expression of her feelings) than to continue to survive in a loveless marriage. While Tolstoy does argue against adultery as an abstract idea, he also represents in Anna a woman whose transgressive behavior is motivated by a desire to fulfill her emotional and spiritual needs with sincerity and honesty.

Adultery is an almost natural by-product of modern culture, Tolstoy seems to suggest. Tragically, it is a by-product that threatens the stabilities and foundations upon which society has been built.

STYLE

Literary Realism

Often viewed as a predecessor to modernism, literary realism found its influential beginnings, most critics agree, in the novels of the Russian writer Tolstoy (including *Anna Karenina*) and the French novelist Honoré de Balzac (*La Comédie humaine*, 1845), as well as the English writer George Eliot (*Middlemarch*, 1871) and the American writer William Dean Howells (*The Rise of Silas Lapham*, 1885). Dedicated to the detailed depiction of life and society as they are rather than as we wish they might be, realism establishes fidelity and truthfulness as key components of the movement while at the same time addressing a set of philosophic assumptions about life (just as *Anna Karenina* does).

Generally, realist writers have been associated with a belief in pragmatism, which connects the truth with a discernible set of consequences and experiences that are at once practical and realistic. Tolstoy's character Lévin, for instance, finds a kind of refuge from the heady intellectualism and intrusive bureaucracy of his day by spending time working his farm. More importantly, he stands as a kind of practical counterpoint to the idealistic and emotionally volatile Anna or the detached intellectualism of his own half-brother Sergéi. Generally, characters within the realist model are isolated (though not always lonely) characters concerned with the workings of everyday life.

Realist writers are also often supporters, if not advocates, of democratic ideas, and prove useful interrogators of the relationship between state institutions and the lives of average citizens. Lévin's interest and concern for the lives of the peasants is a clear example of this stance. Significantly, Tolstoy emphasizes the role of the peasantry at the end of the novel, when the landed farmer (Lévin) reaches his spiritual regeneration through consideration of the virtues and ideals of peasants. Where romantics (like Anna) attempt to transcend the constraints of the immediate to achieve the ideal (in her case, happiness), realistic characters focus their attention primarily on questions in the here and now (to dealing with the immediate), proposing specific actions that can be brought into practice to accomplish visible results.

Interior Monologue

Tolstoy relied heavily on interior monologue as a narrative strategy that brings his characters to life. A type of stream of consciousness writing, interior monologue (sometimes called quoted stream of consciousness) presents a character's thoughts, ideas, impressions, and sensations in the form of a silent inner speech or as a silent form of talking to oneself. It is as if the reader is inside the character's head, and is privy to all that goes on there. The result is meant to mimic the free flow of thought, the free association of ideas, and the jumps (sometimes suddenly and without logic) from one impression to the next.

As in the case of Tolstoy's novel, this strategy brings a vividness to the characters, to the ideas being debated and, in the case of Anna, to the emotions being explored.

HISTORICAL CONTEXT

Economic Crisis and Transition

The late nineteenth century was a time of crisis in Russia. Technology and industry continued to develop rapidly, but lagged in substantive ways to the progress being made in Western Europe and even in North America. New markets, technologies, and theories developed on account of the dynamic powers emerging in a unified Germany, a modernized Japan, and a reunified (post-Civil War) United States. Russia was undeniably a powerful presence on the global scene, but it was also a society marked by deep class divisions, as Tolstoy underscores neatly in *Anna Karenina*. Urban dwellers like Dolly were unaware of, and uncomfortable with, the struggles facing rural farmers; industrial expansion threatened traditional agrarian lifestyles; and political ferment was beginning among the youthful, idealistic intelligentsia. This, to put it simply, was a time of great change and of great opportunity in Russia.

During the 1870s, Russia's economy was developing, as the character of Lévin recognizes, more slowly than the major European nations to its west. This development was hampered in part by a population that was substantially larger than those of the more developed Western countries. More significantly, as Tolstoy points out, was the fact that the vast majority of this massive population still lived in rural communities and still engaged in relatively primitive agriculture. Between 1850 and 1900, for instance, Russia's population doubled, the fastest expansion of all the major countries except for the United States. Yet at the same time the country remained overwhelmingly agricultural, and that practice itself was technologically underdeveloped. As the experiences of Lévin illuminate, control of this sector of the economy remained in the hands of former serfs and peasants. These two groups, in fact, constituted about eighty percent of the rural population. Large estates did account for about twenty percent of all farmland, but few such estates were run according to efficient, large-scale models of production.

COMPARE & CONTRAST

- **1870s:** During the nineteenth century, Russia responds to political and economic pressures with hesitant reforms. The tradition of serfdom is abolished in 1861, which leads to a series of reforms that end with the beginning of World War I in 1914.

  1990s: In 1991, the Soviet Union officially breaks apart, forcing Russia towards a multiparty electoral system. Movement in this direction is sporadic, at best, leading to a constitutional crisis in 1993.

  Today: Russia and the other former Soviet bloc countries continue to struggle with the adjustment to a more democratic system of government. Indeed, in September 2007, Russian President Vladimir Putin surprised the world by dismissing Prime Minister Mikhail Fradkov, dissolving the Prime Minister's cabinet, and then appointing a new prime minister. It is believed that this political maneuver was designed to control the elections for Putin's successor in 2008.

- **1870s:** Russian agriculture is under pressure to adjust to new technologies, and this pressure is even greater due to the breakdown of the serf system and competition from expanding European markets.

  1990s: Following the breakup of the Soviet Union in 1991, large state-run farms must deal with the abrupt loss of government

  subsidies. Livestock inventories go into significant decline, which creates a substantive ripple effect, as the planting and harvesting of feed grain declines by twenty-five percent for a period of ten years.

  Today: Due to good weather during the early 2000s, Russia experiences a rebound in grain harvests and a subsequent increase in livestock production. It is generally believed that grain harvests will continue to gradually improve in the near future. Large farms, many of which were formerly run by the government, continue to dominate grain production.

- **1870s:** Novels about adultery are a relatively new phenomenon when *Anna Karenina* is first serialized. To this point, Russian marriages are frequently arranged by matchmakers, and are built on the assumption of future fidelity. Divorce is difficult to obtain and inevitably leaves a social taint on at least one of the partners. Because divorce is so prohibitive, it is correspondingly rare.

  1990s: Divorce in Russia is actually more liberal than it is in Western countries, which has led to an upward rise in the divorce and remarriage rate.

  Today: The newspaper *Pravda* published an article in 2007 stating that the divorce rate in Russia may be as high as 80 percent.

Furthermore, the still clumsy industrial growth was focused on a small number of urban regions, most notably Moscow and St. Petersburg. But even such a faltering process did make significant impacts on the Russian way of life. By 1890, the country had over 30,000 kilometers of railroads, often used to move the 1.4 million factory workers to and from the textile factories and steel plants that increasingly began to define the landscape.

The Abolition of Serfdom

Following the Crimean War (1854–1856), during which Tolstoy had served in the military, there was a growing movement within Russia for substantive political and social reform. At the forefront of these discussions was a movement to abolish serfdom in Russia, a change that would affect an estimated twenty million or more people. Initiated in 1861, the emancipation of the serfs signaled the end of the aristocratic monopoly over land and economic power. It also set into motion a dramatic reshuffling of traditional class structures and social conventions within the population of Russia. The old ideas and practices were no longer applicable, as newly emancipated workers moved to the industrial cities of Moscow and St. Petersburg in search of work. It was not long before these cities, already overcrowded, became hotbeds for racial and economic tensions as well as home to what might be best described as an underclass ripe for revolution and change.

For those former serfs who decided to remain in the country to work the land, the situation was particularly frustrating. While it was initially thought that they would receive their land as a gift, the freed serfs were forced instead to pay a special and recurring tax to the government, which in turn generously reimbursed the aristocratic landlords for the land that they had lost due to emancipation. In numerous instances, peasants were forced off their land or found themselves left with over farmed plots. Moreover, land that was turned over to the peasants was owned collectively by the village community, which divided the land amongst the peasants. These circumstances provide ample fuel for discussion throughout *Anna Karenina*.

Scene from the 1997 film version of Anna Karenina, *starring Sophie Marceau as Anna Karenina and Sean Bean as Count Vronsky* (Icon | Warner Bros | The Kobal Collection | Keith Hamshere | The Picture Desk Inc.)

CRITICAL OVERVIEW

As A. V. Knowles summarizes in his 1978 essay in the *Slavic and East European Journal*, Tolstoy's reading public reacted to his newest novel with enthusiasm. At the time, comparisons were made to Russian writers (and Tolstoy's contemporaries) Nikolai Gogol and Alexander Pushkin, and the "poet A. A. Fet declared that Tolsto[y] had shown himself to be quite without equal." The novel was discussed widely in the reading public, and everyone inevitably held an opinion about its message, its politics, and its morality. While generally praised, Knowles reports that the novel was chided by some fellow writers as "concentrating only on the genitals", as carrying with it "the idyllic fragrance of babies' diapers," or, as I. S. Turgenev (another writer who was a contemporary of Tolstoy's) charged, showing the unwieldy influence "of Moscow, the Slavophiles, aristocrats, and old spinsters." A critic and scholar openly concerned with how language could be used to express the subtleties of the most powerful relationships defining a culture, Turgenev felt that Tolstoy reinforced too easily the manners of high society. Despite the rejuvenation that defines the close of the novel, Turgenev felt that customs of the peasantry were not portrayed in an authentic or meaningful way.

Knowles further states that critics, as distinct from the more general reading public, "remained unimpressed by, and unsympathetic" to, Tolstoy's newest endeavor. Some were even openly hostile. On a positive note, the novel was praised for its form and structure, and for its attention to such contemporary problems as the relationship between landowners and peasants, state policies towards agriculture and economic disparity, and the role of women in Russian society. Ironically, Knowles claims, some of the harshest criticism argued that the novel was a thinly veiled "protest by the best elements of the upper classes against the inroads being made into society by the new middle and professional classes." According to Knowles, such critiques inevitably suggested that Tolstoy was positioning himself at a distance from mainstream Russian culture, in "a corner of society which led its own life based on traditions that were quite foreign and even antipathetic to the majority" of his readers. Tracing the substantive and tendentious history of the critical views on the novel, Knowles concludes that the main reason that the book was treated so diversely was that it was approached more as a social document than as a literary text. "It was judged," Knowles observes, "from political, sociological, and ethical viewpoints" that, while useful to varying degrees, inevitably clouded the larger picture of the story's literary merits.

Picking up on many of these comments, the prominent Victorian critic Matthew Arnold, in his *Essays in Criticism: Second Series*, praises Tolstoy for "his extraordinary fineness of perception, and his sincere fidelity to it." *Anna Karenina*, he concludes, is not to be considered or evaluated as a work of art. Rather "we are to take it as a piece of life." William Dean Howells concurs, noting in *Selected Literary Criticism* that he sees the novel as "a sort of revelation of human nature."

As the famous critic F. R. Leavis argues in *Anna Karenina and Other Essays*, Tolstoy's *Anna Karenina* is one of "the greatest of novels." Leavis calls the book a story of "magnitude," one in which its "greatness" entails its "largeness." Celebrating the expansiveness of Tolstoy's vision, Leavis goes on to call the novel "the great novel of modern—of our—civilization." *Anna Karenina*, he concludes, "in its human centrality, gives us modern man; Tolstoy's essential problems, moral and spiritual, are ours."

CRITICISM

Klay Dyer

Dyer holds a Ph.D. in English literature and has published extensively on fiction, poetry, film, and television. He is also a freelance university teacher, writer, and educational consultant. In the following essay, he discusses the social pressures brought to bear on Russian married women in the nineteenth century, focusing particularly on

WHAT DO I READ NEXT?

- Readers interested in balancing their reading of *Anna Karenina* with a novel of similar majesty and import would do well to approach Tolstoy's other masterwork, *War and Peace* (1865–1869), an epic exploration of Russia during the Napoleonic era.

- George Eliot's *Middlemarch* (1871) is a seminal example of British realism. Balancing philosophy, politics, and sophisticated narrative structures, it interweaves the stories of various friends, acquaintances, and relations in the fictional town of Middlemarch during the 1830s.

- Gloria Goldreich's novel *Dinner with Anna Karenina* (2006) tells the story of six very different women, all from different backgrounds, who gather over good food and wine as part of a regular book club. The novel traces their discussions of their favorite novels over the course of a year.

- Nikolai Gogol, a Russian writer and contemporary of Tolstoy, to whom Tolstoy is often compared, wrote some of the most influential stories of his generation. *The Collected Tales of Nikolai Gogol* (1999) provides a wonderful overview of his work.

- Marshall T. Poe's very readable *The Russian Moment in World History* (2006) discusses how Russia both integrated and resisted Western influences during the course of its history. As is often a point of discussion in *Anna Karenina*, Russian culture was both fascinated and bothered by questions about what it meant to be Russian and how to keep Russia a distinct social and cultural force in an increasingly homogeneous world.

Dolly (who, unlike Anna, chooses to stay in her loveless marriage).

Reflecting Tolstoy's own intensifying feelings of isolation and alienation from the high society into which he had been born, *Anna*

> AS IS OFTEN HIS STRATEGY, TOLSTOY LEAVES THE FINAL ASSESSMENT OF DOLLY'S DECISIONS TO THE READER. IT IS UNCLEAR WHETHER HER STORY ENDS WITH AN IRONIC ITERATION OF HER WILLFUL BLINDNESS OR IN A CONSCIOUS AND MATURE ACCEPTANCE OF A COMPROMISE MADE IN WISDOM, DIGNITY, AND COURAGE."

Karenina reveals an immediate and personal understanding of the social roles that ultimately shaped the lives of nineteenth-century Russians. Indeed, as the nineteenth century progressed, and with a radical transformation underway following the Crimean War, many of these roles (most notably, those pertaining to class and gender) were increasingly being reconsidered as open to debate and negotiation. With the abolition of serfdom, women also slowly but surely began to raise their voices against their own serfdom, one of subordination, vulnerability, and sexual propriety.

For women readers of the day, stories of female characters whose lives led inevitably toward marriage and toward the often idealized role of wife and mother were commonplace. Such stories reinforced the social status quo and were also a reassuring narrative design, functioning as a kind of moral and social road map that would reveal the path to a happy life. A female character who demonstrated that she valued anything outside of these accepted standards most naturally, it seemed, failed to achieve happiness.

When Tolstoy began to write *Anna Karenina* in the early 1870s, such social codes were already seen in some quarters as powerful impositions upon women's independence. Tolstoy proved himself especially open to exploring the implications of his female characters' physical, mental, and emotional susceptibility to the pressures of social convention. More importantly, he was committed to understanding the consequences of their willingness (or unwillingness, as in the case of Anna) to give in to such overwhelming social pressures. Acutely aware that this complex interrogation of female options within the culture of the day could be read as a powerful threat to tradition, Tolstoy nonetheless made the tensions informing this debate central to his most powerful novel. Obviously, Anna is the most fully realized embodiment of Tolstoy's challenge to the conventionality of Russian culture, a dissident, rebellious woman forced to the margins of her own world and, inevitably it seems, to a tragic death that is her response, at least in part, to a marriage that she cannot escape, and to the punishments that she must endure for even attempting to do so. But what of the other women in the novel, and, more particularly, what of Dolly, whose marital predicament not only opens the novel but indirectly brings about the meeting between Anna and Vrónsky? How does Dolly come to negotiate the consequences of her husband's amorous nature while keeping their marriage intact, and aligned safely within the social expectations of the day?

The very concept of marriage itself is often discussed in the novel. Considered by such a character as Kitty to be a profound source of female happiness, it is recognized by Dolly as an economic and social arrangement, and by Anna as an emotional and spiritual prison. But such a simple contrast is soon proven to be a dangerously false one that collapses under the weight of Tolstoy's argument within *Anna Karenina*. Indeed, Tolstoy indicates that marriage as a social convention leads to the victimization of all the women in the novel. By extension, the story illustrates that women are thus not able to secure a viable position within Russian culture. Through Dolly and Kitty, Tolstoy depicts women as being denied access to any social role beyond that of housewife and mother, while in the more radical Anna he envisions the dismal end to which resourceful, resistant women are inevitably doomed. *Anna Karenina* is, in the end, a novel in which neither conformity nor resistance prove to be reasonable options.

Unwilling to raise her voice against the social institution of marriage, Dolly will go so far as to sacrifice her own sense of propriety, as well as her dignity, by turning a blind eye to Stiva's persistent infidelities. Later, when the couple have moved to the country, readers discover that he has become involved with a ballerina; whether Dolly knows of this affair and ignores it, or whether Stiva has become more adept at hiding his transgressions, is left open to interpretation. What is clear, though, is that Dolly has become acutely aware of how her own decisions in relation to the social conventions of the day reflect not only upon herself but will reflect, ultimately, upon members of her immediate and extended family. To remain silent about such affairs, Dolly understands, is necessary in order to protect the stability, reputation, and future opportunities of her family.

Dolly's concern for social propriety, and by extension her concern for the role into which she has been forced, is so overpowering that despite the fact that her love for Stiva wanes as his infidelities accumulate, she still feels obliged to remain supportive of their union. By the time Dolly goes to visit Anna near the end of the novel, she is no longer interested in marriage for the sake of love and passion, but sees it—somewhat uncomfortably, she must admit—as a necessary means to an end. Supportive of her husband's career, and unhappily bearing the brunt of their financial instabilities, Dolly reimagines her marriage as the only career she can pursue, effectively overlooking any options that might transgress what she considers acceptable standards of behavior, but that might also actually work to circumvent the pressures that bear on her reality. Understanding that her husband remains a key to the financial well being of her family, Dolly silences herself in order to avoid a confrontation that could lead her (or her family) to economic hardship and the loss of social standing.

Knowing of no other viable alternative by which she might sustain her standing in society, Dolly fulfills neatly the conventional role that she has internalized. It is a role that she reinforces for herself later in the novel when she is allowed the opportunity to review the course she has taken (through her observations of Kitty and Lévin) as well as the course she has narrowly avoided (through her observations of Anna's battles with Karénin over a divorce). As she reflects upon Anna's nightmarish battles with her husband, her loss of social standing, and her separation from her son, Dolly finds her reward in knowing that she has not put herself or her family in such dire straights: "She had pitied Anna with all her soul while talking with her," Dolly thinks to herself, "but now she was unable to make herself think about her. Memories of her home and children arose in her imagination with some new radiance, some special loveliness she had not known before.

That world of hers now seemed so precious and dear that she did not want to spend an extra day outside it for anything."

Having seen the perils of the path not taken, Dolly returns to the family that she has helped sustain, often at the cost of her dignity and personal happiness. Setting off from Anna, whom she will never see alive again, Dolly journeys back towards her personal happy ending, one that both circumscribes and defines her. Reimagining herself within a world of precious radiance, Dolly also reimagines herself as a woman in paradise. Unlike Anna, who throws herself under a train as the ultimate statement of her resistance to things as they are, Dolly adapts and learns to survive within her marriage, reconciling her own dreams and passions to conform to the codes and social expectations of Russian culture.

As is often his strategy, Tolstoy leaves the final assessment of Dolly's decisions to the reader. It is unclear whether her story ends with an ironic iteration of her willful blindness or in a conscious and mature acceptance of a compromise made in wisdom, dignity, and courage. Again, this is a distinction that is also left to the readers.

Source: Klay Dyer, Critical Essay on *Anna Karenina*, in *Novels for Students*, Gale, Cengage Learning, 2009.

Amy Mandelker

In the following excerpt, Mandelker discusses the shadow imagery in Anna Karenina, *with particular attention to how it affects the overall meaning of the story. Mandelker also links the themes evoked by the shadow imagery to those found in the story of the Biblical Fall, the legend of Faust, and the myth of Amor and Psyche.*

... The story of the temptation of a woman and the exchange of her shadow for eternal beauty is told in a work with which Tolstoy may have been familiar, a poem by the Austrian poet, Nikolaus Lenau (1802–1850) entitled, significantly enough, "Anna". Anna of the poem appears at the beginning admiring her reflected beauty in a pond, when a supernatural figure appears to offer her eternal beauty in exchange for her shadow and the promise that she will renounce childbearing. The narcissism of this Anna recurs in Anna Karenina, who practices birth control to remain sexually attractive to Vronsky. Thus, the transformation of gender in *Anna Karenina*, from a "man without a shadow"

Scene from the 1948 film version of Anna Karenina, *starring Vivien Leigh as Anna Karenina and Kieron Moore as Count Vronsky* (Hulton Archive / Getty Images)

to a "woman without a shadow" abrogates any straightforward, psychological reading of Tolstoy's use of the "man without a shadow" as a metaphor for the struggle between the rational and the irrational self. When this psychic struggle is enacted by a female protagonist, the motif evokes male anxiety about female sexuality and the desirability of the female body. The shadow (feminine in gender in Russian) is a penumbral, feminine Other, a demonic seductress, an archetypal Eve. Returning to the primary text of original sin reveals the shadow in its originary shape as the Serpent in Eden. When God condemns it to slide along the ground worrying the heel of woman and her offspring, forever crushed beneath her heel, the early conflation of serpent, shadow, and woman is revealed.

Early variants of the novel emphasized the demonic nature of Anna's vitality: the title of the chapter describing Anna's passion for Vronsky was "The Devil" in an early draft, and Anna and Vronsky refer to her jealousy as "the demon." Anna has "something uncanny, demonic and fascinating in her," her face glows "with a bright light, but this glow was not one of joyfulness, but suggested the terrible glow of a conflagration in the middle of a dark night."

Vronsky's role as shadow-demon is implied by imagery which associates Vronsky both with shadow and with Faust: in the early stages of his pursuit of Anna, he is cast as Mephistopheles in the form in which he first appeared to Faust, a dog. Vronsky is repeatedly described as expressing "humble submission," "reverential ecstacy," the look of a dog who wishes to please. It is this "utter subjection, that slavish devotion, which [does] so much to win her." At the scene of their first meeting, the whining of a dog in the luggage

VRONSKY'S ROLE AS SHADOW-DEMON IS
IMPLIED BY IMAGERY WHICH ASSOCIATES VRONSKY
BOTH WITH SHADOW AND WITH FAUST: IN THE EARLY
STAGES OF HIS PURSUIT OF ANNA, HE IS CAST AS
MEPHISTOPHELES IN THE FORM IN WHICH HE FIRST
APPEARED TO FAUST, A DOG."

compartment is audible as Anna's train arrives from Petersburg. In an episode subsequently removed from the novel, Levin is terrorized by a mad dog which exacerbates his obsessive dread of death, and is somehow linked in his mind with the fearful image of a peasant. The emblem of Levin's panic thus connects the demonic Mephistopheles in his incarnation as a dog with Levin's vision of a peasant with a matted beard, undoubtedly the same disheveled peasant who haunts Anna and Vronsky and plays the role in the novel of the "shadow of death." The heirophantic nature of this peasant with matted beard and sack recalls the Tiresias figure of the blind, leprous peasant who fulfilled a similar function in *Madame Bovary*. An enigmatic statement of Anna's may be explained as an obscure reference to Mephistopheles in his canine incarnation and as projection of a troubled psyche: on her final journey to the train station, Anna silently addresses a family embarking on an outing, "The dog you're taking with you will be of no help to you—you can't get away from yourselves." Her observation is immediately followed by recollections of the early days of Vronsky's courtship, and her memories of him as an "abject setter-dog."

In addition to his dog-like servility, Vronsky is repeatedly accompanied by shadows throughout the novel. In the fateful meeting at Bologoe station, as Anna steps onto the platform, "the bent shadow of a man glided by at her feet..." Vronsky then interposes himself between Anna and the light of the lamppost, and stands in the shadow. Anna must "gaze into the shadow" to read his expression. Whenever Vronsky contemplates nature, his vision includes shadows, as when he admires the cloud of midges and the shadow over his carriage "in the already

lengthening shadow of a lush lime tree," or the slanting shadows over the fields as he rides to a rendez-vous with Anna:

> Everything he saw from the carriage window
> ... was as fresh, and gay, and strong as he was
> himself:... the slanting shadows that fell from
> the houses, and trees, and bushes, and even
> from the rows of potatos...

Later, at his estate, his face will be shadowed by leaves as he discusses his relationship to Anna with Dolly: "Daria Aleksandrovna looked with timid inquiry into his energetic face, which under the lime trees was continually being lighted up in patches by the sunshine, and then passing into complete shadow again." After Anna's death, as he waits at the train station to depart for the Balkans, "In the slanting shadows cast by sacks piled up on the platform, Vronsky... strode up and down like a wild beast in a cage."

The definitive association of Vronsky with the shadow figure occurs in the conversation quoted above. In the various redactions of the dialogue, an interesting evolution in grammatical structure suggests a shift in emphasis which resulted from the introduction of the shadow sub-text. In the earlier versions of the passage, before the shadow story was mentioned, the acquaintance states that Vronsky has become Anna's shadow (*sdelalsia eia teniu*). In the final version of the passage, when the reference to the shadow story is introduced, Anna is said to have brought back with her the "shadow of Aleksei Vronsky" (*ten Alekseia Vronskogo*): Vronsky no longer exists; his shadow has been snared by Anna. His diabolical nature is expressed in his exultant acquiescence in the "terror" of their passion: "Our love, if it *could* be stronger, will be strengthened because there is something terrible in it," a demonic statement which was even more villainous in the earlier version, where their love was to be strengthened "by the crime, the evil that we have done to [Karenin]." Tolstoy's revisions minimize Vronsky's role: no longer the primary actor ("he became her shadow"/*sdelalsia eia teniu*), he becomes the passive agent of Anna, who "brings back with her" the shadow of Vronsky.

If we view Vronsky as a shadow and the power relationship of Anna and Vronsky as that of owner and shadow, or a lady and a dog, Anna would appear to be the passive victim who succumbs to, rather than offering temptation, as Princess Miagkaia subsequently argues: "How can she help it if they're all in love with her and follow her about like shadows?" Pursuing this interpretation, it is Vronsky who, having become possessed and yielded to his shadow, now seduces and compromises Anna to gain authority over her soul. In the course of the novel, Vronsky assumes the powerful position, just as the shadow usurps the scholar's position, or the man in gray (Mephistopheles) gains power over Peter Schlemihl. Vronsky's power over Anna gives him the responsibility and culpability for the problematic aspect of their "position." The description of Vronsky as a murderer bending over Anna's body after the consummation of their love affair suggests that he is morally responsible for her fall, just as he is responsible for the death of his horse, Frou-Frou . . .

Has Tolstoy condemned Anna? Or has he presented a tragic vision of entrapment? Within the confines of a life which denies her spiritual growth, Anna's only avenue for the pursuit of complete psychic awareness is through adulterous passion. Thus, Anna's captivation by a shadowy demon lover may be read as a version of the originary myth of the ecstatic lover, who engages in the passionate, erotic pursuit of endless desire ultimately subtended by the death drive. Jung would consider the allure of this type of shadow figure to reflect animus possession, domination by a demonic lover who, like Eros in the Psyche myth, "lures women away from all human relationships and . . . cut[s] a woman off from the reality of life" (von Franz, 202).

Interestingly, casting Vronsky as an animus, or Eros, the erotic death demon, is textually supported by echoes of Apuleius' "Amor and Psyche": Vronsky's role as the dutiful son of a mother reknowned for her beauty and promiscuity reflects the relations of Amor and Venus. Like Venus, Mme Vronskaia is responsible for introducing her son to the woman he will fall in love with and whom she will later persecute. Like Amor and Psyche, Vronsky and Anna have a daughter. The seclusion enforced on Anna by her separation from society encloses her in Amor's dwelling and provokes in her the types of doubt which drove Psyche to violate Amor's edict and examine the sleeping God by candlelight. In a tableau reminiscent of the myth, Anna illuminates the sleeping Vronsky:

> *He was asleep there, and sleeping soundly. She went up to him, and holding the candle above his face, she gazed a long while at him. Now when he was asleep, she loved him so much that at the sight of him, she could not keep back tears of tenderness. But she knew that if he awakened he would look at her with cold eyes . . .*

Anna's illumination of Vronsky follows a scene where, reading by candlelight, she senses the inevitability of suicide as the only escape from her position. Her candle gutters, shadows descend upon her from every direction and plunge her in darkness. Anna's reading by candlelight becomes the controlling metaphor for the entire novel when Tolstoy repeats the metaphor to describe her last hours and death. Thus, lifting her lamp to see, casting shadows and light in order to read and know Love, interconnects every illumination in the novel and suggests the ultimate meaning of the shadow imagery. Anna's candlelight reading of the novel, of love, of life, repeats Psyche's transgression in pursuit of knowledge and her weakness in needing to affirm with the light of reason the intuitive life of passion associated mythologically with darkness and shadow. Yet, it is a light of knowledge which is suppressed by the patriarchy; the transgression consists of lighting a lamp to see the truth, but the light will drive the beloved away.

In the final sequence of the novel's penultimate part, Anna, like Psyche, is cast out of Amor's paradise of love and embarks on a journey as a result of Mme Vronskaia's machinations, recalling Venus' scourge on Psyche . . .

For Anna Karenina, a victim of the oppression and dependent status of women in the 19th century, the pursuit of passionate love is the only channel of action available which will liberate her from social constraints and place the life of the individual spirit above the life of the social body. The quest is Psyche's, who transgressed in her desire to know Love and thus is cast out of Paradise. Psyche's reward and apotheosis, like Ulysses' return, affirms the reader's positive view of Olympus. The death of the hero/ine may seem a punishment in this tradition of the folk tale or romance, where physical and material benefit (beauty rather than ugliness, wealth rather than poverty) reflect the evaluative dimension of good and evil. But mythic figures transcend this dichotomy, constituting an amalgam of oppositions and a restructuration of the material plane according to spritual imperatives. Such a process characterizes the action of myth, where heroes and heroines die in order to be transfigured for a cosmic benefit.

Within the tragic and mythic tradition, Anna's death does not constitute a punishment, but a liberation from her confinement in a social arena where the quest for the development of an autonomous self, emblematized as the acquisition of a shadow, constituted an urforgivable transgression.

Source: Amy Mandelker, "The Woman with a Shadow: Fables of Demon and Psyche in *Anna Karenina*," in *Novel: A Forum on Fiction*, Vol. 24, No. 1, Autumn 1990, pp. 48–68.

Gary R. Jahn

In the following excerpt, Jahn explores the centrality and complexities of railway images in Anna Karenina. *Jahn argues that the railway serves as a touchstone from which most readings of the novel originate, especially readings focusing on Anna's passion or the condition of her society.*

... The idea that the main function of the railroad is to suggest or symbolize death in general may also be criticized on grounds specific to itself for, in fact, the railroad is the agent only of Anna's death. Many characters in the novel are associated in one way or another with the railroad, but only Anna perishes. That the railroad symbolizes upper-class society also seems, upon examination, to be problematical. Logic leads to the conclusion that Anna was killed by (or, more accurately, made herself the victim of) upper-class society, but, as has often been noted, the novel contains many representatives of that very sector of society who, in the morally objective sense, conduct themselves in the same manner as Anna with Vronskij and yet suffer no ill effects therefrom. Stiva Oblonskij, as we have seen, is even portrayed as attractive rather than repellent. It has been argued that there is a qualitative difference between Anna and these other characters which explains why her fate is different from theirs. This difference is said to reside in Anna's much greater genuineness and sincerity as opposed to the hypocrisy and conventionalism of the other characters. If this very cogent idea is applied only in the moral sphere, however, it leads to a fragmentation of the novel's unity. The different fates of the various characters must then be seen as the result of individual differences, as a simple capturing of the diversity of reality without any attempt at finding an underlying unity in the understanding of that reality on a conceptual level; while not unthinkable, this would, at least, be unlikely from the

> THUS, ANNA TRULY IS, AS SHE SAYS AGAIN AND AGAIN, BOTH GUILTY AND YET NOT TO BLAME. SHE IS THE TRAGIC VICTIM OF HUMAN NATURE WHICH CALLS BOTH FOR THE UNHINDERED EXPRESSION OF THE INDIVIDUAL AND THE ANTITHETICAL ACKNOWLEDGMENT OF THE ULTIMATE DEPENDENCE OF THE INDIVIDUAL UPON THE SOCIAL."

point of view of Tolstoj's usual practice. Moreover, if this principle is applied to the overtly parallel stories of Anna and Levin, we are left with a novel in which the two central characters are after all simply different types, involved in different stories, and the links between them (for example, their similar experiences, the slow growth in Levin from his absolute aversion to "fallen women" to his ultimate attraction to Anna) are a failed attempt to unify two stories that are in fact comparable only as opposite poles of the moral compass. The contrast between them becomes evident, but there seem to be no solid grounds for comparison. The novel is not one story with two facets, but two stories connected rather crudely at a single moral interface. Criticism has tended to resist this conclusion, but it seems inevitable in the light of the reasoning just presented.

The difficulties inherent in the interpretation of the railroad as an image of the Russian high society of the time may be overcome by taking the railroad to represent instead the much broader concept of the social aspect of human existence. The railroad is not, after all, uniformly identified with any particular sector of society in the novel, the remarks to the contrary in Levin's book notwithstanding. At the very first appearance of an actual train in the novel (Anna's arrival in Moscow; I, 17) the disembarking passengers demonstrate that the railroad is not the exclusive preserve of the idle rich: a guards officer, a merchant, and a peasant are the first to descend. In addition, the railroad is the connecting link among all the various particular societies presented in the novel: Moscow, St. Petersburg, Levin's estate, the German spa,

Italy, Vronskij's estate, and so forth. Each of these individual societies is developed in some detail and discussed as to its workings, for example, the enumeration and description of the various subdivisions of Petersburg society in II, 4. This close attention to the structure and operation of various concrete social entities suggests that all human activity presupposes a social framework, that the social is an integral and necessary adjunct to the individual. The railroad, as the physical link among the various societies, is an eminently suitable means for the representation of the generalized or abstract link among them also.

If the railroad is the image of the concept of the social, it is no surprise to find that the novel's most social character, Stiva Oblonskij, who is specifically stated to have friends at every level of society and who is at home in any social context (I, 5), is also the character most closely associated with the railroad. He shares with the railroad the operative function of connecting the various social *loci* of the novel (for example, Moscow and Levin's estate, when he goes to sell his wife's forest land [II, 14], Moscow and Petersburg, when he goes to plead Anna's case for divorce to Karenin [VII, 18]). He is present at both the first railway scene and the last (Vronskij's departure for the Balkans; VIII, 2). He is the witness of both episodes involving the children's game of "Railroad." Finally, as though realizing his metaphorical function, he seeks and finally obtains a post in an agency which superintends the operation of the railways.

This interpretation of the railroad image and Stiva's close connection with it explains the anomaly of his belonging to upper-class society and yet remaining relatively free from the stigma of his membership therein. In the same way the association of the children with the railroad may be explained. The railroad, as the symbol of the social, represents a morally neutral force which is the foundation of all actual societies. Particular social groups may, on the whole, be morally better or worse, and, from Levin's point of view, a dependence on the railroad does signify moral laxity. At the same time, however, the railroad is connected to the broader concept of the social in general, and in this respect its function is to illustrate rather than to condemn.

Princess Betsy and her coterie are clearly no more than targets for Tolstoj's invective against the moral shortcomings of a particular social

entity. Stiva's function is more broadly conceived. Through the railroad he is associated with the general concept of the social and he thus escapes, in some measure, the opprobrium heaped upon the others even though his conduct is not, in the objective sense, far different from theirs. Turning to the children, it would seem that in their game of "Railroad" they become familiar with the pressure of the social. As they mature, they gradually leave the spontaneous, self-centered, and natural world of childhood and begin to contend with the inevitable constraints of the social. Thus, although the naturalness and spontaneity of the children is highly attractive, it is also not destined to be fully developed by the adult. Anna, who attempts to indulge the individual, spontaneous, and natural force within her, perishes beneath the train.

Several particular qualities of the "social" are suggested by the use of the railroad as its sign. First, the social involves rules and orderliness as suggested by the tracks along which the train must run and in the mechanical (that is, also, logical) nature of the object. Second, the social is an inevitable part of life. In the children's game passengers are not allowed to sit on top of the train. All must remain inside because it is too dangerous for the passengers to take a position outside the train. If they attempt to ride on top of the train (that is, to be above society) they will surely end by being crushed beneath it, as, in fact, the fate of Anna demonstrates. It seems to be a case of acceptance of the social or death. Third, the social is a powerful force, as suggested by the earth-shaking strength of the engine and the great speed of the train. Fourth, it must be remembered that the social also has its attractive features. These are suggested by the warmth, comfort, and security inside the carriage on Anna's return journey to Petersburg in I, 29. These are especially emphasized by contrast with the cold and howling winds of the storm outside. Furthermore, the interior of the train is associated with the idyll of conventional happiness represented by the novel of English life which Anna reads in the carriage. Fifth, despite (or perhaps because of) its attractions, the social is also clearly shown to be an affront to the individual. This is suggested by the fact that in the children's game the passengers in fact want to leave the train, to be above it by riding on its top. Anna, too, experiences this sensation. She finds the interior of the train not only warm, but hot; not only secure, but stifling. Ultimately, in Anna's case at least, the train is the agent of the extinction of the individual: having left the train for good in response to the demands of the individual, she ends by being crushed beneath it.

The passage in which Anna's return journey from Moscow to Petersburg is described (I, 29–30) is the most extended appearance of the railroad in the novel and provides the clearest model of that conflict between the social and the individual with which the image of the railroad is at a deep level connected. Beyond the interior security of the carriage lies an exterior setting which is fraught with discomfort and danger. A winter storm is raging; its foremost characterisitcs are cold, snow, and a driving, howling wind. The natural (the exterior) is contrasted to the artificial (the interior of the train), and, it is important to note, the natural not in its benevolent aspect but wild, uncontrolled, and dangerous. This exterior setting surrounds the first open acknowledgment of the developing illicit passion between Vronskij and Anna. Thus, there is a pointed contrast between the conventional but somewhat tedious marital happiness presented in the English novel which Anna reads in the carriage and which is associated with the comfort and security of the train's interior and the illicit passion between Anna and Vronskij which develops in the context of the exhilarating danger of the storm and wind.

The wind is the most significant detail of the exterior setting. Immediately following Vronskij's statement of his love for Anna, the text continues: "At that moment the wind, as if it had mastered all obstacles, scattered the snow from the carriage roofs . . . The awfulness of the storm appeared still more beautiful to [Anna] now. He had said just what her soul desired but her reason dreaded." (I, 30). The passage is replete with paradoxical contrasts. The interior of the train is comfortable yet somehow repellent, the exterior is awful but attractive (as shown by Anna's resting her forehead against the cold glass of the carriage window), and these conflicting feelings are bound up with the clearly divided nature of Anna herself: what her soul desires, her reason dreads.

The passage does not suggest that Anna's passion for Vronskij is illicit because it is morally wrong (although there can be no doubt that Tolstoj believed such a passion to be morally wrong), but rather because it is carried on outside of and in defiance of the social. Anna is very quick to realize this as a fact (although not, perhaps, with all its attendant implications) when she tells Vronskij following the consummation of their passion that he is now all that she has (II, 11). She does not at this moment say that she has committed a moral wrong (although she will say this as the novel progresses). Rather, she portrays herself as having forsaken all else, retaining only Vronskij. She has severed her connection with her society, and, on the deep thematic level, she has rejected the claims of the social in favor of the gratification of her individual passion. Her eventual decline and death are clearly and proportionally related to her growing conviction that Vronskij, the single element of the social remaining to her, is tempted to abandon her. Anna's increasing jealousy and possessiveness toward Vronskij are not simply a function of madness. Rather, they signify a recognition of reality: the impossibility of life's continuance in conditions of complete isolation from the general context of the social.

In the scene of her return to Petersburg, Anna's passion is also associated with her often-mentioned characteristic of animation or fullness of life (*oživlennost'*) which had been described as being kept under control and whose presence is bespoken by such superficial characteristics as the recalcitrant curl which continually escapes her coiffure, her shining eyes masked by their heavy lids, and her peculiar, involuntary smile. It is suggested that Anna's suppression of this fullness of life is connected with the feeling of being stifled which she experiences in the railway carriage. Anna's egress from the train suggests a desire to liberate her suppressed sense of the fullness of life, thus explaining the attractiveness of the seemingly unpleasant exterior conditions. The discomfort and danger outside the train go unnoticed by Anna in her hunger for individuality, spontaneity, and unreasoning, natural, passionate action.

Apparently, then, the passage suggests that this highly attractive quality and desire must be, at least to some extent, sacrificed or controlled in order to remain within the train, that is, within the pale of the social, for its full release begins only when the train has been abandoned. The social appears as an insuperable obstacle to the full and gratifying manifestation of fullness of life which Anna desires. Her passion, like the "wind which mastered all obstacles," is the means of this gratification.

The railroad, then, seems to be an image which is fully capable of supporting the various interpretations which it has evoked. It is connected to Anna's passion and her death; it is bound up with the nature of the particular society in which she lived; but at the hub from which these interpretations diverge and by which they are organized is the railroad as the representation of the requirements and privileges of the social in the context of the thematic exploration of the conflict between the desires of the individual and the restrictions placed upon the gratification of those desires by the social. At this basic level *Anna Karenina* is concerned with the representation of a universal human dilemma which is primarily metaphysical and only secondarily moral in its nature. The human being, in the terms of the novel, must live perpetually in the space between the Charybdis of an inescapable (determined) fate as a social being, with its danger of the ignominious loss of individuality and dignity in the swirling whirlpool of social convention and respectability, and the Scylla of unrestrained gratification of the spontaneous ego, of freedom, and of exalted individual worth, with its attendant dangers, discomforts, and ultimate and inevitable disaster. Thus, Anna truly is, as she says again and again, both guilty and yet not to blame. She is the tragic victim of human nature which calls both for the unhindered expression of the individual and the antithetical acknowledgment of the ultimate dependence of the individual upon the social.

The strength of this interpretation of the railroad in *Anna Karenina* is that it allows for the harmonious coexistence of both the attractive and the unattractive characteristics with which the image is endowed in the novel and that it is capable of expressing in some detail that which it represents. As is so often the case with Tolstoj's major images (the sky in *War and Peace*, the black bag in *The Death of Ivan Il'ič*, the snowstorm in *Master and Man*, the races in *Anna Karenina* itself), here again the motif is almost allegorically suited to that which it represents and at the same time is capable of evoking a variety of related responses and intuitions arising from its vivid realization as an object of natural experience in the novel. Thus, despite the neatness and artificiality which seem to inform Tolstoj's major images when they are subjected to an analysis such as that attempted here, they retain the quality of true symbols, signposts on the writer's actual arduous way to the truth and

not mere reductive allegories of his journey. In 1853 Tolstoj wrote in his diary that "Reading a composition, and especially a purely literary one, the main interest is to be found in the character of the author as it expresses itself in the composition. Sometimes the author makes an open affectation of his view ... [but] the best compositions are those in which the author, as it were, attempts to conceal his personal view but at the same time remains always faithful to it wherever it does appear." Tolstoj was clearly an author who felt an obligation to express his "views" in his work, and in *Anna Karenina* he appears to have selected the superior mode described in the passage just cited. His view of the truth about the nature of the conflict between the individual as individual and the individual as social being emerges not in the direct address of the author to his readers but in the telling use of image and symbol and, preeminently, in the image of the railroad.

Source: Gary R. Jahn, "The Image of the Railroad in *Anna Karenina*," in *Slavic and East European Journal*, Vol. 25, No. 2, Summer 1981, pp. 1–10.

Prince Kropotkin

In the following excerpt, Kropotkin explains the moral problems posed in Anna Karenina *and notes that most Russians who read the book when it was first published would not have felt that Anna deserved to meet such a tragic end. Because of this, Kropotkin notes, the novel first provoked an "unfavorable impression."*

... Of all the Tolstóy's novels, *Anna Karénina* is the one which has been the most widely read in all languages. As a work of art it is a master-piece. From the very first appearance of the heroine, you feel that this woman must bring with her a drama; from the very outset her tragical end is as inevitable as it is in a drama of Shakespeare. In that sense the novel is true to life throughout. It is a corner of real life that we have before us. As a rule, Tolstóy is not at his best in picturing women—with the exception of very young girls—and I don't think that Anna Karénina herself is as deep, as psychologiclly complete, and as living a creation as she might have been; but the more ordinary woman, Dolly, is simply teeming with life. As to the various scenes of the novel—the ball scenes, the races of the officers, the inner family life of Dolly, the country scenes on Lévin's estate, the death of his brother, and so on—all these are depicted

> AT ANY RATE, IF THE STORY OF ANNA
> KARÉNINA HAD TO END IN TRAGEDY, IT WAS NOT IN
> THE LEAST IN CONSEQUENCE OF AN ACT OF SUPREME
> JUSTICE. AS ALWAYS, THE HONEST ARTISTIC GENIUS
> OF TOLSTÓY HAD ITSELF INDICATED ANOTHER
> CAUSE—THE REAL ONE. IT WAS THE INCONSISTENCY
> OF VRÓNSKIY AND KARÉNINA."

in such a way that for its artistic qualities *Anna Karénina* stands foremost even amongst the many beautiful things Tolstóy has written.

And yet, notwithstanding all that, the novel produced in Russia a decidedly unfavourable impression, which brought to Tolstóy congratulations from the reactionary camp and a very cool reception from the advanced portion of society. The fact is, that the question of marriage and of an eventual separation between husband and wife had been most earnestly debated in Russia by the best men and women, both in literature and in life. It is self-evident that such indifferent levity towards marriage as is continually unveiled before the Courts in "Society" divorce cases was absolutely and unconditionally condemned; and that any form of deceit, such as makes the subject of countless French novels and dramas, was ruled out of question in any honest discussion of the matter. But after the above levity and deceit had been severely branded, the rights of a new love, serious and deep, appearing after years of happy married life, had only been the more seriously analysed. Tchernyshévsky's novel, *What is to be done*, can be taken as the best expression of the opinions upon marriage which had become current amongst the better portion of the young generation. Once you are married, it was said, don't take lightly to love affairs, or so-called flirtation. Every fit of passion does not deserve the name of a new love; and what is sometimes described as love is in a very great number of cases nothing but temporary desire. Even if it were real love, before a real and deep love has grown up, there is in most cases a period when one has time to reflect upon the consequences that would follow

if the beginnings of his or her new sympathy should attain the depth of such a love. But, with all that, there are cases when a new love does come, and there are cases when such an event must happen [. . .] when, for instance, a girl has been married almost against her will, under the continued insistence of her lover, or when the two have married without properly understanding each other, or when one of the two has continued to progress in his or her development towards a higher ideal, while the other, after having worn for some time the mask of idealism, falls into the Philistine happiness of warmed slippers. In such cases separation not only becomes inevitable, but it often is to the interest of both. It would be much better for both to live through the sufferings which a separation would involve (honest natures are by such sufferings made better) than to spoil the entire subsequent existence of the one—in most cases, of both—and to face moreover the fatal results that living together under such circumstances would necessarily mean for the children. This was, at least, the conclusion to which both Russian literature and the best all-round portion of our society had come.

And now came Tolstóy with *Anna Karénina*, which bears the menacing biblical epigraph: "Vengeance is mine, and I will repay it," and in which the biblical revenge falls upon the unfortunate Karénina, who puts an end by suicide to her sufferings after her separation from her husband. Russian critics evidently could not accept Tolstóy's views. The case of Karénina was one of those where there could be no question of "vengeance." She was married as a young girl to an old and unattractive man. At that time she did not know exactly what she was doing, and nobody had explained it to her. She had never known love, and learned it for the first time when she saw Vrónskiy. Deceit, for her, was absolutely out of the question; and to keep up a merely conventional marriage would have been a sacrifice which would not have made her husband and child any happier. Separation, and a new life with Vrónskiy, who seriously loved her, was the only possible outcome. At any rate, if the story of Anna Karénina had to end in tragedy, it was not in the least in consequence of an act of supreme justice. As always, the honest artistic genius of Tolstóy had itself indicated another cause—the real one. It was the inconsistency of Vrónskiy and Karénina. After having separated from her husband and defied "public opinion"—that is, the opinion of women who, as Tolstóy shows it himself, were not honest enough to be allowed any voice in the matter—neither she nor Vrónskiy had the courage of breaking entirely with that society, the futility of which Tolstóy knows and describes so exquisitely. Instead of that, when Anna returned with Vrónskiy to St. Petersburg, her own and Vrónskiy's chief preoccupation was—How Betsey and other such women would receive her, if she made her appearance among them. And it was the opinion of the Betsies—surely not Superhuman Justice—which brought Karénina to suicide...

Source: Prince Kropotkin, "The Russian Public's Initial Reaction to *Anna Karenina*," in *Ideals and Realities in Russian Literature*, Alfred A. Knopf, 1915, pp. 88–150.

SOURCES

Alexandrov, Vladimir E., *Limits to Interpretation: The Meanings of "Anna Karenina,"* University of Wisconsin Press, 2004.

Arnold, Matthew, *Essays in Criticism: Second Series*, Adamant Media, 2001, pp. 253–99, originally published by Macmillan, 1913.

Caws, Peter, "Moral Certainty in Tolstoy," in *Philosophy and Literature*, Vol. 24, No. 1, 2000, pp. 49–66.

Howells, William Dean, *Selected Literary Criticism*, Indiana University Press, 1993.

Knowles, A. V., "Russian Views of *Anna Karenina*, 1875–1878," in the *Slavic and East European Journal*, Vol. 22, No. 3, 1978, pp. 301–12.

Leavis, F. R., *Anna Karenina and Other Essays*, Chatto & Windus, 1967.

Sansom, Dennis, "Tolstoy and the Moral Instructions of Death," in *Philosophy and Literature*, Vol. 28, No. 2, 2004, pp. 417–29.

Schefski, Harold K., "Tolstoy's Urban-Rural Continuum in *War and Peace* and *Anna Karenina*," in *South Atlantic Review*, Vol. 46, No. 1, 1981, pp. 27–41.

Seifrid, Thomas, "Gazing on Life's Page: Perspectival Vision in Tolstoy," in *PMLA*, Vol. 113, No. 3, 1998, pp. 436–48.

Tolstoy, Leo, *Anna Karenina*, translated by Richard Pevear and Larissa Volokhonsky, Viking, 2000.

Turner, C. J. G., "Psychology, Rhetoric and Morality in *Anna Karenina*: At the bottom of Whose Heart," in the *Slavic and East European Journal*, Vol. 39, No. 2, 1995, pp. 261–68.

Whitcomb, Curt, "Treacherous 'Charm' in *Anna Karenina*," in the *Slavic and East European Journal*, Vol. 39, No. 2, 1995, pp. 214–26.

FURTHER READING

Orwin, Donna, ed., *Cambridge Companion to Tolstoy*, Cambridge University Press, 2002.

> Tolstoy remains one the most important writers of the nineteenth-century and his work has had an innovative influence on the history of the novel as a literary form. The essays in this collection focus on key dimensions of Tolstoy's life and writing, exploring such issues as his relationship to popular writing, his questioning of gender and sexual politics, and his personal aesthetics.

———, *Tolstoy's Art and Thought, 1847–1880*, Princeton University Press, 1993.

> This insightful study, covering the creative period of Tolstoy's two great novels, discusses *Anna Karenina* and *War and Peace* as a balance of his deeply held beliefs and his changing political and spiritual understanding of human nature.

Wasiolek, Edward, *Tolstoy's Major Fiction*, University of Chicago Press, 1978.

> This is one of the best books on Tolstoy in recent decades in that it offers a relatively straightforward but nonetheless convincing and elegantly argued reading of his novels.

Wilson, A. N., *Tolstoy: A Biography*, W. W. Norton, 2001.

> Considered a landmark biography, this book captures the complexities of Tolstoy's life as a writer, an aristocrat, and as a visionary influence. Wilson sweeps away the long-held belief that Tolstoy's writing provides an exact mirror of his life. However, the biographer suggests that Tolstoy's art speaks very profoundly to his relationship with God, with women, and with Russia.

Cannery Row

JOHN STEINBECK

1945

Cannery Row, which was published in 1945, is composed of portraits of the title location's inhabitants. It evokes the fish canning district in Monterey, California, in the early 1940s. Although the novel takes place during World War II, the only hint of war is the brief mention of soldiers stationed nearby and a snapshot of two soldiers and their dates. This omission is perhaps explained by the fact that Steinbeck wrote *Cannery Row* in response to his dissatisfaction upon his return from the battlefields as a newspaper reporter.

The characters in *Cannery Row* are often troubled, and they experience a great deal of conflict, misery, violence, pain, and grief. Nevertheless, they experience a social harmony in the vicissitudes and torments of life at peace amid the horrors of a distant war. This gave the novel vitality when it appeared. Steinbeck did not write another protest novel like *The Grapes of Wrath*. Instead, he wrote a book that portrayed a spirit of peace and community. That spirit still can be felt in the book and is enhanced by the fact that the novel is now a period piece that nevertheless remains true to characteristics that are essentially and timelessly human.

Cannery Row is a series of thirty-two free-standing chapters (vignettes) that are connected yet independent, which is a point that Steinbeck also makes about nature in the novel. In the prologue, Steinbeck asks how he can convey

John Steinbeck (AP Images)

what Cannery Row is like. He answers using an analogy drawn from the way marine animals are collected, a fitting one since Doc makes his living gathering marine creatures. "When you collect marine animals, there are certain flat worms so delicate," Steinbeck explains "that they are almost impossible to capture whole, for they break and tatter under the touch. You must let them ooze and crawl of their will onto a knife blade and then lift them gently into your bottle of sea water. And perhaps that might be," Steinbeck suggests, "the way to write this book—to open the page and let the stories crawl in by themselves."

A recent edition of *Cannery Row* appears in *Steinbeck: Novels 1942–1952*, which was published in 2001.

AUTHOR BIOGRAPHY

John Steinbeck was born February 27, 1902, in Salinas, California, the third of four children, and the only boy. His father, John Steinbeck, Sr., managed a flour mill and was Monterey County Treasurer. His mother, Olive Hamilton Steinbeck, had been a schoolteacher before she married. The family lived a cultured, comfortable life in a large Victorian house and passed summers in their Pacific Grove cottage or at Steinbeck's uncle's ranch.

While in high school, Steinbeck almost died of pleural pneumonia. While convalescing, he began writing stories. After graduation, Steinbeck enrolled at Stanford University as an English major but left without a degree in 1925, having taken several leaves in order to work as a mountain surveyor in Big Sur, California, and as a carpenter's apprentice in a sugar mill, where he also supervised day laborers and performed chemical tests on sugar beets.

In 1926, while in New York City, Steinbeck worked on the construction crew building Madison Square Garden and was a reporter for the *New York American*. Failing to sell his fiction, Steinbeck returned to California. In 1929, his novel *Cup of Gold* was published. In 1930, Steinbeck married Carol Henning, the first of his three wives. Also that year, he met Edward F. Ricketts, the marine biologist and the owner of the Pacific Biological Laboratory who became the model for Doc (the protagonist of 1945's *Cannery Row*). *Tortilla Flat*, published in 1935, brought Steinbeck fame. He published *Of Mice and Men* in 1937 and *The Grapes of Wrath* in 1939. Bestsellers, both became highly successful movies. *The Grapes of Wrath* won the Pulitzer Prize in 1940 and was also banned by many libraries and condemned in the U.S. Congress by Oklahoma representative Lyle Borden for its denunciation of the inequities of capitalism.

In 1940, Steinbeck went on a marine collecting expedition with Ricketts in the Gulf of California. Later that year, he went to Mexico with his first wife to work on the screenplay for *The Forgotten Village*. Steinbeck also met President Franklin D. Roosevelt and discussed propaganda initiatives against Nazi Germany. In 1941, Steinbeck separated from his first wife and began living with Gwyn Conger, a singer with whom he had begun an affair in 1939 and whom he then married in 1943. In 1942, on assignment for the Army Air Forces to write a book about training bomber crews, Steinbeck visited air bases throughout the United States. In 1943, Steinbeck became a war correspondent for the *New York Tribune*. He returned to New

York with battle fatigue and a burst ear drum. Also in 1943, Steinbeck wrote the story that served as the basis for the screenplay for Alfred Hitchcock's film *Lifeboat*. Although he did not win, Steinbeck was nominated for an Academy Award for best screenplay in 1944, the year he wrote *Cannery Row*.

In August of 1944, Steinbeck and Conger had a son, Thomas; two years later, in June 1946, they had another son whom they named John. In October, Steinbeck and Conger visited Sweden, Denmark, France, and Norway. In Norway, Steinbeck was awarded the King Haakon Liberty Cross. In 1947, Steinbeck wrote *The Pearl*, a tragic morality tale set in Bolivia about longing and greed. That year, he also traveled to the Soviet Union with the photographer Robert Capa. Their collaboration, *The Russian Journal*, was published in 1948. That same year, Conger filed for a divorce, and Ed Ricketts died. Distraught, Steinbeck nevertheless began work on two projects, the screenplay for the Elia Kazan/ Marlon Brando film, *Viva Zapata!*, and the novel *East of Eden*. In 1950, Steinbeck married Elaine Scott. In 1954, he published *Sweet Thursday*, the sequel to *Cannery Row*.

While Steinbeck continued to write novels, a travel book, and newspaper columns, he also undertook a number of "good-will" missions for the U.S. government throughout Western Europe and within the Soviet bloc. He wrote speeches for democratic presidential candidate Adlai Stevenson in 1960, traveled to Europe on behalf of President John F. Kennedy, and wrote parts of Lyndon Johnson's inaugural address. In 1962, he was awarded the Nobel Prize for Literature. Steinbeck, unlike many American writers, supported the Vietnam War. He traveled extensively in Vietnam, even going into battle alongside American forces, and reported back to President Johnson. On December 20, 1968, after a series of strokes and heart attacks, Steinbeck died at home in New York City. Six days later, his ashes were buried in a plot in the Garden of Memories Cemetery in Salinas, California.

PLOT SUMMARY

Prologue
Fishing boats return to Cannery Row at dawn. People arrive for work at the canneries. The narrator wonders how to present his story.

MEDIA ADAPTATIONS

- In 1982, David S. Ward directed a film version of *Cannery Row* that combines *Cannery Row* and its sequel, *Sweet Thursday*. The film stars Nick Nolte as Doc and Debra Winger as Suzy. It was produced by Chai Productions and distributed by MGM.

Chapter 1
Lee Chong rents a large storage shed to Mack and his friends to live in for five dollars a week. From their doorway, Mack and the boys can see across the way into Doc's windows. They want to do something nice for Doc.

Chapter 2
Steinbeck meditates on the value and the costs of worldly success.

Chapter 3
William, a former bouncer at Dora Flood's brothel, is unable to make friends with Mack and the boys. He stabs himself to death with an ice-pick, on a dare, after his confession that he felt like killing himself was ignored or mocked by Dora, by one of the prostitutes, and by the cook at the brothel.

Chapter 4
A mysterious Chinese man "disappeared among the piles and steel posts which support the piers" every evening and reappeared each dawn carrying a "wicker basket." The children, who usually taunt odd characters, are afraid of him. But one child, Andy, taunts him with a racial rhyme. As he does, he is gripped with a sense of lonely fear that causes him to see a vast, hallucinatory, and weird landscape.

Chapter 5
Doc's laboratory and living quarters are filled with preserved marine and animal specimens. There are prints on the wall and shelves of books. Doc knows the complexities of nature

and the spiritual and intellectual delights of art, culture, and scholarship. He is a teacher for the odd souls populating Cannery Row.

Chapter 6

Doc collects marine animals. Hazel, one of the men living at the Palace Flophouse, assists him. They gossip about Gay, who has moved into the Flophouse to get away from his wife, and about Henri, a painter who is building a boat that he lives in but never finishes. Doc explains that Henri likes boats but does not like sailing.

Chapter 7

Mack and the boys turn the Flophouse into a home, crowding it with discarded furniture and a great chrome-decorated cookstove. Eddie, who sometimes works as a bartender, brings leftover liquor back to the Flophouse. Mack and the boys decide to throw a party for Doc and to collect hundreds of frogs for him.

Chapter 8

Mr. and Mrs. Sam Malloy live in the vacant lot between Lee Chong's store and the Flophouse, in a discarded boiler from a local cannery factory. They quarrel when she wants to hang curtains and he cannot understand why since "we got no windows." She complains men do not understand women; he rubs her back until she falls asleep.

Chapter 9

Mack offers to gather frogs for Doc at a nickel a frog. Doc agrees, but will not lend Mack his car. Doc must drive to La Jolla to collect octopi. Mack thinks Lee Chong will let them use his truck. Doc gives Mack a note for Red Williams at the gas station authorizing Red to fill their tank with ten gallons. Lee Chong's truck is broken but Gay fixes it.

Chapter 10

The boy, Frankie, has been expelled from school. He hangs around the edges of Doc's laboratory. After three weeks, he approaches Doc's worktable. He tells Doc he is beaten at home by the men who come to see his mother, or they give him a nickel and send him away. Doc has him wash his filthy hands, clips and cleans his lice-infested hair, and shows Frankie how to sort fish specimens by size, although the task is daunting for him. When Doc has guests, Frankie accidentally spills a tray full of beer on one. He

retreats to the cellar, curls up in a box of excelsior, and whimpers. Doc follows him, hears his whimpers, and goes back upstairs because "there wasn't a thing in the world he could do."

Chapter 11

Gay fixes Lee Chong's Model T, and the men set out to catch frogs. Mack tries to get Red Williams to put five instead of ten gallons in the tank and give him change in cash. Red, warned of Mack's tricks by Doc, refuses.

The Model T will not take hills in first gear. But it can, turned backwards, in reverse. The needle valve of the carburetor breaks; Gay takes it to get it fixed. The car he hitches in breaks down. Gay fixes it. The grateful owner takes him to a bar. After a drunken brawl, Gay is arrested and put in the county jail, a comfortable place, where he stays for six months. When Gay does not return, Eddie hikes over to a construction site to see if he can find a Model T to steal a carburetor needle from.

Chapter 12

Monterey can boast about its concern for the honor of its writers. After embalming the body of the American humorist Josh Billings, the embalmer tossed the organs into the bay. A boy and his dog found the liver and intestines and would have used them for fishing bait had not an alert man passing noticed they were dragging what looked like a man's liver. The embalmer was made to collect and clean the parts, put them in a leaden box, and bury them inside the coffin with the body.

Chapter 13

Eddie returns before dawn with a carburetor. In the morning, the boys set out and reach a sandy edge of the Carmel River. They decide to wait till nightfall to catch frogs. They nap. Hazel cooks a rooster they have run over. The owner of the land approaches with his gun and dog. He orders them off his property. Mack ingratiates himself, addressing the man as Captain, by praising his pointer. The man agrees it is a fine dog but notes that Nola (the dog) is ill from an infected wound. Mack asks to look at Nola's wound, immediately makes friends with her, and when Mack suggests an Epsom salts compress, the Captain asks him to go home with him to tend to the dog. Mack tells the others to clean up the campsite.

Chapter 14

Early morning, Cannery Row hardly stirring, two soldiers and their girls walk tired and happy through the streets. The girls are wearing the boys' hats; the boys have their dates' hats on. They stop on the beach, drink some beer and the soldiers lay their heads in their girls' laps. A watchman comes to shoo them away, but one of the soldiers smiles at the watchman and tells him, colorfully, to get lost, and the watchman does.

Chapter 15

Mack treats the dog. The Captain offers him one of her litter and goes frog-catching with the boys in his own pond. They catch hundreds of frogs. Since the Captain's wife is away, they get drunk together, and the boys leave for home glad they are doing something nice for Doc.

Chapter 16

Dora and the prostitutes take care of the sick during an outbreak of influenza and at a time when the brothel is exceptionally busy because a new regiment of soldiers has arrived at the nearby army base. The canneries are employing as many workers as possible because of a bountiful sardine catch, which also helps to keep the brothel busy.

Chapter 17

Even when he sees the curtains drawn and hears Gregorian chant being played on the phonograph, and knows Doc has a woman with him, Mack is sensitive to Doc's loneliness. Doc drives to La Jolla for octopi. Mack and the boys are collecting frogs. Henri, from Red Williams's gas station, watches a flagpole skater who has installed himself atop the flagpole at Hollman's Department Store. Doc stops for food and picks up a hitchhiker. He stops for a beer and asks the hitchhiker if he wants one. When the hitchhiker lectures Doc about drinking and driving, Doc orders him out of the car. Curious to see what it tastes like, Doc orders a beer milk shake, telling the waitress he is sick and drinks it on his doctor's orders, having discovered that people prefer lies to the truth.

Chapter 18

Collecting octopi, Doc discovers a drowned girl underwater. Shaken by the sight, he tells a passing stranger. The stranger says he will get a bounty when he reports it. Doc leaves in disgust, telling the stranger to make the police report and take the bounty himself.

Chapter 19

Dr. Merrivale shoots an air gun at the flagpole skater. Richard Frost cannot figure out how the flagpole skater goes to the toilet. Driven from his bed by curiosity one night, he calls out the question to the skater on his perch and learns, as he tells his wife when he gets home and slips back into bed, that "he's got a can up there."

Chapter 20

Mack and the boys return the truck to Lee Chong and make a deal to trade frogs for groceries. The Flophouse gang decide to have the party for Doc at Doc's lab because Doc has a record player and because they can surprise him when he returns. They decorate Doc's place and bring over the crate of frogs. They begin the party without Doc, and it ends after one in the morning, but before Doc's return. The party turns into a melee. The case of frogs is broken open and all the frogs escape. The place is a mess and the damage is considerable.

Chapter 21

In the morning Doc returns, exhausted. The lab is a shambles; animals are in panic; records, phonograph, glass cases, and instruments are broken. Mack, waiting for Doc, admits the mess is his making. Doc punches him in the jaw twice and calls on him to fight; Mack says he had "it coming." Once his anger is spent, Doc calmly asks Mack to tell him what happened. Mack explains that they planned a surprise party for him, thinking he would be back in time for it, but that it "got out of hand." Mack tells Doc he is sorry and adds that saying that "don't do no good," and that he has been "sorry all my life," and that whenever he tries to do something good it turns out badly. He promises Doc that he and the boys will pay for the damage and clean up the place. Doc tells him that even though he means to pay, he never will and that he [Doc] needs to clean up by himself. Mack leaves. Doc has forgiven him.

Chapter 22

Henri lives in his boat, often with a female companion. His girlfriends keep moving out because the cabin is too small. One night, alone, feeling sorry for himself, Henri sees a handsome young man and a beautiful boy sitting across from him.

The man cuts the baby's throat with a straight razor. Henri goes over to Doc's place in fright, hoping Doc will go back to the boat with him to see if he sees what Henri saw. Doc declines, explaining it will not help Henri whether Doc sees the apparition or not. As they talk, a woman visitor appears. She has a date with Doc. Doc tells Henri to tell her his story. She goes home with Henri and stays for five months until she moves out, like the others, because of the cramped quarters.

Chapter 23

After the party at the lab, "gloom settled over the Palace Flophouse." Mack takes to his bed. The boys are ostracized by everyone in Cannery Row. Only the dog, Darling, seems to keep her cheer. The rest of the town also suffers. The Malloys fight. A group of women effect the temporary closing of Dora's brothel. Doc has to borrow money to pay for the damages to the lab. One of the townsmen loses his legs when he falls asleep on the railroad tracks and a train runs over him. The town loses convention business because the brothel is closed. Some boats get free of their moorings and are tossed, broken, onto the beach.

The gloom begins to lift when Darling gets sick. Hazel and Jones go to see if Doc can help. He protests he is not a veterinarian, but he looks at Darling and prescribes a course of treatment. Following his instructions, the boys take the dog through her illness and restore her to health. With her return to health, everything in Cannery Row begins to get better. The brothel is allowed to reopen. Lee Chong resumes friendly relations with the boys.

Mack visits Dora and tells her how the party was actually a result of good intentions, no matter how badly it turned out, and asks her what he can do for Doc. Her answer—"You gave him a party he didn't get to. Why don't you give him a party he does get to"—greatly impresses Mack and sets the direction for the final section of the book.

Doc and Richard Frost drink beer on the Fourth of July, waiting for the parade to come by. Across the way, they see the Flophouse guys sitting outside their door. Doc compares them to people driven by ambition, and considers the boys to be truly the wise men of the age in their detachment.

Chapter 24

Mary Talbot is rumored to be descended from witches. Sometimes she has alley cats to tea. She loves to give parties. Her husband, Tom, is a writer who lives on hope even as his stories are rejected by major magazines. Finally, he is overcome by despair at his failure. When Mary sees one of the cats in the yard tormenting a mouse, and screams, Tom kills the mouse and shoos the cat away. Through this divertissement he escapes his gloom. Mary says she understands how cats are, but she will have difficulty liking the predatory cat. The chapter ends with the suggestion that she is pregnant.

Chapter 25

Good cheer spreads throughout Cannery Row. The boys decide to give Doc another surprise party, but not to force it to happen. They decide, too, that they need an occasion for the party. Mack goes over to Doc's to find out when his birthday is. Not wanting to make him suspicious, he leads up to his question with talk about astrology and horoscopes. But Doc recognizes a ploy and suspects a hidden motive and says October 27 is his birthday when, in fact, it is December 18.

Chapter 26

Joey's father killed himself with rat poison after a year of unemployment. Willard taunts and teases him and challenges him to fight without being able to get a rise out of him or compromising Joey's dignity.

Chapter 27

Mack and the boys make preparations for the party. No one is formally invited; the news of the party just spreads through Cannery Row. Everybody prepares for it. The women at Dora's make Doc a silk patchwork quilt out of old lingerie. Mack and the boys decide to have the party at Doc's, but not if he does not show up. Doc overhears a drunk in a bar mention it. Realizing that everyone will bring liquor but no one will think of food, he buys food as well as wine and whiskey. As a gift, Mack and the boys trap tomcats for Doc, and keep them at the Flophouse. Although the cats are caged, they make Darling skittery.

Chapter 28

Frankie sees a clock in a jewelry store window and longs to give to Doc. He breaks the window at night and flees with the clock and is apprehended. Despite Doc's request that Frankie be paroled in his custody, Frankie is confined to a mental hospital.

Chapter 29

The afternoon of the party, Doc finishes his work, locks away valuable, breakable, or dangerous objects and animals, and takes a shower. Mack and the boys bathe and decide not to bring the cats over to the lab. The prostitutes dress in street frocks rather than in the elaborate gowns of their trade. Everyone waits for the time of the party to begin.

Chapter 30

The party is a ritual release of repressed energy in celebration of life's messiness; it is a great success, with eating, drinking, dancing, noise, and festive brawling. Even the police, called by a woman five blocks away because of the noise, stay to take part. The squad car is commandeered for a liquor run. At the center of the chapter, Doc reads a Sanskrit poem in translation about lost love.

Chapter 31

A gopher finds a perfect spot to make his home, far from gardens, so that there is no fear of traps. After burrowing a fine domicile beneath the earth, the gopher waits for a female companion. When none arrives and the gopher grows lonely, he seeks a mate at another gopher hole only to be attacked by the male gopher who lives in it. The injured gopher returns to his home, but when no female companion appears, he moves "to a dahlia garden where they put out traps every night."

Chapter 32

Doc is in a melancholy mood. Amid his caged specimens of rats and rattlesnakes, he eats, listens to Gregorian chant, and looks at the poem he read at the party, reciting lines that celebrate the illumination brought to the poet by his past, now lost, experiences.

CHARACTERS

Horace Abbeville

Horace Abbeville is a minor character who deeds over a building to Lee Chong in order to pay off a cash debt. Lee Chong allows Mack and the boys to live in it. They call it the Palace Flophouse and Grill.

Alfred

Alfred is the watchman and bouncer at Dora Flood's brothel, the Bear Flag Restaurant.

Andy

Andy is a boy who teases the mysterious Old Chinaman, and as he chants his racially disparaging rhyme, he experiences a frightening hallucination.

Captain

This is what Mack calls the man who comes to shoo Mack and his friends off his land when they are camping out waiting to catch frogs. The man is won over when Mack takes care of his ailing dog. He lets them catch frogs in his pond, and, since his wife is away, the house is a mess and he and the boys get drunk.

Mr. Carriaga

Carriaga appears in an anecdote about an actual writer, the American humorist Josh Billings. He discovers that, after Billings's body was embalmed, the embalmer threw Billings's organs into the bay.

Kitty Casini

Kitty Casini is a cat that Mary Talbot has befriended. Mary is disturbed when she sees the cat tormenting a mouse.

Lee Chong

Lee Chong is a Chinese grocer who owns the general store. He is a shrewd but honorable businessman, hard-nosed on the one hand, yet good-hearted and even generous on the other.

Darling

Darling is a dog that Mack and the boys adopt as a puppy and care for. She is loved by all of them. Darling serves, in the plot, to bring Mack and the boys back into the community of Cannery Row after the disastrous party they throw at Doc's.

Doc

Doc is the hero and central figure of *Cannery Row*. There is an air of integrity, melancholy wisdom, and stoicism about him. He runs a biological laboratory and collects marine specimens that he sells to experimental laboratories. He is a popular and loved figure, yet he is still lonely. He respects the boundaries between individuals but also is attentive to all human need. Despite his title of "Doc," he is not a physician. Nevertheless, when necessary, he attends to human patients and to sick animals.

Eddie

Eddie sometimes lives at the Flophouse. He works as a replacement bartender and keeps jugs behind the bar and fills them with a mix of leftover drinks to bring back to the Flophouse.

Eric

Eric is a barber, a friend of Henri the painter. He gives Doc a rowing machine as a birthday present.

Flagpole Skater

As an advertising ploy, this man skates on a platform built atop a flagpole outside Hollman's Department Store.

Eva Flanegan

Eva Flanegan is one of the prostitutes at Dora Flood's. She attends church and tends to drink. When William, Dora's bouncer, tells her he feels like killing himself, her response is to yell at him and berate him.

Dora Flood

Dora Flood runs the brothel on Cannery Row. She is a tough and shrewd businesswoman but also a good boss and an active and willing participant in the community. This is illustrated best by Dora having the women who work for her sit by the bedsides of the sick during an influenza epidemic, but it is also illustrated by the amount of her charitable contributions—necessarily large payoffs because her business is illegal.

Frankie

Frankie is a troubled boy who does not attend school. His mother is sexually promiscuous, perhaps even an independent prostitute. The men who visit her either hit the boy or give him a nickel to leave. Frankie is drawn to Doc and hangs around his lab trying to be helpful. He steals a clock to give to Doc but is caught and sent to an asylum.

Richard Frost

Richard Frost appears briefly as a drinking companion with whom Doc bets that Mack and the boys will not even glance at the Fourth of July parade as it passes.

Gay

Gay moves into the Flophouse because of difficulties with his wife. He beats her and she hits him while he is asleep. He is an excellent mechanic. He spends most of the time in the county jail for having committed drunken mischief.

The Greek

He is the cook at the brothel. When William tells him he feels like killing himself, the Greek does not think he really means it and hands him the ice pick with which, to the Greek's troubled astonishment, William stabs himself.

Hazel

Hazel is a man. He was the last of seven children and his overburdened mother did not discover his gender until after she had named him. He lives at the Palace Flophouse. He is a simple man who asks Doc questions because he likes being spoken to.

Henri

Henri is a painter, but he does not paint. He makes art out of chicken feathers or broken nutshells or pins and pincushions. A Francophile, he is not French and his name is not really Henri. He lives in a boat he is always building and never completes. In a disturbed moment, he hallucinates a man slitting a child's throat. He is fascinated by the flagpole skater.

The Hitchhiker

When Doc stops for a beer, the hitchhiker to whom he is giving a lift lectures him about the dangers of drinking and driving. Doc orders him out of the car.

Hughie

He lives at the Palace Flophouse.

Mr. Jacobs

He owns the jewelry store from which Frankie steals the clock to give to Doc.

Joey

Joey is a gentle boy. His father committed suicide and Willard teases him about it.

Jones
He lives at the Palace Flophouse.

Mack
Mack is one of the principle characters of the novel. He is a loser in terms of social success and his projects often go terribly wrong. Still, he is a good-hearted, generous man, rough but tender. He lives in the Flophouse and is paterfamilias to the other men living there.

Phylis Mae
She is one of the prostitutes at Dora's brothel.

Sam Malloy
Malloy lives in an old, discarded boiler on a vacant lot across from the Flophouse. He rents the hollow pipes in the vacant lot to hobos as places to sleep.

Mrs. Sam Malloy
Mrs. Malloy quarrels with her husband when he is insensitive to her desire to put curtains up in the windowless boiler.

McKinley Moran
Moran figures in a conversation about him between Mack and Hughie. He was a deep-sea diver, paid by the government to find buried liquor and at the same time paid by a bootlegger not to find the liquor.

Nola
Nola is the Captain's dog. Mack treats her tick wound. She is Darling's mother

An Old Chinaman
He is the mysterious figure Andy taunts. He collects things in the bay at night. One of the soles of his shoes is loose and flops as he walks.

Kitty Randolph
Kitty Randolph is a cat that Mary Talbot has befriended

Mr. Randolph
Mr. Randolph is on the board of directors of one of the canning companies. He decided to discard the old boiler in which the Malloys live.

Mr. Ryan
Ryan appears in the Josh Billings anecdote as the man Carriaga speaks to about Billings's death.

Mary Talbot
Mary is Tom's wife. She tries to keep gloom away from him, loves parties, is rumored to be the descendant of witches, and has tea parties for the neighborhood cats.

Tom Talbot
Talbot is a discouraged writer living in Cannery Row. His manuscripts come back to him with rejection notes and he is often behind in paying his bills.

Willard
Willard is a cruel boy with a streak of bully in him. He teases Joey about Joey's father, who has committed suicide.

William
William is dead at the time of the narration of *Cannery Row*. He had been the bouncer/watchman at Dora's but grew depressed because of his inability to make friends with Mack and the boys. William kills himself after complaining that he wanted to be friends and no one he told took what he said seriously.

Red Williams
Williams owns a gas station in Cannery Row.

THEMES

Detachment
Although never indifferent to events or individuals, Doc has the kind of quietness about him that suggests detachment. While concerned about the welfare of others, whether the boy Frankie, the painter Henri, or the dog Darling, he also maintains a distance from others. Before treating Darling, Doc protests that he is not a vet. But once he examines the dog, he gives as good treatment as a veterinarian would. When Henri comes to him overcome by fright after his murderous hallucination, Doc keeps his distance and helps Henri by sacrificing his own pleasure for Henri's. Doc does not welcome Frankie when the boy starts to hang around his laboratory but waits until the boy has become comfortable enough to come close to him. When Frankie retreats to the cellar and remains there whimpering, Doc does not go near and comfort or support him. Rather, his attitude is reflected in the narrator's remark that "There wasn't a thing in

TOPICS FOR FURTHER STUDY

- Doc follows Frankie to the cellar in chapter 10, after the boy has accidentally spilled beer on one of the guests. Doc listens to him crying but then goes back upstairs. The narrator writes: "There wasn't a thing in the world he could do." In an essay of at least 500 words, explain why you agree or disagree with the narrator's conclusion.

- Doc makes his living by supplying animals to testing laboratories. This once-common practice has since been criticized as inhumane by many advocates of animal rights. After careful research, present a twenty-minute report to your class examining the issue of animal experimentation, its current extent, and the arguments for or against it. In cases where experimentation on animals has stopped, discuss what has replaced it and the effectiveness of the newer procedures.

- In chapter 20, the narrator reports that Lee Chong sold "felt pennants commemorating 'Fighting Bob.'" Fighting Bob refers to Robert LaFollette, Sr. (1855–1925). Using the library and the Internet for your research, prepare a fifteen-minute presentation discussing who Robert LaFollette was, what he did, and why he was important. Explain why he is mentioned in *Cannery Row*.

- Doc listens to music throughout the novel. He is particularly fond of Gregorian chant, the music of Beethoven (he listens to the *Moonlight Sonata* and to the *Great Fugue*, commonly called by its German name, the *Grosse Fuge*), and of Maurice Ravel (he listens to the "Pavane for a Dead Princess" and to *Daphnis and Chloe*). After listening to these pieces of music yourself, prepare a lecture for your class and describe how these musical works illuminate or reflect Doc's character.

- Choose a chapter from *Cannery Row* and rewrite it so that it is narrated by Dora Flood.

the world he could do," reflecting the idea that fundamentally each person is alone, even when in need of another. When he cannot save Frankie from incarceration after Frankie has stolen a clock, Doc is moved, but shows it only by getting back to his work. The same idea of detachment is evident in Mack's attitude regarding the second attempt at giving Doc a party. Overeager the first time, Mack comes to realize that he cannot force the event but must let it happen on its own. Similarly, the Flophouse boys are shown as admirable because they remain outside the excitement of the July Fourth parade. A particularly touching example of detachment is presented in the chapter concerning Joey and Willard, as Joey rebuffs Willard's bullying without responding to it. The flagpole skater represents an austere version of isolation and detachment.

Interconnectedness of All Life in Nature

Cannery Row itself, although named for the sardine canning industry located there, takes its identity not from that industry but from the particular ecology of the region, from the interconnected relationships within and between nature and culture. The natural resources of the region determine the industrial culture and that industrial culture affects the social culture. As a marine biologist, Doc depends on the natural environment as much as the canneries do. Dora and Lee Chong, too, both cater to the natural requirement for food and sexual release, respectively. In the first chapter, the narrator draws a connection between marine life and human life when he reveals his story-telling strategy. He wants his stories to "crawl" into his book "by themselves" the way "You must let" marine life "ooze and crawl ... onto a knife blade and then lift them gently into your bottle of sea water." In chapter 21, Steinbeck first describes the behavior and attitudes of the animals in Doc's lab and immediately afterward describes the behavior of the people on Cannery Row. Philosophically, the narrator repeatedly draws a distinction between denatured people, people who sacrifice their natural disposition for the sake of worldly success and become ill, and people, like Mack and the boys, who remain loyal to their natures, even when the price is the lack of worldly success. Mack, for example, senses Doc's loneliness. After Mack's unsuccessful party for Doc, the whole town falls into gloom. Even Darling's health and the health of the town are linked.

Loneliness

A sense of fundamental loneliness or individual isolation runs through *Cannery Row*. Gay would rather be in jail than at home with his wife. Mrs. Malloy feels isolated in her sensibility because she is a woman. Her husband, although a good husband who comforts her, is alone in his emotional separation from her, and his goodness appears more as a result of sympathetic duty rather than real connection. The Captain wishes he were not married. Mack lives with a sense of his inability to connect with others, whether his lost wife or Doc. The prostitutes embody loneliness and Dora has made a virtue of it in her role as a Madam. William, the brothel watchman who committed suicide, is an emblem of lonely isolation. Doc, connected as he is to nature and the life of the town, is a deeply isolated man. He lives in a flow of ever-passing experience.

Love in Varied Form

Except for Frankie's overt declaration of hopeless love for Doc, the theme of love is implicit although pervasive. There are varieties of love. With regard to the prostitutes, love appears as lust. In several situations, for Sam Malloy, for example, love appears as domestic duty. In Doc and Mack, it is shown to be a generosity of the spirit. In the Sanskrit poem Doc reads, it appears as a nebulous sense of something lost.

Respectability versus Nonconformity

Steinbeck overtly criticizes the conventions of respectability by the nature of his main characters—Doc, a loner, Mack, a loser, and Dora, a Madam. Most of the secondary characters, too—characters the reader is meant to like, whether the prostitutes, Mack's companions, Lee Chong, Henri, or the Malloys—are marginal to society and live in unconventional ways. Steinbeck also states that the qualities that are valued, like understanding, generosity, gentleness, openness, and kindness, are associated with failure. The characteristics that are associated with success are those generally held in lower esteem: "sharpness, greed, acquisitiveness, meanness, egoism, and self-interest."

studying, just as Doc collects specimens and injects them with several colored fluids so that their characteristics will be highlighted and the specimens can be studied. The narrator establishes himself in the first chapter not so much as a man who makes up stories using his imagination but as a man who gathers them from the world around him.

Stereotypes

Naturalist rather than psychologist, the narrator draws characters as types rather than as individuals, and relationships as typical rather than as specific. Lee Chong is the familiar Chinese merchant, considered inscrutable and shrewd. Dora is the very portrait of a Madam with her mix of a hard exterior and a tender inside. Mr. Malloy and the Captain are stock characters, henpecked husbands. Mack is a prototypical hobo. Henri is a standard caricature of an unsuccessful artist. And Doc is an exemplary man of the first half of the twentieth century, strong, silent, self-sufficient, sensitive, in touch with nature, and yet lonely.

Vignettes

Cannery Row, a novel of approximately 130 pages, is divided into 32 chapters. Although there is a thread connecting the chapters, sometimes because of an ongoing story being told and sometimes because the events or persons described are part of the ambience of Cannery Row, each chapter is a vignette, a free-standing portrait of one or another aspect of life or nature. Even episodes in the larger story—Mack and the boys going frogging (frog hunting), or the story of Frankie—can stand alone. Chapters like those devoted to the Talbots, to the two soldiers and their girls, to the gopher, or to Josh Billings, might be removed from the book without a reader ever suspecting their absence despite the fact that their presence enriches the totality of the narrative.

STYLE

Narrator as Naturalist

Not only is the force of Nature a theme of *Cannery Row*, and not only is Doc a naturalist, but the narrator of the novel is also presented as if he were a naturalist. His characters are presented as specimens that he has collected and is

HISTORICAL CONTEXT

Flagpole Sitting

Flagpole sitting, the practice of sitting on a small platform set upon the top of a pole for as long as possible, was a fad that reached its peak in the 1920s. Although an apparently frivolous activity, it resembles the discipline some religious

COMPARE
&
CONTRAST

- **1940s:** Animals are regularly used in laboratories to develop and test medicines and cosmetics. The practice goes largely unchallenged.

  Today: The use of animals in laboratories continues, although it has become somewhat less common due to social views. Animal advocacy groups regularly protest the practice and lobby to have animal testing outlawed.

- **1940s:** Monterey is one of the major centers of fish canning.

  Today: After the fishing industry collapsed in the 1950s, Monterey's Cannery Row, a street located on the waterfront, became a tourist center. It currently attracts fishermen, scuba divers, and visitors to the Monterey Bay Aquarium. Literary tourists, people drawn to Cannery Row because of Steinbeck's novel, also visit frequently.

- **1940s:** The United States recovers from the Great Depression because of the boost given to the economy (brought on by increased production in the industrial-military complex) by World War II.

  Today: The wars in Iraq and Afghanistan are draining resources from the American economy (brought on by increased military spending) and the country's infrastructure and social services suffer because of it.

hermits imposed upon themselves when they sat in isolation upon tall columns. The most famous of these is hermits St. Simeon, who sat for thirty-six years upon a column in Turkey during the first part of the fifth century C.E. Flagpole skating is a whacky variation of flagpole sitting.

The Great Depression

The exact time in which *Cannery Row* takes place is not given, but the story seems to be occurring just as the Great Depression is ending and World War II is beginning, so one can pinpoint the era as early 1940s. While the influence of the war is hardly visible in the novel, the culture of the depression is obvious. People are poor and live in makeshift dwellings. The Great Depression started at the end of 1929 when the stock market crashed. It lasted until the beginning of World War II. There was massive unemployment; people lost their homes, and itinerant poor traveled throughout the United States on railroad boxcars and lived in hobo encampments.

Taoism

Unlike the 1960s, which saw an outbreak of interest in Asian culture, Zen Buddhism, and Taoism, in 1944, when Steinbeck was writing *Cannery Row*, Taoism was quite arcane. Taoism is a Chinese philosophy of non-attachment to the things of the world. It teaches the cultivation of emptiness and the belief that any way that can be called *the* way is not the way. Its defining text is called the Tao Te Jing or the Way of Life. Its author is believed to be the Chinese sage, Lao Tse, born around 604 B.C.E.

World War II

Although World War II is not mentioned in *Cannery Row*, its presence haunts the book by its absence, for at the time of the novel's composition, not just the United States but the entire world was mobilized and involved in strenuous battle. The United States, England, the Soviet Union, and their allies, fought against the Germans, the Japanese, and the Italians. *Cannery Row* presents a picture of a society that functions peacefully despite human weaknesses and conflicts. It presents a vision of the world as an organism composed by the balanced interaction of interdependent parts, a vision distinctly in contrast with the nature of war in which part is set against part as if they were not mutually dependent upon each other.

Monterey Canning Company, the old warehouse for the fish cannery, now serves as a landmark in Monterey, California. It was made famous by John Steinbeck's book Cannery Row *(© Carl & Ann Purcell / Corbis)*

CRITICAL OVERVIEW

Cannery Row puzzled critics when it was first published, particularly because of the circumstances of the world around it. It was written and published as World War II raged, but gave hardly a word to the war. Peter Lisca traces first responses to the novel in *The Wide World of John Steinbeck*. Lisca reports that F. O. Mathiessen, reviewing the novel in the *New York Times*, declared that "it's a puzzler why Steinbeck should have wanted to write or publish such a book at this point in his career." Lisca also states that Edmund Wilson, writing in the *New Yorker*, said that among Steinbeck's works, it was the one he "most enjoyed reading." Nevertheless, Wilson also reportedly found it "sentimental" and simple-minded in its "philosophy." Lisca further relates that the critic Orville Prescott declared that, with *Cannery Row*, Steinbeck "did not just write a trivial and seemingly meaningless and purposeless novel. He wrote with all his usual professional felicity of expression, a sentimental glorification of weakness of mind and degeneration of character."

Notably, the initially critical reception did not affect the novel's popularity, and later critics were far more accepting of the book. Indeed, in his 1986 book, *John Steinbeck's Fiction: The Aesthetics of the Road Taken*, John H. Timmerman focuses on the problems of civilization, consumerism, and nature in *Cannery Row*. Kevin Hearle, in a critique in *After The Grapes of Wrath: Essays on John Steinbeck*, suggests that despite "Steinbeck's formidable talent for describing actual places" *Cannery Row* is "profoundly concerned with the power of discourse—literary and non-literary—to shape our understanding of the world."

CRITICISM

Neil Heims

Heims is a writer and teacher living in Paris. In the following essay, Heims examines Steinbeck's depiction of women in Cannery Row.

WHAT DO I READ NEXT?

- Ernest Hemingway's 1952 novella, *The Old Man and the Sea*, like *Cannery Row*, is a story of a man isolated within and by his own powers, and of this man's relation to nature. Whereas Steinbeck contemplates the unity of all things, Hemingway explores the conflict and struggle he sees as being at the heart of survival.

- Steinbeck's 1939 novel about the Dust Bowl, *The Grapes of Wrath*, unlike *Cannery Row*, is one of the major social novels of the twentieth century. It also established Steinbeck as one of the greatest American writers of the twentieth century.

- The popular radio performer and author Garrison Keillor wrote *Lake Wobegon Days* (1985). Very much in the spirit of *Cannery Row*, the book weaves a number of vignettes into a portrait of a fictional town in Minnesota.

- Thornton Wilder's 1938 classic depiction of small-town America, *Our Town*, explores the organic connections between individuals and the interplay of life and death in human life.

- Elie Wiesel's memoir, *Night* (1958), relates events that were happening in the same time period as that in which *Cannery Row* takes place. *Night*, however, discusses Wiesel's experiences in the Auschwitz concentration camp, not in the more humane setting Steinbeck evokes. Nevertheless, the connection between individuals and their environment that Steinbeck seeks to explore in *Cannery Row* can also be found in Wiesel's book.

After giving a sense of the ambience and surface of the setting in *Cannery Row*—Steinbeck mentions its people, but only to identify them by type. They may be considered equally as "whores, pimps, gamblers, and sons of bitches," or as "saints and angels and martyrs and holy men."

> CANNERY ROW, AS STEINBECK PORTRAYS IT AND VALUES IT, IS A MAN'S WORLD."

In other words, he is asserting that it is nearly impossible and certainly mistaken to see people or to understand their actions from only one perspective. Nevertheless, in *Cannery Row*, one perspective is privileged over another, the perspective that celebrates the culture of men and dismisses or gently disparages the culture of women.

Although the prologue speaks of "the town men and women [who] scramble into their clothes and come running down to the Row to go to work," and of the "upper classes" (the "superintendents, accountants, [and] owners who disappear into offices"), neither the workers nor the bosses appear in the novel. *Cannery Row* is not about class differences. With its focus on a group of marginalized men and women, Steinbeck presents a story implicitly concerned with the tension between male and female perspectives on the condition of being alive and how to regard that condition. Cannery Row, as Steinbeck portrays it and values it, is a man's world. It is a world of men who live their lives separately from women, even those men who are married. For these men, women serve as a diversion, an object of longing, or a restraint on natural liveliness. Women are not depicted as socially subordinate to men but as temperamentally other. The Captain's wife is a politician. Dora Flood, the madam of the brothel, is a strong and shrewd businesswoman. Nevertheless, women are portrayed as being either an enhancement or a restraint to the men around them. Their existence, even Dora's, powerful and canny as she is, is contingent on male existence and male need. Male existence, on the other hand, even among the most marginal of the men, is absolute in and of itself. When men are needy, it is not a sign of their contingency but of their human condition.

Steinbeck's narrative stance is that of a scientific naturalist, not a psychologist. Fittingly, then, *Cannery Row* shows both men and women as types rather than as complex individuals immersed in, and influenced by, cultural and social forces. Doc is a prototypical combination of the hard-bitten but profoundly sensitive man, secure and sufficient even if he is also gnawed at by loneliness (something like God before he created Adam). Mack is a similar man, although he lacks Doc's composure. He is a grown-up boy who has fallen short of being a man in his social accomplishments. But he is a terrifically resourceful and honest boy. And he is the leader of a benevolent gang of men called "the boys." Lee Chong, the stereotypical Chinese grocer, is canny, suspicious, shrewd, and calculating, but he is fundamentally decent and good-hearted. He is also self-sufficient.

The men in the novel who are married (Sam Malloy, Gay, the Captain, and Tom Talbot), are all portrayed, in one way or another, as hampered by their wives. And the women, apart from Dora, are portrayed fundamentally as children. Mrs. Malloy goes into hysterics when her husband cannot understand how she is going to hang curtains in the windowless iron boiler they live in. Gay's wife, who is only mentioned, but never portrayed, waits for Gay to fall asleep and then begins hitting him. He then beats her. Married life is such that Gay prefers life in the county jail, where he can play checkers with the sheriff. Mack was married, but he could never do anything right, according to his wife. According to him, however, he was always trying to. He has much better luck with Doc. Although he makes mistakes, he and Doc deal with Mack's failings man to man. After the ill-conceived party, Doc punches Mack twice, and then listens compassionately to Mack's explanation. Mary Talbot, Tom's wife, is shown as slightly daffy and slightly demented. Rumored to be descended from a witch, she loves to give parties and routinely serves tea to the neighborhood cats, with which she converses. She is oblivious to the manly sorrows of her husband, but is often his delight. She lessens his cares because of her girlish naïveté.

Furthermore, Mack and the boys have a grand time with the Captain. Because his wife is away, he can go frogging with them. He can also unplug a cask of whiskey, an act that his wife prohibits. His absent wife, the Captain says, "is a wonderful woman," and he gives her what may be for some men the highest compliment that can be given to a woman: She "ought to of been a man." Then he gives the compliment a spin and reveals his feeling about being married:

"If she was a man I wouldn' of married her." The Captain's wife is felt to be at fault for having her own career and for not keeping the house from becoming a mess while she is away from home. She is also characterized as being a killjoy for imposing restraint on the Captain: no drinking, no mess, no fun.

The women who are presented in a positive light are those who are available to men when they are needed and who make no demands upon them. Interspersed between the two chapters devoted to the Captain, there is a utopian interlude. Two soldiers and their girls are seen in the very early morning, "very tired and very happy," after a long night on the town. The scene ends on the beach; the soldiers lie with their heads in their girls' laps. The soldiers and the girls look, smiling, into each other's eyes, sharing a "peaceful and wonderful secret." This is the interval that transcends reality. The soldiers will go back to the war. The girls will go back to their lives. Years later, when they all get married, whether to each other or to others, their marriages, as *Cannery Row* seems to suggest, will be nothing like this early morning idyll.

Then there is Dora Flood. As the successful proprietor of a brothel, she is an independent woman who is strong, shrewd, and wise to the ways of the world and to the men to whom she caters. Dora is an exception because her career is dedicated to catering to men, and her success is that she knows how to do it. She earns the highest praise from Mack, and it is not the backhanded praise that the Captain gives his wife. Mack means to give Dora tribute when he says: "Now there is one hell of a woman. No wonder she got to be a madam. There is one hell of a woman." What Dora has done to earn such tribute is to offer the kind of advice that no respectable wife inside the covers of *Cannery Row* would offer. When Mack tells her about his ill-conceived and disastrous party for Doc, and about his wish to do something for him that will succeed, Dora says: "You gave him a party he didn't get to. Why don't you give him a party he does get to?" The narrator, as well as Mack, likes and respects Dora. So does Doc. Nevertheless, she is not of their world. She caters to it. That she does so for cash is all the better. It keeps the transactions between her world and the world of the men free of the encumbrances or restraints that accompany involvement with "high-minded ladies."

The only womanly figures that exist in the men's world are mere shadows. Doc is attractive to women. The boys notice that Doc frequently has women visitors who stay through the night. But these women are shadows to the reader, figures that run through Doc's fingers like the water that he probes when harvesting marine specimens. At the core of the second party, and in the concluding chapter of the book, Doc recites out loud a poem embedded in an awareness of a lost beloved. The poem offers the possibility of attaining the spiritual elevation associated with love. These are suppressed romantic symptoms in Doc and in the book. There is no woman who can realize them. Those women who are congenial to men are comforting to their complex masculinity, like Dora and her prostitutes. The prostitutes, when one or another is brought forward, are shown as quirky, not quite stable in themselves, but efficient in their work and relatively good-natured. The deep emotional tensions and relationships in the novel exist only among the men.

But there is a lasting malaise haunting the book that focuses on Frankie and on Doc's inability to do anything for the miserable boy. Frankie is the boy who insinuates himself shyly into Doc's life, whom Doc accepts when no one else will. Nevertheless, Doc is unable to rescue Frankie after he breaks into Jacob's Jewelry Store and steals a clock, which he wants to give to Doc as a token of his love and respect. While Doc can replace the boy's dead father, he cannot replace Frankie's mother. She is not dead, but she is absent, visited continuously by men who either hit Frankie or give him a nickel to disappear. Frankie becomes, in consequence, a figure through which the absent female is suggested.

Source: Neil Heims, Critical Essay on *Cannery Row*, in *Novels for Students*, Gale, Cengage Learning, 2009.

Robert S. Hughes, Jr.

In the following excerpt, Hughes takes an in-depth look at Mack and the boys to show the moral values that Steinbeck extols via their example.

. . . Why do Mack and the boys accommodate themselves so easily to life on Cannery Row, while several less-fortunate characters die? As we have seen, the Palace Flophouse boys pursue simple pleasures and contentment as advocated by Taoism; and, unwittingly following Christ's counsel in the New Testament, they live with fewer material goods than their

> THE PALACE FLOPHOUSE BOYS NONETHELESS REMAIN CRUCIAL TO THE NOVEL'S INVERTED MORALITY. THEY RENOUNCE THE GREED AND SICKNESS OF THEIR TIME, REFUSING TO SELL THEIR SOULS 'TO GAIN THE WHOLE WORLD.'"

contemporaries. Hence Frederick Bracher has observed that "Mack's real strength, like Thoreau's, comes from renunciation. . . . [M]ost of the things valued by the middle class—mechanical gadgets, security, cleanliness, prestige, comfort—Mack finds too expensive." In other words, Mack and his friends enjoy a durable, single-sex community, free from the financial, legal, and emotional commitments of middle-class life. They are neither sick from having too much money nor despondent from having too little. Based on the inverted moral perspective of the novel, then, the Palace Flophouse boys live more enlightened lives than the "respectable" Monterey with whom Steinbeck compares them.

The boys' comfortable adaptation to life is illustrated by their frog-hunting expedition into the Carmel Valley. They camp by the "lovely" Carmel River on the sandy shore of a deep, green pool, stewing a chicken (a windfall from their trip) over an open fire, as "around them the evening crept in as delicately as music." Mack and his friends blend so harmoniously with their surroundings that Steinbeck uses the word "happy" to describe their encampment. During this frog-hunting scene, Mack and the boys demonstrate not only their adaptability but also their talent for relaxation. Steinbeck more than condones this talent; he becomes its active champion. While "respectable" Monterey condemns the Palace Flophouse boys for being loafers, we know that in *The Log from the Sea of Cortez* (1951) Steinbeck (along with Ed Ricketts) views loafing as a sign of wisdom and strong survival value. "Only in laziness can one achieve a state of contemplation which is a balancing of values, a weighting of oneself against the world and the world against itself. A busy man cannot find the time for such balancing. We do not think a lazy man can commit murders, nor great thefts, nor lead a mob. He would be more likely to think about it and laugh."

Just as laziness fosters contemplation, according to Steinbeck and Ricketts, so too does alcohol provide innumerable benefits. In *The Log* Steinbeck and Ricketts argue that the "theory that alcohol is a poison" is "too blindly accepted." Actually "our race has a triumphant alcoholic history," they counter, in which liquor has served as an "anodyne, a warmer of the soul, a strengthener of muscle and spirit." This philosophy—or at least its outward manifestation—certainly carries over into Cannery Row, where drinking is a universal pastime. Eddie's infamous wining jug provides a centerpiece in the Palace Flophouse. Dora's Bear Flag Restaurant, among other things, is a favorite watering hole. And Doc—admirer of eighth-century Chinese poet of inebriation Li Po—daily imbibes several quarts of beer. Thus Cannery Row has its own cult of alcohol which attributes considerable powers to its consumption. Mack, for example, peers into an empty whiskey glass "as though some holy message were written in the bottom." But just how many of the collateral benefits of drinking mentioned by Steinbeck and Ricketts the Palace Flophouse boys receive is difficult to tell. Perhaps liquor promotes their laziness, whose advantages have been outlined above. One might also conclude that they drink simply because it makes them feel good or helps them forget.

Nonetheless, Ed Ricketts (the model for Doc in *Cannery Row*) believed that the real-life prototypes of Mack and the boys were "the Lotus Eaters of our era, successful in their resistance against the nervousness and angers and frustrations of our time." As Steinbeck explains in "About Ed Ricketts," "Ed regarded these men with the admiration he had for any animal, family, or species that was successful in survival and happiness factors." Ricketts contended that bums like Mack and his friends would *"deliver* our species from the enemies within and without which attack it" (italics mine). Doc's most succinct statement about the Palace Flophouse boys comes when a "Black Gloom" has settled over them after their disastrous first party in Doc's lab. In a conversation with Richard Frost, Doc calls Mack and his cohorts "true philosophers" and then repeats the inverted moral perspective introduced earlier in the book: "In a time when people tear themselves to pieces with ambition and nervousness and covetousness, they are relaxed. All of our so-called successful men are sick men, with bad stomachs, and bad souls, but Mack and the boys are healthy and curiously clean. They can do what they want. They can satisfy their appetites without calling them something else."

This glowing appraisal is tempered somewhat by Mack's earlier admission to Doc: "I been sorry all my life.... Ever'thing I done turned sour." Lewis Owens points out this darker side of the "flophouse castaways, a sad and less pleasing dimension of failure, rejection, and withdrawal." Owens argues that rather than adjusting well to life, Mack and his buddies represent severe maladjustment. "Mack is in retreat from the world outside of the Row; he has failed in love and in any kind of deep commitment and has come to hide out from further commitment on Cannery Row." The Palace Flophouse boys nonetheless remain crucial to the novel's inverted morality. They renounce the greed and sickness of their time, refusing to sell their souls "to gain the whole world." That they may be viewed as mere hedonists, on the one hand, or as saviors of mankind, on the other, reflects the moral ambiguity of these intriguing characters.

Helping Mack and the boys survive comfortably on the Row is their occasional reluctant benefactor, Lee Chong. Steinbeck associates the humane and astute Chinese grocer with Taoism, yet also with the "abacus and cash register." Thus Lee Chong combines Oriental inaction and contentment with Western striving for material prosperity. He is not avaricious, though "if one wanted to spend money, he was available." Lee never presses those who owe him money, yet he cuts off credit when the bill becomes too large. He is a realistic man in the details of business, yet sympathic in matters of the heart—"a hard man with a can of beans—a soft man with the bones of his grandfather." One of Lee's finest qualities is that he sees beyond his own immediate profit or loss. While a conventional grocer would hardly bargain with bums like Mack and the boys, Lee does so, often to his own apparent financial disadvantage. For example, when he reluctantly "rents" the old Horace Abbeville place to Mack and his friends, Lee has the foresight to know that although they will never pay rent, at least the building will not mysteriously go up in flames, as it might if he refuses them. In addition, he gains several steady customers in his store, the loss in rent being more than compensated for by money they spend and goods they don't steal. Thus Lee Chong belies the stereotypical business "success" (condemned through the inverted morality of the novel) by combining seemingly incompatible traits of character. He manages not only to remain healthy and prosperous but also to avoid destroying others on his way to financial security...

Source: Robert S. Hughes, Jr., "'Some Philosophers in the Sun': Steinbeck's *Cannery Row*," in *The Short Novels of John Steinbeck: Critical Essays with a Checklist to Steinbeck Criticism*, edited by Jackson J. Benson, Duke University Press, 1990, pp. 119–31.

Peter Lisca

In the following essay, Lisca argues that the twin themes of Cannery Row *are escape from material values and from belief in activism. As part of his thesis, Lisca discusses Eastern philosophy.*

Between *The Grapes of Wrath* and *Cannery Row*, Steinbeck's next major work of fiction, came a period of five years during which he was occupied with a variety of writing. During the last two of these years this writing was directly related to America's involvement in World War II, ending with Steinbeck serving five months abroad as a war correspondent. The war experience left Steinbeck so depressed that he refused even to edit his dispatches for publication in book form, and they were not published until 1958 (*Once There Was a War*). Instead, in less than two months he produced *Cannery Row*, the first of three works of fiction written in quick succession, varying widely in materials and techniques but each exploring some reaction toward a world whose basic values had plunged it in turn from eleven years of severe economic depression into the massive aggression and destruction of a world war.

In *Cannery Row* (1945) this reaction is one of escape into a counterculture superficially reminiscent of *Tortilla Flat*, except that the earlier novel is a light, tongue-in-cheek affair, and the new novel—for all its humor—is a philosophically based and impassioned celebration of values directly opposed to the capitalist ethic dominant in Western society. Looking through "another peephole," Steinbeck discovers that what normally might be called "thieves, rascals...bums" may just as truly be described as "saints and angels and martyrs and holy men." For as Doc, the central character, expresses it, the traits leading to success

> *CANNERY ROW* OFFERS NEITHER A DETAILED ANATOMY OF SOCIETY'S 'MANGLED CRAZINESS' NOR A PROGRAM FOR CHANGING IT."

in our society are frequently "greed, acquisitiveness, meanness," whereas failure may be the result of "kindness, generosity, openness, honesty, understanding and feeling."

The book is short and episodic, made up of thirty-two little chapters totaling only 181 pages. The setting is the section of Monterey, California, characterized by its sardine canneries (Cannery Row), and the time is just before World War II. Its numerous and varied characters include Doc, the biologist who runs the one-man Western Biological Laboratory; Dora Flood, madam of the Bear Flag Restaurant (a whorehouse); Lee Chong, owner of a grocery store; Mack and the boys (Hazel, Eddie, Hughie, Jones), who live in a storage shed they call the Palace Flophouse and Grill; Gay, who lives with the boys or in the jail to escape his wife; Henri, an avant-garde painter; Mr. and Mrs. Malloy, who live in an abandoned boiler; Frankie, a retarded juvenile whom Doc befriends; and many others, some of whom appear only briefly. The book's narrative line is a very thin one, consisting of Cannery Row's two attempts to give a surprise party for Doc, whom they all admire. The first one turns out to be a glorious failure, resulting in the wrecking of the laboratory and ending before Doc even arrives. After a period of gloom, a second party is launched and proves a riotous success. The novel closes with Doc washing the dishes the following morning.

Cannery Row offers neither a detailed anatomy of society's "mangled craziness" nor a program for changing it. Rather, it brings into being a new world to replace the one that is in the process of self-destruction. It is a world not of whole cloth but of bits and pieces, varying in chronology, recollected in nostalgia, and lovingly assembled, like the patch-work quilt presented to Doc by the girls of Dora's whorehouse, or one of the fantastic collages done by Henri, the novel's eccentric artist. Thus, while one episode concerns the death of the American humorist Josh Billings (1885), in another, Model T Fords are in common use; while Henry follows "feverishly … in periodicals the latest Dadaist movements and schisms," Sam Malloy's historically contemporary Chalmers 1916 piston and connecting rod is valued as a rare antique; elsewhere in the book, the year 1937 is clearly referred to as in the past. In addition to this free intermingling of various time levels, there is also a haunting effect of timelessness, achieved in part by the relative lack of plot (movement) and in part by the recurrence of specific descriptions and acts. A mysterious old Chinaman goes down to the sea each evening at five thirty and returns each morning. The rhythmic flopping of the loose sole on his shoe, normally a very temporary condition, through its presumed continuance accentuates that timelessness. These two qualities of the novel's time sense—its blurring of chronology and the sharp recurring detail—are the very essence of homesickness, out of which Steinbeck said he wrote the book; his close friend Ed Ricketts, the original of Doc, described it as "an essay in loneliness." *Cannery Row* brings together again in the unchanging world of art those qualities of life that—hastened by the war—had passed never to return, and for which Steinbeck felt a deep nostalgia. In this respect the novel is firmly in the pastoral tradition.

In the novel's preface, addressing himself to the problem of setting down Cannery Row "alive," Steinbeck proposes an analogy that resonates through all aspects of the work, for as its time sense is in free flux, so also are its other qualities. His comparison of the writing of this book to capturing whole fragile and delicate sea worms extends to both content (stories/sea worms) and method or form ("let the stories crawl in by themselves"/"ooze by themselves"). And as the seawater in which the specimens are held has no shape except that imparted by its container, so the novel seems equally arbitrary in form. Only about half of the thirty-two chapters pick up the tenuous narrative thread. Alternating almost regularly with these are "the little inner chapters" (as Steinbeck once called them) that sometimes add to our knowledge of the main characters and sometimes introduce material of no causal relationship. Generally, however, all these inner chapters serve in some way as comment or contrast to the novel's major theme.

The openness and freedom of the novel's structure is a formal expression of those same qualities in the Cannery Row community itself, upon which no convention or authority imposes conformity or direction. It has instead the natural order of a biological organism, manifesting its own inner dynamics. The lines of interaction between individuals and even between institutions proliferate in all directions—Frankie and Doc, the laboratory and the whorehouse, the Chinese grocery store and the Palace Flophouse, the idealized women in Doc's poetry books (Petrarch's Laura, the girl in "Black Marigolds") and Dora's practical prostitutes. Those relationships normally expected to be exploitative or repressive are mutually beneficial—the jailor and Gay, McKinley the diver and the Prohibition agents and the bootlegger, a landowner and trespassing bums, the police and a riotous party, even the whorehouse and the Ladies' Anti-Vice League. This rich variety of viable relationships is possible because all elements of the community share a quality that is most explicit in Steinbeck's description of Mack and the boys. He calls them "the Beauties, the Virtues, the Graces" because in a world of greed and rapacity—"ruled by tigers with ulcers, rutted by strictured bulls, scavenged by blind jackals," they "avoid the trap" of ambition. To this imagery of maimed animals is opposed a version of the Peaceable Kingdom, in which Mack and the boys "dine delicately with the tigers, fondle the frantic heifers, and wrap up the crumbs to feed the seagulls of Cannery Row." Their lack of material gain is not seen as lack of ability. Doc is certain that these "bums" can "get money." But "they just know the nature of things too well to be caught in that wanting." To Hazel's observation that Mack could have been President of the United States had he wanted to be, Jones replies, "What could he do with it if he had it?"

The novel's informing spirit is the *Tao Teh Ching* of Lao-tzu, a Chinese philosopher of the sixth century B.C. Like *Cannery Row*, the *Tao Teh Ching* was written in a time of brutal war ("Period of the Fighting States") and, in reaction to those conditions, presented a system of human values devoid of all those qualities that had brought on that war. It is interesting in this connection to quote from the prefatory remarks of two well-known editions of the *Tao* published just before *Cannery Row*:

> For Laotze's book … teaches the wisdom of appearing foolish, the success of appearing to fail, the strength of weakness … if I were asked what antidote could be found … to cure this

contentious modern world of its inveterate belief in force and struggle for power, I would name this book...[Lao-tzu] has the knack of making Hitler and other dreamers of world mastery appear foolish and ridiculous

(Lin Yutang, *The Wisdom of China and India* [1942])

And the Western world might well temper its characteristic faults by taking Laotzu to heart... "Laotzu is one of our chief weapons against tanks, artillery and bombs."

(Witter Bynner, *The Way of Life* [1944])

That Steinbeck was familiar with Lao-tzu's little text of forty or so pages is certain, and most probably he was familiar with it in the Lin Yutang translation, although several others were also available. In *Journal of a Novel* (1951) he listed Lao-tzu along with Plato, Christ, and Buddha as "the great ones." Significantly, Ed Ricketts, to whom *Cannery Row* is dedicated, was much attracted to Taoism and refers to it several times in his letters and unpublished papers. In chapter 2 Steinbeck speculates that Lee Chong, who takes up most of the first chapter and with whose name (which is similar to that of Lao-tzu's famous disciple Chuangtse) that chapter begins, is "more than a Chinese grocer. He must be. Perhaps he is evil balanced and held suspended by good—an Asian planet held to its orbit by the pull of Lao-Tze and held away from Lao-Tze by the centrifugality of abacus and cash register..." Doc himself sometimes reads aloud to Lee Chong in English from the poetry of Li Po, a figure associated with Taoism. In this context even the novel's ancient and mysterious Chinaman is suggestive.

Taoism rejects the desire for material goods, fame, power, and even the holding of fixed or strong opinions—all of which lead to violence. Instead, man is to cultivate simple physical enjoyments and the inner life. To be obscure is to be wise; to fail is to succeed; in human relationships force always defeats itself; even laws are a form of violence; the moral life is one of inaction.

These principles are generally visible throughout *Cannery Row*; frequently the consequences of their absence are illustrated in the "little inner chapters." In addition, however, much of the novel seems to exemplify specific passages in the *Tao*. Sometimes there is even a similarity of expression. Steinbeck writes in chapter 2: "The word is a symbol and a delight which sucks up men and scenes, trees, plants, factories, and Pekinese. Then the Thing becomes the Word and back to Thing again, but warped and woven into a fantastic pattern. The World sucks up Cannery Row, digests it and spews it out, and the Row has taken the shimmer of the green world and the sky-reflecting seas." Surely Steinbeck's meditation upon his own creative act is reminiscent of the Gospel according to Saint John, but its similarity to the very first passage of the *Tao Teh Ching* is even more striking:

Existence is beyond the power of words
To define:
Terms may be used
But are none of them absolute.
In the beginning of heaven and earth there
      were no words,
Words came out of the womb of matter;
And whether a man dispassionately
Sees to the core of life
Or passionately
Sees the surface,
The core and the surface
Are essentially the same,
Words making them seem different
Only to express appearance.
If name be needed, wonder names them
      both:
From wonder into wonder
Existence opens.

(Witter Bynner, *The Way of Life*)

There are other correspondences of statement between the two works. Steinbeck's "Virtues and Graces" live with "no money, no ambitions beyond food, drink and contentment" whereas most men "in their search for contentment destroy themselves and fall wearily short of their target." Lao-tzu says,

There is no greater curse than lack of
      contentment.
No greater sin than the desire for possession.
Therefore he who is contented with content-
      ment shall always be content.

(Lin Yutang, XLVI)

Steinbeck's "another peephole," through which Mack and the boys are seen in different perspective, may be a version of

Who understands Tao seems dull of
      comprehension;
Who is advanced in Tao seems to slip
      backward;
... Great character appears like insufficient;

Solid character appears like infirm.

(Lin Yutang, XLI)

When Mack and the boys will not even turn their heads to look at the Fourth of July parade because "they know what will be in the parade," they illustrate the Taoist principle that "Without stepping outside one's doors, / One can know what is happening in the world" (Lin Yutang, XLVII).

Doc himself clearly embodies the traits of a Taoist sage. He is free of all ambition. He is a consummate "wordless teacher" to the entire community. In listening seriously to Mack's schemes or to Henri's illusions, he illustrates the Taoist principle that by not believing people you turn them into liars. His involvement in the welfare of Cannery Row demonstrates that "the Sage is good at helping men"; his care and kindness toward Frankie shows that for the sage "there is no rejected (useless) person" (Lin Yutang, XXVII). In his study of a tide pool or even a stinkbug, he conforms to the Taoist precept that one should look to Nature to know oneself, one's real human nature. "He didn't need a clock . . . He could feel a tide change in his sleep." He is at one with his total environment—including the whorehouse, Lee Chong's, the Palace Flophouse—and thus in communion with the harmonious balance of Tao. At the height of his birthday party, Doc is seated calmly on a table, cross-legged in the Oriental posture of meditation.

> The Sage dwells in the world peacefully, harmoniously.
> The people of the world are brought into a community of heart
> and the Sage regards them all as his own children.

(Lin Yutang, XLIX)

The world into which *Cannery Row* escapes is not a perfect one; not everyone lives according to the *Tao*. There is a series of misfortunes on Cannery Row, caused seemingly by some vague natural force about which "there is no explaining." But there is little in *Cannery Row* of the kind of evil men bring upon themselves through "greed, acquisitiveness, meanness, egotism and self-interest"; or through the desire to impose one's own standards on others; or even a single standard on oneself. And these incidents serve as contrasts to the book's theme. The poet Wallace Stevens could have been quoting Lao-tzu in his well-known line, "A violent order is disorder"; and his corollary statement, "A great disorder is an order," could be

the epigraph for *Cannery Row*. For Steinbeck's created world is characterized by its rich variety, its benevolent chaos: "Cannery Row is a poem, a stink, a grating noise, a quality of light, a tone, a habit, a nostalgia, a dream . . . tin and iron and rust and splintered wood, chipped pavement and weedy lots and junk heaps, sardine canneries." The same rich variety is evident in all its parts: Lee Chong's grocery store, with its hodgepodge of every conceivable commodity ("but one," Dora's), in and out of season; the Carmel River, which, though short, has a long and varied list of characteristics—"everything a river should have"; Doc's lab, with its scientific apparatus, double bed, phonograph, cookstove, poetry books, and lady visitors; Eddie's "wining" jugs, containing bourbon, wine, scotch, beer, and even grenadine mixed together; the great tide pool (a microcosm of "the cosmic Monterey") in which Doc collects his specimens and in which is found such a variety of life forms and modes of survival. All are patterns of the rich community of Cannery Row and of the novel itself—both its form and content.

In this light, Steinbeck's prefatory analogy of letting the stories ooze into the book by themselves, like delicate sea worms into a collecting jar, rather than forcing them into an order, becomes also a moral statement. (There is no formal order in the *Tao Teh Ching*, either.) Mack learns that the first party failed because "we forced her," and that the second will succeed if they just "let it happen." Steinbeck tells us that those celebrations that are "controlled and dominated" are "not parties at all but acts and demonstrations, about as spontaneous as peristalsis and as interesting as its end product." William, the first bouncer at Dora's Bear Flag Restaurant, commits suicide because, unlike Alfred, his successor, he tries to force himself on people and is rejected. Henri can love boats and be happy because he does not drive himself to the logical conclusion of finishing his boat and thus having to go out upon the water, which he fears. On the other hand, Mrs. Malloy is unhappy because she wants to do such things as "force" lace curtains upon the windowless boiler in which she lives. The ambitious wife of the landowner in the hilarious frog-hunting episode fails as a wife because she forces her compulsive neatness upon her husband. The hitchhiker is ejected from the car because he expects everyone to hold the same principles about drinking that he does. Doc knows he is a "free man" because he can indulge the rich variety of his inclinations without fear of contradictions—Bach and Debussy, *Faust* and "Black Marigolds"; even, and at the same time, Palestrina masses and sexual intercourse. In fact, he himself looks "half Christ, half satyr."

The twin themes of *Cannery Row*, then, around which the novel's characters and events casually but effectively arrange themselves, are the escape from Western material values—the necessity to "succeed" in the world—and the escape from Western activism—the necessity to impose order or direction. Like Lao-tzu, Steinbeck elaborates these two escapes into a system of "Virtues and Graces."

Source: Peter Lisca, "*Cannery Row*: Escape into the Counterculture," in *The Short Novels of John Steinbeck: Critical Essays with a Checklist to Steinbeck Criticism*, edited by Jackson J. Benson, Duke University Press, 1990, pp. 111–19.

Jackson J. Benson

In the following excerpt, Benson identifies Cannery Row *as a "folk" novel and compares it to another classic folk novel, Mark Twain's* Huckleberry Finn.

...It is my contention that Steinbeck has really taken Twain's place during the last few decades as the major spokesman for the "folk tradition." And the thematic complex I spoke of above finds its last major expression in his work. To trace this expression in any detail would require a book, but briefly note the importance of "Westering" in his work (and the interpretation, overdrawn but still valid, of *The Grapes of Wrath* as a "wagons West romance" by Bernard Bowron). That Steinbeck has assumed this position is, I think, the essential basis for his popularity, as well as the reason for the antipathy expressed toward him by Eastern intellectual criticism.

There are a number of striking parallels between Twain's and Steinbeck's careers. Both were fascinated by medieval literature, in particular Malory's *Morte d' Arthur*, and both were fond of allegory, the tall tale, and travel literature. Both wrote a wide variety of things during their careers, moving from form to form; and both wrote a great many things of very dubious literary value. And despite a large output, both writers are known primarily for having written one major novel. However, almost everything they wrote, even their most important works, was deeply flawed in one way or another. Both in their heart of hearts were satirists—disillusioned romantic idealists. Twain and Steinbeck

> IF DOC IS NOT THE DISGUISED PRINCE AMONG PEASANTS, WHO IS HE IN THE PASTORAL SCHEME? THE MOST LIKELY ANSWER, IT SEEMS TO ME, IS THAT HE IS THE SHEPHERD. WHO OR WHAT ARE HIS SHEEP?"

have been classified as "funnymen," yet each of them had at times a very black vision of man's nature. No two American writers have had a firmer sense of the ordinary man and of ordinary life, and both maintained the common touch even after they became rich and successful. Yet each moved to the East after becoming rich and successful, and while in the East, each became more and more pessimistic and moralistic in his work. Both were very fond of metaphysics and philosophical discourse, and both were notably unsuccessful at reaching any profound level of philosophical thought.

What ties *Cannery Row* to *Huckleberry Finn* is primarily the deep antagonism at the center of both novels toward respectability and "proper" society. Steinbeck's Monterey (the town itself above the Row), with its civilized corruption, takes roughly the same position as Twain's Mississippi shore, with its shabby values. Whenever Doc leaves the Row, he encounters hostility, hypocrisy, and greed. And whenever the town reaches in to touch the Row, hypocrisy and greed are expressed. Dora and her establishment, for example, are tolerated as long as she is more law-abiding than everyone else and as long as she gives several times more to charity than everyone else. In both novels nature is the cleansing agent, so that Huck can rid himself of the taint of civilization on the river, and Doc can renew his spirit by periodic immersions (feet only) in the Great Tide Pool.

One of the main qualities that ties Doc and Huck together is a fundamental honesty, but in each case the character finds he must abandon his honesty in the face of pressure from society. Huck must tell lies and disguise himself in order to protect Jim, while Doc found as a young man on a walking trip through the South that he could not simply say that he wanted to enjoy the countryside, but had to lie and say he was "doing it on a bet." When he finally decides to try out his beer milkshake, he finds he must invent "doctor's orders" to justify his whim to a suspicious waitress. Both Doc and Huck have a certain openness, even vulnerability, which makes them particularly appealing and which contrasts with the hard façades erected by the respectable people they encounter.

Huckleberry Finn and *Cannery Row* are primarily satiric in mode, episodic in structure (both the escape of Jim and the party for Doc are secondary to the material developed along the way), and range in emotional tenor from light humor at one end of the scale to horror and black satire at the other. The central satiric device in each novel is the confrontation between the good people outside of conventional society, whom society frowns upon as criminals or bums, and those people within society who have been corrupted by respectability and made humorless, inflexible, and blind, with little or no ability to enjoy life.

The two most common image groupings in the two novels are death and money—thus exposing those two pillars of frontier settlement life, violence and the "hard cash" mentality. A third pillar, loneliness, is only slightly exposed in Twain's novel in the separation of Jim from his family, but it is revealed in some detail in Steinbeck's book. Whereas greed is somewhat more frequently satirized in *Huckleberry Finn*, there are also instances in *Cannery Row*: for example, there is the man on the beach at La Jolla who can think only of the bounty paid for the discovery of a body, in the face of Doc's complex vision of beauty and death. Money is the tool by which civilization tries to enforce conformity in both novels. Huck rejects the fortune held for him by Judge Thatcher to take off for the territory, and throughout the novel he resists the temptation of the bounty put on Jim's head. Mack and the boys, in the Steinbeck novel, solve the problem of enforced behavior through petty theft, fits of work (usually through the kindness of Doc), and the reluctant cooperation of Lee Chong.

There are a number of other connections, but all are rather generalized; they arise out of the value system behind the novels rather than out of the specific materials of the novels themselves. Subject, technical point of view, and specific characterizations are all different, of course. The most important point, beyond the kinship of the values involved, that can be made by using *Huckleberry Finn* as an analogy to illuminate *Cannery Row* may be that both books are products of vital,

likable personalities. And it is the personality of the author in each case, as it is reflected in the tone and vitality of the narration, that appears to be the main factor in making each novel successful.

The folk position that Steinbeck shares with Twain is, as we have seen, heavily infused with what have been called "frontier values" as well as the literary conventions which have evolved from those values. Some of these values, such as the evils of civilization, are endorsed by Twain and Steinbeck. Some, such as the feud in *Huckleberry Finn*, are satirized, while others are the source of good fun. No one has paid much attention to the fun that Steinbeck gets from these values as they have been translated into the conventions of popular Western literature.

By changing the Row and its canneries to Dodge City and its stockyards, the Row can be viewed as the very model of the main street in a town of the old West. Doc becomes the kindly, wise, and patient general practitioner. He is the "fountain of philosophy and science and art," the only educated man, the only professional among the frontier ruffians. Dora is, of course, the saloon owner and madam, a combination practical businesswoman and mother to the entire male community. And Lee Chong runs the town's general store, a store which stocks nearly anything anyone would want, but which tends to sell more whiskey, beer, and chewing gum than anything else. Even the kids, who haunt the store when they are not throwing rocks or taunting each other or strangers, have a ragtag, frontier-town quality.

Henri is the crazy old prospector who rummages around in vacant lots looking for boat parts and who, like his Western counterpart who would be at a loss if he ever did find gold, never wants to complete his boat. Mack and the boys could just as well be living in the bunkhouse on the B-Bar-B Ranch as in the Palace Flophouse; and it is a nice touch to have the ranch foreman, Mack, taking his men to round up cats rather than cattle, and wild frogs rather than wild horses. The tactics of stampeding the frogs from one end of the "valley" into a trap are familiar.

As usual, the settlers—in this case the Malloys—are ridiculous with their chintz curtains. Then there are the inevitable knock-down-drag-out fights (all in fun and made up in good fellowship later) and the community crisis (the flu). When there is a party, the main ingredients are steak and whiskey. That Steinbeck has these conventions in mind is certified in the ending of the sequel, *Sweet Thursday*, wherein Doc gets the girl (a reformed saloon girl, of course) and the two of them ride his bucking car off into the sunset.

Steinbeck's parody of the Western is not the "secret" of *Cannery Row*; it joins a number of other modes and themes which in various ways comment on man's relationship to nature. Adjacent to the Western, another aspect of the novel concerns its pastoral elements. The pastoral does not extend throughout the novel nearly as far as the Western parody, but a few elements are obviously present and appear to work together with the parody on the lighter side of the novel. The only long-standing major article about *Cannery Row* is one which develops the pastoral—Stanley Alexander's "*Cannery Row*: Steinbeck's Pastoral Poem." Unfortunately, Alexander is caught in the trap that catches most critics at one time or another: he takes the pastoral material and pushes it too hard, trying to force the entire novel into his pattern on the basis of only a few pieces of evidence. The novel really only hints at the pastoral, and usually in an inverted way.

Alexander's first mistake, I think, is to bring William Empson's *Some Versions of Pastoral* to bear on *Cannery Row*, probably because he sees Steinbeck inaccurately as a Marxist. He refers to Empson's view that the pastoral is the "primary literary convention which reflects the characteristic class relations of western society," bringing "together in rural or even wilderness scenes representatives of (relatively) exalted social classes and (relatively) low social classes." If we try to apply this to *Cannery Row*, we are in trouble already, for only one out of three criteria applies. We do not have a rural scene, nor do we have a representative, except by distant implication, of exalted social classes. (There are no wealthy Monterey citizens in the novel except by distant reference to the man who gains "the whole world" and comes "to his property with a gastric ulcer, a blown prostate, and bifocal[s]."

Trying to put Doc into this role simply does not work. According to Alexander, the form of *Cannery Row* approximates the Renaissance pastoral because of Doc, who represents "the secure, educated, powerful class from which he comes 'down' to operate the Western Biological Laboratory." Nonsense. No one could read "About Ed Ricketts" in *The Log* and think such a thing. (The language used in *The Log* to describe Ed is almost precisely the same language used to describe Doc in the novel—the

model is extremely close to the fictional character.) However, if one wants to avoid the biographical fallacy, one only has to look at Doc's role in the novel. He is almost classless, an eccentric among other eccentrics and iconoclasts. True, Doc does bring the arts and sciences to the Row, as well as a certain wisdom. But these are presented as the peculiar facets of Doc's character, not the badges of class. He may be the intellectual who has dropped out and joined the counterculture, but he has not dropped out of wealth, power, and security.

Alexander gets closer to the real uses of the pastoral in the novel when he admits that the locale is "neither sylvan dale nor frontier ranch nor family farm; it is instead an industrial slum." That may be putting it a bit strongly (for those who remember the Row in its heyday, it is difficult to think of as a "slum"), but we should keep in mind the fact that the Row is dominated by factories which house machines which cut up animals and stick them in metal cans, and that Mack and the boys have been finding shelter in the discarded pipes of the canneries. The fact that they can only exist on vacant lots and among the refuse of factories suggests what the sylvan dale has finally come to.

The setting suggests that this is the reversal of the pastoral, or the pastoral corrupted. Alexander seems to recognize this temporarily when he talks about Doc sharing the scene with "mock-pastoral bums and whores who in better days were swains and maids." Indeed, if *Cannery Row* must be referred to as a pastoral, it surely should be called a "mock-pastoral," playing upon the original form as it does by reversing many of the pastoral conventions. And if we must refer to Empson, it would be more appropriate to consult his chapter on the mock-pastoral, which examines *The Beggar's Opera*. While Mack and the boys may not have a great deal in common with Mac and his gang, surely Newgate with its rogues and whores is closer to the Row with its rogues and whores than the Renaissance's "another part of the forest" with its disguised nobility.

If Doc is not the disguised prince among peasants, who is he in the pastoral scheme? The most likely answer, it seems to me, is that he is the shepherd. Who or what are his sheep? Well, one possibility is that all the inhabitants of Cannery Row are his flock. Or he may be the shepherd of the sea animals. Doc, who is described by Steinbeck as having a face "half Christ and half satyr" (no doubt in part a private joke between Steinbeck and Ricketts), may be an exaggerated version of the swain who is traditionally thought of as half connected to humanity and half to nature. But I agree with Peter Lisca, who suggests that Doc can be seen as a sort of "local deity" (not, again, that he is powerful so much as he is more accepting, wiser, and more concerned with the welfare of others than anyone else around him—that is, he is Christ-like). If he is meant to resemble a god, he would appear to resemble Pan, who was the god of the shepherds and patron god of the pastoral and who was half man, half goat. Doc is constantly connected with music throughout the novel, and in the most striking pastoral interlude in the book, he hears a "high thin piercingly sweet flute" as he experiences a vision of great beauty. Also like Pan, Doc is "always in love with one nymph, or another, but always rejected." Since Pan eventually became the god of all nature for the Greeks, it is fitting that Doc represent him in the universe of Cannery Row, wherein, as described by Steinbeck, "Our Father" is in nature.

Northrop Frye has said that "the pastoral of popular modern literature is the Western story," which seems to imply that all that is needed for a pastoral is people in a rural setting with animals. Actually, the conventions of both the Western and the pastoral are more complex than that, and such a statement really does not mean much. Nevertheless, although the amount of overt pastoral material in the novel is meager, we can say that the mock-Western, which we reviewed earlier, and the mock-pastoral in *Cannery Row* form a kind of community of parodic commentary on man's changing perception of his relationship with nature.

Source: Jackson J. Benson, "*Cannery Row* and Steinbeck as Spokesman for the 'Folk Tradition,'" in *The Short Novels of John Steinbeck: Critical Essays with a Checklist to Steinbeck Criticism*, edited by Jackson J. Benson, Duke University Press, 1990, pp. 132–42.

SOURCES

Hearle, Kevin, "'The Boat-Shaped Mind': Steinbeck's Sense of Language as Discourse in *Cannery Row* and *Sea of Cortez*," in *After The Grapes of Wrath: Essays on John Steinbeck*, edited by Donald V. Coers, Paul D. Ruffin, and Robert J. DeMott, Ohio University Press, 1995, pp. 101–12.

Lisca, Peter, *The Wide World of John Steinbeck*, Rutgers University Press, 1958, pp. 197–98.

Steinbeck John, *Cannery Row*, in *Novels, 1942–1952*, Library of America, 2001, pp. 101–225.

Timmerman, John H., *John Steinbeck's Fiction: The Aesthetics of the Road Taken*, University of Oklahoma Press, 1986, pp. 133–65.

FURTHER READING

Astro, Richard, *John Steinbeck and Edward F. Ricketts: The Shaping of a Novelist*, University of Minnesota Press, 1973.

Ricketts was the model for Doc in *Cannery Row*, and the man to whom Steinbeck dedicated the novel. This book explores the relationship between Steinbeck and Ricketts.

Parini, Jay, *John Steinbeck: A Biography*, Henry Holt, 1994.

This literary biography reconstructs Steinbeck's, life as a writer.

Riesman, David, *The Lonely Crowd*, Yale University Press, 1955.

This landmark sociological study of the challenge to individuals living in a mass society, pays particular attention to the various adaptations possible, focusing on three particular responses that Riesman calls tradition oriented, inner directed, and outer directed, categories that well describe the characters in *Cannery Row*. Doc, for example, is an inner directed man.

Sinclair, Upton, *The Jungle*, Grosset & Dunlap, 1906.

This landmark novel focuses on the meat packing industry in Chicago at the beginning of the twentieth century. Unlike *Cannery Row*, it is not only a novel of local character but is also a work of propaganda that is meant to incite social change.

Steinbeck, John, *Steinbeck: A Life in Letters*, edited by Elaine Steinbeck and Robert Wallstein, Penguin Books, 1975.

This is an extensive, comprehensive collection of Steinbeck's letters, whether to his wife or to the president of the United States. The letters are dated from 1923 until right before Steinbeck's death.

Cat's Cradle

KURT VONNEGUT, JR.

1963

Cat's Cradle by Kurt Vonnegut, Jr., was published in 1963. While Vonnegut felt that science fiction was too limiting a genre description, *Cat's Cradle* probably fits in that genre most accurately. It is an imaginative fantasy, in which the exact date and time are not clearly established, as is common with science fiction. The novel's plot reflects the cold war atmosphere of the early 1960s, when it seemed that any minute the escalating march toward larger and more deadly weapons might lead to war and the possible massive destruction of whole cities and populations. The title of the novel is taken from a children's game, for which there is no solution. This title reflects the novel's focus on the nature of so-called scientific progress, which puts the world at risk for annihilation. Vonnegut uses satire, irony, and parody to question the integrity and responsibility of scientists who create weapons with no thought to their destructive powers or how they might be used. He also parodies religion as a cure-all for the people and a means by which leaders are able to calm their subjects and allow them to exist happily amid poverty, disease, and destruction. Even the location that serves as a setting for Vonnegut's novel, San Lorenzo, is a parody of the island nations of the Caribbean that are ruled by ambitious wealthy men.

In *Cat's Cradle*, Vonnegut's fourth novel, the careless use of *ice-nine*, a weapon capable of destroying all life, serves as a warning about the drawbacks of technology. Although Vonnegut's

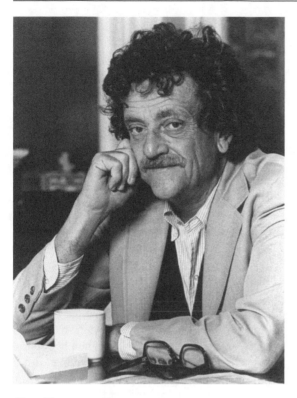

Kurt Vonnegut, Jr. *(AP Images)*

1969 novel, *Slaughterhouse-Five*, made him a bestselling author, *Cat's Cradle* has remained a favorite of readers, who find that in this novel, Vonnegut's warning that truth is only an illusion, captures the essence of 1960s social rebellion. Dial Press has begun reissuing Vonnegut's novels, including *Cat's Cradle*, which was reissued in 2006.

AUTHOR BIOGRAPHY

Kurt Vonnegut, Jr., was born on November 11, 1922, in Indianapolis, Indiana. His father, Kurt Vonnegut, Sr., was a successful architect. His mother, Edith Sophia Lieber, was the daughter of a brewer. Vonnegut was the youngest of the family's three children. Vonnegut grew up not knowing that the family was originally from Germany. Even though they were fourth generation Americans, anti-German sentiment following World War I caused Vonnegut's family to hide their heritage. Vonnegut graduated from Shortridge High School in Indianapolis in 1940. Although he wanted to study journalism in college, he enrolled at Cornell University in Ithaca, New York, as a biochemistry major. Vonnegut's father felt that his son would have a better future in biochemistry than as a writer. While at Cornell, Vonnegut became a writer and editor for the university newspaper. In the middle of his junior year at college, Vonnegut dropped out of school and enlisted in the army. It was 1942 and the United States was at war. Vonnegut was assigned to an infantry battalion and trained as a mechanical engineer. He returned home on Mother's Day 1944, to discover that the evening before, his mother had committed suicide by swallowing sleeping pills. Three months later, Vonnegut was sent overseas, and in December 1944, he was captured by German troops during the Battle of the Bulge. As a prisoner of war, Vonnegut worked in a slaughterhouse in Dresden. On February 13, 1945, Dresden was annihilated by a firestorm of bombs that killed 135,000 people in about two hours. Vonnegut and other prisoners of war survived because they were locked in a cold meat locker three stories beneath the slaughterhouse. After the night of bombing, the prisoners emerged from their shelter to discover that the city and all its people had vanished in the firestorm. Vonnegut spent the next several weeks helping to recover the burned corpses of Dresden's population.

When he returned to the United States in 1945, Vonnegut went back to college, studying anthropology at the University of Chicago. He married his high school sweetheart, Jane Marie Cox, with whom he had three children between 1947 and 1954. In 1947, Vonnegut began working as a publicist for General Electric in Schenectady, New York. He also supplemented his income writing short stories, the first of which was published in 1950 in *Collier's* magazine. Vonnegut's first novel, *Player Piano*, was published in 1952. A second novel, *The Sirens of Titan*, was published in 1959, followed by *Mother Night* in 1961. *Cat's Cradle*, published in 1963, brought Vonnegut more attention than his previous works but not much money. After the publication of his fifth novel, *God Bless You, Mr. Rosewater* (1965), Vonnegut began a two-year residency at the University of Iowa Writer's Workshop. A Guggenheim Fellowship allowed Vonnegut to return to Dresden in 1967, where he began doing research for his most famous novel, *Slaughterhouse-Five*, published in 1969. Vonnegut's master's thesis at the University of Chicago had been rejected by the Anthropology Department in 1947, but it was awarded in 1971, after he had become a successful and quite famous writer. He used *Cat's Cradle* as the subject for his anthropology thesis. Vonnegut published several more novels, collections of short stories, collections of essays and speeches, plays, and a variety of other works. Vonnegut's first marriage ended in divorce in 1979. He married Jill Krementz in 1979, with whom he adopted a child. In addition, Vonnegut adopted his sister's three children after her death from cancer. Vonnegut attempted suicide with sleeping pills and alcohol in 1984, but recovered. He died on April 11, 2007, from brain injuries sustained several weeks earlier in a fall at his New York City apartment.

PLOT SUMMARY

Chapters 1–20

Readers are introduced to the narrator, John, in the first of 127 very brief chapters, most only a page or two long, that make up Vonnegut's *Cat's Cradle*. On the first page, John explains that when he was younger he began to write a book, *The Day the World Ended*, about the day that the atomic bomb was dropped on Hiroshima. John explains that he was a Christian then, but he is now a Bokononist. Bokononism is a religion that is little known outside of one location, the Republic of San Lorenzo. Bokononism's followers believe that humanity is organized into teams who inadvertently, without either knowledge or intent, do God's will. Each of these teams is called a *karass*, which explains how strangers can become connected, even when there seems to be no explanation for how the connection was established. John will discover the members of his *karass* as the book progresses and the story is told. Bokonon, who founded the religion that bears his name, claims that people should not try to understand what God is doing; they are fools if they try to do so. John admits that this is true, but regardless, he intends for the book that he is now narrating, *Cat's Cradle*, to offer an explanation for what God is doing in the world.

John next explains that his own *karass* includes the three children of Dr. Felix Hoenikker, one of the fathers of the atomic bomb. John also explains how he became connected to the

MEDIA ADAPTATIONS

- *Ice-9 Ballads*, by Dave Soldier, was released by Mulatta Recording in 2001. The album features a selection of spoken text, some of it set to music, from *Cat's Cradle*.

Hoenikker family. After he discovered that the youngest Hoenikker son, Newt, has pledged to his old college fraternity, John writes to Newt asking for his recollections of August 6, 1945, the day the bomb was dropped. When he replies, Newt tells John about his father playing with a piece of string the day the bomb was dropped. A man who was in prison had sent Newt's father a novel about a bomb that would destroy the whole world. There was string wrapped around the novel, and Newt's father began to use it to play the children's game cat's cradle with his son. Because his father never played any games with anyone, Newt was frightened of his father, who seemed very large and scary when he came that close. In his letter to John, Newt explains that his father was very hurt that his son was frightened and ran away from him. Newt also tells John that when he told his sister, Angela, that he hated his father and that he was ugly, Angela slapped him and told him that his father was a great man who won the war the day the bomb was dropped. In one of his many postscripts to this letter, Newt explains that he is a midget and his brother, Frank, who has disappeared, is a criminal wanted by the police. Chapter 8 ends with the information that Newt was in love with a forty-two-year-old Russian midget, Zinka, who rejected him.

A year later, John is traveling through Ilium, where the Hoenikker family lived, and decides to stop and ask about the family. There he meets a woman, Sandra, whom he describes as a whore, and who used to attend school with the middle child, Frank Hoenikker. While in Ilium, John makes an appointment with Asa Breed, Dr. Hoenikker's old boss at the Research Laboratory. Asa relates a story to John about how one morning on the way to work, Dr. Hoenikker had gotten tired of driving in traffic and simply abandoned his car in the middle of the road. After the police towed the car, the doctor's wife, Emily, picked the car up, and on her way home was in an accident. The injury from that accident ultimately led to her death in childbirth. This story is meant to illustrate Dr. Hoenikker's carelessness and his lack of concern for even his own family.

Asa next gives John a tour of the Research Laboratory, where one of the secretaries explains that she does not understand what she types, just that it is about a bomb that will turn everything inside out or upside down. When John finally sits down in Asa's office and begins asking him questions, Asa thinks that all of the questions are an attack on scientific discovery, especially the kind of discoveries that lead to bombs and other weapons. Asa then becomes angry at John's perceived attack on all scientists. Asa defends the scientists at the Research Laboratory as the only people who are doing pure research, simply seeking more knowledge for the sake of knowledge and not for commercial use. Asa explains to John that Dr. Hoenikker was asked to solve the problem of mud that bogs down Marines in combat. Asa hypothesizes that quite by accident scientists might discover a way to use a very small seed of some kind that would freeze the water in mud so that mud becomes solid. This hypothetical seed would be called *ice-nine*.

Chapters 21–40

In the first chapter in this section, Asa emphatically states that no such seed exists, but John is frightened, realizing that a seed of *ice-nine* could set off a reaction that would freeze all streams and rivers and eventually oceans, until all water on Earth was frozen solid. John's interview with Asa ends at that point, when an angry Asa almost throws John out of his office. The narrator, John, then briefly explains that Dr. Hoenikker had discovered *ice-nine* before his death. Before his death, he told his children about the discovery, which he had with him. When he died soon after this revelation, his children divided the sample of *ice-nine* evenly among the three of them. The narration then returns to John's contentious visit at the Research Laboratory. As he is being escorted off the property, John prevails upon his escort to show him Dr. Hoenikker's personal laboratory and office. John discovers that Dr. Hoenikker's laboratory remains exactly as it was at the time of his death, filled with cheap

toys, typical laboratory equipment, and stacks of unanswered mail. The laboratory is very disorganized, representing Hoenikker's lack of interest in everything but his own scientific discoveries.

After he leaves the Research Laboratory, John decides to go to the cemetery and photograph Dr. Hoenikker's grave. Once he arrives, he discovers that the tallest memorial in the cemetery is in the Hoenikker family plot. The memorial is for the doctor's wife, Emily, with the word, MOTHER, carved on its surface. The doctor's monument is a simple cube, with the word, FATHER, carved on it. After he leaves the cemetery, John visits a local tombstone establishment. The owner is Marvin Breed, Asa Breed's brother. Marvin tells John that the Hoenikker children used the doctor's Nobel Prize money to buy the monument for their mother a year after her death. It never occurred to the doctor to put a monument on his wife's grave. Marvin also tells John that when they were in high school, he and Emily had dated and later became engaged, but then his older brother came back to town, stole Emily from Asa, and promptly married her. According to Marvin, though, Hoenikker had no interest in people and neglected his wife, never showing her any love. Marvin tells John that Frank Hoenikker walked out of the cemetery during his father's funeral, not even remaining until it was over. Frank moved to Florida, got caught up with a group of car thieves, and is presumed dead. Marvin also explains that while Newt might be a four-foot tall midget, his sister, Angela, is six feet tall. Dr. Hoenikker had forced Angela to quit high school at age sixteen and stay home to keep house for him. She had no friends and only an isolated, lonely existence in her father's home. As John is leaving the tombstone office, he asks about a carved angel on display and is told the story of how it was ordered many years earlier but not paid for, since the immigrant who bought it for his wife's grave was later robbed. The name carved on the bottom of the angel is John's last name, which is not revealed to the reader. The discovery of the angel, however, is further evidence of the link that John has to the Hoenikker family and Ilium.

Before he leaves Ilium, John stops by Jack's Hobby Shop, where Jack shows John the model of a small country that Frank Hoenikker created in the basement. The model is carefully detailed, the result of thousands of hours of meticulous work. Jack is heartbroken that Frank might be dead at the hand of some gangsters and all his talent lost. The great irony here is that Frank, who never cares how his actions might affect others, was having an affair with Jack's wife. This is John's last stop in Ilium, and after it is over he returns to his New York apartment, where he discovers that the poet who sublet the place has completely trashed the apartment, run up a huge phone bill, and killed the cat. Rather than be angry, John decides that the damage done by the poet is meant to turn him from his nihilistic beliefs, and so the poet has done John a favor.

An indeterminate period of time later, John notices a supplement in the Sunday *New York Times*. The supplement, which is meant to attract investors and tourists, promotes the Republic of San Lorenzo, which is undergoing a building boom. John immediately falls in love with the girl pictured on the cover of the insert. Mona is the daughter of the dictator, Miguel "Papa" Monzano, who is pictured on a page inside the supplement. John also notices that the man standing next to the dictator is identified as General Franklin Hoenikker, the Minister of Science and Progress of the Republic of San Lorenzo. The supplement explains that Frank is responsible for the revitalization and building plan currently under way in San Lorenzo. In a separate section of the supplement, Frank explains that he was lost at sea and starving when he was literally washed up on the shore of San Lorenzo. Because he had no passport, Frank was immediately jailed, but then "Papa" Monzano visited and asked if Frank was the son of Dr. Felix Hoenikker. Once he was identified as Dr. Hoenikker's son, Frank found that he was welcomed everywhere. Sometime later, John is assigned to write a story about Julian Castle, who abandoned his life as an American millionaire to build a free hospital in San Lorenzo.

Chapters 41–60
John quickly decides to fly to San Lorenzo, where he can meet with Philip Castle, the proprietor of the hotel and Julian's son. The bigger motivation for going to San Lorenzo, however, is Mona, with whom John has been in love since he first saw her photo on the cover of the Sunday *New York Times* supplement. On the plane trip to San Lorenzo, John meets the Mintons, an elderly couple so involved with one another that they manage to exclude John from even

the most casual conversation. John also meets H. Lowe Crosby and his wife, Hazel, who are moving their bicycle business to San Lorenzo, where the government does not interfere as much in commerce. Crosby complains that back in Chicago, where their original business was located, the government interfered constantly and made it nearly impossible to run a business. Hazel is pleased that John is also from Indiana, since Hoosiers from Indiana are always the most successful people. John decides that Hazel is a *granfalloon*, a term that Bokonon applies to people who find false affinity to others based solely on some vague connection. Every single person who has ever lived in Indiana is connected, according to Hazel.

Hazel's husband admires the dictatorship in place in San Lorenzo, where there is absolutely no crime. There is no crime because the punishment, regardless of the kind of crime, is to be impaled on a giant hook and left to dangle from a gallows. While Crosby thinks that the hook might be a bit extreme for a democracy, such as in the United States, he does think that public hangings might work well to stop juvenile delinquents from committing crimes. Crosby tells John that Minton was fired from his last diplomatic assignment after his wife wrote a letter that was published in a newspaper, in which she was critical of Americans for being self-centered and egocentric. Minton was accused of being soft on communism, a label that Crosby agrees is accurate, since anyone who does not love America and Americans is clearly a traitor. Minton's reassignment to San Lorenzo is a punishment and demotion.

The Mintons encourage John to read a history of San Lorenzo that they have with them on the plane. This is when John learns about Bokononism for the first time. He learns that Bokononism claims that evil is necessary, since the conflict between good and evil creates a tension that is important because the existence of evil makes good so much better. A biography of the founder of Bokononism explains that Bokonon's real name was Lionel Boyd Johnson who, after many journeys, was washed ashore naked in San Lorenzo, where he re-created himself as Bokonon, the founder of a new religion. Also washed ashore was Edward McCabe, a marine deserter, who had been shipwrecked with Bokonon. While John is reading the book about San Lorenzo, he discovers that Angela and Newt Hoenikker have boarded the plane and are also on their way to San Lorenzo, where Frank is to be married to Mona. Angela and Newt are eager to share photos and stories about their father, whom Angela idolizes as a great scientist. Angela tells John that she married a very handsome man who heads a company that manufactures weapons. He came to Ilium and sought her out after the death of her father. They married within two weeks of their first meeting. John then returns to his seat on the plane and continues reading the book about San Lorenzo's history, which details all of the times that this small country has been conquered and the many rulers who have controlled it. San Lorenzo has never been independent, and the people, who live in terrible poverty, have always been exploited in some way. Although fictional, San Lorenzo is similar to any number of small countries in the Caribbean that are exploited by larger and wealthier countries. Countries like San Lorenzo are often referred to as banana republics.

Chapters 61–80

When the plane finally lands in San Lorenzo, John learns that Bokononism is outlawed in San Lorenzo. Anyone caught practicing the religion will be executed by the hook. Bokonon has disappeared, but there are posters seeking his capture, dead or alive. San Lorenzo is supposed to be a Christian country and no other religion is to be tolerated. Vonnegut describes the people of San Lorenzo as oatmeal colored, mostly naked, and very thin, with missing teeth; they are also very quiet. John then meets the dictator, "Papa" Monzano, who is obviously very ill. "Papa" names Frank Hoenikker his heir because Frank is a man of science. All of the passengers are then taken to their accommodations. On the way to the hotel, John learns the story of the Hundred Martyrs to Democracy. This is the story of how, after the attack on Pearl Harbor in 1941, San Lorenzo declared war on Japan and Germany and drafted 100 young men, who with no real training were put aboard a submarine and promptly massacred in an attack by a German submarine in San Lorenzo's harbor. After Crosby insults Philip Castle and is in turn insulted by Philip Castle, Crosby insists that he and his wife must be given accommodations in the embassy. John, then, is the first and only person to stay at the hotel, where Philip is creating a twenty-foot high mosaic of Mona. It is obvious that everyone is in love with Mona, who is revealed to be a secret practitioner of Bokononism. Philip also believes

in Bokononism, but as an American, he is exempt from the hook. John is no sooner shown his room than Frank calls and demands to see John, immediately.

John takes the island's only taxi to Frank's house, where he discovers Newt dozing on the Terrace. Newt has been painting and has created a childlike canvas of black marks that he later tells John is a picture of a cat's cradle. According to Newt, the cat's cradle is not real, since there is no cat and no cradle. This is true of many other things, says Newt, such as religion, which is only an illusion. Angela, who has been touring the free hospital that Julian Castle established, next arrives with Castle, who is an especially unpleasant man. Castle declares Newt's painting meaningless and throws it off the balcony. Castle explains to John that everyone on San Lorenzo is a Bokononist. The religion is all that gives them hope, in the midst of their miserable poor lives. Bokonon arranged with McCabe to disappear and have his religion outlawed, so that it would be more attractive and have more zest. Bokonon also suggested the hook as a punishment for anyone caught practicing his religion. For some time, McCabe played along with this game and staged ritual searches for Bokonon, which were more about bringing food to the exiled religious leader. The people were happy with this new arrangement, although they were still just as poor. Their belief in Bokononism, however, gave them hope and they forgot their hunger and disease. Eventually, though, Bokonon and McCabe forgot that they were playing a game and each became the prey and the hunter for real, and so finally each went mad.

Chapters 81–100

After Castle finishes his story, Angela and Newt rejoin them on the terrace, where Angela and Newt get very drunk. Once she is drunk, Angela begins to play the clarinet. Her playing is beautiful and frightening in its passion. After dinner, Frank has still not appeared, but he calls and tells John that Papa is nearly dead of his cancer. Frank also tells John that it is his destiny to continue to wait for Frank to return to his home. Soon a convoy of soldiers arrives and begins to build fortifications to protect the home of San Lorenzo's next president. Given the fear of the hook, it is not clear why the president would need protecting. John finally goes to sleep but is awakened in the middle of the night and discovers that Frank has returned.

John and Frank walk to a cave to talk, and John quickly realizes that Frank only speaks in clichés. Frank explains that he realizes that he has no public persona, and so he offers John the job of president of San Lorenzo. The only catch is that the president must marry Mona, the woman with whom John has been in love since he first saw her photo.

Mona and John have their first meeting and perform *boko-maru*, the ritual touching of the soles of each person's feet by the feet of another. John immediately orders Mona not to perform this intimate ritual with another person, but she refuses and says she will not marry him if she cannot follow the rituals of her religion. John quickly agrees, and his first attempt to rule Mona is ended. The following morning, John and Mona are betrothed, and he is taken to see "Papa" before he dies, so that he can have the formal blessing of the former president. When he arrives at the president's castle, the first thing that John sees is the huge hook and the scaffold, which is designed to intimidate all visitors. John is escorted into "Papa's" bedroom, where the dying man lies with a small cylinder attached to a chain around his neck. Inside the cylinder is a sliver of *ice-nine*, although John does not know this yet. "Papa" tells John to try and kill Bokonon and to tell the people that science is truth. After "Papa" is given last rites according to the rituals of Bokononism, John begins to write his first speech as the new president and decides that, rather than reform San Lorenzo in any way, he will leave things as they are.

Chapters 101–120

At the reception to honor the Hundred Martyrs, where John will announce that he is to be the next president, everyone of importance on the island gathers to hear speeches and watch a display by the six Air Force planes that the United States has given to San Lorenzo. The food and drink are uniformly terrible. After John eats a piece of albatross meat he is violently ill and makes his way to a bathroom. He is stopped by Dr. von Koenigswald, who is hysterical. The doctor exclaims that "Papa" has committed suicide by ingesting the contents of the cylinder that hung around his neck. As soon as John sees "Papa's" body, he realizes that the cylinder contained *ice-nine*. Within minutes, the doctor also dies, after touching "Papa's" lips and then touching water, which when it comes into contact with *ice-nine*

solidifies, thus quickly solidifying von Koenigswald as well.

This chapter begins with John accusing the three Hoenikker children of keeping *ice-nine* for their own use and risking the lives of everyone on Earth. Frank used *ice-nine* to buy his job on San Lorenzo, and he reminds his siblings that they each used *ice-nine* to buy what they wanted, whether it was a handsome husband for Angela or a Russian dancer for Newt. John immediately understands that the U.S. military has *ice-nine*, courtesy of Angela's husband, and the Soviet Union has *ice-nine* courtesy of Newt's Russian dancer girlfriend. The cold war standoff between the two countries is the only thing that has kept the world from self-destructing. As John and the three Hoenikker children clean up the mess of spilled *ice-nine*, Frank, Angela, and Newt tell how they divided up the *ice-nine* after their father died that Christmas Eve so many years ago. After the death scene in "Papa's" bedroom is cleaned, John rejoins the reception to honor the war dead, which has continued in his absence. The new ambassador is supposed to give a formal speech to honor the Hundred Martyrs, but instead begins to talk about the killing of children in war. Minton is referring to the young men who die as soldiers in times of war, and who are sacrificed by the stupidity of old men who do not go to war. After Minton completes his speech, everyone begins to watch the air show that is scheduled as the evening's entertainment. As the air show begins, one of the planes appears to have smoke billowing from beneath it. This plane crashes into the castle, and a large portion of the castle and the surrounding battlements collapse into the sea. The Mintons are among the first to be killed, and they disappear into the sea with dignity, standing upright and holding hands. In a moment, another section of the castle collapses into the sea, this portion containing the dead body of "Papa." Immediately, the sea becomes solid with the effects of *ice-nine*. Changing the seas from liquid to solid affects the weather patterns and soon terrible tornados fill the air.

As everyone begins to flee the castle, Mona takes John to the manhole cover that conceals an oubliette that leads into the dungeons under the castle, where they take cover in a carefully constructed bomb shelter. John decides that their forced isolation is the perfect opportunity to consummate his relationship with Mona. After seven days, John and Mona emerge from their shelter to find the world covered with *ice-nine*. They soon find stacks of dead people, all of them victims of ritual suicide. A note left under a rock explains that many of the local people had survived the freezing of the sea and the winds that followed. They had captured Bokonon and asked him what God was doing and what they should do. Bokonon told the people that God must want all the people dead, and so they should kill themselves, which they did. The note is signed by Bokonon.

Chapters 121–127

Although John is angry at what he reads in Bokonon's note, Mona laughs and explains that the people are better off dead. She then touches the ground, then her lips, and dies instantly. John is found by the Crosbys and Newt, and is taken to Frank's cave, which is all that remains of his former house. Frank has also survived, but Angela died when she attempted to play her clarinet, which had *ice-nine* on the mouthpiece. Julian and Philip Castle had also died as they tried to make their way through the tornados to their hospital. After six months, John feels that the small group of survivors is like the Swiss Family Robinson, carving out their survival completely isolated and alone in the world. As John ponders what he is supposed to do with his life, he sees Bokonon and asks the old man what he should do. Bokonon tells John that if he were younger, he would write a history of humankind's stupidity, climb to the top of the nearby mountain, thumb his nose at God, and kill himself with the poison that turns men to statues. The novel ends with Bokonon's words. Thus, it is not clear if John will take the religious leader's advice to kill himself.

CHARACTERS

Bokonon

Bokonon's real name is Lionel Boyd Johnson. After many journeys, he is washed ashore naked in San Lorenzo, where he decides that he can be reborn. He feels that San Lorenzo is his destiny. Johnson sees the poverty and disease on San Lorenzo and initially thinks he can turn the island into a utopia; when he sees that he cannot change things, Johnson reinvents himself as Bokonon. Bokonon realizes that there is no

reality strong enough to combat the terrible existence of the people of San Lorenzo, and so he decides to create a religion based on lies. Although he is supposedly on a Wanted, Dead or Alive poster, no serious attempts have ever been made to arrest Bokonon. Likewise, although Bokononism is outlawed, nearly every resident of San Lorenzo follows that religion. Bokonon survives the disaster caused by the release of *ice-nine*. When asked by the people what caused this disaster, Bokonon tells them that God wanted all the people to die and that everyone who has not yet died should commit suicide. As a result of this statement, almost everyone in San Lorenzo commits suicide.

Asa Breed

Asa Breed was Felix Hoenikker's supervisor at Research Laboratory. He was also in love with Emily, the woman who would become Hoenikker's wife. John initially interviews Asa when he is planning on writing a book about the day the atomic bomb was dropped on Hiroshima. When John learns about Dr. Hoenikker's work on *ice-nine*, he asks Asa if Dr. Hoenikker was successful in creating this weapon. Asa becomes very defensive and denies that *ice-nine* exists. Asa also takes offense at John's questions about the responsibility that scientists owe to mankind. Asa then throws John off Research Laboratory property.

Julian Castle

When he was younger, Julian Castle was like every other entrepreneur who moved to San Lorenzo. He planned to exploit the local labor and make himself even richer. Although he hoped to make money with his Castle Sugar Corporation, he never turned a profit. In fact, he lost money if he paid the local workers even the lowest wages. As a young man, Castle had been ruthless, had been married numerous times, and had exploited many people, whenever the opportunity to do so presented itself. He was also an alcoholic draft dodger who freely spent money without contributing to the world in any way. Then at age forty, Julian decided to build a free hospital in the jungle and named it the House of Hope and Mercy in the Jungle. For the next twenty years, Castle was a reformed multi-millionaire, who provided free medical care to the poor who lived in San Lorenzo. No reason is given for Castle's transformation from selfish millionaire to philanthropist.

Philip Castle

Philip is the only child of Julian Castle. Philip wrote a book about San Lorenzo's history, which John reads on the plane ride to San Lorenzo. Philip opens a hotel, but has no guests. Like everyone in San Lorenzo, Philip is in love with Mona and creates a twenty-foot mosaic of her in the hotel lobby.

Harrison Connors

Harrison Connors is described as a very handsome scientist and the head of a weapons company. He seeks out Angela after the death of her father and marries her within two weeks. Later in the novel, readers learn that he married her only to obtain *ice-nine*. After their marriage, he cheats on Angela. Although he does not appear in the novel and is only mentioned briefly, he is important because he provides the U.S. government with *ice-nine*, the same weapon that the Soviet Union also possesses, thus maintaining cold war equality between the two countries.

H. Lowe Crosby

John first meets Lowe on the plane to San Lorenzo. Lowe is traveling to San Lorenzo to investigate whether he can move his bicycle manufacturing business to this small country, where he can take advantage of the poverty and lack of government labor restrictions to make his bicycles for less cost than in the United States. Lowe is an opportunistic drunk, who is bombastic and insulting to nearly everyone. He and his wife survive the contamination by *ice-nine*. As one of the few survivors, Lowe becomes the primary cook for the small group.

Hazel Crosby

Hazel and her husband, Lowe, are fellow passengers with John on the same flight to San Lorenzo. Hazel is fixated on being a Hoosier, a native of Indiana, and insists that everyone else who is a Hoosier should call her Mom. She exemplifies the Bokononist idea of the *granfalloons*—people who think that they are closely connected to others, simply because they have a common interest, religion, or place of origin. Like her husband, Lowe, Hazel represents the worst possible image of Americans abroad as loud, obnoxious, and pushy. Hazel is one of the few to survive the end of the world by *ice-nine* contamination. She begins to sew an American flag after the end of the world and is determined that the United States will remain an important

force after *ice-nine* kills almost everyone in the world.

Angela Hoenikker

Angela is the only daughter and the oldest child of Felix and Emily Hoenikker. She was taken out of school at age sixteen and turned into a full-time housekeeper, cook, and nanny after her mother died. Angela is described as six feet tall and having the face of a horse. She plays the clarinet very well, and uses music to escape the loneliness of her life. After her father died, Angela shared the *ice-nine* that her father invented equally with her two siblings. Within weeks of her father's death, the very lonely and vulnerable Angela marries Harrison Connors, a very handsome weapons researcher, who marries her only to gain access to her inheritance of *ice-nine*. Angela is convinced that her father was an underappreciated heroic figure. She is blind to his failings and proudly tells everyone of her father's many triumphs. Angela initially survives the destruction caused by the release of *ice-nine* but dies after she tries to play her clarinet, which has been contaminated with *ice-nine*.

Dr. Felix Hoenikker

Dr. Felix Hoenikker is one of the scientists who created the atomic bomb. He is long dead when Vonnegut's novel begins, but his research and the neglect of his children—who use *ice-nine* to buy the happiness they never had as children—play a central role in the events of the novel. When he was alive, Hoenikker was completely removed from the reality of ordinary day-to-day life, and as a scientist, he took no responsibility for anything he created. Dr. Hoenikker thought of his research as a game to be played. This allowed him to make *ice-nine*, without ever considering the disaster that would unfold if the material was ever used or if it ever escaped from its container. Hoenikker existed only in his own personal space, never considering the lives of anyone else, including the lives of his neglected wife and three children.

Franklin Hoenikker

Frank is the second child of Felix and Emily Hoenikker. After his father died, Frank shared the *ice-nine* that his father invented equally with his two siblings. Frank is like his father in that he has no social skills and is unable to interact well with other people. As a teenager, he built an elaborate model of a small country at a local hobby shop, but the primary reason for spending so much time building the model was mostly to disguise the affair he was having with the hobby store owner's wife. After Frank gets into some trouble with a group of car thieves, he takes refuge on San Lorenzo and gives *ice-nine* to the country's dictator. Just as his father took no responsibility for his scientific inventions, Frank takes no responsibility for the devastating effects made possible by *ice-nine*. Frank survives the destruction of almost all life in the world after the accident with *ice-nine*. Even after he has caused all this destruction, Frank takes no responsibility for what he has unleashed. Like his father, Frank lives in his own little world, in which the lives of others have no role or consequence.

Newton Hoenikker

Newt is a four-foot tall midget and the youngest child of Felix and Emily Hoenikker. Newt's mother died during childbirth, and he was raised by his older sister, Angela, who continues to treat him like a small child, even after he has become an adult. After his father died, Newt shared the *ice-nine* that his father invented equally with his two siblings. John corresponds with Newt as a way to learn more about Dr. Hoenikker and his response to the dropping of the bomb on Hiroshima. Newt's affair with Zinka, a Russian midget spy, puts *ice-nine* into the hands of the Soviet Union. Newt creates paintings of a cat's cradle that are mostly ugly black canvases. He survives the destruction created by *ice-nine* and continues to paint.

John

John is the narrator of Vonnegut's novel. His last name is never revealed to readers, although there is a suggestion that it is somehow important. As the novel begins, he plans to write a book about the day the atomic bomb was dropped on Hiroshima, which is how he becomes mixed up with the Hoenikker family. His research leads him to Ilium, the original home of the Hoenikker children. While visiting with Dr. Hoenikker's former supervisor, John learns about *ice-nine* and immediately recognizes the danger this weapon presents. On a flight to San Lorenzo, where John is to interview Julian Castle for an article he is writing, John meets two of the Hoenikker children and learns about San Lorenzo's history. With the dictator, "Papa," near death, Frank Hoenikker asks John to be president, and John agrees, only because the president gets to marry

the very beautiful and erotic Mona Monzano. After *ice-nine* is released upon the world and nearly all life dies, John is one of the few to survive. He survives when Mona leads him to an oubliette under "Papa's" castle. When they are trapped, John sees their isolation as an opportunity to have sex with Mona. They hide for seven days and emerge to find that Bokonon has told his followers that God was trying to kill them, and so they should do as God wishes and kill themselves. Mona also kills herself, leaving John as one of only a few survivors. John's own ending is ambiguous, but Bokonon in the final sentences says that he would climb to the top of the mountain and lie down and commit suicide by eating *ice-nine*. Since John has become a follower of Bokonon, readers can assume that he does as Bokonon suggests and commits suicide.

Claire Minton

Claire Minton is the wife of the new ambassador to San Lorenzo. John meets Claire and her husband on the plane ride to San Lorenzo. Because of an earlier letter that Claire wrote criticizing Americans as self-centered, egocentric people who expect everyone to love them, her husband lost his former post as ambassador and is punished by being sent to be the new ambassador to San Lorenzo. Claire and her husband are so close that they seem to function as a single entity. John labels their unity a *duprass*, a *karass* composed of only two people, who are so close that no one else can invade their unity. Claire dies with her husband, the two holding hands and facing death with dignity.

Horlick Minton

John meets Horlick Minton on the plane to San Lorenzo. Horlick and his wife, Claire, form a *duprass*, a *karass* composed of only two people, who are so close that no one else can invade their unity. As the new ambassador to San Lorenzo, Horlick gives a speech at the celebration of the Hundred Martyrs that condemns war and the governments that send young men off to die as heroes. Horlick labels these young men murdered children and reveals that his only child died in war. He also says that, rather than honor wars with speeches and celebrations, people should despise the stupidity of a society that kills soldiers. Just after he completes his speech, Horlick and his wife die in an accident, the two holding hands and facing death with dignity.

Miguel Monzano
See "Papa"

Mona Aamons Monzano
Mona is the adopted daughter of "Papa" Monzano. She is a native of San Lorenzo and is the natural daughter of a Finnish architect, who died before her birth. Mona was adopted to boost "Papa's" popularity and then turned into an erotic symbol of the country as a way to boost tourism and investments. According to the writings of Bokonon, Mona must marry the next president of San Lorenzo, which at various times is either Frank Hoenikker or John. John only agrees to be president after he learns that Mona will marry the next president. Although John falls instantly in love with Mona when he sees her photo, she has no special love for him, beyond the love that she feels for all human beings, as a practitioner of Bokononism. Mona initially survives the contamination of *ice-nine* that brings about the end of the world. She and John spend seven days in an oubliette under "Papa's" castle. While they are trapped, John sees their isolation as an opportunity to have sex with Mona, but later she tells him that the world is not a good place to create children. After Mona and John leave the oubliette, she commits suicide by eating *ice-nine*.

"Papa" Monzano
See "Papa"

"Papa"
"Papa" is the dictator of San Lorenzo. In exchange for *ice-nine*, "Papa" gives Frank the title of Major General and a job as Minister of Science and Progress in the Republic of San Lorenzo. "Papa" is in his seventies and is dying of cancer. He uses the *ice-nine* to commit suicide, which triggers the deaths of most of the rest of the world, when his body is propelled into the sea after a portion of the castle collapses. "Papa" emphatically believes in the power of science, but his illness reveals that he is also a follower of Bokononism.

Dr. Schlicher von Koenigswald
Von Koenigswald is a former Nazi doctor, who murdered many people at Auschwitz. He began to work for Julian Castle at his free hospital as a way to atone for his crimes. It is estimated that he would have to work for more than a thousand years to atone for the many lives he took while working for the Nazis. Von Koenigswald is "Papa" Monzano's doctor, and after "Papa" dies, von Koenigswald accidentally touches the spilled *ice-nine* and dies instantly.

Zinka
Zinka is a midget, a Russian dancer with whom Newt is in love. She is also a Russian spy. Zinka pretends to love Newt only long enough to steal *ice-nine* from him. Although she appears only very briefly in the novel, she is important because she gives the Soviet Union the same weapon that the United States also possesses, thus maintaining cold war equality between the two countries.

THEMES

Life as a Game
Vonnegut makes several references to games in his novel. The primary reference is to cat's cradle, a game played by children in all cultures. It is a game without a cat and without a cradle. It is also a game with no end or solution, a puzzle without meaning. The string in the game creates a series of X's that offer no real shape. The game is a metaphor for the lack of meaning in the characters' lives in this novel. The cat's cradle is an illusionary game, but so is life, in this novel. Newt claims that the game is like much of life, offering the illusion of reality but with no substance. Vonnegut also mentions that Felix Hoenikker saw the creation of weapons as a game. In other words, the creation of an atomic bomb, which is capable of terrible destruction, loss of life, and lasting effects on the environment and on people's lives, was just a game to the scientists who created it.

Religion as Thought Control
The religion of Bokononism is, as Vonnegut makes clear in his novel, formulated on lies. The purpose of Bokononism, as described by Bokonon, is to give the people false hope and help them to forget the abject poverty and disease that permeates their lives. Since there is no way to eliminate the terrible poverty and disease of their country, giving the people religion allows them to feel more hopeful about their existence. The larger implication is that all religions are a collection of lies used to keep the masses satisfied in times of great poverty, disease, and disaster.

TOPICS FOR FURTHER STUDY

- John's initial contact with the Hoenikker family is a result of his interest in the bombing of Hiroshima. Research the bombing of Hiroshima and the decision that was made to bomb Japan. Create a poster presentation that lists the arguments for and against the dropping of the atomic bomb.

- The Republic of San Lorenzo is a fictional country, but it is meant to represent any number of small countries, such as Nicaragua and Haiti, where a long history of political and military influence by larger imperial countries has had an impact on the lives of the inhabitants. Research the history of Haiti under President François "Papa Doc" Duvalier and write a paper in which you discuss Duvalier's rule.

- Vonnegut's novel makes reference to the McCarthy era and the hunt for Communists. Research McCarthyism and its effect on writers, who were often targets of the McCarthy hearings. Prepare and deliver a speech in which you briefly outline the history of McCarthyism and then explain whether you think something similar could happen now.

- Vonnegut's book questions the responsibility that scientists should assume for the weapons they create. A number of the scientists who worked to develop the atomic bomb wrote about the experience and about their feelings concerning the bomb's destructive force. Robert Oppenheimer, Edward Teller, Leo Szilard, and Otto Frisch are only a few of the scientists who were involved. Research at least one of the scientists who worked on what was then called the Manhattan Project (the development of the atomic bomb) and write a paper in which you discuss ways in which the scientist whom you chose either took responsibility for his or her contribution or failed to do so.

- Bokononism is not a real religion, but there are similarities to bits and pieces from other religions. In the Caribbean, where the action of Vonnegut's novel takes place, Catholicism and Voodoo are the two most common religious forces. Write an essay that compares Bokononism with these two real religions. In addition to explaining what Bokononism borrows from other religions, you should argue what each religion might offer to people who live in extreme poverty.

Although Bokononism is a fictional religion, there are elements of other religions present, such as the idea that destiny guides people's actions. Many people who define themselves as Christians will state that whatever happens was meant to be. Both Bokonon and the narrator, John, express a similar belief about destiny as the force that brought them to San Lorenzo. Religion is only one of many things that Vonnegut attacks using humor. From the wanted posters that call for the arrest of the religious leader, Bokonon, which he has created himself, to the threat of the hook for those who practice Bokononism—and it turns out everyone does practice Bokononism—the whole basis for religious belief

on San Lorenzo is a sham. Like charlatans crying out in a marketplace, religion in Vonnegut's novel is about illusion and not reality. The purpose of Bokononism is for readers to think about religion in a more critical fashion.

The Pitfalls of Scientific Advancement

As Vonnegut makes clear in his novel, scientists often fail to take responsibility for their actions. Felix Hoenikker creates *ice-nine* without giving any thought to why doing so might not be a good idea. He is presented with a challenge and solving the challenge becomes the only motivation that he needs. Hoenikker is so careless in handling this weapon that he takes it with him on a brief vacation for Christmas. While his children are gone, he essentially plays with it in his kitchen, and then goes to sit down, where he dies. He gives no serious thought to the danger created by a substance that can freeze all water on the earth. He is so unconcerned that he does not even bother to clean up the mess that he made playing with *ice-nine* before going to sit down and rest. John does something similar on San Lorenzo when "Papa" Monzano dies. He also allows the Hoenikker children to take a break from cleaning up the mess created by their misuse of *ice-nine*, and as a result, Hoenikker's invention is allowed to contaminate the world, killing nearly all life. Just as their father never gave a thought to whether he should have invented such a substance, his children give no thought to whether they should use the material. Vonnegut suggests that this is too often the result of technology: scientists give no thought to whether an invention is a good thing, and they give no thought to who might use their invention and whether it will be used responsibly.

The Search for Happiness

The three Hoenikker children were all terribly neglected as children. After the death of their mother, the oldest child, Angela, became a surrogate mother, cook, housekeeper, and nanny. The neglect by their father leaves each one to search for happiness wherever it can be found. The neglected Angela, who was too tall and too unattractive to actually form any friendships, was pulled from school at age sixteen and further isolated from the rest of the world. She has had no opportunity to meet a young man to marry. Thus, when she is briefly courted by the incredibly handsome Harrison Connors immediately after her father's death, she willingly trades her *ice-nine* inheritance for the chance of marital happiness. The middle child, Frank, who as a teenager created models and seduced the wife of the town hobby store owner, used his *ice-nine* to buy a place in "Papa" Monzano's government. However, Frank is so scared of living that he begs John to take the presidency and the beautiful Mona, who comes with the job. For the youngest child, Newt, *ice-nine* provided a brief fling with a Russian dancer, Zinka. While *ice-nine* could buy Angela a handsome husband, it could not guarantee he would be faithful and she would be happy. Nor could Frank be happy as president of San Lorenzo, since *ice-nine* could not give him the ability to fill the role that it

purchased. Similarly, Newt found only very brief happiness with Zinka, who quickly left him humiliated and feeling used, as so many newspaper accounts were only too happy to relate. Ultimately the three Hoenikker children's search for happiness put their father's invention of *ice-nine* into the hands of unscrupulous individuals and governments.

STYLE

Black Humor

Black humor is the use of satire and irony to transform serious topics into absurd topics. In black or dark comedy, the author parodies things that might ordinarily be considered sacred, such as religion. For instance, Vonnegut's treatment of religion is an example of black humor. Bokononism is a fictional religion based on lies, in which the creator, Bokonon, says that God had no reason for creating mankind, and since God has no interest in mankind, humans are instructed to try and figure out their purpose for existing. In another humorous twist on religion, the seven days to create the world that form the beginning of the biblical Genesis story are rewritten by Vonnegut to become the seven days Mona and John hide in the oubliette under the castle. Although not a Garden of Eden, the makeshift bomb shelter has plenty of food and fresh water, and John is finally given the opportunity to engage in a sex orgy with Mona. It is not the biblical Garden, but it is, instead, a parody of paradise. Although black humor is intended to be entertaining for the reader, it is also supposed to prompt questioning of those social entities that are often taken for granted, such as the role of religion in society.

Invented Words

Vonnegut fills his novel with made-up words that have no meaning, except that which he gives to them. The most obvious example is his creation of the word, Bokononism, which is defined as a religion of lies in which humans are organized into teams who unintentionally do God's will. Other invented words include *karass* (members of an individual's "team"), *sinookas* (tendrils of an individual's life that become entwined around the tendrils of those who are on his or her team), *wampeters* (the pivot or common object of an individual's

Mushroom cloud from an atomic bomb (*Hulton Archive / Getty Images*)

team), *vin-dit* (the idea that God has some plans for each individual, which will be revealed in good time). All of these newly created words allow Vonnegut to parody religion through the use of words that have no meaning, just as religion in this novel has no real meaning.

Single First-Person Narrator

When the narrator is a single character, like John, the story is limited to only that character's point of view. John tells the story and interprets it for the reader. The reader learns about the experiences of other characters, but only as John has experienced their stories. The single first-person narrator is limited to only the details experienced by or told to him. John lacks the omniscient view of a third-person narrator, in which the author serves as the narrator offering all views. In some cases, authors use multiple narration, in which several characters tell their stories. This gives the reader the opportunity to see the characters from multiple perspectives. In *Cat's Cradle*, John is told several stories by other characters, which allows the readers to have a more encompassing view of events. Because John is writing *Cat's Cradle* as his own personal memoir, he is able to interject information that he learned long after

some of the events occurred, and so in this case, first-person narration is not as limited as it typically would be.

Science Fiction

Cat's Cradle is an example of the science fiction genre, positing fantastic possibilities based on scientific advancements. As is common for this genre, the exact date of the events narrated is never clearly stated. The novel is set in a vague sometime after the atomic bomb was dropped on Hiroshima and Nagasaki in August 1945, but whether that date is in the late 1940s, during the 1950s, or the early 1960s, is never clearly stated. Since the dropping of the atomic bomb on Hiroshima, science fiction, whether in novels or in films, has often explored the destructive force of scientific advancement spinning out of control. Vonnegut presents a fantasy of a future destroyed by science, which is a common theme of this genre. Although the creation of the atomic bomb was a real event, Vonnegut takes one of the supposed fathers of the bomb, a fictional Felix Hoenikker, and uses him to create the ultimate weapon to destroy all of mankind. While the story is fantasy, the threat presented is a possibility; while most science fiction offers the opportunity for redemption, Vonnegut's novel ends with no such rescue.

HISTORICAL CONTEXT

The Cold War

Vonnegut's novel *Cat's Cradle* is set against the concern of imminent destruction that the events of the cold war created in people's minds. The horror of an estimated 150 million dead during World War II and fears that technology was capable of creating even more terrible destruction defined the period after World War II. This fear of war became known as the cold war. The United States and the Soviet Union, two former allies who had never been friendly even before their mutual hatred for the Nazis united them, emerged from World War II as superpowers, but they were superpowers who distrusted one another. In addition, each of the two superpowers was allied with groups of smaller countries. The Soviets allied with many of the Eastern European countries that formed their western border, while the United States allied with western European countries. This animosity spilled

COMPARE & CONTRAST

- **1960s:** In 1957, the first efforts to end nuclear weapons testing begin. The following year, President Eisenhower proposes a conference to discuss test ban verification. Over the next few years, several proposals are made to end nuclear testing. The first limited ban on testing is implemented in 1963.

  Today: Although there have been several comprehensive test ban treaties since 1963, a more comprehensive ban has not yet been approved. The United States government has consistently refused to ratify and sign such an agreement and instead argues for the right to maintain stockpiles without testing such weapons.

- **1960s:** Air travel is still relatively unusual in the early 1960s, but gains in popularity throughout the decade.

  Today: Air travel has become so ordinary that people no longer dress up for the experience, as they once did. The convenience of getting somewhere quickly continues to outweigh the inconveniences of air travel, such as increased security and travel restrictions.

- **1960s:** The peace symbol—three lines pointing down, with one line pointing up, enclosed in a circle—is used for the first time in 1958. It is introduced as the symbol for nuclear disarmament by English philosopher Bertrand Russell, at an Easter march in Aldermaston, England.

  Today: The peace symbol now stands for far more than nuclear disarmament, and it is used to protest war and violence of all kinds. Although technology still poses threats to peace, the prominence of the peace symbol since 1958 suggests that there will always be people who actively seek the end to war.

---

over into the Middle East, when the United States championed Israel, and the Soviets became allies with the Arab countries. While neither group wished to go to war again, the threat of war motivated the actions of both groups. The use of the atomic bomb in Hiroshima and Nagasaki revealed that, not only did the United States have such a weapon but also there was a demonstrated willingness to use it against an enemy. By the early 1950s, both countries had nuclear weapons, and both countries were using frequent nuclear tests as an implied threat. As a result, the United States and the Soviets competed against one another in the developing and stockpiling of weapons. As each country developed larger, more deadly weapons, the other was forced to match that development. For instance, in 1952, the United States exploded the first hydrogen bomb, which was smaller than the bomb used at Hiroshima, but it was 2,500 times more powerful. The following year, the Soviet Union tested its first hydrogen bomb. When the Soviets launched Sputnik into space in 1957, it became clear that the Soviets could also launch their nuclear bombs to the United States, using a similar rocket system. By 1961, when Vonnegut was writing his novel, it was estimated that there were enough bombs stockpiled to destroy the entire world. The theory of Mutually Assured Destruction, developed in the early 1960s, made certain that the arms race might well be a race toward the destruction of the world.

The Cuban Missile Crisis

All of the escalating rhetoric of the cold war nearly led to a very real war during a very long fourteen days in October 1962. In events that came to be called the Cuban Missile Crisis, the world held its breath and waited to see if the two superpowers would finally unleash nuclear war upon the world. Anyone who was a child in the early 1960s probably still remembers the Duck and Cover exercise that all children in school practiced during that period. In the event of a nuclear bomb, schoolchildren were taught to duck down and hide under their desks. Many parents built bomb shelters in their back yards, as well. All of this preparation reached a climax in mid October 1962, when aerial photographs showed that the Soviets had installed missiles in Cuba. These missiles were aimed at the United States. For a week, President Kennedy conferred with advisors and then announced in a televised speech that any attack on the United States coming from Cuba would be considered to be an attack by the Soviets. Kennedy put the United States military on alert for all possible eventualities, which most observers took to mean a possible nuclear attack. A week later, the Soviets backed down, but the fear and panic caused by the Soviet missile scare was not soon forgotten. The idea that any country could so easily start a nuclear war and destroy one another became the topic of books, such as Vonnegut's, but also films, such as *Dr. Strangelove or: How I Learned to Stop Worrying and Love the Bomb* and *Fail-Safe.* The cold war and the Cuban Missile Crisis made it clear that technology and weapons had created a dangerous world in which to live.

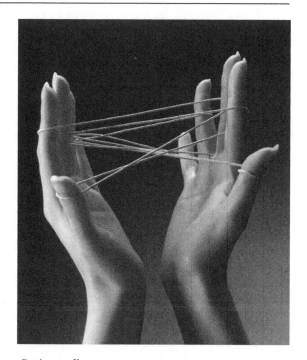

Cat's cradle (© Patrick Blake | Alamy)

CRITICAL OVERVIEW

Upon its release in 1963, Terry Southern reviewed *Cat's Cradle* for the *New York Times.* In his review, Southern states that the novel is a "work of a far more engaging and meaningful order than the melodramatic tripe which most critics seem to consider 'serious.'" Vonnegut's earlier novels had not drawn much interest, and in fact, the initial printing of *Cat's Cradle* was only 500 copies. This was a novel, though, that seemed to reflect the concerns that many people had about nuclear weapons at the time. As Southern notes in his review, Vonnegut's novel "is an irreverent and often highly entertaining fantasy concerning the playful irresponsibility of nuclear scientists."

C. D. B. Bryan observes in his 1969 *New York Times Book Review* article, "Kurt Vonnegut, Head Bokononist," that there are recurring messages in Vonnegut's writing. One message is "Be Kind," and the second message is that "God doesn't care whether you are [kind] or not." Vonnegut's writing, according to Bryan, is "quiet,

humorous, well-mannered and rational," the kind of writing that creates "an articulate bridge across the generation chasm." Indeed this ability to span the generations is best captured by a tribute written after Vonnegut's death. The student Kara Caldwell writes in the *University News* that Vonnegut's passing is personally "devastating" to her, but it is made worse knowing that so many people have not yet read his work. Caldwell hopes her column will inspire readers to pick up a Vonnegut book, and so she points out that Vonnegut's "life was one of a kind," and his "writing was even more unique." As Caldwell's tribute makes clear, one of Vonnegut's legacies remains his ability to inspire college students.

Indeed, the best indication of the lasting influence of Vonnegut's writing is found in the many obituaries and columns written after his death in April 2007. Gary Sawyer writes in the *Herald & Review* that, although Vonnegut wrote about depressing subjects, such as war, the end of the world, and suicide, he remained "a humanist." He could take the most difficult subjects and write about them "with humor and gentleness," because he "believed in the basic decency of mankind." The exact opposite view was take by Lev Grossman in his tribute in *Time* magazine. While Grossman celebrates "Vonnegut's sincerity, his willingness to scoff at received wisdom" and that "something tender in his nature" that he was unable to suppress, Grossman does not agree completely with Sawyer's claims of Vonnegut's humanism. Grossman says of Vonnegut that his "opinion of human nature was low," and that the author was "endlessly disappointed in humanity." It is characteristic of Vonnegut's appeal that two people could read his work and emerge with such differing opinions. One of the most important and unique tributes to Vonnegut was published in the *Chemical & Engineering News*. Rudy M. Baum says of Vonnegut that he was a writer "who knew that words are powerful." His fiction is "free-form, raw, repetitive, and bursting with ideas, emotions, and anger, much like the rock and roll we were listening to" at the time of his writing. Baum explains that Vonnegut taught him that "skillfully wielded words are powerful, that irony and sardonic humor can prick the smug self-assurance of the powerful, and that a writer's work can help unite dispossessed individuals in their collective response to power." As many Vonnegut admirers would agree, Baum's words serve as a testament to the enduring power and legacy of Vonnegut's work.

CRITICISM

Sheri Metzger Karmiol

Karmiol has a doctorate in English Renaissance literature. She teaches literature and drama at the University of New Mexico, where she is a lecturer in the university's honors program. Karmiol is also a professional writer and the author of several reference texts on poetry and drama. In this essay, Karmiol discusses the message of moral responsibility that Vonnegut delivers in Cat's Cradle.

In many ways, *Cat's Cradle* is an expression of Vonnegut's belief that writers have a responsibility to alert their readers to injustice, danger, and the need for social change. In a 1973 *Playboy* magazine interview with David Standish, Vonnegut argues that writers are "expressions of the entire society," and "when a society is in great danger, we're likely to sound the alarms." Sounding the alarm is what Vonnegut does in this novel; he takes on the scientific community, the ideology of truth, and the pursuit of knowledge, all of which he fears have created danger in a world without a social conscience. Being able to do something, according to Vonnegut, does not mean that that ability should necessarily constitute

WHAT DO I READ NEXT?

- Vonnegut's *Palm Sunday: An Autobiographical Collage* (1981) is a collection of autobiographical writings. Students interested in the author will find the book a valuable read.

- Vonnegut's bestselling novel *Slaughterhouse-Five* (1969) is a fictionalized account of the author's experience as a prisoner of war during the firebombing of Dresden, Germany, in 1943.

- *The Bible according to Mark Twain* (1996), by Joseph B. McCullough, is a collection of Twain's humorous retellings of biblical stories, including diaries of Adam and Eve. Vonnegut was most often compared to Twain, both in appearance and in writing style. Like Twain, Vonnegut thought that the topic of religion was a good target for parody and sarcasm.

- Ken Kesey's *One Flew Over the Cuckoo's Nest* (1962) is an example of dark humor by one of Vonnegut's contemporaries. Kesey's novel of a mental ward in which the inmates rebel against authority has long been considered an anthem of the 1960s.

- *Lucky Jim*, by Kingsley Amis, is considered a classic of the twentieth century. This 1954 novel, in which Amis parodies the stuffy academic life of a British university, remains a fine example of the kind of sarcastic humor that appealed to Vonnegut.

- *The Nuclear Muse: Literature, Physics and the First Atomic Bombs* (2000), by John Canaday, is one of the very few books that attempts to bridge the gap between science and literature by examining the literary texts written by scientists who worked on the development of the atomic bomb.

action. In other words, possessing the knowledge of how to create destructive technology does not mean that one should create such technology.

" VONNEGUT, OF COURSE, GOES BEYOND QUESTIONING AND CHALLENGING IN *CAT'S CRADLE*. WHAT HE DOES, INSTEAD, IS IMAGINE A WORLD IN WHICH ACCOUNTABILITY IS NO LONGER RELEVANT."

Vonnegut believed that writers have an obligation to serve as "alarm systems" who can challenge their readers to confront injustice and create change, and so he made cold war technology and naïve, foolish scientists the target of his 1963 novel. The fictional, irresponsible scientist, Felix Hoenikker, whose work destroys human life in *Cat's Cradle*, was based on a real person, a scientist with whom Vonnegut's brother worked. In his interview with Standish, Vonnegut explains that, historically, scientists were so focused on their work that they never considered what use might be made of their discoveries. He says that "it used to be that scientists were often like Irving Langmuir" (a Nobel Prize-winning scientist who served as the model for the childlike, innocent Felix Hoenikker). Vonnegut explains that Langmuir claimed that "he was simply unearthing truth, that the truth could never hurt human beings." Langmuir was not "interested in the applications of whatever he turned up," according to Vonnegut. The fictional Dr. Hoenikker also lacks any awareness of the dangers posed by his inventions. He is so unaware that he takes his invention, *ice-nine*, on his Christmas vacation and spends time playing with the compound. He dies as a result of handling the compound without taking care that the material does not fall into the equally careless and irresponsible hands of his children. During the time that Langmuir was working, scientists paid more attention to the search for knowledge than to any use that might be made of that knowledge.

The development of atomic weapons was one field, however, that led to a greater awareness of the social and moral responsibility that scientists must assume. In a 1950 letter to the Society for Social Responsibility in Science, Albert Einstein wrote: "In our times scientists and engineers carry particular moral responsibility, because the development of military means of mass destruction is within their sphere of activity." Einstein

felt that scientists would need the backing of a strong social and scientific organization to withstand the pressures placed upon scientists, who "face difficulties" in following their conscience. Einstein clearly understood that scientific advancement in weapons research could pose a danger to the world. As if to confirm Einstein's fears, scientists continued to develop larger, more powerful, and more deadly nuclear weapons in the decade that followed his letter. The possibility of mass destruction became a reality, and literature became one way to sound the alarm that it was time for someone to take responsibility for the development and use of all this dangerous technology.

Vonnegut's treatment of the scientific community in *Cat's Cradle* presents an argument for the need for someone to assume moral responsibility for this technology. In particular, Vonnegut uses the development of *ice-nine* to illustrate his worry that scientists are only concerned with solving problems and creating products without any thought about how these discoveries might be used. Vonnegut has Felix Hoenikker's boss at Research Laboratory present the argument that all scientific discovery is good because science is truth. A fictional scientist, Asa Breed, tells the narrator, John, that scientists at the facility that he oversees work unsupervised on whatever interests them. The work of these scientists is solely concerned with the pursuit of knowledge, which to the scientific community is absolute truth. In his essay in the *Hastings Center Report*, Michael J. Selgelid acknowledges this same kind of belief among real scientists, who "commonly believe that knowledge is good in itself and that both freedom of inquiry and the free sharing of information are essential to the purity and progress of science." Selgelid quotes Robert Oppenheimer, who helped develop the atomic bomb, as saying that "it is good to turn over to mankind at large the greatest possible power to control the world." Oppenheimer's words are so similar to the argument put forth by Asa Breed that they represent the kind of warning that Vonnegut's novel suggests should not be ignored.

The period during which Vonnegut was writing *Cat's Cradle* was a time when the technology-fueled arms race between the United States and the Soviet Union was putting the world at great danger from nuclear war. Naturally, Vonnegut was not the only person worried about nuclear technology. In his essay in the *Journal of American*

History, Paul Boyer notes the obsession that Americans had with nuclear weapons, during the 1950s and early 1960s. According to Boyer, during this period, "the nation had been gripped by profound nuclear fears," in part due to the cold war arms race between the United States and the Soviets to create bigger and more deadly weapons. Boyer argues that "nuclear fear was a shaping cultural force in these years. Books, essays, symposia, and conferences explored the medical, psychological, and ethical implications of atomic weapons." In 1961, President Kennedy gave a televised speech in which he urged Americans to participate in a national bomb shelter program. As a result, many people built bomb shelters in their back yards, and even "Papa" Monzano has a bomb shelter built under his castle in Vonnegut's novel. At the same time, the Federal Civil Defense Administration, which had been created in 1951 as a response to the Soviet Union's first atomic bomb test, created evacuation plans, radio alert systems, warning sirens, school air raid drills, and films on how to survive a nuclear attack. What was missing from all this planning was any sense of responsibility for the creation of the weapons that made such planning necessary. This lack of demonstrated moral responsibility is the issue that Vonnegut addresses in *Cat's Cradle*.

Vonnegut is not alone in claiming that writers have an artistic responsibility to serve as alarmists who can alert readers to risks they may not understand or to dangers of which they might be unaware. In his essay in *Symploke*, Robert L. McLaughlin discusses the ethical and moral responsibility of literature. He laments a world in which publishers and big-box booksellers seem only interested in bestsellers and profits. This is also a world in which potential readers are only interested in reality television. Because of a changing environment for writers, McLaughlin argues that the kind of literature that embraces social responsibility is no longer being written or read. In his contemporary world, fiction functions as occasionally challenging "our culture's values, raising consciousnesses, occasionally transforming individual lives." McLaughlin does not see these occasional possibilities for change as sufficient. Like Vonnegut, McLaughlin argues that literature's role "is to question, challenge, and reimagine the ideological status quo." Vonnegut, of course, goes beyond questioning and challenging in *Cat's Cradle*. What he does, instead, is imagine a world in which accountability is no longer relevant. In Vonnegut's fictional world,

no one takes responsibility for his or her actions. Felix Hoenikker cannot envision a world where his inventions would not be valued, and his children are so busy searching for long-denied happiness, they never consider the results of their actions. Vonnegut makes sure that readers understand that the Hoenikker children are neglected, unloved, and unhappy. In creating these children as victims, as well as perpetrators, the author asks his readers to consider any possible excuses for their actions. Ultimately, Vonnegut proposes a world in which excuses cannot suffice to exonerate blame.

The search for reasons, for excuses, or for answering the question of why people behave as they do is a common query of philosophers. Philosophy professor Elinor Mason, writing in *Philosophical Books*, explores what kinds of situations might excuse an individual from accepting moral responsibility for his or her actions. As noted above, this is an important point to consider, with regard to the Hoenikker children, who were starved for affection as children and who each subsequently bartered *ice-nine* to buy a brief chance at happiness. Mason says that there are debates in the philosophical community about the kinds of conditions that "excuse someone from responsibility for something they have done." In particular, Mason notes that there are "debates about whether a deprived childhood is an existing condition" that absolves someone of responsibility. Vonnegut's position on this argument is clearly established in *Cat's Cradle*. After the release of *ice-nine* and the destruction of almost all life in the world, the middle Hoenikker child, Frank, spends his time creating an ant farm, where he observes that the ants have devised a system of cannibalizing one another to create water. Frank, whose *ice-nine* destroyed the world, is oblivious to his role in the destruction. No amount of baiting by the narrator, John, can get Frank to accept or admit any moral responsibility for the devastation he has caused. In fact, his response to John's comments is to say that he has grown up since the release of *ice-nine*. John's disgust with Frank's actions and his disavowal of responsibility illustrate Vonnegut's dismissal of the philosophical debate about whether there are excuses that negate actions. These excuses only camouflage a more serious issue—the absence of moral responsibility by those who fail to safeguard their fellow man. As a result, in *Cat's Cradle*, Vonnegut reimagines a world in which the collapse of social and moral responsibility can have destructive consequences for the world.

Cat's Cradle is an example of how imaginative, socially responsible literature can function in the world. The ending is bleak; nearly all life is destroyed, and there is no hope that the world can survive. Still, the ending argues that readers cannot just sit back and ignore the looming disaster presented by cold war technology. Although McLaughlin expresses concerns that modern writers have not taken up the baton of social responsibility, there are still writers willing to accept the challenge of changing the way their readers think about the world. Some novels, such as those in J. K. Rowling's Harry Potter series for example, continue the effort of writers to reimagine a world in which a few responsible people try to combat the carelessness of governments who fail to protect their citizenry. In Rowling's world, people reimagine a world in which the status quo of discrimination and hate are no longer tolerated. Although on the surface Rowling's adolescent novels might seem vastly different from Vonnegut's *Cat's Cradle*, both authors hope to inspire their readers to meet the challenge presented by socially and morally responsible literature.

Source: Sheri Metzger Karmiol, Critical Essay on *Cat's Cradle*, in *Novels for Students*, Gale, Cengage Learning, 2009.

Michael Bland

In the following essay, Bland argues that the game of cat's cradle has anthropological and cultural significance that reveals superstitious meanings about death, and that this device is a mechanism to provide continuity in Vonnegut's novel.

Why did Kurt Vonnegut choose *Cat's Cradle* as the title of his novel, and what is the significance of the children's game? The answers are perhaps to be found in anthropology, Vonnegut's major as a graduate student at the University of Chicago (Vonnegut, *Fates Worse than Death*. [NY: Putnam, 1991], 122).

The cat's cradle probably originated as a primitive pastime in ancient China (Sigmund A. Lavine, *The Games Indians Played*. [NY: Dodd, 1974], 86). The game most likely came to America via the Eskimos, who in turn taught it to the American Indians (Lavine [,] 87). The tea trade brought cat's cradle to Europe from China in the 17th century (Camilla Gryski, *Cat's Cradle, Owl's Eyes: A Book of String Games* [NY: Morrow, 1984], 62). For many centuries the cat's

cradle has been played and passed on from adults to children in almost every culture (Carolyn F. Jayne, *String Figures and How to Make Them*. [NY: Dover, 1962], xiv).

In his letter to Jonah [sic, et al.] in *Cat's Cradle*, Newt Hoenikker mentions the first and only time his father Felix tried to play a game with him. A prison inmate had just sent Felix a novel about the end of the world which was bound with a length of string that Felixb [sic] began to play cat's cradle with. Beyond the game's significance to the Hoenniker's personal relationship is the fact that Felix has continued the tradition of teaching the game to another generation.

Many cultures believe that the cat's cradle has magical properties. In Germany it is called *hexenspeil*, "witches game" (Gryski, 65). Before an Eskimo father leaves on a seal hunt, he tells his son not to play at home because he fears that the son's play may cause his fingers to become caught in the harpoon ropes (Lavine, 88). In the novel, Newt refers to Eskimos who play cat's cradle (113).

But the most relevant superstition belongs to the Navajos, who claim that cat's cradle was taught to them by the spider people and that it is to be played only in the winter, when the spiders are asleep. Legend says that if a spider sees a Navajo child playing cat's cradle, the child will have a horrible death (Lavine, 87).

The book that Felix Hoenikker receives from the inmate is *2000 A.D.*, a title suggesting both Christ's first and second comings. Here, Christ will appear on earth ten seconds before a nuclear holocaust. The apocalypse must anticipate, however, that Felix knows that ice-9 not atom bombs will end the world. Thus, when he uses the string that bound up the book to teach Newt cat's cradle, which resembles Christ's manger (Jayne, xiii), Felix joins the Eskimo and Navajo fathers who use the game as a superstitious way of protecting themselves and their children.

A number of images from *Cat's Cradle* echo the ominous superstitious beliefs cultures have attached to the string game. The lattice work holding up Papa Monzano's house resembles a cat's cradle. Jonah says the painting which Newt is working on resembles a spider's web, another reference to a cat's cradle and the possibility of horrible death. When asked what his painting is, Newt does not know, just as Felix does not know the terrible implications of his doomsday devices when he creates them.

The Eskimos played cat's cradle in the fall to catch the sun in the strands of the weave to delay the long winter night (Gryski, 72). In Vonnegut's novel eternal winter falls over the earth after an airplane crashes into the cradle-like lattice work of Papa Monzano's house and causes a sliver of ice-9 to fall into the ocean.

Vonnegut uses the cat's cradle image to [hold] his novel together in the same way that the prison inmate uses the string game to bind Felix's copy of *2000 A.D.* Because the novel also links the game to destruction, Vonnegut, the former anthropology student, appears to be using ancient superstition to render a futuristic world.

Source: Michael Bland, "A Game of Black Humor in Vonnegut's *Cat's Cradle*," in *Notes on Contemporary Literature*, Vol. 24, No. 4, 1994, pp. 8–9.

William S. Doxey

In the following article, Doxey suggests some possible sources for the characters' names in Cat's Cradle.

While some attention has been given to Vonnegut's use of names in *Cat's Cradle* (see Stanley Schatt, *Kurt Vonnegut, Jr.* [Boston: Twayne, 1976]), several important names remain unexamined, specifically those of Felix Hoenikker, Lionel B. Johnson, and Earl McCabe.

In Latin, "felix" means happy. "Hoenikker" may be pronounced the same as "Hanukkah," which is a Jewish holiday (also known as the "Feast of Lights") celebrated for eight days beginning on the 25th day of Kislev (3rd month of the Hebrew year corresponding to November–December). Hanukkah is marked by the exchange of gifts. The holiday commemorates the Jews' victory over the Syrians led by Judas Maccabeus, who reconquered Jerusalem and restored the temple in 165 B.C. "Hanukkah" is derived from the Hebrew *hānakh*, to be dedicated. Nobel Laureate Hoenikker is most certainly that, though it is through game-playing and following his curiosity that he makes his great discoveries.

Felix dies on Christmas Eve, and ice-nine—his most recent, and most lethal, formulation—is his gift to his children. "Some Happy Hanukkah!" Vonnegut seems to be saying.

As Bokonon, Lionel B. Johnson is a spiritual leader for the inhabitants of San Lorenzo. His message, cast in the form of calypso verses, is based upon his admonition that, "'All of the true

things I am about to tell you are shameless lies.'" The significance of his name seems to be in the fact that as "Johnson" he is a "son of John" who offers spiritual leadership as did his namesake John, author of the Book of Revelation which deals with "last things." It is Johnson-Bokonon who makes the last gesture of the novel by stating that were he a younger man he would "write a history of human stupidity" and then go up on the mountain and freeze himself into a statue "thumbing" his nose"—but at whom? Surely God; but rather than speaking the name of the [unnameable], he says "'at You Know Who.'"

The name of Earl McCabe—a deserter from the U.S. Marine Corps who, with Johnson, took control of San Lorenzo in 1922—may have no significance beyond itself. It may, however, contain an ironic reference to the Judas Maccabeus who, by leading his people to victory over the Syrians, caused the occasion for which the Hanukkah celebration was created. A parallel in *Cat's Cradle* may be seen in Felix Hoenikker's Hanukkah gift to his children eventually being used in San Lorenzo to freeze the world solid. The connection between the two characters seems to exist only on the level of names, but in accordance with Bokononist belief this in itself may be good evidence that the scientist and the deserter belonged to the same *karass*, a structure analagous to the checkerboard yet "as free-form as an amoeba."

Vonnegut's humor is of a cosmic type which, ultimately, enables the reader to smile at fate and perhaps even laugh. The extended significance of the names of Felix Hoenikker, Lionel B. Johnson, and Earl McCabe adds to one's realization of the comedy that is *Cat's Cradle*.

Source: William S. Doxey, "Vonnegut's *Cat's Cradle*," in *Explicator*, Vol. 37, No. 4, Summer 1979, p. 6.

Wayne D. McGinnis

In the following essay, McGinnis argues that Vonnegut's invention of ice-nine is not a device of science fiction. Instead, ice-nine serves as a metaphor to discuss the social problem of evil.

One of the more fascinating elements of Kurt Vonnegut's novel *Cat's Cradle* (1963) is its fictional scientific discovery *ice-nine*, a seeded form of water which crystallizes or stays frozen at extremely high temperatures. Vonnegut fans and critics have long pondered the source and implications of *ice-nine* and have naturally turned to science for help; one of the first dissertations on Vonnegut contains this footnote: "I am indebted to Dr. William Brown, Professor of Chemistry at the University of Southern California, for pointing out to me that Russian scientists have isolated an 'ice-two' and 'ice-three.' This is further evidence that Vonnegut is a social critic who is dealing with problems of the present and foreseeable future." The bubble burst for this kind of speculation, however, when the "polywater" controversy was permanently shelved in 1973. The Soviet scientist Boris V. Deryagin, discoverer of what was taken to be the prototype of *ice-nine*, announced in that year that there was in reality no such form of dense water with "polywater's" amazing physical properties, properties of such interest to cold war-minded officials that a "polywater gap" had been declared in the mid to late '60's. Deryagin confirmed what some Western scientists had suggested all along, that polywater's properties could be attributed to contamination of ordinary water by outside agents such as dissolved quartz or even human sweat.

Had Vonnegut followers known the *real* source of *ice-nine*, all the speculation about this science fiction "invention" and its implications of social criticism could have ended long before, too. In 1969 Vonnegut addressed the American Physical Society in New York City and told of how he came upon the idea for *ice-nine* when he was working for General Electric in Schenectady, N.Y., during the early '50's. While working as a public relations man for GE, Vonnegut heard a story about H. G. Wells' visit to Schenectady in the '30's. Irving Langmuir, the Nobel Prize winning chemist (1881–1957), was recruited to entertain the dean of science fiction and thought up a story he hoped Wells would want to write: "It was about a form of ice which was stable at room temperature." Wells didn't take to the idea, and as Langmuir and Wells were both dead when he began writing *Cat's Cradle*, Vonnegut considered it his "found object." He tested the idea by suggesting an ice with such stability to a crystallographer at a cocktail party and was told that *ice-nine* was scientifically impossible (this episode antedates Deryagin's "confession" by ten years). Vonnegut still liked the idea: "Be that as it may, other scientific developments have been almost that horrible. The idea of Ice-9 had a certain moral validity at any rate, even though scientifically it had to be pure bunk" (*Opinions*, p. 97).

Given this overriding moral validity, to insist on the mere contemporary social implications of *ice-nine*, or to make it some amazing science fiction contraption is to distort Vonnegut's purpose for basing a fiction on it. Because God speaks to Job from out of a whirlwind, we do not call the book of *Job* a piece of science fiction, nor do we treat the exposition of Job's problems as a piece of social criticism of the Old Testament era. Like *Job* and *Candide* and *Ra[s]selas* and many other parables, *Cat's Cradle* uses extraordinary devices as metaphors for age-old, universal problems. The *ice-nine* metaphor is closest to the poetic metaphor Frost uses in his poem "Fire and Ice"; morally, it represents an embodiment of the destructive principle or "evil." Scientifically, *ice-nine* is perhaps closest related to the Second Law of Thermodynamics' proposition of the concept of entropy, the final inert amalgamation of all matter and energy in the universe, as much a philosophic as a physical concept. Vonnegut has been robbed long enough of his poetic mantle by well meaning but misguided science fiction addicts and social critics. Since we have the origin of *ice-nine* from Vonnegut himself, let us place the writer of *Cat's Cradle* in the universal moral arena where he belongs.

Source: Wayne D. McGinnis, "The Source and Implications of Ice-Nine in Vonnegut's *Cat's Cradle*," in *American Notes & Queries*, Vol. 13, No. 3, November 1974, pp. 40–41.

SOURCES

Baum, Rudy M., "Kurt Vonnegut," in *Chemical & Engineering News*, Vol. 85, No. 17, April 23, 2007, p. 3.

Boyer, Paul, "From Activism to Apathy: The American People and Nuclear Weapons, 1963–1980," in the *Journal of American History*, Vol. 70, No. 4, March 1984, pp. 821–44.

Bryan, C. D. B., "Kurt Vonnegut, Head Bokononist," in the *New York Times Book Review*, April 6, 1969, p. 2.

Caldwell, Kara, "A Tribute to Kurt Vonnegut," in *University News*, April 16, 2007, http://media.www.unews.com/media/storage/paper274/news/2007/04/16/Forum/A.Tribute.To.Kurt.Vonnegut-2844051.shtml (accessed December 19, 2007).

Einstein, Albert, "Letter to Society for Social Responsibility in Science," reprinted in "Social Responsibility in Science," in *Science*, Vol. 112, No. 2921, December 22, 1950, pp. 760–61.

Grossman, Lev, "Kurt Vonnegut, 1922–2007," in *Time*, April 12, 2007, http://www.time.com/time/arts/article/0,8599,1609650,00.html (accessed December 19, 2007).

Jennings, Peter, and Todd Brewster, "Into the Streets 1961–1969," in the *Century*, ABC Television Group, 1998, pp. 373–75.

Mason, Elinor, "Moral Responsibility," in *Philosophical Books*, Vol. 46, No. 4, October 2005, pp. 343–53.

McLaughlin, Robert L., "Post-Postmodern Discontent: Contemporary Fiction and the Social World," in *Symploke*, Vol. 12, Nos. 1–2, 2004, pp. 53–68.

Sawyer, Gary, "Vonnegut's Work Will Be Read for Ages," in *Herald & Review*, April 15, 2007.

Selgelid, Michael J., "A Tale of Two Studies: Ethics, Bioterrorism, and the Censorship of Science," in *Hastings Center Report*, Vol. 37, No. 3, 2007, pp. 35–43.

Southern, Terry, "After the Bomb, Dad Came Up with Ice," in the *New York Times*, June 3, 1963.

Standish, David, Interview with Kurt Vonnegut, Jr., in *Conversations with Kurt Vonnegut*, edited by William Rodney Allen, University Press of Mississippi, 1988, pp. 76–110; originally published in *Playboy*, Vol. 20, July 1973.

Trager, James, *The People's Chronology: A Year-By-Year Record of Human Events from Prehistory to the Present*, Henry Holt, 1992, pp. 958–87.

Vonnegut, Kurt, Jr., *Cat's Cradle*, Dial, 2006.

FURTHER READING

Diederich, Bernard, *Papa Doc: Haiti & Its Dictator*, Marcus Weiner, 1990.
    Vonnegut modeled San Lorenzo and its dictator, "Papa" Monzano, on Haiti and its dictator, François "Papa Doc" Duvalier. This book examines Duvalier's metamorphosis from country doctor to ruthless dictator.

Kelly, Cynthia, ed., *The Manhattan Project: The Birth of the Atomic Bomb in the Words of Its Creators, Eyewitnesses and Historians*, Black Dog & Leventhal, 2007.
    This book is a collection of essays, excerpts from books, and articles that creates a picture of the people who developed the atomic bomb, the policy that led to its use, and the ethical implications of its use.

Klinkowitz, Jerome, *The Vonnegut Effect*, University of South Carolina Press, 2004.
    This book is a study of how Vonnegut's work reflects the cultural and social changes from 1964 to 2004.

Walker, J. Samuel, *Prompt and Utter Destruction: Truman and the Use of the Atomic Bombs against Japan*, University of North Carolina Press, 2004.
    This book is an analysis of the events that led the United States to decide to use atomic bombs against Japan.

Weeramantry, C., *Nuclear Weapons and Scientific Responsibility*, Springer, 2000.
    This book explores the responsibility that scientists must assume in agreeing to hire themselves out to whatever nations offer employment. The author tries to alert scientists to the importance of conscience and legality as essential issues of their work.

The Dew Breaker

EDWIDGE DANTICAT

2004

The Dew Breaker (2004) is a novel by Edwidge Danticat, an American writer who was born in Haiti. Haiti is a small, impoverished country that occupies the western third of the island of Hispaniola; Haiti is bordered by the Dominican Republic, which occupies the eastern two-thirds of the island. Haiti is located in the Caribbean Sea between Cuba and Puerto Rico, and is 700 miles from the coast of Florida.

The Dew Breaker consists of nine linked stories. The stories are set either in the Haitian-American community in New York, or in Haiti during the time of the brutal dictatorships of François Duvalier, known as Papa Doc, and his son, Jean-Claude Duvalier, who ruled Haiti from 1957 to 1986, during which time thousands of people were tortured and killed. The torturers, members of the Duvaliers' militia known as the Tonton Macoutes, were also known as dew breakers because of their practice of coming for their victims before dawn. The novel focuses on one dew breaker in particular, a man who committed horrible crimes in Haiti in the 1960s and who has since lived an unremarkable life in New York with his wife and daughter. But as the novel shows, the crimes he committed have left a terrible legacy that still haunts the Haitian-American community in New York so many years later. Is it possible that he could ever be forgiven or redeemed? Danticat's subtle treatment of this theme makes *The Dew Breaker* a compelling exploration of the mind of a torturer and the limits of compassion.

Edwidge Danticat *(Francois Guillot / AFP / Getty Images)*

AUTHOR BIOGRAPHY

Edwidge Danticat was born January 19, 1969, in Port-au-Prince, Haiti, to poor parents. When Danticat was two years old, her father immigrated to the United States, working as a taxi driver in New York. Two years later, Danticat's mother joined her husband in New York, leaving Danticat and her younger brother Eliab to be raised by their uncle. In 1981, when Danticat was twelve, she joined her parents in New York.

Raised speaking Creole and French, Danticat learned English by reading the works of African-American novelists such as James Baldwin, Richard Wright, and Alice Walker. As a recent immigrant attending a high school in Brooklyn, she felt isolated from her classmates and took to writing about her homeland as a way of escape.

After high school, Danticat attended Barnard College in New York, graduating in 1990 with a degree in French literature. Although her parents wanted her to pursue a career in medicine, she chose not to enroll in nursing school. Instead she pursued a Master of Fine Arts degree

at Brown University, graduating in 1993. Her thesis was an early version of her semi-autobiographical novel, *Breath, Eyes, Memory*, a revised version of which was published in 1994. The novel was well received and became a bestseller when it was selected by the Oprah Winfrey Book Club in 1998.

Danticat followed her success with *Krik? Krak!* (1995), a collection of short stories that was nominated for the National Book Award. Danticat's second novel, *The Farming of Bones*, was about a 1937 incident in which thousands of Haitian farm workers were massacred by soldiers in the Dominican Republic. The novel won the American Book Award.

After she wrote *Behind the Mountains* (2002), a book that takes the form of the diary of a teenaged Haitian girl, Danticat published *The Dew Breaker* (2004), her most critically acclaimed novel. It was nominated for the National Book Critics Circle Award in 2004, and received a PEN/Faulkner Award nomination in 2005.

In addition to her fiction, Danticat has written *After the Dance: A Walk through Carnival in Haiti* (2002), a nonfiction account of Haiti's annual Carnival celebrations. She has also edited *The Butterfly's Way: From the Haitian Dyaspora in the United States*, a collection of stories, poems, and essays by Haitian writers living in the United States.

In 2007, Danticat published a memoir, titled *Brother, I'm Dying*. As of 2008, Danticat lived in Miami, Florida.

PLOT SUMMARY

The Book of Ka

The first of the nine interconnected stories in *The Dew Breaker* is set in Lakeland, Florida, and is narrated by Ka, a young female Haitian immigrant who lives in New York. She has traveled to Florida with her father, also a Haitian immigrant, in order to sell her mahogany sculpture of her father to Gabrielle Fonteneau, a Haitian-American television star and art collector.

Ka and her father stay in a hotel, but when Ka wakes in the morning her father has vanished, and the sculpture is gone, too. Her father finally returns at sunset, without the sculpture. He drives Ka to a lake and indicates that he

MEDIA ADAPTATIONS

- An unabridged audio CD of *The Dew Breaker* was published in 2004 by Recorded Books.

threw the sculpture in the water. Ka is angry, and her father explains that he did not feel worthy of the statue. His daughter has always been told that her father had been imprisoned in Haiti, but now he confesses that he was never in prison; instead he was responsible for killing and torturing many people who were prisoners. He says he would not do such things now.

When they return to the hotel, Ka calls her mother, wanting to know how she could love her husband, knowing what she knows about him. Her mother responds that she and Ka have saved him; it was when he met his future wife that he stopped torturing others.

The next day, Ka and her father visit Gabrielle for lunch. When asked where in Haiti he comes from, Ka's father lies, in order to reduce the possibility of being identified. When they leave the Fonteneaus' house, Ka dreads the long journey home, knowing that she must come to terms with what she has learned about her father's dark past.

Seven

A Haitian immigrant in New York is about to be reunited with his wife, whom he has not seen in seven years, since they were married in Haiti. He has spent those years working, saving, and acquiring a green card so that he can bring his wife to the United States. The man, who works two jobs as a janitor, shares a basement apartment with Michel and Dany, two other Haitian immigrants. They rent the apartment from a Haitian immigrant couple (who later turn out to be Ka's parents).

The man greets his wife at JFK airport and drives her home, pleased that she has taken trouble with her appearance in honor of the occasion. That night they make love. He goes to work

the next morning, leaving her at home, where she listens to Haitian radio stations. She spends an entire week in the apartment, fearful that she would get lost if she ventured outside. She passes the time cooking and listening to the radio, which informs her of the troubles of being a Haitian immigrant in New York. She also writes letters home. On the weekend, her husband takes her to a park in Brooklyn, and she thinks back to times they spent in Haiti together. She is conscious of being in a strange land where she does not speak the language.

Water Child

Nadine is a thirty-year-old Haitian immigrant who lives alone in Brooklyn and works as a nurse in the Ear, Nose and Throat department of a hospital. Her parents in Haiti write to her, urging her to call more often, but she feels disinclined to do so. Having split up with her boyfriend, she still suffers mental pain from the abortion she had seven months ago. She lives an isolated life.

Nadine has to deal with the distress of a patient in the ward, Ms. Hinds, a woman who has had a laryngectomy, leaving her without the ability to speak. Nadine has to train Ms. Hinds to write down what she wants to say.

That night, Nadine tries to call Eric, her ex-boyfriend, but finds that he now has an unlisted number. (Eric is the man in "Seven," who has now been reunited with his wife.) She calls her mother instead, but they are unable to talk of anything important.

The next day, after she says good-bye to Ms. Hinds, Nadine sees a distorted, enlarged reflection of herself in the metal of the elevator doors, which reminds her of her aborted pregnancy and the fact that the baby would have been born that week.

The Book of Miracles

This story is narrated by Anne, the wife of the dew breaker, as she, her husband, and their daughter drive to a Christmas Eve Mass. Anne is the only member of the family who believes in miracles and is eagerly anticipating the midnight Mass, which is the only time she and her family go to church together. During the Mass, Ka spots a man she thinks is Emmanuel Constant, who is wanted for murder and torture committed when he led a death squad in Haiti. Fliers have been posted in the neighborhood with his picture on them. Anne worries that one day her husband's face may appear on a similar flier. She also worries that one day her daughter may find out about her father's past. As she goes to take Holy Communion, Anne looks at the man and realizes he is not Constant. But she decides never again to attend Mass for fear that someone might recognize her husband.

Night Talkers

Dany, the tenant in "Seven," returns to the Haitian countryside to visit his blind aunt, Estina Estème, who lives in a one-room house in a valley. Dany wants to tell her that he has found in New York the man who killed his parents and was also responsible for blinding her. When Dany tries to tell his aunt his story he is interrupted by a visitor, but that night he dreams about the conversation he wants to have with her. He recalls the night his family's home was blown up and his parents shot. He was six years old, and he remembers seeing the man responsible for the carnage, who threatened to shoot him as well. After Dany found himself living in the house of the guilty man in New York, he once went to the man's bedroom at night, intent on killing him. But he lost the desire to kill out of fear that he might be mistaken about the man's identity. Dany does not get the chance to tell his aunt the full story because one night she dies in her sleep.

The Bridal Seamstress

Aline Cajuste, a young Haitian-American who is an intern journalist with a Haitian-American periodical, interviews Beatrice Saint Fort, who is retiring from her job as a bridal seamstress. Beatrice is also originally from Haiti. After the interview, they walk in the neighborhood, and Beatrice points out the house where a Haitian prison guard lives. She tells Aline that, when she was young and still living in Haiti, this man, angry that she refused to go dancing with him, took her to a prison where he whipped the soles of her feet. Intrigued by Beatrice's story, Aline later takes a close look at the house, but a neighbor tells her that no one lives there. She goes back to Beatrice and says the house is empty, but Beatrice replies that the man always lives in empty houses, otherwise he would be caught and sent to prison. She thinks that he is always able to find her, wherever she lives. Aline concludes that the woman's anguish over what she suffered has left her mentally unbalanced.

Monkey Tails

Michel, the tenant at the dew breaker's house in New York, looks back at a traumatic day in Haiti in 1986, when he was a fatherless twelve-year-old boy. The dictator Jean-Claude Duvalier has just been driven from power, and members of the dictator's once-feared militia, the Tonton Macoutes, are being attacked in the streets by the angry populace. Michel seeks out his friend Romain, an older boy, who was abandoned by his father, Regulas. Regulas is a militia member who is being sought by the local people because of the crimes he committed against them. Romain and Michel decide to escape the chaos by going to a hotel, but they are unable to get a room. It turns out that Romain thought he might find his father at the hotel. While they are there, Romain lets slip that Michel's father is a local man named Christophe. Michel had suspected this but had never been willing to acknowledge it. Romain then says he is fleeing the country, and Michel is to go home to his mother. The next day Michel discovers that Regulas shot himself to avoid being captured. Michel never hears of Romain again.

The Funeral Singer

Rézia, Mariselle, and Freda, three young female Haitian immigrants in New York in the 1970s, become friends when they are the only Haitian students in an English class. They tell one another their stories. Freda, the narrator, used to be a professional singer at funerals in Haiti. Her father was arrested and beaten by the authorities and, after being released, he vanished at sea. Later, Freda refused to sing at the dictator's palace and then fled the country at her mother's insistence. Mariselle's husband was killed because he painted a portrait of the president that the government disapproved of. Rézia was raped by a member of the militia. Now these women are trying to imagine a better future for themselves in their new country.

The Dew Breaker

The final narrative begins in 1967, when the dew breaker was a member of the militia group known as the Volunteers. He is waiting in his car outside a church, where he plans to assassinate a popular Baptist pastor who has been preaching against the government. He joined the militia a decade ago, when he was nineteen. As he rose in the hierarchy, he gained a reputation for enjoying the psychological and physical tortures he would inflict on the prisoners at Casernes, a military barracks.

The preacher is a man without fear. His wife is dead, poisoned at the order of the authorities, and he knows he will soon be assassinated, too. Against the wishes of his deacons, he goes to the church that evening. His stepsister Anne is there but she leaves early. During the sermon, the dew breaker and his gang of thugs burst in, seize the preacher, and take him to prison, beating him severely. However, later, the dew breaker is told by his superior, a woman named Rosalie, that the preacher is to be released. The government does not want him to become a martyr. The preacher is brought to the prison office, where he encounters the dew breaker. During the interview, the chair the preacher is sitting on collapses. He takes a broken piece of wood and strikes the dew breaker's cheek with it and then draws the wood down the man's face, badly injuring him. The dew breaker shoots him dead. Fearful that he will now be arrested himself for breaking orders, he starts to go home. He encounters Anne on the street, who is rushing to the prison to see her stepbrother. But instead, she accompanies the dew breaker home and tends to his wounds. She appears to thinks he is a victim who has escaped the prison. When he recovers, the dew breaker arranges for them both to fly to New York. He never harms anyone again. They never fully discuss what happened the night the preacher was murdered, but they both find a kind of redemption through their mutual love for their daughter, Ka.

CHARACTERS

Anne

Anne is the wife of the dew breaker. She loves him in spite of his brutal past, believing that he has now become a decent man. She thinks that she and Ka, their daughter, have saved him. Anne is a religious woman who has always believed in miracles. Originally from Haiti, her early life was full of tragedy. Her younger brother was drowned, and both her parents died when she was young. She moved to the city to be with her stepbrother, the preacher who was later killed by the dew breaker. On the night of her stepbrother's death, she helped the dew breaker recover from the wound the preacher inflicted on him, without knowing how the dew breaker had sustained the injury. Then she traveled with

him to New York, where they married and later had their daughter. Anne never investigated the full story of what had happened the night her stepbrother was killed, and she cannot fully explain to her daughter why she loves her husband. One thing she does know is that the epileptic seizures she used to suffer from ceased after she met the dew breaker. But she is worried about how Ka will react now that she has learned about her father's past. In addition, Anne feels the insecurity of her life: "This pendulum between regret and forgiveness, this fright that the most important relationships of her life were always on the verge of being severed or lost."

Aline Cajuste

Aline Cajuste is a young Haitian woman living in New York who works as an intern at a Haitian-American magazine. She is sent to interview the retiring seamstress, Beatrice Saint Fort. Aline is a lesbian who has recently been jilted by a girlfriend thirty years older than she is.

Monsieur Christophe

Monsieur Christophe appears in "Monkey Tails." He is the owner of a tap station in Port-au-Prince, and he sells water to the local people. He is the father of Michel, but he refuses to acknowledge it.

Claude

In "Night Talkers," Claude is a young Haitian man who immigrated to the United States but has been deported after killing his father. Claude is happier back in Haiti than he ever was in New York. He shows no remorse for killing the father who tried to stop him from using drugs. But Claude also believes that he was rehabilitated while in a U.S. prison.

Dany

Dany is one of the two Haitian immigrant men who live in the basement of the dew breaker's house in Brooklyn. He recognizes the dew breaker as the man who killed his parents, and at one point Dany wants to kill the dew breaker, but then changes his mind. Dany returns to visit his Aunt Estina in Haiti to inform her of what he has discovered.

The Dew Breaker

The dew breaker is never named. He came from a family of landowning peasants and was educated at a school run by Belgian priests. But the family's land was confiscated by army officers after

Papa Doc came to power in 1957. After this, the dew breaker's father became insane and his mother vanished. At the age of nineteen, the dew breaker joined the militia, the Volunteers for National Security. Over the next decade, he killed and tortured many people at Casernes, the military barracks. He would devise the most cruel tortures and enjoy carrying them out.

In 1967, the dew breaker kills the Baptist preacher, but not before the preacher badly injures the dew breaker's face, leaving him scarred for life. But then the dew breaker's life changes. Escaping possible arrest himself, he flees to the United States with Anne. They begin a new life, settling in Brooklyn; he works as a barber, and renounces his violent past. His daughter, Ka, describes him as a "quiet and distant man." He likes museums and frequently takes Ka to the Brooklyn Museum, where his particular interest is in the Ancient Egyptian rooms. But the dew breaker can never really escape what he did. He suffers from nightmares because of it and has a guilty conscience. He fears detection, which forces him to live almost as a fugitive, not having close friends, never inviting anyone back to the house, and never teaching his daughter anything about Haiti. After Ka is born, however, he seems to believe that in some way he has been redeemed from his past, and he tells her "Ka, no matter what, I'm still your father, still your mother's husband. I would never do those things now."

Aunt Estina Estème
Aunt Estina Estème is Dany's aunt who lives in the Haitian countryside. She has been blind since the dew breaker and his accomplices set fire to the house where she was living with Dany's parents and then six-year-old Dany. Aunt Estina dies before Dany can fully explain that he has found the dew breaker in New York.

Gabrielle Fonteneau
Gabrielle Fonteneau is a young Haitian American who is a television star and art collector. She lives in Florida and has agreed to buy a sculpture from Ka.

Freda
Freda is the narrator of "The Funeral Singer." She is a twenty-two-year-old Haitian immigrant in New York who used to sing professionally at funerals in Haiti. But after her father was beaten by government thugs and was then lost at sea,

she refused an invitation to sing at the dictator's palace and immigrated to the United States.

Ms. Hinds
In "Water Child," Ms. Hinds is a patient in the Ear, Nose and Throat department of a Brooklyn, New York, hospital. She is frustrated and angry because she has just had a laryngectomy and is unable to speak.

Josette
Josette is a nurse in the Ear, Nose and Throat department of a Brooklyn, New York, hospital. She is a young Haitian immigrant who came to the United States as a girl and so, speaks English without an accent.

Ka
Ka is the daughter of Anne and the dew breaker. She narrates "The Book of the Dead" and also appears in "The Book of Miracles." Unlike all the other major characters in the book, she was born and raised in the United States—in East Flatbush, Brooklyn. She has never been to Haiti. Ka is artistic and creates wood sculptures of her father. Unlike her religious mother, she professes to be an atheist. She is angry at her father when he throws away her sculpture of him in Florida. She is utterly dismayed when he confesses to her that he was not imprisoned for a year in Haiti, as she had always understood to be the case, but was in fact one of the notorious killers and torturers in that country.

Mariselle
In "The Funeral Singer," Mariselle is one of the three young Haitian immigrants who meet at an English class in New York. She left Haiti after her artist husband was killed by government assassins and is now trying to establish a new life for herself. She gets a job at an art gallery.

Michel
Michel is one of the two Haitian immigrants who live in the basement apartment of the house owned by the dew breaker in New York. In "Monkey Tails" he looks back at his childhood in Haiti, especially the day in 1986 when the dictator fled the country.

Nadine Osnac
Nadine Osnac is a young Haitian immigrant who works as a nurse in a hospital in Brooklyn. She lives in a one-bedroom condo and is a

solitary figure without friends. She keeps the television on all day just to have human voices in the room. Her parents in Haiti want her to keep in touch with them more frequently, but she puts off calling them. Nadine recently had an abortion and the memory of it troubles her. She has erected a shrine to the aborted baby in her apartment.

The Preacher
The preacher, who is never named, appears in "The Dew Breaker." He is a fearless Baptist minister who preaches against the government. He willingly courts martyrdom and is killed in prison by the dew breaker in 1967, after being arrested at his church while giving a sermon. The preacher is not cowed by his attackers or his jailers, however, and manages to inflict a severe wound on the face of the dew breaker before he is shot dead.

Regulus
In "Monkey Tails," Regulus is the father of Romain. He abandoned Romain when the baby was only one month old. Regulus is a member of the militia that has committed atrocities against the local people. He tries to hide from the mob and then shoots himself to avoid capture.

Rézia
Rézia is one of the three Haitian immigrant women in "The Funeral Singer." She owns a Haitian restaurant in Manhattan. In Haiti, when she was young, she was sent by her parents to live with her aunt, who ran a brothel. Threatened with imprisonment by a militia member, her aunt allowed the man into Rézia's room one night, where he raped her.

Romain
Romain in "Monkey Tails" is a friend of Michel's. Abandoned by his father, he is an only child. He is some years older than Michel, who looks up to him. Romain is quite worldly, sophisticated, and intellectual, with a habit of quoting from the books he has been reading.

Rosalie
Rosalie is a short, stout woman in her fifties who occupies a senior position at the military barracks. She is the dew breaker's superior and reproaches him for the clumsy way he arrested the preacher.

Rosie
In "Monkey Tails," Rosie is a distant cousin of Michel's. She is employed as cook and cleaner by Michel's mother. Michel is in love with her.

Beatrice Saint Fort
In "The Bridal Seamstress," Beatrice Saint Fort is a seamstress in Queens, New York, who makes bridal gowns. She is a small woman in her fifties, and is about to retire from the job she has done almost all her life. As a young woman in Haiti, she was tortured by a prison guard and has never forgotten the experience. She believes that the guard is living in her neighborhood in Queens, although this is not really the case.

Vaval
In "Monkey Tails," Vaval is Michel's cousin. He watches the chaos on the streets and tells Michel about it.

THEMES

Redemption and the Weight of the Past
The dew breaker is a man who has committed horrible crimes that weigh on his conscience still, thirty-seven years after he left Haiti. He is haunted by his shameful past and still fears that he may be recognized by someone he has harmed. But since he feels remorse for his actions and has tried in his way to make amends by loving his wife and daughter, he is not presented as irredeemably evil. He is in fact a rather ordinary man who in a violence-prone society was unable to resist his worst impulses. His wife is a religious woman who believes in miracles and loves telling stories about them. She believes that her love for the dew breaker has helped to save him. For her, it is a miracle that he has been transformed. The dew breaker tries hard to believe this himself, naming his daughter Ka, meaning "good angel," as a sign that he had been changed and blessed. But his redemption can at best be only partial. The scar on his face is a reminder that he will always be marked by what he did, and Ka sees how troubled he remains, all those years later. He does not like being photographed, and when she tries to take a snapshot of him, he holds his hands up, hiding his face. He literally must hide from the world. His guilt also affects his wife, since she must live with the fear that he may be discovered, and she

TOPICS FOR FURTHER STUDY

- Write an essay in which you describe U.S. policy toward Haiti from the 1960s to the 1980s and up to today. How has it changed over the years? What has caused the changes? What can the United States do to help Haiti, the poorest country in the Western Hemisphere?

- Research the incidents referred to in "Seven," concerning the Haitians Abner Louima and Patrick Dorismond. What difficulties have Haitian immigrants encountered in New York and Florida? What difficulties do they have in common with other immigrant groups, and in what ways are their problems distinctive? Conduct a class presentation in which you discuss your findings.

- Imagine Ka's feelings at the moment she hangs up the phone on her mother in "The Book of the Dead." Write a poem in which she relates her thoughts and feelings at that moment—about her father, her mother, and herself.

- Conduct a class presentation in which you discuss the issue of torture. How is torture defined? How can it best be prevented internationally? What is U.S. government policy regarding torture? Can torture ever be justified?

---

will lose him. She also fears that Ka, having learned his secret, may reject them both.

Redemption from the misdeeds of the past is also a theme in the story "Night Talkers," in the character of Claude, who killed his father while in the United States. He is deported to Haiti, but finds himself at peace there. He tells Dany: "I'm the luckiest fucker alive. I've done something really bad that makes me want to live my life like a fucking angel now." Like Dany and Aunt Estina, Claude is a "night talker" who is able to talk in his sleep about his troubles. Not only that, Claude is "able to speak his nightmares to himself as well as others, in the nighttime as well as in the hours past dawn." Speaking out his story is a healing experience for Claude, and he does it without apparent feelings of guilt or remorse, something that the dew breaker is unable to do. Unlike Claude, the dew breaker remains tied to his past, in spite of all his efforts to transcend it.

The Struggles of Haitian Immigrants

In addition to the horrific picture the novel gives of life in Haiti under the Duvalier regimes, many of the narratives give insight into the difficult lives led by Haitian immigrants in New York, living in society that is so different, in everything from language to climate, from their own. Some, like Beatrice the seamstress, are still haunted by the torture inflicted on them in Haiti; others, like the man in "Seven," are compelled to work two low-paying jobs as a janitor so that he can send money back to his wife in Haiti. Long family separations are frequent, as for Dany and Michel, who feel the loss keenly. When their roommate's wife arrives, they enjoy the meals she cooks for them, which "made them feel as though they were part of a family, something they had not experienced for years" (p. 46). Nadine Onesco in "Water Child" also experiences loneliness, cut off from her family but unable to create lasting ties of her own. Like her married ex-boyfriend Eric, she sends half of her salary back to Haiti, to support her parents.

There are also references to the perils of being a Haitian immigrant in New York. To illustrate this, the author twice draws on real incidents. In "Seven," it is reported that Dany and Michel used to frequent the Cenegal nightclub but stopped going there after a Haitian man named Abner Louima was arrested and beaten at a police station. In the same story, Eric's wife hears on the radio about another real-life incident in which a Haitian American named Patrick Dorismond was shot by a policeman in Manhattan.

Yet there are also success stories among the Haitian immigrants. The three young women in "The Funeral Singer," all of whom fled persecution in Haiti, show every sign of having the strength and the resources to succeed in their new country. That success is possible for Haitian immigrants is shown by the example of Gabrielle Fonteneau. As the dew breaker says to Ka: "A Haitian-born actress with her own American television show. We have really come far."

Symbols of Redemption

At the nadir of the dew breaker's life, the night following his killing of the preacher, he dreams of his childhood. It is like a dream of paradise. He is working with his mother in the garden, and for a while his father watches them unobtrusively. Pristine nature touches all the boy's senses, and he notices that the seeds he and his mother planted have sprung into trees and "healing weeds." It is a scene of peace and perfection, suggesting that even in the midst of evil, some sense of beauty lives on and carries within it the possibility of healing from all wounds. The dream, which the dew breaker wants to tell Anne about, thus forms part of the redemption theme.

If the dream contains the idea of redemption through images of nature, a similar theme is conveyed through art in the form of the sculpture that Ka creates of her father. It shows him kneeling, eyes downcast, a humble posture that, although it is based on a false idea of her father in prison, nonetheless conveys the regret that he feels about his past life and, ironically, his feeling that he does not deserve to have a sculpture made of him. In that sense, he is redeemed from his former arrogance.

The Use of Multiple Languages

The Haitian immigrants belong in two worlds, and these worlds are marked out by language. Ka's mother, Anne, whose native language may be Creole or French, speaks ungrammatical English. "He come back," she says of her husband, intending to use the future tense but omitting the word "will." The dew breaker is also caught between two linguistic worlds. Sometimes he uses Creole phrases, saying that he wants "Yon ti koze, a little chat" with Ka. He cannot express his deepest thoughts in English, and when he tries to explain his past to Ka he says will have to speak in Creole, while she continues to speak in English. This shows the gulf that has suddenly opened up between them.

In "Water Child, " when Eric leaves a telephone message for Nadine, Nadine notices that he manages in three words to speak Creole, French, and English: "Alo, allo, hello," and then speaks English in a heavy accent for the rest of his message. The three Haitian women in "The Funeral Singer" all struggle with their English, which suggests the difficulty they are having in adjusting to

Jean-Claude Duvalier, former president of Haiti
(Giovann Coruzzi | AFP | Getty Images)

their new country. On the other hand, Josette in "Water Child," who has been in the United States since she was a young girl, speaks perfect English. However, she uses Creole words from time to time because, like many immigrants, she still has a need to remember her origins. "She's so upset and sezi" she says of a patient, and she also uses the word "banbòch" to refer to a party.

Haiti from the 1960s to the 1980s

In 1957, François Duvalier, a country doctor who became known as Papa Doc, was elected president of Haiti. He proved to be a ruthless leader who quickly cemented his own power, and he declared himself president for life in 1964. To curb the power of the Haitian army and the influence of the Catholic clergy, he created the militia called the Volunteers for National Security, also known as the Tonton Macoutes, that was entirely loyal to him. (This is the militia the dew breaker joins in the story.) The Macoutes had the power to arrest anyone they chose and were entirely above the law.

COMPARE
&
CONTRAST

- **1960s:** The first wave of modern emigration from Haiti to the United States takes place. Many Haitians, fleeing from political repression and poverty, seek a better life in the United States.

  1980s: As conditions in Haiti remain turbulent, thousands of Haitians attempt to immigrate to the United States. However, the U.S. government, apprehensive about large-scale immigration from Haiti to Florida, imposes severe restrictions on the number of Haitians who are allowed to stay.

  Today: According to the U.S. Census conducted in 2000, there are 419,317 foreign-born Haitians living in the United States. Most of them live in Florida (43.5 percent) and New York (29.9 percent).

- **1960s:** The murderous and corrupt regime of President François Duvalier in Haiti creates a dark decade in Haitian history. Thousands of Haitian citizens are tortured, killed, or driven into exile.

  1980s: After the dictatorship of Jean-Claude Duvalier is overthrown in 1986, Haitians hope for a new democratic era, but elections in the later part of the decade are marred by intimidation and violence.

  Today: In May 2006, Haiti inaugurates René Préval as president after a fair and democratic election. A democratically elected parliament is also inaugurated.

- **1960s:** Haiti is the poorest country in the Western Hemisphere and one of the poorest countries in the world. Eighty percent of its population lives below the poverty line.

  1980s: In a population of 5.5 million, 50 percent of Haitians are unemployed.

  Today: In 2006, helped by the International Monetary Fund, the Haitian economy grew by 1.8 percent. It is the first year of economic growth since 1999.

The Duvalier dictatorship brooked no opposition and was responsible for killing as many as 30,000 people and forcing many more into exile. Torture was routine. As Elizabeth Abbott describes in her book *Haiti: The Duvaliers and Their Legacy*, "even [Duvalier's] splendid palace had a torture room, its walls painted rusty-brown to camouflage blood spattered from its victims." Duvalier himself would watch the torture sessions through peepholes in the walls.

After Duvalier died in 1971, his son Jean-Claude Duvalier, known as Baby Doc, was appointed president for life at the age of nineteen. He proved to be almost as ruthless as his father, curbing the press and eliminating political opposition. Baby Doc was also financially corrupt, enriching himself and his family by the misuse of government revenue. Nothing was done to address the fundamental inequality in Haitian society, in which a tiny French-speaking elite owned about half of the country's wealth at the expense of the Creole-speaking majority who were kept in poverty. Popular discontent with the Duvalier dictatorship gathered force in the 1980s, helped by a 1983 visit of Pope John II, who publicly called for change. In 1986, as protests continued to grow, Duvalier was forced by the army to resign. He fled with his family to France. From 1986 to 1990, Haiti was ruled by a series of governments in which the military played a large role. In 1990, Jean-Bertrand Aristide, a former Roman Catholic priest and champion of the poor, was elected president with 67 percent of the vote in a free election.

Haitian Immigrants
The twenty-nine-year long brutal dictatorship of the Duvaliers resulted in a large increase in the

A burned human skull in a graveyard reportedly used as body dump by the Tonton Macoutes in Port au Prince, Haiti (© WorldFoto | Alamy)

number of Haitians coming to the United States, both by legal and illegal means. This occurred especially during the 1970s. In 1972, hundreds of Haitians fleeing the country by sea landed in Florida. They, and subsequent Haitians arriving by the same means, became known as "boat people." Many found asylum in the United States and later became U.S. citizens. Communities of Haitian Americans sprang up in South Florida, in cities such as Miami (where the Haitian enclave became known as Little Haiti), Fort Lauderdale, and West Palm Beach. Other Haitian immigrants settled in New York, forming communities in areas such as East Flatbush, Brooklyn (where the dew breaker and his family live). Many Haitian immigrants went into business for themselves, opening barbershops (the dew breaker earns his living as a barber) and restaurants specializing in Haitian cuisine (as Rézia does in "The Funeral Singer"). Most first-generation Haitian immigrants were poor, but second-generation immigrants born in the United States achieved higher educational and income levels.

CRITICAL OVERVIEW

The Dew Breaker received very favorable reviews, with critics praising Danticat's skill and insight. In *Time*, Pico Iyer comments that "Danticat's gift is to combine both sympathy and clarity in a moral tangle that becomes as tight as a Haitian community." Referring to the ubiquitous sense of loss that the characters experience, Iyer argues that "all these scarred characters are looking for, in effect, is a way to mourn their dead properly, as in the rambunctious, storytelling wakes of home." In *Booklist*, Donna Seaman refers to the novel as "Danticat's beautifully lucid fourth work of fiction: the baffling legacy of violence and the unanswerable questions of exile." Seaman concludes: "Danticat's masterful depiction of the emotional and spiritual reverberations of tyranny and displacement reveals the intricate mesh of relationships that defines every life, and the burden of traumatic inheritances: the crimes and tragedies that one generation barely survives, the next must reconcile."

One of the few reservations about the quality of the book was expressed by the reviewer for *Publishers Weekly*, who suggests that "some readers may think that what she gains in breadth she loses in depth; ... Danticat does not always stay in one character's mind long enough to fully convey the complexities she seeks." However, the reviewer acknowledges that "the slow accumulation of details pinpointing the past's effects on the present makes for powerful reading, however, and Danticat is a crafter of subtle, gorgeous sentences and scenes."

CRITICISM

Bryan Aubrey

Aubrey holds a Ph.D. in English. In this essay on The Dew Breaker, *he discusses some key aspects of Haitian history, as well as how Danticat presents the character of the dew breaker.*

Few readers will put down Edwidge Danticat's *The Dew Breaker* without being haunted by the stories that it tells in such an elliptical fashion. They strongly evoke the two extremes of the human condition: the capacity of human beings to inflict extreme physical suffering on other human beings; and the human capacity to love what seems unlovable, and in doing so to offer a kind of redemption to those who seem scarcely to deserve it. And yet *The Dew Breaker* also shows how the shadow cast by those who torture other human beings spreads dark and long over many years and many miles, reaching out even to touch those unborn at the time of the crimes. The novel also shows that redemption from such inhuman acts of cruelty and sadism will always remain, at best, tentative and incomplete.

In practical terms, Danticat's interest in writing about a torturer who immigrates to the United States and lives among some of those he once tortured, or their relatives, was stimulated by a real-life case in New York in the 1990s, a case that also found its way into "The Book of Miracles," one of the stories in *The Dew Breaker*. It concerns a man named Emmanuel Constant. In Haiti in 1993, Constant founded a militia, The Front for the Advancement and Progress of Haiti (FRAPH), which raped, terrorized, and killed supporters of ousted Haitian president Jean-Bertrand Aristide. Like the dew breaker in the novel, members of the FRAPH death squad would swoop on their victims at dawn. In one

WHAT DO I READ NEXT?

- Danticat's memoir *Brother, I'm Dying* (2007) tells a story that will sound familiar to readers of the *The Dew Breaker*. Her life story is one of tragedy and hope intermingled.

- *The Butterfly's Way: Voices from the Haitian Dyaspora in the United States* (2001), edited by Edwidge Danticat, is a collection of thirty-three essays and poems by Haitians living in the United States. Many of the writers explore the theme of being an outsider in the United States but no longer belonging in Haiti either.

- *Walking on Fire: Haitian Women's Stories of Survival and Resistance* (2001), by Beverly Bell and with a foreword by Danticat, is a collection in which thirty-eight Haitian women of varying backgrounds tell their stories of arrests, beatings, torture, and sexual abuse suffered at the hands of the Haitian authorities. The common thread is that they all chose to resist their oppression and lived to tell their tales, becoming voices for justice.

- *Haiti in Focus: A Guide to the People, Politics, and Culture* (2002), by Charles Arthur, is a concise guide to the history and culture of Haiti. Arthur examines topics such as how the country first became independent in 1804 and the U.S. occupation of Haiti from 1915 to 1934. He also describes all aspects of the country as it is today, offering visitors advice about what to do and see.

notorious incident in the town Cite Soleil, FRAPH gunmen set fire to houses, forcing victims, including children, back into burning buildings and killing fifty people. (This incident is eerily similar to the one recorded in "Night Talkers," when Dany's parents are shot by the dew breaker and their house is burned down.) After Aristide was restored to power by the United States in 1994, Constant fled to New York, where he became a real estate agent and

> DANTICAT DELVES INTO THE LIFE AND THE THINKING OF THE TORTURER, AS IF TO ANSWER THE QUESTION THAT IS SURELY ON THE READER'S MIND: WHAT MANNER OF MAN IS THIS? THE ANSWER IS BOTH ILLUMINATING AND DISTURBING."

lived in plain sight in Queens, not very far from a Haitian immigrant community. In 2000, he was convicted, as noted in "The Book of Miracles," in absentia by a Haitian court for his part in a massacre in 1994.

Many Haitians in New York recognized Constant but were too scared to speak out, fearing that he still had the power to harm them. A woman in a New York train station nearly fainted when she recognized him from a photograph, according to an article published in the *New York Times* in 2006, when Constant had finally been arrested and charged with defrauding banks. This recalls the incident in "The Dew Breaker" when an old woman who had been tortured was interviewed about her experience thirty years later. She "would stammer for an hour before finally managing to speak, pausing for a breath between each word." The psychological effects of torture remain long after the physical wounds have healed, as evidenced also by Beatrice, the woman in "The Bridal Seamstress," who is mentally unbalanced by her experience of torture that happened probably thirty or forty years ago. Another example is that of Dany, whose parents were killed by the dew breaker, and who by some grim coincidence has ended up living in the same house as the torturer. Even after the passage of many years, Dany still has a fear that the man will make good on the threat he made to shoot Dany when Dany was six years old.

With the example of Emmanuel Constant in mind, well-wishers of Haiti will note with regret that torture and random killings by militias did not end with the departure into ignominious exile of Jean-Claude Duvalier in 1986. It may be scant comfort to know that at least Haiti during the 1990s was not as bad—as far as state-instituted violence and torture was concerned—as the era

of the Duvaliers, which was truly a hideous chapter in Haiti's troubled, violent history. For the most part, *The Dew Breaker* approaches the Duvalier years obliquely, but readers of Elizabeth Abbott's *Haiti: The Duvaliers and Their Legacy*, will find enough revolting details of the dictators' murderous practices to keep them awake at night. Abbott describes conditions inside Fort Dimanche during Papa Doc's rule. This is the prison mentioned in "The Dew Breaker" as being "literally a sepulcher from which no one was ever expected to resurface." Abbott reports that at Fort Dimanche the cells were so overcrowded that the prisoners slept in shifts. "Gruel was slopped twice daily onto the floor. . . . Sanitary facilities consisted of a foul, overflowing bucket." Malnourished prisoners died every day, and the corpses were taken away by the jailers on the same carts that were used to deliver the food. And then there was the torture itself. One punishment was to confine a tortured prisoner to a device known as a *cachot*: "A tiny coffin-like cell without room to move where prisoners slated for especially lingering deaths were confined and given no food or water until they died of their injuries, infections, dehydration, starvation, and the absence of all hope."

Abbott also mentions that some of the prisoners at Fort Dimanche would try "to cure their diarrhea by scraping lime from the walls and mixing it with food. Flesh, beaten and sore, was bathed with lime and urine, soothing it, preventing infectious eruptions that would kill." This small detail describing the resourcefulness shown by those who were forced to endure such horrific treatment finds its way into "The Dew Breaker," when the recently arrested preacher awakes to find that the other prisoners are urinating on him. He discovers that they believe "their urine could help seal the open wounds on his face and body and keep his bones from feeling as though they were breaking apart and melting under his skin." This incident movingly dramatizes the presence of mercy, empathy, and humanity in the midst of callousness and brutality.

It is in "The Dew Breaker," the final story in the book, that Danticat confronts head-on the terrifying details of Papa Doc's Haiti and the atrocities carried out by the Tonton Macoutes. Danticat delves into the life and the thinking of the torturer, as if to answer the question that is surely on the reader's mind: what manner of man is this? The answer is both illuminating and disturbing. The dew breaker turns out to be not so different from the ordinary man. He could be almost anyone. In fact, he and his family started out as victims themselves, when their land was taken over by the army after Papa Doc came to power in 1957. With his father driven insane and his mother disappearing, it is easy to see how a nineteen-year-old might have been seduced into joining the militia after attending an impressive presidential rally in Port-au-Prince. After that, the steady accumulation of power in immature hands in the service of a brutal government led to all-too-predictable results.

A decade into his career as a torturer and murderer, as he waits in his car for the opportunity to kill the preacher, the dew breaker reveals at least some of the mental processes that allow him to carry out such acts. He convinces himself that he is in fact doing a good thing, since he dislikes the Protestant church and thinks that the preacher has brainwashed his followers. He, the dew breaker, will help to liberate them by slaying the preacher. It is likely that many men throughout history who have committed crimes against humanity have assuaged their consciences with similar logic, however lame their reasoning might appear to others.

In another deft touch that provides insight into the torturer, Danticat shows him, as he waits to carry out his mission, sending a boy who is studying his schoolbooks under a tree to get him some cigarettes. He offers the boy some extra money because he recognizes in him something of his own former self. As he engages the boy in conversation he shows that he is not entirely devoid of human feelings: "There was a part of him that wished he could buy that child a future, buy all children like that a future."

To this insight into the mind of the torturer, one might add what can be gleaned about him from the first story in the book. "The Book of the Dead" reveals that the dew breaker, in the thirty years or so that he has spent in the United States, is a quiet, insignificant, ordinary man; the kind of man no one would suspect of committing such horrific deeds. It appears that he has been a good husband to his wife and a father who inspires devotion in his daughter. In fact, Ka admires and idealizes him so much that she depicts him in noble postures in her sculptures. *The Dew Breaker* is as much about the sudden shattering of Ka's tranquil life as it is about her formerly

murderous father. Innocent of any wrongdoing, she must now deal with the painful knowledge that her beloved father is not the man she thought he was. Thus, as Shakespeare's character Feste puts it in *Twelfth Night*, "the whirligig of time brings in his revenges." The physical agony that the dew breaker inflicted on his innocent victims has crossed the ocean and transcended time; it is now manifested as the mental pain of his own daughter—and who can say when, or if, that pain, that stain on her happiness, can ever be removed?

Source: Bryan Aubrey, Critical Essay on *The Dew Breaker*, in *Novels for Students*, Gale, Cengage Learning, 2009.

Robert McCormick
In the following review, McCormick critiques the book's structure, which he feels leaves too many aspects of the story unexplained.

"Ka, your father was the hunter, he was not the prey." With those words, Ka's father reveals the truth to his daughter in "The Book of the Dead," the first section of Edwidge Danticat's recent work, *The Dew Breaker*. One vaguely intuits then why he threw Ka's wooden sculpture of him, called "The Prisoner," into one of Florida's innumerable artificial lakes. We don't understand completely, however, the significance of his prominent facial scar, although we sense as was the case in Danticat's 1998 novel *The Farming of Bones* (see WLT 73:2, p. 377), that it is the scar of Haiti, the badge Haitians wear as a visible sign of their collective suffering.

Danticat's latest fictional work starts slowly. One suspects the author may have made too many concessions to reality in her photographic representation of the flatness of American life with its newly enriched Haitian American television stars; its motel culture; its police officers from Lakeland, Florida, who don't know the geography of the New World; the social pressure in East Flatbush to put up Christmas decorations, et cetera. There is, too, a bit of the sociologist in her detailing the folklore of Haiti: the ritual "branding" of the clothes of those soon to be buried, her presentation of the "palannits," or the "night talkers, people who wet their beds, not with urine but with words." By the end, however, we understand why Ka's Haitian American parents choose to remain on life's surface.

I wish I could say this text was well constructed. Its powerful final chapter explains certain mysteries, such as the origin of Mr. Bienaime's scar. It also illuminates certain ironies of the lives of Ka's parents, such as Anne's patrolling the aisle at midnight mass on Christmas Eve to inform her daughter that a stranger they see there is not the Haitian assassin whom his daughter thinks she recognizes from posters. Or the fact that the son, whose parents were victims of the former "dew breaker," rents a basement apartment from the unobtrusive Mr. Bienaime, who, in Brooklyn, has become a barber. Some of the nine segments don't seem to belong, though. In fact, almost all the chapters were published previously as short stories.

Unlike *The Farming of Bones*, which focused on Haiti and the Dominican Republic in the late 1930s, this text is grounded in the 1960s but also relates the last few minutes in Haiti of "Baby Doc" Duvalier in 1986 and the subsequent vigilantism directed against the henchmen he left behind. It also vaguely evokes Aristide, because Ka's father, in his last official act, abducts from his church in Bel-Air and then kills a converted Baptist clergyman (Aristide is Catholic), the same clergyman who, in the Casernes Dessalines military barracks, will scar his interrogator's face with the splintered wood of a broken chair in his last defiant act. Running away, bleeding, the torturer encounters the pastor's stepsister outside the barracks, ignorant of his role as her stepbrother's murderer, even of the clergyman's death, she nurses the facial wounds of the Tonton Macoute. The National Palace, however, wanted the preacher alive, so the next day Ka's future parents obtain seats on a plane for New York.

Ultimately, one understands why the father always covers his face and never wants it photographed. We understand why Anne goes to mass regularly and why she must view the "'transformation" of her husband as a quasireligious miracle in which she plays the primary role. We understand their unobtrusive lifestyle, why they don't put up Christmas decorations. What we don't know, though, is just as important, for, although Anne ultimately learns her stepbrother was killed, it is not clear whether she ever learns that her husband was the preacher's murderer.

The text presents two levels of truth. One is the father's admission to Ka at the beginning that he was the "hunter." After having read the final chapter, though, we wonder how much he really told his daughter. Did he tell her he killed

the preacher? Danticat doesn't tell us how Ka will react to what she has learned after she hangs up on her mother.

Source: Robert McCormick, Review of *The Dew Breaker*, in *World Literature Today*, Vol. 79, No. 1, January–April 2005, 2 pp.

Robert Birnbaum
In the following excerpt from an interview, Danticat discusses life in Haiti and her writing process for The Dew Breaker.

... RB: *Haiti used to manufacture baseballs.*

ED: They don't make them anymore, that's moved on. Even when they were, that was something like 10 cents a day. People were being paid that, with no benefits and ruining their health. But there's not many opportunities in the city and fewer now in the country. For example, someone who would spend a couple of months growing a chicken and now you can buy chicken legs from Miami that arrive the same day [as they are slaughtered] for less than that, so who is going to waste their time doing that? We had a *cochon oui*, the local pig, and that was, for a lot of people, that was a bank account. You grew your pig and if your child has to go to school, you sell the pig or you slaughter it and sell the meat. And in the 1990s the U.S. had a campaign where they eradicated all the pigs because the FDA decided they had swine fever. So there was a complete eradication of that whole population. One of the last indigenous animals to this island.

RB: *No replacement?*

ED: There were replacements of these pigs from Iowa who couldn't live there. [both laugh] They had to build houses for those pigs. They had to buy grain from the U.S. So they killed the

> BUT HOW DO YOU WRITE A BOOK ABOUT HAITI? AND THIS PARTICULAR BOOK, LIKE A LOT OF THE OTHER BOOKS I HAVE WRITTEN, CAME FROM A KIND OF DESIRE TO GO BACK TO HAITI AND TO REVISIT AND MAYBE TO UNDERSTAND BETTER SOME THINGS FROM THE PAST."

pigs and now you have to buy the Iowa pigs from the same people, buy the grains to feed them because they couldn't eat what local pigs had eaten. And it took more than a decade to replace some of them—now you see more of them because they also came from Jamaica and other places. But it was a valuable resource that was completely depleted.

RB: *That kind of arrogance reminds me of a story I read recently [in Todd Balf's* The Darkest Jungle *] about a plan to cut another canal from the Atlantic to the Pacific in the Darien Gap, the area in Panama that borders what is now Colombia. Apparently in the '70s the plan was to cut the second canal using eight nuclear devices to blow up the channelway. This was a reserve that was inhabited by 40,000–50,000 indigenous people whose roots are prehistoric. And, of course, these people would be resettled.*

ED: Yeah, yeah, it's collateral damage. And all the people who starved because their pigs were killed, they were collateral damage.

RB: *I don't know if this is an apocryphal story but I was told that the border between the Dominican Republic and Haiti is clearly demarcated, with the Haitian side being barren and foreboding and the Dominican side being lush and green.*

ED: That's true in a lot of places where you have the boundary. There was a very large program behind that. Trujillo, who was a president [of the Dominican Republic] for many decades, had a program specifically aimed at that, sprucing up a lot of the border towns in order to contrast them from Haiti—it was a very conscious effort. Haiti has a larger population, in a smaller area. Not that there isn't poverty in the Dominican Republic, but aside from that you have more tourism, so part of whatever preservation has been connected to that, too. Trujillo was interested in the contrast. And even for myself when I have had to go there, if I am staying in Cap-Haitien, which is on the Haitian side close to the border, there are times when I, shamefacedly, need to make a phone call or something, [and] I have had to cross the border.

RB: *And now what about the writing of a book about Haiti? Some parts of* The Dew Breaker *have appeared before, what was the very first story you wrote?*

ED: The very first story was 'The Book of the Dead.'

RB: *Did you know that you were going to write this as an interwoven collection of stories?*

ED: No, I had just finished my book *The Farming of Bones*, the book about the Dominican Republic and Haiti, and I was going back to writing stories. I didn't feel like I could go into a novel just then. So I went back to writing stories and I started this one story about a father and a daughter who went on a trip. And the father makes this revelation to his daughter, that he was not a prisoner, as his family had thought, but was a 'dew breaker,' a sort of a torturer.

RB: *That is an interesting phrase for such an odious thing.*

ED: It comes from the Creole. It's an expression *choukèt laroze*; it really means somebody who breaks or shakes the dew. That's where that comes from. Creole is very forgiving of things like that. There is also an expression on the other side, *gouverneurs de la rosée*, people who govern the dew, who are kinder people, people of the land who nurture the land and try to control their destiny through the land. But that was the first one I wrote and I was very intrigued by the father so I started writing the very last story, which talked about his past and the last time he was in Haiti.

RB: *That story that is called 'The Dew Breaker.' And so the stories in between?*

ED: The stories in between really came in between. The third one was in the middle, which involved the family. So I was always circling around this family. But how do you write a book about Haiti? And this particular book, like a lot of the other books I have written, came from a kind of desire to go back to Haiti and to revisit and maybe to understand better some things from the past. I am very much intrigued by Haitian history and the way it is connected to current struggles. So the book is an attempt at exploring that.

RB: *The notion of Creole being very forgiving is fascinating. In the very first story the father does something and—without giving it away—the daughter is clearly angered and she gets around to getting angry but first she says something to the effect that she had always thought anger was not a useful thing. I thought, 'Oh really?'*

ED: [laughs]

RB: *All through the stories I have this sense of the Haitian ethos having so little malevolence— [pause]*

ED: I'll give you an example of something very real and similar. In the 1990s we had a man who, again, was backed by the CIA and he was on *60 Minutes*, Emmanuel Constant, he started an organization called FRAPH. There was a point in the late '90s in New York where people would say, 'Guess what? I was at party...' and they would mention his name. For me, that was always extraordinary. How forgiving are we? Even the fact that people think now that they would accept Jean-Claude 'Baby Doc' Duvalier coming back. How either forgetful or forgiving that Emmanuel Constant—whose organization killed 5,000, and if you hear 5,000 in a Haitian estimation it's probably double that number—that he can feel safe to walk in the community, some of whom are wounded people. That to me was the kind of lack of malevolence—

RB: *Danny [sic] in one of the stories has an opportunity to harm the dew breaker and doesn't.*

ED: But he didn't want to be wrong—like many of the characters that felt they would want to repeat exactly this thing. Because on one level they were wrong about his parents—that there was a mistake made and his parents shouldn't have been killed.

RB: *I have been thinking about forgiveness. I caught some piece of Elie Wiesel's speech at Auschwitz, where he said something like, 'No, you cannot forgive these people'—*

ED: Umm—

RB: *My sense of the conditions in Haiti with these predatory dictators and their elite killers, the Tonton Macoute, sustains my sense of the horrific. You do mention one instance of a Tonton Macoute having gasoline poured down his throat and then ignited.*

ED: There were many cases like that after the dictatorship ended in 1989. There was a term that was created around that—*dechoukaj*—'uprooting.' Many of these Tonton Macoutes were killed. What interested me in the stories and in these people and in this era because it was the last era that I lived consistently in Haiti was to understand these people so at least to try to get as close to understanding these people as possible. The country and other countries, too, where things are difficult, keeps repeating or keeps recreating this environment that creates these kind of people. Now we have a phenomena with young men who are deported, many from

the United States and were returned to Haiti and became what is called chimé—

RB: *Like Claude?*

ED: Yeah, they are stranded there. And they have assembled together [in gangs] to survive and some of them, not all of them become involved in crime and are labeled this way in the country. The greatest of ironies is that you have some American soldiers from the country that deported them, some will be killing them. So you have this situation that keeps opening this opportunity to allow these types of people to be created or recreated. First you had the *Macoutes* under Duvalier then in FRAPH and now the Chimé. There are people, I am sure, that have gone from group to group because they don't have work. Because they don't have other things. So there is this culture and the lack of infrastructure that perpetuates this kind of system.

RB: *What are you going to do next?*

ED: I am taking it easy for a little while. I am doing a young adult book that I am almost done with [about] Anacaona, who was actually one of the few female indigenous leaders before Columbus came and she was a very powerful leader and known to be a poet and she was one of the last ones. She was hung by Columbus's people a couple of decades after they landed on the island. She hung in there and fought and was a true warrior-queen. I don't like to use the word 'queen' but a true warrior and leader in our history.

RB: *And you chose to make this a young-adult story?*

ED: Yeah, it's my first attempt at dealing with this story. It will be in a series called 'Royal Diaries' that sort of positions it with other women who were leaders but it concentrates on a particular time, like their teens. Maybe I will do something later with her later but this was a way to approach it in a manageable way.

RB: *Well, I hope we talk again.*

ED: Likewise, thank you.

Source: Robert Birnbaum, "Birnbaum v. Edwidge Danticat," in *Morning News*, April 20, 2004, 11 pp.

Rhonda Cobham

In the following review, Cobham applauds The Dew Breaker. *The critic feels that the novel expertly shows the struggle to retain humanity in even the worst of circumstances.*

> FOR THESE SILENT CHARACTERS, THE ISSUE IS NOT ONE OF AUTHENTICITY—WHICH CHOICE OF LANGUAGE IS MOST POLITICALLY CORRECT FOR DESCRIBING THEIR PAIN—BUT OF ONTOLOGY—HOW DOES ONE BEGIN TO DESCRIBE A PAIN THAT EXISTS BEYOND LANGUAGE?"

Aristide's desperate struggle to govern in Haiti is barely mentioned in Edwidge Danticat's new novel. Her focus is mostly on the ways in which events in the 1980s, near the end of the Duvalier regime, continue to haunt Haitians who have since migrated to America. Nevertheless, the nagging uncertainties surrounding Haiti's recent crisis reverberated like the shadow pain of an amputated limb all through my reading of *The Dew Breaker*. The narrator in Danticat's last novel, *The Farming of Bones*, bore witness to the genocide of Haitians at the hands of their Dominican neighbors in the mid-1930s. This time, however, both hunter and prey are the monstrous progeny of Haiti itself.

The narrative line in *The Dew Breaker* is strung across a series of linked short stories that leads to a single question: Can the tales we tell about our past offer us any alternatives in the future other than those of becoming either hunter or prey? The answer, like the answer to the riddle about trees and their shadows with which the book closes, depends on perspective: the angles from which the multiple plots illuminate character; the chronology the entire narrative imposes on events; the quotidian details—a stone in a glass of water, an overflowing ashtray, three snippets of fabric—through which the stories locate or sublimate pain. Danticat's unexpected juxtapositions intensify the quiet tragedies on the periphery of the action. Thus, a casual sexual liaison one story mentions in passing seems merely ornamental in a plot that focuses on the protagonist's reunification with his newly arrived wife. When the same liaison resurfaces at the margins of another story, from the perspective of the woman whose happiness it destroyed, we discover that the small cruelties we easily forgive

in fictional heroes and close friends may be susceptible to the same scrutiny as the enormities of which we accuse our most sadistic enemies.

Danticat's use of language raises the stakes in the wider debate over the most effective way to represent the Creole voice on the page. Unlike Patrick Chamoiseau's Martinican Creole in his Prix Goncourt-winning novel Texaco, which acquires a patina of innocence in response to the corrupting dominance of colonial French, Danticat's Haitian Creole is used by state officials as well as ordinary Haitian people. Consequently, her narrators cannot claim to speak a language that has no alliances with institutional authority. Moreover, Danticat sees Caribbean Creoles as vital, increasingly metropolitan, phenomena that change continuously in response to new political and linguistic challenges. The title *The Dew Breaker*, for example, is one translation of shouket laroze, an expression that refers to the silent, magical way in which dew "falls," or "breaks," as they say in Haitian Creole, on the early morning leaves. As Danticat explains, Haitians under Duvalier's regime often used the term ironically to name the state-sponsored torturers who typically descended upon their victims in the silence before dawn. But Danticat's title also signifies on Jaques Roumain's 1946 novel, *Les Gouverneurs de la rosee*, translated into English by Langston Hughes as *Masters of the Dew*. Roumain co-opts the picturesque, rural imagery of shouket laroze into his novel's rewriting of Romeo and Juliet as Haitian pastoral. His translation of the Creole phrase allows him to connect Haiti's feudal past to his utopian vision for a triumphant proletariat future in a modern nation state, where men will be masters of the elements, capable of transcending narrow allegiances to family and clan. At the time Roumain was writing, nationalism in Europe already had demonstrated a sinister proclivity for co-opting "authentic" folk customs and language to support the agendas of totalitarian regimes. However, Roumain's translation of shouket laroze elides that possibility in the Creole context. Danticat's alternative translation suggests violence as well as mastery. It makes visible the excesses of the nationalist, socialist, and capitalist ideologies that have stunted Haiti's growth during the six decades that separate *The Dew Breaker* from *Masters of the Dew*.

Freed from the myth of a morally untainted Creole, as well as from the assumption that Creole-speaking subjects never think or speak on their own behalf within the discourse of modernity, Danticat can use any language register she chooses to carry her message. All the registers available to her characters make their appearance in the stories. The text indicates their presence by meticulously documenting the media through which these multiple languages are filtered. There are New York AM talk radio broadcasts in French and Creole; answering machine cassettes containing messages in stilted English that start off with "Alo!"; notebooks crammed with English sentences in barely decipherable script; tables bearing food or drinks over which American English is peppered with Haitian expressions like sezi—the Creole word for crazy—or Kennedy—Creole slang for secondhand American clothes. Much of this linguistic variety is transcribed onto the page in English, but Danticat alerts the reader each time the language shifts. In one tense exchange between the protagonist, Ka, and her father, for example, the three language registers represented are crucial to the emotional nuance of the passage. Ka's continued identification with the father she can no longer trust; his need, after year's of silence, to explain himself to her; the necessity and impossibility of their communication—all are indicated in their awkward shifts between Haitian English, Haitian Creole, and American English:

> "I say rest in Creole," he prefaces, "because my tongue too heavy in English to say things like this, especially older things."
>
> "Fine," I reply defiantly in English.
>
> "Ka," he continues in Creole, "when I first saw your statue, I wanted to be buried with it, to take it with me into the other world."
>
> "Like the Ancient Egyptians," I continue in English.
>
> He smiles, grateful, I think, that in spite of everything, I can still appreciate his passions.

And then there are the endless, empty silences that leave their bearers scarred and bloated: A reflection in a shiny metal elevator door grotesquely inflates the body of a woman who can speak to no one about the pregnancy she has aborted. The bruised, calloused hands of a child bear silent witness to the daily torture of the classroom. Like the novice journalist who interviews a wedding seamstress in one story, the reader is challenged to imagine "men and women whose tremendous agonies filled every blank space in their lives. Maybe there were hundreds, even thousands, of people like this, men and women chasing fragments of themselves long lost to others." For these silent characters, the issue is not one of authenticity—which choice of language is most politically correct for describing their pain—but of ontology—how does one begin to describe a pain that exists beyond language?

The answer, for Danticat, seems to be that stories must be told with whatever words we have—even the stories about their victims that torturers revisit in their dreams. One crucial moment of storytelling occurs deep in the Haitian countryside. The scene is reminiscent of Joseph Zobel's 1955 novel *Rue Cases-Negres*, better known to American audiences in its 1983 adaptation for the screen by Euzhan Palcy as *Sugar Cane Alley*. The film follows the conventions of the Caribbean narrative of childhood, in which Creole communities figure as sites of rural innocence that the boy protagonist celebrates, even as he moves away from femininity, orality, and pastoral freedoms towards masculinity, text, and the disciplines of modernity. Danticat's story inverts this paradigm. Instead of sitting with the child protagonist at the feet of a wise old griot who instructs us in the myths of his people's origins, we lounge with the teenager Claude, as he imports the hip-hop idiom of Flatbush Avenue into a new myth of origins about a son who destroys his father in order to feed his drag habit. Claude cannot speak Creole, yet he is one of the few protagonists in the novel who comes close to achieving absolution through narrative. Another man writes down his story in a formal letter addressed to his unborn child. A woman learns how to "parcel out [her] sorrows" in stories and songs among her friends, "each walking out with fewer than we'd carried in."

Like Danticat's previous novels, *The Dew Breaker* succeeds in transforming Haiti and its diaspora from an abject spectacle to a symbol of the persistence of human dignity in the face of terror. Even the hunters in this grim passion play seem to struggle for redemption through the penance of speech. Like their prey, they carry on their bodies the scars left by the indignities they have suffered and inflicted. And yet those same bodies continue to yearn for beauty and order and the possibility of love. There is nothing sentimental about Danticat's novel. It has etched into my imagination images I would prefer to think have no basis in reality. But, like the mouth that contains both speech and silence in the *Egyptian Book of the Dead*, from which Ka gets her name, this novel's unlikely combination of shadows, rhythms, and silences captures the aspirations all immigrants bring with them, the nightmares we are trying to escape, and the fantasies of joy, loss, and longing that tie us inextricably to imagined homelands in the Caribbean, in Brooklyn, and beyond.

Source: Rhonda Cobham, "The Penance of Speech," in *Women's Review of Books*, Vol. 21, No. 8, May 2004, 3 pp.

Richard Eder

In the following review, Eder explores how The Dew Breaker *could or could not be considered a horror novel.*

Archimedes held that he could lift the earth if he had a lever long enough, and an extraplanetary fulcrum to rest it on. There are horrors so heavy that they seem untellable. To bear to tell them so that we can bear to read them, a writer must find somewhere outside—peaceful, unmarked—to project them from. Atrocity enters the imagination not as the violating point of the knife but as the fair flesh violated.

That is how the Haitian-American writer Edwidge Danticat has managed over the past 10 years to portray with such terrifying wit and flowered pungency the torment of the Haitian people. In one of the stories in *Krik? Krak!*, a National Book Award finalist, a maid to a rich Haitian family finds a dead baby, names it Rose, keeps it for days, washing it to dissipate the smell, and finally buries it. It is discovered by the gardener, her lover, who calls the police.

So much for horror; but what locks it in is the maid's irony: "We made a pretty picture standing there, Rose, me and him. Between the pool and the gardenias, waiting on the law."

Or in *The Farming of Bones*, a novel about Trujillo's 1930's massacre of Haitian workers in the Dominican Republic, no awful detail precipitates the bloody swirl so clearly as the lilting innocence of the word "parsley." "Pesa" in Creole, "perejil" in Spanish; but Haitians can't manage the Spanish "r" and its guttural "j," so those unable to say "perejil" were killed and parsley stuffed in their mouths.

The final and title story of *The Dew Breaker*, Danticat's new collection, makes a more direct approach to horror. Set in the 1960's during the

> IN HER OTHER STORIES AND IN THIS COLLECTION DANTICAT OFTEN USES THE HAITIAN COMMUNITY IN THE UNITED STATES AS THE HORROR-SPARED SITE FOR HER FULCRUM. DESPITE DIFFICULTIES, STRANGENESS AND UNCERTAINTIES, THESE CHARACTERS ARE SWIMMERS PULLED FROM THE DEPTHS."

reign of François Duvalier, it recounts, dry-mouthed, the hours spent by a Tonton Macoute (one of Duvalier's murderous agents) as he waits in his car for a dissident preacher to arrive at church.

The agent bursts in after the sermon, throws the priest into a truck, tortures him and takes him to headquarters to kill him. Word mysteriously comes—the regime's terrors were always mysterious—that he is to be released instead. Before the agent can obey, the priest gouges his face with a shard of wood; the agent shoots him dead.

Yet even this story, with its headlong darkness, has strangely flickering lights that permit us to see it by. Waiting, the agent sends a loitering schoolboy to buy cigarettes; when the boy returns, the man questions him paternally about his schoolwork. There is the street scene itself. Among the kiosks purveying tobacco, trinkets and food, the waiting car is one kiosk more, purveying death; and as much part of daily neighborhood life as the others.

When the priest is dragged into prison, bleeding and burned with cigarettes, his cellmates urinate on him. It is a work not of contempt but of corporal mercy, since they believe urine to heal and soothe. Haiti lives at depths where contempt cannot grow; down there, mercy straggles but persists.

In her other stories and in this collection Danticat often uses the Haitian community in the United States as the horror-spared site for her fulcrum. Despite difficulties, strangeness and uncertainties, these characters are swimmers pulled from the depths. Nitrogen bubbles course agonizingly in their bloodstream, memories rack them; yet there is an uncertain daylight, and it is by this that darkness is called up and told.

In "The Funeral Singer," the telling is light but painful. Three Haitian women meet regularly at a restaurant one owns on the Upper West Side. She'd fled after being forced to have sex with the Tonton Macoutes; another, after her painter husband was shot for a caricature of Duvalier. The third, the narrator, was the daughter of a fisherman who drowned, perhaps deliberately, after his fish stall was taken over. At his funeral she sang "Brother Timonie"—the name means "steersman"—so affectingly that soon she was in demand at other funerals. Now, with the slow rock of a fishing boat on a sea swell, the women talk, remember, try to look ahead. Lubricated with rum, the narrator sings "Brother Timonie," the steersman's song learned from her father. The others join in; tableware is smashed. "And for the rest of the night," the story concludes, "we raise our glasses, broken and unbroken alike, to the terrible days behind us and the uncertain ones ahead."

In "Monkey Tails," an immigrant groping at the edge of security and perhaps happiness lies in bed with his pregnant wife and tapes, for their unborn child, his own childhood memories of chaos and betrayal. In "Seven," a man preparing for his wife's arrival from Haiti, after seven years apart, gets his bachelor housemates to agree not to sit around in their underwear.

Venturing from their room on her first night, the wife reports "two men playing dominoes in the kitchen...dressed in identical pink satin robes." It is the lightest of the stories yet shadowed with the marital uncertainty that follows long separation.

In a breathtaking displacement, Danticat starts the collection with the aftermath, 25 years later, of the prison murder story recounted at the end. A young Haitian-American artist drives to Florida to deliver a carving. Her father comes for the ride, a quiet man who has worked as a barber in Brooklyn since he fled Haiti. She adores him; in fact, he is her sole subject so far, rendered kneeling, naked and disfigured by a facial scar inflicted in a Haitian jail. Her intention was to symbolize the torment of their country; soon we see the terrible complexity of the torment.

One morning the father sneaks out of their motel and throws the sculpture into a lake. He doesn't deserve a statue, he tells her. "Your father was the hunter, he was not the prey." His

years in prison were spent as torturer and killer. As for the nightmares he often complained of, they were "of what I, your father, did to others."

To the reader—who has not yet been plunged into the terror of the final story—it is a whiplash, searing yet oddly cauterized. This is America, not Haiti, and the daughter can own the confidence to feel horror and express it. "How do you love him?" she demands of her mother, who always knew the truth and who also knew a different one. Her husband had indeed fled a nightmare. "You and me, we save him," the mother says. "When I meet him, it made him stop hurt the people. This how I see it. He a seed thrown in rock. You, me, we make him take root."

A different truth and one impossible, perhaps, for an American daughter to accept. Hard for the reader, as well. And almost certainly for Danticat. She has written a Haitian truth: prisoners all, even the jailers. With neither forgiveness nor contempt, she sets it upon a fulcrum from where she's had the courage and art to displace the world even as she is displaced by it.

Source: Richard Eder, "Off the Island," in *New York Times Book Review*, March 21, 2004, p. 5.

SOURCES

Abbott, Elizabeth, *Haiti: The Duvaliers and Their Legacy*, McGraw-Hill, 1988, pp. 133–35.

Danticat, Edwidge, *The Dew Breaker*, Alfred A. Knopf, 2004.

Iyer, Pico, "When Life Is a Ghost Story: In Edwidge Danticat's Collection of Interwoven Tales, Haitians Try to Mourn Their Bloody Past," in *Time*, Vol. 163, No. 10, March 8, 2004, p. 79.

Kilgannon, Corey, "To His Compatriots' Relief, Haitian Exile Is Arrested," in *New York Times*, July 11, 2006.

Newland, Kathleen, and Elizabeth Grieco, "Spotlight on Haitians in the United States," in *The Migration Information Source*, April 2004, http://www.migrationinformation.org/USfocus/display.cfm?id=214 (accessed December 12, 2007.)

Review of *The Dew Breaker*, in *Publishers Weekly*, Vol. 251, No. 8, February 23, 2004, p. 49.

Seaman, Donna, Review of *The Dew Breaker*, in *Booklist*, Vol. 100, No. 12, February 15, 2004, p. 1033.

Shakespeare, William, *Twelfth Night*, Methuen, 1981, p. 152.

FURTHER READING

Farmer, Paul, *The Uses of Haiti*, Common Courage Press, 2005.

Farmer, a physician who has worked in rural Haiti for many years, offers a critique of U.S. policy toward Haiti, pointing out among other things that the United States supported the dictatorship of Papa Doc Duvalier.

Galembo, Phyllis, *Vodou: Visions and Voices of Haiti*, Ten Speed Press, 2005.

Galembo examines vodou, or voodoo, the spiritual beliefs of Haitian people as they are practiced today. Based on interviews as well as the author's participation in voodoo rituals, the book includes over eighty color photographs.

Girard, Philippe, *Paradise Lost: Haiti's Tumultuous Journey from Pearl of the Caribbean to Third World Hotspot*, Palgrave Macmillan, 2005.

Girard argues in this survey of 200 years of Haitian history, that Haitians themselves must take some responsibility for their country's continuing poverty.

Greene, Graham, *The Comedians*, Vintage Books, 2005.

Set in Haiti and the Dominican Republic during the time of Papa Doc Duvalier's rule, this novel was first published in 1966. Not surprisingly, it paints a dark portrait of life in Haiti, so much so that Papa Doc himself was moved to denounce Greene as a liar.

The Good Soldier

FORD MADOX FORD

1915

Ford Madox Ford's *The Good Soldier* (1915) is considered to be his best work, as well as one of the best novels of the twentieth century. The book tells the story of two wealthy couples, one from England and one from America, who befriend each other at a resort town in Germany and return there over more than a decade to continue their friendship. Over the course of the novel, the narrator, John Dowell, finds out more and more details about the complexities of his friends' marriage, and of the strains and responsibilities that life imposes on those who have been born to a life of privilege.

Ford's original title for this book, *The Saddest Story*, captures the sense of melancholy that surrounds the events that he relates. When it was published in 1915, however, his publishers rejected that title. The final title resounded strongly with audiences when it came out during World War I. If readers expected to find a book about war, though, they were bound to be disappointed. Though Edward Ashburnham, the English husband, does hold a commission in the army, Ford never relates any combat experience. The title ironically refers to the propensity of Edward, and of all members of his social set, to behave according to the implied rules of social behavior and not their emotions.

The Good Soldier has remained in print since its first publication. It is currently available in several editions, including one from Broadview Press published in 2003.

Ford Madox Ford (E. O. Hoppe / Getty Images)

AUTHOR BIOGRAPHY

Ford Madox Ford was born Ford Hermann Hueffer on December 17, 1873, in Merton, Surrey, England. His father, Francis Hueffer, was a well-known music critic and writer on music. His mother, Catherine, was the daughter of the famous Pre-Raphaelite painter Ford Madox Brown. Eventually, after working on a biography of his maternal grandfather, Ford adapted his subject's name and took it as his own.

When he was growing up, Ford's family acquaintances included such literary luminaries as Algernon Swinburne and Dante Gabriel Rossetti and Christina Rossetti. Ford was educated at the Praetorius School, Folkstone. Though he never attended college, he was fluent in several languages and was a prolific writer. His first novel, *The Brown Owl*, was published when he was eighteen: it was a folk story illustrated by his grandfather. He was married in 1894, at the age of twenty-one, to Elsie Martindale. The marriage was not good from the start and was steeped in scandal. Ford was notoriously unfaithful, at one point having an affair with Elsie's sister, the stress of which caused him to have a nervous breakdown in 1904, leading to his hospitalization. Although he and Elsie separated in 1908, they did not divorce, possibly because of the tenets of Catholicism (Ford had converted to that religion when he was nineteen). They went on instead to lead separate lives, with little connection between them.

In the early years of the twentieth century, Ford met the author Joseph Conrad and formed a friendship. They collaborated on two books: *The Inheritors* in 1901 and *Romance* in 1903. Ford went on to write several novels on his own, most notably those in his trilogy *The Fifth Queen*, about one of Henry VIII's wives. He also started the *English Review* in 1908. Though he was able to persuade some of the country's most recognized literary stars to publish in it, Ford was forced from his position with the magazine in 1910. That same year, unable to pay child support to Elsie, he spent eight days in prison. Soon after, he started work on *The Good Soldier*, which was published in 1915.

Ford served in World War I until he suffered shell shock at the Battle of Somme, and was sent home in 1917. He moved to Paris and started another publication, *The Transatlantic Review*, working on it with the Lost Generation writers, including Ernest Hemingway, Ezra Pound, Jean Rhys, and Gertrude Stein. Ford's poetry was frequently published, and he was included in the Imagist movement that was started by Pound.

After becoming involved with an American artist, Janice Biala, Ford began dividing his time between Europe and the United States. He was a Visiting Lecturer at Olivet College in Michigan in 1937–1938, and began friendships with Allen Tate, Caroline Gordon, Robert Lowell, and Katherine Anne Porter. It was on a trip back to the continent with Biala that Ford fell ill. He died in Deauville, France, on June 26, 1939, at the age of sixty-six.

PLOT SUMMARY

Part One

The Good Soldier begins with its narrator, John Dowell, telling readers that he and his wife, Florence, were acquainted with Captain and Mrs. Ashburnham for nine years. During that time they would all meet at the German resort town of Bad Nauheim. To the Dowells, the Ashburnhams, Edward and Leonora, seemed the ideal British couple: he owned a large estate

MEDIA ADAPTATIONS

- A 1983 adaptation of the novel made for Granada Television under the same title was aired on American television as part of the Masterpiece Theater series on PBS. The television movie was directed by Kevin Billington and stars Robin Ellis, Vickery Turner, Jeremy Brett and Susan Fleetwood. A DVD of the film from Acorn Media includes a biography of Ford Madox Ford.

that had been in his family for generations, and came to Bad Nauheim for treatment for his weak heart, which had recently caused him to give up his military commission in India. The Dowells had been coming to the resort for four years already because Florence had a weak heart too: she came from a family with heart problems and was too ill to travel from continental Europe.

Dowell gives details out of chronological order. He relates, for instance, the fact that he had returned to America after Florence's death in 1913, and then been asked to come to England and join the Ashburnhams at their estate; after that he tells the story of how the two couples met in 1904, at Bad Nauheim, when they were seated together in the spa's restaurant. He then tells a story about the time before he even met Florence, when she and her uncle and her boyfriend, Jimmy, traveled to Europe, careful of the uncle's own heart ailment. For years, the Dowells and the Ashburnhams associated with each other every year at Bad Nauheim, taking day trips to nearby cities and going out to restaurants.

On one such trip, Florence arranged a visit to an ancient city where Martin Luther once stayed, and where a piece of his original Protest was kept in a glass case in a castle. When they viewed it, Florence touched Edward Ashburnham on the wrist, pointing out that it was this document that separated the English from the lowly Irish, Italians, and Poles, indicating that Edward's Protestantism made him superior to others. Leonora raced from

the room in tears; when John caught up with her, she blurted out that she had been insulted because she was an Irish Catholic. John was relieved to find that she was upset about having her religion insulted, having thought the problem stemmed from the touch that passed between his wife and Edward.

He explains how, as he later came to understand, the Ashburnhams came to Bad Nauheim. It was not that Edward had a heart problem after all. Their travels there came as a result of Edward's continuing pattern of infidelity. First, he had made improper advances at a young woman in a railway car, and had been taken to court, dragged through the newspapers, and paid a fine. That incident led him to an affair with an exotic dancer, which caused Edward to spend a large part of his vast estate. To save on expenses, the Ashburnhams left England for India, where Edward took up a military position. There followed an affair with the wife of an army officer, who went on to blackmail Edward. In Burma, he formed an attraction to Maisie Maiden, a young married woman with an actual weak heart. It was when Maisie went to Bad Nauheim, leaving her husband behind, that Edward made up his own heart condition, to follow her.

One morning, Leonora caught Maisie in the hall outside of Edward's room and hit her across the face, thinking that she had spent the night there when in fact she had just gone in while Edward was out to return a grooming kit she had borrowed. Florence, who was already having an affair with Edward, saw Leonora hit Mrs. Maiden, and that night, to show that they were not as wild as they might have seemed, the Ashburnhams sat at the Dowells's table and introduced themselves.

The day that they saw the Luther Protest document was the day they found out, upon returning to Bad Nauheim, that Maisie Maiden had died. She had heard Edward and Florence talking earlier that day and had come to the conclusion that the Ashburnhams had paid her passage to Bad Nauheim for her to be Edward's mistress, in effect purchasing her from her husband. In packing to leave while the party was away, she'd had a heart attack.

Part Two

Part Two of the book opens with rumination of the significance of August 4. On August 4, 1899, Florence set off on her world tour with her uncle and Jimmy. On August 4, 1901, she married John Dowell. On that date in 1904, Maisie Maiden died. And on August 4, 1913, Florence died.

Dowell explains that his courtship of Florence was more of a competition with her other suitors. Her aunts and uncle were opposed to their marriage, and so he came to her house with a ladder and they eloped. After running away together they boarded a ship to Europe, and as soon as the ship was out to sea it was caught in a storm: the turbulence supposedly caused a strain on Florence's weak heart. Because of her heart condition, she never slept with Dowell, and kept her bedroom door locked at night to keep thieves out. Later, though, he found out that she had lovers in her room while he was locked out, including Jimmy, who had been living in Europe and extracting blackmail money from her for years. When they arrived in Paris, ostensibly for their honeymoon, she locked John Dowell out and took up with Jimmy again.

Florence began her affair with Edward Ashburnham in 1903, and he chased Jimmy away. Knowing that he was interested in Maisie Maiden, Florence interfered, driving Mrs. Maiden to suicide. In 1913, the Ashburnhams came to Bad Nauheim with Nancy Rufford, a teen-aged girl who was the daughter of a friend. Leonora, knowing that Edward was growing interested in Nancy and that she could fall for him, was careful to not leave them alone together. She also knew that Edward was having an affair with Florence, though, so she sent Florence along with them the one time that she let them go off into a darkened garden together. Florence, thinking that she had come across Edward and Nancy in each other's arms, ran back into the hotel, upset; there, she encountered her husband in conversation with a man who looked up, recognized her, and blurted out that she was the woman he had seen years ago, coming out of the bedroom of a man named Jimmy at five a.m. Florence went to her bedroom and was later found dead. Dowell assumed that she'd had a heart attack, and that the medicine found in her hand was a heart cure: it was only later that Leonora told him that the vial in her hand contained poison. He then found out that she'd never had a heart condition.

Part Three

One of the few things John Dowell remembered from the evening Florence died was telling Leonora that he was now free to marry Nancy Rufford, whom he had not even thought about much before. After Florence's death, Dowell returned to the United States, but soon received a telegram from Edward, asking him to come to England. Right after that, he received another telegram from Leonora with the same request.

Dowell recounts much about the history of the Ashburnhams' life together, including how they came to be married and how Edward's affairs made him vulnerable to blackmail, as well as how Leonora was able to rebuild his financial stability following blackmail and scandal. The events of this section are all alluded to in other parts of the book and are gone over in greater detail here.

Part Four

The mood at Branshaw House, the Ashburnhams's estate, was grim. Leonora knew that Edward loved Nancy, and she loved him. Edward, sick in love but not willing to break social conventions, drank heavily. Nancy looked up to Edward but did not think that he, a married man, could ever think romantically about anyone but his wife. However, Nancy's understanding of marriage changed after she read a newspaper article about a neighbor couple's divorce. Once she realized that she could possibly one day have Edward, she went to his bedroom. He rejected her, and wrote to her father, a military officer in India and an abusive parent, to arrange to send Nancy to live with him. John Dowell, knowing that Nancy was being sent away, asked Leonora if he should offer to marry her, but she knew that he planned on buying a home nearby and could not stand the thought of having the girl Edward loved living so close, so Leonora persuaded Dowell to wait another year. They all said goodbye to Nancy at the train, with no mention of the underlying loves or jealousies. That night, Edward slit his throat with his pen knife.

Leonora ended up marrying a man who had been interested in having an affair with her when she was married. John Dowell traveled to India to find Nancy, only to discover that she had been driven insane when the news of Edward's suicide reached her. He moved her back to Branshaw House and, as the novel ends, he lives with Nancy and some servants, although, in her madness, Nancy never acknowledges his existence.

CHARACTERS

Edward Ashburnham

Edward's official title is Captain, Fourteenth Hussars, of Branshaw House, Branshaw Teleragh. He is thirty-three in 1904, when he meets the Dowells. "Teddy," as his wife Leonora calls him, is the "good soldier" referred to in the novel's title: not only has he recently been active in the military in Burma, but he also displays the characteristics one would expect of a British officer regarding his compassion toward those in need and his willingness to suppress his own desires in order to do what is considered socially proper.

Edward has a weakness for women. He married Leonora at an early age, before he understood his own desires, and suppressed his feelings for other women in order to behave as was expected of an officer. His trouble begins when he tries to console a woman he sees crying on a train and ends up being sued for making improper advances. The negative publicity puts the thought of being unfaithful into his head, and he goes on to have an affair in Monte Carlo with the mistress of the Grand Duke. He gives her large sums of money, and drunkenly gambles away even more when she refuses to see him. In order to avoid bankruptcy, Edward gives control of his estate over to his wife, and agrees to take up active military service and move to India, but there he becomes involved with another woman, Mrs. Basil, whose husband blackmails Edward for years to come. When Edward becomes protective of young, frail Maisie Maiden, he pretends to have a heart problem, and he and Leonora go to the spa at Nauheim. There, Florence Dowell, who has always wanted to marry a titled Englishman, begins an affair with him.

Edward kills himself when he realizes that he is in love with Nancy Rufford, the daughter of a family friend who thinks of him as "Uncle Edward." Unable to live without her but unwilling to corrupt her with an affair, he sends her away to India and slits his throat.

Leonora Ashburnham

Beside John Dowell, who was oblivious to most of what his wife and Edward were up to, Leonora is the one main character who survives at the end of the novel, and so Dowell learns much of what he knows from her. Leonora grew up as one of seven daughters. Her father was an Irish military captain, acquainted with Edward Ashburnham's father but not of his same social class. Edward was given the choice of which Powys daughter he wanted to marry and he chose Leonora, possibly because of a shadow that crossed her face in the group photo he saw of the seven sisters, making her look mysterious.

Because Leonora is an Irish Catholic, she does not believe in divorce. When she becomes aware of Edward's involvements with other women, she does what she can to either separate them (as in the case of Mrs. Basil) or to keep them close, so that she can control their social impact (as with his involvement with Maisie Maiden). She also takes control of his financial affairs when she finds out that he has lost large sums of money, having him sign control of his English estate over to her. She treats the tenants on Edward's estate much more strictly than he ever did. Having come from a poor family, she understands how to economize much more than Edward does.

Bagshawe

Bagshawe is the man John Dowell happened to be idly conversing with when Florence passed by: unaware that she was his wife, Bagshawe blurts out her maiden name in surprise and tells Dowell, in his amazement, that he once saw her coming out of a man's bedroom at five in the morning.

Mrs. Basil

Mrs. Basil was a woman that Edward had an affair with in India. As the wife of an army officer, she was often left alone and bored, and Edward developed a sympathy for her. After their affair ended, her husband, Major Basil, blackmailed Edward, extracting from him a sum of three hundred pounds annually.

Rodney Bayham

Early in the novel, John Dowell relates a conversation in which Leonora tells him that she once tried to have a lover, Bayham, but could not go through with the affair. When she and Edward move back to England at the end of the novel, Rodney Bayham, the man who was nearly her lover, starts giving Florence attention, and by the end of the book she is married to him. Dowell summarizes Rodney's pure ordinariness with the fact that ready-made clothes fit him perfectly.

Carter

Carter is the only relative that is mentioned by name in the book; he is a second nephew, twice removed. Dowell hires investigators to look into Carter's past because he senses that other relatives are apprehensive about it, but it turns out that they find him strange because he is a Democrat. When he dies, Dowell intends to leave his vast fortune to Carter, whom he judges to be a nice, hardworking young man.

Florence Dowell

Florence comes from the Hurlibird family of Philadelphia. She was raised by her maiden aunts, Florence Sr. and Emily. A few years before John Dowell met her, she and her then-current boyfriend, Jimmy, joined her retired uncle on a world cruise. Jimmy stayed in Paris, and Florence continued to send him money. When she returned to Paris on her honeymoon she and Jimmy continued their affair, and he ended up blackmailing her.

Her aunts tried to prevent John Dowell from marrying Florence by hinting at her sexual activity, but he only thought they meant that she was a little bit of a flirt. When they sent her away to their brother's house, he followed, brought a ladder, and Florence eloped with him. Having seen how cautious her uncle was about his own heart condition, she made up a story about being stricken during the honeymoon crossing of the Atlantic, and told Dowell her weak heart would prevent her from crossing the ocean again or ever sleeping with her. She became trapped in her lie because it prevented her from leaving the continent and crossing to England, which was her dream. When she met Edward Ashburnham she became his mistress because he was the type of British nobleman she always wanted to marry.

Having carried on her affair with Edward right under his wife's nose, Florence is destroyed by it. On the same night that she sees Edward walking in private with Nancy Rufford and thinks that he is leaving her for Nancy, she runs into her husband talking with a man whose house she once stayed at with Jimmy. Knowing that the man can make Dowell finally see how promiscuous she is, Florence swallows a poison that she has carried with her for years, ready for such an occasion. Florence lives for the excitement of lies and sexual conquest and dreams of being an English noblewoman, but her false heart disease, which keeps John Dowell attached to her, ends up breaking her lies apart.

John Dowell

John Dowell is the book's narrator, trying to piece together what happened to his wife and friends after the events have already passed him by. Dowell was independently wealthy from inherited money when he met Florence Hurlibird and decided, in a competitive spirit, to outdo her other suitors and convince her to marry him. Naïvely, he did not realize that she was sexually active with other men, and he did not question her when she claimed to have come down with a heart problem on their honeymoon. For years, John lived with Florence but slept in a separate bedroom and was never intimate with her.

Dowell sees the Ashburnhams as the ideal of the English couple, and he thinks that he and his wife make a fine set of friends, not realizing that his wife has been sleeping with Edward Ashburnham throughout the nine years of their friendship. The moment in which he realizes what a sexually promiscuous woman Florence is occurs right before her death: Dowell happens to be talking to a man who recognizes her and says, unaware that Dowell is her husband, that he once saw that woman come out of a man's room at five in the morning. Dowell thinks that she died trying to save herself with heart medication, and has to be told by Leonora, much later, that his wife committed suicide.

Within hours of Florence's death, still in a daze, Dowell announces an ambition that he did not even know he had, to marry young Nancy Rufford. When he later joins the Ashburnhams at their English estate, he is as oblivious as ever, planning to marry Nancy without realizing that there is a crisis in the house, since she and Edward are in love. Even after Edward arranges to send her away, in order to prevent himself from destroying his marriage and her life, Dowell intrudes with the innocent question of when Edward thinks he should ask her to marry him. In the end, Dowell is left as a caretaker for Nancy, though she is in a catatonic state. John Dowell is used by his friends and used by his wife, and when there is nobody left, he voluntarily devotes his life to a woman who cannot acknowledge his existence.

John Hurlibird

Florence's Uncle John is a wealthy, generous man. After retiring, he takes a world cruise, and takes his niece and her boyfriend along with him. He takes cases of oranges along with him on the cruise ship, and he gives an orange to almost everyone he meets, as a goodwill gesture. Uncle John believes that he has a heart condition, and is treated for one by a number of physicians: when he dies, his body is donated to a medical college, where it is determined that his heart was fine all along.

Jimmy

Jimmy was Florence's lover when she was young and single. He traveled to Europe with Florence and her uncle, then stayed in Paris, allegedly to write. For years Florence sent him money. When she returned to Europe after she was married to John Dowell, she continued her affair with Jimmy. Dowell believes that Jimmy only went away after Edward Ashburnham became Florence's new lover and beat him up.

Julius

Julius was an old African American who worked for John Dowell when he was single. As Dowell and Florence are leaving for their honeymoon, Julius drops one of Florence's bags, and Dowell goes into a rage; for the rest of their marriage, Florence, who does not understand the relationship between Dowell and Julius, fears that Dowell can be sparked to an uncontrollable temper.

La Dolciquita

In Monte Carlo, Edward has an affair with the mistress of a Grand Duke, who is referred to in the book only as "La Dolciquita." She demands masses of money from him in payment for the money that she would not make if the Grand Duke found out about their affair and cut her off. After she stops seeing him, Edward wastes even more money at the gambling tables, drunk and in despair, until she agrees to have one last fling with him with whatever he has left.

Maisie Maiden

Maisie Maiden is a young woman that Edward Ashburnham developed a romantic interest in, with tragic results. She and Edward met in India, where her husband, Charlie Maiden (whom she refers to as "Bunny"), is serving in the army. She was too poor to go to Bad Nauheim for treatment for her weak heart, so Leonora Ashburnham, thinking that it would get her out of Edward's system, paid for Maisie's passage. Later, though, upon realizing that Edward's past affairs are causing him to pay blackmail, Leonora turns furious upon running into Maisie in the hall outside of her room and strikes her in the face. When Maisie realizes that her expenses were paid so that she could be Edward's mistress, she rushes to return

home to her husband, but she has a heart attack while packing and dies. The narrator says that he does not believe that there was ever an actual affair between Maisie and Edward.

Nancy Rufford

Nancy Rufford is a young girl recently out of a convent school. Her father is abusive, and so her mother sends her to live with her old friend Leonora Ashburnham and her husband, Edward, whom Nancy is so close to that she refers to them as her aunt and uncle. While living with the Ashburnhams and traveling with them, Nancy does not realize that Edward is falling in love with her. When his lover Florence Dowell sees Edward and Nancy together, she realizes how he feels toward Nancy and runs away in tears, later committing suicide.

Living at the Ashburnham's estate after Florence's death, Nancy starts to realize that she is falling in love with her "Uncle Edward." She dismisses the idea because he is married to Leonora, but a news article about a local couple becoming divorced makes her realize that couples can break up. She goes to Edward's room one night and offers herself to him, but he turns her away. Immediately afterward he writes to her father in India to take her back. When she is in India, Nancy hears that Edward committed suicide right after she left England, and she is driven mad, unable to recognize who or where she is, repeating the word "shuttlecocks" or expressing her faith in God when she speaks at all.

THEMES

The Confines of Religion

The subject of religion comes up frequently in *The Good Soldier*. The most relevant place is when religion is used in a climactic moment of the first book, when Leonora, after listening to Florence talk disparagingly about Catholics, races from the room and later exclaims to John Dowell that she is upset because she is a Catholic. The most obvious significance of this event is that Florence has used stereotypes about religions to bait Leonora, insulting her subtly. In the rigid social structure of Edwardian England, Protestantism was considered the "proper" religion, associated with fine breeding and social manners. Catholics, on the other hand, were viewed as being socially inferior. Some of this came from the idea that Protestantism celebrated rationality while the Catholic Church,

TOPICS FOR FURTHER STUDY

- Write two stories about something that happened to you: one in direct chronological order, and the other in the disjointed style of reminiscence that Ford uses in *The Good Soldier*.

- One of the main causes of friction in the Ashburnham marriage stems from their different religions; namely, Leonora's Roman Catholic upbringing forbids her from being divorced. Pick a religious group that you are not familiar with and write a report on its position on divorce.

- Two World Wars involving Germany have been fought since this novel was written. Write a history of the town of Bad Nauheim, where much of the novel's action takes place, and how it has changed throughout the twentieth century as a result of World Wars I and II.

- This story takes place in a time when transportation and communications were much more limited than they are today. Choose one aspect of modern technology (such as air travel, instant messaging, or web-based medical information) that you feel would have most affected the events of the Dowells' and Ashburnhams' lives, and write a report explaining how you think the plot would have been changed because of it.

with its emphasis on saints, relics, and the moral authority of the Pope, emphasized mysticism. Also, Catholicism was associated with poverty: some of this had to do with the fact that Catholicism flourished in countries that had higher rates of poverty, which some viewed as being caused, at least somewhat, by the church's doctrines against birth control (Catholic families, like Leonora's, tend to have many children) and divorce.

The church's position on divorce served to make Florence's jibe at Leonora even more effective. In telling Edward that the Protest is an important part of his character, she sends her lover an implied message: that Protestants like himself are not as trapped in unwanted marriages as a Catholic like Leonora might think. Florence uses this occasion to pretend to talk about a historical document, knowing that the ability to divorce is an issue that separates Edward and Leonora.

The subject reappears later in the book, controlling Nancy's relationship with Edward. Having gone through the same Catholic training as Leonora—they were educated at the same convent—she originally views Edward's marriage to Leonora as an immutable fact. They are a couple in her mind, and so she does not even think of Edward as a potential lover. It is only after she reads about the divorce of the Brands in the paper that she realizes that divorce is in fact a part of life, that the Church of England was formed by Henry VIII to make divorce an acceptable practice. Once she goes beyond her Catholic training and sees divorce as a possibility, Nancy thinks that she and Edward could have a future together, and she goes to him in the night and offers herself to him.

Shades of Infidelity

Ford shows several levels of infidelity in this novel. The lowest level is the characters who are reluctant about breaking their marriage vows. Leonora, for example, tries to have an affair with Rodney Bayham but finds that she cannot go through with it, while Maisie Maiden is swept up by Edward's charms and nearly succumbs to him before racing back to her husband. At the other extreme are characters like Florence and Jimmy, who have an affair, leave it when it is inconvenient, and then resume it when she returns to Europe on her honeymoon, showing contempt for her new husband.

Edward Ashburnham represents the range of types of infidelity in this book. He is sentimental and caring with Maisie Maiden; he is direct and almost business-like when he is seeing Mrs. Basil; and he conducts a wild sexual relationship with the Grand Duke's mistress. When it comes to Nancy Rufford, though, he struggles to avoid an affair, even after she comes to his bedroom at night to offer herself to him. Edward's behavior might have less to do with respect for his marriage than with his respect for Nancy's purity.

Sickness, Real and Imagined

In this novel, there are four characters who are said to be suffering from heart disease, but only one, Maisie Maiden, actually does have a weak heart. Among the others, two use their supposed infirmities as excuses to manipulate others.

Florence's uncle, John Hurlibird, honestly believes that he has a heart problem. He retires from business and would like to live a life of leisure, but he feels forced to take a trip around the world so that his sisters will not view him as being lazy. Throughout the trip he takes precautions to care for his heart and follows the medical advice of his physicians. It is only after he is dead, when he leaves his heart to science, that it is discovered that his heart was fine.

Florence, on the other hand, having learned about heart disease from watching her uncle, pretends that she has a heart problem. This allows her to shut her new husband, John, out of her life immediately, telling him that the physical strain of sex might kill her. He leaves her alone at night, and her lovers come to her room. Her phony heart disease works against her, though, when she is not able to fulfill her life's ambition and cross the Channel to England because she has already spread the story that a boat ride would strain her too much.

Maisie Maiden's weak heart forces her to leave her husband in India and go for treatment to Bad Nauheim. This separation leaves her vulnerable to the romantic interests of Edward Ashburnham, who feigns his own heart disease in order to follow her to the spa. When Maisie finds out that the Ashburnhams paid her husband to finance her trip, she feels that they have set her up to be Edward's lover: in her haste to pack and leave, she strains her weak heart and dies. True illness makes one weak and vulnerable, but false illness gives the socially powerful the opportunity to be even more pampered than they normally are.

STYLE

Limited Point of View

Most of the structure of this novel stems from the fact that its narrator, John Dowell, is trying to piece together the significance of events that happened in his life. As he understood things up until his wife Florence's death, he had been involved in a stable marriage for years with a woman

suffering from heart disease. Every year, at the Bad Nauheim spa, they renewed their acquaintance with the Ashburnhams, a British couple of old wealth and sturdy, dependable character. It is not until the Ashburnhams have telegrammed him to cross the ocean again and join them at their estate that he learns the realities of his life, including that during their marriage his wife was sleeping with her old boyfriend Jimmy, and had been sending him money for years; that her alleged heart disease was a willful, malicious lie; that Edward Ashburnham would have lost his money and all of his prestige if his wife had not taken control of his life; and that Florence did not die taking medicine that would save her life, but instead poisoned herself. Over the course of the book, these details unravel, forcing readers to readjust their understanding of John Dowell's situation gradually, as Dowell himself does.

Uneven Chronicle

If readers find this novel confusing, it might be because it is told out of chronological order. Ford uses the novel's structure to simulate the experience of, as the narrator describes it, a man sitting in a room and telling the events to a friend. As a speaker might do, the narrator, Dowell, skips backward and forward in time, going over the same stories again and again after details are filled in. A point like Edward's near-financial ruin might be explained once when Dowell is telling readers about how the Ashburnhams came to Bad Nauheim, for instance, and then told again, with more background, when he is talking about Leonora's personality and her need to control her husband's life.

The order is less chronological than thematic, as if the teller of the tale is being reminded of things while he is speaking. Maisie Maiden, for instance, is mentioned several times before readers know her actual place in the sequence of events. Dowell's marriage to Florence, which could be argued to be the beginning of the whole series of events, comes in the middle of the tale, after readers have seen them as a contented couple of tourists and have then had a chance to piece together Florence's deceitful nature. To some extent, Dowell's style of referring to events long before they are actually explained could be thought of as a form of foreshadowing, but he does not make them seem like clues about what is to come. Instead, the jumps in his narrative forward to the future then back to the past simulate the feeling of memory.

COMPARE & CONTRAST

- **1915:** Florence Dowell can see the coast of England from the shore of France, but she cannot go there because of her imagined heart ailment. Indeed, the only means of transportation between the coast of France and the coast of England is by taking a boat across the English Channel.

  Today: Since the Channel Tunnel was completed in 1994, trains run regularly between the two countries.

- **1915:** Divorce is available, but very uncommon in upper-crust British society.

  Today: The social stigma against divorce is practically forgotten. The Prince and Princess of Wales were divorced in 1996 and the Duke and Duchess of York were divorced in the same year.

- **1915:** A person could convincingly fake a chronic heart condition simply by learning to mimic the symptoms of such a condition.

  Today: Advanced diagnostic testing allows doctors to examine the heart itself, and not have to rely only on the patient's word.

HISTORICAL CONTEXT

The Edwardian Era

The Edwardian Era is that period in English history when Edward VII, the son of Queen Victoria, ruled England. It is seen as a bridge between the worldview of the Victorian Era and the harsh reality that came with the outbreak of World War I, in 1914.

Queen Victoria ruled the United Kingdom of Great Britain and Ireland for a long time, from 1837 to 1901. Characteristics of her personality came to define the cultural mood of the time. To this day, the word Victorianism is used to describe a rigid class system; vast economic chasms between the rich and poor; repressed sexuality; and a strict code of manners. While the Industrial Age took place during Victoria's reign, bringing great technological advances, the era is still characterized as one when social attitudes looked to the past and toward conserving tradition.

By contrast, the Edwardian Era is looked at as a time when England sought to shake off tradition and embrace the future. After having the same monarch for nearly sixty-five years, more than most people's lifetimes, the dawn of the new century brought a fresh face to the British Empire: although change of the country's mood was not overnight, there are still particular elements that make the Edwardian Era distinct.

Unlike Victoria, who, especially in her later years, remained very narrow in her contacts with the world, Edward loved travel. As such, newspapers reporting on his travels introduced British citizens to the ways of peoples all over the globe, and people in foreign lands became acquainted with the British. This curiosity about the world coincided with advances in travel technology that had developed at the end of the nineteenth century: rail lines were extended to remote areas that were previously unreachable; ocean liners gained in weight, capacity, and speed, culminating in the historic launch of the *Titanic*, which sank on its maiden voyage in 1912, killing 1,500. The quick development of the airplane after the Wright Brothers' first flight in 1903 further prodded interest in travel.

While the Edwardian period was marked by social progress, it was also a time of strict class divisions. People born "of society" could expect to hold their social positions throughout their lives, barring any great catastrophe, while those who were born of the lower classes found that even the accumulation of wealth did not guarantee them admission to the upper social echelon. The unwritten rules about who one associated with and how one behaved oneself were drilled into some people from birth, leaving others to wonder what it would take to become socially prominent.

The Edwardian Era did not necessarily end with Edward's death in 1910. The mood of the times continued. Most historians use the term Edwardian to talk of the period right up to the beginning of World War I. The war changed much that had been stable about the British Empire through Victoria's and Edward's reigns. Colonies changed hands, and in the bombing of England, fortunes were lost. Children born to wealth and privilege found themselves faced with the horrors of the new weapons of war, including new, powerful bombs dropped from planes and chemical warfare. The lines between classes blurred during the war, which brought suffering to all.

The Great War

The social stability of the Edwardian Era was irretrievably broken in 1914, when the world exploded into the first of two World Wars in the twentieth century that changed western civilization. The political structure across Europe had been in place for almost a hundred years, since the reign of Napoleon. By 1914, governments across the globe had allied themselves with other governments, dividing into two basic groups: the Triple Entente, composed of France, Russia, and Great Britain, and the Central Axis, which was led by the German Empire, the Austro-Hungarian Empire, and the Ottoman Empire. Tensions between these political factions was high when, on June 28, 1914, a Bosnian Serb student assassinated Archduke Franz Ferdinand, the heir to the Austro-Hungarian throne. Austro-Hungary demanded that Serbia find those responsible for the assassination, and, soon, determining that Serbia was not moving the investigation along quickly enough, Austro-Hungary declared war on Serbia. Due to a mutual defense pact, Russia began mobilizing its troops, and as it did, Germany, an ally of Austro-Hungary, declared war on Russia, and then on France. Soon all of Europe was involved. By August, the navies of opposing armies were fighting each other as far away as the Pacific Ocean, and ground troops were in conflict across Africa. Italy entered the war in 1915, and the United States became actively involved in 1917.

The scope of the Great War, as it was known at the time, is hardly imaginable today. Approximately twenty million people died as a result of the fighting, and slightly more suffered serious injuries. The Austro-Hungarian, German, Ottoman, and Russian empires were broken up. A number of countries, notably Czechoslovakia, Estonia, Finland, Latvia, Lithuania, and Poland, became independent states for the first time in a century. Great Britain prospered in the period after the war ended in 1918, taking control of several African colonies from Italy. But the treaties that ended the fighting were unstable and eventually led to the rise of the German Nazi party in the 1920s and 1930s, resulting in the Second World War, which was even more traumatic to international order.

CRITICAL OVERVIEW

The Good Soldier is generally considered to be Ford's best work, as well as one of the best novels of the twentieth century. At the time of its publication in 1915, though, there were some critics who disliked aspects of the novel. Some reviewers found the structure too confusing, while others objected on moral grounds, feeling that it promoted promiscuity. Theodore Dreiser, himself one of the enduring novelists of the twentieth century, wrote in a 1915 *New Republic* article (reprinted in *Ford Madox Ford: The Critical Heritage*) that he feels "with all its faults of telling, it is an honest story, and there is no blinking of the commonplaces of our existence which so many find immoral and make such a valiant effort to conceal." That same year, novelist Rebecca West praised the book in a *Daily News* article (also reprinted in *Ford Madox Ford: The Critical Heritage*), noting that "it is as impossible to miss the light of its extreme beauty and wisdom as it would be to miss the full moon on a clear night." West goes on to praise the novel's cleverness and "the obvious loveliness of the color and cadence of its language."

The novel's literary importance has grown over the years, and in 1951, there was a resurgence of interest in Ford marked by the release of new editions of all of his major works. Critic Mark Schorer, in an introduction to a reprinted edition of the novel (reprinted as a stand-alone piece in *Critical Essays on Ford Madox Ford*),

A mineral spring spa in Jugendstil in the style of art nouveau in the cur treatment facilities of Bad Nauheim, Hessen, Hassia, Hesse, Germany (© superclic | Alamy)

poses the question of whether *The Good Soldier* should be considered a "novelist's novel," or something that would be more pleasing to writers than to members of the general public. Schorer's own answer to the question is that the book's power is not limited to writers: "*The Good Soldier*, like all great works, has the gift of power and remorse."

The enduring power of this book is evident in the fact that critics continue to return their attention to it. Critic and novelist A. S. Byatt wrote in *Passions of the Mind* (1991) that she considers the tone of Ford's prose in *The Good Soldier* to be particularly powerful, noting that the "combination of the precisely, evocatively lyrical, or vivid, with the flat tone of normality . . . is one of the glories of the book. The others are the manipulation of the time-shift, and the difference between revelation by dialogue and terrible act."

CRITICISM

David Kelly

Kelly teaches literature and creative writing at two colleges in Illinois. In this essay on The Good Soldier, *Kelly examines the significance of the book's brief final segment and how it affects the reader's understanding of all that came before it.*

In the last few pages of his 1915 masterpiece *The Good Soldier*, Ford Madox Ford presents a strange little coda that is not anticipated and seems unnecessary. Yet, if one thinks about it, the coda serves to give new definition to the entire story that precedes it. At this point, the novel seems over, strategically and emotionally, with nothing more to tell. The characters who are going to die have died, and the futures of those who are going to live have been accounted for. Leonora Ashburnham is widowed, remarried, and expecting a son; the book's narrator,

WHAT DO I READ NEXT?

- Written as a companion piece to a Public Broadcasting Service series of the same name, Juliet Gardiner's *Manor House: Life in an Edwardian Country House* (2003) provides insight into the sort of life led by Edward and Leonora, and aspired to by Florence.

- Another novel by Ford, *Parade's End*, is often considered one of the finest novels ever written about World War I. It is a large, sprawling book, a compilation of four distinct novels, brought together to document the vanishing pre-war generation. Originally published in separate editions from 1924 through 1928, the complete volume is most recently available in a Carcanet Press edition of 2007.

- Arthur Mizener's biography of Ford, *The Saddest Story* (1971), is one of the most complete chronicles of the author's life ever written.

- Ford is just one of the many towering literary figures profiled in Ernest Hemingway's memoir of life in Paris during the 1920s. *A Moveable Feast* (1964) was the last book published during Hemingway's lifetime.

- In his 2000 book, *Modernism*, Peter Childs refers frequently to *The Good Soldier*, as well as other works by Ford, to explain the shift in literary sensibilities that came about in the post-war era.

John Dowell, is also widowed, living in his ancestral land of England, and once more caring for a beautiful invalid who can never be a true companion to him. Florence and Edward, the spouses who habitually betrayed Leonora and Dowell, have both committed suicide. The story lines have come to an end, and yet the narrator decides to add a description about Edward's death.

This abrupt turn, and the brief segment of not quite two pages that it introduces, is significant on several levels. For one thing, it would

> IF DOWELL HAD DIRECTLY EXPLAINED THAT HE SAW HIS FRIEND'S INTENTION TO COMMIT SUICIDE, READERS COULD FIND THIS LACK OF ACTION MORALLY QUESTIONABLE, ESPECIALLY IF THE LINK ESTABLISHED IN THE LAST SCENE WAS NOT PRESENTED."

have to be significant in any story to have the death of one of the four principle characters brought up, especially when the narrator brings it up casually, as an afterthought. Of course, Edward Ashburnham's death could not be insignificant: a good case could be made that, as the character who brings the most conflict into the lives of his wife and the Dowells, Edward is the most significant figure in the book. The novel centers around him. Dowell, the passive narrator, is a man so incurious about life that his wife is able to carry on affairs for years right under his nose, without his knowledge, keeping him locked out of her bedroom. Edward, on the other hand, is thirsty for life. He goes from one woman to the next, but he also is bound by a moral code so strong that it makes him send the one true love of his life, Nancy Rufford, back to her abusive father, knowing that her fate would be even worse if she stayed with him. In short, Edward is simply not a forgettable character, and for Dowell to pretend that he nearly forgot the night that Edward cut his throat is quite a stretch of credulity.

Given Edward's prominence in the novel, it would be more likely that his suicide would be the climax of the book than an afterthought. The entire book, though, works against that effect. For one thing, there is no element of surprise about his death. Rather than keeping readers wondering what fate will befall Edward Ashburnham, Ford has Dowell talking about him in the past tense throughout the story, and he is referred to as a dead man in the first pages of the first chapter; the fact that he will slit his own throat is largely out in the open.

In the final chapters of the book, readers can see his foretold fate approaching as Edward lives his final weeks in wretched misery. The question of his death is one of "when," not "if." In this sense, his actual death is irrelevant enough to slip by without notice: not his death itself, really, but the moment that it occurred. Edward's demise is such a strong presence throughout the book that the fact of its actual arrival seems a petty, minor detail.

What the story lacks, though, up to those closing pages, is a strong display of Edward Ashburnham's dignity. He is seen throughout the book as a user of women and a pawn of women, a drunk, a blowhard, a foolish gambler and a sentimental landlord, and, most prominently, as a man who only retains his self-esteem when he submits himself to the wife he betrayed. He kills himself because of his longing for the girl who calls him "Uncle Edward." Readers know that much by the time they reach the end of the book. What they do not guess from the long journey through Dowell's narrative is that John Dowell, at their last meeting, would come to see himself and Edward Ashburnham as virtually one and the same.

In this coda of the last two pages, Dowell reveals such absolute empathy with Edward that he understands, with just a glance, Edward's intention to kill himself. Even more significantly, he knows that Edward's decision is the right one. This is not necessarily a foregone conclusion. The life of a British lord, after all, does still have its value. Edward is still very wealthy; he has his marriage to Leonora, which, flawed and limp as it is, at least is not openly hostile; he has a mission, even, in protecting the tenants whose families have been on his land for generations from falling victim to Leonora's heartless efficiency.

Of course, by this point in the novel, Edward has admitted that he will never have Nancy Rufford as his own—not because of law or social pressures or objections from his wife or even resistance from Nancy herself, but due solely to his own sense of moral propriety. Loss of a love does not necessarily, though, lead to a life that is not worth continuing. Edward apparently feels that it does. It might seem like a melodramatic view, but meek, cuckolded John Dowell, who spent years held at a distance from his own wife and will spend eternity held at a distance from young Nancy, agrees with him completely.

What this brief section about Edward's death does, ultimately, is to make the reader empathize with Edward's choice, and understand above and beyond all reason that his choice to take his life is a reasonable one. Edward, the mechanistic "good soldier," is humanized here, at last. He becomes flesh and blood, and not just a staid, repressive tool of duty. In these last two pages, Ford creates an actual scene, with descriptions of Edward's voice, his skin, his hair. Actual lines of dialog are exchanged. The handwriting on the telegram is rendered with detail, as is Edward's suit and his penknife.

The depth of this last scene is best understood in contrast to the shallowness of the narrative in the previous two hundred and seventy pages. The novel's narrative is styled to resemble the musings of a man sitting in a country cottage and telling his story to a friend, interrupted by the wind and the roar of the sea, and it does this job so well that it comes out being just as insubstantial as such a conversation would be. Lines of dialog, when they do occur, are isolated, very seldom coming in pairs or following the back-and-forth flow that a normal conversation would. Objects and people are described, sometimes in great detail, but the narrative does not stay with any of them for long, and is likely as not to jump backward a decade or two in the next paragraph.

Throughout most of the book, Ford is telling the general story of the lives of his main characters. In the last scene, however, he has an important event to relate: it is a small, quiet moment, but that is all the more reason that he tells the story of Dowell's last meeting with Edward with such care and delicacy. There is just one scene earlier in the book that can compare in its attention to detail, and to moment-by-moment attention: the scene when the two couples, Dowells and Ashburnhams, take an excursion out to the town of M—, where they visit the castle that holds a fragment of Luther's Protest. Like the final scene, this one flirts with mystery, being ruled by passions that are left unspoken. Florence's dig at Leonora is patently offensive to anyone who is aware of what it would mean to a Roman Catholic like Leonora to hear her praise the Anglican split from the Catholic Church—an awareness that Edward, apparently, lacks. For those aware of its significance, it seems just as portent, as fraught with significance, as Edward's taking out his penknife when his life is clearly over. In the first case, Leonora runs away, filled suddenly with the horrifying realization that Florence is flaunting the fact that she is Edward's mistress: it is the most spontaneous action in the book. In the final scene, Dowell is flooded just as instantly with the realization that Edward intends to kill himself, but he doesn't move a muscle. He does nothing. Dowell is as passive a character as they come.

And it is Dowell's passivity that allows Ford to make readers feel what it is like to be Edward Ashburnham. The link between the two men, as Dowell notes it in the book's final paragraph, is that they are both sentimental people. The meaning of this is unclear, though it seems to have something to do with the fact that they are each willing to behave according to emotions that they cannot, and will not, ever express. Whatever it means, the main significance is that it is something they have in common: a moral code. If Dowell had directly explained that he saw his friend's intention to commit suicide, readers could find this lack of action morally questionable, especially if the link established in the last scene was not presented. Dowell can let Edward die because he knows exactly how he feels.

If not for this final coda, the story would end at the most recently recorded point of John Dowell's life, leaving readers to think about his sad relationship with Nancy, doting on her in ways she can never appreciate, having been driven mad by love for another man. This would be a sad ending. But in bringing attention back to Edward Ashburnham, and establishing him as the man John Dowell would be if he had the courage of his convictions, Ford has made a sad story that much more depressing.

Source: David Kelly, Critical Essay on *The Good Soldier*, in *Novels for Students*, Gale, Cengage Learning, 2009.

Julie Gordon-Dueck

In the following article, Gordon-Dueck takes a psychoanalytical approach to interpreting the characters in The Good Soldier.

In *The Good Soldier* John Dowell, as narrator, struggles to understand what has transpired in his relationships with his wife, Florence, and their friends, Edward and Leonora Ashburnham, over a nine year period. Dowell's quest for this knowledge is precipitated by discoveries of infidelity and suicide which challenge his long-standing belief that the upright appearances of these individuals represented their genuine natures. Baffled by the incongruence between appearances and internal motives, Dowell desires to know what truly lurks

> OVERALL, DOWELL BECOMES MORE CAPABLE OF INCREASINGLY ACKNOWLEDGING HIS SHADOW BY PROJECTING ELEMENTS OF HIS SHADOW, OR INFERIOR SELF, ONTO EDWARD."

in the "heart" of human nature. More specifically, however, Dowell is struggling to come to terms with Carl Jung's concept of the "shadow." The shadow is broadly known as the deepest, most primitive part of the psyche, an archetype inherited from prehuman ancestors which exists in the unconscious and contains all the animal instincts and respective tendencies toward immorality, aggression, and passion. This essay will explore aspects of Dowell's arduous journey with the shadow by discussing his initial encounter with the shadow, his experiences with the shadow in others, and the gradual synthesis of his own shadow into his psyche which provides him with greater insight into himself and others.

The nine year Dowell/Ashburnham friendship provides a natural catalyst for Dowell's encounter with the shadow, for it is a "young-middle-aged affair" which occurs while Dowell is 36–45, Florence is 30–39, Edward is 33–42, and Leonora is 31–40. Jung posited that middle-age, which he believed begins between the ages of 35–40, marked the time of life when one most fully encounters the shadow. Prior to mid-life, the individual is typically focused on establishing a role in society in order to survive. Most of one's [energy] is consciously invested in building the "persona," the archetypal public self, while stifling the instincts of the unconscious shadow. Although the shadow is frequently identified by its destructive/ aggressive potential, it equally serves as a dynamic reservoir of creativity, passion, and imagination. By making the shadow conscious, enriching opportunities for improved insight, awareness of the larger world, and personality synthesis are possible. As a result, prior ideals and beliefs are often challenged and replaced by new ones. Jung compares middle-age to the sun's position at noon: "At the stroke of noon the descent begins. And the descent means the reversal of all ideals and values that were cherished in the morning. The sun falls in contradiction to itself. It is as though it should draw in its rays, instead of emitting them" (Jung 106).

As he begins to write his story, Dowell, at 45, is overwhelmed by his encounter with the features of the shadow he has discovered through Florence's and Edward's affair. Being confronted with the primal in these persons forces him to begin considering his own shadow, even if initially at an unconscious level. While this encounter would be difficult for anyone, it is especially difficult for Dowell, for he presents with what Jung referred to as an "inflation of the persona," the over-identification with the persona at the expense of under-developed parts of the personality, such as the shadow. John Sanford discusses the manner in which Jung compared initially facing the shadow with alchemy. When one first perceives the shadow, it is like the stage of "melanosis" in which "everything turns black inside the vessel containing all the alchemical elements" until eventually there is movement toward the creative center of the self, a more realistic self-awareness is gained, and the "false persona" begins to dissipate (qtd. in Miller 23). Dowell reflects this process through the repeated phrase, "it is all darkness," which is especially prominent toward the beginning of the story but resurfaces throughout the narrative along with continual images of darkness and light as Dowell plunges deeper into his encounter with the shadow. Dowell also acknowledges that meeting the shadow is a type of "paradise lost" when he describes the date of Florence's suicide as "the last day of absolute ignorance and perfect happiness."

Dowell's inflated persona is revealed in his lifstyle and perceptions of himself and others. Dowell is initially a rather dull and amorphous character. His personality exemplifies that when the shadow is sacrificed to the persona, there is a cessation of spontaneity, creativity, strong emotions, and deep insights. Dowell seems to have no motives, ambitions, or passions. He describes himself as having no job, no family connections, and no real passion for Florence. He simply wanders into her life and marries her. He does whatever Florence wants, and while there is some nobility in his loyalty and care for her, he does not give the impression that his commitment was an active choice, but rather something to fill his time and give him an identity within the conventions of society. Dowell's lack of awareness of his shadow and his inflated persona can

be seen in his early description of himself as completely noble: "For I solemly avow thst not give him an identity within conventions of society. Dowell's lack of awareness of his shadow and his inflated persona can be seen in his early description of himself as completely noble: "For I solemly avow that not only have I never so much as hinted at an impropriety in my conversation in the whole of my days; and more than that, I will vouch for the cleanness of my thoughts and the absolute chastity of my life."

Dowell's naive perceptions of others, which he compulsively reviews throughout his story, suggest that he has spent most of his life relying on the personas of other individuals to define his world view as much as he relies on his own persona to define his total identity. Particularly in the first few sections of the novel, Dowell consistently refers to himself, Florence and the Ashburnhams as "good people." He describes the Ashburnhams as "the model couple," Florence as "too good to be true," and frequently refers to Edward as "perfect." He further confirms their civility by elaborately describing their respective backgrounds of wealth and privilege.

Several literary qualities in *The Good Soldier* reflect Dowell's struggle to accept and synthesize the shadow more fully into his personality. The story's full title, *The Good Soldier: A Tale of Passion*, already embodies Dowell's central conflict. The word "good" connotes the concept of the persona, while "passion" suggests the shadow. Indeed, it is the confused exploration and eventual acceptance of these polarities that Dowell confronts on his journey toward self-knowledge throughout the novel. Dowell's choice to write his story signifies his willingness to take action, something he has not done before in his life. Furthermore, it is a creative process which can tap into his imagination and thereby lead him into the further depths of the shadow. The loose chronology by which Dowell conveys his story parallels the non-linear time dimension of the shadow and the unconventional manner by which its contents seep into Dowell's consciousness. The movement between different perspectives as Dowell tells his story mirrors his intrapsychic movement from complete darkness toward greater awareness and integration. The limited, first person view conveys the intimacy of Dowell's interior journey of the mind.

Dowell's use of various images describe how his confrontation with aspects of the shadow in

Florence and the Ashburnhams initially disrupt his psychic equilibrium. He compares his discoveries of infidelity and suicide to witnessing "the sack of a city or the failing to pieces of a people." He notes that the "breaking up of our little four-square coterie was such another unthinkable event," while the seeming relational stability "vanishes in four crashing days at the end of nine years and six weeks". Still in shock, and struggling with the cruel deception of appearance in the relationships, he states: "It was like a minuet... yet I can't believe it's gone... it was a prison—a prison full of screaming hysterics..." Overall, Dowell's distress is actually positive, for his psyche must become somewhat dismantled in order to acknowledge and begin to accept the presence of the shadow.

Dowell also asks many questions, hesitates making any definite statements, and contradicts himself several times, especially in the early stages of his story when he is experiencing the most shock and psychic disarray. He knows the Ashburnhams "with an extreme intimacy... and yet, in another sense, we knew nothing at all about them." Dowell also poses his question regarding basic human nature in dichotomous, extreme terms at the end of the first section of part one: "Am I no better than a eunuch or is the proper man—the man with the right to existence—a raging stallion forever neighing after his neighbor's womankind?" Dowell uncharacteristically weeps "for eleven miles" when Leonora confesses, during a carriage ride in the dark, that she tried to have an affair while still married. Obviously, the revelation of Leonora's shadow greatly threatens the security of Dowell's persona and world view.

The numbers four and nine appear symbolic of Dowell's quest to comprehend the shadow. "Four" is used frequently to describe the Dowell/Ashburnham affiliation. Dowell refers to the friendship as "our little four-square coterie," whose rational stability "vanished in four crashing days." Dowell also emphasizes the precise duration of the friendship as nine years several times throughout the story, particularly in the beginning. While his compulsive focus on time serves to help him analyze the tragic events which have occurred, the significance of the numbers cannot be overlooked. The symbolic meanings of both nine and four suggest Dowell's evolving psychic process of discovering and integrating the shadow into his personality. Nine is considered to be the symbol of truth and

the "symbolic number 'par excellence,' for it represents triple synthesis on each plane of the corporal, the intellectual and the spiritual" (Cirlot 234). Four is symbolic of "the human situation, of the external, natural limits of the 'minimum' awareness of totality, and finally, of rational organization" (Cirlot 232). Taken together, these numbers suggest Dowell's limited perspective in comprehending the "hearts" of others and even his own (four), yet acknowledge his journey toward a greater synthesis of the shadow in himself (nine). Dowell's frequent statement, "I don't know," underscores the limits of his knowledge of other persons' "hearts," despite his gradual willingness to synthesize the shadow into his consciousness.

The scene in which Dowell laughs at the black and white cow lying on its back in the middle of a stream signifies the deepening of Dowell's encounter with the shadow in himself and others. First of all, Dowell is "off duty" as Florence's nurse and ironically believes she is free from excitement while educating Edward about Ludwig the Courageous. This loosening of Dowell's persona allows his shadow to emerge through his laughter at the cow. While Dowell realizes his cruelty and knows he should pity the cow, he experiences you [sic] in viewing this odd scene, stating, "It is so just exactly what one doesn't expect of a cow." Although unaware, Dowell is actually laughing at his own unexpected and evolving internal conflict, for the cow represents both the shadow (black) and the persona (white) which are literally being turned upside down within Dowell's psyche. The mere fact that Dowell laughs at this scene indicates an emergence of his shadow, for "humor is often a manifestation of shadow truth," and laughing at another's misfortunes often indicates "repressed sadism" (Miller 42).

The black and white cow also, foreshadows Dowell's future conflicts with the shadow and persona in his wife, the Ashburnhams, and himself. Following the cow scene, Dowell's shadow rises closer to consciousness and he is more sensitized to at least a vague sense of primitiveness and evil in those around him, particularly, in Leonora. After Florence touches Edward's wrist during her lecture about the Protestants, Dowell observes, "I was aware of something treacherous, something frightful, something evil in the day." During Leonora's outburst after she sees Florence touch Edward's wrist, Dowell perceives her running "her hand with a singular clawing motion upwards over the forehead . . . her face was exactly that of a person looking into the pit of hell and seeing horrors there." In regard to Leonora's vigilance over Edward's potential love interests, Dowell describes her as "watching Edward more intently and with more straining of ears than that which a cat bestows upon a bird overhead . . ."

Dowell develops an increasingly negative view of Leonora and admits he actually dislikes her at the end of his story. Through Leonora, Dowell senses the negative price which is paid for an over-developed persona. He seems to realize that Leonora's persona is so false and rigid that it contains a very nasty shadow personality of its own, underneath. John Sanford notes that the shadow is not inherently evil, but that the ego, or persona, "in its refusal of insight and its refusal to accept the entire personality, contributes much more evil than the shadow." Leonora's repression of her shadow impulses in the service of her religious and reserved persona is conveyed through her denial of femininity, avoidance of expressing passion for Edward, and her refusal to nurture and encourage him. When Leonora's persona falters, she is at the mercy of a ruthless shadow which is out of control from being ignored for so many years. Dowell perceives many cruel behaviors in Leonora during this time. Leonora talks to Florence about her affair with Edward in "short, explosive sentences, like one of the damned." She threatens to divorce Edward, repeatedly curses him for his past affairs, feels extraordinary hatred for Edward, tortures him with Nancy Rufford's presence, and even wishes to "bring her riding whip: across the girl's face." Her immersion into the shadow is best captured in the image of her wearing black one night and stumbling over "the tiger skins in the dark hall" on her way to Nancy's room while a "sudden madness possessed her, a desire for action, a thirst for self-explanation."

Dowell also displays more of his own shadow instincts as his story progresses. In stark contrast to his description of her as "poor" during the first part of the novel, Dowell eventually admits he "hates" Florence and calls her a "whore." Later, he refers to her as "vulgar" and as "a flirt." He moves from describing Leonora and Florence as "good people" to "good actresses" and also refers to Edward, Leonora, and Florence as "three gamblers." Following Florence's death, he makes a "slip of the tongue" and says he wants to marry

Nancy, unaware that he "had the slightest idea even of caring for her." He adds, "It is as if one had a dual personality, the one I being entirely unconcious of the other." Later he admits to being greedy with certain foods and also admits that he had been attracted to Maisie Maiden.

Overall, Dowell becomes more capable of increasingly acknowledging his shadow by projecting elements of his shadow, or inferior self, onto Edward. Since Dowell's persona appears upright and unadventurous, it is likely that he projects his more masculine and passionate shadow side onto Edward. Robert Bly notes that projection is often a positive movement toward psychic growth, for it is a crucial means of finally seeing one's shadow material (Bly 12). What is unconscious must be projected outward into the world in some form before it can be owned and recognized. Dowell's projection of his shadow onto Edward seems to account for both his admiration and disdain of Edward. Until the end of the story, Dowell both admires yet criticizes Ashburnham. While he frequently refers to Edward's "perfect" features and kindness, he also refers to him as "dull," "stupid," and as a "sentimental ass." He accuses him of breaking up "the pleasantness" of his life and of killing Florence. Nonetheless, Dowell's admiration for Edward increases as the story progresses. Dowell admires the strong emotions and passion of Edward's shadow which Edward makes an effort to acknowledge, unlike Leonora. It is possible that at some level, Dowell can see that Edward's willingness to confront both the destructive and creative elements of his shadow, as seen in his affairs yet his generosity and concern for others, make him a more interesting and authentic person than Leonora. Although Edward obviously cannot cope with the middle-age task of integrating his shadow more fully into his self, and commits suicide, Dowell perceives Edward's life as the more authentic, spirited, and humane.

By the end of his story, Dowell has had much time to reflect on the tragedies which have affected him over a two year period. He moves from an amorphous, overwhelmed, defensive, and disoriented posture to an increasingly accepting, committed, and insightful individual who has wrestled with and synthesized his shadow more fully into his consciousness. The movement of his interior journey is symbolized by his outward journeys which are longer, more extensive more in depth, and more purposeful than his shallow travels with Florence, who only wanted to view sites superficially. Two of his major travels include going across the Atlantic to meet Edward during his final days, and then retrieving Nancy after her breakdown in Ceylon months later. Unlike his former passive posture, he expresses devout love for Edward and Nancy. In answer to his initial dichotomus question regarding which type of person has the right to an existence —"the eunuch or the stallion?"— Dowell seems to comprehend the inevitable existence of both the persona and shadow in all persons, but definitely sides with those who will explore their shadows, even if unsuccessfully, like Edward and Nancy. Dowell's growing acknowledgement of the inseparability of good and evil in all persons is reflected in one of his last questions: "Or are all man's lives like the lives of us good people—like the lives of the Ashburnhams, of the Dowells, of the Ruffords—broken, tumultuous, agonized, and unromantic, lives punctuated by screams, by imbecilities, by deaths, by agonies?"

By the end of the story, Dowell also reveals more extreme features of his shadow. He admits he is jealous of Leonora's life, and would like to be a polygamist, even if he has only pursued these fantasies vicariously through the life of Edward. He denounces society for idealizing the persona, and notes that Nancy's and Edward's formal display as she leaves Branshaw would have been "better in the eyes of God if they had all attempted to gouge out each other's eyes with carving knives." Dowell has definitely learned to value elements of his shadow by owning the inferior self he has projected onto Edward:

> I love him because he was just myself. If I had the courage and virility and possibly also the physique of Edward Ashburnham I should, I fancy, have done much of what he did. He seems to me like a large elder brother who took me out on several excursions and did many dashing things whilst I just watched him robbing the orchards, from a distance. And, you see, I am just as much of a sentimentalist as he was...

While Dowell admits he can never know the true nature of anyone's heart, he has learned a great deal about his own by confronting the persona and shadow in himself. Even though his life may not have been what he would have desired, Dowell has learned to make choices, feel passion, and know himself more fully while accepting the limits of human knowledge.

Although virtually alone, he achieves insight in ways the other characters in the story do not. His solitary existence also highlights the rarity of the honest introspection and insights he has achieved. As Carl Jung notes: "One does not become enlighted [sic] by imagining figures of light, but by making the darkness conscious. The latter procedure, however, is disagreeable and therefore not popular" (qtd. in Zweig 4).

Source: Julie Gordon-Dueck, "A Jungian Approach to Ford Madox Ford's *The Good Soldier*," in *Journal of Evolutionary Psychology*, Vol. 25, No. 1, March 2004, pp. 40–45.

Marguerite Palmer

In the following essay, Palmer examines the significance of Nancy's use of the word "shuttlecock" to describe her situation, pointing out how the word was used to describe women's clothing with religious significance in colonial India, where Nancy lived.

Dowell, in Ford Ma[d]ox Ford's *The Good Soldier*, retrieves the deranged Nancy from India, and she is reduced to two utterances: "Shuttlecock" and "Credo in unum Deum Omnipotentem." Dowell casts back in his mind and constructs an explanation, which recalls a conversation with Leonora.

> I know what was passing in her mind, if she can be said to have a mind, for Leonora has told me that, once, the poor girl said she felt like a shuttlecock being tossed backwards and forwards between the violent personalities of Edward and his wife. Leonora, she said, was always trying to deliver her over to Edward, and Edward tacitly and silently forced her back again. And the odd thing was that Edward himself considered that those two women used him like a shuttlecock.

Dowell's reflection on Nancy's meaning has aroused no critical discussion; it is generally accepted. Yet Dowell is demonstrably a most unreliable narrator of events of which he is a direct witness. His experience of colonial India is negligible and secondhand; he talks glibly of having picked Nancy up from India, but she was in fact in another country, Ceylon.

In colonial India, shuttlecock had passed into the language (Urdu/Hindi and colonial slang) as descriptive jargon for the indigenous Muslim women when they appeared in their burkahs. The burkah is a single full circle of material some ten feet in diameter, the center of which is placed over the head, thus completely covering the woman in swathes of material. A woman thus covered may look out of her confinement by means of a "grille" embroidered over a small aperture in front of her eyes. For three centimeters' depth around the sides and the back of the head, the material is smocked or rouched, giving an appearance similar to the "head" of the badminton shuttlecock; about a foot from the bottom of the garment, it is horizontally pleated, which weights it and prevents the cloth from blowing around, when windy, in any provocative way. The combination of smooth "cap," rouching, heavy pleating, and a full length of usually white material was reminiscent of the badminton shuttlecock to the colonial British. The term burkah has been retained in modern Pakistan; the garment is still commonly worn all over modern Pakistan, especially in the North West Frontier Province, which borders Afghanistan and the former USSR. The term has been claimed, and transliteration has now corrupted it to "shatal cock."

The term and the image would have been instantly recognizable to any ex-colonial of the Indian part of the Empire, and especially to both Leonora and Edward Ashburnham: Edward had served in the area of Chitral, in the sensitive border area of the North West Frontier Province, where the burkah is worn to this day.

Our understanding of the term shuttlecock as a statement of Nancy's predicament is facilitated by its context. It underlies the colonial, patronizingly humorous paternalism of the British, which Ford may have been criticizing. The burkah is also an icon of religious fundamentalism, implying adherence to religious mores and folkways, as well as the concomitant sexual unavailability, reminiscent of a Christian nun. The Nancy that Dowell is left with is a "forever-unavailable" woman. Their religious backgrounds will never overlap no matter how Dowell may fantasize about his willingness to "compromise" for Nancy. He fails to recognize the impossibility that she would ever be likewise disposed: Dowell is willing to surrender his religious heritage, and he wrongly assumes that Nancy is, too; Nancy is a Roman Catholic, to whom it is anathema to marry outside the faith. He has retrieved her only to be left alone, not comprehending the full implication of either his own actions or those of the others.

Source: Marguerite Palmer, "Ford's *The Good Soldier*," in *Explicator*, Vol. 56, No. 2, Winter 1998, 2 pp.

SOURCES

Byatt, A. S., "Accurate Letters: Ford Madox Ford," in *Passions of the Mind*, Vintage International, 1993, p. 104.

Dreiser, Theodore, "'The Saddest Story': Theodore Dreiser on *The Good Soldier*," in *Ford Madox Ford: The Critical Heritage*, edited by Frank MacShane, Routledge, 1997, p. 49; originally published in the *New Republic*, June 12, 1915, pp. 155–56.

Ford, Ford Madox, *The Good Soldier*, Vintage International, 1989.

Schorer, Mark, "*The Good Soldier*: An Interpretation," in *Critical Essays on Ford Madox Ford*, edited by Richard A. Cassell, G. K. Hall, 1987, p. 49; originally published in *The Good Soldier*, by Ford Madox Ford, Alfred A. Knopf, 1951.

West, Rebecca, "Rebecca West on *The Good Soldier*," in *Ford Madox Ford: The Critical Heritage*, edited by Frank MacShane, Routledge, 1997, p. 44; originally published in the *Daily News*, April 2, 1915, p. 6.

FURTHER READING

Cheng, Vincent J., "English Behaviour and Repression: 'A Call: The Tale of Two Passions'," in *Ford Madox Ford: A Reappraisal*, edited by Robert Hampson and William Anthony Davenport, Rodopi B.V., 2002, pp. 106–31.

> In this essay, Cheng reviews the moral complexities that Ford explores in *The Good Soldier*.

Haslam, Sara, "Novel Perspectives," in *Fragmenting Modernism: Ford Madox Ford, the Novel and the Great War*, Manchester University Press, 2002, pp. 41–64.

> Haslam uses this novel as a specific example of how World War I affected Ford's writing style, and fiction in general.

Moser, Thomas C., "Impressionism, Agoraphobia, and *The Good Soldier*," in *The Life in the Fiction of Ford Madox Ford*, Princeton University Press, 1980, pp. 122–95.

> Moser provides a psychological examination of Ford's life and work, following his writing career from beginning to end.

Snitow, Ann Barr, *Ford Madox Ford and the Voice of Uncertainty*, Louisiana State University Press, 1984.

> This book traces Ford's career as it evolved from the peaceful early years to the turbulence of the war, with a central climactic chapter devoted to *The Good Soldier*.

The Hound of the Baskervilles

The Hound of the Baskervilles by Sir Arthur Conan Doyle was published in serialized form from August 1901 to April 1902 in the British magazine the Strand. The novel was wildly popular with the public, which had been waiting for a new Sherlock Holmes story for eight long years. The story's Gothic setting in Dartmoor, England, the murky depths of the Grimpen Mire bog, the supernatural overtones of the spectral hound, and the legend of a curse upon the Baskerville family all combined to make the novel one of the most loved Sherlock Holmes tales of all time. For over one hundred years, the book has never been out of print, and numerous film and stage versions have been produced worldwide.

The book was inspired by Conan Doyle's friend Fletcher Robinson, a Dartmoor native who told the author of the local legend of a huge phantom hound that haunted the foggy moors. Originally, the novel was not a Sherlock Holmes story. Conan Doyle had killed off the Holmes character in "The Final Problem" seven years earlier, but he decided the case was a perfect match for Holmes and Watson. However, Conan Doyle set the story two years before Holmes's tragic "death," thereby frustrating fans who had hoped the detective would be brought back to life. The Hound of the Baskervilles is narrated by Dr. John H. Watson, Holmes's faithful sidekick, and is reconstructed from his notes and recollections. The story is unusual in that Watson plays a central

SIR ARTHUR CONAN DOYLE

1901–1902

Arthur Conan Doyle (Imagno / Getty Images)

rolc in thc plot, while Holmes is off stage for much of the action. The book was illustrated, as were many Holmes tales, by Sidney Paget, whose depictions of the detective and Dr. Watson have become famous in and of themselves. The novel's success indeed prompted Conan Doyle to resurrect Holmes for subsequent adventures.

A recent edition of the novel may be found in *The New Annotated Sherlock Holmes*, W. W. Norton, 2006.

AUTHOR BIOGRAPHY

Sir Arthur Conan Doyle was born in Edinburgh, Scotland, on May 22, 1859. His father was an architect who illustrated magazines and children's books in his spare time; his mother had been educated in France and was a voracious reader. Conan Doyle graduated from Edinburgh University in 1881 with a degree in medicine and received his doctorate from Edinburgh University in 1885. Despite several attempts to establish a medical practice, Conan Doyle was an unsuccessful doctor; in 1891, he gave up the medical profession to concentrate entirely on writing. One of his professors in medical school, Dr. Joseph Bell, was renowned for his ability to make accurate assumptions about people by observation alone. Bell was the inspiration for the character of Sherlock Holmes, along with C. Auguste Dupin, the inspector created by Edgar Allan Poe in what is commonly regarded as literature's first mystery story, "The Murders in the Rue Morgue."

Conan Doyle was an adventurer. Upon receiving his medical degree in 1881, he embarked on a six-month whaling voyage to the Arctic, serving as the ship's doctor. Several years later he sailed to the west coast of Africa, and in 1900 he traveled to South Africa during the Boer War to serve as a physician in a British field hospital. Despite his penchant for adventure and love of sports (he was rumored to have introduced downhill skiing to Switzerland), he was a devoted family man and made his living primarily as a writer.

Following his activities in the Boer War, he returned to London and wrote *The Hound of the Baskervilles*, which was promptly published in serial form in the *Strand* from August 1901 to April 1902. That same year he was knighted for having written a propagandist pamphlet supporting the British position in the Boer War. The author's steadfast support of the British Empire, his staunch belief in stratified social classes, and his distrust of female suffrage, labor unions, and Mormons are evident in his fiction, especially in the character of Sherlock Holmes. Conan Doyle was uncommonly prolific, his sixty Sherlock Holmes stories amounted to a sliver of his oeuvre—an insignificant one, in his own estimation. He wrote them primarily for money and because he was unsatisfied with the inferior quality of his contemporaries' mystery stories. Holmes's reliance on logic and reason in solving crimes was a new idea, as was the idea of presenting enough clues for the reader to theoretically be able to figure it out for him or herself.

Conan Doyle wrote many other forms of fiction, from supernatural tales, science fiction, adventure, domestic comedy, horror, and historical novels, in nearly all formats, including plays, poetry, stories, and novels. His stories featuring the character of Brigadier Gerard, who was based on the real-life French General Baron de Marbot, are highly regarded, as are several other of his adventure novels, including *The Lost World*. None of these, however, matched the popularity of his Holmes stories, and he often bristled under the fame they brought him.

Conan Doyle was equally prolific in nonfiction. He wrote many works of history, biography, and spiritualism. Indeed, spiritualism—the belief that the dead can communicate with the living through a medium—was the central preoccupation in the last twenty years of his life; he was one of the movement's staunchest devotees in England. Having built his reputation on a belief in scientific advancement, rationality, and intellectualism, he lost considerable credibility among the public for his unwavering belief in the paranormal, especially after he was found to have been duped by the Cottingley fairy hoax, in which two Yorkshire girls were photographed cavorting with supposedly real fairies that allowed themselves to be photographed.

Conan Doyle married twice, fathered five children, and died of a heart attack on July 7, 1930, in Sussex, England. Interest in Sherlock Holmes has remained strong throughout the years, with many fans dubbed "Sherlockians" involved in organizations that promote the conceit that Holmes and Watson were real people and that Conan Doyle was merely Watson's literary agent. The Sherlockians' published criticism both pays homage to Conan Doyle's illustrious detective and provides the academic world with a healthy dose of gentle humor.

PLOT SUMMARY

Chapter 1: Mr. Sherlock Holmes

Sherlock Holmes and Dr. Watson start the day at 221B Baker Street with an exchange regarding a walking stick left behind the day before by an unknown visitor. Holmes astounds Watson by determining that the stick belongs to a country doctor who received it as a retirement gift from Charing Cross Hospital. His pronouncement is verified by the appearance of Dr. James Mortimer, who returns for his walking stick and to consult the detective regarding the strange circumstances surrounding the death of his patient and friend, Sir Charles Baskerville, the baronet of an estate located in the Dartmoor region of Devonshire. Mortimer

MEDIA ADAPTATIONS

- A silent film version of *The Hound of the Baskervilles* was made in 1920. It was directed by Maurice Elvey and stars Eille Norwood as Sherlock Holmes and Hubert Willis as Dr. Watson. The novel was adapted by William J. Elliott and Dorothy Westlake.

- A 1939 film adaptation of *The Hound of the Baskervilles* by Ernest Pascal was directed by Sidney Lanfield and stars Basil Rathbone as Sherlock Holmes and Nigel Bruce as Dr. John H. Watson.

- A 1959 film adaptation of *The Hound of the Baskervilles* by Peter Bryan was directed by Terence Fisher and stars Peter Cushing as Sherlock Holmes and André Morell as Dr. Watson.

- An abridged audiobook of *The Hound of the Baskervilles* was released by HarperCollins Audiobooks in 2000.

- A Canadian television production of *The Hound of the Baskervilles* by Muse Entertainment Enterprises was filmed in Montreal and aired on Canadian and U.S. television in the fall of 2000. It was directed by Rodney Gibbons and stars Matt Frewer as Sherlock Holmes and Kenneth Walsh as Dr. Watson.

- A 1968 unabridged audio recording of *The Hound of the Baskervilles* from a Canadian Broadcasting Corporation radio production was released by Random House Audio in 2000.

- *The Hound of the Baskervilles* was produced for the Public Broadcasting Service television series "The Return of Sherlock Holmes" in 2003. The adaptation is written by T. R. Bowen, directed by Brian Mills, and stars Jeremy Brett as Sherlock Holmes.

- A humorous stage version of *The Hound of the Baskervilles* was written by Steven Canny and produced by the Peepolykus Theater Company at the West Yorkshire Playhouse in England in 2007.

inadvertently insults Holmes by calling him "the second highest expert in Europe."

Chapter 2: The Curse of the Baskervilles

Dr. Mortimer produces a letter, dated 1742, outlining the legend of the Baskerville curse. The letter was written by Charles's ancestor, Hugo Baskerville, and recounts the legend of his great-grandfather, also named Hugo. The elder Hugo fell in love with a farmer's daughter, kidnapped her, and held her captive at Baskerville Hall. While Hugo and his cronies drank the night away downstairs, she climbed out a window and ran across the moor toward her home. Hugo quickly discovered her escape and chased after her in a drunken fury. His cronies followed in an attempt to prevent him from killing her. They stumble upon a shepherd who claims to have seen the young woman being chased by Baskerville, who was riding his black horse and was accompanied by a spectral "hound of hell." Soon after they find both the maiden and Baskerville dead; tearing at Baskerville's throat is "a foul thing, a great, black beast, shaped like a hound, yet larger than any hound that ever mortal eye has rested upon." Since that day, the writer claims, subsequent generations of Baskerville men have suffered untimely sudden deaths.

Dr. Mortimer explains that his recently deceased friend was a philanthropist and childless widower who had moved to his inherited estate only two years earlier after returning from South Africa where he had sought his fortune in the region's gold mines. Sir Charles was terrified of the Baskerville curse and suffered from a weak heart; one evening he was found dead of a heart attack in an alley of the estate that bordered the moor. Dr. Mortimer, a man of science, was summoned by Baskerville's groom to examine the body and was terrified to discover nearby "the footprints of a gigantic hound!"

Chapter 3: The Problem

Holmes asks Mortimer a few questions about the weather on the night Sir Charles died, the position of his body, and characteristics of the hound's paw prints. It becomes apparent that Holmes does not believe in the curse but that Mortimer does. Furthermore, Mortimer states, several people have previously seen the spectral hound wandering along the moor at night. However, Mortimer states that he does not want Holmes's help in discovering what happened to Charles, but rather to counsel him on what to do about Henry Baskerville. Henry is the

last of the Baskervilles, and Mortimer fears that if he meets a similar untimely demise, then the Baskervilles' long tradition of philanthropy in the region will come to an end. Holmes advises Mortimer to return in twenty-four hours with Sir Henry Baskerville, and then he will decide what to do.

Holmes spends the rest of the day contemplating the case and consulting detailed maps of Devonshire. That evening Holmes announces to Watson that Charles Baskerville must have been waiting for someone. He says little else, though it is apparent to Watson that Holmes knows more about the case than he lets on.

Chapter 4: Sir Henry Baskerville

Dr. Mortimer returns to 221B Baker Street with Sir Henry Baskerville, who brings with him a mysterious letter delivered to him at the Northumberland Hotel. The note is composed of words cut from a newspaper: "As you value your life or your reason keep away from the moor." Holmes believes Baskerville is being followed; no one—not even Baskerville—knew he was going to be at that hotel until he arrived in London. Baskerville is also flummoxed by the theft of a brand new boot that he had set out to be polished. After Mortimer and Baskerville leave, Holmes and Watson follow them and discover Baskerville is being tailed by man disguised by a fake beard. Holmes hires a messenger boy, Cartwright, to scour through the garbage near the Northumberland Hotel in search of the cut-up newspaper.

Chapter 5: Three Broken Threads

Holmes and Watson meet Mortimer and Baskerville for lunch at the Northumberland Hotel. Baskerville is furious—another one of his boots has been stolen. Baskerville states that he intends to travel to Baskerville Hall that week; the curse does not faze him. Holmes informs Baskerville that he is being followed and asks if there are other possible heirs to Charles's considerable fortune. Charles's younger brother is presumed to have died childless in South America. Thinking that Mr. John Barrymore, Charles's loyal butler, may be attempting to scare Henry Baskerville from assuming his inheritance in an effort to obtain the manor for himself, Holmes sends Barrymore a telegram that must be hand delivered to the butler. If it does not reach him, they have uncovered the bearded man tracking Mortimer and Baskerville in London. Holmes announces he is working on a case and will not be able to accompany Baskerville to Dartmoor. He sends Watson instead with instructions to submit detailed reports of all goings-on.

Chapter 6: Baskerville Hall
Holmes bids Watson adieu and tells him the culprit behind Charles's death will be found among his acquaintances in Dartmoor. Holmes limits the pool of suspects to the Barrymores, the stable groom, the neighboring farmers, Dr. Mortimer and his wife, the naturalist Mr. Stapleton, his sister Beryl Stapleton, and Mr. Frankland. Watson, Mortimer, and Baskerville arrive in Dartmoor to find armed soldiers searching for an escaped murderer, Selden. When Baskerville arrives at his estate, Barrymore introduces himself and announces that shortly he and his wife will seek employment elsewhere or go into business for themselves with the money Charles has bequeathed to him.

Chapter 7: The Stapletons of Merripit House
The next morning Watson and Baskerville discuss having heard a woman's sobs during the night. They quickly discover it was Mrs. Barrymore, whose red, swollen eyes are apparent as she serves them breakfast. Afterward, Watson visits the postmaster and discovers the telegram Holmes sent was delivered to Mrs. Barrymore—not Mr. Barrymore as was instructed. On his way back to Baskerville Hall, Watson is greeted by name by Mr. Jack Stapleton, a neighbor and naturalist who is out scouting butterflies. Stapleton grills Watson about whether or not the new baronet is superstitious or believes in the legend of the hound. Stapleton asks Watson point blank if Sherlock Holmes will be visiting to investigate the legend; Watson is taken aback by his directness. Stapleton seems relieved to hear that Holmes will remain in London, and he invites Watson to Merripit House to meet his sister. Watson obliges. Along the way Stapleton delights in telling Watson about Dartmoor's dangerous moors, its Neolithic stone ruins, and the nearby Grimpen Mire, a vast bog known to swallow large animals whole. Just then, an ominous howl from a distant, unseen creature rolls across the landscape. Stapleton explains the townspeople believe it is the hound of the Baskervilles, but that he, a man of reason, believes it is settling mud or a rare bird. Watson finds Stapleton's explanations insufficient.

Stapleton rushes off after a butterfly and Miss Beryl Stapleton appears, a dark beauty wholly unlike her brother. She issues Watson a dire order: "Go back! ... Go straight back to London, instantly." When Stapleton reappears, he introduces Watson to his sister and she apologies profusely, explaining that she thought Watson was Henry Baskerville.

Chapter 8: First Report of Dr. Watson
The chapter takes the form of Watson's letter to Holmes from "this most God-forsaken corner of the world." He tells Holmes that Henry has become enamored of the exotic Miss Stapleton, who seems equally interested in him. Her brother, however, seems upset by their attraction and tries to keep them apart. Watson writes of Mr. Frankland of Lafter Hall, a litigious landlord whose spiteful lawsuits prove entertaining. Frankland is an amateur astronomer and has lately used his telescope to scan the moor for evidence of the escaped convict. Then Watson explains the peculiar behavior of the Barrymores. In the middle of the night, Watson witnessed Barrymore sneak into an unused room and send candle signals through a window to someone on the moor.

Chapter 9: Second Report of Dr. Watson
Watson writes of his theory that Barrymore was sending signals to a lover, which would account for why Mrs. Barrymore has been so upset lately. Watson and Baskerville agree to spy on him the following evening to verify their hunch. Also, Henry is planning to expand the manor and is thinking of asking Miss Stapleton to marry him. Watson had promised Holmes he would guard Henry steadfastly, but Henry has begun strolling the moor alone, ostensibly to rendezvous with Miss Stapleton. Watson follows Baskerville during one such occasion and discovers the couple is also being tracked by Stapleton, who rudely interrupts the couple's dalliance. Watson reveals himself to Henry, and Henry states that Stapleton is out of his mind to prohibit his marriage to Miss Stapleton.

Later that day Stapleton appears at Baskerville Hall to apologize for his outburst, explaining that if his sister were to marry, he would be unbearably lonely. Then Watson relates what happened the night he and Henry confronted Barrymore about his midnight candle signals: Barrymore refused to come clean in the matter, and Henry fired him. But then Mrs. Barrymore appeared, horrified at the trouble she had caused and admitting that her brother is Selden the murderer, and he is hiding out on the moor. Barrymore's signals alert Selden to the food they have left for him. Henry, convinced the Barrymores were not plotting against him, for-gave the couple and reinstated their employment. Nevertheless, Henry and Watson, alarmed that a murderer was in their midst, armed themselves and took off across the moor to capture the criminal. They were stopped cold by the bloodcurdling howl of a beast coming from the Grimpen Mire. Eventually they found Selden, a savage hulk of a man, but he escaped. As they made their way back to Baskerville Hall, they spotted a tall, lone figure upon the tor; Watson was inclined to believe he had seen the ghost of Hugo Baskerville. Watson con-cludes his letter asking Holmes to join him and stating that "the moor with its mysteries and its strange inhabitants remains as inscrutable as ever."

Chapter 10: Extract from the Diary of Dr. Watson

The chapter takes the form of Watson's diaries and are augmented by his recollections. He con-siders rational explanations for the hound he has heard twice on the moors. He is not as gullible as the "poor peasants" who believe in a superna-tural, fire-breathing fiend-dog. But he wonders, where is the dog during the day and what does it eat? As for the stranger he saw on the tor, he believes it is no one he has met before. Henry and Barrymore argue over whether or not Selden should be turned over to the authorities. They agree to let Selden remain until he can escape on a ship to South America. In gratitude, Barrymore reveals what he knows about the night Charles Baskerville died. Having recov-ered a partially burned letter from Sir Charles's study, Barrymore learned that Sir Charles was to meet a woman with the initials L. L. by the gate at 10 o'clock that night.

Watson writes Holmes immediately about this development, and wishes once again the great detective were at Baskerville Hall to make sense of the matter. He also wonders why Holmes's correspondence has been so vague and sporadic. Later, Watson braves the rain and searches the tor for signs of the man he saw the previous night. He finds nothing, but Dr. Mortimer happens by and offers him a ride back to Baskerville Hall. Watson asks him if he knows an L. L., and Mortimer mentions Laura Lyons, who happens to be Mr. Frankland's daughter, whom he has disowned because he disapproved of her marriage. That eve-ning Barrymore tells Watson that Selden has seen a second man on the moor, camping out in the Neolithic ruins and having food brought to him by a boy from Coombe Tracey.

Chapter 11: The Man on the Tor

Watson visits Laura Lyons the next morning. The woman is wary of Watson's motives and his supposed connection to her father. She denounces her father and states that her only friend was Charles Baskerville. She is incensed with Watson's questions regarding her relation-ship with Charles; he merely gave her financial assistance to spare her from becoming destitute. She finally admits to having written Charles with a request to meet him in the Yew Alley the night he died. All she wanted was his assis-tance in paying off her estranged husband so she could get a divorce. Time was of the essence; Baskerville was leaving for London the next morning. However, she states that she never showed up at the appointed time. Watson can-not get her to explain why.

On his way to investigate the man on the tor, Watson is intercepted by Mr. Frankland, who invites him to Lafter Hall for a drink. Frankland then tells Watson that through his telescope he has spied a boy taking food to the convict on the moor. Watson realizes it is not the convict the boy is helping, but his mysterious intruder. Watson leaves Lafter Hall and proceeds to Black Tor, which he has just viewed through the tele-scope. He locates the ancient stone hut that is sheltering the stranger; he also finds a sheet of paper on which is written "Dr. Watson has gone to Coombe Tracey." Watson realizes that he—not Henry—is being followed. He hears footsteps behind him. The man speaks: "It is a lovely eve-ning, my dear Watson." It turns out that the man on the tor is Sherlock Holmes.

Chapter 12: Death on the Moor

Holmes has nearly all the information he needs to solve the case. Yet Watson complains that Holmes has simultaneously used him and not trusted him. Holmes assures Watson that his detective work has not been in vain. Indeed, Holmes has already divined that Laura Lyons holds the key to solving the puzzle and that Miss Stapleton is really Mr. Stapleton's wife, not his sister. Thus, it was she who warned Henry in London to stay away from the moor. Furthermore, Stapleton led Laura Lyons to believe he was a bachelor and would marry her once she obtained a divorce.

Holmes tells Watson to return to Baskerville Hall and guard Henry. Just then the two men are interrupted by a piercing wail that shatters the twilight stillness. Fearing the hound, they sprint across the moor and discover a body sprawled out on the ground, the man's head bashed in from a fall off a cliff. It appears to be Henry Baskerville. They begin dragging the body back to the manor when they discover it is not Baskerville—it is Selden the convict, dressed in Baskerville's old clothes, which the Barrymores gave him. Stapleton appears, and his disappointment is palpable when he learns the man is Selden, not Baskerville. He asks if the two had heard the spectral hound that so haunts the locals' imaginations. Then Stapleton calls Holmes by name, even though the night is dark and he has never before met the detective. After they part, Watson wants to turn Stapleton into the police. Holmes refuses, saying they have not yet sufficiently established their case.

Chapter 13: Fixing the Nets

Back at Baskerville Hall, Sir Henry welcomes Holmes and Watson breaks the news about Selden's death to the Barrymores. Holmes is entranced by a portrait of Hugo Baskerville and later tells Watson that the portrait bears an uncanny resemblance to Mr. Stapleton. It is the last piece of evidence Holmes needs to put the pieces together: Stapleton is Charles Baskerville's previously unknown nephew, and he has come to England from South America to get rid of Charles and Henry and to claim his inheritance. Holmes laughs as he realizes "the nets are all in place, and the drag is about to begin."

The next morning Holmes tells Henry that he and Watson must return to London and that Henry must drive to Merripit House, have dinner with Stapleton, and then walk home alone across the moor. Being a man of courage, he agrees. Meanwhile, Holmes calls for Lestrade, a Scotland Yard detective, to meet him in Coombe Tracey with an unsigned warrant.

Chapter 14: The Hound of the Baskervilles

That evening Holmes, Watson, and Lestrade sneak over to the grounds of Merripit House. They watch Henry and Stapleton through a window. At one point, Stapleton leaves the room, and soon the three men hear footsteps on gravel. Stapleton, unaware he is being watched, unlocks an outbuilding and enters it. "A curious scuffling noise from within" ensues, and several minutes later Stapleton reemerges and returns to the house. Finally, Henry appears and nervously makes his way to the moor for the long walk

home. Suddenly, "an enormous coal-black hound" emerges galloping from the fog. "Fire burst from its open mouth, its eyes glowed with a smouldering glare, its muzzle and hackles and dewlap were outlined in flickering flame." Holmes and Watson fire their guns simultaneously. The beast is struck, howls, yet pounces on Henry. Holmes fires five shots at it. The dog dies and Henry is spared. They gather around the dead animal. Its glowing eyes and fiery muzzle are due to a prepared concoction of phosphorus.

Holmes orders Henry to stay put and the three men run to Merripit House in pursuit of Stapleton, where they discover Mrs. Stapleton bound and gagged. They untie her, and she shows them the bruises that prove Stapleton abused her. She says he may have escaped to an abandoned mine on an island in Grimpen Mire. The fog is too dense for them to chase after him and they must wait until morning. When at last they search the bog, they discover Henry's lost boot, but uncover no trace of Stapleton. "Somewhere in the heart of the great Grimpen Mire, down in the foul slime of the huge morass which had sucked him in, this cold and cruel-hearted man is for ever buried."

Chapter 15: A Retrospection

As an epilogue, Watson provides Holmes's summary of the case. In conversations with Mrs. Stapleton, Holmes learned that Stapleton was indeed the son of Rodger Baskerville and the nephew of Charles Baskerville. Rodger had fled England, emigrated to South America, married, and sired a son, also named Rodger. Rodger was as nefarious as his father; he married a Costa Rican beauty, Beryl Garcia, and absconded to England with stolen money and changed his name to Vandeleur. For a while he ran a school in Yorkshire, but when he had courted enough trouble he changed his name to Stapleton and moved to Devonshire. He disguised his wife as his sister in order to use her as a decoy in an elaborate scheme to inherit Baskerville Hall. When he learned of Charles Baskerville's weak heart and his fear of the Baskerville curse, he procured a big dog, hid it on Grimpen Mire, and waited for the proper time to carry out his plan. When Stapleton learned that Henry Baskerville was the next heir to the manor, he traveled to London—taking his wife with him because he no longer trusted her—possibly for the purpose of disposing of Henry before he reached Baskerville Hall. Stapleton was the bearded spy; Mrs. Stapleton was the author of the note. Holmes admits the tip-off was the note's jasmine scent, which would only be worn by an exotic woman of good standing. Thus, he suspected the Stapletons before he even reached Devonshire. However, because Stapleton had already seen Holmes with Mortimer in London, the detective knew he could not be seen in Devonshire—Stapleton was already on to him. So Holmes sends Watson instead. As for how Stapleton would claim his inheritance after Henry's death, Holmes offers several suggestions but concludes that "what a man may do in the future is a hard question to answer."

CHARACTERS

Mrs. Eliza Barrymore

Mrs. Barrymore is the housekeeper of Baskerville Hall, the wife of Mr. Barrymore, and the older sister of Selden, the escaped murderer. She is secretly aiding her brother with the help of her husband, but comes clean when Henry Baskerville threatens to fire her husband for his subterfuge. She takes pity on her brother and his plight. Her nocturnal sobs are Watson's first indication that something is amiss at Baskerville Hall.

Mr. John Barrymore

The butler of Baskerville Hall, Mr. Barrymore is faithful to the recently deceased Sir Charles Baskerville and tells Henry Baskerville that he and his wife intend to leave their positions as soon as replacements are found. Barrymore's midnight activities look suspicious to Watson and Baskerville, who follow the butler one night and discover him sending signals to the escaped convict on the moor.

Sir Charles Baskerville

The former head of Baskerville Hall, Charles's suspicious death sets the events of the novel in motion. Charles Baskerville was a philanthropist who assisted many residents of the local village with the fortune he acquired from investing in South African gold mines. He had a weak heart and was extremely superstitious, especially when it came to the supposed curse of the Baskervilles. As a rule, he did not wander beyond the gates of the estate at night, which made his presence in the Yew Alley the night of his death suspicious.

Sir Henry Baskerville

Sir Henry Baskerville is a robust, outdoorsy man around 30 years old who has inherited Baskerville Hall upon the death of his Uncle Charles. He has just arrived in England from Canada, where he was a farmer. He quickly becomes embroiled in the mystery when his boot disappears from his hotel the first night he is in London. He is not superstitious and readily assists Watson in the investigation into Charles's death. He becomes nervous only when Holmes instructs him to walk home from Merripit House alone in the dark along the moor. Henry falls in love with Beryl Stapleton, believing her to be Stapleton's sister, and considers proposing to her. He is an honest man of enterprising spirit who appreciates the Dartmoor landscape of his ancestors. He is also a forward-thinking man who hopes to modernize Baskerville Hall with electric lights.

Sir Hugo Baskerville

Hugo Baskerville is the unscrupulous ancestor responsible for the curse of the Baskervilles. As the legend goes, in the 1640s Hugo became infatuated with a young maiden from a nearby farm and kidnapped her. He imprisoned her in a locked room, but she escaped. On horseback, Hugo pursued her and was later found dead—along with the girl—in a shallow ravine, his neck gnawed on by a "great, black beast" with "blazing eyes and dripping jaws."

Cartwright

Cartwright is the messenger boy Holmes pays to track down the newspaper used in the threatening message to Baskerville. Holmes brings Cartwright to Coombe Tracey in Dartmoor as his errand boy and charges him with keeping tabs on Watson. Cartwright disguises himself as an urchin and delivers goods to Holmes when he is camped out in the ruins of the stone huts on the moor.

Mr. Frankland

Mr. Frankland is a litigious landlord who serves as the story's comic relief; he lives in Lafter Hall and is an amateur astronomer who uses his telescope to spy on a man hiding out on the moor. He is a bitter man intent on suing people out of spite. He has disowned his daughter, Laura Lyons, because he disapproved of her marriage to an artist.

Mr. Sherlock Holmes

An eminent detective, Sherlock Holmes of 221B Baker Street in London is sought after for his considerable skills of deduction, logic, and reason. He does not believe for a minute that the Baskerville curse has anything to do with the supernatural. He is an intellectual, a connoisseur of tobacco and violins who enjoys astounding his friend and partner, Dr. John Watson, with his investigative skills. He examines Dr. Mortimer's walking stick—not knowing who had left it behind the previous day—and determines it belongs to a doctor who left London's Charing Cross Hospital to establish a country practice, someone who is "a young fellow under thirty, amiable, unambitious, absent-minded, and the possessor of a favourite dog, which I should describe roughly as being larger than a terrier and smaller than a mastiff." Holmes enjoys the status quo, is cultured nearly to the point of snobbery, and does not like to share his thoughts regarding cases currently in progress. In fact, he tells Watson that he will remain in London while Watson travels to Baskerville Hall to investigate Sir Charles's death; instead Holmes also travels to Dartmoor in order to collect evidence on the case without being seen. He has a healthy ego and can be somewhat prickly; when Dr. Mortimer refers to him as the "second highest expert in Europe" Holmes cuts him off mid-sentence and says "I think, Dr. Mortimer, you would do wisely if without more ado you would kindly tell me plainly what the exact nature of the problem is in which you demand my assistance."

Conan Doyle modeled Sherlock Holmes on a professor from his medical school, Dr. Joseph Bell, and on Edgar Allan Poe's character C. Auguste Dupin. Holmes is courageous, as shown by his bravery in taking down the giant hound, and he persists in solving his cases logically, waiting until all the evidence is collected before making allegations. On the other hand, Holmes likes to work alone; he frequently does not tell Dr. Watson what he is up to, especially when he has Watson believe he is in London working on a case, when in fact Holmes is in Dartmoor collecting evidence. He is able to spend an entire day in solitude, as he does after Dr. Mortimer approaches him with the strange death of Charles Baskerville, doing nothing more than smoking and looking at maps.

Inspector Lestrade

Inspector Lestrade is the Scotland Yard detective whom Holmes summons from London to assist with the plan to capture Stapleton. On the night they plan to capture Stapleton after he releases his hound on Henry Baskerville, Lestrade assures Holmes he is armed, but instead of a gun he carries a flask in his pocket. When the hound appears he hits the ground; he is not as brave as Holmes.

Mrs. Laura Lyons

Laura Lyons is the disowned daughter of Mr. Frankland. Having married an artist against her father's wishes, Laura has been abandoned by her husband and lives alone in the nearby village of Coombe Tracey. She makes a meager living as a typist and seeks a divorce from her husband so she can marry Mr. Stapleton, whom she believes is a bachelor. Stapleton, acting as Charles Baskerville's financial consultant, has Laura arrange a secret meeting with Baskerville the night he dies to ask for the money she needs but makes sure she does not keep the appointment. Thus, she becomes an unwilling pawn in Stapleton's game.

Dr. James Mortimer

A country doctor in Dartmoor, Dr. Mortimer was Charles Baskerville's personal physician and friend. Knowing that Charles was much too fearful about the Baskerville curse to wander alone on the moor at night, Mortimer is instantly suspicious of Charles's death. Convinced foul play is involved, he seeks out Sherlock Holmes when he travels to London to welcome Henry Baskerville, who has just arrived from Canada. Even though Mortimer presents himself as a man of reason and science (like Holmes himself), it is clear that he is rattled by the seemingly supernatural appearance of "the footprints of a gigantic hound" at the scene of Charles Baskerville's death. Mortimer is also an amateur phrenologist who believes he can determine a person's character from the shape of his skull.

Selden

Selden is the infamous Notting Hill murderer who has escaped from prison and is presumed to be hiding out on the moor. Selden is Mrs. Barrymore's younger brother, and she and her husband supply him with food and clothing while he plots his escape to South America. In preparation for the journey, Selden disguises himself in one of Henry Baskerville's old suits, which proves fatal when Stapleton's hound tracks Henry's scent to Selden and causes his death. Holmes believes that Selden's misshapen head reveals his evil nature, and Mrs. Barrymore herself admits that Selden was spoiled as a child and has always wanted more from life than a person from his social class had a right to expect. His sense of entitlement above his social status caused him to turn to a life of crime.

Mrs. Beryl Stapleton

Beryl Stapleton is Stapleton's wife, a natural beauty and a native of Costa Rica, whose exotic jasmine perfume tips off Holmes that she is the author of the note warning Henry Baskerville to stay away from the moor. She is forced to pose as Stapleton's sister as part of his plan to inherit Baskerville Hall. She is physically abused by her husband, who ties her up in Merripit House the night he sets the hound loose on Henry Baskerville. Mrs. Stapleton is sympathetic toward Henry Baskerville; knowing that her husband plans to kill him, she composes a note to scare him away from Dartmoor. When Dr. Watson arrives in Dartmoor, she mistakenly believes he is the new heir to Baskerville Hall and beseeches him to escape before it is too late. She seems genuinely interested in Baskerville when he courts her, only to be cut off from him when her husband becomes jealous. She is a woman trapped, and yet she does what she can to change her situation.

Mr. Jack Stapleton

Jack Stapleton is the alias of Rodger Baskerville, Jr., the son of Charles Baskerville's younger brother Rodger, a ne'er-do-well who fled to South America as a young man and was presumed to have died childless. Rodger married Costa-Rican-born Beryl Garcia, absconded with a large amount of money, immigrated to Yorkshire, assumed the name Vandeleur, and started a private school. When the school went bankrupt, he moved to Dartmoor and began anew with the name Stapleton, posing as a naturalist. Upon learning of the Baskerville curse, he came up with a plan to scare Charles Baskerville to death and somehow assume his inheritance as the last remaining member of the Baskerville family. He uses his knowledge of nature and animals to learn the ins and outs of the moors and the great Grimpen Mire, where he stashes a vicious hound he has trained to kill. Thus, Stapleton is intelligent but cocky, befriending the Baskervilles while plotting to kill them. His intelligence, however, makes him a good match for Holmes, who uses all of his deductive reasoning skills to capture Stapleton in the act of trying to murder Henry Baskerville.

Stapleton is a villain without any redeeming qualities. He kills without remorse, abuses his wife, lies, and assumes fictitious identities to get what he wants. In the end, after his plan to kill Henry Baskerville goes awry, Stapleton disappears into the Grimpen Mire, never to be seen again. He is presumed to have drowned in the bog.

Dr. John H. Watson

Dr. Watson is Sherlock Holmes's informal business partner and the narrator of *The Hound of the Baskervilles*. Though he is ostensibly married and has his own medical practice, Watson eagerly decamps for Dartmoor to collect evidence on Holmes's behalf. Watson represents a typical middle-class Englishman, someone who is intelligent, good-natured, hard-working, loyal, but no match for Holmes' superior intellect. Watson, however, realizes he will never be Holmes's intellectual equal and is content to play second fiddle to the master, exhibiting bravery, stamina, and understanding in the process. For example, when waiting for the hound to appear on the moor as the fog rolls in, Watson is right behind Holmes with his gun drawn and readily fires at the beast in order to save Henry Baskerville.

Watson is eager to please Holmes, constantly amazed at the detective's skills, but irritated when he discovers Holmes has been in Dartmoor all along. He feels that Holmes does not trust him. All the same, the events that mark his stay at Baskerville Hall baffle him. Watson is almost child-like in his allegiance to Holmes. Though annoyed that Holmes has not taken him into his confidence regarding his plan to travel to Dartmoor, when Holmes praises Watson's investigative efforts: "I must compliment you exceedingly upon the zeal and the intelligence which you have shown over an extraordinarily difficult case," Watson writes that "the warmth of Holmes's praise drove my anger from my mind."

Watson acts as a sort of Greek chorus for the audience, highlighting the astonishment the reader is supposed to feel over Holmes's genius. At the same time, he comes across as slightly naïve and fawning.

THEMES

Science versus Superstition

The main theme of *The Hound of the Baskervilles* is the superiority and triumph of science—represented by Sherlock Holmes—over superstition, which is

TOPICS FOR FURTHER STUDY

- After reading *The Hound of the Baskervilles*, name three instances in which Holmes's deductive reasoning relies on stereotypes. In an essay, note what each instance reveals about Holmes himself.

- Mystery writer Ronald Knox formulated "The 10 Commandments for Detective Novelists," in 1928. Number nine on the list is, "The stupid friend of the detective, the Watson, must not conceal any thoughts which pass through his mind; his intelligence must be slightly, but very slightly, below that of the average reader." Name three instances in *The Hound of the Baskervilles* in which Watson's intelligence could be deemed below that of the average reader. Lead a class discussion to determine whether this helps or hinders the plot.

- Jack Stapleton exploits the legend of a supernatural, fire-breathing beast by using a phosphorus compound to achieve the effect of blazing eyes and jaws. Research phosphorus and its properties. Would it really have been possible for Stapleton to have concocted such a substance? List three dangers that such a substance might have presented, either to Stapleton or the dog, and present your findings to the class.

- The Great Grimpen Mire of the story is a fictional bog modeled on the Fox Tor Mire near the Grimspound ruins in Dartmoor. List three ecological characteristics of an English mire, or bog. Create a visual aid that illustrates and discusses these traits.

---

represented by the Baskerville curse. Sir Charles Baskerville was so consumed by superstition that he is manipulated into an untimely death. Holmes, in contrast, states definitively from the outset that a logical explanation is possible to explain Charles's death and "the footprints of a gigantic hound."

Holmes's sense of logic and reason, while evident in the way he handles cases, is also repeatedly pointed out by the narrator. In the beginning of chapter 15, Watson writes of Holmes: "he would never permit cases to overlap, and ... his clear and logical mind would not be drawn from its present work to dwell upon memories of the past." Holmes solves much of the case while secluded in his study, poring over detailed maps. He draws upon his vast knowledge of perfume to uncover Beryl Stapleton's complicity in the case, and he uses his knowledge of newspaper fonts to determine the origins of the note that threatens Henry in London.

Trust and Betrayal

Though Stapleton, as the villain, dishes out a fair amount of betrayal—against his wife, Charles Baskerville, Laura Lyons, and nearly everyone else he comes into contact with—the theme of trust and betrayal is most evident in the relationship between Dr. Watson and Sherlock Holmes. Holmes, claiming business in London prevents him from traveling to Dartmoor, instructs Watson to travel to Baskerville Hall to gather information on the case and has him send progress reports back to 221B Baker Street. He does not tell Watson he will also be in Dartmoor, working undercover while camping out in the Neolithic ruins on the moor. However, this apparent lack of trust is necessary in order for the mysterious "man on the tor" portion of the story to work. If Watson knew Holmes was in Dartmoor, that Gothic element of the story would not work, and the cliffhanger at the end of chapter 11 would not be possible, thus robbing the story of much of its atmosphere.

When Watson realizes Holmes's failure to disclose his whereabouts, he feels slightly betrayed: "'Then you use me, and yet do not trust me!' I cried with some bitterness. 'I think that I have deserved better at your hands, Holmes,'" Watson writes. Even after Holmes explains his reasoning for the deception at length, Watson is perturbed but able to convince himself, once again, that Holmes is the better man:

> I was still rather raw over the deception which had been practised upon me, but the warmth of Holmes's praise drove my anger from my mind. I felt also in my heart that he was right in what he said, and that it was really best for our purpose that I should not have known that he was upon the moor.

Appearance versus Reality

The spectral hound, with jaws and eyes ablaze, at first appears otherworldly. But as a man of reason, Holmes knows that appearances can be deceiving. Even Dr. Mortimer is inclined to believe in the Baskerville curse; having a man of science taken in by superstition makes that element of the story particularly convincing.

The story's other elements of deception heighten its Gothic tone: Mr. Stapleton appears to be a cheerful naturalist who lives with his sister; Selden falls to his death while appearing to be Henry Baskerville; the Barrymores' strange behavior appears to link them to Charles's death; Beryl Stapleton appears to be a fetching maiden but is really an abused wife. In the end, Holmes uses logic to decipher reality hiding behind false appearances, thus revealing how ordinary events masqueraded as supernatural occurrences.

Social Class

Sherlock Holmes is firmly entrenched in Victorian society and is comfortable with the status quo. He respects those of the professional class, such as medical doctors like Watson and Mortimer, and is inclined to hold their opinions in high esteem. As for members of the landed gentry, such as the Baskervilles, he is likewise inclined to give them the benefit of the doubt and take their concerns seriously. Conversely, servants such as the Barrymores receive cordial but distant regard from Holmes, as do cab drivers, street urchins, and even Lestrade—a Scotland Yard detective. Both Beryl Stapleton and Laura Lyons are endangered by Stapleton's scheme, but Holmes does not go out of his way to express his sympathy or to aid them. Selden, as a member of the lower class—a murderer and a convict to boot—is destined to pay for his sins. By assuming Henry Baskerville's clothing in an attempt to pass himself off as a member of a higher class, he pays the ultimate price—his life.

Holmes is satisfied when the case is solved and social order is restored to its previous state; he and Watson can return to London and Henry Baskerville can live in peace. Those of the lower classes—Beryl Stapleton, Laura Lyons, and the Barrymores—are regarded as weak. Beryl Stapleton is imprisoned by her husband; Mrs. Barrymore aids a criminal and cries at night; Laura Lyons pays for marrying beneath her by being deserted and forced to work for a living. After Holmes solves the case and order is restored to Baskerville Hall, the fate of these characters is of no interest to him.

STYLE

Gothicism

The Gothic novel, which relies heavily on elements of horror and romance, originated in 1764 with Horace Walpole's *The Castle of Otranto*, flourished in 1818 with the publication of Mary Shelley's *Frankenstein*, and culminated in the 1847 publication of both Emily Brontë's *Wuthering Heights* and Charlotte Brontë's *Jane Eyre*. In the late Victorian era, Gothic literature was popularized by lurid "penny dreadful" stories, published serially in cheap booklets and magazines. But, in the emerging literature of the United States, Gothicism was gaining a new foothold. Edgar Allan Poe, whom Conan Doyle greatly admired, filled his writings, such as the 1839 story "The Fall of the House of Usher" with Gothic overtones, unexplained phenomena, strange noises, and characters descending into madness.

The Hound of the Baskervilles exhibits many Gothic elements, including a decrepit ancestral home, a local legend, supernatural elements, and a sense of doom and danger evoked through detailed descriptions of time and place, and the disintegration of both physical surroundings and the characters' mental states. Gothicism is perhaps most notably apparent in the description of the desolate Dartmoor landscape, with its rocky tors, thick fog, prehistoric stone ruins, the mysterious "man on the tor," and the dangerous Grimpen Mire—a bog so treacherous that it traps and drowns a horse. Baskerville Hall itself is also described in Gothic tones:

> The whole front was draped in ivy, with a patch clipped bare here and there where a window or a coat-of-arms broke through the dark veil. From this central block rose the twin towers, ancient, crenellated, and pierced with many loopholes. To right and left of the turrets were more modern wings of black granite. A dull light shone through heavy mullioned windows, and from the high chimneys which rose from the steep, high-angled roof there sprang a single black column of smoke.

Despite these trappings, the novel remains firmly in the world of logic and reason, as good detective stories must. Every seemingly inexplicable happening ultimately has a logical explanation. Conan Doyle, then, uses Gothicism purely as a way to enhance the mood of his story and to demonstrate that Holmes's talent for reasoning is superior to ignorant superstition.

Cliffhanger

Conan Doyle wrote his Holmes stories for the masses, and *The Hound of the Baskervilles* was no exception. Because the novel was published serially in the *Strand*, it was important to keep readers excited enough to buy the next issue. Hence, the cliffhanger. Conan Doyle ended each chapter with an exciting revelation that made readers want to know what happens next. The most famous of these cliffhangers comes at the end of chapter two, after Dr. Mortimer has recounted the legend of the Baskerville curse for Holmes and Watson. When Holmes asks Dr. Mortimer about the footprints Mortimer found at the scene of Charles Baskerville's death, he replies: "Mr. Holmes, they were the footprints of a gigantic hound!" Chapter eleven, "The Man on the Tor," also includes another famous cliffhanger. As Watson is investigating the hiding place of the mysterious stranger on the moor, the stranger returns: "'It is a lovely evening, my dear Watson,' said a well-known voice." The unexpected appearance of Sherlock Holmes startles the reader and raises many questions that will be answered only in the next installment—readers must buy the next issue.

Cliffhangers are common practice in contemporary literature; authors must use every trick they can to keep readers turning the page or risk losing them to other forms of entertainment. However, in the Victorian era, when the emerging leisure class had considerable time on its hands and literacy rates were steadily increasing, novels were a primary source of entertainment and tended to be long, rambling works filled with many characters, subplots, and lengthy descriptive passages. Contrary to that, nearly all the Holmes stories are just that—stories. Conan Doyle wrote only four Holmes novels, and it is no surprise that he used the traits common to short stories—brevity, clarity, and a fast pace—in those four books. A cliffhanger serves to set up the next installment and to maintain the story's forward momentum.

Folklore

The Black Dog is a mainstay of British folklore, a beast who signifies evil and imminent death. The Black Dog is invariably nocturnal and sometimes associated with storms or the sea; often it is said to have red eyes. Different regions have developed different myths, many of which probably arose from ancient Celtic or Germanic traditions. In Yorkshire the black dog is named *Barghest*, in Lancashire *Gytrash*, and in Wales *Gwyllgi*. The central mystery of *The Hound of the Baskervilles* concerns a real-life legend of a devil hound that was said to haunt the foggy moors in Devonshire. The legend was recounted to Conan Doyle by Fletcher Robinson, a friend from his sea-faring days who was a native of the area. Conan Doyle credited Robinson with the inspiration for the story in the foreword to the first printing of the novel. A supernatural black beast with blazing eyes was believed to be an omen of misfortune for anyone unlucky enough to encounter the creature. Some believe that small horses native to Devonshire, heath ponies, when viewed through the fog that often blankets the region, appear to be large dogs—a possible logical explanation for the supernatural legend.

Conan Doyle borrowed the Baskerville name from Robinson's groom, but the house, the curse, and Hugo himself are strictly figments of the author's imagination. Many folktales, however, include elements of ruthless ancestors, pacts with the devil, and curses that plague subsequent generations. By building his story on such time-honored traditions, and in including the stone ruins of prehistoric peoples in a windswept region far removed from civilized London, Conan Doyle signaled to readers that the story would be a Gothic ghost story, steeped in the unpredictable elements of nature (fog and the Grimpen Mire) that harkens back to the oral tradition.

Neat Resolution

Many mysteries are not solved until the final chapter, sustaining suspense and interest throughout the entire story. *The Hound of the Baskervilles* is notable for citing the guilty party in chapter twelve, three chapters before the end of the book—and even by the end of chapter four Holmes is fairly certain of the culprit. The last two chapters are more of a thriller, focusing on the capture of Stapleton and his dog.

The final chapter consists entirely of resolution, providing a myriad of background details that flesh out the story and provide motive for Stapleton's elaborate scheme. This long resolution provides satisfaction to the reader in neatly tying up all loose ends (except for the question of how Stapleton planned to claim Baskerville Hall after Henry's death). The resolution takes place in the cozy environs of 221B Baker Street, back in rational, modern London where everything has a logical explanation; Gothicism has been vanquished and fanciful legends left behind in rural England. Conan Doyle has shown that superstition is no match for civilization.

Mystery Conventions and the "Locked Room" Mystery

The Hound of the Baskervilles belongs to the Golden Age of detective fiction, a period that also includes works by Agatha Christie, Ellery Queen, and P. D. James. They are among the most well-known writers of the "locked room" genre—traditional mysteries that usually involve a small pool of suspects thrown together in a particular setting (in this case the area around Baskerville Hall). Suspects emerge, motives are uncovered, and the brilliant detective is the only one who can make sense of it all. Crime writer Fr. Ronald Knox, a writer and charter member of the Detectives Club, a group of writers who promoted the emerging genre, developed the "The 10 Commandments for Detective Novelists" in 1928, first published in his book *Essays in Satire*. Though the list postdates most of Conan Doyle's Holmes stories, it is evident that Knox and the other members of the club were inspired by many conventions that Conan Doyle established over the course of his career. Rule number one reads "The criminal must be someone mentioned in the early part of the story, but must not be anyone whose thoughts the reader has been allowed to follow." Though Conan Doyle violated this rule in his first Holmes novel, *A Study in Scarlet*, while the detective genre was still evolving, he later adhered to it faithfully. Rule number two reads "All supernatural or preternatural agencies are ruled out as a matter of course" and seems almost to have been inspired by *The Hound of the Baskervilles*.

HISTORICAL CONTEXT

The Victorian Era and the Rise of the Popular Novel

The Victorian era in England commonly refers to the reign of Queen Victoria, which lasted from 1837 until 1901. The period coincided with the Industrial Revolution and the emergence of a middle class in England that enjoyed more leisure time and wealth than at any previous time in history. During this era, social stratification was strictly enforced. Wealthy people—the landed gentry especially—did not socialize with those who labored for a living. The underclass, mainly those

who toiled in factories or who worked as servants, remained marginalized by the social order and rarely escaped from their station in life. Sherlock Holmes adhered to these social conventions. Though he sometimes relies on the Baker Street Irregulars, a group of urchins, to do favors for him (and in *The Hound of the Baskervilles* he pays Cartwright to be his gopher), Holmes keeps his social circle tight, preferring instead the company of Dr. Watson and Dr. Mortimer, middle-class men such as himself, and Henry Baskerville, whose title of baronet automatically confers status upon him. The Barrymores, Selden, and Laura Lyons, however, as members of a lower class are beneath Holmes's concern apart from being suspects in his case. Holmes is nothing if not a purveyor of the status quo.

In the Victorian era, the growing middle class spawned a new interest in mandatory education for their children. In 1870, the Education Act required all children between the ages of five and thirteen to attend school. This resulted in a rising literacy rate and a better educated population overall. As a result, novels and magazines became a popular form of entertainment for a wide cross-section of people. Charles Dickens and many poets were popular, as were magazines featuring "light" fiction. Light fiction was designed merely for entertainment, not moral teaching, and Conan Doyle's detective stories, with their accessible language, lack of dogma, and thrilling plots, were immensely popular with the literate middle class, who eagerly purchased successive editions of the *Strand* and other magazines that featured his work.

New Scotland Yard and the Rise of the Detective

By 1890, Scotland Yard was well established as the headquarters of the metropolitan London police, and it had just moved to larger quarters, a brand-new Victorian-style building just down the street from the Houses of Parliament. The organization employed many inspectors, or detectives, and prided itself on adopting the state-of-the-art Bertillon procedure used to identify criminals, which was based on anthropometry, a series of bodily measurements designed to eliminate unreliable eyewitness reports. Despite this, Scotland Yard detectives had not been able to solve the Whitechapel murders, attributed to Jack the Ripper, that ceased in 1889. As an independent investigator, Sherlock Holmes has an ambivalent relationship with Scotland Yard

COMPARE & CONTRAST

- **Late 1800s:** The premiere U.S. research and publishing firm for the study and practice of phrenology (the interpretation of character through studying the shape of the skull), Fowler & Wells in New York City, closes after more than fifty years in business. The firm's founders, brothers Orson and Lorenzo Fowler and their partner Samuel Wells, promoted phrenology as a way to gain self-knowledge.

  Early 1900s: London psychiatrist Bernard Hollander publishes *Scientific Phrenology*, an influential book that established the methodology for measuring the skull.

  Today: Though phrenology has been long discredited, it is still considered a significant theoretical development because it initiated the belief that the brain contains certain areas that control various human functions and emotions. Contemporary disciplines such as cytoarchitecture, which examines the arrangement of cell bodies in the cerebral cortex, can trace their origins to phrenology.

- **Late 1800s:** French criminologist Alphonse Bertillon's system of anthropometry, a scientific method of identifying criminals based on measurements of the head and body along with identifying tattoos and scars, is used in France and England to help identify criminal suspects.

  Early 1900s: The United Kingdom Fingerprint System, known as the Henry Classification System, is adopted by Scotland Yard as a forensic tool for investigating crimes.

  Today: Fingerprints are still used to gather evidence at a crime scene, but DNA profiling, also known as genetic fingerprinting, is used increasingly to identify suspects in criminal cases.

- **Late 1800s:** Queen Victoria reigns in Great Britain and the British Empire extends across five continents, including Canada, where Henry Baskerville has been a farmer, and portions of Central America and the Caribbean, where Rodger Baskerville lived.

  Early 1900s: Queen Victoria—England's longest reigning monarch—dies, and her son becomes King Edward VII, ushering in the Edwardian era. The British Empire is still growing and peaks in land mass around 1918.

  Today: Queen Elizabeth II, has reigned for fifty-five years, second only to Queen Victoria and George III. The British Empire is much smaller than in Queen Victoria's time, consisting of sixteen countries and a total of 128 million people.

and believes his talents are superior to their sometimes bumbling behavior. He gives a backhanded compliment to Inspector Lestrade when he says to Watson, "he is the best of the professionals, I think."

In 1901, the year *The Hound of the Baskervilles* was serialized in the *Strand*, Scotland Yard adopted the United Kingdom Fingerprint System, known as the Henry Classification System, as a forensic tool for investigating crimes. But Scotland Yard detectives were not required to carry a revolver until 1898, which may account for Holmes inquiring whether or not Lestrade has a gun as they prepare

to face the hound. Wanting to appear professional, Lestrade assures Holmes he does but it is almost certainly a flask of liquor he is hiding, not a weapon.

The British Empire

The Hound of the Baskervilles takes place during the height of the British Empire's power, which spanned so many countries that, literally, the sun never set on it. Among the British upper class, this position of political superiority fostered great pride and often arrogance. Criminals, such as Selden, or wayward members of the ruling class, such as Rodger Baskerville, freely

Scene from the 1939 film version of Sherlock Holmes: The Hound of the Baskervilles, *starring Basil Rathbone as Sherlock Holmes and Nigel Bruce as Dr. Watson* (20th Century Fox | The Kobal Collection | The Picture Desk Inc.)

traveled to foreign lands such as Canada, Australia, or South Africa in order to escape persecution at home or seek their fortune by plundering resources or establishing exploitive business ventures. Henry Baskerville was a resident of Canada, which had been part of the British Commonwealth since 1867. This would have made his immigration back to England to claim his inheritance from the motherland a natural, expected occurrence.

In their conquest for Africa, British troops won the Second Boer War, during which Conan Doyle, who was too old to serve in the military, volunteered as a field hospital doctor in South Africa. In the novel, Charles Baskerville gained his fortune in the gold mines of South Africa, a fortune that he used benevolently upon returning to Dartmoor. He supported the less fortunate residents of Coombe Tracey, such as Laura Lyons, who, abandoned by her husband and forced to work for a meager living, would have been seen as a charity case.

Stapleton, the son of Charles Baskerville's brother, was born and raised in Central America, where he met and married the fiery Latin beauty Beryl Garcia. Though the British controlled several Caribbean islands, Beryl Stapleton's native Costa Rica was a Spanish colony, which may account for her reputation as an exotic (i.e., not British) beauty, prone to unpredictable behavior as opposed to characteristic British reserve. Selden, the murderer who dresses in Henry Baskerville's clothes in preparation for his escape to South America, would most likely have escaped British law and culture altogether if he had been successful. Much of South America was under Spanish, Portuguese, and French influence; only Guyana was ruled by England. It would have been easy for Selden to disappear into the vast continent.

CRITICAL OVERVIEW

The Hound of the Baskervilles remains as popular in the twenty-first century as it was when it was first published. Holmes himself has proven to be one of the most enduring characters in modern literature, more famous even than his creator. Indeed, Holmes's cap, houndstooth coat, Calabash pipe, and magnifying glass have entered the popular consciousness as representative of the clothing for a stereotypical English detective. Watson's discovery of the mysterious "man on the tor" is one of the genre's most famous moments, as is Dr. Mortimer's exclamation of having found "the footprints of a gigantic hound!"

Admirers have praised the book's Gothic setting, the supernatural elements that turn out to have a logical explanation, and Conan Doyle's deft use of Watson's narration to create suspense and provide the public with a Holmes story even after the great detective's supposed death at Reichenbach Falls. Indeed, the only serious criticism of the book comes from those who note chronological inconsistencies within the story's timeline. It is thought to take place around 1889, but that date conflicts with the timeline of previous Holmes cases, none of which are alluded to in the text. Conan Doyle affixed no date in the story, so its place in time must be deduced from hints given within the text. Critics give estimates as early as 1886 and as late as 1900, according to Leslie S. Klinger's chronology chart in *The New Annotated Sherlock Holmes*.

Furthermore, many Sherlockians, those Holmes fans who create mock criticism based on the fallacy that Holmes and Watson were real people, have long argued over the supposed whereabouts of Baskerville Hall and the identity of its diabolical ancestors. Writer James Branch Cabell claimed that his ancestor Richard Cabell, a British Lord from Buckfastleigh, Devon, was the model for Hugo Baskerville, reports Klinger in *The New Annotated Sherlock Holmes*. Klinger also observes that the Conan Doyle expert William S. Baring-Gould argues that Lew Hall at Lew Trenchard in Devon was the model for Baskerville Hall because its features match those described in the novel. Others dispute this theory on the basis that Lew Hall was too far from Grimspound and Fox Tor Mire, which are thought to be the inspiration for Grimpen Mire, comments Howard Brody in the *Baker Street Journal*. According to Brody, these critics believe the real Baskerville Hall was Hayford Hall, due to its proximity to Fox Tor Mires and to the fact that the manor boasts its own hound legend. Another inconsistency concerns the *Cyclopides* butterfly that Stapleton chases; it would not have been found in the Dartmoor region of Britain, claims Klinger.

As for the story itself, *The Hound of the Baskervilles* is a favorite with critics. Critic Donald J. Watt, as quoted by Benjamin F. Fisher in *English Literature in Transition 1880–1920*, summarizes the story as "a ripping good yarn, which is related by means of some astutely manipulated conventional literary devices ... [including] structure, mood, and metaphor." Author and critic Francis O'Gorman believes that the novel represents Conan Doyle's ambivalence about the supernatural world, having been written while the author was involved in spiritualism. "At the height of his career, neither intolerant nor wholly a believer," says O'Gorman in the *Yorkshire Post*, "Conan Doyle was sufficiently immersed in a search for reliable facts about 'the other side' and some now argue *The Hound of the Baskervilles*, written from the midst of this process, is an emblem of these beliefs."

CRITICISM

Kathleen Wilson

Wilson is a freelance writer and editor. In the following essay, she comments on the discrepancy between the male characters in The Hound of the Baskervilles, *who represent rationality and self-involvement, and the female characters, whose moral dilemmas give their conflicts more nuance but who are nevertheless pushed to the margins of the story.*

Among critics and fans alike, *The Hound of the Baskervilles* is praised for its Gothic, foreboding setting in which superstition and legend ultimately give way to logic and reason. In the figures of Sherlock Holmes, Dr. James Watson, Henry Baskerville, and Dr. Mortimer, Sir Arthur Conan Doyle exhibits his superlative grasp of characterization; he places these upstanding Victorian men in the "locked room" of Dartmoor to make sense of Charles Baskerville's death and the legend of the spectral hound. Shunted to the margins of the story are the women: Beryl Stapleton, Laura Lyons, and to a lesser extent Mrs. Barrymore, all of whom suffer at the hands of men and yet remain powerless to help themselves. Holmes seems less interested in their misfortune than he is in demonstrating his own tremendous powers of deductive reasoning. Indeed, he spends more time analyzing Beryl's perfume than he does trying to save her.

It may be asking too much that Beryl Stapleton and Laura Lyons muster the fortitude to escape their predicaments. As Victorian women they are constrained by laws both social and legal. Social constraints mire them in a psychological struggle between what they want (freedom from the men who control them), and their desire to adhere to Victorian norms that discourage such freedom. Along with Mrs. Barrymore, whose familial devotion to her brother—an escaped convict—leads to her nocturnal wailing and the hand-wringing crime of aiding and abetting a murderer, Beryl and Laura are the only characters in the novel who suffer cognitive dissonance due to their moral entrapment.

Conan Doyle was adept at creating fallible characters, even those who served as heroes and protagonists. Sherlock Holmes is one of the most loved characters in all literature, and yet he is not necessarily lovable. He is egotistical and presumptuous in a way that connotes a sense of masculine entitlement. He is confident in his abilities—he balks when Dr. Mortimer refers to him as the second greatest detective—and he sees no need to tell Watson of his plans to travel surreptitiously to Dartmoor. His failure to disclose this crucial information under the guise that he is "protecting" Watson is demeaning, because it presumes that Watson, a medical doctor and a gentleman, needs to be protected.

WHAT DO I READ NEXT?

- "Murders in the Rue Morgue," published by Edgar Allan Poe in 1841, is commonly regarded as the first detective story, even though the work predates the concept of a "detective" as such. The detective figure in the story, C. Auguste Dupin, on whom Conan Doyle modeled Holmes, is an aristocratic and brilliant eccentric who lives in Paris and astounds the unnamed narrator, a close friend, with his powers of deductive reasoning.

- *A Study in Scarlet*, published in *Beeton's Christmas Annual* in 1887, was Conan Doyle's first Sherlock Holmes story—and one of only four Holmes novels—and introduced the characters of Dr. Watson and Scotland Yard inspector Lestrade. Because the book predates established conventions of the detective novel, it violates many of these stylistic rules and relies partly on supernatural events. In the story, Holmes pays homage to Edgar Allan Poe's C. Auguste Dupin. The story concerns two murders in England that are linked to a Mormon settlement in the United States.

- *The Coming of the Fairies*, published in 1922 by Arthur Conan Doyle, reprints the Cottingley fairy photographs that depict miniature winged fairies cavorting with two girls from Yorkshire. Conan Doyle, an ardent spiritualist, outlines evidence for the photos' authenticity with the methodical detail for which he was known. Conan Doyle, however, had been duped; the photos were later proven to be a hoax.

- *The Moor* (1998), by award-winning author Laurie R. King, is a continuation of *The Hound of the Baskervilles*. In this sequel, Mary Russell, Holmes's plucky young wife, a detective herself and narrator of the story, travels with Holmes to Dartmoor in 1924 to investigate yet another murder attributed to the spectral hound.

- *Sayers on Holmes* (2001) is a collection of essays by critic and detective novelist Dorothy L. Sayers. Among other topics, the book includes pieces on the importance of Holmes to the detective genre.

- *The Science of Sherlock Holmes: From Baskerville Hall to the Valley of Fear, the Real Forensics Behind the Great Detective's Greatest Cases* (2007) was written by forensics expert E. J. Wagner. Using Conan Doyle's various stories, Wagner traces the rise in forensic science from the turn of the century onward, delving into cases that may have inspired Conan Doyle and later crimes that may have been inspired by Conan Doyle.

- *Head Masters: Phrenology, Secular Education, and Nineteenth-Century Social Thought* (2005) was written by Stephen Tomlinson, a professor of education studies. The book covers the rise of phrenology, such as is practiced by Dr. Mortimer, and how it sparked a beneficial education reform movement in Europe and North America, but also lent a false scientific credibility to racism and eugenics.

- *The Final Solution: A Story of Detection*, by Michael Chabon, is a novella first published in the *Paris Review* in 2003. Sherlock Holmes, living out his days in Sussex, England, as a beekeeper during World War II, becomes involved in the case of a stolen parrot that belongs to a mute boy.

- *Walk Dartmoor* (2006), by Kate and Alan Hobbs, presents numerous walking tours around the Devonshire region, most taking several hours. The tours take hikers past notable landmarks, from the highest tors to the deepest mires, to various bridges, waterways, ancient ruins, and abandoned quarries. In addition, the book presents many historical details and maps.

" ONE HEART-TO-HEART TALK WITH BERYL STAPLETON AND THE WHOLE CASE WOULD BE SOLVED. WATSON SQUANDERS HIS OPPORTUNITY TO BEST HOLMES, IN PART BECAUSE HE IS UNWILLING TO LISTEN."

Watson himself is a bit too eager to please; Dr. Mortimer is forgetful and not particularly hard-working; and Henry Baskerville is unnecessarily harsh on Beryl Stapleton when her real marital status is revealed.

Interestingly, Holmes's masculinity does not necessarily entail chivalry. He exhibits no particular sympathy toward Beryl Stapleton or Laura Lyons though they too are victims of the nefarious Jack Stapleton, the mastermind who procures a big black dog and co-opts the curse of the Baskervilles to drive Sir Charles to an early grave. Holmes's natural habitat is the male bastion of 221B Baker Street, and his avocational pursuits are solitary: cocaine, tobacco, rare violins. That his detective skills might rescue a woman from a life of misery is beside the point, the point being the ego boost that comes from solving the mystery.

If Holmes's solipsism is his flaw, the women of the story suffer the opposite affliction. Beryl, forced by her husband to pose as his sister and to seduce Henry Baskerville, suffers public humiliation and worse when Henry takes the tantalizing bait. But Beryl does what she can. She puts herself in danger by selflessly constructing a warning letter to Henry—a complete stranger—upon his arrival in London. She then accosts Watson in Dartmoor, thinking him to be Henry, and begs him to leave England at once to spare his life. She apologizes when the mistaken identity is revealed, but as clear as her message is—and the fact that she obviously knows something about what is going on—Watson is more interested in her peculiar behavior than in what she is saying. One heart-to-heart talk with Beryl Stapleton and the whole case would be solved. Watson squanders his opportunity to best Holmes, in part because he is unwilling to listen.

Instead, Watson clings to his role of second banana while Holmes crafts a risky caper to catch Stapleton in the act of setting his hound loose. After they (and Inspector Lestrade) slay the hound and rescue Henry, they proceed to Merripit House in search of Stapleton, only to discover a bound and gagged Beryl. Her rescue is merely a happy accident in their quest to bring down her husband; once her gag is removed, she reveals that Stapleton has probably escaped onto his island in the Grimpen Mire, and they are off and running. Holmes shows more compassion to the terrified Henry Baskerville, whom he reassuringly tells to stay put on the moor until help arrives. Beryl merits no such comfort.

Though Stapleton is never found and is presumed dead, thereby freeing Beryl to marry Henry, the otherwise reasonable bachelor simply cannot forgive her sins. Instead, he teams up with Dr. Mortimer and travels the world. Having been dragged across the Atlantic Ocean from her home in Costa Rica and abused mentally and physically by a sociopath, all while trying to warn those targeted by said sociopath, Beryl's heroism is invalidated by her gender and thus she is of no interest to Holmes, Watson, Mortimer, or Baskerville. Her fate as a widow without the means to support herself is not their problem, even though they have caused it. Henry, especially, has reason to thank her for her valiant effort to spare him and no reason to believe her affection toward him was not genuine. Yet his masculinity necessitates saving face in the matter by shunning her.

Laura Lyons suffers a similar fate. She has been abandoned twice, first by her father—the litigious Mr. Frankland of Lafter Hall—and then by her husband, a ne'er-do-well artist. She has no means to obtain a divorce from her absent spouse and is thus forced into a life of workaday drudgery as a typist, albeit a proper one who is alarmed and cautious when strange men show up at her door. Such a precarious social position makes her prime fodder for Stapleton's evil plan. He prompts her to arrange the ill-fated meeting with Charles Baskerville, ostensibly to seek his financial help in obtaining a divorce (which at the time would have cost more than she would have made in a year), by implying that he will marry her afterward. Desperation renders her blind to his manipulation, and she arranges a late-night rendezvous with Sir Baskerville in the Yew Alley. Stapleton then makes sure she backs out of the meeting so he can send his "spectral" hound in her place. One is almost surprised that Stapleton spares her life; after all, the original Baskerville curse included two bodies—Hugo's and the escaped maiden's—a reprise with Sir Charles and Laura might have proven irresistible.

In the end, both Beryl and Laura gain some measure of freedom, but it is only a collateral effect of Holmes having solved the case. The detective exhibits no outward pleasure in having made the women's lives better. He is mostly concerned with triumphantly revealing that the hound was a mortal canine dowsed in phosphorus. Conan Doyle keeps his male characters firmly in the realm of rationality and objectivity (the exception being Watson's girlish irritation upon discovering Holmes's subterfuge). The author delegates emotions, particularly stormy feelings of hopelessness and doom, to his female characters who, in concordance with Victorian values, are by turns hysterical and skittish. The tempestuous Gothic moors, with their foggy nights, mysterious animal howls, and treacherous terrain, are personified in the book's female characters, who themselves are moody, forbidding, and temperamental. In the end the glory goes to the men, while the struggles of the women elicit as much interest as the forgotten ancient ruins scattered along the Dartmoor hills.

Source: Kathleen Wilson, Critical Essay on *The Hound of the Baskervilles*, in *Novels for Students*, Gale, Cengage Learning, 2009.

Jesse Oak Taylor-Ide

In the following excerpt, Taylor-Ide examines Sherlock Holmes's ability in The Hound of the Baskervilles *to deftly cross the line between mysticism and rational Victorian ideals. According to Taylor-Ide, he does this through a symbolic ritual transformation on the moor.*

The Late-Victorian Period presented the need to confront an increasing dissolution of boundaries that had once been more concretely defined. In 1859 (the year Conan Doyle was born) Darwin published *The Origin of Species*, removing the concept of a solid divide between humans and animals. Similarly, the increasing flow of people to and from the far reaches of the globe turned London, the seat of British power, culture, and identity, into what Watson called a "cesspool in which the loungers and idlers of empire are inevitably dredged." Many

Illustration of The Hound of the Baskervilles *by Sidney Paget* (Public Domain)

of these "loungers and idlers" were British, many were foreign, and many seemed to blur the line between these two categories, either being of mixed blood, or having acquired foreign tendencies through sojourns in Marlow's "dark places of the earth." Within this "cesspool" of ontological uncertainty, Sherlock Holmes is generally understood, and indeed presents himself, as the ultimate rational being—the champion of the solid, masculine, British mind in the face of foreign mysticism and irrationality...

Unlike many of the criminals he pursues, Holmes rarely leaves Britain. Instead he highlights the degree to which "Britain" was becoming an increasingly hybridized entity through the influx of foreign influences. In order to counter these threats, Holmes goes through transformations similar to those associated with sojourns abroad through the use of ritual process. Social theorist Victor Turner describes such ritual processes as symbolic dissolutions of the self, departures from the societal structure. This leads to a period of liminality, or anti-structure, where the individual is "betwixt and between" worlds. Eventually, a reintegration into structured society

"THE HOUND OF THE BASKERVILLES

ILLUSTRATES HOW HOLMES'S PASSAGE BETWEEN THE

WORLD OF SOCIETY AND THE DARK, POLLUTING

WORLD OUTSIDE IT THROUGH RITUAL

TRANSFORMATION IS IN FACT THE CENTRAL THEME

THAT ENABLES HIS SOLVING OF THE MYSTERY."

follows, with the individual assuming a new identity and role within that structure. The liminal world into which one crosses is often seen as somewhat magical, certainly polluting, and in this case analogous to the "dark" foreign spaces of the empire. The individual is altered by this transition, and is often seen as somehow tainted by the experience, bringing back shards of the darkness like the dust clinging to a traveler's clothes.

The Hound of the Baskervilles illustrates how Holmes's passage between the world of society and the dark, polluting world outside it through ritual transformation is in fact the central theme that enables his solving of the mystery. By contrast, in *The Sign of Four*, similarly ritualized scenes are given an inverted position in the structure of the narrative, framing the main action, which takes place within the societal structure of London. Despite their distinctions, both of these novels pit Sherlock Holmes in an explicit battle with figures corrupted by time spent in foreign lands. In this light they may be read as allegories of the Victorians' battle to affirm their civilization, and by extension their humanity, in the face of dark, regressive influences that threaten to drag them back into a precivilized state...

Nowhere is Holmes's ritual transformation as apparent or as fully developed as in *The Hound of the Baskervilles*, arguably the most complex and deeply allegorical of the Holmes stories. The mystery of the hound is brought to Holmes's attention by Dr. James Mortimer. Mortimer is continually referred to as a "man of science," in distinction to Holmes "the specialist in crime," thus highlighting both the degree to which pure science is unable to come to terms with the threat of the hound, and the degree to which Holmes's methods are something other than scientific. Mortimer in fact attempts to

cover his inadvertent offence in calling Holmes "the second highest expert in Europe" by saying, "To the man of precisely scientific mind the work of Monsieur Bertillon must always appeal strongly." Bertillon was a criminal anthropologist who devised a complex system of measurement to identify "criminal types"—an area of study very similar to Mortimer's own passion for phrenology. The unscientific elements of Holmes's methods are further illustrated immediately upon Mortimer's departure. Holmes suggests that Watson leave him alone for the rest of the day, a request which Watson honors immediately, noting: "I knew that seclusion and solitude were very necessary for my friend in those hours of intense mental concentration during which he weighed every particle of evidence, constructed alternative theories, balanced one against the other..." Watson's observation is true in many instances, but here it is erroneous. Holmes repeatedly notes the danger of forming theories when one does not have enough evidence. Since the amount of evidence that he has been presented with at this point is quite small, hardly enough fodder to sustain his immense reasoning power through an entire day of intense concentration, it would contradict his own counsel to spend the afternoon engaged as Watson suggests. Holmes spends the day collecting evidence, not weighing it.

The room is so choked with heavy smoke upon Watson's return that he can barely get through the door. It is not only the smoke that isolates Watson from the rooms at 221B, however. Holmes is barely visible—"a vague vision ... coiled up in an armchair with his pipe between his lips." Terms like "vague vision" and "coiled" characterize Holmes as otherworldly, almost reptilian. He seems to have undergone a ritual transformation—passed into a dark, liminal world outside the societal structure, and has returned cloaked in that darkness, which is manifested in the close, smoky atmosphere of the room. Though both this and the cocaine ritual take place in their shared rooms, Watson seems removed from the scene in both cases. This distance is maintained as Holmes alludes to his changed state of mind in direct opposition to Watson's immersion in the solid British masculinity of his club:

"Where do you think I've been?"
"A fixture also."
"On the contrary, I have been to Devonshire."
"In spirit?"

"Exactly. My body remained in this arm-chair and has, I regret to observe, consumed in my absence two large pots of coffee and an incredible amount of tobacco. After you left I sent down to Stamford's for the Ordnance map of this portion of the moor, and my spirit has hovered over it all day."

This is an ambiguous statement—especially in Holmes's use of the word "it." Does "it" refer to the moor or to the map? Based on Holmes's use of the word "spirit," "it" can be read in reference both to the moor and to the map; or, more precisely, to the moor through the map. According to the *OED*, spirit can, among other things, refer to the soul, essence, or immaterial part of a corporeal being, to the immaterial intelligent part of a person, or a matter of the mind or mental activity. These are closely related, but subtly and significantly different connotations—the difference lying in the faculty of reason.

The spirit as the soul is the place of religion and mysticism, the realm that traditionally defies reason. Spirit also means, however, the aspect of a person that is sentient, thoughtful, and reasoning. Holmes employs both of these meanings in the above passage. It is the incredible reasoning faculty of his mind that hovers over the map all day. It is his essence, the immaterial aspect of himself that perceives on a level other than reason, which travels to Devonshire, aided in its liberation from his body by huge quantities of caffeine and strong tobacco in Doyle's version of a shamanistic trance.

Holmes's preoccupied state in pondering the map is quite similar to Buddhist monks who meditate over mandalas, spiritual maps that serve as guides on the journey to enlightenment. A literary example can be seen in Rudyard Kipling's *Kim*, in which the lama is one of the few still living that can both draw and explicate the mandala, "the Wheel of Life." Distinctly different from a scientific use of the imagination, this "mental mapping meditation" involves a literal projection of the spirit through the mandala. Holmes in his fashion adopts the principal and applies it to a British Ordinance map: "Yes the setting is a worthy one. If the devil did desire to have a hand in the affairs of men—." He trails off, unable or unwilling to finish the sentence and convey what his spirit encountered on the moor, and then says, "The thing takes shape Watson. It becomes coherent. Might I ask you to hand me my violin, and we will postpone all further thought on this business ... " This ability to detach his mind from cases at will, usually through his hypnotic violin playing, is another characteristic that Watson marvels at on numerous occasions. Holmes's solitary, tobacco-filled vigils may often provide the solutions to his cases; these periods of musical self-hypnosis provide the tranquility to allow him to recognize understanding when it comes to him. This sense parallels a yogic tenet: "knowledge is not something external to us to be received like a gift, nor a mental construction either, to be built up from scratch by logical reasoning. ... it is in reality a hidden treasure, something waiting in the very depths of ourselves to be discovered." Holmes certainly does not carry his detachment this far and would be appalled at the dismissal of logical reasoning, but the idea that too much reasoning could obscure the truth that will come in tranquility speaks to yet another connection to Eastern religion ...

Like the foreign lands of the empire, [the Dartmoor] landscape is not unpopulated. Nor are the hound, with its disembodied cry like the voice of the moor itself, and the escaped convict, Selden, the only mysterious figures loose upon the moor. The night that Watson and Sir Henry attempt to capture Selden, Watson catches sight of "the figure of a man upon the Tor": "He stood with his legs a little separated, his arms folded, his head bowed, as if he were brooding over that enormous wilderness of peat and granite which lay before him. He might have been the very spirit of that terrible place." This figure is, of course, Sherlock Holmes. It is not enough for Holmes to ponder the case from Baker Street, amassing clues like puzzle pieces until he eventually fits them all together. In order to solve the mystery of the hound he must enter into its domain on the moor, not merely as a visitor as Watson does, but as one who lets the moor permeate his own being. He must live in the ancient dwellings, meditating on the roots that connect civilized humanity to its darker origins. He must breathe the air tainted by Grimpen Mire, and listen to the call of the hound. He must, in short, pass through a ritual transformation and become the "spirit of the moor" that Watson saw that night on the Tor.

Holmes seems to be eerily unaffected by the harshness of the moor. Watson notes, "he had contrived with that cat-like love of personal cleanliness which was one of his characteristics, that his chin should be as smooth and his linen as perfect as if he were in Baker Street." Christopher Clausen writes that this is the moment when we know that civilization must ultimately triumph. There is certainly something reassuring in the ease with which Holmes seems to be able to transport the civilization of Baker Street out onto the moor, fulfilling an ideal which caused British explorers to sacrifice their lives in order to carry dress uniforms and fine china on expeditions deep into the Arctic. But it also calls Baker Street's solidity into question—if civilization can be so easily carried into the darkness, could the reverse not also be true? If the boundaries between these worlds are so permeable, how easy might it be for another such figure, one more affected by the darkness, to transport that darkness back to civilization?

These fears are central to the significance of the hound, and indeed to many of the crimes that Sherlock Holmes investigates. Stapleton is just such a figure, who returns from South America to conjure the hound. Jonathan Small's return from the Andaman Islands with the devilish Tonga is another example, as are "*The Devils Foot*" and "*The Speckled Band*," in which knowledge attained overseas, of an African poison and an Indian snake respectively, is put to murderous purposes. Similar power and danger surround other figures such as Stoker's *Dracula* and even Coleridge's *Ancient Mariner*. The most obvious example of the danger of the moor provided here, however, is the convict, Selden.

Given the allegorical connection between the moor and foreign lands, Selden is placed in a very similar situation to the "poor whites" of the empire, who often return home as the criminals (or apparent criminals) in the Holmes stories . . .

Just when Holmes's liminality as "the man upon the Tor" has been highlighted, Selden's death illustrates the precariousness of that liminality. Holmes's reaction upon realizing the identity of the dead man they had believed to be Sir Henry establishes an instant connection: "It is not the baronet—it is—why, it is my neighbor, the convict!" Claiming the convict as a neighbor reminds us of the similarity between Selden's position on the moor and his own. Both have been living in the abodes of pre-civilized humanity in this world of darkness. This fits within Turner's description of the interconnectedness between people who inhabit the ritual space of anti-structure, something

he refers to as "communitas." Selden's demise, being literally overrun by the spirit of the darkness manifest in the hound, strikes home the danger lurking around those who exist outside the social order. An even more specific warning in Selden's death clarifies this danger: "'Then the clothes have been the poor devil's death,' said he. 'It is clear enough that the hound has been laid on from some article of Sir Henry's—the boot which was abstracted in the hotel in all probability—and so ran this man down." It is putting on Sir Henry's clothes that leads the hound to Selden, a fact that speaks directly to the explanation given for the origins of his criminality. His sister, Mrs. Barrymore, says that he felt entitled to more than his due because he was spoiled as a child. This feeling of entitlement is literalized in his assuming garb far above his lower-class station in order to escape to Latin America. In doing so he presents an even stronger challenge to the social order than he has up to this point, and it brings his doom upon him. The attempt to rise above one's social standing outside the societal structure of the metropole brings about ruin and death—a clear warning to Sherlock Holmes or anyone else who passes into the dark space outside structured society.

The threat presented by Selden, however, is dwarfed by that of the other figure in the novel who has been corrupted by the darkness—Stapleton. Before his guilt (and identity as a illegitimate Baskerville) is revealed, Stapleton represents an imperial icon—the European naturalist/ explorer. Since he (supposedly) acts only out of the desire to gain knowledge, the scientific researcher is often viewed as one of the noblest and most benign of colonial figures, one whose explorations are removed from the exploitive elements of his capitalist or military counterpart. Holmes demonstrates a similar fixation on knowledge, and is himself an amateur scientist—often occupying himself with chemical experiments unrelated to his professional investigations.

In Stapleton, however, this ideal is perverted to malevolence through the witchcraft and voodoo associated with his Latin American roots, an association seen in the novel through his frequent sojourns and comfort on the moor. Especially as it immediately follows the discussion of Selden's death, Stapleton's appearance, strolling nonchalantly across the moor on the heels of his hound while contentedly puffing a cigar, mimics Holmes's civilized appearance on the moor, and presents yet another instance of Turner's "communitas." Thus we see a similar marriage of the scientific and the mystical, the British and the foreign, and the ability to move between them, in both Holmes and Stapleton. In challenging Stapleton, then, Holmes is in effect serving almost as a conscience, reigning in a dark doppelganger that he might become himself if, like Conrad's Kurtz, he succumbed to the darkness.

The degree to which Stapleton has been absorbed by the darkness, meanwhile, is fully revealed as his dark power seems almost indistinguishable from that of the moor itself as the final scene unfolds. The fog moves in off the moor, shrouding the path as if the devil's own breath is behind it—suggesting that Stapleton may be only a pawn in the power of a deeper evil. It is from this deathly shroud that the apparition bursts:

> A hound it was, an enormous coal-black hound, but not such a hound as mortal eyes have ever seen. Fire burst from its open mouth, its eyes glowed with a smouldering glare, its mussle and hackles and dewlap were outlined in flickering flame. Never in the delirious dream of a disordered brain could anything more savage, more appalling, more hellish be conceived than that dark form and savage face which broke upon us out of the fog.

The hound is a manifestation of all the fears at work throughout the novel. It is an animal seeming to cross the boundaries between myth and reality, conjured from the days before science had explained that no such creature could possibly exist. The hound is all the more terrifying, because while it seems so other-worldly, it is also so very British. It was born in London, and turned to evil by the foreign-born but British-blooded Stapleton. Unlike Stoker's *Dracula*, it is not a foreign being that must be invited in—it is only coming home.

Watson's portrayal of the hound reflects the ambiguity seen in his depiction of Holmes in his liminal state, both when he is sitting in Baker Street enveloped in smoke, and when he sees him as "the figure of a man upon the Tor." In each of these instances, the figure portrayed cannot be fully defined—"a vague image," "the figure of a man," "not such a hound as mortal eyes have ever seen," "the delirious dream of a disordered brain...." The similarities between these characterizations return to Holmes's connection with both Selden and Stapleton through the moor, and reflect Turner's "communitas," the affinities between figures inhabiting the darkness that is

central to Holmes's success. Both Watson and Lestrade are petrified with amazement and fear. It is only because Holmes has been prepared and transformed through ritual of his time on the moor like a priest before a sacrifice that he can kill the hound.

In fact, the ritual is even completed by a sacrifice—Sir Henry is offered up to the hound and then resuscitated once it is dead. Holmes's emptying his revolver into the hound's body with a fervor bordering on possession, meanwhile, is an inverse of the common image of a witch or heathen priest using ritual to bring a magical force into the rational world. In this case, Holmes's ritual transformation brings his technological British weapon into the darkness...

Source: Jesse Oak Taylor-Ide, "Ritual and the Liminality of Sherlock Holmes in *The Sign of Four* and *The Hound of the Baskervilles*," in *English Literature in Transition 1880–1920*, Vol. 48, No. 2, Spring 2005, pp. 55–71.

James Kissane and John M. Kissane

In the following excerpt, Kissane and Kissane argue that The Hound of the Baskervilles *portrays Sherlock Holmes as a folk hero—one who uses scientific reasoning instead of brute strength to vanquish seemingly supernatural evil.*

It is no mystery why Conan Doyle's *The Hound of the Baskervilles* should be regarded as a classic of its genre. Most of its elements have since become virtual requirements for a satisfactory detective novel, and nowhere else do these characteristic features appear in such distinguished, one might say quintessential, form. The bizarre crime is not only conceived with ingenuity, it exudes the mystery and horror of the supernatural. The circumscribed society confines suspicion within strict limits; and Doyle not only keeps the list of suspects to a daring minimum but comprises it of such classic types as the Family Doctor (Mortimer), the eccentric (Frankland), the Naturalist (Stapleton), and of course the Butler (Barrymore). There are not one but three atmospheric settings: London, a gloomy ancestral hall, and a desolate moor. Doyle stages his climax, at which evil is at last confronted and exposed, with great showmanship. As Holmes, Watson, and Lestrade await the appearance of the murderous hound, the threat of a concealing fog adds a full measure of suspense to the unique uncertainty of the peril. Finally, there is the master detective—or rather detectives, for in addition to Holmes, whose supremacy among the breed

> THE SCIENTIFIC CHARACTER OF HOLMES'S FAMOUS METHOD IS PERFECTLY EVIDENT IN ANY OF HIS NUMEROUS ADVENTURES, BUT WHAT *THE HOUND OF THE BASKERVILLES* ALMOST UNIQUELY PRESENTS IS THE HERO-DETECTIVE ACTING SPECIFICALLY AS THE CHAMPION OF EMPIRICAL SCIENCE, FACING ITS CRUCIAL CHALLENGE, THE CHALLENGE OF THE SEEMINGLY SUPERNATURAL."

finds no serious challenge, Watson also qualifies, since in this adventure he plays an unusually important role by doing much of the sleuthing himself.

Doyle's specific achievement, however, argues for more than mere representative status. *The Hound of the Baskervilles* stands above its author's other works at the same time that it stands for his predominance in the field of detective fiction. One obvious feature that sets this tale apart offers a clue to its particular excellence. Anyone familiar with the Holmes stories will recognize *The Hound of the Baskervilles* as the only one of the four novel-length works that includes no separate, retrospective narrative. In each of the others the events underlying the mystery and leading to the crime form a distinct tale—a tale that does not involve Holmes and Watson and has its setting far from Baker Street and even outside England. In *A Study in Scarlet* it is the account of Jefferson Hope and the Mormons; in *The Sign of Four* it is Jonathan Small's story of the Agra Treasure; and in *The Valley of Fear* there is the episode of labor union terrorism among the Allegheny coal miners. In each case the purpose of the "flashback" is to provide colorful incident and exotic atmosphere beyond that contained in the crime and its solution. In *The Hound of the Baskervilles* the Baskerville legend which Dr. Mortimer reads to Holmes and Watson may seem similar to the episodes mentioned, but in fact it performs a quite different function. The legend is a beginning to the action rather than a clarification at the end; it is essential to the actual crime, and its atmosphere permeates the enveloping mystery.

What this means, of course, is that by developing his tale out of the "west country legend" mentioned in the acknowledgment Doyle created a work of greater unity than he managed to do in his other longer efforts. The difference in effect is obvious. In *A Study in Scarlet*, for example, our interest in the solution of the crimes and the apprehension of the criminal has been satisfied before the account of Hope's adventures among the Mormons begins. In *The Hound of the Baskervilles*, on the other hand, the exposure and thwarting of Stapleton's scheme is also, in a sense, the last chapter to the Baskerville legend. The melodrama and the problem in detection are woven into a single narrative; in the other novel-length adventures they are separate.

The unified fable that results is a classic embodiment of the abstract form of the detective story as it has been entertainingly and instructively delineated by W. H. Auden ("The Guilty Vicarage," *Harper's*, May, 1948). In essence the fable concerns the freeing of an ancestral house from a contaminating curse. The crime, Sir Charles's death, is identified with the curse that has plagued the Baskerville family, and it jeopardizes the heir, Sir Henry, and casts suspicion upon the society gathered around Baskerville Hall. In solving the crime and exposing the criminal, Sherlock Holmes performs the traditional heroic function of purging the hall of its ancestral blight and the society of the presence of guilt. Conan Doyle brings out these elements of his fable with thoroughness and solidity and rises to heights of mastery in the way he uses this material to dramatize a struggle of scientific reason against superstition and irrationality. It is common to regard the detective story as having been born of nineteenth-century "scientism"; *The Hound of the Baskervilles* is the example of the genre in which the implications of that origin are given their most vivid and their richest artistic realization.

The murder of Sir Charles Baskerville confronts us with the family curse in two ways. Most immediately the death, because of its circumstances, raises the spectre of the legendary hound; but it raises also the question of the fate of the new heir. Doyle gives careful emphasis to Sir Henry's situation. A Canadian, he is really a newcomer as yet untouched by the sinister aspects of his inheritance. Still, he accepts his role as the "last of the old race" and Baskerville Hall as "the home of his fathers" (chapter iii). We are clearly made to feel that there is a family as well as a personal fate involved in the mysterious circumstances Sir Henry encounters. Indeed, Stapleton's scheme to gain the inheritance makes explicit the connection between the personal peril and the family one. Moreover, the effect of the Baskervilles' fortunes upon the more general welfare is also stressed. The revival of the Baskerville legend causes "a reign of terror in the district" (chap. iii), and were Sir Henry to avoid the curse by remaining away from the Hall the results would be still more serious: "'... the prosperity of the whole poor, bleak countryside depends upon his presence'" (chap. iii). Even Sherlock Holmes in all his rationalism cannot help seeing the successful completion of the case in the context of the Baskerville curse. Over the body of Stapleton's giant dog Holmes pronounces his version of the hero's vaunt: "We've laid the family ghost once and for ever" (chap. xiv).

Thus in this particular adventure Sherlock Holmes earns in a special sense the title "folk hero" that one recent writer has given him (Dwight Macdonald, "A Theory of Mass Culture," *Diogenes*, Summer, 1952, p. 11). One has in fact only to substitute Grendel, Hrothgar, and Heorot for the Hound, Sir Henry, and Baskerville Hall to see Holmes playing Beowulf's epic part. Naturally these heroes' methods are as vastly different as their personalities. Holmes, who concedes that "in a modest way I have combatted evil" (chap. iii), does so mainly by his powers of observation and reason rather than by the strength of his hand, and he overcomes his inhuman adversary by showing that what appears to be supernatural is but the agent of a human master whose designs can be discovered and foiled by scientific deductions. The scientific character of Holmes's famous method is perfectly evident in any of his numerous adventures, but what *The Hound of the Baskervilles* almost uniquely presents is the hero-detective acting specifically as the champion of empirical science, facing its crucial challenge, the challenge of the seemingly supernatural. Hence, in solving this case Holmes does more than expose crime and defeat a criminal, he expunges heroically a family curse and demonstrates reassuringly the sufficiency of reason.

Doyle takes pains to emphasize that the Baskerville crime is an especially severe test of Holmes's method. The detective himself repeatedly remarks upon the unmatched complexity of the case, but its formidableness is chiefly suggested

through the agency of Dr. Mortimer, who brings the affair to Holmes's attention. Many times Holmes stresses the similarity between Mortimer and himself with respect to their devotion to science. "This is a colleague," he remarks to Watson, "after our own heart" (chap. iii), and he compares Mortimer's knowledge of human skulls to his own ability to identify newspaper type (chap. iv). Thus when Mortimer reflects that "There is a realm in which the most acute and most experienced of detectives is helpless" (meaning the supernatural), it carries considerable dramatic weight. Holmes's reaction adds to this effect. He is struck that "a trained man of science" should entertain a supernatural explanation of Sir Charles's death: "I have hitherto confined my investigations to this world ... to take on the Father of Evil himself would, perhaps, be too ambitious a task" (chap. iii). Holmes is speaking facetiously of course, but the scene does place squarely before us the possibility that there may be limits to the ways of reason.

Dr. Mortimer puts Sherlock Holmes on trial in yet another way. At the outset Mortimer does not seem quite ready to grant Holmes's scientific pretensions. In the delightfully comic conclusion to the opening chapter he offends Holmes by referring to him as "the second highest expert in Europe."

> "Indeed, sir! May I inquire who has the honor to be the first?" ...
> "To the man of precisely scientific mind the work of Monsieur Bertillon must always appeal strongly."
> "Then had you not better consult him?"
> "I said, sir, to the precisely scientific mind. But as a practical man of affairs it is acknowledged that you stand alone. I trust, sir, that I have not inadvertently—"
> "Just a little," said Holmes.

Throughout the novel Conan Doyle is careful to show that his detective is as "precisely scientific" as Dr. Mortimer and to free him from the stigma of being merely "a practical man of affairs." Watson's description of Holmes's procedure is unmistakably the traditional portrait of an experimental scientist in action:

> ... hours of intense mental concentration during which he weighed every particle of evidence, constructed alternative theories, balanced one against the other, and made up his mind as to which points were essential and which immaterial (chap. iii).

Holmes himself defends one of his conclusions against Mortimer's charge of "guesswork" by labeling it "the scientific use of the imagination" (chap. iv). And when Inspector Lestrade arrives on the scene he is designated "the practical man" as contrasted to Sherlock Holmes, "the reasoner" (chap. xiii).

But if the case is a test of Holmes personally, it is even more a test of what his method ultimately represents: that is, the ability of reason to reduce even the most baffling mystery to a commonplace. This theme is presented in miniature in the very first page of the novel. Watson is scrutinizing Dr. Mortimer's stick. "Well, Watson," says Holmes, who has his back to him, "what do you make of it?" Watson is, of course, astonished and affirms that his companion must have eyes in the back of his head. But Holmes's explanation is, as usual, elementary: "I have, at least, a well polished silver-plated coffee-pot in front of me."

This little exchange may be seen as a kind of synecdoche for the Holmes-Watson relationship. The detective is perfectly in character here, but his friend is not less so. It is Watson's regular function to register bafflement in the face of mystery and to express wonder as Holmes solves it. Perhaps it should be emphasized, however, that though Watson is a foil he is not a burlesque character, as the radio and motion picture dramatizations have portrayed him. His bewilderment is intended not so much to reveal him as the butt as to add luster to Holmes and his deductions. If Watson does play Sancho to Holmes's Quixote, the joke, when there is one, is as likely to be directed toward the eccentric knight of nineteenth-century rationalism as made at the expense of his faithful squire. It is probably most accurate to regard Watson as a kind of chorus. We may patronize him somewhat, but we also take our cue from him on how to react.

But, as has been mentioned, Watson's role in *The Hound of the Baskervilles* demands special notice. Throughout the middle section of the novel it is he, not Holmes, whom we observe conducting the investigation. This is in one sense an entertaining turnabout, similar in effect to those two adventures in which Holmes, acting as narrator, becomes his own Watson. More important, however, Watson's activities as investigator neatly solve a major technical problem faced by all detective-story writers who depend upon hero-detectives. How is one to

preserve mystery through the length of a novel without casting doubt upon the superior intelligence of the master sleuth? The detective must remain in the dark nearly as long as the reader, for to have him reach a solution early and not disclose it is both irritating and implausible. Yet to fill a book with clues which the detective fails to penetrate until near the end implies a certain amount of ineffectual groping in the part of the hero. In *The Hound of the Baskervilles*, however, Holmes yields the stage to Watson and withdraws behind the scenes. Thus when the reader must experience uncertainty he shares it with Watson as he follows his diligent but rather unenlightened maneuvers; when the time comes for an *éclaircissement*, Holmes, his supreme intellect uncompromised, reappears to provide it.

The suddenness of Holmes's return to the action is the dramatic anticipation of the decisiveness with which reason triumphs over mystery. His virtuosity in unraveling the web in which Watson has been toiling dazzles us as it does the good Doctor, but there is no mistaking the source of Holmes's power. "The world is full of obvious things which nobody by any chance ever observes," he remarks to Watson on one occasion (chap. iii). This, then, is the explanation of all mystery and wonder; and it is through his refusal to acknowledge any other and by a steadfast pursuit of his rigorous empiricism, as the "scientific expert," that Holmes's particular heroism is defined . . .

The figure of Selden, a Cain-like outcast from society, adds an important note to the novel. It is significant that he is a brother of the harmless domestic, Mrs. Barrymore, to whom "he was always the little curly-headed boy that I nursed and played with" (chap. ix), for we are thus shown the unexpected emergence of malignant and retrogressive tendencies in the very midst of an innocence that cannot even recognize them. Selden exemplifies this dark side of human nature in a way that the actual villain Stapleton, as long as he must remain unidentified with the crime, cannot. But Stapleton, at the proper point, completes the picture of a vaguely yet fundamentally imperiled civilization. After all, he is not less a descendant of the Baskerville line than is Sir Henry; and although the brutishness of Hugo Baskerville may be refined in him, the marks of violence upon Mrs. Stapleton show it is still present. The scene in which Stapleton's Baskerville blood is revealed makes this clear.

The portrait of Hugo is discovered by Holmes to bear a resemblance to the naturalist Stapleton, and the detective's comment on the similarity places the whole matter in a specifically biological context. "It is," he says, "an interesting instance of a throw-back, which appears to be both physical and spiritual" (chap. xiii). Legend, as Doyle's contemporary Henrik Ibsen also knew, is not the true source of the ghosts that haunt humanity: man's natural inheritance furnishes its share . . .

Source: James Kissane and John M. Kissane, "Sherlock Holmes and the Ritual of Reason," in *Nineteenth-Century Fiction*, Vol. 17, No. 4, March 1963, pp. 353–62.

SOURCES

Brody, Howard, "Location of Baskerville Hall," in *Baker Street Journal* Vol. 29, No. 4, December 1979, pp. 229–34, 247.

Cavendish, Richard, "Publication of *The Hound of the Baskervilles*: March 25th, 1902," in *History Today*, Vol. 52, No. 3, March 2002, p. 57.

Clausson, Nils, "Degeneration, Fin de Siècle Gothic and the Science of Detection: Arthur Conan Doyle's *The Hound of the Baskervilles* and the Emergence of the Modern Detective Story," in *Journal of Narrative Theory*, Vol. 35, No. 1, Winter 2005, pp. 60–87.

Conan Doyle, Arthur, *The Hound of the Baskervilles*, in *The New Annotated Sherlock Holmes*, edited by Leslie S. Klinger, W. W. Norton, 2006, pp. 383–627.

Favor, Lesli J., "The Foreign and the Female in Arthur Conan Doyle: Beneath the Candy Coating," in *English Literature in Transition, 1880–1920*, No. 4, April 2000, pp. 398–409.

Fisher, Benjamin F., "*The Hound of the Baskervilles* 100 Years after: A Review Essay," in *English Literature in Transition 1880–1920*, Vol. 47, No. 2, Spring 2004, pp. 181–91.

Frank, Lawrence, "The Hound of the Baskervilles, the Man on the Tor, and a Metaphor for the Mind," in *Nineteenth-Century Literature*, Vol. 54, No. 3, December 1999, pp. 336–72.

———, "Reading the Gravel Page: Lyell, Darwin, and Conan Doyle," in *Nineteenth-Century Literature*, Vol. 44, No. 3, December 1989, pp. 364–87.

Hall, Jasmine Yong, "Ordering the Sensational: Sherlock Holmes and the Female Gothic," in *Studies in Short Fiction*, Vol. 28, No. 3, Summer 1991, pp. 295–303.

Kendrick, Stephen, "No Ghosts Need Apply," in *Holy Clues: The Gospel According to Sherlock Holmes*, Pantheon Books, 1999, pp. 89–96.

Kissane, James, and John M. Kissane, "Sherlock Holmes and the Ritual of Reason," in *Nineteenth-Century Fiction*, Vol. 17, No. 4, March 1963, pp. 353–62.

Klinger, Leslie S., ed., *The New Annotated Sherlock Holmes*, W. W. Norton, 2006.

Knox, Ronald, "The 10 Commandments for Detective Novelists," http://www.ronaldknoxsociety.com/detective.html (accessed June 20, 2007).

O'Gorman, Francis, "A Whole New World in the Story of Conan Doyle's Famous Hound," in the *Yorkshire Post*, February 27, 2006.

Taylor-Ide, Jesse Oak, "Ritual and the Liminality of Sherlock Holmes in *The Sign of the Four* and *The Hound of the Baskervilles*," in *English Literature in Transition 1880–1920*, Vol. 48, No. 2, Spring 2005, pp. 55–71.

FURTHER READING

Baring-Gould, William S., ed., *The Annotated Sherlock Holmes*, Crown, 1967.

This book is the definitive edition of Holmes stories and novels, annotated by a notable expert.

Harrison, Michael, "As Famous as Baker Street," in *In the Footsteps of Sherlock Holmes*, Drake Publishers, 1972, pp. 36–39.

This piece demonstrates the minutia with which Holmes fans are consumed. Building on the mention of the Northumberland Arms in *The Hound of the Baskervilles*, Harrison presents the factual information of the real Northumberland Hotel in London and how it meshes with the events of the story.

Moss, Robert A., "Old Frankland: A Case of Identity," in *Baker Street Journal*, Vol. 52, No. 1, Spring 2002, pp. 27–32.

This essay attempts to connect the character of Mr. Frankland with the British chemist Edward Frankland.

Schama, Simon, *A History of Britain: The Fate of Empire 1776–2000*, Hyperion, 2002.

The third volume of Schama's work focuses on the transition of Britain from an oligarchy to a more participatory government, especially during the Victorian era.

Weller, Philip, ed., *The Hound of the Baskervilles: Hunting the Dartmoor Legend*, Devon Books, 2001.

This book offers an exploration of the novel's setting, with details regarding real legends and locations that may have inspired Conan Doyle, along with other tidbits of interest to fans of the story.

Hullabaloo in the Guava Orchard

KIRAN DESAI

1998

Kiran Desai's debut novel, *Hullabaloo in the Guava Orchard* (1998), made the author an instant success at the age of twenty-seven. She is the voice of a younger generation of Indian writers who write in English, many of whom live in self-exile. Indeed, many expatriate Indian novelists have gained international attention, including Salman Rushdie, Arundhati Roy, and Anita Desai (Kiran Desai's mother).

India is home to many religious groups, including Hindus, Buddhists, and Muslims. It also has a history of political strife among those groups, exacerbated by the interference of British colonialism and modern globalization. Desai, like other Indian writers in English, combines these elements of India's traditions and history with a secular emphasis on storytelling. Her work explores the toll that these cultural divides have taken on India's population.

Desai's work is known for its rich and colorful language, and detailed presentations of setting and character. *Hullabaloo in the Guava Orchard* presents a fictitious small town called Shahkot in North India. The town has a mixed culture of traditional Indian social norms and of modern life, wherein the runaway Sampath Chawla, who just wants to be left alone, is forced into being a holy man in spite of himself.

Given its popularity, the novel was still in print as of 2008; it was reissued as an Anchor paperback in 1999.

Kiran Desai *(The Guardian Hay Festival 2007. David Levenson /
Getty Images)*

AUTHOR BIOGRAPHY

Kiran Desai was born on September 3, 1971, in
New Delhi, India, the youngest of the four children of Anita and Ashvin Desai. Her mother,
Anita Desai, whose own mother was German
and whose father was Indian, is one of the most
respected and famous Indian writers today.
Ashvin Desai is a Delhi businessman. Kiran's
parents are now separated, due to the nature of
Anita's career and travel. Kiran's early life was
spent in Delhi, and sometimes in a family house
in Kalimpong in the Himalayas, the scene of
much of her second novel, *The Inheritance of
Loss.*

Kiran was educated at a convent in Kalimpong, and at the age of fifteen, accompanied her
mother to England when her mother got a temporary teaching position there. When Anita Desai
moved to the United States to teach and write,
Kiran went with her, for she has remained closest
to her mother, as a friend and fellow writer. In

America, Kiran went to high school in Massachusetts and then to Bennington College in Vermont.
At first she planned on studying science, but
because of her natural talent for writing and her
mother's encouragement, she soon switched
majors. After graduating from college, she
enrolled in writing programs at Hollins University
in Virginia and then Columbia University, where
she got an M.F.A. in writing. She began *Hullabaloo in the Guava Orchard* while at Hollins and
completed it as part of her M.F.A. work at Columbia. The novel was published in 1998, when she
was twenty-seven. The book was well received by
critics, and the book received the Betty Trask
Award from the British Society of Authors.

After this success, Desai secluded herself for
eight years to write her second novel, *The
Inheritance of Loss* (2006). While the first novel
introduces social problems, it does so in a light
comic or satiric mode and does not linger on
them. The second novel takes up the more tragic
theme of the loss of tradition, and the difficulties
faced by immigrants who try to make a new life.
For this novel, Desai won the Booker Prize for
fiction. At the age of thirty-five, she was the
youngest woman ever to win it.

In addition, *The Inheritance of Loss* was
selected as a *Publishers Weekly* Best Book of
the Year in 2006; as one of the *New York Times
Book Review* 100 Notable Books of 2006; finalist
for the National Book Critics Circle Award for
Fiction in 2006; short-listed for the Orange Prize
in 2007; and long-listed for the Dublin IMPAC
Award of 2008.

As of 2008, Kiran Desai lived in Brooklyn,
New York, but spent time regularly with family
in India. She is close to her family and especially
to her mother. Indeed, mother and daughter
have given readings of their novels together.

PLOT SUMMARY

Chapter 1

In the Himalayan foothills, in the small north
Indian town of Shahkot, during a very hot
summer, many proposals are made to induce
the monsoon. By September the situation is so
bad that famine relief camps have to be set up.
This is the year Sampath Chawla is born. His
mother, Kulfi, is only twenty-one and just married to Mr. Chawla. She gets bigger and hungrier
as the drought gets worse, but none of the relief

MEDIA ADAPTATIONS

- *Hullabaloo in the Guava Orchard* was adapted as an unabridged audiobook read by Madhav Sharma and produced by Isis Audio Books on six tapes (1999).

planes coming with supplies reach them. Kulfi is so hungry, she obsesses about food and sells everything in the house. Finally, she draws pictures of food on the walls, and when there is no more wall space, Sampath is born. It is the day the monsoon rains finally come. In the storm, Kulfi gives birth, and Sampath has a brown birthmark on his cheek. As if by miracle, a Swedish relief plane drops a crate in front of the Chawla house with food in it. Kulfi thinks her baby looks like he came from another planet. The baby is named Sampath, Good Fortune.

Chapter 2

Twenty years have passed. Sampath has grown into a thin and oversensitive young man, unable to sleep with the noisy breathing of his family around him, all sharing the one ceiling fan: father, mother, grandmother Ammaji, and sister Pinky. He rushes to the roof of the house where it is just as hot. He sings and walks back and forth all night, wishing he had somewhere else to go; he feels suffocated in his life. When morning comes and the town begins to wake up, he sees his father come out with a yoga mat. His grandmother goes for morning milk. She worries that Sampath did not sleep.

Chapter 3

Mr. Chawla is a man of habit and performs morning exercise. He is forty and head clerk at the Reserve Bank of Shahkot. He shouts orders to his family as he readies for the day. Ammaji and Pinky try to keep up with his demands. Mr. Chawla reads bits from the newspaper. Kulfi is uninvolved with what is going on and sits by the window thinking of food. She has grown more and more peculiar, and the grandmother has to

do all the work. Pinky is disgusted by the political scandals her father reads and wants him to read the story about the Cinema Monkey who attacks ladies outside the cinema, stealing food and pulling at their saris. Mr. Chawla lectures Sampath on how to be a success. Sampath had been happily idle until his father found him a job at the post office. The father and grandmother argue about Sampath's future, and the sister joins in.

Chapter 4

Sampath bicycles in the morning traffic of Shahkot, among children, clerks, beggars, holy men, animals, and cars. Pinky gets off the back of his bicycle and goes to the public bus. She is pretty, and removes a hairpin to stab any man who hassles her. The post office is a gloomy building, and Sampath crawls under the barbed wire fence. He hears the flirting between two postal workers, Mr. Gupta and Miss Jyotsna. She describes an incident with the Cinema Monkey who ripped her clothes and ran off with her peanut cone. Sampath is fascinated by her beautiful red toenails. They speak of the wedding of the daughter of their boss. When the boss, Mr. D.P.S., arrives, they jump to attention. Sampath tries to add up the wedding accounts, but all the bills look alike, and his mind gets dizzy. As soon as the boss leaves, the two clerks flirt again, and Sampath begins reading the mail. He is supposed to sort the letters, but he likes to read about the lives of the people of Shahkot. At the end of the day, Sampath has finished none of his work and is scolded.

Chapter 5

Later, the whole office staff is on duty at Mr. D.P.S.'s house to help with his daughter's wedding. Curious, Sampath wanders into rooms of the house and looks in drawers. He is drawn by the expensive perfumes, even dressing up in wedding clothes. He becomes drunk on the various scents. He looks at jewelry and gems, lights a candle and looks at himself in a mirror. He feels transported. He had always been attracted to beauty and imaginative stories and thus, failed his examinations and his job. He goes out and dances up and down in front of the marriage tent. His boss and the crowd stare at him, but Sampath is floating in his own world. He jumps into the fountain and disrobes, singing, as the audience shrieks. He is fired on the spot, and his father is furious, saying he will have to find another job. Sampath feels trapped in a life he hates. Looking at a guava, he wishes he could have its quiet beauty. The guava fills him with sweetness, and he dreams of freedom.

Chapter 6

When his family is gone the next day, Sampath runs away, catching a bus. He rides past the outskirts of town. When an old woman on the bus insists on talking to him, he jumps from the bus. The passengers see him race to an old orchard on a hill. Sampath runs until he finds an old tree that looks inviting. He climbs it and settles in. It is a guava orchard, part of the university research reserve. Sampath feels peaceful. Life is sweet and uncomplicated. He feels at home and falls asleep in the branches.

Chapter 7

The Chawla family go to the police to search for their son, and the whole town makes the most of the drama. The watchman of the university forest reserve bicycles into Shahkot and announces there is a man in a guava tree who won't come down. Mr. Chawla feels sure it is Sampath, and the family catches the bus and gets off at the old orchard. They find Sampath in the tree, eating a guava. Sampath thinks of excuses, but in the end says nothing. His mother alone seems to understand why he is in the tree. The family calls in Dr. Banerjee from the bazaar clinic, who tries to get Sampath to come down, but Sampath is afraid of being locked up for being insane. Dr. Banerjee hoists himself into the tree with his stethoscope and pronounces Sampath indeed crazy. The family tries all kinds of remedies that don't work. Then they visit a holy man, who says Sampath just needs to get married.

The Chawlas can only find an ugly girl for Sampath. The girl arrives with her family on the bus, which is full of pilgrims singing. The bride, her family, and the pilgrims arrive at the tree. While Sampath has romantic fantasies about beautiful women, he is horrified by the ugly girl, as the pilgrims lift her into the tree in her billowing sari. When she tries to touch Sampath's feet in devotion, he yells, and she falls out of the tree. He wants to shout to the people to leave him alone, but instead, he calls out to Mr. Singh, whose letters he has read in the post office. He asks if his jewelry is still hidden beneath the tulsi plant? Then he asks Mrs. Chopra about the lump in her throat. Sampath goes on revealing the secrets he has read in letters, and the people assume he has

divine powers. Soon a newspaper article proclaims him to be a holy man in a tree.

Chapter 8

Mr. Chawla suddenly realizes that Sampath might make the family rich. People no longer laugh at his son; they arrive in growing numbers to consult him. The Chawlas take over the watchman's shed and move to the orchard to manage Sampath. They make him comfortable with food, a cot, and an umbrella. Sampath delivers his Sermon in the Guava Tree to all the pilgrims who come to the orchard. He answers their questions with witty and nonsensical aphorisms. Among the first to arrive are his old co-workers, Miss Jyotsna and Mr. Gupta. Sampath enjoys his new position of power, and is in great humor. When he is tired of the questions, Sampath goes to sleep in his tree. His simplicity and directness are counted great spiritual virtues. Kulfi, totally inspired by her son, begins cooking masterpieces in the orchard in her outdoor kitchen. She too likes the freedom of being in the forest. Sampath grows fat, nourished by the exotic food cooked only for him.

Chapter 9

Pinky is worried that her life is being disrupted by her family's orchard life. She is reduced to once a week trips into the bazaar for supplies. Mr. Chawla is on leave from his regular job and has plans of getting rich managing the pilgrim trade to his son's tree. Pinky feels alone, with no family to support her social ambition. She has to plan her own elaborate outfits and overdresses for the market, as though she is a movie star. She insists that she is being followed by men in the street. Mr. Chawla believes she invents situations because she is starved for drama, and he makes her go to the market in plain dress. On a trip to town to buy Ammaji new dentures, Pinky and Ammaji are attacked by the Cinema Monkey while buying ice cream after seeing a movie. When Ammaji takes a bite of ice cream, her dentures stick in the cone, the cone drops, and the monkey runs off with it. The Kwality Hungry Hop Ice Cream boy frightens off the monkey and recovers the dentures. Having been rescued in front of a cheering crowd by the Hungry Hop boy lights a flame in Pinky's romantic heart. She had thought the boy unremarkable before, but suddenly, he is a hero.

Chapter 10

Mr. Chawla has made the watchman's shed comfortable, with electricity and running water. Mr. Chawla opens a bank account for a proposed temple to which the devotees could donate. He approaches merchants to put up ads in the orchard. Buses make detours so passengers can visit the new Baba in the tree. Ammaji operates a tea stall. Mr. Chawla sells garlands and fruit to pilgrims, then collects them and sells them again.

Sampath is charmed by the visitors who ask him questions on the nature of life. One is a spy from the Atheist Society and Branch to Uncover Fraudulent Holy Men (BUFHM). Some of Sampath's answers make sense and some don't, but they have the ring of truth, so the pilgrims are satisfied. The spy takes notes in a notebook; he writes that Sampath avoids questioning by pretending to be otherworldly. Sampath's rejection of a bride is the final proof to the crowd that he is a true hermit. Miss Jyotsna sings a hymn, and Sampath thinks how pretty she is. He sings with her, and the people join in. The spy wonders how he can fool the people. He plans his investigation into Sampath's life.

Chapter 11

Kulfi searches the forest for exotic things to cook for her son. She kills game found in traps. She is completely exhilarated by the outdoors, fearlessly rounding up the ingredients, and coming back muddy from her forays. Tough from all the exercise, she cuts up the game herself in her outdoor kitchen, in ecstasy. The smells drive the pilgrims mad. Sampath is filled with desire for her food. The spy tries to collect a specimen of Sampath's food in a bottle to see if he is being drugged, but Kulfi hits him on the head with a broom. Mr. Chawla decides to limit visiting hours, and Sampath becomes even more popular.

Chapter 12

Then the monkeys arrive. The Cinema Monkey follows Pinky to the orchard and brings his friends. Sampath is delighted with the monkeys that are a nuisance to everyone else. He plays with them, acting like a monkey himself. They become his bodyguard, sleeping and eating with him in the tree. Now all food has to be locked up, for they are thieves. When her family is distracted, Pinky dresses up and escapes to town, with the spy following her. When he takes the bus with her, she jabs him with a hairpin, and he

has to see a doctor. The Hungry Hop boy is slow but good humored. He does not notice Pinky's deliberate attentions, so she becomes more direct. She bites a piece of his ear off. He screams for help, and Pinky is taken to the police station. When they find out she is the Monkey Baba's sister, they escort her back to the orchard. Once a photo of Sampath is published in the *Times of India*, he gets enormous amounts of mail in the orchard. The spy makes a case to the BUFHM: Sampath is mad and should be locked up, but instead he is famous. It is people like this who obstruct the progress of the nation!

Chapter 13

The monkeys eventually find some bottles of rum and become drunk. When it is discovered they are drunk, Sampath defends them with a proverb no one can understand. The monkeys become addicted to alcohol and forage for it among all the pilgrims' bags. The pilgrims are afraid of being bitten, and a war with the monkeys begins. Sampath alone is forgiving, but the monkeys have gone too far.

Chapter 14

Mr. Chawla worries that their scheme may fail, just when his bank account was getting fat enough to buy shares in the VIP Hosiery Products company. He tells his son that he should have a proper hermitage inside a concrete structure that will keep the monkeys out. He starts to give Sampath advice on how to handle the crowds. The monkeys throw apples at him. Sampath is worried but immediately forgets his trouble by watching the beautiful insects on the tree. When Kulfi brings him dinner, he complains about the conspiracy to get him out of the tree. She says cheerfully that they could poison everyone! Sampath feels his mother and the monkeys are the only ones who understand him. The monkeys get more and more wild, even going to the bazaar to steal alcohol. One day, they rip up everything in the orchard, and the next day Mr. Chawla goes to town to appeal to the officials about the problem.

Chapter 15

The Chief Medical Officer is in constant fear of his ulcers flaring up. When Mr. Chawla arrives to discuss the crisis, the Chief Medical Officer realizes the trouble that could ensue if he got involved. He reminds Mr. Chawla of the sacred nature of monkeys, who were god Rama's followers. The Chief Medical Officer calls the biology department at Lady Chatterjee University to handle the problem. Verma, the head of the biology department, has his own theory he would like to test: killing the lead monkey and hanging him in view of the others. His wife tires of his theories and warns him the Hanuman Monkey Temple will be after him if he tries to interfere. In the local army post, the Brigadier picks up the phone. It is Verma, who gets him by mistake. The Brigadier watches birds through binoculars to relax. His goal is to find a green pigeon. He calls the Police Superintendent, who is not available because he is getting his shoes shined. When the Brigadier tries to call the Public Health Department, he gets several wrong numbers. The Brigadier gets in a jeep to visit the CMO. The CMO had gone with Mr. Chawla to see Verma at the university. All the officials missed each other that morning and were not able to discuss the monkey menace. In the orchard, Sampath scolds the monkeys, who have hangovers, but he forgives them.

Chapter 16

In his family's house, the Hungry Hop boy nurses his ear, bitten by Pinky Chawla for no reason that he knows. He is babied by his family of twelve women and three men. Sampath thinks the end is coming. Either the monsoon season or the monkey problem will force his removal from the tree. He loves his monkey friends, even when they behave badly. He wants to stay in the orchard to become part of its beauty. Pinky writes a note of apology to the Hungry Hop boy. She tries to deliver it, but the house is guarded by his female relatives. She sees him sitting in the bathroom window, and taking aim with the note in a stone, hits him in the jaw. He is knocked out, and when he comes to, reads the note and is confused with feelings of love. She comes every day. His family thinks he has lost his mind and decides to marry him off, sending a message to Mr. Chawla to keep his daughter at home. Mr. Chawla lectures Pinky and orders Ammaji to be her chaperone. Ammaji has to wear tennis shoes to keep up with Pinky. After a while, Ammaji gives up. Pinky continues stalking the Hungry Hop boy, bribing the milkman to carry their notes.

Chapter 17

Sampath writes a poem, inspired by his memory of Brother John at the missionary school. He only feels close to his mother and the monkeys. The spy follows Kulfi around and begins to wonder why his mind is so full of Sampath's teachings. He feels

he is being seduced. Kulfi is bored, and keeps searching for new ingredients, realizing she has never cooked monkey! The spy loses her as she climbs into the wild mountain country, daydreaming she is a royal cook conquering the world for whatever ingredient she wants.

Chapter 18

The war with the monkeys escalates; many devotees are injured. The monkeys go freely in orchard or bazaar, and it is not safe to be out alone. There are articles on the danger of monkey bites in the papers, and the Hanuman Temple protests on behalf of the monkeys. The officials realize they are in for a severe problem. There are two camps of devotees: one that wants the monkeys destroyed, and one that wants them protected. Sampath is forgotten in the controversy. Meetings and arguments all over town disrupt the once peaceful town of Shahkot.

Chapter 19

Verma at the university works on his plan to kill the Cinema Monkey and display its carcass. He delivers this plan to the CMO and sends a copy to the new District Collector, who has not yet arrived. Verma's wife plots a separation from him because she does not approve. The Brigadier also has a plan: a firing squad of a hundred men combing the bush and discharging rifles to scare the monkeys. The CMO suggests revoking all liquor licenses. The Superintendant of Police does nothing because he is lazy. The officials go to Sampath to get his blessings for their projects; crowds of outraged citizens go along with them. Sampath cannot understand their hysteria. He can only speak to a crowd when he is happy, so he says nothing. The ugliness of the situation makes him vomit in their midst, and they leave.

Chapter 20

The new District Collector, who has authority from the central government, arrives from Delhi. Mr. Gupta, who used to work with Sampath in the post office, is appointed his secretary. Mr. Gupta meets the new District Collector at the train. He tries to explain the situation and takes the D.C. to his new home. The new D.C. is a young, untried civil servant, and his first posting was supposed to be easy. But suddenly, he is thrust into an emergency for which he is ill prepared.

Chapter 21

The D.C. is engaged in meetings with all the officials. He is terrified to look out his window and see the crowds. The evening before, he had gone to the orchard to see Sampath. Sampath and the D.C. both felt equally vulnerable to the crowd and sympathetic to one another. The Monkey Protection Society puts pressure on the D.C., who makes the Brigadier stop firing on the monkeys. Then the CMO calls, followed by angry shopkeepers who do not want their liquor licenses revoked. They hear the crowd shouting Sampath's slogans. The monkeys make another raid. Mr. Chawla approaches the D.C. with an idea to catch the monkeys and truck them off to another forest. The D.C. agrees, and adds that the Baba will have to descend from the tree temporarily while they clean up the orchard. A date is set, but Sampath says he will not descend or abandon the monkeys. Kulfi gets the strange idea of cooking a monkey on this day of clean up. Everything in the orchard now looks like the town: garbage, advertisements, people. Sampath again feels caught in a trap.

Chapter 22

The Brigadier trains his men to catch monkeys. The police are preparing the nets. In the orchard, Sampath is wondering how to escape. He is nervous and unable to sleep or eat. His mother cannot tempt him with food. On April 30, the day of the attack, she begins her great feast. Sampath stares into the mountains where there is a waterfall and no people. The monkeys play in the tree, unaware of the plotting against them.

Chapter 23

The Hungry Hop boy is trapped in his room, guarded by his relatives, who are plotting his marriage. He gets a note to Pinky, and she sends a note back proposing they escape in the Hungry Hop van on April 30 when everyone is catching monkeys. They should meet at 5 a.m. under the tamarind tree. He agrees. Pinky packs and offers to take her brother with them, but Sampath refuses. Meanwhile, the Hungry Hop boy is introduced to his bride, who turns out to be very pretty. His family promises him a car and a television, and he begins to have doubts about Pinky. On the fateful morning, he gets in his truck, still undecided, and heads to the rendezvous but is cut off in the streets by the cars and people heading toward the orchard.

Chapter 24

The D.C. gets up at 4 a.m. to join the army to go to the orchard where they plan to meet the police. When he tries to go out of his driveway, it is blocked by the belongings of the disgruntled cook, who is leaving his job. Just as the Brigadier is pulling out with his troops, he spots the green pigeon he has been looking for. He gets a net, but the pigeon gets away. He thinks this a bad omen. The D.C. catches up to the Brigadier, and they run into the CMO, who is trying to leave town on vacation. The D.C. wishes he had gone into computers instead of civil service. The Brigadier is warned not to go by Verma's house, for his wife is moving out. The cavalcade proceeds slowly until they all get blocked by the Hungry Hop van.

Chapter 25

In the orchard, Kulfi sleeps near a boiling pot, ready for the day's catch. She wakes early and goes to the forest for a spice to flavor the pot, passing the spy. Sampath is awake all night watching the beauty of the orchard. The darkness is better than human company. He sits like a Buddha, holding a perfect guava in his hand. In the van, the Hungry Hop boy is still trying to make up his mind as he drives. Pinky sees the van approach, and then, it goes away. It is weaving in and out of the traffic that is trying to get to the orchard. The spy climbs the tree right over Kulfi's pot, so he can see better. In the back of the Brigadier's jeep, the Hungry Hop boy has been tied up to keep him out of the way, as the cars and trucks go to the orchard. Mr. Chawla shouts to Sampath that they are coming. The monkeys get excited, ready to escape. The soldiers get into battle formation. Pinky finds the Hungry Hop boy tied up by the army. She is scornful, for he has let her down. Mr. Chawla goes to the tree to rescue Sampath, but it is empty. Everyone crowds around, but all they see where Sampath used to be is a large guava with a mark like Sampath's birthmark on it. The Cinema Monkey picks up the guava and leaps from the tree with the other monkeys. The monkeys travel higher and higher up the mountain. In the orchard, there is the crack of a tree branch and the spy falls into the cauldron.

CHARACTERS

Ammaji

Ammaji is Mr. Chawla's mother and Sampath's grandmother. She takes over the duties of her son's wife, since Kulfi seems to be incompetent. She does not mind this, for she does not lose her place of power in the house. Ammaji fusses over

Kulfi when she is pregnant, trying to get her to take herbs, or to sing to the baby and watch the planetary configurations. She represents the older traditional habits and lore of India, while her son is the modern trained colonial servant. She defends Sampath to the other family members, and once her son makes a business of Sampath's spiritual role, she joins in with a tea stall. She is proud of her grandson's success, which she once predicted. She is the kind of grandmother who is traditional and supportive to the younger generations, going along with her son, or granddaughter who wants to go to a movie—anything to keep the family together. In the orchard, Ammaji covers for Sampath's lapses, telling stories of his spiritual tendencies to the pilgrims.

Atheist Spy

The spy is a schoolteacher who hates his job in Shahkot and hopes to win fame as an undercover agent. Sampath Chawla is his first assignment from the Branch to Uncover Fraudulent Holy Men (BUFHM). The spy hangs around listening to Sampath's answers to questions, writing them down in his book and trying to make sense of them. He grew up in poverty and thinks he will one day win fame in the papers as an intellectual on TV. He interprets everything as a fraud because he begins in that frame of mind. He believes the country is held back by beliefs in crazy holy men, and he personally wants to champion intellectualism over religious fraud. Because he came from a poor background, he likes to identify with the upper classes. He decides to persecute Sampath because of the emptiness of his own life, but he traps himself by falling into Kulfi's cauldron while spying on her cooking.

Dr. Banerjee

Dr. Banerjee is the doctor from the bazaar clinic who tries to get Sampath down from the tree. He writes an article about monkey bites causing rabies, forcing the CMO to counter with an article saying that rabies is not a problem, so he will not have a crisis on his hands.

The Brigadier

The Brigadier is head of the local army post. He sits on a western style toilet, using his binoculars for bird watching, which soothes him. His goal, more important than his job, is to spot a green pigeon. Each morning he methodically washes a different part of his body. His soldiers seem the least interesting part of his concerns, but he does enjoy shouting at them. In the crisis, he plans a firing squad to shoot in the bush and scare off the monkeys.

Kulfi Chawla

Kulfi is the eccentric mother of the main character, Sampath. She is beautiful but comes from a crazy or eccentric family and appears to be mentally unstable herself. Mr. Chawla's mother, worried that her son would not have a wife, was responsible for the match. Kulfi had been married off in a hurry when young so her family would not be left with a mad woman. She had begun sleepwalking while eating melons and fruit. Kulfi's family marries her quickly to the Chawlas, who are a lower class. Mr. Chawla resisted the marriage at first, but his mother liked Kulfi and the dowry that would enable them to buy a refrigerator. Kulfi's hunger while pregnant is enormous and does not abate, even after she gives birth. She has dark passionate eyes, but people are uneasy looking at her. Kulfi's obsession with food, oddly enough, does not lead to her cooking or doing anything around the house. She seems bored with domestic life and sits by the window, as though she is in a cage and would like to escape. She lets Ammaji run the house. She rarely cooks; only wild and exotic food will satisfy her. She is a sort of food artist. In watching her son's retreat to the orchard, she remembers her own youth when she felt the need to escape. She knows why he is sitting in a tree; Kulfi and Sampath are the only ones in the family who understand one another. Inspired by what she takes to be Sampath's wisdom, she begins finally to cook the masterpieces that have been in her mind. Her early attempts had been foiled when she tried to steal and cook pheasants from the zoo, but in the orchard, her creativity is unleashed and she is a wild woman when she rounds up the ingredients, such as seeds, eggs, and animals. While the forest pacifies Sampath, Kulfi is stimulated and ignores warnings about snakes and scorpions. She daydreams of being a royal cook. Mr. Chawla thinks her crazy and would like to have her committed but does not do so to protect the family name. When he threatens to build a cement hermitage for Sampath, Kulfi confides her idea to Sampath that all of them could be poisoned! Sampath suspects that she once purposely made him sick on her food to get him out of school. She cooks one of every kind of creature in the forest and has to search harder and harder for new ingredients; finally, she comes up with one ingredient she has never used before: monkey!

Pinky Chawla

Pinky, the younger sister of Sampath, is a rather empty-headed teen Indian girl interested in clothes, appearances, and romance. She is embarrassed by her brother initially and only gradually feels sympathy for him. She is pretty and likes to get her own way; she is not afraid to ride the bus and stab aggressive men with her hairpin. She resents living in the orchard with her family because she cannot be part of the social scene in town. She is a dramatic and emotional young woman who insists that men follow her around. After she is rescued from the Cinema Monkey by the Hungry Hop ice cream vendor, she has more sympathy for Sampath, thinking they are both victims of life. She luxuriates in her romantic despair under Sampath's tree. She pursues the Hungry Hop boy, not sure in her adolescent confusion whether she likes him or not. She bites through his ear but is not arrested because she is the Baba's sister. She pursues the Hungry Hop boy until he agrees to run away with her but scorns him when he is unable to live up to her demands.

Mr. R. K. Chawla

Mr. R. K. Chawla is Sampath's prosaic father; he has the opposite personality of Sampath or Kulfi. He is a finicky and exact bureaucrat, the head clerk of the Reserve Bank of Shahkot. He does not like irregularities in life, so he hardly knows what to make of his wild wife and son. He gives advice to his pregnant wife, who ignores him. He has a slight build but feels a need to throw around his authority. He does everything by the clock and by the book; he is a modern Indian bureaucrat. Early on, he gives up trying to influence his crazy wife and tries to mold Sampath, which proves equally impossible. Once Sampath moves into the guava orchard, Mr. Chawla first tries to get his son healed or married, then gives up and makes a business out of the orchard holy man. He sees only the materialistic aspect of the situation, yet he believes himself to be honest. For instance, he tells himself that the bank account for his son's temple would not be for embezzling, and yet later it turns out he has been using it for personal investments. He becomes desperate when the monkeys invade and his son starts to withdraw after he proposes a cement hermitage. Mr. Chawla feels vulnerable in all the hullabaloo and comes up with the final plan to catch the monkeys.

Sampath Chawla

The son born to Kulfi and Mr. Chawla during the monsoon is the main character. He is born with a brown birthmark on his cheek and, because he came with the rains, he is called Sampath—Good Fortune. Kulfi is soothed by him. He grows up a strange boy, imaginative, and attracted, like his mother, to sensuous beauty. Also like her, he seems to get lost in the objects of his perception, becoming one with them. Thus, at the wedding of his boss's daughter, he takes the colors and textures of the wedding clothes into himself until he is drunk on the beauty and sings naked in the fountain. He could be seen either as mad or as an ecstatic mystic. Thus, in a key moment while eating a guava, he becomes the guava's sweetness and has the desire to run away. He cannot make himself do the tiresome tasks of the world any more and has little control or social sense. He climbs and stays in the guava tree in the orchard as a bid for freedom and feels this is the way life should be, peaceful and beautiful. However, soon his family and neighbors arrive to get him down. His inspired trick of telling all the people their secrets, found out from the letters he has read in the post office, leads to his being pronounced a clairvoyant holy man. People arrive to ask questions of the so-called Monkey Baba, and he obliges with aphoristic riddles that don't make complete sense but leave people satisfied with the profound wisdom. Sampath is suddenly turned around from a fool to a respected wise man, and he can't help enjoying it at first. He prefers the monkeys who settle in his tree, however, as more his type. His taming of the monkeys is seen as another miracle, for monkeys are dangerous and can wound or kill a person. When the monkeys become a drunken nuisance, everyone wants to get rid of them except for Sampath. He thinks to himself that the only people who make sense are his mad mother, the wild monkeys, and himself. He seems part monkey himself, enjoying naughty pranks and spontaneous behavior. He feels the tree in the orchard represents the first time he has truly seen life as it is—he is at one with its beauty. If he could only stay long enough, he could melt into it. As the people converge on the orchard in a moment of maximum chaos, Sampath apparently disappears as he holds a guava; like a Buddha, he is absorbed into its life force. The fruit bears a mark exactly like Sampath's birthmark.

Chief Medical Officer (CMO) of Shahkot

The Chief Medical Officer is a hypochondriac, worried about his ulcers. When they flare up, he drinks onion juice. He does not want to deal with the monkey crisis and passes it off to the biology department at the university. He is a satire on the Indian civil servant, more concerned with his own benefits than with helping the public. He wants to get promoted to get out of Shahkot, and proposes to solve the monkey problem by revoking all liquor licenses, which is a very unpopular move.

D.C.

The D.C., or District Collector, comes from Delhi to the backwater of Shahkot as his first posting. He is quiet and firm in his ideals, and is still young to government service. He is thin and weak. His father is influential in the Indian Administrative Service. He is afraid of getting a black mark on his record if he doesn't handle the crisis in Shahkot carefully without offending any group. Each official pushes his own plan to get rid of the monkeys in hopes of winning glory. Mr. Gupta from the post office becomes his secretary. It doesn't look hopeful for him; the first thing that happens is he offends his old cook, who resigns because the D.C. won't eat British chops.

District Collector

See D.C.

Mr. D.P.S.

Mr. D.P.S. is the head of the post office and is Sampath's boss. He fires Sampath during his daughter's wedding, when Sampath drops his pants in the fountain in front of the wedding guests.

Mr. Gupta

Mr. Gupta works in the post office with Sampath, and is sympathetic to Sampath when Sampath is fired. He later becomes secretary to the new District Collector, advising him on the tense situation in Shahkot.

Hungry Hop Ice Cream Boy

The Hungry Hop boy sells Kwality ice cream from a cart in front of the cinema and rescues Pinky Chawla and her grandmother from the Cinema Monkey. He is described as slow but good natured, so he doesn't understand Pinky's romantic attentions until she bites his ear in frustration. He recuperates at home, guarded by his female relatives. Pinky manages to deliver notes to him and kindle a romantic attachment. They plan to run away together, but his family tries to bribe him by marrying him off to a pretty girl. He is confused because, if he stays, life will be simple for him, but Pinky is exciting and forbidden. He sneaks out to the rendezvous with Pinky, only to be sabotaged by the forces marching on the orchard to capture the monkeys. Pinky gives up on him in disgust because he doesn't know how to play his part as the hero.

Brother John

Sampath remembers this missionary teacher of literature as his favorite teacher, dismissed for pinching the bottom of a sweeper woman. He gave Sampath his only good experience at the school by reading beautiful poetry with passion. Sampath loves the words in the poem Brother John read, and thus writes his own poem.

Miss Jyotsna

Miss Jyotsna is the pretty employee in the post office with Sampath. He was always attracted to her beauty and liked to watch her flirt. He knew from the contents of her purse how much she owed stores and used this knowledge when telling the secrets of the townspeople. Believing he is clairvoyant, she becomes a devotee of the Monkey Baba, singing hymns and telling stories of his post office days to the other devotees. She delivers his fan mail to the orchard. In the controversy over the monkeys, she sides with protecting the monkeys and hits the atheist spy with her purse.

Superintendant of Police

The Superintendant of Police loves Shahkot and accepts it as it is. He is lazy and likes to associate with his town cronies and his sexy wife, rather than wasting time in dealing with the monkeys.

Verma

Verma is the head of the Biology Department at Lady Chatterjee University, who has theories on everything, including how to solve the monkey problem by killing the leader to frighten off the others. His theories usually fail, such as the time he tried to feed sleeping pills to the monkeys, and the street urchins ate the food instead. His wife decides to leave him because she is fed up with his self-importance and his useless theories.

THEMES

Freedom from the Mundane

The primary motivation of the main character, Sampath, is to be free of the forced and false manners of life. He hates his job in the post office and goofs off, unable to make himself focus on things he doesn't like. When he loses his job for his indecent and high spirited antics at his boss's daughter's wedding, his father angrily says he will have to find him another job. Mr. Chawla is an ambitious civil servant and has no idea what ails his son or why his son is such a failure. Sampath feels everyone is conspiring to keep him in a net. "It was a prison he had been born into." He wants a natural and free life: "He wanted open spaces. And he wanted them in large swathes, in days that were clear stretches he could fill with as little as he wished."

Many of the characters have similar urges, for instance, Kulfi, Sampath's half mad and repressed mother. From the moment she is made to marry, Kulfi refuses to cooperate or perform her duties unless she wants to. As sensuously aware as Sampath, she loves color, texture, taste, and paints the walls of the house while pregnant. She imagines and cooks sumptuous dishes once she is set free from the house and can live in the forest near Sampath.

Kulfi and Sampath seem extreme in their need to be free, but other characters have needs as well. The Chief Medical Officer wants to get out of Shahkot, so he can have peace and quiet. The wife of Verma leaves him to be free of his domineering theories. The Hungry Hop boy wants to be free of his female relatives, and Pinky wants to run away from boredom.

The most freedom loving creatures are the monkeys, that come and go as they will, and create havoc, for they cannot be caught or tamed. Sampath sees them as a symbol of his own joy, swearing he will not live without them. Sampath represents the human urge to be free of constraint, without social conformity. The two conflicting urges of freedom and conformity have to be kept in balance by most adults. Sampath, however, lacks any social sense, like the monkeys. He finally runs away from home when he tastes the sweetness of a guava and feels its wildness within, thus shedding his last social conditioning. He takes up his home in a guava tree as the most natural home for him: "This was the way of riches and this was a king's life, he thought."

TOPICS FOR FURTHER STUDY

- Research the influence of English colonization in India. In terms of *Hullabaloo in the Guava Orchard*, give a class presentation in which you discuss examples of the English legacy that can be found in the town of Shahkot.

- Research the role of women and marriage customs in ancient India. Write a paper showing how ancient ideas about women are still evident in modern India and how those roles are changing. Discuss this topic in terms of the female characters in *Hullabaloo in the Guava Orchard*. Focus particularly on Pinky, Kulfi, and Ammaji, three generations of Indian women.

- Have different class members report on the various religions of India: Hinduism, Buddhism, Islam, and Christianity. Discuss the conflicts in Indian life due to religious differences, as well as the religious concepts and customs brought up or implied in the book. How do these concepts of worship and devotion differ from Western ideas? Compile a group paper on the topic.

- Write a paper on the Independence Movement in India under Mahatma Gandhi. Are any of Gandhi's values of peaceful civil disobedience innocently reflected in Sampath's behavior? Give examples from the book.

- Watch one or more of the films from Satyajit Ray's masterpiece, the "Apu Trilogy," such as *Pather Panchali*. Write an essay in which you comment on the issues of Indian life shown in the films, comparing them to those that are also mentioned in Desai's novel.

The narrative shows the forces civilization uses to keep people from having such freedom: religion, family, economics, social beliefs, and politics. Sampath simply walks away from it all. Only two kinds of people are bold enough to do this: a madman or a holy man. It is a matter of debate which one he truly is.

The Joys and Sorrows of the Imagination

Both Kulfi and Sampath suffer because they have too much imagination for the ordinary world. They find that, to get along, they have to suppress their extraordinary sensibilities, for they are aware in ways that others are asleep. Sampath has the perception of a poet or artist. He gets lost in his studies, distracted by the sound of words, or the shapes of maps.

Kulfi processes the world through taste and cooking. She is a culinary artist, searching each day for new herbs and spices, driving everyone in the orchard mad for her delicately flavored dishes. In the orchard, she alone understands Sampath's urge to live in a tree. For it is in the outdoors that her own imagination is set free: "She felt she was on the brink of something enormous." She daydreams of being a royal cook who could command the world to supply her with endless ingredients.

By contrast we have Mr. Chawla, who knows nothing in an orchard but how to make money from his son's career as a holy man. The Hungry Hop ice cream boy is similarly ignorant of the romantic interests of Pinky Chawla, who he thinks hates him when she bites his ear. She has to become the aggressor in the romance, for he does not have the imagination to keep up with her. Most of the townsfolk are interested in mere advancement in life, like the civil servants, who have their own comforts in mind and cannot see farther than their noses.

Tradition versus Modernity

The many layered life of India provides the setting of the story. The grandmother, Ammaji, is pushing traditional remedies and astrological lore on Sampath, while the father, proud of his modern banking career, and a product of the English system, castigates his mother's ignorance. He performs yoga exercises at home, then puts on Western manners and goes to work. Pinky is a teenager caught between old and new images of marriage. She wants to look like the Indian movie stars she sees on screen, and have a romantic affair, but her father wants her to be secluded, modest, and shy, like the ideal Indian woman. He cannot decide whether he wants her to go to business school or stay home. She has her own ideas; she rides the bus and pokes men who pinch her, and pursues the Hungry Hop boy.

The small town of Shahkot, like much of rural India, has electricity intermittently and an antiquated phone system that rings the wrong numbers. The barbed wire fence around the post office is vandalized and used by people who scrounge for what they need. The town moves slowly in its ways, though it has its modern face with movie house, buses, cars, and a university. If the traditional desire for religious gurus makes people see Sampath as a holy man, it also produces a modern atheist who wants to debunk the fraud and save India from the dark ages. These contradictions of old India and modern India, side by side, provide much of the humorous satire.

The Limitations of Point of View

The problem of interpretation or multiple points of view becomes a comic issue in the story as everyone has a version of who Sampath is and what to do about the monkeys in the orchard. Shirley Chew, writing in the *Times Literary Supplement*, concludes that Desai has "in hilarious and subtle ways, taught us to look again and with fresh eyes at the world we make for ourselves."

At first Mr. Chawla treats Sampath's desire to live in a tree as a sickness or madness, and he calls in a doctor, then tries Tibetan medicine, homeopathy, Ayurveda, and finally tries to marry his son off. As soon as Sampath is pronounced a holy man, Mr. Chawla changes his tune, seeing his son as a success and the orchard a commercially lucrative shrine. Miss Jyotsna, a former post office employee with Sampath, suddenly becomes Sampath's devotee; she sings hymns under his tree, and begins believing in his proverbs. By contrast, the atheist spy tries to gather evidence of a hoax. There is Pinky's point of view of her brother as a fellow sufferer in life, and the mother's and grandmother's maternal sympathy. The bureaucrats in town have different points of view on how to rid the orchard of the monkey problem, from military attack to poisoning. Sampath, on the other hand, views the monkeys as his only friends, the only creatures that make sense to him. The narrator concludes: "Sampath himself was forgotten in the fray, although his name was bounced back and forth between the warring factions like a Ping-Pong ball."

The point is that no one can comprehend the wild and free life that Sampath and the monkeys represent, because they see it from their own narrow perspective. Desai makes clashing points of view funny and demonstrative of the postcolonial

Gray Langurs perched on a tree limb (© *Theo Allofs | Corbis*)

condition of India; at the same time, she shows it is a universal trait of the human condition.

STYLE

Folk Literature

Hullabaloo in the Guava Orchard has some characteristics of folklore, part of the long tradition of oral literature that was passed from generation to generation before stories were written down. Folklore includes folk tales, fairy tales, fables, proverbs and legends. A fable is a short narrative, often with animal characters, or of a fantastic nature, that teaches morals or ethics. Examples are Aesop's fables, which contains familiar tales such as the Tortoise and the Hare (the race is not always won by the swift). India has a rich legacy of folklore and fables in the *Panchatantra* and *Jataka Tales*, for instance. The *Panchatantra* of Bidpai is set in a framework as lessons in the art of politics for princes but includes animal characters to illustrate the points. Similarly, the *Jataka Tales* teach Buddhist ethics through

animal characters, like the greedy crow. Desai's novel is set in modern India but feels like a fable with fantastic characters, the monkeys, and the hero turning into a guava. Sampath teaches in proverbs from his tree, and some of the sayings play on platitudes familiar to an Indian audience.

Satire and Folly Literature

Satire is a kind of literature using absurdity, fantasy, and nonsense to criticize society. The fool is a character who, through lack of virtue or balance, reveals the vices of society. In European tradition, the novel *The Ship of Fools* by Sebastian Brandt (1494) presents society as a collection of fools, each with a different vice. *Gulliver's Travels* by Jonathan Swift (1726) and *Candide* by Voltaire (1759) are works in the same vein. Desai, familiar with both eastern and western literature, uses this kind of narrative to create a string of fools. The administrators and citizens of the town of Shahkot, such as the Brigadier, the CMO, Verma, the biologist, the chief of police, the Hungry Hop boy, Mr. Gupta, and Sampath's father and sister all have eccentricities deemed in the normal range by society, whereas Sampath's desire to live in a tree is judged extreme. One of Desai's Indian predecessors is R. K. Narayan, who had written novels about humorous local characters in a fictional town called Malgudi, a model for Shahkot. Sampath is the name of one of Narayan's characters in his 1949 book *Mr. Sampath, A Printer of Malgudi.*

The Religious Quest

Indian literature is full of characters who leave home, like the Buddha, in search of enlightenment. In this tradition, Sampath's running away to the forest is a familiar motif, for the Indian pilgrim would renounce the world and seek a teacher or retreat. In the great Indian epic, *The Ramayana*, the prince Rama is banished to the forest to live as an ascetic for a certain number of years. In the forest, Rama and his wife meet many holy men who impart wisdom and blessings. When a demon abducts Rama's wife from their hermitage, Rama seeks help from the monkeys. Hanuman, a monkey general who is a god in disguise, helps him win a war against the demons with an army of monkeys. Once the war is won, the monkeys get drunk and tear up the forest. Hanuman is forever the sworn and devoted friend of Rama. This universally known and loved story of India has some humorous echoes in Desai's novel, with the bond between Sampath and the monkeys, and his excusing their drunken rampages. Sampath's quest for freedom ends in a sort of symbolic enlightenment as he becomes one with all life by turning into a guava. The poetry and rich appeals to the senses in traditional Indian literature are delightfully adapted by Desai in her style.

The Indian Novel in English

There is a long tradition of English writing from Indian authors, and a very rich heritage of vernacular literature as well in India's beautiful languages, such as Hindi, Urdu, Bengali, Marathi, and Tamil. Since India gained its independence in 1947, however, its writers have used the novel in English more extensively as an artistic vehicle to express the contemporary condition of their country. English, the language of their former oppressor, Great Britain, has the advantage of being a common second language for India's millions. Through the vehicle of a novel written in English, writers from diverse backgrounds, languages, and styles have been able to share their vision and memory of India. In particular, Salman Rushdie in 1981, with the publication of *Midnight's*

Children, for which he won the Booker Prize, announced a new international awareness for the secular, Indian postcolonial novel. The name of his novel refers to the children born after midnight on the day of Indian independence into a different world than the old India, and it has stuck as a name for a whole generation of writers and their way of seeing the past through critical and personal lenses. This type of novel has been used by many famous authors since the 1980s and includes such works as Arundhati Roy's *The God of Small Things* (1996) and Anita Desai's *Fasting, Feasting* (1999).

These novels have in common that they are in English, and though they use traditional references, they are secular in emphasis (without a particular religious bias), and they speak mostly of colonial or postcolonial (after independence in 1947) events. They probe the political, psychological, and historical confusion of a people who are both traditional and modern at the same time. Rushdie made famous a nonlinear style of magical realism (a blend of realism and fantasy) that could imitate the large and mythic canvas of the traditional Indian epic, while peppered with the incongruities of modern life. Other novelists use other styles, and Desai, though her tale is mythic in nature, eschews the label magical realism being applied to her work. Kiran Desai's younger generation of Indian writers is sometimes dubbed as Midnight's Grandchildren because they are a later generation than Rushdie's. This group has not only Indian tradition to draw from, but also earlier models in the Indian-English novel, from such authors as Rushdie and Kiran's mother, Anita Desai. The town of Shahkot, though made humorous with fantastic characters, still clearly exhibits the clashing values of postcolonial India.

HISTORICAL CONTEXT

Ancient India

India contains remnants of the oldest civilizations on earth; an example is, the Indus Valley Civilization dating to approximately 3,000 B.C.E. in Northern India and Pakistan, in the valley of the Indus River. It was a sophisticated urban trading culture (Harappa and Mahenjo-daro were notable cities), with developed agriculture, arts, and science. This was followed by the Vedic period when the major Hindu religious texts, the Vedas, were composed in Vedic Sanskrit during the second and first millennia B.C.E. The Vedic civilization centered around the Ganges River and the northern plains of India, producing the most familiar cultural practices of India today. Society was divided into four groups: Brahmins, or religious priests; the Kshatriyas, rulers and warriors; the Vaishyas or citizens; and the laborers or Shudras. Modern India has abolished the caste system, but there are plenty of references in Desai's novel to the lingering class distinctions. For instance, Mr. Chawla does not want his daughter Pinky to associate with the Hungry Hop boy, as he is beneath her. Kulfi was married to someone beneath her station because she was considered mad and hard to marry off.

In traditional India, the desire for the soul's liberation from its earthly rounds of reincarnation led pilgrims to renounce the world as a trap and seek a religious teacher, as the citizens of Shahkot believe Sampath to be. Such historical religious teachers as the Buddha who founded Buddhism, or Mahavira, a major figure in Jainism, are deeply revered models of non-attachment to the material world. Sitting at the feet of an enlightened teacher was considered a way to come out of suffering, and the pithy proverbs of great masters in the collection known as *Upanishads* are the familiar background for Sampath's clichés and platitudes in the guava orchard (as in the Sermon in the Guava Tree, Chapter 8).

This ancient India is still very alive in India today and pictured in the novel in the marriage customs, the family and traditional feasts, the religious beliefs, and the holy men that can still be seen everywhere, sitting under trees, by rivers, or begging for their food. The Society for the Protection of Monkeys in the novel is a humorous hit at a fundamentalism that would claim all monkeys as divine because the god Hanuman was. The ancient Indian epic, *the Ramayana*, depicts the gods coming down from heaven in the form of monkeys to help the hero Rama win a war against evil. The monkey god Hanuman was a friend of Rama's, and Hanuman is still worshipped in India today, so monkeys, like cows, could have a religious significance for some Hindus. Buddha was also said to have had an incarnation as a monkey.

British Rule

The British East India Company was given permission by a Mughal emperor in 1617 to trade in India. In protecting its trading interests, Britain used more and more military force, until it took over large areas of India and its administration, with the cooperation of local rulers. The British used the policy of Divide and Rule, thus playing off the local enmities of individual Indian states against each other, to gain a foothold. In 1857, after the rebellious Indian Mutiny, the English Crown took over the country, adding India to its empire. The British ruled in India with many trained Indians as part of their administrative staff. The upper classes of India lost their traditional power, and in order to gain advancement in the new system, Indians had to have an English education and training to get positions in the British Raj.

India's Independence

From the 1920s, leaders such as Mohandas Gandhi sought to rouse the Indian people from their colonial stupor. Gandhi taught the people to boycott English products and to make their own cloth and salt. He used the principle of non-violence to protest the presence of the British and gained a following of millions. He was miraculously able to unify all the religious factions of India, particularly the Hindus and Muslims, who were rivals. Independence was granted in 1947, with the partition of the country into largely Muslim Pakistan and Hindu India. India today retains its many religions and cultures but is a secular state, a parliamentary democratic republic modeled on the British system.

Postcolonial India

Desai's novel takes place in contemporary India as a postcolonial nation. Postcolonialism has a special meaning for the former territories of European nations. All of the countries in Africa, Asia, or the Americas that were held by European powers were drastically changed by the dominant and foreign culture. The Indian Civil Service, for example, is a remnant of the British Administrative System, and is subject to Desai's satire. The British system of administration is often seen as completely unsuitable, rigid, and laughable when applied to Indian life. All of the officials in Shahkot are ridiculous and incompetent, retaining the air and mannerisms of British lackeys. There is a chain of command, from the Police Commissioner to the District Collector, who arrives from Delhi to straighten out the hopeless mess of the locals.

The postcolonial nations often exhibit symptoms of displacement, shock, and mixed values,

Guava trees in an orchard (© *Dinodia Images* / *Alamy*)

amounting to a modern identity crisis. Because of the globalized western economy, they cannot go back to the way things were, and they cannot forget their origins. Mr. Chawla is on one side, for instance, with his Western business values, and the atheist spy is part of the secular group in India who wants to drop the old religion and be part of the modern world. The Hanuman Temple Group, on the other hand, is part of an older religious view, and the people who want to worship Sampath as a guru hark back to their sacred roots. These confusions of the old and new are made fun of in this novel. In her second novel, *The Inheritance of Loss* Desai spells out the tragic cost of fractured values to millions of postcolonial people today.

CRITICAL OVERVIEW

There was a good deal of advance publicity for *Hullabaloo in the Guava Orchard* because of Kiran Desai's literary connections. Part of the novel was

pre-published in the *New Yorker* and in Salman Rushdie's anthology of Indian writing in English, *Mirrorwork: 50 Years of Indian Writing 1947– 1997* (1997). Rushdie's pronouncement in the introduction to that anthology, that the forthcoming book was "lush and intensely imagined," set the tone for reviews when the book came out in 1998.

Zia Jaffrey, writing in the *New York Times*, was, like many, disappointed in the linear plot and ending. Nevertheless, she states that the "characters are juicy morsels" in this layered parable of India that feels like "a medieval tapestry." A reviewer writing in *Publishers Weekly* calls the author "a masterful satirist of human foibles, vanities and self-delusions." While the reviewer agrees that the plot fizzles out at the end, the critic praises Desai as "an impeccable stylist." Indeed, Desai's prose is universally admired for its beauty and sensuous detail.

Many critics cannot decide how to categorize Desai in the tradition of the Indian novel—whether she is closer to her mother, Anita Desai, or to R. K. Narayan, to Salman Rushdie, to Arundhati Roy, or whether she is a writer whose work exists apart from that of her cultural peers. Matt Condon, writing in the *Sun Herald* claims the reader may start by "groan[ing] with the familiarity" of the motifs, but that later on, the book "takes flight into often ludicrous fancy and becomes something unique." Nurjehan Aziz, writing in the *Globe and Mail*, agrees that the book presents a romantic picture of India, but the critic likens "the fabulist nature of the story and its clean lines" to R. K. Narayan's novels. Regardless, critics generally appreciate the *Hullabaloo in the Guava Orchard*'s funny and imaginative treatment of India.

CRITICISM

Susan Andersen

Andersen holds a Ph.D. in English and teaches literature and writing. In this essay on Hullabaloo in the Guava Orchard, *she discusses the main character of the novel as an example of a literary device, that of the wise fool.*

Hullabaloo in the Guava Orchard highlights all sorts of foolish characters in Desai's satirical look at a small town in contemporary North India. Everyone from the Brigadier to Pinky Chawla represents some sort of human illusion or folly. Sampath Chawla is also a fool, yet he is a wise fool. In his naïveté, his thoughts and actions are unwittingly clever. Sampath shows, through his innocent bid for freedom, how unnecessarily binding the constraints of society truly are. He is the touchstone that reveals the hypocrisy of his culture.

Sampath's flight from his society to a guava tree is humorously treated by Desai, yet there is a serious core to it that puts Sampath in the company of other wise fools. The tradition of the spiritual quest is both parodied and taken seriously, for it has much in common with the artist's quest. Furthermore, Sampath is certainly a religious humbug (as the spy from the Atheist Society tries to show), though the role of a holy man has been forced upon him. Sampath prefers to be left alone. He articulates a genuine human aspiration for freedom and joy, as well as simplicity in life and the ability to live in the present moment.

Sampath's yearning to be rid of the distractions of life is interpreted variously as religion,

WHAT DO I READ NEXT?

- *The Empire Writes Back: Theory and Practice in Post-Colonial Literatures* (2nd edition; 2002), by Bill Ashcroft, Gareth Griffiths, and Helen Tiffin, has chapters defining post-colonial literature (a term applying to literature produced by the citizens or former citizens of countries that were once colonized by the British) and proposing models for cross-cultural criticism. It includes discussion of postcolonial works, such as those by V. S. Naipaul and R. K. Narayan.

- Anita Desai's *Clear Light of Day* (2000), a Booker Prize finalist, is a novel by Kiran's mother about the process of self-understanding. It is set in India and tells the story of four children in the Das family who have grown up and grown apart.

- Kiran Desai's second novel, *The Inheritance of Loss* (2006), won the prestigious Booker Prize for fiction. It is set in both New York and Nepal in the 1980s, and it follows the lives of characters who immigrate to New York, as well as those who stay in their volatile homeland of Nepal.

- Jerzy Kosinski's *Being There* (1970) portrays Chance, the simpleton gardener who is reminiscent of Sampath. Chance's gardening advice is seen by other characters as profound wisdom.

- R. K. Narayan's *The Guide* (1958) is a predecessor for Shahkot's hullabaloo. The novel portrays Raju, a corrupt Indian tourist guide who has just been released from prison. Raju is mistaken by a peasant for a holy man, thus obliging him to play the part.

rebellion, madness, or illness by the other characters. Indeed, Sampath's interactions in the village of Shahkot present a humorous critique of many Indian institutions. All the contradictions of religious and social boundaries that keep the people, as Sampath feels, in a prison, are rejected

> SAMPATH SITS SERENELY IN THE MIDDLE OF THE HULLABALOO WHILE THOSE AROUND HIM SELF-DESTRUCT IN THEIR OWN ILLUSIONS. IN THIS WAY, HE IS TRULY A WISE FOOL."

by him: "He thought of how he was leaving the world, a world that made its endless revolutions towards nothing." Because of this, Sampath is perceived as either a holy man or a lunatic. The pronouncement of his holiness depends on a series of funny misunderstandings, including the assumption that he is celibate when in reality he merely feels that the woman foisted on him for a wife is repulsive. His true malady is totally missed by everyone except Kulfi, who suffers from the same claustrophobia as her son.

Kulfi's protest against her own stifled life is simply to withdraw. She does not participate in the household chores but leaves them to the grandmother, Ammaji. Sampath, however, reaches a crisis in which he must do something more, for he cannot bear another job after he gets fired. Kulfi tries to soothe him by offering to make him an egg. Sampath replies: "I do not want an egg ... I want my freedom." After Kulfi has put a guava in his hand, "he wished he could absorb all its coolness, all its quiet and stillness into him." And then in a fantastic moment, he gets his wish and begins to expand "with a cool greenness" and "wild sweetness." This is his inspiration to run off to the guava orchard.

There, his quest to become a part of beauty continues, as he sits in his tree, despite the hullabaloo with his family, the pilgrims, and the monkeys below. Though none of the characters are seen as evil, most are petty and unimaginative. There are, for example, the town officials who come up with lame schemes to get rid of the monkeys, and the Hungry Hop boy, who can think of nothing more than selling ice cream or having a TV set and a new car. Sampath, however, is the fool who wants the freedom to become a guava, a feat which he accomplishes in the last scene.

From Sampath's point of view, his quest to become one with beauty is fulfilled. In his tree "he felt weightless ... rocked by this lambent light." He is more and more thirsty for the world's loveliness, but the more he reaches for it, the more it escapes from him. He decides it must "reach out and claim him instead." And it finally does. In the last night in the orchard, Sampath seems to have what might be called Buddha's experience of *samadhi*, or oneness with the universe. He is the Buddha in the tree, instead of beneath the tree: "He could let all [the dark's] whisperings, all its shades of violet, float into him. This impersonal darkness could be comforting as no human attention ever was." Then he picks a guava with a "Perfect Buddha shape." In the morning, he is gone, and only the guava bearing Sampath's birthmark remains. Is Sampath's transformation simply a foolish parody, or the echo of ancient Indian stories?

Sampath's proverbial non sequiturs highlight his role as a wise fool. When a pilgrim asks about the best way to realize God, Sampath answers: "Some people can only digest fish cooked in a light curry. Others are of a sour disposition." The people accept his sayings as allegorical truth, but they puzzle over the interpretation of such difficult maxims as "first a chikoo is raw ... if you do not pick and eat it quickly, it will soon rot and turn to alcohol." The narrator records the confusion: "What was he saying? That the time of perfection passes, that you should eat a chikoo at the right time only?" In addition, Sampath's protection of the monkeys is seen by the religious fanatics as support for the divinity of monkeys. On the other hand, the atheist spy, hoping to prove that Sampath is a fraud, can only repeat Sampath's wacky sayings, thus appearing to be foolish himself. Sampath sits serenely in the middle of the hullabaloo while those around him self-destruct in their own illusions. In this way, he is truly a wise fool.

The contrast of Sampath's world of imagination and the petty ugliness of modern Indian life becomes more and more glaring as the orchard is turned into a commercial nightmare with ads, blaring PA systems, busloads of visitors, drunken monkeys, and the constant interruption by people asking Sampath questions about their lives. Chapter 19 goes back and forth between Sampath as he looks at the precious objects in his tin can—a spider, feathers, seeds, a moth—and the soldiers and officials who surround the orchard in this perceived crisis, one which has been created by their own folly. Sampath is part monkey, part guava; he is a fool, but he is wiser than the fools he leaves behind.

Source: Susan Andersen, Critical Essay on *Hullabaloo in the Guava Orchard*, in *Novels for Students*, Gale, Cengage Learning, 2009.

Amitava Kumar

In the following excerpt, Kumar discusses Desai's Hullaballoo in the Guava Orchard *in the context of other well-known Indian writers.*

Paul Theroux once complained that in V. S. Naipaul's *India: A Million Mutinies Now* (1990), "There is no smell, no heat or dust, no sweating men, no lisping saris, no honking traffic, nothing except the sound of yakking Indians." There are by now nearly one billion of those "yakking Indians" in the world—although Theroux's long, entertaining, damning book about Naipaul is hardly the best place to hear them.

In *Sir Vidia's Shadow* (1998), Indians utter charming phrases like, "I am not knowing, sir"; I don't recall a single Indian from Theroux's book who didn't speak in funny, *babu* English. While Naipaul often wrote about intriguing and sophisticated people like Mallika, the Muslim widow of the Dalit poet Namdeo Dhasal, Theroux seems to think that India is best glimpsed in endless descriptions of urban clamor. In fact, Theroux rarely bothers to talk with the Indians he meets, and his conclusions about them always have to do with caste. He follows this rule with everyone; Naipaul himself is no more exempt than the Brahman beggar by the roadside. In a passage that would shame even the colonial anthropologist of a bygone era, Theroux—undaunted by the nuances of personality, or even culture—perceives an essential Indian identity in his literary hero. "It had taken me a long time to understand that Vidia was not in any sense English, not even Anglicized, but Indian to the core—caste conscious, race conscious, a food fanatic, precious in his fears from worrying about his body being 'tainted.'"

Theroux's cartoonish visions of India stay with him no matter how far he journeys from the subcontinent. In London, his erstwhile mentor seems suddenly pathetic:

> *Vidia on a London street was less likely a Nobel Prize candidate than a shopkeeper, the very dukawallah he despaired of: a London news-agent hurrying from the bank back to his shop, where he hawked cigarettes, chewing gum, and the daily newspapers, keeping the tit-and-bum magazines an the top shelf. That place was now a national institution, known throughout Britain as "the Paki shop."*

BUT DESAI—LIKE RUSHDIE—LACKS ANY SENSE OF SOCIAL ENGAGEMENT, AND SHE IS QUICK TO PATHOLOGIZE KULFI'S NONCONFORMITY."

By forcefully recreating the well-known British stereotype of the indian shopkeeper, Theroux shows his sympathy for Naipaul's troubled encounter with the West. But this seemingly compassionate description conceals an ambiguous insult: in sketching the portrait of an anonymous Indian scuttling along, is Theroux bringing down the writer or the shopkeeper? Or both?

Theroux's brand of casually chauvinistic insight is actually a sign of willful and obstinate ignorance. It's almost enough to make the reader nostalgic for Naipaul's arrogant knowingness: even in his most uncharitable moments, Naipaul has never presumed to speak for anyone else. In one passage from *Sir Vidia's Shadow*, Naipaul expresses his contempt for the writer who would try to serve as a spokesman. "He is just bringing news," Naipaul says. "That is what he does. Brings news from Nottingham, from working-class people. It's not writing, really. It's news. Don't be that sort of writer, bringing news."

That's not bad advice. Many writers would do well to take it to heart—especially the new generation of Indian writers whose faces are so resolutely turned toward the West. In simply bringing news, these writers produce bad books. Worse still, forgetting the manners taught in the English-language convent schools that they all no doubt attended, these writers reveal their distaste for the poor and weak around whom they cannot help but wrap the eight arms of their narratives.

In the summer of 1998, India—and then Pakistan—suddenly exploded on the front pages of the newspapers around the world. The nuclear bomb tests were the culmination of a heady season of self-assertion, a year during which the fiftieth anniversary of Indian and Pakistani independence came to life in a flurry of literary acclaim. By December, it was clear that South Asia's literary stable was even more fearsome than its atomic arsenal. Breathless, magazines like the *New Republic* almost begged for mercy:

Macaulay, who said that "a single shelf of a good European library is worth the whole native literature of India," has been paid back for his ignorant denigration of Indian literature: he has been pelted with masterpieces. His punishment has taken a form which he could not have imagined, the vivid prosperity of an Indian literature, and a Pakistani literature, written in Macaulay's own language.

This sudden attention was certainly not unwelcome. In the ice-cream parlors of New Delhi, a lot of Indians were happy to receive so much notice in the pages of the *New Republic*, the *New Yorker*, or the *Atlantic*. The literary magazine *Granta* even saw fit to send a reporter to my own little-noticed hometown, Patna. There, an intrepid Brit found Mistah Kurtz in the figure of our chief minister, Laloo Prasad Yadav. Apparently, "Laloo" took *Granta*'s emissary for a walk through his vegetable garden and offered friendly dietary information: "'This is satthu,' he said. 'Very good for wind.'"

Such characters also appeared in the Indian fiction that appeared in the same magazines at around the same time. As these magazines are all published in English, the Western reader could be forgiven for believing that Indians write only in English. In fact, some Indians seem to believe this, too: Salman Rushdie added grist to the anglophone mill with his infamous claim that Indian literature in English far exceeds in quality Indian literature in all other languages. He has admitted that he doesn't know those other languages, and that there have been problems with translation, but none of this troubles him overmuch. Rushdie fervently believes "that India's encounter with the English language continues to give birth to new children," and as proof he offers Kiran Desai's debut novel, *Hullabaloo in the Guava Orchard* (1998). Her book has lots of heat and dust, sweating men, lisping saris, and honking traffic, as well as plenty of yakking Indians. Too many, perhaps: in order to escape them, Sampath—the novel's verbose, daydreaming hero—climbs up a tree and finds himself suddenly transformed into a holy man. Salman Rushdie, meet Deepak Chopra.

Sampath wants to escape the "ugly sea of humanity" and find refuge in a world "where there was not a trace of civilization." He offers mindless platitudes, some of which were culled by the author from *Bhargava's Standard Illustrated Dictionary of the Hindi Language*: "Dab your mouth with honey and you will get plenty of flies ... Sweep before your own door ... Many a pickle makes a mickle ...

Talk of chalk and hear about cheese." Eccentrics are numerous in the novel, and all events remain odd but harmless. Like the reporter from *Granta* visiting Patna, Desai offers the reader a comforting assortment of quaint folks: no poets or historians, union leaders, female doctors, teachers, people filled with purpose. Desai's characters lead sheltered lives, far removed from the unsightly world of GATT debates and nuclear bombs. Mainly inoffensive and mildly cretinous, the Indians in her novel pose no threat to anyone, least of all to the West.

Even before she published the novel, Desai (along with her mother, Anita, and, of course, Salman Rushdie) was among the eleven writers tagged as "India's leading novelists" in a group portrait in the *New Yorker*'s 1997 Indian Fiction issue. Now that we have the book, we may well ask: Where's the hullabaloo? Indeed, there is nothing in her novel that exceeds the mannered fabulism of R. K. Narayan, a style that charmed readers for decades before Rushdie gave it the poison of history to drink and—overnight!—it grew a tail and claws. *Hullabaloo in the Guava Orchard* never quite escapes this monstrous moral economy of the pleasant.

In spite of her Narayan-like fascination with the pastoral, Desai—like Rushdie—seems most interested in social dysfunction. She zeroes in on Sampath's mother, Kulfi, who is suffocating beneath flowering neuroses and private grief. The novel even offers a couple of remarkable passages on the institution of marriage and the demands it can make on women in India; on the two or three best pages of her novel, Desai mocks both Jane Austen and the *Manu Smriti*, the antiquated Hindu code of law. At this point, the reader might eagerly anticipate a moving story about the perils of gender in India. But Desai—like Rushdie—lacks any sense of social engagement, and she is quick to pathologize Kulfi's nonconformity. Like Sufiya Zenobia Shakil in Rushdie's *Shame* (1983), Kulfi is quickly condemned to murderous zeal and madness. It is soon revealed that Kulfi's whole family is plagued by mental illness; the narrative finally tames her by giving her a stove of her own. Don't worry, cook curry.

Desai also borrows Rushdie's unease about the people who inhabit the subcontinent: in *The Moor's Last Sigh* (1995), Rushdie portrayed a rural populace thirsty for blood. In his strange, dreadful India, anyone who lives outside the city's civilizing walls is condemned to a life of barbarity. Indian villagers are portrayed as zealous Hindus who worship the god Ram, even though all the recent riots in India have taken place in urban areas:

> In the city we are for secular India but the village is for Ram. And they say Ishwar and Allah is your name but they don't mean it, they mean only Ram himself, king of Raghu clan, purifier of sinners along with Sita. In the end I am afraid the villagers will march on the cities and people like us will have to lock our doors and there will come a Battering Ram.

This can only be understood as the dismay and ignorance of a distant cosmopolitan. Desai, on the other hand, avoids this problem by evading the issue entirely: *Hullabaloo in the Guava Orchard* is too serene to touch, on riots or anything else more raucous than a *tamasha* caused by drunken monkeys on a rampage. If Rushdie's fantasies betray his fears, Desai's novel is a bit too sanitized not to raise suspicion. Where have all the people gone?

With the masses missing in action, can language itself—delicate and lyrical, filling a cupboard with spices and fauna—provide safe haven from the rough forces of social upheaval? Desai's language, in any case, is not quite up to the task; her characters seem asphyxiated in their unlikely, pretty, empty India. When he feels cornered at the novel's end, Sampath pukes on his cot. And, then, like the fabled Indian performing his rope trick, he vanishes into thin air. His mother Kulfi keeps on cooking, bent on completing her quest to find a monkey to put in her pot. The one person who remains skeptical of Sampath is identified only as "the atheist." At the novel's conclusion, he meets his end by accidentally falling into Kulfi's simmering vindaloo. The critic, in effect, is shown to be a monkey.

This was the only lesson I could retrieve from Desai's novel: when it comes to deciding the fate of critics, even genteel plots can take a surprisingly chilling, brutal turn.

... Last summer, I watched Farhad Asghar perform at the Papp Public Theater with South Asian youth from Elmhurst, Queens. Asghar's skit was about the Number Seven Train in New York City, a train that "starts out in Flushing, Queens, a very Asian community, picking up more Asians and other people of color along the way ... My trips on the train," Asghar says, "showed ... me how the city was segregated." In "The Seven Right before Seven," Asghar treats us to a kind of travel narrative that is strikingly different from Paul Theroux's concoctions:

> We stand here waiting for a train to take us somewhere where we can make someone else rich, the physical manifestation of the Marxist argument, I see brown, yellow, black and even a little white ... waiting ... for this metaphorical train to take us into the fulfillment of the American dream... Knowing all too well we'll just be coming back nine, twelve, sixteen hours later, too tired to dream at all.

In words like these, literature that has its history in the Indian subcontinent comes into its own, even when describing something as alien to those distant origins as the New York City subway. Unlike so much Indian writing in the West, "The Seven Right before Seven" asserts its links with the Safdar Hashmis and Paul Gomras of the Indian subcontinent—both murdered on the highway, going somewhere else.

I've been told that in postcolonial writing, as in real estate, location is everything. In both cases, the aphorism holds true, but only insofar as your location determines your neighbors. It's not so much whether you are writing in New Delhi or New York; it's for whom and with whom you are writing that truly matters. One of my favorite parts of Theroux's *Sir Vidia's Shadow* was an account of Naipaul talking about himself and his brother, the late Shiva Naipaul:

> If we were addressing audiences of people like ourselves, we would have been different writers. I am always aware of writing in a vacuum, almost always for myself, and almost not having an audience. That wonderful relationship that I felt an American writer would always have with his American readers, or a French writer with his French readers—I was always writing for people who were indifferent to my material.

Ah, readers ... to think that a literate critical mass could have saved us from the truth of those words, however disingenuous they may be. To think that an audience of "people like ourselves" could have made Theroux's easy disdain for yakking Indians so much more superfluous! Perhaps only an audience of "ourselves" can relieve us from the shopworn mannerisms—and from the desperate yearning for authenticity—that characterizes so much of what passes for Indian writing in the West.

Source: Amitava Kumar, "Louder Than Bombs," in *Transition*, Vol. 79, 1999, pp. 80–101.

Philip Marchand

In the following article, Anita and Kiran Desai are interviewed as they prepare for a joint reading of their novels in Toronto. Marchand also provides biographical detail on Kiran Desai and discusses Hullaballoo in the Guava Orchard.

Literary history is full of father-son novelist pairings, and various combinations of siblings who wrote novels. So far, however, there have been few cases of a mother and a daughter who both happen to be novelists.

Certainly the appearance of novelist Anita Desai and her daughter Kiran Desai tonight at 8 at the Brigantine Room, 235 Queens Quay W. is a first for the Harbourfront Reading Series.

Relations between father and son novelists—Kingsley and Martin Amis are an instance—are usually coloured with at least a hint of Oedipal rivalry. Anita and Kiran Desai, however, seem completely comfortable appearing together. The soft-spoken Anita Desai, 60, one of India's foremost novelists writing in English, gives new meaning, in fact, to the over-used words "nurturing" and "supportive."

She encouraged her daughter, who initially was a science major at Bennington College in Vermont, to venture into literature. "I've been telling her for years that she wrote so well, and that she should take up writing, but she wasn't interested at all," she says. That disinterest ended when Kiran took a creative writing course at Bennington— "just as a change," Kiran says— and discovered she really did love literature.

On her part, Kiran Desai, 26, author of the recently published novel, *Hullabaloo In The Guava Orchard* (Publishers Group), not only feels no pressure being the daughter of a famous writer, but candidly admits the family name was a help getting published. "In some ways, it's been easier for me because of the connection," she says. People know the name."

Indeed they do. The novels of the elder Desai, including *Cry, The Peacock* and *The Clear Light Of Day*, were among the first to show readers outside India the inhabitants of that country from the point of view of someone who was not a part of a dying British Raj. Desai's female characters were particularly vivid, and something of the mother's feminism informs Kiran's novel, as well—there are numerous reminders in the story of the country's cultural bias in favour of males.

But *Hullabaloo In The Guava Orchard* is a comedy and not a polemic. Its hapless hero, one Sampath Chawla, climbs a guava tree one day in search of a quiet retreat, and immediately gains a reputation as a holy man. Crowds flock to hear his wisdom. A member of the national Atheist Society attempts to expose him as a charlatan.

The novel sides neither with the religious seekers nor the would-be debunker. "I wanted to show as many angles as I could, to allow everyone his or her own voice," Kiran says. "It's such a complex business. I don't have any right answer or any kind of simple answer. I certainly don't want to come out with a statement at the end of it all. I don't want to write a moral tale."

Many critics have used the label "magic realism" to describe the narrative, and there is something akin to the mythic, larger than life touches of a Gabriel Garcia Marquez in many of the characters and incidents. Kiran concedes that she likes the work of Marquez, but avoids the magic realist label—if there is a connection between her novel and the works of Marquez, it is the link between the cultures of India and Marquez's Colombia. Both are permeated with the supernatural and the preternatural. "The novel isn't as surreal or bizarre a book as it seems to western readers," Kiran says. "I think a lot of it is taken from reality."

"It's very realistic," her mother points out. There was a real hermit who sat in a tree in India. People used to go to him from all over. He would put his foot on their heads as a form of blessing."

Kiran laughs incredulously. "He put his dirty feet on their heads?"

"Even Indira Gandhi went to him," Anita says.

"One time a man was going to ask him a blessing, and he was in a bad mood, he wanted to be left alone, and he just opened his mouth and let out a stream of filthy abuse."

"That's in the (Hindu) tradition, too," Kiran adds.

"There's a temple in India you can go to, not to pray, but to abuse and curse the gods."

Although the Desais keep a home in Delhi, India, and travel on an Indian passport, both mother and daughter are thoroughly cosmopolitan.

Anita Desai, whose mother was German, teaches a creative writing course at the Massachusetts Institute of Technology.

Kiran, who was raised in India, has also studied abroad since she was an adolescent, returning to her native country during school vacations.

Currently she is finishing a master's degree in creative writing at Columbia University in New York City—*Hullabaloo In The Guava Orchard* is the equivalent of her master's thesis.

This has contributed to a sense, on the part of both mother and daughter, of being of an outsider in their native India—a sense that is often an essential part of a writer's equipment.

Certainly Kiran feels that her distance from India helped her to write the novel.

"I think it freed up my imagination," she says.

"The reality of life in India can be very overwhelming."

Source: Philip Marchand, "Writer Inspired by Mom," in *Toronto Star*, June 10, 1998, 2 pp.

Elizabeth Renzetti

In the following interview and profile, mother and daughter novelists Anita and Kiran Desai converse about characteristics of India and Hullaballoo in the Guava Orchard.

On a busy street in downtown Toronto, vendors peddle small bits of India—mehndi skin-painting kits, ornate silver earrings—to liven up the drab Western palette.

Inside a nearby restaurant sits the real thing. Two women wrapped in glowing saris—teacher and student, mother and daughter, novelists both—are discussing the exotic allure of their homeland. Or, more precisely, their homeland doesn't seem very glamorous at all when viewed through the lens of long acquaintance.

"What's exotic here is not exotic in India," says Kiren [sic, et al] Desai, 26, who has just produced her first novel, *Hulabaloo in the Guava Orchard*. "People might think, 'Oh, a guava is so exotic.' But in India it's nothing. You eat it all the time."

Next to her, listening carefully to every word, sits her mother, novelist and teacher Anita Desai. Anita published her first book, *Cry, the Peacock*, when she was 25, long before Kiren was born. Now, at 62, she has four children, nine novels, two Booker Prize nominations, one professorship in creative writing at Massachusetts Institute of Technology, and no advice for her daughter.

"Oh no, no," she says in her silk-quiet voice, when asked if she gave Kiren the benefit of her professional wisdom. "She went around asking how she should end the book. We said all the

most predictable, banal things. But her ending was something specific to her. It took me completely by surprise."

The ending of *Hullabaloo*, a satirical fable about religious devotion and domestic strife, will take most people by surprise—unless they read the piece in The Wall Street Journal proclaiming it one of the must-read books of the summer. (The article gives away the surreal ending.)

Kiren has not heard that she's been lauded in the pages of the foremost business paper in the United States, but it is only the latest turn in the great publicity wheel on which she hopes she won't be broken.

"I'm not a natural performer," she says with a sigh as she contemplates having to read publicly tonight. "It's so totally different from the writing life. I feel sometimes as if I'm in a whole different incarnation. When you're writing you live so quietly, like a mouse."

Anita, watching her daughter, nods: "It's two different worlds that you have to live in—the completely private, almost secret one, when you're writing, then this public one. It can be quite against the grain."

Especially for these two, as shy and soft-spoken as they are. Kiren, who interrupted her studies in creative writing at Columbia University in New York to finish her novel, is somewhat more giggly and vocal, and vibrant in her silver earrings and emerald sari.

They have never read together before: tonight's performance at Harbourfront in Toronto will be their first. "I am so terrified of reading," Kiren says. She gets little consolation from her mother, who adds, "so am I." When it's suggested that perhaps they can provide comfort for each other, Anita raises one eloquently skeptical eyebrow.

Anita will read from her 1997 novel, *A Journey to Ithaca*, the tale of a mismatched young European couple on a thwarted quest for enlightenment in India. The spiritual journey, the overwhelming need to believe—even in its most fraudulent form—is also at the heart of Kiren's novel, though hers is told with a more surreal, comic bent.

It's a preoccupation that can't be avoided in India, says Kiren, even in an non-religious household like the Desais' (both mother and daughter split their time between the United States and Delhi). "My family isn't religious," says Kiren, the youngest of four. "That's very unusual in India, so I think I was always very aware of this big secret I was not part of."

Adds her mother, "There's such feeling that if you're writing about India, about contemporary India, you have to tackle contemporary themes like politics. But really, every move you make in India is based on religion and philosophy."

Also, apparently, on the fantastic, other-worldly nature of much of Indian folklore and literature. Kiren's novel draws heavily on this tradition, although she swears that the some of the novel's most absurd passages—like the pack of monkeys who become alcoholics and rampage through the countryside—are absolutely true. There appears to be some debate between mother and daughter about whether the drunken mammals were in reality monkeys or elephants—although the debate itself sets them laughing.

Says Anita, "There was an elephant tribe that was notorious because it got very addicted to alcohol. They would go to the army barracks, break into the bar and drink their rum."

During the writing, the young novelist was far removed from the lush guava orchard in which her first novel is set. Kiren, who is single, wrote much of her book at her mother's kitchen table in Boston; Anita's early writing years were squeezed into the few hours when her four children were at school. "When you have so little time, it's precious. I wrote much more in those years than I do now." She smiles at her daughter. "Now the urgency is gone."

When Anita set out to hook a publisher, she had to cast her line as far as Britain, because "there weren't Indian publishers interested in what we were doing... They weren't interested in finding Indian writers. Now, there are so many publishers." Indian literature has become so hot, Kiren laughs, that everyone she talks to in Delhi claims to be writing a book.

Source: Elizabeth Renzetti, "'Like Mother, Like Daughter In Person,'" in *Globe and Mail*, June 10, 1998, p. E3.

SOURCES

Anandan, Prathima, Review of *Hullabaloo in the Guava Orchard*, in *Contemporary South Asia*, Vol. 8, No. 3, November 1999, pp. 386–87.

Aziz, Nurjehan, Review of *Hullabaloo in the Guava Orchard*, in the *Globe and Mail*, June 13, 1998, p. D14.

Chaudhuri, Amit, Introduction, in *The Picador Book of Modern Indian Literature*, Picador, 2001, pp. XVII–XXXI.

Chew, Shirley, "The Wise Man Sitting in a Tree," in *Times Literary Supplement*, May 15, 1998, p. 21.

Condon, Matt, Review of *Hullabaloo in the Guava Orchard*, in the *Sun Herald* (Sydney, Australia), September 5, 1999, p. 31.

Desai, Kiran, *Hullabaloo in the Guava Orchard*, Atlantic Monthly Press, 1998.

Jaffrey, Zia, "The Prophet in the Tree," in the *New York Times*, July 19, 1998.

Marchand, Philip, "Writer Inspired by Mom," in the *Toronto Star*, June 10, 1998, p. E1.

Review of *Hullabaloo in the Guava Orchard*, in *Publishers Weekly*, March 23, 1998, p. 77.

Rushdie, Salman, Introduction, in *Mirrorwork: 50 Years of Indian Writing 1947–1997*, edited by Salman Rushdie and Elizabeth West, Henry Holt, 1997, p. XX.

Smith, Dinitia, "Kiran Desai's India and Its Great Divides," in the *International Herald Tribune*, October 25, 2006, p. 9.

Stevenson, Helen, Review of *Hullabaloo in the Guava Orchard*, in the *Guardian*, June 6, 1998, p. 10.

FURTHER READING

Buck, William, *Ramayana: King Rama's Way: Valmiki's Ramayana Told in English Prose*, University of California Press, 1974.
   This very readable novel version of the most famous story in India is about the exile of King Rama and his alliance with the monkeys against the forces of evil.

Gandhi, Mahatma, *The Essential Gandhi: An Anthology of His Writings on His Life, Work, and Ideas*, edited by Louis Fischer, Vintage, 2002.
   The philosophy of peaceful resistance to tyranny is both wise and foolish, like Sampath's protest. Nonviolent resistance was so powerful in Gandhi's hands that it helped India gain its independence in 1947 and later inspired Dr. Martin Luther King Jr.'s course of action during the Civil Rights Movement in the United States.

Mehrotra, Arvind Krishna, ed., *The Illustrated History of Indian Literature in English*, Permanent Black Publishing, 2003.
   This book contains a discussion of major authors and periods, bringing a great deal of perspective to Indian writing in English.

Radhakrishnan, Sarvepalli, and Charles A. Moore, eds., *A Source Book in Indian Philosophy*, Princeton University Press, 1967.
   Along with explanatory notes, this collection provides an overview of the ancient Hindu ideas that inform Desai's novel.

Nervous Conditions

TSITSI DANGAREMBGA

1988

Nervous Conditions, a novel by Zimbabwean author Tsitsi Dangarembga, was first published in 1988, and is currently available in a 2004 edition. Set over a period of about ten years, from the 1960s to the early 1970s, *Nervous Conditions* takes place in Zimbabwe before the country had attained official independence from Britain and while it was still known as Southern Rhodesia or simply Rhodesia. The novel is semi-autobiographical; the author draws on her own experience of growing up in Rhodesia during that period. *Nervous Conditions* centers around the experience of several female characters as they either challenge, or come to terms with, the traditional patriarchal structure of their society. The young narrator, Tambu, must show great determination as she overcomes all the obstacles to her progress in life. She also has to learn how to understand, largely through the difficult experiences of her cousin Nyasha, the negative effects that British colonialism has had on her society.

One of the few novels written by a black Zimbabwean about this transitional time in Zimbabwe's history, *Nervous Conditions* gives valuable insight into the traditional life of the country's native Shona-speaking people. The novel is an important contribution to postcolonial literature, a term that refers to works by authors from countries formerly colonized by European governments.

AUTHOR BIOGRAPHY

Tsitsi Dangarembga was born in 1959 in Mukoto, in the African country then known as Southern Rhodesia, and now known as Zimbabwe. At the time, Rhodesia was a British colony. At the age of two, Dangarembga moved with her family to Britain, where she remained until she was six years old, after which she returned to Rhodesia and attended a missionary school in the city of Umtali, which is now called Mutare.

In the 1970s, Dangarembga returned to Britain, attending Cambridge University, where she studied medicine. However, Dangarembga became homesick in England and returned to her home country in 1980, the year in which Zimbabwe finally attained its independence from Britain. Dangarembga continued her education, studying psychology at the University of Zimbabwe and becoming active in the student drama club. She found she had a talent for writing plays, and a number of her plays were produced at the university. These included *The Lost of the Soil* (1983), which she also directed. Dangarembga then became involved in a theater group called Zambuko. In 1987, Dangarembga's play *She No Longer Weeps* was published in Harare.

Dangarembga had also developed an interest in writing prose fiction. In 1985, her short story "The Letter" was published in *Whispering Land: An Anthology of Stories by African Women*. Her major success followed three years later with the publication of her semi-autobiographical novel, *Nervous Conditions*, which was the first novel to be published in English by a black woman from Zimbabwe. It was published in England in 1988 and in the United States in 1989. In 1989, the novel won the African section of the Commonwealth Writers Prize.

Following this success, Dangarembga pursued an interest in film, studying film direction in Berlin at the Deutsche Film und Fernseh Akademie. Also during this period, Dangarembga made a documentary for German television. Then she made a film called *Everyone's Child* (1996), about the fate of four siblings after their parents die of AIDS. The film was another landmark in the cultural history of Zimbabwe, since it was the first feature film directed by a black woman in that country. *Everyone's Child* was shown at many film festivals around the world.

In 2006, Dangarembga published *The Book of Not*, a sequel to *Nervous Conditions*. As of 2008, Dangarembga lived in Harare, Zimbabwe.

PLOT SUMMARY

Chapter 1

Nervous Conditions is set in the African country then known as Rhodesia in the early 1960s. The narrator and protagonist is a young black woman named Tambu, who looks back on her experiences as a child and adolescent. She begins by mentioning that she was not sorry when her elder brother Nhamo died in 1968, when she was thirteen. Since 1965, he had been attending a Protestant Christian mission school some twenty miles from the family's village. His English-educated uncle, Babamukuru, is the headmaster of the school and wanted Nhamo to attend it so he could have a good education and then raise his family up from poverty. But after Nhamo began attending the mission school, he did not like coming home, and he was reluctant to take on chores such as helping in the fields or with the livestock or firewood. The only times he would willingly help were when his uncle came to visit.

Tambu relates how she did not get along with her brother, who used to try to get his sisters, including the younger one, Netsai, to do errands for him. He felt he had more power and authority than they did. Tambu preferred life when he was not around but she felt guilty about her dislike of him. What she really disliked was the fact that her brother's education had received priority over her own. This was the norm in her family; the concerns of the males were considered more important than those of the females.

Chapter 2

Tambu tells of how the family is so poor soon after she starts school at the age of seven that they cannot afford the school fees. Her mother manages to scrape some money together by selling eggs and vegetables, but this is only enough to continue Nhamo's schooling. Disappointed, Tambu had to remain at home. Her father told her she should not mind since, as a girl, all she needed to know was how to cook and clean. Tambu protests, and refuses to give up her goal of going to school. She grows her own maize, hoping to sell it to raise money for school fees, but when the crop is ripe, her brother steals it. Furious, Tambu fights Nhamo during the games that take place after Sunday School. They are separated by the teacher, Mr. Matimba, who rebukes them both but then listens patiently to Tambu's story and offers to help her. Two days later, Mr. Matimba drives her to the city of Umtali in the school truck, where he helps her to sell her maize cobs on the street. An old white lady named Doris gives her ten pounds toward her school fees. Mr. Matimba suggests that she give the money to the headmaster of the school for safekeeping. Tambu's father is annoyed by this and claims that the money is his, since Tambu is his daughter.

Tambu goes back to school the following year and for the next two years she comes top in her class. During her second year, the big event in the family is the return of Tambu's uncle, Babamukuru, from studying in England.

Chapter 3

The extended family celebrates the return of Babamukuru, his wife Maiguru, daughter Nyasha and son Chido. Babamukuru is treated like returning royalty, but Tambu is upset because she is not allowed to go to the airport to greet her uncle because she is a girl. There is a big family meal, which Tambu helps to prepare, followed by dancing and singing. Tambu is disturbed by the fact that her cousins speak English most of the time and seem to have forgotten their native Shona.

A family discussion led by Babamukuru results in a decision to transfer Nhamo to the mission school so he can have the best education possible and later be able to provide for the family. Nhamo is thrilled by the news and regards himself as very important. Tambu is jealous, and they quarrel. As a result, Tambu no longer speaks to her brother. Instead, she tries to befriend her cousin Nyasha, who has changed as a result of her stay in England. Nyasha, however, is rather uncommunicative.

In November 1968, Nhamo is due to return home for a visit. But instead, Babamukuru returns with the news that Nhamo was taken ill and died within a few days, possibly of mumps. Babamukuru decides that Tambu should be given an opportunity to attend the mission school in Nhamo's place.

Chapter 4

Tambu is excited as her uncle drives her to the mission school. She is expecting to be transformed into a new person and is looking forward to living in greater comfort, since she will be in her uncle's house. She is very impressed by the grandeur of the white house, especially the large, elegant living room. Everything is such a contrast to the modest home she grew up in. Tambu's aunt, Maiguru, is gracious to her, offering her anything she might want in the way of food or drink. Nyasha is excited to see her cousin, which surprises Tambu. But Tambu also thinks that Nyasha speaks disrespectfully to her mother, and disapproves of her for it. The English-educated Nyasha appears glamorous to Tambu in a way she finds disturbing.

Chapter 5

Tambu shares a room with Nyasha, and they become friends. Tambu becomes fond of Nyasha, even though she does have her disagreements with her cousin. The first night of Tambu's stay, the family has supper together. Nyasha shows that she is unwilling to act submissively toward her parents, and she is dismayed because they have confiscated a novel she was reading because they thought it was unsuitable. She abruptly leaves the dinner table and returns to her room. Tambu is shocked to discover that Nyasha also smokes cigarettes.

Later that evening, Babamukuru gives a fatherly talk to Tambu. He tells her she is fortunate to have this opportunity to continue her education, and that it is not only for herself but also for her family, who would in the future be able to depend on her.

The next day, Tambu attends the mission school for the first time. She is fourteen years old. She excels at the school. She reads widely and is very diligent. The teachers like her, as do the students, who elect her as class monitor at the beginning of the third term. She continues to get to know Nyasha, who fascinates her, Anna the housegirl, who bores her, and her aunt Maiguru. Tambu is surprised to find out that Maiguru has a master's degree, and is disturbed that her aunt has sacrificed an independent career in order to support and look after her husband and family.

Chapter 6

Tambu discovers that she likes the white missionaries at the school, especially the young ones. She makes friends with Nyaradzo, a white girl who is the daughter of a missionary. Meanwhile, Chido, her other cousin, wins a scholarship to a multi-racial private school in Salisbury, the capital city, and Nyasha excels at her exams. On the last night of the semester before she returns with her family for the Christmas vacation, Tambu, Chido, and Nyasha attend a dance at the mission. Tambu normally prefers going to debates and films, but to her surprise she enjoys the boisterous atmosphere of the dance. When they return home, Babamukuru is angry with Nyasha who has stayed out later than the others and for a while was alone outside with a boy. The two of them engage in a bitter argument, and Babamukuru, after accusing Nyasha of behaving like a whore, hits her twice across the face, knocking her to the floor. He hits her again and she fights back. He spits at her and disowns her as his daughter for challenging his authority. Nyasha walks out of the room. Within the next few days, Babamukuru gives his daughter a formal punishment of fourteen lashes, while her mother looks on. Tambu is sympathetic to the conflict Nyasha is experiencing, while Nyasha insists that her father has no right to treat her the way he does. Tambu admires her resilience.

Chapter 7

Tambu, her uncle, aunt, and Nyasha return home for two weeks at Christmas 1969. Tambu is shocked at how run-down the home in which she grew up now seems, since she has gotten used to living at the mission. At home, she is surprised to find her Aunt Lucia (her mother's sister), who has a reputation for loose morals, and Uncle Takesure, a distant cousin of Babamukuru's who is the father of Lucia's as-yet-wifeunborn child, even though he already has a wife. Babamukuru despises them both and has ordered them to leave, but they have not responded to his request. Another aunt and uncle, Gladys and Thomas, are also present at the family reunion. It is crowded, with twenty-four people in all. Eight people sleep in the kitchen; some of the boys sleep in the back of a truck. Tambu and Nyasha work hard at all the domestic chores that are necessary, as does Maiguru.

During the vacation, Babamukuru and the other male members of the family demand to know of Takesure why he has not gone back to his own home. Takesure says that he would have done, but Lucia refused to go. Not admitted to the conference, Lucia is angry, fearing that her reputation is being slandered and she is being blamed for the situation. Maiguru refuses to offer an opinion, saying it is none of her concern, since Takesure and Lucia are not her relatives. This response angers Tambu's mother, who insults Maiguru after she has left the room and also lambastes her sister Lucia, accusing her of sleeping with her husband.

Lucia then overhears Takesure defaming her at the family conference, saying that she is a witch who wants to get Jeremiah, Tambu's father, to marry her. Furious, Lucia enters the house, drags Takesure to his feet, and has her say. She says that Jeremiah tried to seduce her and that she is going to leave the house, but she will take her sister, Tambu's mother, with her. Then Lucia walks out. As the family conference continues, there is some discussion about the general misfortunes of the family. Jeremiah wants to hold a cleansing ceremony involving the sacrifice of an ox, but Babamukuru declares that their troubles are due to the fact that Jeremiah has never been married in a church before God. He is therefore living in sin, and this must be remedied.

Chapter 8

The guests depart after the Christmas vacation. Lucia and Takesure remain for the time being. Lucia is ready to leave but says that she is waiting for her sister to decide whether she will come with her. Life returns to the normal routine and in a little while Tambu returns to the mission for the start of the new semester. In March, Tambu's mother has a baby boy in the mission hospital. Lucia says she wants to find a job so she can be more useful, and Babamukuru arranges for her to work as a cook at the girls' hostel. Lucia is elated. Tambu is very impressed by how her uncle manages his responsibilities to his family, but Nyasha thinks that women should not have to depend on men to help them out. In the last week of September, the church wedding of Tambu's parents takes place. Tambu, however, regards the wedding as ridiculous and refuses to attend. Babamukuru is furious at her for being disobedient. The day after the wedding he calls her into the sitting-room, tells her he is disappointed in her, and gives her fifteen lashes, one for each of her fifteen years. She is also made to take over the duties of Anna, the housemaid, for two weeks. Babamukuru's wife, Maiguru, rebels against her husband's domineering manner and leaves the home, going to stay with her brother. But after five days, she returns home.

Chapter 9

Some Catholic nuns come to the mission. They are recruiting two of the brightest students for scholarships to their rather elite, multiracial convent school, the Young Ladies College of the Sacred Heart. The girls sit an entrance examination, and

Tambu excels and wins a scholarship to attend the school. She is excited because she knows that the convent offers a superior education. At first, however, Babamukuru refuses to allow her to go to the convent. He thinks her future is well provided for as things stand. But Maiguru wants her to attend the convent. Babamukuru eventually changes his mind and gives his permission so that Tambu can receive the finest education in the country. Tambu is overjoyed, but her mother is disappointed that her daughter will be going even farther away. Also, some of Tambu's friends at the mission act coolly toward her, resenting her success. Nyasha, however, says that she will miss Tambu. Nyasha continues to have conflicts with her father, and she develops an eating disorder.

Chapter 10

Babamukuru drives an excited Tambu to the convent for the start of her first term. Nyasha promises to visit, but she does not. However, she does write long letters, complaining that she feels like an outsider at her school. She also explains that she has not visited because Babamukuru will not permit it. Tambu does not see Nyasha again for several months, but when she does return on vacation she is shocked at how thin her cousin has become. Nyasha eats little, and after supper at night she goes to the bathroom and induces vomiting. One night she explodes in anger, tearing her books and breaking mirrors. Her parents take her to a psychiatrist, and Nyasha is put in a clinic for several weeks. Slowly, her condition improves. Tambu's mother blames all the trouble on the young people becoming too influenced by English ways, and she warns Tambu to be careful. Tambu takes the warning seriously and decides to no longer accept everything she is taught at the convent without questioning it.

CHARACTERS

Anna

Anna is the housemaid for Babamukuru and Maiguru.

Babamukuru

Babamukuru is Tambu's uncle, he is married to Maiguru, and is head of the entire Sigauke clan. From an early age, Babamukuru was a hard worker and was also ambitious. He attended the Christian mission school and then received a government scholarship to study in South Africa. After that he won another scholarship, this time to study in England, where he attained a master's degree. He spent five years in England, from 1960 to 1965, with his wife and two children, Chido and Nyasha. When the story begins, Babamukuru is in a responsible position as headmaster of the mission school and is also Academic Director of the Church's Manicaland Region. He has a strong sense of duty and sees it as his responsibility to help ensure the prosperity of every branch of the Sigauke family. He also plays a leading role in mediating family disputes. A much-admired man, Babamukuru "inspired confidence and obedience. He carried with him an aura from which emanated wisdom and foresight." However, because he takes on a lot of responsibility he is often weighed down by it, becoming irritable and difficult to deal with. He is also a disciplinarian with an authoritarian attitude, especially toward his female dependents. He is used to be being obeyed and does not permit any argument. When Nyasha shows she is willing to stand up to him, he loses his temper and strikes her across the face and has to be restrained from hitting her again. He is disappointed that she does not behave exactly as he expects her to, and his relations with his daughter remain strained. Babamukuru gets along better with Tambu because she is more willing to accord him the respect he thinks he deserves as the head of the family, although he inflicts corporal punishment on her after she refuses to attend the wedding of her parents.

Chido

Chido is Tambu's cousin, the son of Babamukuru and Maiguru. Thanks to the intervention of a white benefactor, Mr. Baker, Chido wins a scholarship to a high-quality multiracial boarding school in Salisbury, where he makes friends with two white boys. After starting at the boarding school, he likes to spend his time with his friends rather than going back home for the holidays. Tambu describes Chido as "big, athletic and handsome," and he is confident with girls. He likes to tease Tambu and she enjoys it.

Aunt Gladys

Aunt Gladys, also referred to in Shona as Tete Gladys, is Tambu's aunt, her father's older sister. She is a large, formidable woman.

Jeremiah

Jeremiah is Tambu's father. He is an amiable, agreeable but weak man who does not have the education or the ambition to lift his family out of poverty. He always defers to his brother Babamukuru, who has a much stronger personality. Jeremiah also likes to ingratiate himself with Babamukuru, who helped Jeremiah out financially, sending him money for his children's school fees. Although he is not a successful man, Jeremiah does possess a certain cunning. He is good at begging and getting other people to lend him money. He also has very traditional attitudes about the way things should be organized. He thinks that girls should stay at home and cook and clean rather than get an education, an attitude that irks Tambu.

Lucia

Lucia is Tambu's aunt, her mother's sister. She is several years younger than Mainini, and is known for her beauty. Tambu describes her as a "wild woman." She is bold and physically strong. When she was young, she acquired a reputation for being promiscuous and was even called a witch by the villagers. After Mainini lost Nhamo and became pregnant, the still-unmarried Lucia was sent by her parents to help look after her. Lucia soon became pregnant by Takesure, and she also may have had sexual relations with Jeremiah. Eventually Lucia, who has more ambition than her passive sister, is given a job by Babamukuru as a cook at a girls' hostel, and she also enrolls in school. She has never been to school before and is proud of herself for achieving this goal. So Lucia manages to attain a measure of independence, which greatly pleases her.

Mainini Ma'Shingayi

Mainini, which means "mother" in Shona, is Tambu's mother. Her given name, which her husband sometimes uses, is Ma'Shingayi. Her family of origin was extremely poor, but she has not fared much better with Jeremiah, and her nineteen-year-old marriage is not a happy one for her. For the most part, however, she is resigned to her fate and the restricted life of poverty she leads, and she counsels the young Tambu to accept her lot as a woman. Occasionally Mainini, who becomes pregnant with her third child, gives expression to her frustrations. She resents the fact that Maiguru is rich and educated and that, as a result, people pay more attention to her. Mainini even blames Maiguru for the death of her son Nhamo, saying that it happened because Nhamo was taken away from her and sent to the mission. Mainini fears she is losing Tambu for the same reason and thinks that Tambu now scorns her for her poverty.

Maiguru

Maiguru is Babamukuru's wife. She is an intelligent, educated woman, having earned a master's degree when she and her husband both studied in England. She works as a teacher at the mission school but has not pursued an independent career as fully as her qualifications would permit her to do. Maiguru always defers to her husband; she rarely offers an opinion of her own, since she places family harmony above self-assertion. Toward the end of the novel, however, she starts to chafe at the restrictions of her life and tells her husband she is not happy. She says she is tired of being a housekeeper for his relatives when they come to stay and tired also "of being nothing in a home I am working myself sick to support." This is one of the few occasions when she speaks up for herself. When her husband shows no interest in listening, Maiguru decides to walk out on him. She leaves the home for five days, staying with her brother, and when she returns she seems happier after her brief show of partial independence.

Mr. Matimba

Mr. Matimba is a teacher at the local elementary school. He helps Tambu by taking her to Umtali to sell her maize.

Netsai

Netsai is Tambu's younger sister.

Nhamo

Nhamo is Tambu's older brother by one year. He excels at primary school even though he is one of the youngest students, coming top of the class two years running. He attends the mission school for three years, beginning in 1965. Nhamo is ambitious and intelligent, but he and Tambu do not get along well. She thinks he is puffed up with his own importance. He gets his sisters to run errands for him and, on one occasion, he beats Netsai with a stick. Tambu does not like him because of the ideas he acquires when he goes to the mission. In her eyes, Nhamo thinks he is superior simply because he is a boy; he deserves to have an education but his sister does not. After he steals her maize, Nhamo and Tambu have a vicious physical fight, and they continue to grow apart. Eventually, Tambu does not even speak to him because of what she regards as his elitist attitudes. Nhamo dies in 1968 after a brief illness, possibly mumps. Tambu does not mourn his death.

Nyasha

Nyasha is Tambu's cousin, the daughter of Babamukuru and Maiguru. She spends five of her early years in England with her parents, attending an English school. When she comes back to Rhodesia, she speaks more English than Shona, which Tambu finds disturbing. Nyasha remains thoroughly influenced by the sophisticated ways she picked up abroad. When she and Tambu become roommates at the mission school, Tambu admires Nyasha because she is unconventional and "glamorous in an irreverent way," but she is also wary of her because of Nyasha's more radical and rebellious nature. Nyasha, for example, reads books that her parents consider unsuitable, and she secretly smokes cigarettes; she definitely has a mind of her own, wants to act independently, and refuses to accept traditional gender roles. She sees no reason why women should always play a subservient role to men. Like Tambu, Nyasha is an excellent student and reads voraciously, anxious to inform herself about history and current affairs so she can develop her own opinions. "Everything about her spoke of alternatives and possibilities" is what Tambu says of her cousin.

Nyasha soon comes into conflict with her father because she talks back to him; she does not accept his absolute authority over her life, an attitude that infuriates him and results in a beating for her. Eventually Nyasha becomes so full of emotional conflicts connected with her need for independence from her authoritarian father that she develops an eating disorder. She eats very little and becomes weak and thin. When she forces herself to eat, she immediately goes to the bathroom and vomits the food up. Obstinate and rather idealistic, Nyasha refuses to compromise her views. She always wants to fight back and try to get her father to see things from her point of view rather than meekly accepting his.

Mainini Patience

Mainini Patience is Tambu's aunt, married for eight years to Babamunini Thomas. She still has some independence of thought, and she sides with Mainini in the family dispute about what to do with Lucia.

Rambanai

Rambanai is Tambu's youngest sister.

Uncle Takesure

Uncle Takesure is a distant cousin of Babamukuru's. He has two wives but it seems that he is happy with neither of them, since he jumps at the chance to leave them and help work on the land at Jeremiah's homestead. Shortly after he arrives, he makes Lucia pregnant. Babamukuru orders him to leave but he does not go. Takesure is an amiable scoundrel, dominated by the more aggressive Lucia.

Tambu

Tambu, or Tambudzai, is the narrator of the story. She is the daughter of Mainini and Jeremiah, and is the sister of Nhamo. Tambu is a sensitive, highly intelligent girl who early in her life finds that being a girl deprives her of some of the privileges that are automatically enjoyed by boys. She resents the fact that, in her family, her education is less of a priority than that of her brother. But Tambu shows great enterprise and determination in growing her maize crop in order to sell it to raise money for her school fees. At an early age she decides not to let the limited expectations others have of her to affect her ability to forge the life she wants for herself. After her brother's death, Tambu is given the opportunity to attend the mission school, an opportunity that she makes the best of. A diligent and conscientious student, she eventually wins one of only two scholarships available to an elite multiracial convent, where she continues her education.

Tambu's nature is to be dutiful and respectful. She respects the authority of Babamukuru, her uncle, and is grateful to him for giving her educational opportunities. She regards him "as nearly divine as any human being could hope to be." In this she differs from Nyasha, who continually questions his authority and the traditional ways of doing things. Tambu's preference in life is for order, for things to be settled, and Nyasha's unconventional ways disturb her. However, Nyasha has a marked influence on Tambu.

Eventually Tambu learns not to take everything she is taught at face value but to evaluate it for herself. She describes this as "a long and painful process." Part of her growth comes when she plucks up the courage to defy her uncle and refuse to go to her parents' wedding, which she regards as a ridiculous spectacle. She begins to realize that the reverence with which she regards her uncle "stunted the growth of [her] faculty of criticism." By the end of the novel, therefore, she is well on the way to becoming a mature young woman, one who has had the courage and the perseverance to grow beyond the limited role that was prescribed for her in the poor rural family in which she grew up.

Babamunini Thomas

Babamunini Thomas is one of Tambu's uncles, the younger brother of Babamukuru and Jeremiah, married to Patience. He is trained as a teacher and, as a result, his family is well provided for.

THEMES

Destructive Effects of Colonialism

Rhodesia, as Zimbabwe was known during the time the story takes place, was a British colony. It was ruled by Rhodesian whites who traced their ancestries to England, and white Christian missionaries set up schools to provide a Western, Anglicized education for African children.

Although the novel does not centrally confront the issue of racism, it does contain many allusions to the destructive effects of colonialism on traditional African life. Tambu hears about the precolonial days from her grandmother, who refers to the whites as "wizards well versed in treachery and black magic," who forced the prosperous Africans, including Tambu's great-grandfather, off their land and into less fertile areas. Some of the Africans found themselves in virtual slavery, working on the farms of the whites. Others went south to work in the gold mines.

The whites do set up their mission schools to educate the Africans they rule over, but they have a paternalistic attitude toward their pupils. As Tambu comes to learn, "whites were indulgent toward promising young black boys in those days, provided that the promise was a peaceful promise, a grateful promise to accept whatever was handed out to them and not expect more." In other words, whites are helpful to blacks only on the condition that the blacks

TOPICS FOR FURTHER STUDY

- Write an essay in which you analyze the way white people are portrayed in the novel. Are they hostile to blacks or sympathetic to them? Do they regard blacks as their equals? Have they brought anything of value to the country or is their presence entirely harmful?

- Tambu comes of age during the period of Rhodesia's Unilateral Declaration of Independence (UDI). Research what this period was like in the history of the nation. Why was UDI declared? What course did the subsequent civil war take? How did the white minority government plan to hold on to power? What led to its eventual defeat? Make a class presentation based around a timeline of events ranging from 1965 to 1980.

- Research the eating disorders of bulimia and anorexia, both of which afflict Nyasha. What causes eating disorders? Who suffers from them? What is the cure for them? Present your findings to the class.

- Imagine that you are Tambu. Write a letter to Netsai, your younger sister, advising her about how to approach her life as a woman and how to deal with difficulties along the way. Based on your knowledge of the novel, is Netsai likely to have the same opportunities as Tambu? What pitfalls do you think Tambu would advise Netsai to avoid?

accept the status quo and do not threaten the whites' position of superiority.

One problematic aspect of education by the missionaries is that it teaches the Africans to speak English rather than their native tongue, which in that region of the continent is Shona. This encourages the Africans to forget their origins and the traditional ways of their culture. This is the case with Nhamo, to the extent that his mother thinks someone at the mission has bewitched him. In the case of Nyasha, because she spent five of her early years in England, she has learned little of her own cultural tradition and is in effect alienated from her own people. This is why she is unpopular at the mission school, where the girls taunt her for thinking "she is white." Even her own mother thinks that Nyasha picked up "disrespectful ways in England" and no longer knows how to behave toward her relatives. Nyasha is herself aware of the situation and refers to herself and her brother, Chido, as cultural "hybrids." The divisions brought by the intrusion of foreign ways is well illustrated in the incident when Babamukuru enters the room as his family sit down to dinner. Babamukuru's wife greets him in Shona, Nyasha greets him in English, and Tambu greets him in a mixture of the two languages. At the end of the novel, Tambu's mother complains that the more time the African children spend in the Anglicized educational system, the more they are lost to their true selves, and this is a cause of deep distress to her.

Children and teachers in a school playground, Rhodesia, 1971 (© Paul Almasy / Corbis)

Challenging Traditional Gender Roles

Tambu states clearly in the opening paragraph of the novel that her story is principally about herself and the other females in her life, and how they were either emancipated from the restrictions imposed by traditional gender roles or continue to be trapped by them. She and Lucia escaped, she says, while her mother and Maiguru did not. Nyasha rebelled, and because her rebellion has made her seriously ill, her ultimate fate hangs in the balance.

Of all the women, it is Mainini, Tambu's mother, who seems to fare the worst. Condemned to a life of poverty with a man she has no respect for, she is unable to influence the course of her life. No one listens to her because she is a woman. To give one example of many: when she complains that she does not want her son to be speaking English all the time, her husband tries to reassure her that he needs to receive an education. Mainini does not argue with him and says nothing more about it, but she remains unhappy and resentful about the way her wishes are always ignored.

Maiguru has the advantage of having had an education, and she lives a comfortable life in material terms, but she does not use all her talents and qualifications because she must first serve her husband. She rarely speaks up for herself, and even when she makes a belated bid for freedom by leaving home, she has nowhere to go and no means of supporting herself. She can only show once more her dependence on men by staying for a few days with her brother.

The outspoken Lucia is less intimidated by the patriarchal structure of traditional society than the other women. She has not been enslaved by marriage and has never learned to be deferential to men. In a society where only men make the important decisions, she defies the rules by storming into a family conference that had been discussing her relationship with Takesure without even inviting her in to defend herself. By the end of the novel, Lucia has won some independence for herself and has started to go to school, but it is independence of a limited kind since she secured her job as a cook at the hostel only through the intervention of Babamukuru, the family patriarch.

STYLE

First-Person Point of View

The story is told entirely from Tambu's point of view, in the first person. This means that nothing can be related that she does not either participate in directly or hear about from someone else. Also, information about all the other characters is filtered through her consciousness. Readers only know what Tambu knows about the other characters and therefore readers only see them through her eyes. What this means is that given Tambu's interest in gender issues, the male characters, especially Nhamo and Babamukuru, tend to get presented in an unflattering light. Babamukuru, for example, for all his accomplishments and sense of duty, comes across as a domestic tyrant. Given the author's decision about how the story is to be narrated, the reader cannot be given direct insight into Babamukuru's own thoughts, which might have made him a more sympathetic character. In contrast, the female characters, such as Tambu's mother, Lucia, Nyasha, and Maiguru, are presented with greater understanding of their plight. Had the story been told by an omniscient narrator in the third person, or by one of the male characters, the effect on the reader might have been quite different.

Language

One of the themes of the novel is the loss of the native language Shona in favor of English, the language of the colonizers, and this theme is also reflected in the book's style. The English influence can be found of course in the fact that the novel itself is written in English, with British English spellings of words such as "apologise" (instead of the American "apologize"), and "mum" for the American "mom." The smattering of Shona words that occur throughout the text convey the fact that the language is disappearing. These words include "pada" and "nhodo," both referring to games played by the children, and "dare," a family conference. However, the fact that the characters, even the most Anglicized of them, refer to one another in forms of address rooted in Shona terms shows the survival of tradition in spite of colonialism. For example, "mukoma" refers to an older sibling of the same gender, which is why Jeremiah uses it to refer to Babamukuru. "Baba" is a term of respect used of a man who is also a father, and "Sisi," as Netsai refers to Tambu, is the Shona term for sister. "Tete" is Shona for aunt.

HISTORICAL CONTEXT

Rhodesia in the 1960s

Although the novel does not emphasize it, during the 1960s and 1970s, Rhodesia was in a long political crisis that set the stage for a civil war that only ended with independence in 1980. Southern Rhodesia, as the country was officially known, was a British colony that had been self-governing since 1923. Whites composed approximately 5 percent of the population but had all the political power. Blacks were not permitted to vote. However, as Britain gradually granted its African colonies independence, the pressure for establishing majority black rule grew. Britain insisted that no independence would be granted without majority rule. This led the white government of Rhodesia to make what was known as a Unilateral Declaration of Independence (UDI) in November 1965. In the novel, only Nyasha takes any interest in UDI, wanting to know "why UDI was declared and what it meant."

Neither Britain nor any other nation in the world formally recognized Rhodesian independence. Britain regarded the UDI as an act of treason, dismissed the Rhodesian government, and imposed economic sanctions. The United Nations also imposed sanctions. Rhodesia received limited support from South Africa, at that time also ruled by a white minority government. In 1970, Rhodesia, which had until then claimed to be loyal to the British Crown, declared itself a republic.

In the early 1970s, the Zimbabwe African National Union (ZANU) based in Mozambique and led by Robert Mugabe, and the Zimbabwe African People's Union (ZAPU), based in Zambia and led by Joshua Nkomo, began a guerrilla war aimed at overthrowing the white minority regime. During the 1970s, the position of the Rhodesian government became progressively weaker, and in 1979, negotiations took place in London to end the war. In 1980, the country became the independent Republic of Zimbabwe, with Mugabe installed as president.

Postcolonial Literature

Nervous Conditions is an example of what is called postcolonial literature, meaning literature written by authors from mostly African and Asian nations that were former colonies of the European powers, such as Britain, France, Belgium, and Portugal. Such works often foreground the indigenous culture of the nation that was devalued, and sometimes almost obliterated, by the colonizers. Often the characters in postcolonial literature must deal with their sense of possessing a dual identity, having absorbed much of the colonial culture at the expense of their own. Nyasha in *Nervous Conditions* would be an example of this. Postcolonial literature, according to Peter Barry in *Beginning Theory: An Introduction to Literary and Cultural Theory*, goes through three stages, beginning with the adoption of European models of literature and

COMPARE
&
CONTRAST

- **1960s:** Rhodesia declares unilateral independence from Britain in 1965 and tries to preserve white minority rule.

  1980s: The newly independent Republic of Zimbabwe establishes black majority rule for the first time, under the leadership of President Robert Mugabe. Although Mugabe promises that change will be gradual and minority rights respected, about two-thirds of the white population leaves the country during the 1980s.

  Today: Economic mismanagement by the government, including a land redistribution program that began in 2000, has impoverished the country. According to the CIA World Factbook, the inflation rate was 585 percent in 2005, and nearly 1,000 percent in 2006. The number of whites in the country has fallen to less than 1 percent of the population.

- **1960s:** Because Rhodesia is ruled by a white-minority government, blacks are mostly excluded from government schools. Christian mission schools take up the challenge of educating black children, but are only able to admit a fraction of the children who are in need of an education.

  1980s: After Zimbabwe wins its independence, many of the Christian mission schools are taken over by the government.

  Today: Because of the continuing economic crisis in Zimbabwe, many of the church schools that the government took over following independence have been returned to the churches. Christian schools, the majority of them run by the Roman Catholic Church, account for one-third of the schools in the nation.

- **1960s:** In Rhodesia, African women are restricted in their rights, not only by the government, but also by the traditional patriarchal structure of African society. Women do not enjoy equal opportunities in either education or employment.

  1980s: Following independence, the government of Zimbabwe officially advocates more rights for women, creating the Ministry of Community and Cooperative Development and Women's Affairs in 1981. This agency works toward eliminating discrimination against women.

  Today: Zimbabwe is in a continuing economic crisis and the government represses human rights. According to a report by Amnesty International in 2007, women's groups are at the forefront of the movement to defend human rights, but many women who peacefully protest government policies are arrested and detained.

writing within that tradition. The second stage is when the writer "aims to adapt the European form to African subject matter, thus assuming partial rights of intervention in the genre." The final stage is when the postcolonial writer uses forms and genres native to his or her own culture, without feeling the need to defer to European standards. *Nervous Conditions* would belong in the first and second categories, since it is written largely in the form of a traditional coming-of-age story in Western literature, but the setting is entirely African and some importance is attached to traditional African culture.

CRITICAL OVERVIEW

Tsitsi Dangarembga's *Nervous Conditions* attracted considerable favorable attention from reviewers when it was first published in 1988. A reviewer for *Publishers Weekly* calls it a "skillful" beginning to Dangarembga's writing career and notes that Tambu shows "an uncanny and often critical self-awareness" as she challenges the role she is expected to adopt as a woman. The reviewer concludes that the novel is "a resonant, eloquent tribute to" her family. Charlotte H. Bruner, writing in *World Literature Today*, gives another positive response to the

Mrs. L. F. Parriss demonstrates aginst unequal schooling in Salisbury, Rhodesia, in the 1960s
(© INTERFOTO Pressebildagentur | Alamy)

novel, which "provides a fresh and original treatment of themes common to some earlier African novels." Commenting on the characters of Tambu and Nyasha, Bruner writes that "with considerable humor and insight, [Dangarembga] makes their crises of self-fulfillment in today's Zimbabwean world the focus of her novel." The reviewer's conclusion is that Dangarembga's "excellent style and power of characterization make the book outstanding."

For P. Alden, writing in *Choice*, the novel is "an important addition to the female bildungsroman." ("Bildungsroman" is a German term referring to a novel that shows the protagonist growing from childhood to maturity.) In Alden's view, Dangarembga "combines complex analysis of ideological pressures with insight into the formation of adolescent personality." The novel also possesses some "finely comic scenes, as when the family patriarchy attempts to sit in judgment on Tambu's rebellious and pregnant aunt Lucia."

WHAT DO I READ NEXT?

- Dangarembga's *The Book of Not: A Sequel to Nervous Conditions* (2006) continues Tambu's story as she lives at the convent boarding school and further encounters the problems in Rhodesia created by colonialism.
- *Zimbabwe: The Rise to Nationhood* (2006), by economist Jacob W. Chikuhwa, is a comprehensive history of Zimbabwe that goes from prehistory to the present. The book presents detailed analysis of the Unilateral Declaration of Independence in the 1960s, the guerrilla war that followed, and the emergence of the modern republic of Zimbabwe in the 1980s. The book includes maps, illustrations, a glossary, and an index.
- *Half of a Yellow Sun* (2006), by Nigerian novelist Chimamanda Ngozi Adichie, is set in the late 1960s during the three-year civil war in Nigeria caused by the desire of the Igbo people in eastern Nigeria to secede and form the independent nation of Biafra. The epic story is told partly through the eyes of a thirteen-year-old boy who is conscripted into the Biafran army, and is partly told by his twin sisters.
- *Changes: A Love Story* (1993), by Ghanian-born writer Ama Ata Aidoo, takes a sometimes-satirical look at the attempt of two contemporary African women, Esi and Opokuya, to balance their feminist aspirations for successful careers with their obligations to their husbands and families, who are less than sympathetic to their ambitions. This is an African novel with a theme that will be easy for Western readers to understand.

CRITICISM

Bryan Aubrey

Aubrey holds a Ph.D. in English. In this essay, he discusses Nervous Conditions *as a coming-of-age story, a critique of colonialism, and a protest against patriarchal society.*

Rhodesian family (*Bert Hardy / Picture Post / Getty Images*)

Tsitsi Dangarembga's *Nervous Conditions* is at once a coming-of-age story, a critique of colonialism, and a protest against a traditional patriarchal society that predates colonization. The book's most important theme is the development of Tambu, the story's adolescent narrator. Tambu is a semi-autobiographical figure who reflects Dangarembga's own experience of growing up in Southern Rhodesia in the 1960s and early 1970s. The Anglicization and alienation of Tambu's cousin Nyasha is also an important theme in the novel.

As the first novel written in English by a black woman from Zimbabwe, *Nervous Conditions* gives a fascinating picture of traditional rural and familial life in that country during the last decade or so of white minority rule. Tambu grows up in poverty, in a house without running water or electricity. She relates how the children would wash themselves in cold water in an enamel basin or in the nearby river; light at night was provided by candles and home-made paraffin

lamps. In their homestead, the trappings of modern life, even down to knives and forks, were absent. People would eat using their fingers. Tambu also got used to hard physical work at an early age, rising at dawn with the rest of the family to work in the fields.

However, Tambu's upbringing was not an unhappy one, since the extended family structure of the Sigauke clan is a strong one, and the description of the family gathering when Babamukuru returns from England in 1965, when Tambu is still only ten years old, gives valuable insight into the rituals and traditions of this Shona-speaking African family. As Tambu carries the water dish for people to wash their hands, she has to make sure that she knows everyone's status in the family hierarchy, because she must first give the bowl to those who are highest in seniority and then move down to those with progressively lower status. At first she makes a mistake, kneeling before her uncle Babamukuru, who is the most educated of the family and its de facto leader. But seniority is

"

THE PROBLEM FOR NYASHA IS THAT SHE IS SO ANGLICIZED—BY THE TIME SHE SPENT IN ENGLAND, AND BY THE BRITISH-DESIGNED EDUCATION SHE HAS RECEIVED AT THE CHRISTIAN MISSION SCHOOL—THAT SHE HAS NO KNOWLEDGE OF HER OWN CULTURAL TRADITIONS."

ascribed by age, so she should first have gone to her grandfather Isaiah, the oldest member of the family, and then to all her male relatives in order, before doing the same with her female relatives, beginning with her grandmothers and then her aunts. The family relationships are complicated and Tambu gets confused: "This uncle was that uncle's tezvara by virtue of his marriage to that one's sister, but also his brother because their mothers were sisters." ("Tezvara" is a Shona word that means father-in-law.)

Only later, after Tambu starts to attend the mission school and lives at Babamukuru's house, does she become ashamed of the humble family home that she returns to visit during vacations. By this time, as all adolescents do, she has begun to develop a more mature understanding of how the world works, and she perceives the main obstacle to her happiness and success to be the firm structures of the patriarchy that prevent female advancement. This is not an entirely new thing for her to realize, since at a very early age she was counseled by her mother to learn to accept the burdens that she would inevitably carry as a woman. For Tambu's mother, being a woman involved making sacrifices for the family; her daughter should not even think of getting an education. And being black, according to her mother, would ensure her poverty. But Tambu is determined not to let such obstacles hold her back. It is interesting that, even though she can have had no knowledge of the second wave of the feminist movement that was at that time (the mid- to late 1960s) beginning to have a large impact on Western culture, she nonetheless conceived the same goals that Western feminists were calling for: that she should be allowed to live the life she wants for

herself, in accordance with her talents, abilities, and inclinations, rather than have a life prescribed for her by what may well have been centuries of tradition—certainly it was not introduced by the white colonizers—in which the male will dominated female lives.

Tambu, it must be said, is one of the fortunate ones. Although she had admirable determination, intelligence, and common sense, as well as an ability to analyze her own experiences, she must have been one of only a few African girls from a poor rural background in Rhodesia who were able to overcome the many obstacles to their progress, including, in Tambu's case, the indifference of her mother and father to her education. There is also an irony attached to Tambu's educational career because she is in fact helped along her way by patriarchal influence— that of her English-educated uncle, Babamukuru, who, despite his authoritarian ways does not seem to have any prejudices about education for women. Later, through her outstanding scholastic achievements, Tambu is admitted to a white-run convent with high educational standards. Thus she is eventually helped out by the very structures— patriarchal, colonial—that have otherwise failed to acknowledge women's rights and ambitions outside the home, and have also in a sense divided the black Africans in Rhodesia from themselves by ensuring that many of them develop a dual cultural identity.

If Tambu has a relatively smooth path of advancement in life, largely because of her deferential attitude toward her uncle, who is her benefactor, the same cannot be said of the spirited Nyasha, her cousin. It is Nyasha who has the daring to challenge the patriarchal structure of Rhodesian society directly in the family, where the patriarchal influence begins and manifests itself most forcefully. The scene in which father and daughter become so enraged with each other that they come to blows, with Babamukuru losing all control and having to be restrained after his own daughter punches him in the eye, is the most dramatic in the entire novel. Nyasha differs from Tambu partly in the fierceness of her temperament, which makes her less willing to compromise, and partly in the fact that, unlike Tambu, she spent five of her most formative years in England.

The Anglicization of Nyasha, as well as that of her brother, Chido, raises the important issue of colonialism. Rhodesia at the time of the novel was a self-governing colony of Britain, but those who ruled it were the white minority who possessed strong cultural and kinship ties to England. Colonialism, as practiced by the European powers in some cases up to the second half of the twentieth century, had negative consequences for the colonized population. One of the first books to bring attention to this, and which effectively began the practice of postcolonial literary criticism, was *The Wretched of the Earth*, by Frantz Fanon, published in 1961, which took as its subject the French colonization of Africa. The title of *Nervous Conditions* is taken from this book, and Dangarembga uses a passage from it as an epigraph for her own novel. Fanon urged colonized people to recover a sense of their own cultural history and identity, which is usually obliterated by the colonizers who, in effect, teach that the history of the colonized country began with their arrival. All civilization and progress is presented as the result of what the colonizers have brought. It is interesting in this respect that Rhodesia was named after the British businessman and politician Cecil Rhodes, who in the late nineteenth century acquired the territory (including modern-day Zambia) for the British Crown. The naming of the territory after a white businessman who was interested in exploiting its material resources might well be seen as an arrogant assertion of colonial power and an invalidation of the true nature and history of the country, which pre-dates the coming of the British by thousands of years.

The problem for Nyasha is that she is so Anglicized—by the time she spent in England, and by the British-designed education she has received at the Christian mission school—that she has no knowledge of her own cultural traditions. She is trying to find a way for herself, fighting against the authoritarian rule of her father, but with no firm moorings, no path laid out for her in life. She does not fit in with the other girls at the mission school. As she writes to Tambu: "They do not like my language, my English, because it is authentic and my Shona, because it is not!" This shows the irony of her position. Her native language, Shona, now seems inauthentic to her, and the language of the colonizer, English, has become her natural way of communicating. Tellingly, in the same letter, Nyasha informs Tambu that she is beginning a diet, and when Tambu next sees her she is looking thin. The desirability of slimness in a woman is a largely Western ideal, so it is

significant that Nyasha adopts it as her goal. The illness she develops is anorexia, which again is something that afflicts Western women and must have been very uncommon in Rhodesia, especially for black Rhodesians in the early 1970s. But Nyasha also shows sufficient historical awareness to understand what has happened to her and her country, and to be angry about it. In a rage she tears up one of her history textbooks, calling it "their history. ... Their bloody lies," and adding: "They've trapped us. But I won't be trapped." She succinctly describes her own situation when she tells her father: "I'm not one of them but I'm not one of you." There, in a nutshell, is the postcolonial conflict: people of the colonized nation become divided against themselves, fully belonging to neither culture, but, at least in Nyasha's case, determined to forge their own path.

Source: Bryan Aubrey, Critical Essay on *Nervous Conditions*, in *Novels for Students*, Gale, Cengage Learning, 2009.

Carolyn Martin Shaw

In the following excerpt, Shaw compares the feminist threads in Nervous Conditions *to those in Dangarembga's play* She No Longer Weeps.

... In the case of the novel, though the female characters learn from each other, each woman is expected to act in accord with her own sense of integrity, to honor her own belief and conscience, and to speak up, if not for her own ends, then because her sense of self demands it. I suggest that this representation of feminist consciousness in *Nervous Conditions* could be seen as a paean to Audre Lorde, who in her essay "The Transformation of Silence into Language and Action," famously said, "Your silence will not protect you" (41). In *Nervous Conditions*, women and girls fail to contain themselves; they speak out. But speaking out in and of itself is not a surefire solution to the problem of sexism. Lorde never suggested that it was, but rather that using language to define oneself, to act with integrity, and to recognize the power within oneself are all crucial to women engaged in life-threatening battles. Dangarembga does not parrot this slogan, but examines and interrogates it. Speaking out does not automatically bring victory, as is made apparent through Tambu's disassociative state and Nyasha's anorexia-bulimia. With these acts, Dangarembga probes the limits of Lorde's dictum.

While speaking up may confirm agency by its very intonement, Dangarembga's use of Lorde reveals both the vulnerabilities of speaking up as well as its power. Silence will not protect you; but speaking, in and of itself, does not redress gender inequality. Yet despite persistent obstacles, Dangarembga's protagonists work with personal integrity toward "the transformation of silence into language and action."

Two other important elements of 1980s feminism were best articulated by Audre Lorde: "the master's tools can never dismantle the master's house"—replacing men with women without changing patriarchal structures is not liberating— and "the erotic as power"—the celebration of feelings, of the erotic, as a means of liberation for women and society (Lorde 110–13; 53–59). The narrator of *Nervous Conditions* understands that the master's tool are double-edged, but Mainini, Tambu[']s beleaguered mother, feels this most deeply as she blames "the Englishness" for killing her son and taking her daughter away from her. By remembering her grandmother and the women and girls whose story she tells in the novel, Tambu, as the adult narrator of the novel, argues against Lorde's maxim, "the master's tools can never dismantle the master's house." Like her grandmother, Tambu believes that she can and should harness the master's power, in this instance, education in English. She can continue her education in Mission schools and not be destroyed by "the Englishness." Rather she sees writing the novel itself as a part of her own (and by implication) other women's liberation.

Without falling into a hackneyed dichotomy of male is to mind as female is to feeling, Lorde exhorts women to see "living as a situation to be experienced and interacted with, we learn more and more to cherish our feelings, and to respect those hidden sources of our power from where true knowledge and, therefore, lasting action comes" (37). The narrator's memory of the luxuriousness of Tambu's dance movements, her celebration of her aunt Lucia's sexual appetite, and representation of Nyasha's desire for bodily pleasure all suggest a well-spring of erotic power that can fuel social change.

She No Longer Weeps, written before the novel, helps the reader to appreciate the undercurrents of *Nervous Conditios*. The following passage from the play, Martha to her mother, is a clear example of the powers of the erotic:

> NAMING MALE POWER 'PATRIARCHY' AND RECOGNIZING ITS ROOTS AS WIDESPREAD IN SOCIETY AND CULTURE WERE MAJOR ACHIEVEMENTS OF THE SECOND WAVE OF FEMINISM IN THE 1970S AND 1980S. IN THIS REGARD, DANGAREMBGA'S USE OF THE TERM 'THE PATRIARCHY' IN *NERVOUS CONDITIONS* IS A SIGN OF HER ENGAGEMENT WITH WESTERN FEMINISM."

> I don't want to feel ashamed of myself because my mind is free—it's the celebration rather than marriage that becomes the important thing. I like to feel my life in every cell of my body-pleasure and pain, pleasure and pain, pleasure and pain … I like to shudder with pleasure, and sob with desire … (*SNLW* 31; ellipsis added).

Martha in *She No Longer Weeps* and Nyasha in *Nervous Conditions* both show desire for bodily pleasure, but the ontogeny of this desire is not developed in either work. The desire is strong and seemingly socially productive, given its associations with the other progressive causes each young woman embraces. Their feminism is not a liberal feminism that would establish equality of access and opportunity, but it includes recognition of women as out-spoken, pro-active, and lusty. *She No Longer Weeps* differs from *Nervous Conditions* in that the play begins with a feminist protagonist. Though the convention-shattering opening line of *Nervous Conditions* suggests a woman-centered consciousness, the work of the novel is to show how that consciousness was developed. From early on in the play, Martha's stakes in feminism are clear and her explicit goals are quite congruent with those that I am using Audre Lorde to represent. Martha wants women to define themselves outside of their relations to men; she wants to capture the power of the erotic for the new Zimbabwe; she wants to make the personal political; and she wants women to have control over their own bodies, their labor, and their children.

Naming male power "patriarchy" and recognizing its roots as widespread in society and culture were major achievements of the second wave of feminism in the 1970s and 1980s. In this regard, Dangarembga's use of the term "the patriarchy" in *Nervous Conditions* is a sign of her engagement with Western feminism. She employs this term to describe the men and women responsible for making decisions for the Sigauke clan. Is there a Shona word that she could have used? Not to put too fine a point on an old debate in language and culture, but to what extent is this group's salience marked in the culture by a distinctive linguistic term? I put this question to a linguist at the University of Zimbabwe in the African Languages and Literature Department, who answered in two parts. First, on the inclusion of women in the patriarchy, he noted that women in positions of authority over the speaker, especially father's sisters, can be addressed as baba, the Shona term for father. Secondly, there is no distinctive term for "the patriarchy," but he gave a Shona sentence that summarizes patriarchal practices, which he translated as follows: Customs that give anyone perceived as being in one[']s father's or husband's line respect or higher status (Mashiri, personal communication). More generally, Masasire (43) indicates that such a group might be called Vana Vanyamunhu, children of one man. In *Nervous Conditions*, this one man would be the narrator's grandfather, whom we know of only through the grandmother's stories.

Father's sisters (paternal aunts) by all accounts then are in "the patriarchy." My experience in Zimbabwe, in the 1980s and two decades later, corroborates Dangarembga's impression of the place of power of father's sisters, who are typically called by an honorific that distinguishes them from mother's sisters. And true to the portrayal in *Nervous Conditions*, I noted that a brother's wife is often an underappreciated handmaiden to her husband's sisters. Dangarembga's use of the term "the patriarchy" picks up on the one familial position in which women have the most power in Shona society and underscores that it comes by virtue of patrilineal descent. Representing this patrilineal group as male and female shows the subtlety of Dangarembga's knowledge of her own culture, while using "the patriarchy" to nominate it signals the influence of Western feminism.

Also embedded in *Nervous Conditions*, and more explicitly in *She No Longer Weeps*, is a call for social recognition of the value of women's labor, whether in the farms and homes of the rural areas or the schools, offices, and homes in the townships. A socialist feminist approach to women and production holds that if women had power and authority over their labor, both production and reproduction, then they would have

commensurate power and position in their societies. Several critics have noted Dangarembga's portrayal of women's work in her novel (Andrade 28; Creamer 352–53, and Wixson 223): women find value in the labor itself, whether turning out a family feast or working as a teacher, but that labor is not esteemed by the men in the family. Moreover, working women's wages are often controlled by men. Turning from productive labor to reproductive labor, Dangarembga seems to hold that if women had ultimate power and authority over their children, patriarchy would diminish, if not dissolve. Calling on women to do just that, in *She No Longer Weeps*, Martha says,

> So we women must be strong and give the men nothing. They should not even be allowed to see the children otherwise they will in their simplemindedness be happy because they can have the pleasure without the responsibility. It is up to us women. We must take sole responsibility for everything we produce. (*SNLW* 49)

Dangarembga's choice of the term "produce" is deliberate. Part of her process of being "conscientized" during the early postcolonial period was to study the rhetoric of socialism: "with all this rhetoric going on about socialism: I didn't know much but at least I could listen to the rhetoric and read all the correct texts to make my own decision as to what I thought about these people who were giving out these phrases and this jargon" (Veit-Wild 105). The above passage from the play echoes 1980s' debates in Zimbabwe, which had hollowly declared itself a socialist state, with little change in the relations of production in the country. During the first five years of independence, Zimbabwean intellectuals promulgated scientific socialism, but no socialism took root. The constitution negotiated at independence maintained much of the colonial economy, including ownership of land and industry. The socialist agenda was left to be reached through under-funded cooperatives and re-settlement schemes. The redistribution of resources from the colonial rulers to the masses could not (and would not later) take place ...

Source: Carolyn Martin Shaw, "'You Had a Daughter, but I Am Becoming a Woman': Sexuality, Feminism and Postcoloniality in Tsitsi Dangarembga's *Nervous Conditions* and *She No Longer Weeps*," in *Research in African Literatures*, Vol. 38, No. 4, Winter 2007, 18 pp.

Kwame Anthony Appiah

In the following foreword to Nervous Conditions, *Appiah argues that, unlike most African novels, this story is not specifically addressed to a Western reader. Instead, the novel is written in such a way as to make it universally accessible.*

'*I was not sorry when my brother died.*'

What an arresting first sentence! As readers (whether or not we come from Zimbabwe, the setting of this novel) we respond to these words in the light of the knowledge that the speaker, like the author, is a woman. Isn't there something especially shocking—something inhuman, unnatural—in a sister's coldness in the face of a brothers'[sic] death? Reactions such as these are plainly anticipated, for the book continues:

> Nor am I apologising for my callousness, as you may define it, my lack of feeling. For it is not that at all. I feel many things these days, much more than I was able to feel in the days when I was young and my brother died, and there are reasons for this more than the mere consequence of age. Therefore I shall not apologise but begin by recalling the facts as I remember them that led up to my brother's death, the events that put me in a position to write this account.

This is a first-person narrative, addressing the reader in the second person. And since, of course, the narrator knows nothing of you and me, it is natural to ask: Who is it that 'may define' our protagonists as callous? To whom, in other words, does our protagonist decline to apologize?

Well, to answer that question I must say a little more about our protagonist and her story. She is Tambudzai—Tambu for short—and we learn swiftly that her uncle is headmaster of the mission school in Umtali, to which he has taken her brother for his education. There her brother learns to despise the village, just as he had learned in the village to despise his sisters.

Understanding that her brother's education is a way out and up, and knowing that her uncle's wife, Maiguru, has completed an education abroad, Tambu begins to ask her father why she, too, cannot be educated. He replies, 'Can you cook books and feed them to your husband?' And Tambu goes to complain to her mother:

> '*Baba says I do not need to be educated,*' I told her scornfully. '*He says I must learn to be a good wife. Look at Maiguru,*' I continued, unaware how viciously. '*She is a better wife than you.*'

> My mother was too old to be disturbed by my childish nonsense. She tried to diffuse some of it by telling me many things, by explaining how

NEVERTHELESS, WHILE NOT SPECIFICALLY ADDRESSED TO A WESTERN READERSHIP, THE PROBLEMS OF RACIAL AND GENDER EQUITY THE TEXT RAISES ARE NOT IN ANY WAY UNFAMILIAR TO US."

my father was right because even Maiguru knew how to cook and clean and grow vegetables. '*This business of womanhood is a heavy burden,*' she said. '*How could it not be? Aren't we the ones who bear children? When it is like that you can't just decide today I want to do this, tomorrow I want to do that, the next day I want to be educated! When there are sacrifices to be made, you are the one who has to make them. And these things are not easy; you have to start learning them early, from a very early age. The earlier the better so that it is easy later on. Easy! As if it is ever easy. And these days it is worse, with the poverty of blackness on one side and the weight of womanhood on the other. Aiwa! What will help you, my child, is to learn to carry your burdens with strength.*'

But Tambu is not persuaded, preferring to ask for seed to grow maize to sell at the market, so that she can pay the fees that her father will not pay.

This struggle for learning is transformed when her brother is carried away by disease. Because she has no other brothers, education into a Western modernity is suddenly available to Tambu, the oldest girl. The situation is very clearly set up: the brother's death is the condition of the sister's emancipation. From now on we watch as Tambu, grateful to her Western education for her transformation from a peasant girl to an educated 'sophisticate,' struggles to integrate the moral order of her village upbringing with a constantly growing sense of the injustice of her position as a woman. This developing awareness is driven not only by her own experience but by the lives of the women around her: her mother, fatalistic and self-giving; her uncle's wife, an educated woman frustrated by her husband's inability to respect her opinions; her mother's sister, an adult who follows her own way, negotiating between Tambu's father and her lover.

And through this process of discovery, Tambu is guided by her cousin, Nyasha, whose experiences in England (where both her parents acquired their post-graduate degrees) have forever alienated her vision: Nyasha rejects the absoluteness of her father's claims to authority and believes that her educated mother is wasting herself as the helpmate of her domineering father. Yet Nyasha's resistance has a price: In her search for bodily perfection (conceived of in a most un-Shona way in terms of an ideal of thinness) she becomes first bulimic and then anorexic, ending up in the hands of a white psychiatrist in Salisbury.

Tambu's mother, Mainini, has a diagnosis:

'It's the Englishness,' she said. 'It'll kill them all if they aren't careful ...'

The anxiety that her mother may be right worries Tambu for a few days. True, she has triumphed again, receiving one of the two places in the highly competitive (and largely white) convent school of the Sacred Heart, where she is being trained by nuns. And she enjoys its challenges, and is looking forward to returning. But she has nights of bad dreams about her dead brother and about Nyasha and Nyasha's brother, who have both 'succumbed' to Englishness. Finally, however, she 'banishes' the suspicion that the Englishness she is acquiring at the convent will place her, too, in a nervous condition.

There is a common critical view that the modern African novel is implicitly addressed to a Western reader. Here, according to that familiar response, is what we might call a 'safari moment': a Zimbabwe constructed for the moral and literary tourist. The story I have sketched seems too easy for us to enter into; shouldn't the life of a Shona village girl be harder for us to make sense of? And doesn't its accessibility undermine its claim to speak authentically in a Zimbabwean voice?

To approach an answer let us start with the fact that Tsitsi Dangarembga's novel lacks the telltale marks of an author addressing an Other from Elsewhere. The Shona vocabulary, including the titles assumed by various members of the family, the food, and the greetings are not presented with an explanatory gloss. Indeed, the author goes to considerable lengths to make it plain that Tambu, far from addressing a Western Other, is not even particularly at ease with that Other. 'Another thing that was different about the mission was that there were many white people there.' So begins Chapter Six. And later on the same page:

Today there are fewer white people on the mission. They are called expatriates, not missionaries, and can be seen living in unpainted brick houses. But they are deified in the same way as the missionaries were because they are white so that their coming is still an honour. I am told that whether you are called an expatriate or a missionary depends on how and by whom you were recruited. Although the distinction was told to me by a reliable source, it does not stick in my mind since I have not observed it myself in my dealings with these people.

These are not the words of a character talking to an Other; indeed, though Dangarembga's irony here presupposes a reader who knows, unlike Tambu, how to use the words 'expatriate' and 'missionary'—and thus draws attention to the possibility that it will be read by a foreign reader—this is a passage that is not exactly friendly to that reader.

As important as these signs in Tambu's language of her distance from a reader from 'outside,' is the fact that the central moral issue of the book—the question of how the postcolonial Western-educated woman and her sisters, daughters, mothers, and aunts, peasants or workers, wage earners or wives, shall together find ways to create meaningful lives, escaping the burdens of their oppression as women, but also as black people, as peasants, and as workers—does not directly concern Euro-American readers, whether women or men, because this question is so richly embedded in a context those readers do not know. Dangarembga's novel assumes that these concerns, which arise from that specific situation, are shared in an immediate and concrete way between the protagonist and her silent and invisible hearer, the 'you' to whom Tambu speaks.

Nevertheless, while not specifically addressed to a Western readership, the problems of racial and gender equity the text raises are not in any way unfamiliar to us. Our narrator never suggests that her readers, whoever they may be, should judge her life by standards different from their own: despite the distancing of her first paragraph—'Nor am I apologizing for my callousness, as you may define it'—she does not presuppose that she lives in a separate moral sphere. She challenges us to hear the story that leads up to her brother's death because she believes that once we have heard it, we—whoever we are—will not find her callous or unfeeling.

Tsitsi Dangarembga writes with the confidence that the story she has to tell will make sense to readers from many places, with many preoccupations, and that she can tell it without betraying the authenticity of Tambu's voice. Tambu has not been shaped to make her accessible to any specific audience, whether inside Zimbabwe or outside. She is fully imagined: a character who reveals her concerns as she tells her story, with all the details specific to its time and place. Because that world is made real in the language of the novel, it does not matter if you know nothing at all of Zimbabwe's cultures, politics, and history. Everything you need waits for you in Tambu's narration.

Each novel is a message in a bottle cast into the great ocean of literature from somewhere else (even if it was written and published last week in your home town); and what makes the novel available to its readers is not shared values or beliefs or experiences but the human capacity to conjure new worlds in the imagination. A fully realized novel provides readers with everything they need for their imaginations to go to work. It is because the world Tsitsi Dangarembga opens up in this novel is so fully realized, so compelling, that Tambu has found so many friends in so many places around the planet.

Source: Kwame Anthony Appiah, "Foreword," in *Nervous Conditions*, Seal Press, 2004, pp. iii–viii.

Supriya Nair

In the following excerpt, Nair shows how Tambu uses her colonial education to raise her social status and achieve her personal goals.

. . . It is, of course, possible to read Tambu's desire for colonial education as a correlative desire for bourgeois status and colonial capital. But the tendency to conflate easily bourgeois feminism and colonial education simplifies the options of women in the so-called Third World. In a discussion of the "inauthentic native," Rey Chow critiques intellectuals who are disturbed by people from the Third World choosing the impurity of capitalism over the revolutionary potential of Marxism (27). The latter apparently have no business to be making this choice, particularly if, as in the case of China, the state officially sanctions Communism over capitalism. Within the privileged confines of the United States academy, it seems easy for us to disapprove of non-Marxist natives while we enjoy the benefits of a capitalistic world, even as we claim radical unease in our positions. The Third World can then be romanticized as the

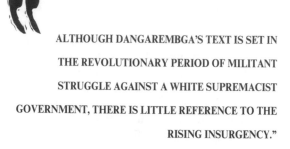

ALTHOUGH DANGAREMBGA'S TEXT IS SET IN THE REVOLUTIONARY PERIOD OF MILITANT STRUGGLE AGAINST A WHITE SUPREMACIST GOVERNMENT, THERE IS LITTLE REFERENCE TO THE RISING INSURGENCY."

"true" revolutionary space that still holds out the promise of Marxism while we live, as best as we can, in the contaminated States. Since these categories have been drawn up as absolute binaries, all choice has subsequently been reduced to an either/or one.

Rather than lamenting Tambu's "selling out" to the forces of bourgeois capital, I would historicize her decision and underline it as a determined choice to transform the homestead while at the same time being aware of her limited options. "If you were clever, you slipped through any loophole you could find. I for one was going to take any opportunity that came my way. I was quite sure about that; I was very determined . . . I would go," she resolves. In her case, one assumes that Ngugi's broken line of harmony from peasant background to formal colonial school will be a fissure that she desires, not just because she is a peasant but because she is a black female adolescent in former Rhodesia, and views this identity without romanticization. What follows is a brief survey of the homestead that Tambu views ambivalently, with both attachment and detachment. Smoky kitchens that cause watery eyes and bronchitis; wood fires that either burn furiously or indifferently, leaving carbon monoxide suspended in the air; trips to the river, Nyamarira, quite a distance from her home, carrying water-drums which press into her spine; a lavatory that stinks and that infects the food through the passing flies. Our narrator relentlessly catalogs life during festival, joyous occasions when the extended family gathers: "Twenty-four stomachs to fill three times a day. Twenty-four bodies for which water had to be fetched from Nyamarira daily. Twenty-four people's laundry to wash as often as possible" (the lack of technological tools to ease these laborious chores goes without saying) . . . and all this woman's work.

Given these living conditions, Tambu is able to resist attempts to keep her from continuing her education because she sees education as one way, however impure and treacherous, of altering her vulnerable status. Her uncle's reluctance to let his niece join a white school is morally inspired. While the colonial school offered material benefits, it was also a dangerous site for a growing girl who would lose her sense of place in the traditional family structure, a lack of mooring that would apparently lead to the woman's looseness or immorality. Tambu's cousin, the rebellious Nyasha, suggests that Tambu refrain from convent education on intellectual and political terms. Here the contamination is a cultural one as Nyasha argues that entry into the locus of colonial civic control will make a puppet out of her cousin. Tambu's mother's protest, expressed by a complete withdrawal from domestic functions as she proceeds to mourn the impending loss of her daughter to white people, marks the threat to the domestic work structure, since she will lose not just a daughter but a companion and helper. Ironically, it is the core of women around Tambu who influence her decision and help her identify what she finally regards as the main threat—not education but the patriarchy itself.

The arguments against education, particularly colonial education, were often played out through binaries of tradition versus modernity, national pride versus cultural imperialism, and where women generally stood in this divide is obvious. The supposed clash with modernity would involve the perils of colonial education: a change in the old ways, a threat to traditional symbols of power, a passive student being worked over by the Western world, confusion and vacillation, exile and alienation, and so on. These were the problems raised when considering the negative aspects of a cultural transformation that some people recognized as much more than an imposed one, and one that grew out of the demands of the changing indigenous cultures. To use these arguments against women, as they often have been, would serve to keep them in their place, which, within the colonial patriarchy, was usually subservient.

Although Dangarembga's text is set in the revolutionary period of militant struggle against a white supremacist government, there is little reference to the rising insurgency. Nationalist histories of independence movements reduce the struggle to a Manichean one, the natives against the colonial settlers. But unrest in the colonies has been a result of dissatisfaction not just with colonial rule, though that was certainly significant. Local grievances were also a contributing factor. As Norma Kriger argues, "unmarried peasant children challenged their elders, women battled their husbands, subject clans sometimes tried to usurp power from ruling clans, and the least advantaged attacked the better-off" (8). In such cases, the various agencies of the colonial state were often strategic elements manipulated in the internal struggles of groups that forged alliances where they could. This is not to suggest that peasant resistance to colonial inequalities was only incidental or oblique, but that the struggle was a multifaceted one.

In the already rigid inequalities perpetuated by the colonial government, rural women had fewer jobs and were paid less. Health and educational issues were grossly ignored. Kriger reports that in 1967 "nearly 80 percent of Africans never finished more than five years of schooling." Most of those who did go and remained in school were males (62). Given such deep unequal development structures, the issue of a native elite isolated from the masses in the case of Zimbabwe (then Rhodesia) was a practically non-existent one.

The gender inequalities of the Shona in the period of the sixties were just as discriminatory. In a system of legal and social structures that favored men, the women were expected to serve their husbands and their families. Tambu's decision to leave for the mission school will have to be read in this context. It is not just the colonial school that she fears will weaken her. Observing the almost divine power that her uncle holds over the women in the family, she confesses: "My vagueness and my reverence for my uncle, what he was, what he had achieved, what he represented and therefore what he wanted, had stunted the growth and faculty of criticism, sapped the energy that in childhood I had used to define my own position." Her emphasis is on returning to a critical position, rather than blindly following the path set for her.

Tambu is also a witness to the struggle between her cousin, Nyasha, and her uncle, in which Nyasha is subsumed both by the burden of colonial history and by her father's unyielding sovereignty. It is interesting that in a larger context of severe malnutrition, Nyasha suffers from anorexia nervosa and bulimia, disorders generally associated with white, middle class women. Nyasha's use, or misuse of food, as the case may be, does come from having enough to throw up, but her illness cannot easily be dismissed as culturally inappropriate. Her struggle against the forces that dictate her life is performed orally, exaggerating and sometimes distorting the daily rituals of domestic interaction as expressive metaphors. Every instance of bulimic purging comes after a verbal argument with her father, who forces her to eat in order to assert his control. Nyasha's violent purging in the privacy of the bathroom is also indicative of the indigestibility of patriarchal order and discipline, which she nevertheless internalizes in her anorexic condition, the exercise of her will reduced to disciplining and punishing her body. But her violent rending of colonial textbooks by tearing into them with her teeth, calling them "bloody lies," is also emblematic of the ideological diet of colonial history that literally sickens her. Her internal and physical disruptions signal severe psychological trauma—a trauma that goes entirely unrecognized until several hysterical ravings, violence against her father (she punches him back), and a skeletal body are finally taken seriously. The available psychiatric help is unable to cure her, however, recommending instead the usual remedies prescribed for emotionally unhealthy women. She is sick but she catches the infection from the alienating structures that are themselves too sick to prescribe a cure.

Even as Nyasha manifests the ills of colonialism, her gendered identity is also constantly in torment. Seeking the respect of her father and desiring a more respectable position for her mother than she sees possible, Nyasha at the same time hates her parents and herself for all their inadequacies. Her sharp insights into their collective devaluation and her discursive eloquence come at a high cost, typical of the melancholic condition. Consumed as she is by her loss, she fills the emptiness within her and then vomits it up in the privacy of the bathroom, unable to position herself productively outside the closeted domestic space.

Tambu, I think, serves as a foil, as an optimism of the will to Nyasha's pessimism of the intellect. She is constantly guarding against the possibility of alienation, articulating her decisions by means of her narrative, willing herself to think critically. At one point, tired of all the injunctions to remember her past, her culture, her identity in the amnesia-provoking atmosphere of the mission school, she wonders, "If I forgot them, my cousin, my mother, my friends, I might as well forget myself. And that, of course, could not happen. So why was everybody so particular to urge me to remember?" Her act of narrating the story is a conscious attempt to inscribe her memory, an undramatic yet meaningful assertion of agency and struggle:

> Quietly, unobtrusively and extremely fitfully, something in my mind began to assert itself, to question things and refuse to be brainwashed, bringing me to this time when I can set down this story ... the story I have told here is my own story, the story of four women whom I loved, and our men...

Unlike Nyasha, who is largely disgusted with the status of the women in the family, Tambu senses their strength in their particular methods of resistance and learns from each one while forming her own distinct identity. But what makes the narrative even possible is, according to the novel's conclusion, Tambu's growing critical consciousness of both the forces that eventually destroy her cousin. While she continues her education, she stops revering her uncle and romanticizing the colonial school.

If Nyasha's story stereotypically presents the destruction of the colonial/exiled student, the response Tambu's "own story" makes to Ngugi's text is that the colonial student need not necessarily be a passive receptacle, reified by the experience of colonial education. Indeed, Ngugi's own work with Gikuyu peasants counters cultural anxieties about mass hypnosis. His contribution as an organic intellectual, or as Fanon's intellectual who engages in a dialogic and dynamic relationship with other peasant intellectuals, is itself a mediated critique of the anxiety recorded in *Decolonising the Mind*. As Tambu demonstrates, while melancholia is often an unavoidable condition of postcolonial intellectual history, it is not inevitably, tragically self-defeating.

Source: Supriya Nair, "Melancholic Women: The Intellectual Hysteric(s) in *Nervous Conditions*," in *Research in African Literatures*, Vol. 26, No. 2, Summer 1995, 10 pp.

SOURCES

Alden, P., Review of *Nervous Conditions*, in *Choice*, Vol. 27, No. 3, November 1989, p. 492.

Barry, Peter, *Beginning Theory: An Introduction to Literary and Cultural Theory*, Manchester University Press, 1995, p. 195.

Bruner, Charlotte H., Review of *Nervous Conditions*, in *World Literature Today*, Vol. 64, No, 2, Spring 1990, pp. 353–54.

Dangarembga, Tsitsi, *Nervous Conditions*, Seal Press, 2004.

Fanon, Frantz, *The Wretched of the Earth*, translated by Richard Philcox, Grove Press, 2005.

Review of *Nervous Conditions*, in *Publishers Weekly*, Vol. 235, No. 5, February 3, 1989, p. 102.

"Zimbabwe," in *CIA: The World Fact Book*, https://www.cia.gov/library/publications/the-world-factbook/geos/zi.html (accessed November 25, 2007.)

FURTHER READING

Ashcroft, Bill, Gareth Griffiths, and Helen Tiffin, *The Empire Writes Back: Theory and Practice in Post-Colonial Literature*, 2nd edition, Routledge, 2002.
    First published in 1989, this is one of the most important books of postcolonial criticism. The authors examine the historical forces that determine how language is used in postcolonial texts, and how such texts form a devastating critique of Eurocentric ideas about the universality of Western literature.

Hill, Janice E., "Purging a Plate Full of Colonial History: The 'Nervous Conditions' of Silent Girls," in *College Literature*, Vol. 22, No. 1, February 1995, pp. 78–90.
    In this analysis of *Nervous Conditions*, Hill shows how the alienation of Shona women from their cultural traditions results in real or feigned sickness, which is used as the only means of rebellion available to them.

Memmi, Albert, *The Colonizer and the Colonized*, expanded edition, Beacon Press, 1991.
    This book was first published in English in 1965 and has become a classic exploration of the effects of colonialism, not only on subject populations but also on the colonizers themselves.

Said, Edward W., *Culture and Imperialism*, Knopf, 1994.
    Said demonstrates how Western literature has been a powerful force in establishing Western dominance over other cultures. In this light, he examines Western literature from the nineteenth and twentieth centuries, as well as contemporary mass media.

Northanger Abbey

JANE AUSTEN

1818

Though it was published posthumously in 1818, Jane Austen's *Northanger Abbey* was written in 1803 and it was the first novel she completed. The book is also one of the first of its day to employ realism (depicting the common, often uneventful happenings of everyday life). The work also comments on the novelistic conventions of the late eighteenth and early nineteenth centuries, including conventions related to the sentimental romance, as well as its subgenre, the Gothic romance. Austen both exploits and mocks these forms as she tells the story of young, naïve Catherine Morland, who eagerly enters the world of the country gentry and upper middle class society, only to be overwhelmed, confused, and sometimes disappointed by the people she meets and by the complexities of their social rules. Often picturing herself as the heroine in one of the romantic novels she reads, Catherine is forced repeatedly to test her notions of appropriate behavior. Her adventures take her from her home in Fullerton to the city of Bath, then to an estate in the country (Northanger Abbey), where her novel-influenced imagination runs wild. Inspired by the frightful mysteries that are the mainstay of Gothic romances, Catherine concocts in her imagination a crime where none actually exists. *Northanger Abbey* is a novel about novels, as well as a novel about contemporary society; and with a light, humorous touch, Austen demonstrates the limitations and the value of both. It is often commented that, while Austen parodies the sentimental novel, her writing is so skillful that she is also able to demonstrate how

Jane Austen (Public Domain)

published in her lifetime, they were thematic and stylistic precursors to Austen's later works.

While Austen's brothers received formal educations, she and her sister were educated largely at home. The girls studied for a brief period, from 1784 through 1786, at the Abbey School in Reading, Berkshire, England. Once they returned home, they continued their education in a self-directed manner, and Austen's interests included poetry, politics, and theology.

In 1795, Austen fell in love with Thomas Lefroy, but the courtship was terminated by Lefroy's mother, who deemed Austen unsuitable, as she was the daughter of a clergyman with little wealth.

During the next several years, Austen began writing novels, drafts of which were later revised and sold. Austen began a draft of the novel that would later become *Northanger Abbey* in 1798 and 1799. She completed revisions in 1803, at which time the work was titled *Susan*. It was sold to publisher Richard Crosby who returned the unpublished manuscript in 1816, though it was later published in 1818.

In 1801, Austen's father retired and moved his wife and daughters to the town of Bath. Austen soon met a young clergyman with whom she fell in love, but he died unexpectedly. The following year, she was engaged briefly to the brother of friends, but she broke off the engagement and never married. Following her father's death in 1805, Austen, her sister, and her mother were cared for financially by Austen's brothers, who subsidized a comfortable middle-class existence for the women in Bath. They moved to the country, in Chawton, Kent, when Austen's brother's wife died in 1808.

Settled once again, Austen began writing in earnest, revising an earlier manuscript. The work became *Sense and Sensibility* and was published in 1811. The novel focuses on the courtship of two sisters, and also explores themes relevant to a post-French Revolution Britain, including property rights and gender issues. In 1813, Austen published *Pride and Prejudice*, a novel that again combined romance with political themes, such as the issue of property inheritance. Austen next published *Mansfield Park* in 1814. In this novel, Austen examines British societal mores (typical customs and characteristics of a community). It was followed in 1816 by Austen's *Emma*, which features a beautiful and wealthy heroine who fancies herself a matchmaker. Austen soon began her

the sentimental novel can be written convincingly and movingly. The effect is such that readers who recognize the satirical elements in the work are nonetheless swept up in a warm and touching love story.

Though it was published nearly 200 years ago, *Northanger Abbey* is available in a 2005 edition that is introduced and annotated by Alfred Mac Adam.

AUTHOR BIOGRAPHY

Austen was born on December 16, 1775, into a comfortably well-off family in the town of Steventon, in Hampshire, England. She was the seventh of the eight children of the Reverend George Austen and Cassandra Leigh Austen. The family was closely knit, and Austen's sister Cassandra was her best friend throughout her life. Like many middle class families of the time, the Austens were quite well read, and enjoyed writing and performing plays for each other. These plays were Austen's first forays into writing. Though these youthful works were not next novel, *Persuasion*. It was Austen's last completed novel and in it Austen turns to such political themes as the social reconstruction of Britain in the years following the French Revolution. The work centers on a heroine who was advised to discourage the attentions of an apparently unsuitable suitor, and is at age twenty-seven seen as a spinster.

Austen, becoming increasingly ill at this time, finished the novel quickly and hurriedly began another, which she never completed. She suffered from what some now believe was Addison's disease, a failure of the adrenal glands. Austen succumbed to her illness and died on July 18, 1817, in Winchester, England.

PLOT SUMMARY

Volume I

CHAPTER 1

As *Northanger Abbey* opens, we are introduced to Catherine Morland and her family. The reader is informed that Catherine is a rather plain, unremarkable girl with nine siblings. Her father is a clergyman, well respected with a comfortable income. Catherine is described as somewhat of a tomboy, and rather unheroic, that is, she does not possess the characteristics of the typical heroines of sentimental novels of the time. At seventeen, she is invited by her neighbors, the Allens, who have no children of their own, to accompany them to the spa town of Bath for a six-week stay.

CHAPTER 2

Having arrived in Bath and having settled themselves in their rented lodgings, Mr. and Mrs. Allen and Catherine visit the "Upper Rooms," a ballroom for the assemblage of visitors to Bath who are out to meet acquaintances and be seen. Mrs. Allen finds no one with whom she is sufficiently acquainted to speak with or for Catherine to dance with.

CHAPTER 3

Attending the "Pump-room" becomes part of the regular routine of the Allens and Catherine. The room features a fountain from which the allegedly medicinal waters of Bath pour. Mr. Allen has come to Bath specifically to partake in the waters for health purposes. While he is there, Mrs. Allen and Catherine stroll the Lower Assembly Rooms,

MEDIA ADAPTATIONS

- *Northanger Abbey* was adapted as a television movie with the same title in 1986, and was directed by Giles Foster and produced by A&E Television Networks.

- *Northanger Abbey* was adapted as a television movie with the same title in 2007, directed by Jon Jones and produced by Granada Television for the United Kingdom channel ITV. The same movie aired on the American Public Broadcasting Corporation (PBS) in January 2008.

another assembly place. Here Catherine is introduced by the master of ceremonies to Henry Tilney, with whom Catherine dances and has tea.

CHAPTER 4

Catherine returns to the Pump-room the next day, eager to see Mr. Tilney again, but he is not there. Instead, Mrs. Allen is reacquainted with an old friend, Mrs. Thorpe, who is the mother of John and Isabella Thorpe (as well as four other children). When the Thorpes recognize a familiarity in Catherine's face, it is discovered that Catherine is the sister of James Morland, who attends Oxford University with John Thorpe.

CHAPTER 5

In the next several chapters, the friendship of Isabella and Catherine is established. Catherine attends balls and the theater with the Allens and with the Thorpes. Isabella and Catherine discover their common interest in novel-reading.

CHAPTER 6

A typical conversation between Isabella and Catherine is related by the narrator as evidence of growing affection the young women have for one another. Catherine and Isabella discuss the novel they are reading, as well as Catherine's interest in Mr. Tilney.

CHAPTER 7

John Thorpe and James Morland arrive in Bath. John's interest in courting Catherine is developed. Catherine finds John's manner somewhat unpleasant.

CHAPTER 8

Henry Tilney's sister Eleanor is introduced. Catherine is eager to make her acquaintance. Catherine seeks the company of Henry Tilney and fails to recognize that John is interested in her.

CHAPTER 9

On an outing with Catherine, John presses Catherine about her relationship with the Allens. He believes Catherine to be favored to inherit the Allens' fortune. Catherine discovers that Mrs. Allen has learned some information about the Tilney family and questions her about them.

CHAPTER 10

The Allens, the Thorpes, and Catherine and James Morland spend an evening together at the theater. The romantic attraction between James and Isabella progresses. Catherine converses with Eleanor Tilney, and is pleased to have advanced their friendship. On another evening at a ball, Catherine enjoys dancing with Henry Tilney and she successfully avoids the advances of John Thorpe.

CHAPTER 11

Having made arrangements to walk with Eleanor and Henry, Catherine is disappointed by rainy weather. As the rain clears up, John, Isabella, and James arrive and attempt to persuade Catherine to join them on an outing. Catherine declines, having made the prior engagement with the Tilneys. John lies to Catherine, telling her he has seen Henry and Eleanor out for a drive. Catherine reluctantly accompanies John, with Isabella and James following in a second carriage.

CHAPTER 12

General Tilney, Henry and Eleanor's father, is introduced. Catherine, given her interest in Henry, is intent on making a good impression on the General. At the theater, she meets the General and speaks to Henry. She is somewhat relieved about her status with the family despite her dismay at not having had the arranged outing with Henry and Eleanor.

CHAPTER 13

John Thorpe does his best to continue to discourage Catherine's affiliation with the Tilneys.

John again thwarts, through deception, an engagement between Eleanor and Catherine. Catherine, angry and hurt, is determined to right any false impression the Tilneys have of her due to John's deceptions.

CHAPTER 14

Catherine, Eleanor, and Henry enjoy an outing, hiking around Beechen Cliff.

CHAPTER 15

Isabella informs Catherine that she and James have become engaged. The young women renew a friendship that had become slightly strained. John attempts to ascertain Catherine's feelings for him, and believes she has some romantic interest in him.

Volume II

CHAPTER 16

Henry Tilney's brother, Captain Frederick Tilney, is introduced. Catherine's feelings for Henry grow more intense. Frederick flirts with the engaged Isabella, and she does not reject the attention, much to Catherine's confusion and dismay. Isabella receives a letter from James, in which he conveys the modest terms of the establishment of their household. He and his father settled upon a fair and comfortable allowance for James to provide for Isabella; Mr. Morland has also requested that the couple wait two to three years before marrying. Isabella is disappointed.

CHAPTER 17

General Tilney invites Catherine to retire with his family to the Tilney's estate, Northanger Abbey. Having been asked back to attend to family business, he seeks a companion for Eleanor. Catherine happily agrees. She looks forward to spending time with both Eleanor and Henry, and also eagerly awaits exploring the abbey, which she pictures as a setting similar to the Gothic romance novels she frequently reads.

CHAPTER 18

Isabella informs Catherine that her brother John is in love with Catherine, and that John believes Catherine has encouraged his attentions. Catherine is shocked and denies the claim entirely. The flirtation between Frederick and Isabella continues, and Catherine is jealous on behalf of her absent brother James.

CHAPTER 19

Catherine discusses with Henry the relationship between Frederick and Isabella. Henry is unable to explain his brother's apparent disregard for Isabella's engagement.

CHAPTER 20

The Gothic section of the novel begins with this chapter. In the next several chapters, Austen alludes to many of the motifs characteristic of the Gothic romances of the time. Catherine and the Tilneys depart for Northanger Abbey. On the journey there, Henry teases Catherine about the romantic notions she has already formed regarding Northanger Abbey. He conjures a story about the mysterious objects and events she might discover there.

CHAPTER 21

Upon her arrival at Northanger Abbey, Catherine's imagination, inspired by the novels she has read, begins to run wild. With the stage set by a dark, stormy night, Catherine comes to believe that the ebony cabinet in her room encases mysterious secrets.

CHAPTER 22

The next morning, Catherine discovers that the cabinet contains only old laundry bills. Henry departs for his parsonage in Woodston, while Catherine is taken on a limited tour of the grounds and home. She longs to see the portions of the abbey that General Tilney elects not to show her. Eleanor and Catherine discuss the death of Eleanor's mother.

CHAPTER 23

Eleanor shows Catherine some of the rooms in the abbey that she previously had not been able to view. At the same time, the young women discuss in more detail the events surrounding the death of Eleanor's mother. Determined to find a mystery in the ancient home, Catherine begins to grow suspicious of General Tilney. His demeanor is often stern and gruff; he is reluctant to show her all of the rooms in the abbey; his wife, Mrs. Tilney, died suddenly nine years ago, Catherine learns. She begins to suspect that either the general had some role in his wife's death or that she is still alive and locked in a separate part of the abbey (both scenarios were common plots of Catherine's favorite novels).

CHAPTER 24

Catherine resolves to search the deceased Mrs. Tilney's rooms. When an opportunity presents itself, she enacts her plan, but is soon discovered by Henry. Rather ashamed of herself, Catherine confesses her suspicions. Henry patiently explains what Catherine perceived to be mysteries, and gently chastises her for her wild imaginings.

CHAPTER 25

Privately, Catherine henceforth vows to be guided by common sense, rather than influenced by notions inspired by fiction. Beginning to worry since more than a week has passed and she has not yet heard from Isabella, Catherine receives a letter from her brother that explains the silence of her friend. James in his letter informs Catherine that his engagement with Isabella has been terminated; he implies that she instead favors Frederick Tilney.

CHAPTER 26

A parson in the nearby town of Woodston, Henry is frequently away from Northanger Abbey to handle business there. The General, Eleanor, and Catherine visit Henry in Woodston. The General hints at this time that a match between Henry and Catherine may be imminent.

CHAPTER 27

Catherine receives a letter at Northanger Abbey from Isabella in which Isabella characterizes Frederick's behavior as annoyingly doting prior to his recent departure to rejoin his regiment. She also expresses confusion regarding James's behavior and asks Catherine to speak to him on her behalf. Catherine is appalled, and not fooled by Isabella's show of innocence.

CHAPTER 28

Soon after General Tilney departs on business from the abbey, Eleanor and Catherine (who are there alone, as Henry is in Woodston) receive word that the General has asked Catherine to leave the abbey, the very next morning. Both women are confused and dismayed at the suddenness of this request, and at the rudeness with which it has been executed; Catherine is to leave by hired coach early in the morning without an escort.

CHAPTER 29

Catherine returns home, dejected. She does not reveal to her family the cause of her sadness.

CHAPTER 30

Not long after Catherine's departure from Northanger Abbey, Henry appears in Fullerton, having been informed of her departure when he arrived back home at the abbey. He followed her directly. Henry explains that his father, having initially been informed by John Thorpe that Catherine was well-to-do, and an heiress of the Allens' wealth, encouraged a match between Henry and Catherine. John had inflated his understanding of Catherine's wealth and social standing when he thought his courtship of her might be fruitful. Having been rejected by Catherine, John informed General Tilney what he had recently discovered through his sister Isabella's short-lived engagement to James— that the Morlands were not wealthy at all. General Tilney subsequently ordered Catherine from his home when he realized that Catherine was not the social equal of his son Henry. Henry ignores his father's wishes and proposes to Catherine.

CHAPTER 31

Catherine's parents consent to the match, but only upon General Tilney's approval, which Eleanor is pivotal in acquiring. Shortly after Eleanor's wedding to a viscount, Henry and Catherine wed.

CHARACTERS

Mr. Allen

Mr. Allen is the neighbor of the Morlands'. He is ordered to the spa town of Bath, which is famous for the medicinal qualities of its waters. Mr. Allen has gout, a condition involving inflammation of the joints. He is described as sensible and, while he is somewhat uninvolved in the details regarding Catherine's attachments, he does attempt to guide her in a parental way about matters regarding social propriety.

Mrs. Allen

Mrs. Allen is the wife of Mr. Allen. She has no children of her own and, suspecting that Catherine is both eager for and old enough to seek entertainment farther afield than Fullerton (the village in which the Allens and Morlands reside), Mrs. Allen invites Catherine to go with her and her husband to Bath for an extended visit. She is described as being a rather superficial woman who is primarily concerned with clothes and finery. Although not unkind to Catherine, Mrs. Allen is not particularly engaged in the events of Catherine's life.

Catherine Morland

Catherine Morland is the novel's protagonist. She is one of the ten children of Mr. and Mrs. Morland.

Described has having been a plain tomboy in her youth, but growing into a pretty teenager, Catherine is presented as being pleasant, but somewhat unremarkable. The narrator notes that Catherine is an avid reader, and that she is "in training for a heroine" of the type in the sentimental and Gothic novels she devours. She has read the type of literary works sentimental heroines would have read, and has studied music and drawing. Having prepared herself as best as she is able for her Bath adventure, Catherine is pleased that Henry Tilney is among the first people to whom she has been introduced once in Bath. Catherine feels that she is in "high luck" to have met someone with such a "pleasing countenance, a very intelligent and lively eye" who "if not quite handsome, was very near it." Direct and forthright, she is unable to lie, and is horrified at the thought of anyone misperceiving her intentions or feelings. When John Thorpe misrepresents her to Eleanor and Henry, Catherine is mortified, and feels compelled to instantly right the situation. Upon learning through Isabella that John felt that she (Catherine) had encouraged his courting of her, she immediately implores Isabella to explain to John that she possesses no romantic feelings toward him, and never has. At Northanger Abbey, in a setting that mirrors popular Gothic romances of the time, Catherine indulges her imagination, expecting to find mysteries everywhere. When none present themselves, Catherine conjures one, suspecting the stern General Tilney to have been involved in some violence against his late wife. Henry calmly disabuses her of her fanciful notions, much to Catherine's shame. She acknowledges privately, after Henry asks "What have you been judging from?", that her irrational pronouncements regarding General Tilney's suspected behavior stem from the type of books she had read prior to leaving Bath. It is not these works—books depicting sinister crimes and mysteries designed to frighten readers for entertainment—that one should depend on for information regarding human behavior, Henry advises. Despite her suspicions regarding the General, however, Catherine rarely ascribes anything but good intentions to those whom she believes she knows well. She is therefore shocked and disappointed to learn that Isabella cared more for wealth than for her brother James, and that Isabella would continue to misrepresent herself, even after James had learned the truth about her. Catherine has grown considerably following her experiences in Bath and Northanger Abbey, having shed her naïve notions regarding the motivations of others, and having discarded many of her own misguided ideas about the world. It is a somewhat wiser, more mature Catherine who marries Henry Tilney at the end of the novel.

James Morland

James Morland is Catherine's brother. He attends college at Oxford with John Thorpe; the two are good friends. While visiting Bath with John, James is reacquainted with Isabella, whom he has met previously. James is also pleased to find his sister Catherine in Bath, and is happy that she has been befriended by Isabella. James courts Isabella and proposes to her. The engagement is soon broken off, however, when Isabella discovers with disappointment the limited finances that James has available through his father's income. James is shocked to find that Isabella and Frederick Tilney seem to have become romantically involved during his brief absence. Like his sister, James grows out of his youthful innocence and naïveté with the help of Isabella Thorpe. Protective of Catherine, he warns her to "beware how you give your heart."

Mrs. Morland

Catherine and James Morland's mother, as well as the mother of eight other children, Mrs. Morland is described as being guided by common sense and love for her children. She and her husband allow Catherine to go to Bath with the Allens, knowing that Catherine is eager and ready, as a young adult, to broaden her horizons. Along with Mr. Morland, Mrs. Morland agrees to Catherine's match with Henry Tilney, wanting her daughter to be happy, but does not give her final consent until Henry's father endorses the engagement as well.

Mr. Richard Morland

Richard Morland is the father of Catherine and James, and of the remaining eight children. Happily wed to Mrs. Morland, he is employed as a clergyman and is well respected in the community. He appears to agree with his wife on most matters where their children are concerned. In preparing Catherine for her trip to Bath, Mr. and Mrs. Morland make arrangements with "moderation and composure, which seemed rather consistent with the common feelings of common life" in contrast to the more refined and extravagant manners of families of a higher social class. This characterization could well be applied to the Morlands in general, with the exception of Catherine's romantic fantasies. In all else, as a family, they appear to be ruled by composure and common sense.

Isabella Thorpe

Isabella Thorpe is the daughter of the widowed Mrs. Thorpe. She is four years older than Catherine, and befriends her quickly. Isabella is shown to be rather shallow, interested very much, like her mother and Mrs. Allen, in appearances. Although she professes to be Catherine's good friend, when Catherine's brother arrives in Bath, Isabella showers most of her attention on James. Although Isabella initially encourages Catherine's interest in Henry Tilney, when John and James arrive in Bath, Isabella attempts to turn her friend's attention to John instead. In addition to being shallow, Isabella is depicted as fickle and false as well. When she discovers how little wealth James would bring to their prospective union, she flirts eagerly with Frederick Tilney. When Catherine questions her, Isabella maintains her love for James and denies her interest in Frederick. In the end, Isabella has a relationship with neither James nor Frederick, nor any other prospects. In literary terms, she may be viewed as the foil (a character who directly contrasts another) to the good-hearted Eleanor Tilney.

John Thorpe

John Thorpe is the brother of Isabella and son of Mrs. Thorpe, as well as the friend and schoolmate of James Morland. He takes an immediate interest in Catherine, which is increased when he suspects she will inherit the wealth of the Allens. He asks Catherine if Mr. Allen is rich, and confirms that the couple has no children, and is interested in the closeness of Catherine's relationship to the Allens. "But you are always very much with them?" he asks, and seems pleased when Catherine answers in the affirmative. John is quite a braggart, always going on about his horses and carriages, and his abilities as a horseman, among other things. He is also quite duplicitous, and goes out of his way to thwart Catherine's relationship with Eleanor and Henry Tilney. It is John who, when first attempting to court Catherine, gives General Tilney a false impression of her wealth, and it is also John who later, when discovering that Catherine has no interest in him, speaks disparagingly of her family and their income. He also tells the

General that the Allens have someone besides Catherine in mind as their heir.

Mrs. Thorpe

Mrs. Thorpe, a widow, is the mother of Isabella and John, as well as two other daughters (Anne and Maria) and two other sons (Edward and William) who are only mentioned briefly in the story. Mrs. Thorpe is also an old friend of Mrs. Allen. When the two women become reacquainted in Bath, Isabella and Catherine are introduced to one another; they form a warm and instantaneous bond.

Eleanor Tilney

Eleanor Tilney is the daughter of General Tilney and the sister of Henry and Frederick. She is portrayed as quiet, intelligent, and good natured. In that she and Catherine grow genuinely and steadily more fond of one another, their relationship stands in stark contrast to the shallow one Isabella initially established with Catherine, a relationship that eventually crumbles under the strain of Isabella's unkind and shallow behavior. At the story's end, Eleanor is married to a man whom she had fallen in love with, who had previously been found by the General to be socially inferior to the Tilneys, but who subsequently inherited considerable wealth and the title of viscount (a British nobleman of high rank).

Frederick Tilney

Frederick Tilney is the older brother of Henry and Eleanor. He flirts with Isabella, knowing full well that she is engaged to another man, a fact that confuses and distresses Catherine considerably. Once the engagement between Isabella and James has been broken off, Frederick returns to his regiment, uninterested in pursuing an extended courtship with Isabella.

General Tilney

General Tilney, a widower, is the father of Frederick, Henry, and Eleanor. Catherine often finds him stern and unapproachable, as well as quite particular about such things as meals and mealtimes. If not always affable, the General is often kind to Catherine, and invites her to accompany his family to their country estate, Northanger Abbey. The General's gruff nature and his unwillingness to allow Catherine to see all of Northanger Abbey are inflated in her imagination to the level of a crime; she begins to suspect him of foul play. Catherine convinces herself that the General has either killed his wife (whom Catherine has been told died of a sudden illness nine years earlier), or that he has locked his wife somewhere within the residence. While she soon realizes, with Henry's help, that neither of these wild stories could possibly be true, the General does treat her somewhat cruelly, despite his initial kindness towards her. When General Tilney learns from John Thorpe that Catherine is not wealthy, nor will she become so through inheritance, the General is angry that he has allowed her to stay in his home, and that he has encouraged a match between Catherine and Henry; he immediately evicts her without an explanation. At the story's end, the General is persuaded by Eleanor to consider allowing Catherine and Henry to marry, and he is pleasantly surprised when he discovers that she is not penniless, but that her family does have a respectable income.

Henry Tilney

Henry Tilney, a clergyman, is the son of General Tilney and is the brother of Frederick and Eleanor. He and Catherine first meet when they are partnered for a dance by the master of ceremonies at a gathering in the Lower Rooms in Bath. He is described as good-looking, and possessing "an archness [mischievous sense of irony] and pleasantry in his manner" that interests Catherine "though it was hardly understood by her." After the dance and tea together, Catherine becomes increasingly interested in Henry, who leaves Bath for a short time after their initial meeting. While General Tilney believes Catherine to be of a comparable social standing, he encourages his son Henry to pursue Catherine. Several years older than Catherine (he is twenty-six to her eighteen by the book's end), Henry often appears amused by her imagination and by the good-natured, innocent way she perceives others. His interest in her is fueled by hers in him; Catherine responds to Henry's wit, his candor with her, and his overall pleasant demeanor. After dancing with him one evening, she gives him her full attention, "listening with sparkling eyes to everything he said; and, in finding him irresistible, becoming so herself." The narrator explains near the end of the novel that Henry was drawn to Catherine from the beginning because she seemed so struck by him. When Catherine's imagination gets away from her at Northanger Abbey and she accuses Henry's father of having harmed the late

Mrs. Tilney, Henry is shocked, but not unkind in his reprimand of her. He implores her to keep in mind "that we are English, that we are Christians." While Catherine fears Henry will distance himself from her, he does not. His affection for her appears to deepen, and when he discovers, upon returning from the neighboring town in which his parish is situated, that his father has sent Catherine away, Henry openly defies General Tilney and follows Catherine. Despite his father's objections, Henry proposes to Catherine and persists in his desire to marry her even while his father refuses, for a time, to give his consent.

THEMES

Gender Issues

Women during the late 1700s and early 1800s had little power over their own destinies. Having no access to higher education, they were schooled primarily in the art of making themselves into a desirable mate. Yet Austen offers several examples of choices women could make that had the power to shape their future. As Henry Tilney observes, in marriage, just as in a dance, "man has the advantage of choice, women only the power of refusal." Austen demonstrates the extent of this power through the character of Isabella. Although at the end of the novel, she is unwed, she has nevertheless, through her flirtation with Frederick Tilney, escaped what has become an undesirable engagement to James Morland. Additionally, the narrator notes that Eleanor Tilney weds "the man of her choice," although General Tilney initially disallows this union, until the gentleman inherited both the title of viscount and a fortune. Catherine is something of an anti-heroine when compared with the heroines of her favorite novels; she is pretty enough, but plain, unworldly, not wealthy. Her lack of worldly experience makes her uniquely appealing to Henry Tilney, despite the fact that he is often amused by her in a manner that sometimes appears condescending. Tilney responds to Catherine's strength of character, and it is in this strength that her power lies—power not merely to attract a husband, but the power to withstand the manipulations of society in general and the Thorpes in particular. She is certain, for example, about her affection for both Henry and Eleanor and does not allow the Thorpes' attempts to cast them as aloof and unsuitable to deter her interest in the Tilneys. Additionally, as the relationship between Henry and Catherine develops, one may

see that while he is older, and wiser in some regards, they appear well-suited to one another in that they both have an honest, candid approach to discourse, and they share common interests, such as their enjoyment of Gothic novels. Catherine grew up as something of a tomboy, enjoying time outdoors and physical pursuits, whereas Henry is shown to have some feminine qualities, such as an interest in fabric and clothes. It seems fair to assume that their marriage will be one in which power sharing, rather than power struggles, will be common. Through their union, Austen demonstrates the possibility for women to achieve, within the confines of the social conventions of the day, a life that is not characterized by the subjugation many women endured. Austen further explores issues of gender and power by emphasizing the differences between sentimental romances and literary novels in an effort to both legitimize and elevate writing as an acceptable and respectable profession for women.

British Social and Political Conflicts

Having witnessed the devastation of the French Revolution, some English authors were eager to point out the political and social differences between England and France in order to encourage the notion that the conditions that brought about the revolution in France did not exist in England. Others took the opposite tack, hoping to sound a warning about the possibilities of a similar upheaval by frankly depicting the social and political conflict in England. Most critics agree that Austen was not an overtly political author, although there is some debate regarding her aims in *Northanger Abbey*. At times she appears to take a decidedly nationalistic approach, extolling, through her more favorable characters, the virtues of English society. In other instances, she knowledgeably references political conflicts contemporary to the late 1700s and early 1800s, the time period in which she was writing *Northanger Abbey* (even though it was not published until some years later). One of the passages in *Northanger Abbey* most frequently cited by critics who seek to stress Austen's own emphasis on the praiseworthiness of English society occurs when Henry Tilney gently rebukes Catherine for her outlandish suspicions regarding General Tilney. Henry implores Catherine, at the end of the twenty-fourth chapter, to keep in mind "the country and the age in which" they live, reminding her that they are English, and Christians. He also points to their education and to British law in

TOPICS FOR FURTHER STUDY

- In *Northanger Abbey*, Austen uses parody for comic effect. She references, either directly or indirectly, elements from the sentimental and Gothic romances she is satirizing, but rather than using such elements to advance the plot in her story, she makes fun of them, often by deflating their power. For example, the mysterious cabinet that is a stock feature in Gothic romances typically will yield an object that serves as a clue to a crime; in *Northanger Abbey*, the cabinet in Catherine's room, despite the suspenseful buildup, contains only some laundry bills. This form of humor is dependent on the reader's knowledge of the material the author is satirizing. What other forms of humor does Austen employ in the novel? Does she make use of less-literary devices? How effective is the humor in the novel for today's readers compared to how the novel was received in nineteenth-century England? Write an essay that addresses these concerns.

- In nineteenth-century England, the middle class was composed of professionals and small landowners who were prevented by their lack of greater wealth from being completely accepted by the upper class. Catherine is ejected from the Tilney's estate when the General discovers she has no substantial wealth. Study the growth and power of the middle class in England during this time period. What was the status of this group politically? What scientific or technological advancements contributed to the success of middle class professionals or to that of the laboring class? How did the upper classes react to the growth of the professional and working classes? Present your analysis in a report.

- *Northanger Abbey* provides a glimpse into the forms of entertainment enjoyed by the middle and upper classes in the resort town of Bath. Research these forms of entertainment and share with the class a slice of nineteenth-century living: play a recording of the type of music enjoyed in England during this time; read a selection from one of the Gothic novels that Catherine and her friends discuss; prepare a typical tea service or share another food typical of the day.

- In a scene in *Northanger Abbey*, Eleanor and Henry Tilney discuss with Catherine various artistic techniques for drawing landscapes, with Henry explaining foregrounding and perspective. Research the landscape drawings of the nineteenth century. How were English landscapes influenced by trends in European art at this time? After finding some examples of English landscape drawings, draw your own landscape emulating this style.

---

order to emphasize the ridiculous nature of her beliefs about his father. In short, he earnestly stresses the stability of England and the civility of the English people. Just a couple of pages later, Catherine will, in her own mind, concede the truth and logic of Henry's arguments. She states that other places in Europe might "be as fruitful in horrors" as those represented in Gothic novels. The "central part of England" with its "laws of the land and the manners of the age" offered a degree of security for unloved wives such as the late Mrs. Tilney. While she still believes that in other parts of the world people may have the characters of fiends or angels, in England people were simply a mixture of good and bad. Balancing this benign portrayal of England is the reference Eleanor Tilney makes about riots when she, Henry, and Catherine are out walking near Beechen Cliff. Henry has joked that the publication of a new Gothic novel might cause a riot in London, and Eleanor seems to fear an actual riot, a notion Henry swiftly dismisses. In fact, as Robert Hopkins notes in his 1978 essay on the political elements of *Northanger Abbey*, the English at the

A scene from Jane Austen's novel Northanger Abbey *(© Lebrecht Music and Arts Photo Library / Alamy)*

turn of the century feared an invasion by the French, and were besieged with riots such as those involving protests over the high price of grain. Hopkins observes that Eleanor's "fear of a new riot was a very real one and characteristic of the 1790s."

STYLE

Sentimental and Gothic Romance

In the typical sentimental novel, which came into fashion in the mid-eighteenth century, the entrance into society of a young beautiful woman is the primary plot device. The "distress" the sentimental heroine faces—in the form of her delicate character being placed in a position in which her reputation and her prospects of securing a suitable husband are in jeopardy—is a

common feature, or convention, of the sentimental novel. *Northanger Abbey* employs conventions of the sentimental novel, but in an ironic way, meant to draw attention to such behavior and criticize it. The trials Catherine suffers, which parallel those of the typical sentimental novel, trivialize the "suffering" caused by parties and dancing and the challenges of maintaining social acquaintances. Yet Austen builds on the conventions of the sentimental novel by exploring the details of everyday life in English society and by tracing Catherine's emotional development as she navigates her new relationships. Gothic romances of the mid- and late-eighteenth century were an offshoot of the sentimental novel and were intended to create a heightened, frightened response in the reader. Austen's treatment of Gothic conventions is similar to her treatment of sentimental conventions: she initially points out the limitations of the conventions of the genre, and then she employs them to her own advantage in telling Catherine's story. Henry Tilney offers a litany of Gothic conventions when he, on the way to Northanger Abbey with Catherine, attempts to frighten her, teasingly, with a Gothic-style narrative of his invention. His story features gloomy chambers, an aging housekeeper, a terrific storm, a mysterious chest that cannot be opened. Catherine in fact encounters many of these very things in Northanger Abbey, and here she looses touch with the simple and direct manner with which she usually approaches her world. Her imaginative responses to stormy dark nights and mysterious cabinets and gloomy corridors align her closely with the stock figures of Gothic romances. She willingly indulges her imagination and allows herself the reactions and corresponding suspicions of Gothic heroines, creating in her mind a crime commensurate with those she has read about in her novels (the death or imprisonment of General Tilney's wife at the General's hands). Catherine's time as a Gothic heroine is rather limited, however, for Henry Tilney's gentle rebuke when he learns of her suspicions is a powerful antidote for her unfounded theories.

Parody

Austen employs a style in *Northanger Abbey* that is referred to as parody (also known as burlesque; an imitation of a literary style featuring exaggeration for comic effect) or satire (use of irony and exaggeration for the purpose of criticizing and exposing shortcomings). Through the course of the novel, she points out conventions of romances of the time and gently mocks them by demonstrating their frivolous nature and by showing how a more meaningful effect can be achieved through greater attention to character rather than plot. Austen's narrator repeatedly refers to the differences between Catherine and the typical sentimental romance heroines. In her simpleness, unworldliness, and innocence, Catherine is found lacking as such a sentimental heroine, but as readers, we are intended to find this to be more of a virtue than a character flaw. In addition to satirizing sentimental novels through Catherine and her experiences, Austen offers a similar parody of Gothic novels by including direct references or more subtle allusions to elements from those novels (such as the setting of the medieval abbey, the mysterious cabinets and locked rooms contained there, and the stormy night that inspires many of Catherine's imaginings). Such elements, which often would have produced clues of some horrendous crime in Gothic novels, in fact have ordinary explanations in *Northanger Abbey*. Catherine's transformation of ordinary objects and events into mysteries, a habit inspired by an imagination fed by Gothic novels, is cured both by Henry Tilney's practical explanations and by Catherine's embracing of her own common sense and her rejection of her romantic imagination.

HISTORICAL CONTEXT

French Revolution

While Austen's work is not overtly political, she wrote during a time of economic and social turmoil in England and Europe. The French Revolution began in 1789 and involved violent class conflict as well as the elimination of royal power in France. In 1793, the French King Louis XVI was executed as was his wife, Marie-Antoinette, later that year. As a period known as the "Reign of Terror" began, England declared war on France. Austen's brothers Francis and Charles served in the Royal Navy during this time. Having gained control of the French government and established a military dictatorship in 1799, Napoleon Bonaparte in 1804 crowned himself France's emperor. That same year, Spain declared war on Britain. Additionally, during the close of the eighteenth century and the beginning of the nineteenth century, England was troubled by domestic upheavals. Not only were

there riots over the price of grain, there were also tensions among small landholders and wage workers who were losing common rights when individual Acts of Parliament authorized land enclosures designed to promote more modern farming methods. At the same time, specialized workers and artisans were rebelling against the industrialization of textile production, industrialization that caused them to experience wage losses and reduced standards of living. Austen alludes to some of these riots when Eleanor expresses her fearfulness as Henry jokes that the release of a new Gothic novel will result in riots in London. With the nation at war with France and Spain and experiencing conflict at home, King George III of England, who had been battling mental illness for years, was declared insane in 1811. The Prince of Wales, who would later become King George IV, became regent at this time. Soon after, the fledgling nation of the United States declared war on Great Britain in 1812. Following the restoration of the Bourbon family to power in France, under the leadership of King Louis XVIII in 1813, Napoleon was defeated in 1815, at Waterloo.

Late Eighteenth-Century and Early Nineteenth-Century Women Authors

In *Northanger Abbey*, Austen makes direct reference to the works of other contemporary female authors. These authors include Fanny Burney, Maria Edgeworth, and Ann Radcliffe. Like Austen, these writers featured middle-class and upper-class characters and the struggles involved in navigating societal rules and relationships in the process of finding mates. Although the work of these women is often the target of Austen's parody, she nevertheless praises their prose efforts. While Austen, in *Northanger Abbey*, attempts (through her parody of sentimental and Gothic conventions, and by creating in Catherine a heroine who is the antithesis of traditional romantic heroines) to elevate the novel above the sentimental and Gothic conventions, she applauds women who have successfully created an alternative, professional future for themselves that exists outside the traditional, domestic roles women were typically allotted in late eighteenth- and early nineteenth-century British society. In her praise of her fellow female novelists in *Northanger Abbey*, Austen observes that these women display the highest achievement in observing human behavior and effectively conveying such observations of human nature with wit and humor.

COMPARE & CONTRAST

- **1800s:** Gothic novels such as *The Mysteries of Udolpho* (which was written in 1794 by Ann Radcliffe) are popular with readers.

  Today: Many people seek out forms of entertainment remarkably similar to those enjoyed in the early nineteenth century. Books and movies intended to frighten, like horror novels by Stephen King (and the films based on them), are among the most popular forms of entertainment today.

- **1800s:** Great Britain experiences an explosion of literary creativity during the late seventeenth century and the early eighteenth century. In addition to the sentimental novels of Frances Burney and the Gothic romances of Ann Radcliffe (Austen references the works of both writers in *Northanger Abbey*), English readers enjoy the works of such Romantic poets as William Blake and William Wordsworth, the historical novels of Sir Walter Scott, the philosophy of Dugald Stewart, and the theological writings of William Paley.

Today: The works of British writers are incredibly diverse and reflect the multinational character of Great Britain. Modern British writers of both English and non-English descent include J. K. Rowling, Ian McEwan, Fred D'Aguiar, and Salman Rushdie.

- **1800s:** In England, class tensions exist between the upper classes and the professional middle class. Additionally, conflicts ignite in the ranks of the working classes as they riot over the price of grain or the industrialization of various industries. (Austen references some of these tensions in *Northanger Abbey*.)

  Today: In Great Britain a major source of conflict is the rights of foreign workers in Great Britain. Fearing the unemployment of native British citizens, some groups and members of Parliament are calling for a limit to the number of foreign workers permitted to seek employment in Great Britain.

CRITICAL OVERVIEW

Northanger Abbey is recognized as an early work by Austen, and many critics point to themes and techniques in this novel that she develops and executes with greater finesse in later works. The novel is often praised for its ability to effectively parody the conventions of sentimental and Gothic romances while utilizing and building on some of these conventions to tell an engaging story. The main problems critics identify in *Northanger Abbey* include the question of the consistency of Catherine's character, the apparent disunity of the Gothic portion with the rest of the book, and what is often seen as an unlikely climax of the story. In *Jane Austen and the Didactic Novel*, Jan Fergus stresses that such criticisms about character and plot consistencies are often generated from comparisons of *Northanger Abbey* with Austen's later novels. Fergus maintains that *Northanger Abbey*

has different aims than the other novels and should be judged on its own merits. The work, Fergus stresses, "is one-dimensional, without the flimsiness that implies: immediacy, excitement and thrust are achieved and do in some degree compensate for losses in sustained or accumulated power."

The issue of Catherine's inconsistent character is directly tied to that of the alleged disunity between the two sections of the novel. What is often cited as jarring about the onset of the Gothic section is the change that overcomes Catherine. Throughout most of the novel, Catherine is a rather direct and unsuspicious individual, but when she encounters elements that remind her of her Gothic novels, her imagination gets the best of her. As Douglas Bush observes in *Jane Austen*, Catherine never allows her imagination to override her "good sense and right-mindedness—except in regard to Henry's home and father." Bush additionally finds

Jane Austen's house at Chawton (Public Domain)

that while the Gothic portion of the work does not ruin the effect of the work as a whole, the section may be viewed as "a conspicuous failure." John Hardy, writing in *Jane Austen's Heroines: Intimacy in Human Relationships*, links the problems in the Gothic section with the abrupt change in Catherine, stating that the issue stems in part from the fact that the "style in which Catherine responds to the assumed Gothic paraphernalia is in contrast to the unbookish freshness with which, in other respects, she articulates her feelings." Fergus takes a different approach when examining the Gothic section of the novel, arguing that, as a parody of Gothic conventions, the Northanger Abbey section is more effective than Austen's treatment of sentimental conventions in the early part of the book.

In *General Consent in Jane Austen: A Study of Dialogism*, Barbara K. Seeber charges that too many critics, while allowing that Catherine may have had some justification in being suspicious of General Tilney, seem to agree that Catherine's beliefs about his capacity for violence simply go too far. Seeber offers another way to view this subject, and argues that "domestic tyranny can extend to murder; while critics of *Northanger Abbey* complacently rule this out, the novel does not." The critic asserts that between the

extremes of the Gothic villain that Catherine imagines and the novel's portrayal of the General as not the most amiable of men, lies the possibility that he is capable of domestic violence. The novel, Seeber stresses, does not confirm or deny this possibility.

Given the shifting targets of Austen's parody and her arguably ambiguous aims, critics often attempt to elucidate some aspects of the work while acknowledging the complexities of deciphering other areas of the text. Others dismiss the complications inherent in the work as the result of the novel being one of Austen's earlier efforts. In *Jane Austen and Narrative Authority*, Tara Ghoshal Wallace concludes that "*Northanger Abbey* refuses to yield a stable vision, either moral or aesthetic."

CRITICISM

Catherine Dominic

Dominic is a novelist and freelance editor and writer. In this essay on Northanger Abbey, *Dominic examines the relationship between Catherine Morland and Henry Tilney, demonstrating the way in which this relationship unifies the disparate*

WHAT DO I READ NEXT?

- *Persuasion*, written by Jane Austen and published in 1818 along with *Northanger Abbey*, was the last novel that Austen completed before she died. It is a valuable source of comparison with *Northanger Abbey*.

- *Jane Austen's Letters* (2003) offers a glimpse into the biographical particulars of Austen's life and demonstrates the same wit that is evident in her fiction.

- *The Mysteries of Udolpho* (1794), by Ann Radcliffe, is repeatedly referenced by Austen in *Northanger Abbey* and is an excellent example of the Gothic romance genre.

- *Camilla; or, A Picture of Youth* (1796), by Fanny Burney, is an example of the sentimental romance genre that Austen parodies in *Northanger Abbey*. Like *The Mysteries of Udolpho*, *Camilla* is referenced directly in *Northanger Abbey*.

- *Jane Austen: The World of Her Novels* (2006), by Deirdre Le Faye, provides a detailed historical context designed to aid in the understanding of, and appreciation for, Austen's novels. The author includes coverage of such topics as foreign political affairs, social issues, fashion, and details about everyday living.

---

sections of the novel by virtue of its unsentimental nature.

At the heart of *Northanger Abbey* is the relationship between Catherine Morland and Henry Tilney. The emotional ties developed between them are often lost in critical debates regarding the efficacy of Austen's parody or in attempts to discern her possible political or social criticisms, analyses, and observations. Yet it is the relationship between Catherine and Henry that provides the unity and the broad appeal of the story for both the intellectual reader engaged in the dissection of Austen's irony and for the casual reader seeking to be

> YET IT IS THE RELATIONSHIP BETWEEN CATHERINE AND HENRY THAT PROVIDES THE UNITY AND THE BROAD APPEAL OF THE STORY FOR BOTH THE INTELLECTUAL READER ENGAGED IN THE DISSECTION OF AUSTEN'S IRONY AND FOR THE CASUAL READER SEEKING TO BE ENTERTAINED BY THE NINETEENTH-CENTURY VERSION OF A ROMANTIC COMEDY."

entertained by the nineteenth-century version of a romantic comedy. While Austen parodies many elements of sentimental and Gothic fiction in the course of the novel, a slow and steady constant in the story is the development of the relationship between Catherine and Henry. It is not a relationship based on love at first sight, nor is it sensationalized in any way. Rather, the two characters share warm conversation, often comic exchanges, and an ability to express themselves with candor that few of the other characters in the book share. It is not difficult to see why they are drawn to one another, and despite the abrupt turns and shocks of Austen's parody, the reader is satisfyingly returned on a regular basis to the growing romantic interest Henry and Catherine have for each other.

Catherine and Henry meet early on in the story, at the beginning of the third chapter. In addition to finding Henry's appearance pleasing, Catherine responds to the "fluency and spirit" with which he converses, and it is through their conversations that their initial bond is formed. Henry is the first person in Bath, besides the Allens, with whom Catherine has any extended conversations. Catherine will soon find, when she meets the Thorpes in the following chapter, that Henry is unique in his ability to appreciate her innocent candor and not treat it as deliberate coyness. She becomes frustrated as the novel progresses in the way both Isabella and John either infer that she has motives that she does not in fact possess, or the way in which the siblings misrepresent her to others. But from the beginning, Henry is able to respond to her honesty, and urge her to continue to be frank with him. When she unsuccessfully attempts social artifice, trying to keep some thoughts about him private by telling him she has not been thinking of anything, Catherine cannot avoid blushing. Henry replies that he would rather be told, simply, that she will not tell him what she is thinking, and then comments that now that they are acquainted, he will be able to tease her about this incident, and that "nothing in the world advances intimacy so much."

Catherine's attraction for Henry increases with each minute she spends with John Thorpe, who shows himself to be materialistic and rather annoying in general. Catherine politely accepts his company on occasion to please Isabella, but her thoughts remain with Henry. When Henry and Catherine share a dance at the ball after being interrupted and delayed by John Thorpe, Henry expresses some irritation, and perhaps jealousy, by comparing the dance to a marriage and suggesting to Catherine that as she has agreed to dance with him, he should not have to share her company with another man. While Catherine refuses to concede that his comparison has merit, she assures him that she has no desire to dance with another man anyway. Henry replies that with this admission, she has offered him "a security worth having." A discussion ensues about Bath and the entertainments it offers, and Henry is described as being amused by Catherine's earnest responses. Such instances are sometimes taken as evidence that Henry condescendingly views Catherine as childish. In fact it could be argued that he is delighted to have an opportunity to see Bath and its society through Catherine's more innocent and optimistic eyes. When she asks who could possibly ever tire of Bath, Henry replies: "Not those who bring such fresh feelings of every sort to it, as you do."

Later conversations are also cited as evidence of Henry's patronizing attitude toward Catherine. When they discuss novels in the fourteenth chapter of *Northanger Abbey*, Henry describes how he has enjoyed many Gothic novels, and Catherine replies that, knowing this, she will not be ashamed to like them herself. This is evidence of Catherine's own youth and social inexperience rather than an indication of Henry's personality. The conversation turns to the picturesque scenery and to drawing, and Catherine's feelings of ignorance get the better of her. While Henry does provide an instructional discussion on the topic of drawing landscapes, it is at Catherine's request. While she is uncertain

of herself in some circumstances, particularly when she is not sure what is deemed socially acceptable, Catherine stands up for herself quite forcefully when she feels she has been misrepresented by John Thorpe to the Tilneys. In order to protect her nascent relationships with Eleanor and Henry, she clearly expresses her frustrations to the Thorpes and proceeds as quickly as she can to the Tilneys to right the possibly incorrect assumptions they may have drawn.

That Henry does have moments of condescension cannot be denied, however, as when he makes a jest that he is "noble" enough to explain to Catherine and his sister Eleanor. He later states that "no one can think more highly of the understanding of women than I do. In my opinion, nature has given them so much, that they never find it necessary to use more than half." His backhanded compliment is disregarded by Eleanor as teasing. Yet his views, at times uncharitable though characteristic of the time period, do not undercut his affection for and appreciation of Catherine. When the two converse about Henry's brother Frederick and his flirtation with Isabella, who is engaged to Catherine's brother James, Catherine presses Henry about his brother's feelings. Henry replies to the best of his abilities: his brother can be "thoughtless," and he "can only guess at" his brother's intentions. Henry does attempt to impress upon Catherine the fact that it is Isabella's motivations that perhaps should be a source of greater concern. In this instance, and when Henry disabuses Catherine of her suspicions about General Tilney having killed or locked up his wife, Henry gently attempts to provide Catherine with a means of more accurately ascertaining people's motivations. He advocates analysis over assumption. At the same time, where his father is concerned, Henry is somewhat blinded by familial loyalty to the truth that General Tilney has the propensity for cruelty, although he does concede that, while his mother was alive, she may have suffered from the General's lack of tenderness: "though his temper injured her, his judgment never did," Henry states. In this unwillingness to acknowledge the shortcomings of loved ones, Henry is like Catherine, who assumes that people operate with good intentions (Henry's father being the exception to Catherine's usual rule). Respectfully, Henry does not mention Catherine's suspicions about General Tilney to anyone, or to her, and for this Catherine is grateful. While Catherine's suspicions seem to run counter to her usual nature, and although this is often cited as part of the discontinuous nature of the novel, the sequence as a whole allows for Catherine and Henry to deepen their relationship by allowing the couple to witness flaws in one another, flaws that neither party uses as a basis for rejection.

Not long after this episode, Catherine learns of Isabella's inconstancy, and she finds with some surprise that, although Henry presumes she would feel terribly sad at having lost a friend, she in fact does not feel as "afflicted as one would have thought." Catherine has learned that the loss of false friends provides one with little to mourn, while Henry learns that Catherine will continue to challenge his notions regarding female behavior. Following this incident, Catherine, though fearful she might have to leave the abbey should Frederick return to announce an engagement with Isabella, stays on at the Tilney estate. Henry and Catherine openly express their mutual feelings of disappointment when Henry needs to be away at Woodston (where he serves as a clergyman). On several occasions, Henry hints at an engagement, although Catherine does not seem attuned to these clues. Before he can propose, however, Catherine is expelled from the abbey by General Tilney's orders. As Henry will later explain, the General had learned that Catherine lacked the fortune the General had previously understood her to possess. Henry follows Catherine to her home as soon as he learns of her departure, openly defying the General. In relating the subsequent events, the narrator explains that "Henry was now sincerely attached" to Catherine, "and delighted in all the excellencies of her character and truly loved her society" but that the attraction began because Catherine's "partiality for [Henry] had been the only cause of [him] giving her a serious thought." While the narrator explains that of course this is insulting to the dignity of a heroine, this statement is intended ironically, for Catherine has not fit the mold of the sentimental conventional heroine throughout the course of the entire novel. Prior to this, when Catherine has been compared unfavorably to a typical heroine, it has been clear that Catherine is to be applauded for her avoidance of resembling such a woman. While a vain sentimental heroine might be insulted, it is unlikely that the practical Catherine would be troubled by such knowledge. Furthermore, Catherine's and Henry's relationship cannot be diminished by the observation that Catherine was more attracted to Henry at the onset than he to her, for their feelings deepened

> **THE MAJORITY OF *NORTHANGER ABBEY* DEALS WITH THE COLOR OF CATHERINE'S CHEEKS IN RELATION TO INCREASINGLY EMBARRASSING SOCIAL SITUATIONS AND MIS-READINGS."**

with each subsequent conversation. Regardless of the origin of the initial attraction, a realistic relationship developed in a reasonable fashion over the course of the novel, a relationship aided as much by Catherine's development into a young woman who is able to appreciate the difference between fiction and reality as by Henry's new-found knowledge that not all women conform to his ideas of feminine behavior. Henry recognizes and appreciates that Catherine sees the world differently from most of the women he knows: she is not blinded by social conventions and manners, nor is she sentimental enough to spend too much time grieving the loss of a false friend. It is for forays into realism such as the unsensationalized development of the romance between Catherine and Henry that *Northanger Abbey* is said to anticipate Austen's later works.

Source: Catherine Dominic, Critical Essay on *Northanger Abbey*, in *Novels for Students*, Gale, Cengage Learning, 2009.

Jenna R. Bergmann

In the following excerpt, Bergmann contends that Austen's use of the motif of "the blush" in Northanger Abbey *reveals nineteenth-century notions of gender roles and responses.*

... The blush in Austen's work functions as commentary on the pervasiveness of the ideology that dictates its expression. This ideology distinctly emerges in the following riddle, published in the conservative *Elegant Extracts* in 1803, which offered young women insight into the function and connotation of the blush:

> Roseate tint of purest virtue,
> Bloom ethereal, Blush divine!
> Bidding, by thy sweet suffusion,
> Loveliness more lovely shine!
> More than beauty's fairest feature,
> More than form's most perfect grace;
> Touching the fond heart, and giving
> Softest charms to ev'ry face!

Test of quick-empassioned feeling;
Jewel, in the dower of youth;
Modesty's unquestioned herald;
Pledge of innocence and truth!
Infant passion's varying banner;
Trembling consciousness display'd!—
Lover, seize the fleeting meteor;
Catch the rainbow ere it fade!

In this formulation, the blush, connected to purity and divinity, simultaneously addresses the gaze of a male lover urged to take advantage of the blush's fleeting nature. Austen plays ironically with this ideologically over-determined convention when *Northanger Abbey*'s rake, Frederick Tilney, flirts with the mercenary, husband-hunting Isabella Thorpe, telling her that her eyes are "tormented" because "the edge of a blooming cheek is still in view—at once too much and too little." Isabella's seductively innocent posturing collapses the gap between the blush as a sign of innocent virtue and a symbol of sexual arousal, revealing the problematic nature of the non-verbal gesture and the importance of reading such signs correctly. An especially perplexing sign, the blush connotes widely divergent and culturally weighted meanings. In his writing on Jane Austen and the body, John Wiltshire notes that "The blush is not a straightforward phenomenon of the body, rather one of the acutest signs of the bodily enigma . . . Its phenomenology is puzzling, and its signification is problematic, but it does, in all its varieties, represent clearly a form of the juncture between the body and culture, and functions as a miniaturised version of hysteria, the embodied correlate of a social affect" (19). The blush, then, becomes not only a site of contestation and competing desire, but also a disease that invades the body, as in hysteria. In the verse from *Elegant Extracts*, the blush is a "bloom" which beautifies women by its "sweet suffusion." In this manner, the blush enslaves the somatic system, denying the blusher agency in her own physical expression and possessing her body by a naturalization and internalization of social convention and its resultant neurophysiological response. Consequently, the riddled phrase "Trembling consciousness display'd" (1.14) reveals intimate connections among mind, body, and emotion in the production of the "roseate tint."

The majority of *Northanger Abbey* deals with the color of Catherine's cheeks in relation to increasingly embarrassing social situations and mis-readings. Before Catherine begins her "training for a heroine," she displays "a sallow skin without colour." At this young age, Catherine, not yet inured to the social expectations of her as a woman, lacks the knowledge requisite to effect a blush. Read in terms of the Somatic-Marker Hypothesis, her culture has not yet programmed Catherine with the positive and negative bodily signals that will eventually "teach" her body how to act and react. Catherine is effectively inscribed with the conventions of her culture only when she begins to "read all such works as heroines must read to supply their memories with those quotations which are so serviceable and so soothing in the vicissitudes of their eventful lives." She consciously "creates" her own memory, constructing herself out of the literary platitudes of her time, such as Gray's 'Many a flower is born to blush unseen.'

Once ideology imprints Catherine with what cognitive neuroscience terms a "body-minded brain," analysis of the blush as a somatic response can begin. As Catherine progresses from young girl to self-professed heroine, she remains attentive to her status as such. In an early scene, as Henry Tilney approaches, she responds appropriately with a smile and a blush of awareness at his proximity. Yet Henry does not see her, "and therefore the smile and the blush, which his sudden reappearance raised in Catherine, passed away without sullying her heroic importance." Significantly, Austen uses the word "heroic," recalling a specifically male act of bravery and courage. In this way, Austen implies a connection between the blush and the female; when the narrator notes that Catherine's blush "passed away without sullying her heroic importance," Austen distinguishes between heroism and ideological susceptibility, suggesting the female hero's awareness of the constructs that shape women's behavior in society. As the riddle reveals, blushing, the realm of the female, exists for the male lover to "seize" and possess as he might the woman herself. Catherine displays femininity, in that she has been stamped by the blush, and masculinity, in her evasion of Henry's gaze; she at once embodies the contradictory spaces of innocent purity and desiring sexuality.

Catherine, spotting Henry before he observes her, continues to occupy this ostensibly paradoxical space. Austen implies that had Henry viewed Catherine's blush, she would have become defenseless, objectified, and stripped of any power she might possess. Yet, because Henry does not see Catherine first, she straddles two socially constructed gender roles: female vulnerability and male heroism. By seeing Henry first, Catherine buys herself the time needed to permit the fleeting blush to fade; thus, she retains the power afforded her by spotting Henry before he spots her. Yet exactly what causes the blush remains enigmatic. Does the blush arise because Catherine loves Henry, even at this early stage of the novel? Is she embarrassed because she may eventually become the focal point of his gaze? Does it indicate growing awareness of her own physicality and sexuality? Cognitive neuroscience addresses this type of problematic nonverbal gesture. Clearly, Catherine's mind and body act in a nondualistic manner, engaging in a conversation occurring on an unconscious level. Perhaps, then, Catherine's lack of control over herself and her somatic expression makes her blush significant. Had Henry seen Catherine blushing, he would have observed her shame and embarrassment at the loss of her physical control and power. As a result, she could no longer have remained heroic because heroism precludes vulnerability to social conditioning and constructed notions of femininity. Yet the gender confusion emerges in this scene as a by-product not only of power relations between Catherine and Henry, but also of a system of communication between the mind inscribed with cultural codes and the body which selects the blush as an appropriate, albeit involuntary, response to a particular social situation.

Since Catherine's physical awareness of one blush generates another, its spread mimics the contagion and transmission of disease; effective communication between mind and body becomes integral to combating this "foreign" influence. When Catherine shows Henry a potentially implicating letter, she tries to edit the contents before she hands it over, "recollecting with a blush the last line." Reconsidering, she nearly throws the letter at Henry, "blushing again that she had blushed before." In this sense, the conflict between innocence and sexuality plays out on Catherine's cheeks: her first blush stems from a fear of her own attraction to Henry, while the second comes from a persuasion of her own innocence and purity. Catherine's body has internalized and copied ideologies onto the fibers of her system, causing her to exhibit a second blush, which effectively "colonizes" her body by depriving her of any means of controlling her own bodily expression.

The emotions that Catherine experiences in this particular scene, embarrassment and attraction, function as physical signals. Based on their pervasiveness, Catherine's blushes respond to particular somatic markers; their frequency also owes to the fact that in certain situations, the second blush proves an unavoidable result of the first.

This episode begs the question of how the mind can unconsciously "weed out" undesirable responses. The blush, as a non-verbal response, serves a basic survival function, remaining an oft-viewed involuntary response. I have already discussed how the blush relates to gendered notions of femininity and female sexuality. In both *Northanger Abbey* and the riddle, the blush functions as a sign that makes "Loveliness more lovely shine!" (1.4). The blush makes Catherine more attractive and more desirable to Henry or any other man who happens to see her blush. As in the scene where Frederick Tilney tells Isabella of his torment caused by the slightest view of her "blooming cheek," the blush helps promote the survival of the organism by making the female of the species more attractive to the male. Therefore, when the body processes its signal, it selects the available responses based not only on attention to social convention but also on the survival of the species. The blush functions as an aphrodisiac, a response of almost hypnotic quality.

The mind and body's susceptibility to cultural stimuli makes the system vulnerable to external manipulation. For example, as seen above, the blush functions as a form of disease that opposes mind and body to a "foreign" influence which threatens to enslave the organic system. Yet other external forces, such as erotic play, similarly threaten to disturb the "natural" operation of the system. For example, Henry Tilney sets out consciously to draw a blush from Catherine. Deeply involved with Catherine in a discussion about language, Henry censors one of his own remarks, warning Catherine that should she desire him to speak his mind, "it will involve [her] in a very cruel embarrassment, and certainly bring on a disagreement between [them]." Knowing that Catherine will urge him to tell all, Henry draws her into an erotic game where the blush functions as a subtext. Not surprisingly, when Henry reveals his censored comments as nothing more than a compliment regarding Catherine's "superior good nature," Catherine "blush[es] and disclaim[s], and the gentleman's predictions [are] verified." While cultural discourse suggests that a lady should blush when complimented, Catherine's blush is not entirely devoid of erotic desire; the manifestation of the blush on her cheeks forces Catherine to become aware of her own physicality, and the act of blushing becomes metonymic for intimate physical contact.

As early as 1797, six years before the completion of *Northanger Abbey* and twenty-one years before its publication, Erasmus Darwin noted in *Zoonomia* that "The blush of joy is owing to the increased action of the capillary arteries, along with that of every moving vessel in the body, from the increase of pleasurable sensation" (387). He further remarked that hot skin results from "an orgasm of the cutaneous capillaries" (Darwin 234) and that "In every kind of blush, the arterial blood is propelled into the capillaries faster than the venous absorption can carry it forwards into the veins, in this respect resembling the tensio phalli" (Darwin 60), or, in translation, the erect phallus. Finally, Darwin asserted that "The blush of young girls on coming into an assembly room, where they expect their dress, and steps, and manner to be examined, as in dancing a minuet, may have another origin; and may be considered as a hot fit of returning confidence, after a previous cold fit of fear" (151). Thus, Darwin connected the blush intimately with both self-consciousness and a discourse of male sexuality.

Darwin's male bias focuses on the relation between the blush and male arousal. The riddle also exemplifies this mode of conventional thinking, whereby the male lover's "seizing" the blush is akin to seizing the woman. However, in *Pleasures Taken: Performances of Sexuality and Loss in Victorian Photographs*, Carol Mavor notes that "Although the conduct books and the English novels of the period, which feature the modest woman as a subject for the narrative, often stress the pleasure affected on others when a young woman diffuses crimson on her cheek, there is no reason for us to believe that it could not (and did not) give pleasure to women as well" (112). Thus, while Henry Tilney's "predictions were verified" in Catherine's blush, and while he derives pleasure from her reddened embarrassment, the pleasure Catherine receives from Henry's erotic play complicates conventional thinking. Shortly after her blush, Catherine forgets where she is and loses track of time,

concentrating wholly on Henry's praise and all its possible connotations. As the narrator relates, "There was a something, however, in [Henry's] words which repaid her for the pain of confusion; and that something occupied her mind so much, that she drew back for some time, forgetting where she was." Almost as if experiencing an afterglow, Catherine forgets time and place, an effect stemming from her awareness of Henry's pleasure at his ability to excite a blush from her skin. Thus, Catherine's blush enacts a form of auto-eroticism in that she pleasures herself by pleasing Henry. Therefore, Catherine's blushes become complicated by Henry's manipulation of ideological conventions.

The blush's close connection with both the mind's awareness of social convention and the body's awareness of its own sexuality makes it a striking example of a non-verbal gesture that forces reconsideration of other textual examples of Romantic anti-dualism. While this ideology seemingly bifurcates modesty and sensuality, modesty constitutes the ultimate erotic charge. Thus, although Henry "pleasures" Catherine with something as alien to the organic system as cultural codes and erotic play, read in terms of cognitive neuroscience, these seemingly unrelated influences become integral to understanding the connections between mind and body. The body's internalization of ideology enables the system to use previously "unimportant" and "irrational" experiences such as feelings to produce the "most correct" bodily response. Without this encoding, positive and negative somatic markers would be unable to effect any impact on the mind's process of response selection.

In conclusion, in the Biographical Notice printed in the 1818 edition of *Northanger Abbey*, Henry Austen notes of his sister Jane that "her eloquent blood spoke through her modest cheek." Significantly, while Henry Austen objectifies Jane in the way that the riddle writer subjects women to the male gaze, Austen plays with these objectifications and ideologies, as demonstrated by the final blush of the novel, which belongs to a man. In relaying his father's unfriendly and tyrannical ultimatum to Catherine, Henry "blushed for the narrow-minded counsel which he was obliged to expose." Initially, Austen appears to invert the conventional male/female binary, where women blush and men are heroes. Yet throughout *Northanger Abbey*, she constructs Henry Tilney as the epitome of an effeminate male interested in and knowledgeable about muslin and lace, and able to discourse easily on such topics with Mrs. Allen. As Henry playfully asserts, "I always buy my own cravats, and am allowed to be an excellent judge; and my sister has often trusted me in the choice of a gown. I bought one for her the other day, and it was pronounced to be a prodigious bargain by every lady who saw it. I gave but five shillings a yard for it, and a true Indian muslin." Furthermore, Henry accurately refers to Catherine's dress as "a sprigged muslin robe with blue trimmings," and declares to her, "My dear madam, I am not so ignorant of young ladies' ways as you wish to believe me." Though obviously teasing and ironic, he exhibits unexpected and thorough knowledge about the female realm: When Henry teases the ladies, he cross-dresses by "putting on" the airs of a woman while retaining phallic control; however, when Henry blushes at the end of the novel, the joke is on him—the pedagogical and confident young hero ultimately loses his volition and power. In addition, his disingenuous discussion of ladies garments makes him a tyrant who uses language to gain power and exercise control rather than to express a true interest in muslin and lace. Austen therefore reinforces rather than breaks down the gender binary. Through the use of the blush in *Northanger Abbey*, Austen strives to expose not the falsity of cultural ideology but rather its brutal, universal presence.

Source: Jenna R. Bergmann, "Romantic Anti-Dualism and the Blush in *Northanger Abbey*," in *Wordsworth Circle*, Vol. 33, No. 1, Winter 2002, 5 pp.

SOURCES

Austen, Jane, *Northanger Abbey*, Barnes & Noble Classics, 2005.

Bush, Douglas, Review of *Northanger Abbey*, in *Jane Austen*, Macmillan, 1975, pp. 55–70.

Fergus, Jan, Review of *Northanger Abbey*, in *Jane Austen and the Didactic Novel*, Macmillan, 1983, pp. 11–38.

Hardy, John, "Catherine Morland," in *Jane Austen's Heroines: Intimacy in Human Relationships*, Routledge & Keegan Paul, 1984, pp. 1–18.

Hopkins, Robert, "General Tilney and the Affairs of State: The Political Gothic of *Northanger Abbey*," in *Jane Austen: Critical Assessments*, edited by Ian Littlewood, Helm Information, 1998, pp. 175–85.

McKillop, Alan D., "Critical Realism in *Northanger Abbey*," in *Jane Austen: Critical Assessments*, edited by Ian Littlewood, Helm Information, 1998, pp. 140–49.

Neill, Edward, "The Secret of *Northanger Abbey*," in *Essays in Criticism*, Vol. 47, No. 1, January 1997, pp. 13–32.

Seeber, Barbara K., "'Unnatural and Overdrawn': 'Alarming Violence' in *Northanger Abbey*," in *General Consent in Jane Austen: A Study of Dialogism*, McGill-Queen's University Press, 2000, pp. 116–26.

Wallace, Tara Ghoshal, "*Northanger Abbey* and the Limits of Parody," in *Jane Austen and Narrative Authority*, St. Martin's Press, 1995, pp. 17–30.

FURTHER READING

Mendus, Susan, ed., *Sexuality and Subordination: Interdisciplinary Studies of Gender in the Nineteenth Century*, Routledge, 1989.

> Mendus discusses the construction of gender roles in nineteenth-century Britain and France. The work will provide the reader of Austen's novels with valuable information on traditional constructions of femininity in Britain during this time period.

Payne, Christiana, and William Vaughan, eds., *English Accents: Interactions with British Art c. 1776–1855 (British Art and Visual Culture Since 1750, New Readings)*, Ashgate Publishing, 2004.

> The editors of this volume provide a collection of essays discussing the ways in which British art, such as the kind discussed by Austen's characters in *Northanger Abbey*, was perceived by the international art community in the late-eighteenth and early- to mid-nineteenth centuries.

Reeve, Katharine, *Jane Austen in Bath: Walking Tours of the Writer's City*, Little Bookroom, 2006.

> Austen lived in Bath and set two of her novels there (*Northanger Abbey* and *Persuasion*). Reeve provides descriptions of the places Austen and her characters visited.

Tomalin, Claire, *Jane Austen: A Life*, Vintage, 1999.

> In this biography, Tomalin provides a widely respected and oft-cited account of Austen's life.

Notes from Underground

Zapiski iz podpol'ia, which was later translated as *Notes from Underground* (and also translated as *Notes from the Underground*), is a first-person novel written in a confessional style, and it is one of Fyodor Dostoyevsky's (also known as Dostoevsky) most philosophical works. It is often regarded as a precursor to the existentialist novel. (Existentialism is a school of philosophical thought that stresses the essential freedom of an individual and asserts that truth is subjective and can be arrived at not through rational thought but through personal experience.) The narrator of *Notes from Underground* remains unnamed throughout the novel, and is referred to by critics as "the underground man." The novel is broken into two sections, the first being the underground man's philosophical discussions of such ideas as consciousness, isolation, and inertia. The second section is written as a narrative rather than in the stream-of-consciousness style of the first section, and the events that unfold therein take place prior to the first section. It relates the events that led to the underground man's literal and metaphorical retreat underground. This section focuses on the underground man's feelings of social humiliation and subsequent alienation, and on his encounter with a prostitute whom he implores to seek a better life. *Notes from Underground*, one of Dostoyevsky's earlier novels, anticipates themes of his later works. These themes include alienation, despair, and the questioning of the

FYODOR DOSTOYEVSKY

1864

Fyodor Dostoyevsky (The Library of Congress)

limits of rationality. These themes are prevalent in Dostoyevsky's most famous works: *Prestuplenie i nakazanie* (later translated as *Crime and Punishment*), published in 1866, and *Brat'ia Karamzovy* (later translated as *The Brothers Karamazov*, published from 1879 to 1880).

First published as *Zapiski iz podpol'ia* in serial form in 1864 in the magazine *Epokha* (*Epoch*), a periodical that was edited by his brother, *Notes from Underground* is still in print and available in a 1993 Vintage Classics edition.

AUTHOR BIOGRAPHY

Born in Moscow, on October 30, 1821, according to the Julian calendar, or on November 11, 1821, according to the Gregorian calendar, Dostoyevsky was the second of seven children. (Both the Julian calendar and the Gregorian calendar were used in the nineteenth century. The calendars differ in the way they calculate leap years, though the Gregorian calendar is most commonly used today.) Dostoyevsky's father, Mikhail Andreevich Dostoyevsky, was a doctor. As a child, Dostoyevsky attended boarding school in Moscow. The family left Moscow

in 1828 when Mikhail Andreevich Dostoyevsky was granted the rank of a nobleman and he purchased a village estate. After the 1837 death of Dostoyevsky's mother, Mariia Fedorovna, his father enrolled him in a military engineering school in St. Petersburg. Dostoyevsky's father died in 1839. Dostoyevsky completed his education at the academy as an officer. He then worked as a draftsman but retired in 1843 to pursue his writing.

That year, he began his first work of fiction, *Bednye liudi*, which was published in book form in 1846 and later translated as *Poor Folk*. The critically acclaimed novel centers on a timid man who attempts to save a woman from an unwanted marriage. Dostoyevsky followed this with several short stories that were psychological as well as political in nature. In 1849, Dostoyevsky was arrested for political activities, which included his involvement in a group that discussed socialism, freedom of the press, and other related topics. Dostoyevsky served four years of hard labor in Siberia. Following his release from prison in 1854, he spent several years in army service in the village of Semipalatinsk. He continued to write; his work included the novella *Selo Stepanchikovo i ego obitateli* ("The Village of Stepanchikovo and Its Inhabitants"), published in 1859.

In 1857, Dostoyevsky married the widow Maria Dmitrievna Isaeva. An epileptic, Dostoyevsky's attacks increased following his release from prison, and he used this medical issue as grounds for petitioning for his early return to St. Petersburg. Only gradually were Dostoyevsky's rights—including the ability to retire from the army and the permission to publish—returned to him. He was allowed to return to St. Petersburg in 1859. His feelings of isolation and alienation that developed during his imprisonment and army service informed his subsequent writings. The narrator's paranoia and alienation in *Zapiski iz podpol'ia* are reflective of the intensity of these feelings. The work was published in 1864 in two issues of the journal *Epokha*. (The novel was later translated as *Notes from Underground*). This was also the same year Dostoyevsky lost his wife and his brother.

In 1866, one of Dostoyevsky's best-known works, *Prestuplenie i nakazanie* was published in serial form in the journal *Russkii vestnik*. The work was later translated and published as *Crime and Punishment*. A psychological novel that explores a crime through the criminal's eyes, the novel won immediate critical praise for the precision of its psychological analyses. Dostoyevsky remarried in 1867, this time to a stenographer named Anna Grigorevna Snitkina; the couple had a daughter in 1869. In 1879 and 1880, Dostoyevsky's final novel, *Brat'ia Karamzovy*, was also published in serial form in *Russkii vestnik*. The novel was later translated and published as *The Brothers Karamazov*. The work focuses on the murder of the father of the Karamazov family, and on his sons, one of whom is arrested for the murder. Dostoyevsky died in 1881 (on January 28, Julian calendar; or February 9, Gregorian calendar) of complications from emphysema and epilepsy.

MEDIA ADAPTATIONS

- The film *Notes from Underground*, based on Dostoyevsky's novel and adapted and directed by Gary Walkow, was produced in 1995. It stars Henry Czerny as the underground man and Sheryl Lee as Liza. The cast also includes Jon Favreau and Seth Green. The DVD (by Walkow/Gruber Pictures Production in association with Renegade Films) was released in 1998.

PLOT SUMMARY

Underground

CHAPTER 1

The narrator describes himself as both sick and wicked. Explaining that he is a former civil servant, he contradicts himself repeatedly, taking back what he has said about his wickedness almost as soon as he has said it. He notes "I never even managed to become anything, neither wicked nor good, neither a scoundrel nor an honest man, neither a hero nor an insect." He also informs the reader that he lives in St. Petersburg.

CHAPTER 2

The narrator focuses on the issue of consciousness, particularly his own heightened consciousness. He explains that the more highly developed one's sense of consciousness is, the more one realizes there is nothing to do, to seek, to become. Inertia is the result of heightened awareness. The underground man reveals his perception that his intelligence is superior to that of other people, and that this isolates him from society.

CHAPTER 3

The underground man informs the reader that a normal man is quite stupid, but this fact allows him to be capable of action, such as revenge. A highly conscious individual, like himself, is really more of a mouse. The narrator explores the ways in which this highly conscious mouse could be as deeply offended by the actions of another person, in the same way as the stupid man. Yet the mouse understands that to act on the feeling of offense is impossible. Inertia

remains the state of a highly conscious individual, even though he is plagued by uncertainty and pain.

CHAPTER 4

The narrator uses the metaphor of a toothache to examine how pain, to a highly conscious person, may be seen as pleasurable, and is perhaps the only pleasure he is able to enjoy in his life. The chapter concludes with the question of whether or not a highly conscious individual can respect himself.

CHAPTER 5

The underground man returns to the idea of inertia and its relation to consciousness. He speaks of how he forced himself to fall in love, or start hating, in order to escape the pure boredom of inaction, yet inertia remains the result. Intelligent men like himself are often left with only their own babbling.

CHAPTER 6

The underground man explores the idea of the "beautiful and lofty." The phrase sarcastically refers to the romantic idealism prevalent in 1840s Russian literature. Additionally, the narrator mocks the aesthetics of the 1860s, in his discussion of the artwork in this section.

CHAPTER 7

The notion of self-interest is explored, and the underground man questions whether a person may "act knowingly against his own profit."

Pursuing the idea of man's actions being related to the laws of nature, the narrator demonstrates that scientific explanations for behavior can result in the view that man "will no longer be answerable for his actions." The consequence, he suggests, is that all actions may be calculated mathematically and there will be no action left in the world. He then rejects this notion in favor of the idea that man acts "as he wants, and not at all as reason and profit dictate; and one can want even against one's own profit."

CHAPTER 8

The underground man discusses the nature of human desires, stating that contrary to the arguments that wanting and free will do not exist, and that human actions can be mathematically predicted, it is, rather, that our desires make us human. Wanting encompasses our whole lives, including our reason as well as our desires. The underground man continues to explore the limits of reason.

CHAPTER 9

The underground man assumes his readers interject with the objection that, if man's desires do not conform "with the demands of science and common sense," they need to be corrected. He questions why such a correction would be necessary. Arguing that man is hampered by his fear at accomplishing the goals of science and reason, the underground man explains why men are inclined both to create and to destroy. Achievement of goals means that a man will no longer have anything to search for; he will no longer have a purpose. The only solution, the narrator maintains, is for man to turn to contemplation, yet the result of heightened consciousness is inertia.

CHAPTER 10

The idea of a "crystal edifice" is derided by the underground man. The phrase is used to refer to a metaphorical edifice that is the embodiment of rational ideals, but is also a reference to the Crystal Palace, an actual, physical structure built in 1851 in London to showcase the latest technological inventions of the Industrial Revolution.

CHAPTER 11

The underground man returns to the notion of "conscious inertia," and how this is the only possible course of action. He questions whether it is "possible to be perfectly candid with oneself

and not be afraid of the whole truth." He explains that the reason he has written anything at all is because he is bored, and that writing is like work, and work keeps him out of trouble. Stating that the snow outside has reminded him of an incident from his past, he introduces the next section of the book.

Apropos of the Wet Snow
CHAPTER 1

The underground man states that at the time the events in this section took place, he was twenty-four years old. He reveals the extent to which he thinks himself superior to others, stating that his intellect is highly developed and consequently he feels like "a coward and a slave" to be working in his office, with stupid men. He emphasizes the isolating nature of his intellectual superiority, and expresses a desire for the social equality he feels his coworkers do not extend to him. In his isolation from society, he alternately comforts himself with reading, or with pursuing a bit of "debauchery." One night he comes upon men fighting, and wishes to become involved. He fails to do so but finds himself slighted by an army officer, who moves him out of the way in order to pass; the officer takes no notice of the underground man. The underground man's perception that the officer is too socially superior to notice him leaves him desiring revenge. He resolves to bump into the officer while out walking, and then to take no notice of having bumped him. After concocting a plan to accomplish this goal, he eventually achieves his purpose.

CHAPTER 2

The underground man speaks of sometimes repenting his sins, and feeling hopeful for a little while, and of slipping into a dream state in which he feels incredible love. But when the dreams end (he is "incapable of dreaming for longer than three months at a time") he feels the need to immerse himself into society. In one of these states of mind, the underground man resolves to visit a former schoolmate, Simonov, whom he has not seen for nearly a year.

CHAPTER 3

Simonov and two other friends (Ferfichkin and Trudolyubov) are discussing a farewell party they wish to throw for another friend, Zverkov, who is now an army officer about to leave for an assignment. The four men went to school with the underground man. Feeling as if they are ignoring him, the narrator recalls how everyone at school hated him. As the men discuss the party, the underground man grows annoyed; he is being ignored. While it is common knowledge that the underground man and Zverkov were never on friendly terms, the underground man insists that he be allowed to join the party. The men reluctantly agree to include him. The next morning, he frets over what he will wear to the dinner party, and what the others will think of his shabby clothes.

CHAPTER 4

The narrator arrives at the restaurant an hour before the group does (they had changed the time but failed to notify him). Infuriated with what he perceives to be Zverkov's attempts to embarrass him, the underground man mocks Zverkov to the point that Zverkov does try to embarrass the underground man. The other men join in. Despite the obvious animosity between himself and the group, the underground man does not leave. Eventually, the men decide to adjourn to a brothel, and the underground man begs their forgiveness and also asks Simonov to lend him money so that he may join them. Angrily, Simonov shoves the money at the underground man and departs with his friends.

CHAPTER 5

The underground man follows the group. Resolving to get his revenge, he decides that slapping Zverkov's face is the only thing he can honorably do. When he arrives at the brothel, the men are not there. The underground man expresses extreme relief at not having to slap Zverkov. He sees a beautiful young woman, a prostitute, who has entered the room, and he approaches her.

CHAPTER 6

The underground man asks the prostitute her name, and she informs him that it is Liza; he struggles for something to say. Liza is brief and vague in her responses to his subsequent questions. The underground man tells her a story about a girl from a brothel who died and whose coffin he had seen being carried out of a basement. He tells Liza that she too will one day die like the other girl, sick and alone and unknown. He urges her to change her life so she can still "find love, marry, be happy." Liza's response to his speech is somewhat dismissive. He begins again, condemning Liza's life

as a prostitute, warming to what he describes as a fascinating game. He speaks of morality, poverty, of what drives young women like Liza to live as slaves. While he begins to feel guilty about his manipulation of her, she charges that he seems to speak as if he has learned these things from a book, and he feels mocked.

CHAPTER 7

Driven by his perception of Liza's mockery of him, the underground man begins his speech-making again, attempting to draw out her feelings of shame, attempting to belittle her, accusing her of enslaving her own soul, as well as her body. He tells her another story, more graphic than the first, about a prostitute who dies from illness. Looking at Liza, he finds that she is crying into her pillow. Rushing to leave, he gives Liza his address before he departs.

CHAPTER 8

Once home, the narrator regrets having given Liza his address. He vows to pay Simonov back, and borrows money to do so. He is tormented by thoughts of Liza. As several days pass and Liza does not appear, the underground man begins to feel relief that she will leave him alone, but he imagines the two of them together, in love. The underground man becomes distracted by his servant Apollon, whom the underground man still has failed to pay. He berates Apollon for the servant's pride. As he is yelling at Apollon, Liza appears.

CHAPTER 9

"Disgustingly embarrassed" by her finding him in this state, yelling and wearing a tattered dressing gown, the underground man invites Liza to sit down. He attempts to explain the situation, and succumbs to a fit of despair. Blaming the unpleasantness on Liza, the underground man admits he is angry with himself, but that "naturally, she was going to bear the brunt of it," so he refuses to speak. Liza breaks the silence, informing him that she wishes to leave the brothel permanently. The underground man finally responds by telling her that on the evening they had been together, he had felt humiliated, and that he in turn had humiliated her. "That's what it was," he tells her, then asks "and you thought I came then on purpose to save you, right?" He continues to rant, exposing his own self-loathing to her. He weeps; she comforts him. The underground man realizes that she has become the heroine and he the humiliated one, and as he grasps his need for power over her, Liza embraces him passionately.

CHAPTER 10

After Liza and the underground man make love, he is impatient for her to leave. As she bids him farewell, he attempts to pay her. When he finds the money she let slip from her fingers before she left, the underground man, feeling ashamed, tries to follow her, but the falling snow has covered her footsteps. He stands indecisively, then decides she will be better off without him having "dirtied her soul." He resolves to retreat underground.

CHARACTERS

Apollon

Apollon is the underground man's servant. He speaks little, refusing to ask the underground man about the wages he is owed; the underground man takes this to be an indication of Apollon's pride. Apollon remains calm while suffering the onslaught of the underground's man anger.

Ferfichkin

Ferfichkin is one of the underground man's former schoolmates who is visiting Simonov when the underground man appears. The underground man seems annoyed with him from the beginning. Ferfichkin is described as "short" and "monkey-faced," and as "a fool" who is both ambitious and cowardly. The underground man also comments that Ferfichkin was his worst enemy even when they were young children. At Simonov's, Ferfichkin is openly rude and aggressive toward the underground man. "But we have our own circle, we're friends," he complains to Trudolyubov and Simonov. To the underground man he comments "maybe we don't want you at all." Ferfichkin's manner with the underground man is just as contentious at the farewell party for Zverkov. The underground man challenges Ferfichkin to a duel, but the whole affair is laughed off by all but the underground man.

Liza

Liza is the prostitute with whom the underground man spends the night after he fails to find Simonov, Ferfichkin, and Zverkov after the dinner party. She is described by the underground man as being attractive, but in such a way that the others would not have noticed. Liza endures the underground man's attempts to shame and frighten her away from a life of prostitution. She responds by seeking him out, much to his dismay. Upon her arrival, the underground man is embarrassed that he has been yelling at Apollon, and embarrassed by the shabby condition of the dressing gown he wears. His agitation is obvious, and Liza informs him that she is intent on leaving the brothel. After the underground man rants about his anger with her for having seen him in his current state, Liza runs to him and holds him while they both weep. The underground man cries out: "They won't let me ... I can't be ... good!" When he has finished crying, she embraces him passionately. After they make love, the underground man watches Liza in the bedroom, sitting on the floor, perhaps crying. As she prepares to leave, the underground man attempts to pay her, and she leaves the money behind before disappearing down the street. Liza is often viewed as a catalyst; it is her story that the underground man is reminded of when he sees the snow at the end of the first section of the novel. She represents human connection, and hope and love, all of which the underground man ultimately rejects.

The Officer

An unnamed officer in a bar becomes the object of the underground man's obsession. One night, when the underground man was out hoping to become involved in a bar fight, the officer finds the underground man blocking his way past the billiard table. The underground man relates how the officer "took me by the shoulders and silently—with no warning or explanation—moved me from where I stood to another place, and then passed by as if without noticing." While the underground man fails to protest at this time directly to the officer, he later finds that he cannot avoid thinking about the incident and how he needed to avenge himself for this social slight. For several years after, the underground man would see the officer on the street, and he began to follow him. Eventually, he resolves to bump into the officer while out walking, and he concocts an intricate plan to accomplish his goal. Finally, he succeeds, and though the officer seems not to notice, the underground man is sure he is only pretending not to have noticed. The officer symbolizes the social superiority the underground man assumes other people feel they possess.

Anton Antonych Setochkin

Setochkin is the underground man's department chief at work and is described as "a humble but serious and positive man, who never loaned money to anyone." Despite this, the underground man does ask Setochkin to loan him money; he needs it to buy a new fur collar for his coat, so that he may look respectable when he bumps into the officer whom he feels has slighted him. Setochkin does loan the underground man the money he needs. He is also the person the underground man first turns to when he feels the need to interact socially, and in fact is the only "permanent acquaintance" the underground man has. Setochkin lends the underground man money a second time as well, when the underground asks him for fifteen roubles, in order to pay back Simonov for the money he had lent the underground man the night before.

Simonov

Simonov is a former schoolmate of the underground man. The underground man remarks that, while he does not even acknowledge most of his former schoolmates if he sees them on the street any longer, Simonov seems more open-minded than the others; he is described as independent and honest. The underground man remarks that he suspects Simonov finds him repulsive, but he keeps visiting him anyway. Simonov reluctantly agrees to let the underground man attend the farewell party for Zverkov. At that party, Simonov offends the underground man by acknowledging, without apologizing, that he forgot to send word to the underground man that the time of the party had been changed. He is uncomfortable with the underground man's increasingly rude behavior, but he nevertheless lends him money later in the evening.

Trudolyubov

Trudolyubov is one of the former schoolmates whom the underground man finds visiting with Simonov. The underground man describes him as a cold, military type of personality who is focused on success and promotions. According to the underground man, Trudolyubov thinks quite little of the underground man. Trudolyubov seems confused by the underground man's insistence that he be allowed to attend the farewell party

for Zverkov, observing that the two men were never on good terms with one another. When the underground man begins to cause trouble at the party, Trudolyubov urges him to stop disrupting things, particularly since he invited himself along to the gathering in the first place. By the end of the evening, Trudolyubov has dismissed the underground man as a drunk and as a crazy man.

The Underground Man

The underground man is the narrator of the novel; the story is told entirely from his perspective. He describes himself in the first section of the book as a forty-year-old former civil servant who is sick but too suspicious of doctors to obtain treatment. He has been living alone, "underground," for nearly twenty years. The underground man contradicts himself frequently, and makes it difficult for readers to gauge his sincerity regarding any of the philosophical topics he discusses. Repeatedly he emphasizes his superior intelligence and heightened consciousness. Referring often to the way he presumes he is, or has been, perceived by others, the underground man reveals his deeply rooted sense of paranoia. He additionally describes his intense feelings of alienation and isolation. In the narrative section of the novel, these qualities are demonstrated as well in the underground man's twenty-four-year-old version of himself. Certain that others hate him and seek to offend him, he plots a complex plan to bump into a man who moved him aside at a bar. He invites himself along to a party consisting of men for whom he has no positive feelings, and whom he is certain dislike him immensely. He is almost vicious in the need to cause offense to individuals whom he perceives have offended him (including the unnamed officer, his old schoolmates, and Liza), yet at the same time, he wishes for some sort of social recognition or acceptance from them. After the possibility of some sort of relationship with Liza—a woman who was moved by his words, who sought him out as a friend, perhaps even a savior—is severed by his cruel attempt to pay her for sleeping with him, the underground man finds that he is driven, when in the company of others, to dominate and tyrannize. He longs for peace, to be left alone, he asserts. Having driven Liza away at the end of the novel, he retreats underground.

Zverkov

Zverkov is another former schoolmate of the underground man. He is to be honored at a farewell party that Simonov, Ferfichkin, and Trudolyubov are planning on throwing for him in honor of his promotion and his impending move to another province. Now a successful military officer, Zverkov is described by the underground man as having been a boy whom everyone had liked in school. The underground man notes, however, that he had hated Zverkov, even as a boy, because of his good looks and confidence. When Zverkov and the underground man first see each other at Zverkov's party, the underground man almost immediately feels he is being condescended to. Seeing that Zverkov is being polite and deferential to him, the underground man feels that Zverkov is mocking him deliberately in order to offend him. This sets the tone for the rest of the evening, as the underground man becomes increasingly belligerent with the group, and they become increasingly annoyed with him, particularly since it was he—the underground man—who had insisted on joining them. Zverkov starts to ignore him and begins to entertain the others with stories about women and about his military acquaintances. By the end of the evening, the underground man attempts to apologize to Zverkov, as well as the others, but his efforts are not well received. Zverkov assures the underground man that it is not possible for someone such as the underground man to offend him.

THEMES

Alienation and Isolation

The underground man's sense of alienation and isolation from society is intense. At times it seems as though he has chosen to isolate himself, and on other occasions his extreme paranoia results in his feeling as though society has intentionally alienated him. He is extremely aware of how different he is, or perceives himself to be, from the rest of society, and this is the main reason for his sense of isolation. Certain that his consciousness is highly evolved while most other men are quite stupid, he seems to feel that his living underground, away from society, is inevitable. The effects of this isolation are witnessed by the reader. The reader sees a man who lives in a world of paradox; he repeatedly asserts one thing, and in the next breath states the exact opposite. As an officer, he was wicked, the underground man tells us. Almost directly after, he informs the reader he has lied to us and that he was in fact "never able to become wicked." He then observes that he is aware that

TOPICS FOR FURTHER STUDY

- The underground man is a complex, often abrasive individual. He manipulates people; he seems to seek their company, their friendship, and their respect (as he does with Simonov and his friends, and with Liza), only to push them away again. Write an essay on someone you may know who shares these qualities. Do you feel their interest in friendship is genuine? What might their other motivations be? What personal problems might they have that would prohibit them from developing normal relationships?

- Rewrite the farewell dinner party scene in the first person from the viewpoint of Simonov or one of his friends. How does the individual you selected respond to the underground man and his actions? How does what that character says differ from what he thinks? Does what you wrote significantly change the way the scene would be interpreted? How might the scene be conveyed objectively? Discuss your findings with the class.

- Dostoyevsky's writings were heavily influenced by the philosophical trends and political events of the 1860s. Write a report on Russian Rationalism in the 1860s, paying particular attention to the way this trend grew out of the Romanticism of the 1840s. What types of fiction were other writers, such as Leo Tolstoy (1828–1910) or Ivan Turgenev (1818–1883) publishing at this time? How were these works alike or different from *Notes from Underground*?

- In *Notes from Underground*, the narrator refers a number of times to the "Crystal Palace." Explain in a written or oral report what the actual Crystal Palace in England was, why it was built, what it contained, and what it represented—to the English, to Europe, to the rest of the world. What was the fate of the Crystal Palace?

he possesses elements that are completely opposite of one another. The sense of isolation that inspires manic rants in the first half of the novel actually began developing earlier in his life, during the time that encompasses the second half of the novel. The underground man explains early in the second half of the novel that he is tormented by the idea that no one else was like him, and that he is unlike anyone else. After spending months in isolation, he "would begin to feel an irresistible need to rush into society." This usually entailed a visit to the home of his department chief (Setochkin), where he would also endure the company of Setochkin's daughters and their aunt. Upon returning home after such visits, the underground man seeks nothing more than to alienate himself from society once again, vowing to "put off for a while my desire to embrace the whole of mankind." While he seems internally driven toward solitude, he also feels the force of alienation as an external force. This can be observed in his view of time. In several places in the novel, the underground man notes the unpleasant sounds of clocks. Preparing to leave for Zverkov's farewell dinner, the underground man comments that finally "my wretched little wall clock hissed five." Later, upon waking next to Liza at the brothel, he notes that "Somewhere, behind a partition, as if under some strong pressure, as if someone were strangling it, a clock wheezed. After an unnaturally prolonged wheeze, there followed a thin, vile, and somehow unexpectedly rapid chiming—as if someone had suddenly jumped forward." Back in his apartment, after fighting with Apollon and at the moment Liza arrives, his "clock strained, hissed, and struck seven." Time, in these examples, represented by the painful movement of the clocks, demarks the events of his life. The way time is characterized—as hissing, wheezing, strangled—emphasizes not only the underground man's desire to escape real life and retreat underground, but it also stresses his sense of alienation from the world that other people seem to live in rather comfortably. He is driven to his isolation as much as he seeks it voluntarily.

Inertia

Repeatedly in the first section of the novel, the underground man makes reference to how his highly evolved sense of consciousness, his above average awareness of reality, results in inertia. Action becomes impossible based on the underground man's logic. Being aware of the good in the world, the very act of being conscious of this good, makes the underground man stuck in his "mire." He finds that being stuck in this way actually seemed to him to be his normal state, rather than something he arrived at by chance or decision. He describes feeling humiliated by this condition, certain that he alone experienced it. His awareness of this humiliation leads him to feel as though he has "reached the ultimate wall," and he feels as though even if he possessed the time and the faith necessary in order to change himself, "there is perhaps nothing to change into." The consequence of this line of thinking, the underground man explains, is that "there is simply nothing to do at all." In the second half of the novel, which takes place prior to the first half, the narrator describes the events leading him to this inertia. While he seeks action, it is apparent from the very beginning of this section that the underground man perpetually finds himself in situations that leave him feeling offended and subsequently necessitate the need for revenge. In the course of planning or enacting the revenge, the underground man gets tripped up by his own habit of intellectually dissecting the events that leave him feeling socially slighted. He spends inordinate amounts of time planning to bump into the officer from the bar. He insinuates himself into the group of Simonov and friends in order to prove to them that they are not superior to him; this becomes a lengthy ordeal involving convincing the men to invite him, worrying excessively about the party prior to it, insulting the men at the party only to draw back, silently fuming and pacing for hours, then attacking again, then begging forgiveness. He appears to be taking action, but every action is in fact accompanied by excruciating mental analyses of his actions. In the end, after the underground man's tortured exchange with Liza, which features long periods of pondering what he will say to her and how he will say it and what the likely effect will be, and in which he humiliates her, baits her, sympathizes with her, fears her, confronts her, and humiliates her again, the underground man resolves to abandon almost entirely the bits of action that intersperse his thinking. He longs for peace, for solitude, for the underground, informing the reader that "we've reached a point where we regard real 'living life' almost as labor, almost as service, and we all agree in ourselves that it's better from a book." It is inertia, rather than the real living of life, that he seems to want the most.

STYLE

Confessional Style

Notes from Underground is written in what critics describe as a confessional style. The novel is told in the first person from the underground man's point of view. Although he says he writes only for himself out of boredom and that he never intends to publish the work, he nevertheless addresses the reader directly with some frequency throughout the novel, as if certain the work would indeed have readers. The style allows the reader intimate access into the workings of the underground man's mind. The reader is witness to the full range of his paranoia, his self-loathing, his revenge-seeking, his philosophical rants. A drawback of this style is that reality is filtered through the underground man's apparently disturbed mind, making truth a difficult thing to apprehend. The two sections of the novel differ stylistically in that the first section is presented as a stream-of-consciousness, in which the narrator's thoughts are conveyed seemingly as they occur to the narrator, while in the second section, the underground man's recollections are organized in a narrative format.

Two-Part Structure

Divided into two parts, "Underground" and "Apropos of the Wet Snow," *Notes from Underground* relates events, through the narrator, the underground man, in reverse chronological order. The events of the first section take place after the events of the second. The effect is almost circular. "Underground" dovetails snugly into "Apropos of the Wet Snow" when the narrator, inspired by the falling snow, recalls the events of the second section of the novel. When the penultimate (second to last) paragraph of the second section concludes with the sentiment "But enough; I don't want to write any more 'from Underground'," the reader is aware that of course the underground man did continue to write. Knowing this, we are naturally drawn back to the beginning of the novel. Yet the final paragraph acknowledges this tendency, stating that the underground man "could not help himself and went on. But it also seems to us that this may be a good place to stop." While the distinct sections of the novel are chronologically inverted, and separated

from one another by about twenty years, the effect is not jarring. Rather, there is a definite unity in the way they are linked: the underground man discusses what it is like underground in the first section, and by the end of the second section we learn how he came to take up the underground as he permanent residence.

HISTORICAL CONTEXT

Russian Philosophic and Literary Romanticism and Rationalism

The second half of *Notes from Underground* takes place during the 1840s while the first half takes place during the 1860s. Both time periods are significant in Dostoyevsky's life. He was just beginning his career as a writer in the 1840s. During the 1850s, he was incarcerated in Siberia, and then served out his allotted time in the army. When he returned to St. Petersburg, it was 1859, and Russian literature and philosophy had changed significantly during the time he was away. In the 1840s, the prevailing theme of many of Dostoyevsky's works was focused on the romantic ideals of the time. He was concerned with liberal ideas of a socialist utopia. The thinking of the Russian intellectuals during the 1840s was characteristically sentimental and literary. Prison had not only changed Dostoyevsky, but the times had changed as well by the time he was able to return to St. Petersburg in 1859. Many Russian intellectuals now put their faith not in the "beautiful and lofty"—the romantic ideals of the 1840s that the underground man speaks of with such irony in *Notes from Underground*—but rather in the notion of a spontaneous reason, or rationality, inspired by the moral laws of the Russian Orthodox Church. The more analytical reasoning favored among Westerners at this time was disfavored by many educated Russians, and the idea of Christian Socialism was rejected by some. Rationality among 1860s Russian intellectuals was prized only if its goal remained a spiritual rather than materialistic one. Similarly, in *Notes from Underground*, the underground man rejects the rational quantifying and cataloging and the mathematical formulation of his desires. By contrast, the Russian socialists of the 1860s put their hopes for the advancement of society in the pursuit of materialistic rationality that focused on technical innovations, that is, they put their faith in the idea

COMPARE
&
CONTRAST

- **1800s:** In the mid- to late-nineteenth century in Russia, poverty affects the lives of countless individuals. The underground man is able to keep a roof over his head, but borrows money several times in the book, once to pay a servant, and once to spend an evening out. He is deeply ashamed of his living conditions, and of his tattered clothing.

  Today: Following Russia's transition from socialism to communism to capitalism, many Russians today still struggle with poverty. This struggle continues despite the new wealth being created in some sectors due to the nation's oil reserves.

- **1800s:** Riga and St. Petersburg are among the largest cities in Russia and employ numerous industrial workers. Both Riga and St. Petersburg, as sizable urban centers, have a significant state presence, with military officials regulating urban life under a tsarist regime. Both cities are expensive for working class individuals.

  Today: Riga is now the capital of Latvia, having declared its independence in 1918, although it was later subjected to Soviet domination. By 1994, however, all Russian military troops had left the country. Riga is now becoming an increasingly popular tourist city. St. Petersburg has not been the capital of Russia since 1918; the capital is now Moscow. Referred to as Russia's most European city, as well as Russia's northern capital, St. Petersburg is a major metropolitan center as well as one of Russia's most historic and picturesque cities.

- **1800s:** The nineteenth century is often referred to as the "Golden Age" of Russian literature, meaning that, prior to this time, Russians produced little literature that was read internationally. But in the 1800s, writers such as Dostoyevsky, Leo Tolstoy, Ivan Turgenev, and poet Aleksandr Pushkin produced influential literature that is acclaimed worldwide.

  Today: Russian literature in the late twentieth and early twenty-first century has struggled to distinguish itself internationally. Notable modern talents include Victor Pelevin and Vasily Aksyonov.

- **1800s:** Military officers hold a position of some social prominence and power. The military protects and enforces the imperialist rule of the tsar.

  Today: Russia is no longer an imperialist country, but a capitalist nation ruled by an elected president. Vladimir Putin was elected president of Russia in 2000, and under Putin, the Russian military has been expanded.

---

of the "Crystal Palace" (a metaphorical edifice that is the embodiment of rational ideals, but is also a reference to an actual, physical structure built in 1851 in London to showcase the latest technological inventions of the Industrial Revolution) that Dostoyevsky derides in *Notes from Underground*.

Mid- to Late-Nineteenth-Century Russian Political History

Dostoyevsky returned to a different Russia following his imprisonment and military service in more ways than one. Not only was the philosophical and literary climate transformed, but the political scene was entirely different as well. Tsar Nicholas I was the tsar of Russia from 1825 until his death in 1855. Under Nicholas, the secret police watched for any signs of dissent against the rule of the tsar. Censorship over education and publishing was severe and prevalent. Nicholas was passionate about Russian nationalism; he demanded loyalty to the unlimited authority of the tsar and to the traditions of the Russian Orthodox Church. Nicholas was succeeded by his son Alexander in 1855; Tsar Alexander II ruled until his assassination in 1881. Alexander sought to reform the

Part of the Imperial Palace at St. Petersburg, Russia, 1864 (© *The Print Collector | Alamy*)

government, education, the judiciary system, and the military. Many of Nicholas's restrictive censorship policies were gradually lifted under Alexander's rule. In general his practices have been characterized as liberal, but he avoided succumbing to the utopian aspirations favored by some more revolutionary Russian intellectuals.

CRITICAL OVERVIEW

Dostoyevsky's *Notes from Underground* has been praised as a work of incredible literary complexity and psychological depth. Its influence on the literary and philosophical works of later writers has been the subject of many critical analyses. Critics have also noted the ways in which themes of *Notes from Underground* are developed further in Dostoyevsky's later works. Because the novel is written in the first person, one is invited into the inner workings of the mind of the underground man, and most assessments of the work are in some ways character analyses. Richard Peace, in *Dostoevsky's Notes from Underground* offers an

overview of several of these issues, discussing the way the novel, in terms of theme and construction, is the "typical Dostoevskian novel."

Many critics center their studies on the political and philosophical elements of the work. Louis Breger, writing in *Dostoevsky: The Author as Psychoanalyst* examines the underground man's critique of the romantic and utopian ideals of his youth, demonstrating the ways in which the underground man's views often reflect Dostoyevsky's. Breger also traces the underground man's assessment of rational, materialist utopias. Through it all, Breger notes, the underground man's combination of self-loathing and his insistence on his intellectual superiority is of the utmost interest to many critics. Peter Conradi, in *Fyodor Dostoevsky*, like Breger, focuses on the underground man's assessment of both romanticism and rationality; paradoxically, the underground man appears to condemn both, and in fact the underground man's approach to life is characterized by contradiction and paradox. Conradi observes that not only does the underground man seek the officer's respect, he also desires to fight him in order to win it.

Ralph E. Matlaw, in an essay included in a 1969 edition of the novel, establishes the way in which the two-part inverted chronological structure of the novel is a feature of the underground man's psychological issues. Matlaw explains that "through a complex series of psychological and social motivations" the narrator is "driven to the philosophical position enunciated in the first part." Other scholars attend to the affinity between the themes in *Notes from Underground* and the existentialist thinking of philosophers such as Friedrich Nietzsche (1844–1900) and Søren Kierkegaard (1813–1855). Existentialism emphasizes that in the absence of God, or a transcendent force, humans are responsible for their own existence and what they make of it. Existentialist writings are often focused not only on the freedom of this philosophy but also the dread, boredom, and alienation that often accompany it.

Konstantin Mochulsky, in an essay appended to a 1969 edition of the novel, states that "By the power and the boldness of his thought, Dostoyevsky is second neither to Nietzsche nor Kirkegaard. He is related to them in spirit, one of their tribe." Similarly, Robert G. Durgy comments in his 1969 introduction to *Notes from Underground* that although Dostoyevsky's work preceded the development of existential thought, his writing in *Notes from Underground* introduces the themes of this philosophy. Durgy additionally explains that Nietzsche, having studied the works of Dostoyevsky late in his life, recognized him "as a kindred spirit."

CRITICISM

Catherine Dominic

Dominic is a novelist and freelance editor and writer. In this essay, Dominic studies the characterization of the underground man in Notes from Underground.

Given the often pejorative manner in which Dostoyevsky depicts the underground man, readers may initially be uncomfortable with the narrator, the arguments he makes, and the way he interacts with others. Yet despite the underground man's insistence on his moral superiority, despite his spitefulness and his baiting of Simonov and his friends, and even in spite of the underground man's horrendous treatment of Liza, he nevertheless retains some semblance of a sympathetic character. It may be argued that sympathy for the underground man may be roused by the horror one feels in response to the depths of his paranoia. Robert G. Durgy observes, in his 1969 introduction to *Notes from Underground*, that "psychologists refer to him as the paradigm of the paranoid personality" and that the first section of the novel has been "reprinted in clinical studies of psychotic disorders." It is perhaps easier to sympathize with such an unpleasant individual if we understand that he is, in fact, ill. Furthermore, Durgy notes that the underground man is also of interest to sociologists, who find him "a quintessential expression of urban alienation, a victim of the tragic breakdown in human communication." Whether or not he would admit it, the underground man may be viewed as a casualty of his society. Yet it is not any one of these qualities that makes the underground man an object of sympathy. Rather, the interplay between the underground man's sense of alienation and his paranoia creates a character to whom readers feel drawn (at least as much as they are repulsed by him), and with whom they are able to sympathize. These elements are illuminated in the cycle of events that repeats itself several times throughout the course of the novel. The cycle in which the underground man is

WHAT DO I READ NEXT?

- Dostoyevsky's *Bednye liudi*, which was published in 1846 and later translated as *Poor Folk*, is an interesting read for those who wish to compare his early works (those written prior to his imprisonment in Siberia) with his later works (those published in the 1860s after his return to St. Petersburg).

- *Prestuplenie i nakazanie* (later translated as *Crime and Punishment*), published in 1866, is another of Dostoyevsky's psychological novels. In it, the author draws on themes similar to those in *Notes from Underground*, including the alienation of the narrator. The novel also employs a similar first-person, confessional style.

- *Who Can Be Happy and Free in Russia?* (1917) is a collection of poetry by Nikolai Alekseevich Nekrasov (1821–1878). A poem by Nekrasov is quoted at the opening to the second section of *Notes from Underground*.

- *The Russian Empire: 1801–1917* (1988), by Hugh Seton-Watson, offers a social and political history that illuminates the oppressive atmosphere under which Dostoyevsky wrote.

- *Fyodor Dostoyevsky: A Study* (1921), by Aimee Dostoyevsky, was written by Dostoyevsky's daughter. The biography provides intimate, first-hand accounts of the writer's life.

trapped begins with his intense certainty of his intellectual superiority, leads to his delusional need for revenge, and ends with his alienation and isolation.

As the second half of the novel opens, following the narrator's lengthy discussions of philosophical themes and his assertions of his highly developed consciousness in the first half of the book, the underground man assures the reader of his superior intellectual development. Yet despite this, he also feels a sense of anguish, and consequently "a hysterical thirst for contradictions,

> RATHER, THE INTERPLAY BETWEEN THE UNDERGROUND MAN'S SENSE OF ALIENATION AND HIS PARANOIA CREATES A CHARACTER TO WHOM READERS FEEL DRAWN (AT LEAST AS MUCH AS THEY ARE REPULSED BY HIM), AND WITH WHOM THEY ARE ABLE TO SYMPATHIZE."

contrasts, would appear, and so I'd set out on debauchery." On one such occasion, the underground man finds himself in a tavern hoping to get involved in a fight. Unsuccessful, he is about to leave when an army officer takes him by the shoulder and moves him out of the way in order to pass through the crowded tavern; he does so without even glancing at the underground man. Years pass, and the underground man still thinks of the officer. A revenge is plotted, focusing on the underground man bumping into the officer in the street. Years of resentment, culminating in a bump in the street, result from the underground man's inflating the incident in the bar into an impugnment of his honor. The response is clearly distorted, but the narrator feels as though he has finally established the "equal social footing" he deserves. Despite what the underground man perceives as success in this matter, he once again returns to his isolation to repent his forays into debauchery. Achieving social equality is so important to the narrator because he feels in many ways superior to most of society, despite his obvious self-recrimination. Yet it is not enough that he has won this duel of sorts with the officer, and revenge will continue to not be enough to soothe his soul and assuage his feelings of alienation as the novel continues.

Following a period of several months of self-imposed hibernation, the underground man ventures out into society again, feeling the need "to embrace the whole of mankind." But the acquaintance to whom he usually turns at times like these, his department chief, happens to be unavailable, so he has to content himself with his second choice, a former schoolmate by the name of Simonov. The underground man arrives at Simonov's dwelling just as he and his friends are planning a farewell dinner for another former schoolmate, Zverkov. The underground man has never been friends with Zverkov. Yet, having insinuated himself into the conversation that Simonov and the others are having, the underground man realizes they have no plans to invite him along. He is about to be ignored, unnoticed in the same way he went unnoticed by the officer earlier in the novel. Hypersensitive to being ignored in this fashion, as it intensifies the feelings he already has of alienation from the rest of society, the underground man insists that he will accompany Simonov and the others, he will join the farewell party for Zverkov. Naturally the others are surprised, and even hostile, but the underground man is nevertheless allowed to come along. Although he frets about the impression he will make, he still shows up promptly, only to discover, when the others arrive an hour later, that they changed the time of the party without notifying him. In some ways, this social slighting of the underground man is understandable: he does not even care for any of the men in the group, save, perhaps, Simonov; and he rudely invited himself along. But what the group has done to him is unforgivable in the eyes of the underground man, and he proceeds to spitefully remain with the party to the end, attempting to make everyone as uncomfortable and annoyed as possible. He even spends hours pacing in front of them, loudly clomping his boots, as they drink and laugh together. He is pained at how they misperceive him. Later, the men adjourn to a brothel, leaving the underground man behind, having scoffed at his challenging of one of them to a duel, as well as having refused his apologies. When they depart, the underground man states that he "stood there spat upon." He feels "tormenting anguish" in his heart. While he has arguably earned all the derision of the other men, the underground man's wounds run deep, and he is driven by the pain of his renewed sense of alienation to seek revenge again, determining to find Zverkov and slap his face. He never gets the chance, because the underground man finds not Zverkov at the brothel, but Liza.

Still stung by the way he has been humiliated, has allowed himself to be humiliated, he embraces how low he has sunk, and approaching Liza, he thinks how glad he is to look so wicked, how happy he is for Liza to think he is disgusting. After they make love, he tries briefly to talk to her, to end the awkward silence. Unsure of why he feels unable to leave, he begins a conversation about a coffin he has seen being taken out of a basement; her responses seem to him rude, reluctant, and then "something suddenly began egging me on." The conversation turns into a game for the underground man, an attempt to manipulate Liza and her emotions, to make her feel small and alone, in the same way that he was diminished by Zverkov and his friends. Sensing her vulnerability, he begins to feel powerful, and he is unrelenting in his attack upon her sense of self. When she seems to challenge him, noting that he speaks as if "from a book," he hears mockery in her tone, and a "wicked feeling" takes hold of him. His speech turns cruel rather than simply superior and judgmental. The underground man senses that he "had turned her whole soul over and broken her heart." Although he thinks briefly of continuing his onslaught, in order to finish his "game," he finds now that he only wishes to escape, but not before he asks Liza for forgiveness and gives her his address. He has taken his need for revenge against Zverkov and the others out on her, having found a way, in his broken mind, to assign her some blame, that she might deserve his attack. He reads rudeness and mockery into her tone, and given that she is nothing more than a prostitute, he will not suffer rudeness or mockery from her. Once home, he fears her, and seems ashamed of his own behavior, but then attempts to justify his actions.

For a little while, the cycle within which the underground man seems to be forever trapped appears to have been broken. With Liza, as with Zverkov and company, and as with the officer, the underground man is pained by the discrepancy between his sense of superiority and his being treated as socially inferior; he is either mocked or ignored by these people. His response, with Liza as with the others, is to seek revenge. Finally, his sense of isolation and alienation is revived and intensified with all three encounters. But with Liza, something is different. With Liza, the underground man doubts himself, doubts the necessity of his revenge taking. He is obsessed with thoughts of her, and what will happen to her, and even fantasizes that Liza has been saved by him and rewards him with her love. When she does come to him, though, he is unable to embrace a human emotional connection that is not based on power. The underground man asks Liza, after he has broken down in a fit of crying, if she despises him. Liza hesitates. The underground man reads her reaction as embarrassment, and as an inability to reply. In that moment, all hope for him is lost. In the moment of her hesitation the underground man rejects the possibility that he could live anywhere but underground, that he can hope for anything except isolation. After that brief moment of her hesitation, he orders her to drink her tea. "A terrible spite against her suddenly boiled up in my heart; . . . To be revenged on her, I swore mentally not to speak even one word to her from then on. 'It's she who caused it all,' I thought."

Liza still tries, nevertheless, to connect with him, telling him how she wants to escape the brothel. Her efforts are futile. He tells her that his attempts to "save" her were motivated only by his desire for power over someone. Enraged at her, he reveals that his fear is that she would think he was a hero, but would then "suddenly see me in this torn old dressing gown, abject, vile." Through Liza, the underground man realizes that the sense of superiority his life has been founded on is faulty, and for this, he will not forgive her. Yet she is still drawn to him, and seeing how distraught he is, she seeks to comfort him. In response to her kindness, the underground man seems to pity her and the way that "she considered herself infinitely beneath me." Liza remains by his side as he sobs, and when he stops, the underground man understands that "the roles were now finally reversed, that she was now the heroine, and I was the same crushed and humiliated creature as she had been before me." Realizing that he envies her this power, the underground man admits that without his possessing this same power over someone, without him having the ability to tyrannize, he can not exist, and after they make love again, he wants only for Liza to leave. Furthermore, he attempts to reestablish his power over her by paying her. In the end, she has gone, and he is once again alone. Unable to truly break the cycle, the underground man retreats once again underground, having attempted to avenge the wrongs that he perceives—through the distorted filter of his own disturbed mind—as having been done to him, and having attempted to reset the scales so that his sense of superiority is balanced by a sense of power (rather than outweighed by social inferiority). Pitiable as the underground man is in this state, any sympathy readers may have for him is now fractured, and part of their sense of sympathy must leave with Liza.

Source: Catherine Dominic, Critical Essay on *Notes from Underground*, in *Novels for Students*, Gale, Cengage Learning, 2009.

Rado Pribic

In the following essay, Pribic offers a brief overview of the novel's themes and provides a discussion of Dostoyevsky's characterization of the Underground Man. Pribic additionally assesses the ways in which the opinions and problems of the Underground Man are relevant in today's world.

Ten decades have elapsed since Dostoevski's death, but many of the problems and ideas elucidated in his novels and novellas are still germane to the reality of our time. The same is true of Dostoevski's polyphonic style, which L. Grossman called "a truly brilliant page in the history of the European novel."

Notes from the Underground was written in 1864. It stands at the threshold of Dostoevski's post-Siberian period and includes in rudimentary form the fundamental ideas and aesthetic principles which underlie his subsequent major novels. The protagonist, the underground man, is the archetype of all underground men. His troubles are generated by the predicament of his generation, caught up in the toils of conflicting ideologies, none of which succeeded in fructifying and transforming real life. "Today we do not even know where real life is … we do not know what to join, what to keep up with, what to love, what to hate; what to respect, what to despise," says the underground man at the end of his confession.

Assuming that creative literature constitutes a major expression of thought and response in a given period, the underground man may be considered a socio-historical phenomenon; yet *Notes* itself is, in the first place, a work of art, not an historical document. However, Dostoevski, who throughout the entire novel does not interfere with the underground man's stream of consciousness, adroitly closes the gap between fiction and reality in a footnote which reads: "people like the author of these notes may, and indeed must, exist in our society, if we think of the circumstances under which this society has been formed."

Let us now examine which of the underground man's problems and views are still applicable in our time.

The underground man's most conspicuous traits are acute intellect and heightened self-consciousness. These faculties make the protagonist

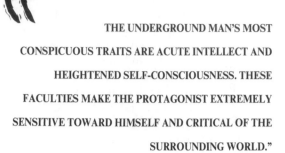

> THE UNDERGROUND MAN'S MOST CONSPICUOUS TRAITS ARE ACUTE INTELLECT AND HEIGHTENED SELF-CONSCIOUSNESS. THESE FACULTIES MAKE THE PROTAGONIST EXTREMELY SENSITIVE TOWARD HIMSELF AND CRITICAL OF THE SURROUNDING WORLD."

extremely sensitive toward himself and critical of the surrounding world. They make him doubt and contradict everything, and, at the same time, they intensify his egocentrism and his vanity to such an extent that he loses the capacity to understand others objectively and begins to judge people only by his own consciousness. "Now, it is absolutely clear to me, because of an infinite vanity that caused me to set myself impossible standards, I regarded myself with furious disapproval, bordering on loathing, and then ascribed my own feelings to everyone I came across," confesses the underground man.

The underground man's solipsism also corrodes his emotional life. He becomes unable to commit himself and can no longer reach out to and affirm the other's self. Thus, from time to time, the underground man retreats into the world of dreams as a substitute for love and friendship. He plays this game so well that he takes it for reality; he sheds tears and suffers. But none of his dreams ever materialize, and the underground man remains an unfulfilled dreamer.

The underground man spends twenty years in self-imposed seclusion; he listens to his own consciousness and torments himself, to the brink of insanity. He indulges in self-destructive analysis; he engages in polemics with himself and other consciousnesses and draws the entire surrounding world into the process of self-awareness. Then he reveals himself and explains his views in a confessional utterance which, according to him, is mercilessly sincere, for the final truth about an individual can be given only by the individual himself. Since the confession is not intended for publication, the underground man does not embellish anything; neither is there a single flash of remorse in the entire work. "Doesn't it seem to you, ladies and gentlemen, that I am repenting of something before you, that I am asking for forgiveness for something? I am sure that seems so . . . But I assure you that I do not care if it seems so to you," says the underground man.

The first part of the *Notes* is a conglomeration of many views and ideas which never develop into a full narrative. Using interior dialogue, the underground man delves into his own consciousness, seeks assessments of himself and anticipates what others will think about him. In the next moment, he annihilates his own definition and shatters the final judgment of his fictitious discussant. He constantly strives to keep one step ahead of his interlocutor and creates loopholes for himself that enable him to continue the dispute as long as he wants and to cut it off whenever it pleases him. His entire train of thought is a vicious circle, consisting of thesis and antithesis without a synthesis.

The underground man begins his confession with a complaint about his poor health. He is aware of his illness but refuses to ask for medical help simply out of contrariness. "I know very well that I am harming myself and no one else. But, it is out of spite that I refuse to ask for the doctor's help. So my liver hurts? Well, let it hurt even more!" The protagonist continues to live in Petersburg, although he knows that he cannot afford it financially and that the climate is unhealthy. He annuls the ruthless sequence of cause and effect with inertia and opposes the mechanistic inevitability of the laws of nature with his whimsical will. "Where are the primitive causes for any actions, the justification for them? . . . I deliberate but the result is that every primary cause drags along another cause that seems to be truly primary, and so on and so forth, indefinitely . . . " And he concludes his reasoning, "The best thing is to do nothing at all, conscious inertia is the best. A toast to the mousehole!" The underground man dreams of a useful and worthwhile life, yet the first thing he does after leaving school is to give up his position and break all ties with the past. He longs for the sublime and the beautiful, but, just when he is most conscious and capable of refinement, he behaves abjectly. In the office, the underground man is rude and mean with people and makes them feel miserable, yet he soon detects that there were many elements in his nature that are just the opposite of wicked.

The underground man painfully senses the disparity between his character and its manifestation under given circumstances, but he goes on destroying his emotions with his intellect and annihilating his rational considerations with his whimsical will. He cannot change, for only a fool can make anything he wants of himself. Finally, the underground man reaches the point where he no longer discerns what is right and what is wrong, whether he believes what he is saying or is just telling a pack of lies. He begins to consider this as the normal state; he even derives pleasure from it. And he draws the conclusion that everything is all right as long as he is aware of it. Thus, the underground man's self-awareness absorbs all other features of his character, dissolves and devastates all concrete traits of his image, until nothing is left but utter inner alienation. But, at the same time, he longs for at least one defining feature. He would not mind if someone were to call him a sluggard. "How awfully pleasant it would be to hear this about myself. That would mean that I am clearly defined, that there is something to be said about me."

The underground man's relationship with his fellowmen is marred by the same contradictory elements that are active in his personality. That brings him into conflict with not only himself but the external world as well. Aware of his keen intellect, the underground man considers himself superior to his fellowmen, yet he immediately develops an inferiority complex and retires into his mousehole when he has to face normal men. In his hole, he plunges into never ending hatred; he thinks up all kinds of humiliation and prepares vengeance, knowing all the time that there has been no humiliation; nor is there anything to be avenged. The vicious circle of these polemics goes on and on, until the underground man brings it to a sudden end.

In his self-absorbed reclusiveness, the underground man rebuts the affirmation of another person's consciousness. There is no "we" in the underground man's thinking; there are only "I" and "the others." The majority of these others is, according to the underground man, stupid and narrow-minded; they resemble one another like a flock of sheep, have no capacity for inventiveness, and think and express themselves in prefabricated patterns.

The others are repugnantly vicious and immoral. They humiliate, hurt, and bully one another; they look down upon others as if they were houseflies and use them as doormats. They judge one another by their clothing and professional success and not by their moral qualities. But, no matter how arrogantly they behave, how deeply they wallow in mud and vices, they will feel no pangs of conscience, for they are not even aware of their depravity.

The others are also hypocrites. They pretend to be honest and sincere, but all they have in mind is trying not to lose sight of the useful. They rave about the sublime and the beautiful but are rogues at the bottom of their hearts. They speak of ideals but would not raise a little finger to actualize these ideals, for they would never jeopardize their careers by standing up against the well-established order of society.

Now, how can an intelligent man function in a society comprised of members who are corrupt, immoral, hostile, and cruel? To this the underground man has three answers to suggest. First, one may, against his better judgment, accept the world, with its inanities and contradictions, and become a spineless creature like the others. Yet, since an intelligent man cannot keep out his conscience, he will loathe himself for this deliberate self-deception. Secondly, one can continue the struggle for truth, although that will entail never ending clashes with the others and with society. Finally, man may realize that there is no remedy to his situation and, as a result, retire into ab[s]olute inertia.

Because of his critical and negative attitude toward his fellowmen, the underground man is unable to establish a close relationship with the others. Love, commitment, and forgiveness are alien concepts to him. He hates his distant relatives who had brought him up, because of their nagging and because they had dumped him in a boarding school[.] He never communicates with his schoolmates, nor does he make friends at work. Once, a nice, yielding boy becomes his friend. But the underground man begins immediately to rule his mind[.] He instills in him contempt for the others and forces him to break with them. When he finally has full possession of the boy, he hates and rejects him. "It was as though I had only wanted his total friendship for the sake of winning it and making him submit to me," says the underground man.

The only person who is capable, at least temporarily, of standing up to the underground man's self-destructive consciousness is the prostitute, Liza. The underground man meets her after a disastrous evening with some former schoolmates and begins to take out his own humiliation on her. The short-lived relationship with Liza is a fine example of the vicious circle in which the underground man's diabolic consciousness spins. In order to intimidate Liza, the underground man concocts a macabre funeral story about a prostitute. Then, noticing that the story does not touch Liza's heart, he shifts the center of gravity to a more sentimental matter. He raves about the beauty of family life, the mystery of love, the rosy cheeks and miniature nails of babies. This time he succeeds. He gives Liza his address, immediately regretting the move, since he is not sure whether he really wants her to come. At home, the underground man daydreams about rescuing Liza and turning her into a fine, intelligent woman who would, of course, fall in love with him. When Liza finally and unexpectedly arrives, she finds the underground man in a rather anti-heroic situation, snapping like a vicious dog at his servant. In a blind rage, the underground man shouts at Liza that he has lied to her, that he wants only power and a role to play. He reveals his perverse and selfish character and then screams that he will never forgive her for having witnessed his nervous breakdown and for having listened to his confession.

When the underground man finally realizes that, despite all he has said, Liza intuitively understands that he is a very unhappy creature, he is furiously drawn to her. In order to shake off Liza's domination, he destroys his image in her eyes with a devilish act. He makes love to Liza and then, sending her away, slips a five ruble bill into her hand.

The underground man explains his stupid and spiteful conduct in a summarizing statement: "I could not fall in love because, for me, loving meant bullying and morally dominating. I have never been able to imagine any other way of loving and have reached a point where I think that love consists of a voluntary concession by the object of my love and my right to bully it."

Liza's departure signals the final break with the outer world. It is symbolized in the squeaking and bang of the heavy apartment door and the dead silence and darkness of the street, which is covered with wet, yellowish snow. The inner and outer alienation of the underground man is now complete.

The underground man's polemics with himself and the others are tightly interwoven with his ideological views. One of the principal ideas set forth in the dispute with socialist utopianism is that man is not a final quantity upon which stable calculation may be made. The equation $2 \times 2 = 4$ is inapplicable to mankind. Man wants to be free and will try to overturn any rules that are forced upon him. He does not want to become a piano key or an organ stop. He will reject the well-engineered crystal palace, because the absolute order of it would destroy his creative freedom. In a world in which everything is planned, life will become extremely boring; there will be no doubts, no suffering, no chaos, no destruction.

The underground man also argues with utilitarianism, which was rather popular in the 1860s. It is self-deceiving to assume that man will do only those things that lie in his best interest. One may shower upon man all earthly blessings, drown him in happiness, and give him economic security. Still, he will give it all up, just to inject his lethal fancies into all the soundness. Man will never stop doing nasty things; he will not become good and virtuous only because it is in his interest to do so. And he will send reason and all things useful and beautiful to hell, just to establish his right to the most abstract wishes.

Another idea propounded by the underground man, on various occasions, is that man has an aversion to seeing his desires fulfilled. He likes to view his objectives from a distance and enjoys the process of achieving more than the goal itself. He is almost afraid of reaching the goal toward which he is working. Achievement means stagnation, the end of desires and wishes. Man is not an ant, which considers the anthill its ultimate goal. His life is an uninterrupted drive for new goals.

The last idea advocated by the underground man is that man does not mellow under the influence of civilization, does not become less bloodthirsty or less prone to war. Through the centuries, man only becomes more vicious, more bloodthirsty, creating an ever greater variety of sensations. In the past, man slaughtered, without any pangs of conscience, those he felt had to be slaughtered. Today, man considers bloodshed terrible, yet he continues to practice it, on an even larger scale. The tyrants of our time are so numerous and familiar to us that they are not even conspicuous. Their methods are so savage and horrifying that they push all the cruelties of barbarous times into the background. Men "fight and fight; they are fighting now, they fought before, and they will fight in the future."

The predicament of the underground man and the problems and ideas he touches upon are all human and universal; they transcend societies and time periods. One has only to look around to find numerous glaring parallels in our century. During the past hundred years, man's intellect has performed miracles in technology and the sciences, but the technical process has not really freed man; it has only brought closer the era of the well-engineered crystal palace. Most of all, man has failed to match his scientific virtuosity with moral and ethical understanding, and little has been done to improve human relationships. As before, man is plagued by divergent ideological, political, and social concepts. The age-old question of good and evil is still a matter of arbitrary interpretation, and the need for truth is not strong enough to prevent man's imagination and train of thought from being perverted into bias and prejudice. Men are still vicious and cruel; they expose one another to unjustifiable hardships and to the most incomprehensible situations, far removed from ordinary life. Finally, if one scrutinizes past historical developments, one might draw the depressing conclusion that man learns nothing from history; he is still fighting, fighting, fighting. And yet, despite physical and spiritual imprisonment, man continues to cherish his individual freedom and employs a great part of his ingenuity to guard against interfering elements. Thus, in conclusion, it can be said that the three possibilities for survival given by the underground man apply to our time as well: agree to everything and become a spineless creature; fight for the truth and one's own views and suffer; or withdraw and retire into the underground.

Source: Rado Pribic, "*Notes from Underground*: One Hundred Years after the Author's Death," in *Dostoevski and the Human Condition after a Century*, edited by Alexej Ugrinsky, Frank S. Lambasa, and Valija K. Ozolins, Greenwood Press, 1986, pp. 71–77.

SOURCES

Breger, Louis, "The Death of Maria: *Notes from Underground*," in *Dostoevsky: The Author as Psychoanalyst*, New York University Press, 1989, pp. 181–209.

Conradi, Peter, "*The Double* and *Notes from Underground*," in *Fyodor Dostoevsky*, Macmillan, 1988, pp. 21–41.

Dostoyevsky, Fyodor, *Notes from Underground*, translated by Richard Pevear and Larissa Volokhonsky, Vintage Classics, 1994.

Durgy, Robert G., Introduction, in *Notes from Underground*, by Fyodor Dostoyevsky, translated by Serge Shishkoff, University Press of America, 1969, pp. VII–XXII.

Jackson, Robert Louis, "*Notes from Underground*: Origins," and "*Notes from Underground*: Analysis," in *Dostoevsky's Underground Man in Russian Literature*, Greenwood Press, 1981, pp. 19–30, and 31–48.

Matlaw, Ralph E., "Structure and Integration in *Notes from Underground*," in *Notes from Underground*, by Fyodor Dostoyevsky, University Press of America, 1969, pp. 181–203.

Mochulsky, Konstantin, "*Notes from Underground*," in *Notes from Underground*, by Fyodor Dostoyevsky, University Press of America, 1969, pp. 129–49.

Peace, Richard, Introduction, "Commentary to *Notes from Underground* Part I," and "Commentary to *Notes from Underground* Part II," in *Dostoevsky's Notes from Underground*, Bristol Classic Press, 1993, pp. V–VIII, 3–35, and 36–68.

Pevear, Richard, Foreword, in *Notes from Underground*, by Fyodor Dostoyevsky, Vintage Classics, 1994, VII–XXIII.

FURTHER READING

Anderson, Barbara A., *Internal Migration during Modernization in Late Nineteenth-Century Russia*, Princeton University Press, 1980.

Anderson studies the patterns of migration in Russia at the end of the nineteenth century, exploring the trends and the reasons for migration. Liza in *Notes from Underground* migrates from the city of Riga to the then-capital of Russia, St. Petersburg.

Flath, Carol A., "Fear of Faith: the Hidden Religious Message of *Notes from Underground*," in *Slavic and East European Journal*, Vol. 37, No. 4, 1993, pp. 510–29.

Flath maintains that within Dostoyevsky's novel is the author's insistence on humanity's need for Christ.

Kaufmann, Walter, *Existentialism from Dostoevksy to Sartre*, Penguin, 1975.

Kaufmann explores the philosophy of existentialism, beginning with the treatment of the subject in Dostoyevsky's *Notes from Underground* and discussing the impact of Dostoyevsky's works on later philosophers.

Meerson, Olga, "Old Testament Lamentation in the Underground Man's Monologue: A Refutation of the Existentialist Reading of *Notes from Underground*," in *Slavic and East European Journal*, Vol. 36, No. 3, Fall 1992, pp. 317–22.

Meerson identifies the similarities between the underground man's speeches and passages in the Christian Bible's Old Testament and explores thematic parallels between the works.

Titova, Irinia, and Paul E. Richardson, "Fyodor Mikhailovich Dostoyevsky," in *Russian Life*, Vol. 49, No. 6, Nov.–Dec. 2006, pp. 52–62.

The authors of this article offer a brief biography of Dostoyevsky that includes discussions of his major works.

So Far from the Bamboo Grove

YOKO KAWASHIMA WATKINS
1986

The events in the autobiographical novel *So Far from the Bamboo Grove*, published in 1986 and still in print, were taken from Yoko Kawashima Watkins's childhood. It took Watkins ten years to write the novel.

When Watkins was young, her father, a Japanese government official, was sent to northern Korea (which was occupied by Japan), where he settled his family. Watkins grew up learning the Korean language and culture while maintaining a grasp of her own Japanese heritage. Later, Russian and Korean armies united against Japan, and along with support from U.S. bombers, forced the Japanese off the Korean peninsula. Watkins's story focuses mainly on her family's journey out of Korea, and on their attempts to reestablish their lives in their war-torn homeland.

So Far from the Bamboo Grove has been both praised and negatively criticized over the years. In 1986, the novel was listed as a Notable Book by the American Library Association. In addition, it received a Best Books for Children designation from the *School Library Journal*. However, more recently there has been some controversy surrounding Watkins's novel. It has been charged that the novel contains an inaccurate or biased account of history, and the suggested rape scene in the story has also been viewed as offensive. Some parents have even tried to have the book removed from school libraries and curriculums. Most readers, however, defend the novel, stating that it is

predominantly a work of fiction, told through the eyes of a traumatized eleven-year-old. For them, this story is a coming-of-age journey.

AUTHOR BIOGRAPHY

Yoko Kawashima Watkins, who is of Japanese descent, was born in Manchuria. Although Manchuria is part of China, and sits on China's eastern seaboard, Japan had invaded Manchuria and controlled the area by 1931. Watkins's family was living there in 1933, in Harbin, when she was born. Later, the family moved to Nanam in northern Korea, possibly thinking they might avoid the conflicts that were threatening between the Japanese and Russian armies. Although the family moved, Watkins's father continued to commute the fifty miles to his station in Manchuria and thus was often away from home. The setting of *So Far from the Bamboo Grove* at the beginning of the story is in Nanam.

As Watkins relates in her novel, when she was eleven, in 1945, it became apparent that Japan was fighting a losing battle in World War II. Her family was warned to leave with just enough supplies and belongings to get them to the port of Pusan on the southern point of the Korean peninsula. After making it to Japan, they discovered that much of their homeland had been destroyed, and they had to survive by eating out of trash cans and earning small amounts of money by selling trinkets door-to-door.

Watkins credits her older sister Ko for encouraging her studies despite the challenges of poverty they faced after their mother died. Watkins would later attend Kyoto University, where she specialized in English. Upon graduation, Watkins worked as a translator for the U.S. Air Force at Aomori, Japan. It was here that she met the man who would become her husband, Donald Watkins. In 1955, Donald was transferred back to the States, where the couple lived in Minnesota, Wisconsin, and then Oregon before settling in Brewster, Massachusetts. Watkins and her husband raised four children, who are now adults.

Watkins has said that she always thought of herself as a writer, but opening herself up to the memories of her escape was very difficult. After publishing *So Far from the Bamboo Grove* in 1986, however, she continued her story in another autobiographical novel, a sequel to the first, called *My Brother, My Sister, and I*. It was published in 1994 and won several awards. In this second story, among other things, Watkins tells of her father's return from a Russian prison camp. Watkins has put together a third book, *Tales from the Bamboo Grove*, a collection of Japanese folktales that was published in 1992. As of 2007, Watkins lived with her husband in Massachusetts and frequently visited schools to talk about her experiences.

PLOT SUMMARY

Chapters 1–3

Watkins's novel *So Far from the Bamboo Grove* begins on July 29, 1945. The Japanese, at this point, still have control of Manchuria. However, Russian troops have gathered along the border and are threatening to advance. Allied troops, especially British and American, have already started bombing industrial sites in northern Korea in their attempts to destroy the economy that Japan has established in that country. Yoko's father has told her mother to have supplies ready should they have to conceal themselves in the bomb shelter they have built. Yoko is the youngest child in the family, and lives with her sixteen-year-old sister, Ko, and the oldest sibling, which is her brother, Hideyo. The children live with their mother in Nanam in northern Korea. Yoko's father takes a fifty-mile train ride to his work in Manchuria and is gone for long periods of time. Although they have supplied the bomb shelter and can hear bombs falling in the distance, Yoko does not have a real sense of the war until Japanese soldiers arrive one day at the family's door, demanding any piece of metal they possess, including her mother's eyeglasses (with their metal frame) and her wedding ring. This angers Yoko so much, she bites one of the soldier's hands. The soldier retaliates by pushing Yoko down and kicking her in the ribs. Yoko's actions showcase both her immaturity and her lack of fear.

Yoko's mother takes her to Dr. Yamada, who announces that Yoko might have one or more cracked ribs. He says it would be best to keep her out of school. This thrills Yoko, because half of the school day is spent collecting old metal cans in the fields or at the ammunition factory, where the students separated good bullets from bad ones. Yoko hated helping the army because she felt she was helping them to kill. One day at school, her teacher, Mr. Enomoto, made the announcement that U.S. planes had dropped two bombs—one on Hiroshima; the other at Nagasaki (August 9, 1945).

To keep Yoko's mind busy, as well as to keep alive the family's Japanese culture, Yoko's mother insists that Yoko study the Japanese arts of calligraphy (artful, brush-stroke writing of Japanese and Chinese characters), the Way of Tea Ceremony (a specialized, formal serving of tea), ikebana (Japanese flower arranging), and Japanese dance. All of these arts are very meditative, clearing and then focusing the mind only on the present moment.

One day when Yoko comes home from school, her mother tells her that she has heard that the Koreans have created what she calls the Anti-Japanese Communist Army. Yoko relates to the reader that, although the Koreans were part of the Japanese Empire, she knew they hated the Japanese. (This part of the story has aroused the negative sentiment in some readers who believe that the author does not tell the reader of the atrocities that the Japanese inflicted on the Koreans. Japan took Korea by force and demanded that they adopt Japanese names, did not allow the Korean language to be spoken, and did what they could to destroy the Korean culture. So the Koreans were part of the Japanese Empire, but it was against their will.)

The subject is quickly changed, as Yoko's mother reminds Yoko of a performance of Japanese dance that is scheduled for the next day. Yoko is a part of this dance group. Yoko does not like to dance, as she feels awkward rather than graceful. However, when she goes to the hospital the next day the patients, who are mostly wounded soldiers, are impressed with her. Major Ryu, who is in charge of the entertainment, asks Yoko if she will go visit some of the soldiers who could not get out of bed to come to see her. One soldier, in particular, is very needy. He is badly wounded and refuses to eat. His name is Corporal Matsumura. When Yoko sees him, Matsumura's head is heavily bandaged, and he cannot see. But he is touched by Yoko's presence. He asks to hold her hand, and then he asks to touch the kimono (traditional Japanese dress) she wears. A month passes, then Corporal Matsumura comes for a surprise visit to Yoko's house. His face is disfigured with raw scars. He thanks Yoko for helping him heal. Yoko dances for him. He comes to visit often after this.

Air raids become more frequent as U.S. planes fly overhead and bomb facilities nearby. Yoko's brother tells his mother that he has decided to join the Yokaren, a student army. He is eighteen, Hideyo tells his mother, old enough to make his own decisions. Yoko's mother is very concerned about her son; she is also worried about the fate of the rest of the family. She fears that if the army is recruiting such young boys, it is a sign that the army is desperate. Although it is not explained, Hideyo is turned down by the army for having flunked their written exam. The family knows that Hideyo was smart enough to pass the test, so they wonder if he flunked it on purpose. Instead of fighting, then, Hideyo works at a nearby ammunitions plant with some other boys his age.

Corporal Matsumura shows up late one night and tells Yoko's family to pack up and leave their home as fast as they can. Yoko's mother is reluctant to leave because Hideyo is not home. Matsumura says that the Russian soldiers have crossed the border and will be there soon. They are specifically looking for Yoko's family because they know Yoko's father is a high-ranking government official. Matsumura has arranged for them to take a train to Seoul, in southern Korea. The mother agrees and leaves notes for Hideyo and for Yoko's father to let them know where they have gone. The train they will travel on is meant to carry only wounded soldiers, so Matsumura gives Yoko's mother a note to give to the station master. The family gathers their things and sets off for the train. When they find the station master, he is reluctant to allow the family to board. Major Ryu, the man who had arranged for Yoko to dance at the hospital, sees the family and tells the station master that Yoko and her family must be put on the train.

Yoko, Ko, and Mother find a small space in one of the boxcars and squeeze themselves in. Wounded soldiers, pregnant women, and sick patients surround them. In the course of one day, a woman gives birth to a dead baby, which an army official takes and throws off the train. Others who die are also pushed off the boxcar. Yoko's mother shares the family's food with everyone. She also helps the nurses administer aid to the patients. On the second day, the train stops for fuel. While there, a group of Korean soldiers inspect the trains. The nurses smear blood on Yoko, Ko, and Mother to make them look as if they are wounded. The nurses know that the soldiers are looking for Yoko and her family and help them hide because they have been so helpful. When the Korean soldiers become suspicious of Mother, the nurse yells at the soldiers, telling them to leave her alone because she has smallpox (a very contagious disease). The soldiers immediately jump off the train. Shortly after the train starts up again, U.S. bombers attack the train. The engine is demolished. Yoko and her family are forced to walk the rest of the way to Seoul, which is forty-five miles away.

They sleep during the day and walk at night so as not to be detected. They have been following the train tracks for eleven days, knowing it will eventually lead them to the southern city. One day, as the women are hiding in a nearby forest, Korean soldiers surprise them and make comments that suggest that they are thinking of raping Ko. U.S. planes fly by and drop bombs nearby. Yoko loses consciousness. When she wakes up, she cannot hear. She is also slightly wounded in the chest. The soldiers are dead.

Yoko's family takes an extra day to rest. The next day, Yoko still cannot hear. When she wakes that day, the first thing she sees is Ko dressed in a Korean uniform. All her hair has been cut off. Mother is likewise dressed. Her hair is also gone. Then Mother cuts of Yoko's hair too. Mother dresses Yoko in another uniform and they resume their journey to Seoul.

Chapters 4–7

Hideyo, Yoko's brother, is working at the ammunition factory with many youths, which include three of his friends: Makoto, Shoichi, and Shinzo. One day, Korean soldiers come in and start shooting everyone they see. The four of them survive the attack either by hiding or pretending to be dead; and then decide to run away together. They all head home, about a day's walk from the factory. Hideyo finds the house deserted and ransacked. He also finds his mother's note, telling him that they are heading for Seoul. He takes what food he can carry and goes off to meet with the other boys. Shinzo's and Shoichi's parents had fled to the south. Makoto, however, found his parents dead. Hideyo suggests that they go to friends of his family to borrow some Korean style clothes. When they

get there, they find these people also dead. But they exchange their Japanese style clothes for the Korean clothes. They too decide to follow the railroad tracks. Later, when they run into some Russian soldiers, the boys are able to convince them that they are Korean. The soldiers tell them they can find food in the next town if they are willing to help the army bury the dead. The boys decide to separate. Hideyo is the only one who wants to continue to Seoul. They promise to meet at the Tokyo Bridge in Japan five years from that day.

The story switches back to the plight of Yoko, her mother and her sister. They have finally arrived at the Seoul station, but they find that conditions have not improved for them. The war is over, but that does not bring them much relief. There are thousands of refugees, not much food, and no place to sleep. There is a medical team that treats Yoko's wounds, which are infected. Yoko spends two weeks in the hospital. Meanwhile, Mother learns that there is a ship that leaves from Pusan, farther south from Seoul, that is taking refugees back to Japan. Mother refuses to leave without Hideyo. She, Ko, and Yoko live at the Seoul station, sleeping on benches and eating food that Ko finds in garbage cans. They watch the trains stop and unload; but Hideyo is never among the passengers. It is not until Ko witnesses the rapes of several young girls that she tells her mother they must leave. It is too dangerous to stay there. So they make signs and place them all over the station, telling Hideyo that they have gone to Pusan and are planning to take the boat back to Japan.

At Pusan, conditions are not much better. Mother wraps Ko's chest to hide the fact that she is a girl. They must wait in line to get on the boat, even long after the boat has left, in hopes that they will make the next boat. They also leave signs in Pusan, telling Hideyo that they will meet him in Japan at the dock.

The story returns to Hideyo's plight. He is starving and freezing in a blizzard. He knows that he dare not fall asleep or he will freeze to death. He sees a red light in the distance and tries to reach it, hoping he will find a family that will take him in.

Chapters 8–11

Mother, Yoko, and Ko finally reach Japan. Japan is suffering from heavy bombardment and the resulting destruction of U.S. attacks. There is a shelter that has been set up for refugees, but there is no food provided. Mother does not feel safe in the shelter as everyone around her family is desperate. People fight for space, and she is afraid what little possessions they do have will be stolen. Despite the challenges and despair, she insists on registering her daughters for school. Then she leaves them to travel north to Aomori to find her parents. While she is gone, Ko takes care of Yoko, making sure she attends classes and bringing food home in the evening. Yoko is constantly humiliated at school by the other young girls there. Yoko's hair is growing out, but it sticks out on top of her head. Her clothes are in tatters and the sole of her shoe is detached. She has no money for supplies and must dig through the trashcans to find pencils and paper that have been discarded. She makes friends with Mr. Naido, the school janitor, who begins to save things like rulers and erasers that he finds. Yoko tells no one about her background. When Yoko complains to Ko about how the other girls make fun of her, Ko tells her that she has to face that same discrimination. She tells Yoko to use these hardships to make her study harder and prove that she is worth something.

Mother returns to tell Yoko that both her maternal and paternal grandparents are dead. They have nowhere else to go. Yoko notices that her mother is extremely tired and does not look well. Ko has not yet returned from school, and since they moved away from the refugee shelter, they have been living in a park in Kyoto. This is where Mother dies.

When Ko finally arrives, after mourning her mother, she makes arrangements for her mother's cremation. A bystander, Mrs. Masuda, steps in when the men who have come with a truck to take Mother's body away tell Ko how much this will cost her. Mrs. Masuda makes other arrangements that cost a lot less and offers the girls a room over her husband's factory.

Ko is learning to sew and makes money selling her wares, which Yoko takes from door-to-door to sell. They also find money sewn in their mother's shawl. It provides them with enough food to get through the winter. Little by little, the girls' lives begin to improve. Yoko writes an essay about her experiences at school and wins a contest that brings in a little more money. The essay is printed in the newspaper and catches the attention of Mr. Matsumura, the soldier whom they met at the hospital in Korea, the one who was refusing to eat. He contacts the girls and promises to help them with whatever they need.

Hideyo is rescued by Mr. and Mrs. Kim, a Korean family. They nurse Hideyo back to health. Hideyo stays with them until the spring, helping them with chores on their farm. Then Hideyo tells them that he must find his family. He makes the journey to Seoul and then Pusan, where he catches the boat to Japan. At the dock in Japan, Ko and Yoko have made sure that messages are posted, so Hideyo will know where they are. When Hideyo lands, he sees their notes to him. The story ends when the three siblings are finally reunited.

CHARACTERS

Mr. Enomoto

Mr. Enomoto is Yoko's grade school teacher in Nanam, North Korea. He teaches his pupils only during half the days. In the afternoons, he has them digging ditches around the school to be used in air raids. He also has them looking for scrap metal in the fields and elsewhere.

Father

See Mr. Yoshio Kawashima

Mr. Fukui

Yoko takes traditional Japanese dance from Mr. Fukui, while she is in Nanam, North Korea. It is Mr. Fukui who directs his dancing students at the hospital when they perform for the wounded soldiers. Mr. Fukui also accompanies the dancers by singing the Japanese songs.

Honorable Brother

See Hideyo Kawashima

Honorable Sister

See Ko Kawashima

Hideyo Kawashima

Hideyo is Yoko's eighteen-year-old brother. He is the eldest of the Kawashima children. Hideyo decides that he wants to join the Japanese army in the student division. He does this without asking his father's permission and against his mother's wishes. However, Hideyo flunks the army exam and is turned down. His mother suggests that Hideyo might have done this on

So Far from the Bamboo Grove

purpose, though it is not explained why she thinks so. Instead, Hideyo offers his help at the ammunitions factory. It is at the factory where Hideyo confronts the war firsthand when Korean soldiers barge in and kill many of the people working there. Hideyo escapes by pretending to be dead. Then he and three of his friends try to make it to Seoul by dressing up as Koreans. Hideyo almost dies along the way but is rescued by the Kim family. He lives with them through the winter, but tells them he must leave when spring comes. He is homesick for his family. Hideyo does not reappear in the story until the end, where he reunites with his sisters. Although Hideyo represents the so-called man of the family in his father's absence, he is separated from his mother and sisters and is unable to help them in their escape. His sister Ko must take on the guise of a male as well as adopting a somewhat aggressive male nature in his absence.

Ko Kawashima

Ko is the elder sister of Yoko. Her character sits somewhat in the background as the story begins, but once the journey to Seoul is under way, Ko takes on a prominent role. Whereas in the beginning, Ko seems insubstantial and sometimes a bit bossy, when the struggle for survival begins, Ko's confidence and her enterprising manner may well be responsible for the family's having made it back to Japan. She is resourceful when having to find food where food does not seem to exist. She does not complain about the hardships they face and is a model for young Yoko to emulate. After her mother dies, Ko takes on an even more impressive role as she does small jobs, such as shining shoes, to make sure Yoko has food and clothing. Ko never bemoans her fate and never allows depression to sap her strength. She is also selfless, ensuring Yoko benefits from her meager earnings. Ko uses her pride in refusing help from others unless she is totally at a loss for what to do. She allows Mrs. Masuda to help with the cremation of her mother and accepts Mrs. Masuda's invitation to use the room above the factory. But Ko refuses help from Corporal Matsumura. Although many of the characters in this story exhibit strength and courage, Ko exhibits outstanding generosity. She becomes the protector, mother, father, and provider for her sister. She is defiant in facing the world and all its tragedies and hazards without boasting. She also never loses her respect for those around her. Of course, Ko is represented through the

eyes of her younger sister, who may well have glorified the experiences; but as told in this story, Ko comes very close to being a saint.

Mrs. Kawashima

Mrs. Kawashima is Yoko's mother and is often referred to in this story as Mother. Though she leads her children to safety during very challenging times, it is not certain that she would have made it if it were not for the courage and strength of her elder daughter, Ko. Mrs. Kawashima understands the world in a way that her children might not. She is more aware of the dangers. She cuts her daughters' hair and makes them dress as young boys, for example. She is a gentle and giving woman who administers to the wounded on the train. But she is not as resourceful as Ko, when it comes to finding food. She carries a knife under her clothes to protect herself and her children. And fortunately, she never comes across a circumstance when she has to use it. Her frailness is hinted at when it is related that her hair turns gray, almost overnight, as she makes the journey from northern to southern Korea. Mrs. Kawashima was smart enough to hide the life savings that she stashed in hidden pockets of her shawl. She is also selfless in wanting to make sure that her son will find them and that her daughters will receive an education, even if she has no food. She knows an education is a key to their survival. But the war and the family's changed circumstances take all her strength. Upon discovering the death of her parents and those of her husband, she is weakened beyond repair. The difference between Mrs. Kawashima and Ko might represent the difference between the generation of Japanese women raised in comfort before the war and the generation that knew little more than war and the challenges of survival.

Yoko Kawashima

Yoko is the narrator of this story. She is eleven years old, the youngest child of the Kawashima family. The author represents the young girl fairly objectively, exposing her weaknesses as well as her strengths. Throughout the story, Yoko is often reluctant to do what is asked of her. As the story unfolds, Yoko exhibits her strengths. She first attempts to protect her mother by biting the hand of a Japanese soldier. Then, in the midst of the family's journey to Seoul, Yoko sustains injuries after a nearby bomb blast. She must continue walking for several days while suffering fever and infection from her wounds, which she does with little complaint.

Once they arrive in Japan, Yoko shows her strengths in different ways. She befriends the janitor, whom all the other students make fun of. Although she wants to drop out of school, Yoko not only meets the challenges of students mocking her poverty, but she also excels at her studies. Yoko never explains why she is dressed so shabbily, never wanting to use her experience as an excuse. Yoko helps Ko sew and then sell the items she has sewn. Instead of buying new shoes, she buys special meals to help nourish her older sister. Of all the characters in this story, it is Yoko who matures the most, because she has so much maturing to do. The story begins with Yoko as a typical pre-teen, who is absorbed in her own world. By the end of the story, she learns to find opportunity where, at first, there looks like there is none. She learns to give, even when there is so little to offer. Yoko might represent the hope of the future.

Mr. Yoshio Kawashima

Mr. Kawashima is Yoko's father. It is because of Mr. Kawashima's job as a Japanese government official that the family is living in Korea. Mr. Kawashima travels fifty miles to go to work in Manchuria. He is seldom home. In this story, Mr. Kawashima never makes an appearance. He is alluded to in stories that are told or in conversations. It is related at the end of the story that Mr. Kawashima was taken prisoner by the Russians and was released six years after his family returns to Japan.

Mr. Lee

Mr. Lee was a Korean friend of the Kawashima family. Hideyo thinks of them as he plans his escape with his three friends. Hideyo knows the boys must change their clothes if they want any chance to escape. So he takes them to Mr. and Mrs. Lee's home, where he finds them dead. He knows they would have given the boys clothes, so they take Korean style clothes they find there.

Mrs. Lee

Mrs. Lee, wife of Mr. Lee, is a Korean woman who befriended the Kawashima family. She is shot and Hideyo finds her dead when he runs to her house to borrow some Korean style clothes.

Little One

See Yoko Kawashima

Makoto

Makoto is a friend of Hideyo's who worked with Hideyo in the munitions factory. Makota hides in the bathroom when the Korean soldiers open fire on the other workers. Later, after the boys escape, Makoto runs home to find that his parents have been killed. Makoto has no other relatives in Korea. He does not follow Hideyo into Seoul. Instead, he goes with Shinzo and Shoichi to another location in southern Korea. He promises to meet up with Hideyo in Japan five years later.

Mrs. Masuda

Mrs. Masuda sees Yoko and Ko in the park in Kyoto after they have arrived from Korea. She witnesses the death of the girls' mother and the struggles that Ko faces in taking her mother's body to be cremated. Mrs. Masuda steps in and keeps the girls from being taken advantage of, she helps them transport their mother's body, and then offers them a room over her husband's factory. Later Mrs. Masuda keeps an eye on the girls, though she is not very forthcoming in offering them food or heat or any other luxuries. Mrs. Masuda might represent the typical relationships among strangers in a war-torn environment in which everyone is fighting to survive.

Corporal Matsumura

Corporal Matsumura is the badly wounded soldier at the hospital in Nanam, North Korea, who has been refusing to eat. His face is heavily bandaged and he cannot see. Matsumura reappears later, when he is mostly healed. He visits the Kawashima house many times. It is Matsumura who comes to tell them that they must leave immediately. He gives them a note that will allow them to ride the train that is evacuating wounded soldiers. Toward the end of the story, Matsumura reunites with Yoko and Ko in Japan. He promises he will do whatever they ask of him.

Mother

See Mrs. Kawashima

Major Ryu

Major Ryu is an army doctor stationed at the hospital in Nanam, North Korea. Major Ryu is the person who asked Yoko and the other dancers at the hospital if they would take the time to visit the soldiers who were too weak to make it to the performance. Later, when Mother is looking for the station master to give him the note that Corporal Matsumura has told her will allow her family to board the train, it is Major Ryu who steps in to assure their safe passage.

Shinzo

Shinzo is one of the friends of Hideyo, who survives by hiding in the bathroom of the munitions factory. His parents are not at home but have left word that they have fled south to relatives. Shinzo parts paths with Hideyo before arriving in Seoul, but promises to meet up with him in Japan one day.

Shoichi

Shoichi is one of the boys who works at the munitions factory and escapes the attack of the Korean soldiers. He has relatives in southern Korea and heads for their homes with Shinzo and Makoto after parting with Hideyo, who heads for Seoul.

Dr. Takeda

Dr. Takeda takes care of Yoko's wounds and infection when the family reaches Seoul. When Dr. Takeda learns of their names, he asks if they are related to Yoshio Kawashima. Mrs. Kawashima says that is her husband. It turns out that Dr. Takeda's father went to school with Yoko's father. He takes good care of Yoko and makes sure the family gets a supply of milk and extra bandages when they leave the hospital.

Dr. Yamada

Dr. Yamada takes care of Yoko in Nanam, North Korea, after a Japanese soldier, who has come to the Kawashima house, kicks Yoko in the ribs, cracking some of them. It is Dr. Yamada who helps Mother to replace her eyeglasses after the soldiers take them from her to use the metal frames.

THEMES

The Effects of War

The author of this novel has become a lecturer on the topic of war. Watkins has stated that one of her main purposes for telling her story was so others would learn of the hardships and cruelties

TOPICS FOR FURTHER STUDY

- Study maps of Korea and Japan, paying attention to where the cities in this story are located. Learn the geography of the land and the typical weather. Then create a class presentation, using maps, images, statistics, and narrative, discussing what the physical journey from northern Korea to Japan must have been like for Yoko and her family.

- There is a lot of controversy about this novel because it is a one-sided version of the Japanese occupation in Korea. Study the history of the Japanese control of Korea and provide a more objective view. What were the motives and needs behind the Japanese attempt to take over Korea? What were their tactics? What hardships did this cause the Korean people? What were the benefits the Korean people experienced, if any? What was the Korean retaliation like? Write your summation in a report and present it to your class. Be prepared to answer questions on the topic.

- This story mentions several items and arts that are enjoyed in the Japanese culture, including the koto, shamisen, kimono, obi, tabi, calligraphy, Japanese dance, flower arranging, and the tea ceremony. Research these items and arts to discover what they are and what they mean to the Japanese people. Write a report on your findings.

- Choose one of the three children in the novel, Yoko, Ko, or Hideyo, and write a short story about the character you've chosen. Consider changing different details from *So Far from the Bamboo Grove.* For example, what would have happened to Yoko if Ko had died? How would the story have differed if Hideyo had been with them during the journey to southern Korea? Be prepared to read your story to your class.

that war can cause not only on the battlefields but also in the daily lives of innocent people. In her novel, Watkins demonstrates that war pits one group against another, which may seem an obvious statement, but the point is that when people are considered in groups, stereotypes evolve. The enemy becomes anyone who looks or dresses or speaks in a certain defined manner. Watkins shows the hatred that develops through these concepts of war as one person can harm or even kill another even though that person never did anything wrong except to be different, even when these lines of difference are hard to depict. For example, is Yoko Japanese or is she Korean? She has lived most of her life in Korea. She knows the language and the culture. And yet, because she was born in Japan, she is considered the enemy, despite the fact that she carries no weapon and has little or no information about the politics and ambitions of the military generals. She is an innocent caught in the crossfire, as are her mother and siblings along with the Korean farmers and all other non-military populations.

Another message from this story is that war turns people into savages, as all social order is either completely destroyed or greatly impaired and everyone must consider his or her own survival. Chaos reigns in these circumstances. Each person must fend for him- or herself. All sense of humanity and compassion are forgotten. People do nothing, for example, when young girls are raped. No one is willing to help because individuals are too concerned for their own welfare. Bodies of dead people are thrown off the train, because they might infect those who remain. There is no time to mourn the dead or even bury them.

Even the soldiers, who are trained to fight for a cause, become confused as to the definition of that cause. Why, for example, were the Korean soldiers specifically searching for the wife and children of Mr. Kawashima? Had they done something wrong? Were they a threat to the Korean government or military? The soldiers' actions were either purely an act of revenge or a false sign of victory over the men who once ruled them. Killing unarmed women and children is not a symbol of power. Watkins's story shows how war changes people, leading many to rely on their most basic animalistic instincts: to kill or to be killed.

The Fight for Survival

The character of Ko represents the most resilient of survivors in this story. Since Watkins dedicates

this novel to her sister, Ko, next to the theme of war, the theme of survival is one of the strongest. Through the character of Ko, Watkins demonstrates how some of the most delicate and unprepared people can become the most capable when forced to fight for their survival. Although raised in a comfortable home with all conveniences provided for her, Ko's instincts for survival kick in when she and her family face danger. Ko is especially aware of what she must do to keep her family from starving. Whether she has to forage for food in garbage bins or polish shoes at the train station to make small change to buy food, Ko is willing to rid herself of false pride in order to help herself and her family to survive. The most interesting aspect of Ko's sense of survival, though, is that she does not forgo her compassion. Despite her need to survive, she realizes that those around her are fighting to stay alive too. So she shares her food with strangers on the train. She finds food and, although her stomach is empty, she brings back the scrubby morsels and distributes them to her sister and mother. The theme of survival is also demonstrated as being reciprocal, as in another scene on the train, when the nurses and other patients conceal the identity of Yoko's family by covering their clothing in blood and lying about their condition. They provide this shelter, it is suggested, because the mother and her daughters helped the patients survive by sharing their water and food with them. There is also the survival of Corporal Matsumura, who was despondent from all his wounds. He had refused to eat, which suggests that he was depressed and might not heal. Yoko and Ko took the time to go see him in the hospital. The family later welcomed him into their home as a friend. Matsumura, consequently, helped the family to escape on the train. Later, in Japan, he continued to offer his help should the girls need it. Hideyo also traded help with the Kim family. He assisted the Kim family on their farm during the winter as war was raging all around them. In return, the Kim family protected him from Korean soldiers, passing Hideyo off as a member of the family. These instances of survival stand in contrast to the theme of war. Although there are moments when one must consider one's own survival, there is often room for compassion, the author shows, even in the most dire of conditions. The fight for survival, in some instances, seems to bring out the best of human instincts.

Loss and Death

With war comes loss, and there is plenty of loss in this story. First the losses appear to be only material. Mother loses her glasses and her wedding ring when the soldiers demand that she give up all metals in her possession. Then when the children visit the hospital to dance, there is the loss of limbs and blood. There is also the loss in separation, as when the family is separated from Hideyo and Mr. Kawashima. And then the loss of the family home. But on the train, when the baby is born dead and then the body is thrown off the train, the seriousness of loss deepens. Not only does death confront the characters, but also the time to even ponder what death means is lost. Hideyo also learns this lesson as he takes a job with the Korean officials, who pack dead bodies in bags and toss them into the river. The greatest loss for Yoko and Ko is the death of their mother. They had relied on their mother for strength, love, and guidance. But here again, circumstances are so stressed that Yoko and Ko have little time to mourn their mother. They must keep moving so they too do not die. There are undercurrents of loss throughout the story also. These are more abstract, thus less obvious. There is the loss of fear, as the refugees face far greater dangers than they ever did before, and they instinctively know that they cannot allow their fear to deter them. The loss of pride is another one, as seen when people must eat food that others have thrown away. There is also the loss of the children's innocence and childhood. This is expressed most clearly by comparing the students in Yoko's and Ko's classes. These students mock the sisters, making fun of their outward appearances because they themselves have no experience nor understanding of what Yoko and Ko have been through. These students have not experienced any such losses and cannot relate to the other girls who do not have the resources they have.

STYLE

Naïve Narrator

Watkins's novel *So Far from the Bamboo Grove* is written from the point of view of the protagonist, Yoko, who is eleven years old. Seeing this story through the eyes of a child has both its strengths and its limitations. The strength of this point of view makes portions of the story more powerful. Yoko suffers many hardships that most adults will never have to endure, such as wounds from bomb blasts. Yoko's ability to learn to endure her wounds makes the experience more painful, as children do not normally suffer so much. She not only endures, she becomes stronger by facing her challenges and in the end acquires the outlook of a much more mature person. She understands the world much better than her classmates, for instance. However, because of Yoko's young and limited vision, the story can sometimes feel flat. For example, more complex issues, such as the reasons for war, the morality of war, or the effects of the long colonization period of the Japanese on the Korean people, are not explored. Instead, the world is very immediate, as a child might witness it. Much of what is considered important is what is happening right now rather than how this might affect the future or how this compares with the past. For instance, take Yoko's attack on the Japanese soldier, when she bites him as he takes her mother's metal-rimmed eyeglasses. This is an act of innocent aggression. Yoko does not consider the fact that the soldier has a gun and might kill her and her mother. Yoko does not even consider her actions wrong. She is attempting to defend her mother. Although the actions of the soldier are terrible in kicking her, in many ways Yoko was lucky that was all the soldier did in retaliation.

This novel has been criticized by Korean readers for not presenting a more balanced presentation. If read with the understanding that this story represents a child's version of the events, the lack of complex understanding of the historical background that led up to the confrontations and hardships that the characters undergo might be more easily forgiven. If the author had written this book through the eyes of the mother or an adult narrator, the story would have been completely different.

Adult Subject Matter at a Young Adult Reading Level

Not only are the concepts kept on a less complicated level, the language is also written in a very simplistic style. The vocabulary is very basic and the sentences are mostly short, making this novel ideal for the young adult reader—aimed at middle school and early high school readers. The story is told in a very matter-of-fact manner with little reflection on the deeper meaning of the actions of the characters. The story reads almost like a journal, as one fact follows another while the story unfolds. Few if any literary devices such as metaphors and similes are used. This may have been

Ruins of Hiroshima after the atomic bomb blast in 1945 (*George Silk | Time & Life Pictures | Getty Images*)

done on purpose, to reflect the vocabulary and thoughts of a child. It might also have been done because the author wanted to aim her story at a younger audience, wanting children to know the atrocities of war in hopes that they would grow up unwilling to partake in such activities. The simplicity of style is also reflected in the emotional displays of the characters. Emotions are expressed but just barely, as if in passing. Yoko, for example, mourns her mother, but she does not dwell on her feelings. This in turn, keeps the reader from fully sharing Yoko's loss. Even physical sensations, such as the cold of winter or the hunger that the characters experience are stated in such simplistic terms that readers are not drawn into them, or if they are, the feelings do not last very long or are not deeply felt.

Autobiographical Fiction

The basic details of Watkins's story are taken directly from her life. For this reason, the novel

is referred to as being autobiographical. However, since the author could not know all the dialogue that took place at times when she was not present (such as during Hideyo's experience), this work is called fiction. The basic details are based on reality, but the specific details come out of the author's memory mixed with her imagination. The author might also have not remembered all the real details and needed to provide incidents that would tie together all the details in a storylike form. Because the author experienced many of the incidents presented in the story, the novel gains authenticity. It feels very real. Because the author manufactured dialogue that might not have actually occurred and maybe tied loose ends together with incidents that happened only in her imagination, the storyline flows and is possibly more digestible for her readers. The other choice would have been for the author to have written this as a memoir, which would have

COMPARE
&
CONTRAST

- **1940s:** After heavy bombing of over sixty Japanese cities, the United States drops two atomic bombs on Japan in August 1945. One is dropped on Hiroshima. The other is dropped on Nagasaki. The bombs destroy the cities and cause over 200,000 deaths. Deaths and poor health from the radioactive fallout continue for many decades.

  Today: Dirty bombs, a combination of explosives and radioactive materials, are reportedly used by terrorists.

- **1940s:** Japan is defeated in World War II and loses its hold on Korea. A decade later, Korea is divided into North and South Korea, with little communication permitted between those who live in either section.

  Today: Leaders of both South and North Korea make historic strides in attempts to ease the strict rules that divide the Korean peninsula. Limited visitation rights are given to families with members on each side of the border. The leaders of both countries meet and try to create better relationships.

- **1940s:** After its defeat, Japan is essentially a broken country. Major cities, including Tokyo, are demolished. The economy is in ruins. The United States offers financial aid to help Japan rebuild.

  Today: Japan, now a leader in automobile manufacturing and electronics, has one of the strongest economies and is considered one of the most successful countries in the world.

---

had to have been totally based on real events. Since she wrote this novel many decades after the actual events, memory and the emotions associated with those memories, might have blurred reality. Writing this story as an autobiographical fiction allows the author a little more poetic license to stretch the truth. This does not mean that the author has told an untruthful story, but rather that she gave herself more room to be creative with it.

HISTORICAL CONTEXT

Brief History of Japanese and Korean Relations

Over the course of its long history, Korea suffered invasions from other countries, including a Japanese invasion that lasted from 1592 to 1598. In more modern times, up to the 1800s, Korea discouraged influence from outside sources except from China, and refused to trade with European countries. But in the 1800s, things began to change. France and the United States

grew more aggressive in their attempts to set up trade. These countries needed markets for their goods and eyed the burgeoning population on the Korean peninsula. They threatened Korea militarily, but Korea was able to thwart their plans.

However, in 1873, the Korean Taewon'gun ("grand prince"), leader of Korea and a great reformer who had worked to strengthen Korean independence, was overthrown. Three years later, Japan, which was then moving fast toward becoming an industrial country far ahead of Korean progress in that direction, forced Korea to trade. China, whose government had worked as a sort of mentor to Korea's modernization efforts, recommended that Korea begin trade with the United States in order to neutralize Japan's effect on Korea. To counterattack this tactic, the Japanese attacked and defeated China in the Sino-Japanese War from 1894 to 1895. To clinch its control on Korea, in 1904 and 1905, Japan also engaged and defeated the Russians, another ally of Korea, in the Russo-Japanese War. With this victory, Japan forced Korea to sign the Protectorate Treaty that same year. Japan thus ruled over Korea's national and international affairs, policing domestic issues as well as relationships with other countries. Complete control ensued with the official annexation of Korea by Japan in 1910.

Limited by space and resources, Japan sought Korean land to use for its agricultural needs. Korean farmers produced crops that were sold to Japan. There have been accounts of Japan using Koreans as slave laborers. Japan also needed Korea's rich natural resources to fuel its manufacturing needs. So minerals were also taken from the Korean land.

The Korean people staged a peaceful rebellion in 1919, called the March First Movement. However, the protestors were no match for the Japanese military and police. Japan clamped down harder on any further protests and as Japan's desires for further military conquests led it into conflicts with China, attacks on Pearl Harbor and other locations in the Pacific, as well as in southeast Asia, stricter impositions on the Koreans were made. Japan wanted the Koreans to assimilate into the Japanese culture, helping to cement its takeover of Korea. Koreans were forced to relinquish their Korean names and adopt Japanese names. The Korean language was also outlawed. These conditions continued until the Japanese were defeated at the end of World War II.

When World War II ended, Russia and the United States, who were allies in that war, divided the Korean peninsula into two parcels: North Korea, which remains under the influence of Communism (as reflected by both the Chinese and Russian governments) and South Korea, which has allied itself with the United States. Today, relationships between Japan and Korea remain strained. Koreans complain that Japan has never apologized for the atrocities that the Koreans suffered during those years of annexation. Some scholars in Japan have sued their own government for tampering with history books, which the scholars claim do not honestly deal with the issues of Japanese control of Korea. There have also been diplomatic problems between the two countries due to Japan's occupation of Korea and Japan's denial of the hardships that were directly caused by that occupation.

Manchuria

Manchuria is a Chinese province located in the northeastern corner of China. Because Manchuria shares a border with Russia, Russia had eyed this land because of the area's resources and the fact that, in controlling this area, Russia would have easier access to Korea. But with Japan's annexation of Korea, Japan, too, eyed Manchuria. Manchuria offered nearly 200,000 square kilometers (about 124,300 square miles) of land, which meant not only more resources but also more acreage on which Japan's growing population could live. So Japan began investing in Manchuria, building manufacturing centers there. Cities were modernized and banking systems were established. To protect those investments, Japan sent regiments of its army to protect its interests in the territory. This all happened around 1929, the same time as the Great Depression in the United States, and the economic nightmare affected Japan as well. Japan's government was weakened by this worldwide depression and was unable to offer its unemployed much help. Japan's army was charged, however, by its conquests of new lands and pushed its agenda of extending its powers into Manchuria as a possible solution to the country's economic problems. In 1931, disregarding its own government edict, the Japanese army invaded and secured the whole province. It set up a puppet government (controlled in all aspects by the Japanese) and renamed the area Manchukuo. When Japan lost World War II, it also lost control over Manchuria. Hundreds of thousands of Japanese were captured by Russia's army and taken to labor camps.

Destruction and Rebuilding of Japan

After Japan's bombing of U.S. ships at Pearl Harbor in Hawaii, in 1941, the U.S. government, along with the Allied forces (except for Russia) declared war on Japan. Japan had also attacked several countries in southeastern Asia, including the Philippines, Thailand, and Hong Kong. The leaders of Japan assumed that Nazi Germany would win control of Europe and that the United States would be forced to negotiate a peace treaty. Instead, the United States decided to wage a fierce war against Japan to ensure an unconditional surrender. Although U.S. ships had taken a beating at Pearl Harbor, there were enough forces and equipment remaining to systematically gain control of the outer limits of Japan's bases and then slowly move in on Japan's major cities. The U.S. airplanes heavily bombed Tokyo, Osaka, and other large metropolitan areas on the main islands in 1945. Despite food and supply shortages, the Japanese were determined not to give up. In July 1945, the

General Yoshijiro Umezu, Chief of the Japanese Army General Staff, signs the surrender document on the U.S.S. Missouri *as Japan accepts defeat to end World War II (© POPPERFOTO | Alamy)*

Japanese government refused an opportunity to sign a declaration of surrender. Shortly thereafter, the United States made the decision to drop the atomic bomb. The first city that was hit was Hiroshima, which was bombed on August 6, 1945. The bomb completely destroyed at least 60 percent of the buildings and damaged most of the rest. An estimated 60,000 people were killed or went missing. Three days later, another atomic bomb was dropped on Nagasaki. On September 2, 1945, aboard the battleship U.S.S. *Missouri*, Japanese government officials surrendered.

An Allied Council, made up of international members, took up the task of restructuring Japan's government. With U.S. General Douglas MacArthur in charge, the Japanese government was remodeled with a new constitution, the Japanese emperor was stripped of powers, and the National Diet was created (a governing body similar to a parliament). The new constitution contained an article that prohibited the Japanese government from ever declaring war again.

CRITICAL OVERVIEW

Although classified as a Notable Book by the American Library Association and placed on the Best Books for Children list by the *School Library Journal*, Watkins's *So Far from the Bamboo Grove* has not received much literary review, except for a discussion about whether the book should be banned from school libraries and curriculums.

In an article on book banning, published by the American Library Association in the *Newsletter on Intellectual Freedom*, an anonymous journalist points out that some parents have objected to the content of Watkins's novel over the years. However, because of this, many educators have come to the book's defense, citing the positive lessons most students learn from the story.

A teacher, Glenda Speyer, writing in the *Boston Globe*, states that she has taught the book to her class and has found the novel to contain powerful themes of love and survival that provide moving lessons for her students. Speyer likens the novel to a "remarkable tool" to teach children how war affects people.

From another article for the *Boston Globe*, Carter Eckert also recommends Watkins's book as a valuable tool, but he points out that what *So Far from the Bamboo Grove* lacks is a historical reference point that Watkins does not delve into. Eckert is making reference to Japan's takeover of the Korean peninsula, which included its attempt to annihilate Korean culture. Eckert does not suggest banning Watkins's book, which he states provides a "heroic personal narrative of survival," but he does suggest that students should read the novel with knowledge of an objective historical context of the times and conditions in which the story takes place. When read in connection with books that offer competing perspectives, Watkins's book can provide students with an understanding, according to Eckert, of "how perspectives vary according to personal and historical circumstances."

CRITICISM

Joyce Hart

Hart is a published author of more than twenty books. In this essay on So Far from the Bamboo Grove, *Hart examines the character development of Watkins's protagonist, Yoko.*

Watkins's *So Far from the Bamboo Grove* has one of the often defined elements of what makes a good story: a character who demonstrates personal growth. As protagonist and narrator of this autobiographical novel, the young eleven-year-old Yoko begins the story as a somewhat typical pre-teen. By the end, although she is not yet twelve, Yoko has matured into a young adult who is emotionally much older than her years. Along the way, Yoko fights and moans, as any child would in her position. But in the end, Yoko's character has been very much changed.

In the beginning of this novel, the author stresses Yoko's youth by first telling readers of the girl's exact age and then by referring to the girl's nicknames, which are Little One, as her mother and older sister call her, and Noisy One, as she is called by her older brother. These terms are both endearing and representative. Yoko also has a propensity for tears whenever she is bothered by something out of the ordinary. But she cries not so much out of fear as out of

WHAT DO I READ NEXT?

- *My Brother, My Sister, and I* (1994) is Watkins's sequel to *So Far from the Bamboo Grove*. In it, the saga of Yoko, Ko, and Hideyo continues.

- Linda Sue Park, a Korean author, has written about her experiences during the Japanese occupation of South Korea. *When My Name Was Keoko* (2004) provides perspective on the Korean experience of the war and is thus a great complement to *So Far from the Bamboo Grove*.

- Banana Yoshimoto's novel *Kitchen* (2002) contains two novellas with two separate narrators. Both are young girls who must face tragedy and the challenge of finding their own identity. Yoshimoto provides readers with a contemporary view of life in Japan.

- *Hiroshima* (1948), compiled by John Hersey, is a collection of stories told by victims and survivors of the atomic bomb attack on Hiroshima. An extra chapter was inserted in the 1989 edition; in it, Hersey recounts what has since happened to the survivors.

displeasure, as when her older siblings tease her. These are not major emotional outbreaks but rather signs of her youth. One positive quality Yoko has, even in the beginning of the story, is her courage. However, readers will note that much of Yoko's courage, though unmistakably bold, comes with a lack of mature understanding of the world around her as well as a lack of comprehension of how adults can easily affect her life. For example, when Japanese soldiers appear at her house, Yoko attacks them when they insist that Yoko's mother relinquish her wedding ring and her metal-framed eyeglasses. Yoko challenges one of the soldiers by biting him. She has no sense of the soldier's greater strength or of the weapon he holds in his hands. Yoko reacts out of anger and fights with the only weapon she owns—her teeth. This may be considered an act of courage, but it is also

"

YOKO HAS BEEN THROWN INTO A WORLD OF
HOSTILITIES SO BRUTAL THAT SHE COULD NOT HAVE
IMAGINED THEM BEFORE."

very immature and foolish. Her attack results in Yoko's receiving a cracked rib; but it could have had much more dire consequences, such as the death of her sister, her mother, and herself.

Later in the story, Yoko complains of trivial affairs. These events are especially meaningless when compared to the events that will soon rule her life. Some examples include her not wanting to collect metal cans for the Japanese army because she does not like the abstract idea of killing that she senses is what war is all about. But she also does not like to practice the more genteel cultural arts of her country, such as calligraphy, the tea ceremony, flower arranging, and dance. In these ways, Yoko is typical of a girl her age, who does not see the bigger picture of the world. The collecting of the metals could save a soldier's life as the metal is turned into weaponry. Wars are hard to support on one hand, but once your country is involved in one, collecting metal could potentially help the war to end. The practicing of cultural arts is a way of understanding where she and her ancestors come from, what her culture is based on and made of. But Yoko comprehends none of this. She wants to do what she wants to do and does not appreciate doing what she is told to do. This rebellion is all a part of growing up, as are the practices that are forced upon her. Through her rebellion, Yoko will learn of the boundaries within which she must define her world. Through learning of her culture, she will gain discipline and the essence of obedience, and she will begin to take part in the world of adults.

In the scenes that follow the opening pages of this story, life is changing all around her, and Yoko has to quickly bear a lot of frightening details that many children never have to even think about. She hears bombs being dropped on buildings not too far from where she lives. She practices air raid drills and must run to specially dug ditches around the school or to the backyard bomb shelter near her home when

a siren is sounded. She also must perform the traditional dances for soldiers, who have lost arms, legs, and parts of their faces when she is forced to visit the army hospital. Yoko is well aware of the war going on around her even before she is pushed out of the safety of her home.

Without much notice, Yoko's mother is told that Russian soldiers are out to kill them because of Yoko's father's role in the Japanese occupation of Manchuria. Yoko's family must leave their home immediately, taking only the bare necessities. Yoko does not fully comprehend the dangers that are rapidly encircling her life. She is sluggish, unwilling to move and considers pencils and pens as items worthy of packing. Although the pressure to leave quickly is apparent in her mother's and her sister's actions, Yoko misinterprets them, stating that both women are acting too harshly toward her. Her mother is impatient with her, Yoko believes, and her sister is too mean.

As the three females begin the first steps of their escape, Yoko is suddenly filled with fear when she first sees Russian and Korean soldiers. This is to be expected. Unable to control her terror, Yoko reacts by vomiting when the soldiers draw near. This reaction makes her feel weak, and she whines when the soldiers leave and her sister makes Yoko run. When they reach the train station and she sees wounded soldiers being loaded onto the train, Yoko comments that she was suddenly awakened. This is the first hint that Yoko is beginning to understand her situation. She begins to understand that this journey is no ordinary trip through the countryside. People are bleeding and dying around her. It is not just other people in danger, she realizes, but she, her sister, and her mother are likewise threatened. Yoko is starting to evolve from young child to a more experienced youth. But she is not quite there. She asks her mother if they will be coming back to their home soon. Her mother, sensing that Yoko needs a child's reassurance and sense of stability, tells Yoko that their departure is only temporary. Readers, however, have a clearer idea that this journey will not include a return. From knowing the details of history, readers know better.

So Yoko relaxes into the safety of false security. She helps the women onboard the train, sharing what little food and water she has, not fully recognizing the shortages of both that are waiting for her. She finds courage, at this stage, because she believes her discomforts are temporary. Her pleasant, leisurely life will return shortly, when she will be allowed to be a child again.

However, as the journey continues, her circumstances only deteriorate further. She is wounded and loses hearing in one ear. She is often close to starving. She sees soldiers blown up by bombs. To stay alive, she must sort through garbage for leftover crusts and rotting fruit. She must dress as a boy, so she will not be raped. These are not the fears or nightmares of an average child in ordinary circumstances. Yoko has been thrown into a world of hostilities so brutal that she could not have imagined them before. On the positive side, though, she learns to appreciate the sacrifices that her sister and mother make to protect her, and she develops a deep respect for them.

Halfway through their journey, after Yoko mourns her mother's death, she develops more fully. She stops waiting for Ko to provide for her and starts to seek ways of taking care of herself. She does her best to shut out the sounds of the jeering voices of her peers, turning her sense of humiliation into inspiration for her own success. She evolves, finally, beyond her sense of self and begins considering the needs of others, especially her sister's needs. This is the final stage of Yoko's rapid development. She sacrifices herself in order to help her sister. She forgoes the luxury of a new pair of shoes and instead buys a nourishing meal for Ko. She finds ways to earn money, sewing dolls and writing an award-winning essay. She learns to make a fire and to cook. She even solves the riddle her mother left in her last words, discovering money sewn in her mother's shawl.

These actions are a sign of maturity. Yoko has broken through the veil of childhood, which usually allows the child to think of no one but herself. It is easy under normal conditions for an eleven-year-old girl to expect to be taken care of. Under such circumstances, there also is no need to think of anything but one's own comfort and to whine when that ease of living is disturbed. But Yoko is forced to grow up quickly, and she responds to those changes in a positive, courageous manner. In the course of this novel, she is transformed from an average child to someone quite extraordinary. Her peers have no understanding of Yoko because their minds are still coddled by normal childhood experiences, their

thoughts are consumed with pretty clothes and well-cooked meals that they assume will always be there for them. To them, Yoko is a tramp—someone too lazy to take care of her appearance. Yoko's poverty is looked upon as a disease, and they shun her, fearful, at least subconsciously, that they might catch her affliction.

Because Yoko once lived in a privileged world, she partially understands the unaffected children around her. But Yoko also understands another, more complicated world—a world of horrific extremes, of blood, pain, and suffering. And she is a survivor of that world. This imbues her with a confidence that no one can take from her.

Source: Joyce Hart, Critical Essay on *So Far from the Bamboo Grove*, in *Novels for Students*, Gale, Cengage Learning, 2009.

Anna L. Griffin

In the following article, Griffin describes a 2003 visit made by the author to speak to students about her book. The article also details Watkins's inspiration to begin writing So Far from the Bamboo Grove.

When Yoko Kawashima Watkins was their age, she was fighting for her life. Perhaps that is the reason why the classroom, filled with 75 pupils at Southeast Middle School, was so quiet during a recent presentation by Mrs. Watkins.

"I wrote this story because I want you to please appreciate what you have," Mrs. Watkins, a Brewster resident, said. "If you can appreciate what you have, then you will look at the world with a different pair of eyes."

Mrs. Watkins is the author of *So Far from the Bamboo Grove*, and *My Brother, My Sister and I*. Children at the school are reading *So Far from the Bamboo Grove*, and because many of the children found that book to be so inspiring the children have chosen the second book. She was recently at the school for a whole day to meet with children, parents and teachers. During that time, she gave several presentations.

So Far from the Bamboo Grove is the story of Mrs. Watkins and her family's flight from the Korean peninsula at the end of World War II.

At that time, Mrs. Watkins was 11 and living in northern Korea with her mother, father, sister and brother. They were from Japan. At the end of the war, the Korean people wanted to regain control of their homeland and to punish the Japanese, who occupied the country for many years.

As a result, Japanese living in the country were forced to become refugees—to leave or face certain death. Some of the Japanese men, including Mrs. Watkins' father, were taken into custody and sent to internment camps. Mrs. Watkins' brother, separated from the family at that time, was able to escape and return to Japan. Mrs. Watkins, her mother and her sister had to make the journey themselves. It was a journey filled with despair, deprivation and danger.

Pupils had prepared many questions for Mrs. Watkins, some dealing with details of her life story and other questions about the writing process.

Mrs. Watkins said she wrote *So Far from the Bamboo Grove* after a visit to the United States. She was staying with a fairly well-to-do family in the Washington, D.C., area and was looking forward to taking a tour of the White House.

"The morning of the tour, I was having breakfast with the woman of the house," Mrs. Watkins said. "Her teenaged daughter comes into the kitchen and does not even say 'good morning.'"

"She proceeds to go to the refrigerator and opens the doors," Mrs. Watkins related. She then told of all of the food located in the refrigerator and the pantry next to the refrigerator.

"After she looked in all of the cabinets, she slammed one of the doors and said, 'There's no food in this house.' She then stomped up the stairs and went into her room and threw open her closet door," Mrs. Watkins said.

She then described all the clothes the young woman had in her closet. "One outfit after the other she took out, tried on, and then threw on the floor," Mrs. Watkins said. "I have nothing to wear," Mrs. Watkins said the young woman exclaimed.

It was this young woman's attitude that prompted Mrs. Watkins to write a 10-page letter to the young woman upon returning to her home. "I outlined what I had been through in Korea and Japan and at the end of the letter I wrote, 'Please appreciate what it is you have, because you don't know what will happen. It may be taken away from you.'"

Following that 10-page outline, Mrs. Watkins was able to write the book, which she said has been well-received The book will soon be translated into the German and Korean languages. "So from this humble beginning, my story has grown," she said.

Mrs. Watkins urged the pupils to be kind to each other and to work with each other. "Imagine what the world would be if we would each be kind to each other and help each other out," she said. "I know this is something that you can do for me and I will do it for you as well. Don't wait to do this. Please for Yoko, do it today. Do it when you leave this classroom and you will see what a better place the world will be."

Source: Anna L. Griffin, "Pupils Get Peek at Past: Japanese Author Speaks at Southeast Middle School," in *Telegram & Gazette*, January 29, 2003, p. 1.

Bradford L. Miner

In the following article, Miner reports on the effect that So Far from the Bamboo Grove *has had on students. He also relates several comments made by the author regarding her childhood, which the book is based on.*

Being thankful.

It's not just a feeling reserved for Thanksgiving Day.

And, as 300 seventh-graders at Quabbin Regional Middle School discovered recently, it's not something one finds in the pages of a textbook.

On a recent morning, spellbound pupils sat on the carpeted floor of Erin Stevens' classroom and listened intently to the soft-spoken Japanese woman who stood before them in traditional dress of kimono and wooden clogs.

It was their first encounter with Yoko Kawashima Watkins, but the 69-year-old author from Brewster was no stranger to any of them.

Mrs. Watkins was thankful just to be there, she told the admiring pupils, grateful for the few minutes she had to share her wisdom and life experiences.

Pupils and teachers were equally thankful for the chance to meet someone they had come to consider a living legend.

A few weeks before her scheduled visit, Mrs. Stevens had read Mrs. Watkins' first book, *So Far From the Bamboo Grove*, published in 1986, to all of the seventh-graders.

The compelling, partly fictionalized autobiography describes the flight of then 11-year-old Yoko Kawashima, her older sister, Ko, and her mother, Saki, from their home in Nanam, in northern Korea near the Chinese border.

Safe during World War II in Japanese-occupied Korea, the surrender of Japan after the bombing of Nagasaki and Hiroshima put the family in imminent danger and set them on the road to the port of Pusan, one step ahead of the Korean Communist Army, in their effort to return to their homeland.

A sequel, which many seventh-graders stayed after school to hear read by Mrs. Stevens, chronicled her brother Hideyo's escape from Korea, and her father's experience in a prisoner-of-war camp in Siberia.

For months now the country has been reminded frequently, in headlines and news broadcasts, of the potential of war with Iraq.

"Right now, this is something we can look at at arm's length, with little if any impact on any of our daily lives, but with Mrs. Watkins, we had in our presence a real survivor, someone who had not only experienced the terror of war, the separation of family, but someone who had overcome seemingly insurmountable obstacles, sharing those experiences with those who read her books," she said.

Mrs. Stevens said a fellow teacher had recommended that she read *So Far From the Bamboo Grove* and when the book showed up among those included in the state's curriculum frameworks for world geography, she decided it would be a bonus to have Mrs. Watkins talk to pupils in her classes.

It wasn't geography, however, that Mrs. Watkins wanted to share. While more than willing to answer questions pupils asked about the events and relationships in the two books, she was equally eager to impress upon pupils the importance of being kind, demonstrating love and respect for one's parents.

Mrs. Watkins brought with her a variety of photographs, Japanese calligraphy and cultural artifacts, to help tell her story and illustrate her lesson in family values.

"I was a spoiled brat of a child and when my mother died, I cried and I cried, and I asked 'What's going to happen to me now?'" she said.

"I was selfish, and the only one I could think of was myself. To this day, the greatest regret in life was that I never thanked my mother for all she had given me."

She told each class in succession that her mother's gifts to her were not measurable by material standards, but in life's most important lessons.

Mrs. Stevens said when the curriculum framework books arrived during the summer, she brought home *So Far From the Bamboo Grove*, read it, and knew immediately that she had to read it to her class.

"We read the book from start to finish over the course of six days, and because the book reads like a good novel, many of the kids wanted to know what happened next. That prompted the after-school reading of Mrs. Watkins' second book," she said.

The teacher said she had her pupils write an essay on "what they gained from the reading of the book that gave them a better understanding of the horrors of war."

"The essays were particularly moving, and we selected the best of them, printed them and gave them to Yoko as a gift for spending the day with us," Mrs. Stevens said.

Many felt personal connections to Mrs. Watkins' story.

One foster child wrote in an essay, "I know how you felt. One time I had to leave in five minutes, I had to leave all my precious belongings behind."

Another pupil wrote, "Now I know I can make it. If Yoko can make it, I can make it," Mrs. Stevens said, noting that in one way or another each of her pupils had been empowered by the book to view their own lives differently.

During her visit with pupils, Mrs. Watkins carefully unwrapped what appeared to be a colorful silk binder.

Removing the contents, she showed the class the original manuscript for *So Far From the Bamboo Grove*. It was written in pencil in Japanese on the back of discarded business forms she had retrieved from a dump container.

"Make the most of what you have. Be kind to others. Love and respect your parents and your teachers. Your life is what you make it," she told pupils.

Mrs. Stevens said she is hopeful that Mrs. Watkins will be a guest at Quabbin Middle School next year and for years to come.

"I cried during each of the class periods. The bell rang and pupils didn't want to leave, but stayed to talk with her. I think I used a whole box of tissues that day," Mrs. Stevens said.

Source: Bradford L. Miner, "War—Upclose, Personal: Pupils at Quabbin Are Left Spellbound," in *Telegram & Gazette*, November 29, 2002, p. A1.

Anne S. Watt

In the following article, Watt discusses the effect that So Far from the Bamboo Grove *had on her niece, Yali, who ultimately began a correspondence and friendship with Watkins. This article is a testament to the transformative power of literature.*

Who would think that a story of desperate escape from northern Korea at the end of World War II would later lead to an intimate friendship between a Japanese woman in her 50s and an adopted Mexican child living in Vermont?

Thanks to Vermont's Dorothy Canfield Fisher Award, Yoko Kawashima Watkins's autobiography came to the attention of my 9 year old niece in Marlboro, Vermont. While looking through the award winning books on the school library shelf, Yali Maria spotted a copy of Watkins's *So Far from the Bamboo Grove* (Lothrop, 1986; Puffin, 1987). She was curious about the picture on the cover of three Asian women huddled fearfully with hands raised against soldiers pointing machine guns, and planes dropping bombs in the distance. Yali brought the book home.

What a surprise! Yali, a competent but not avid reader, could not put this book down. The true story of this Japanese family's grim flight from Korea and from Korean Anti-Japanese Communist Army partisans was unbelievable to Yali. Each night at dinner she would share episodes in the saga with her parents, asking "Is this *really* a true story?"

For several weeks the book became Yali's close companion. She reread it seven times. It went to bed with her, she read it over her breakfast cereal, on the school bus, and curled up on the sofa by the wood stove at night. Never before had Yali (often passionate about people) displayed this kind of a passion for a book!

After several months of Yali's powerful identification with the 11 year old child in this autobiography, Yali's mother finally suggested that she write to the author. My sister got Mrs. Watkins's address from the dust jacket, and Yali wrote Yoko her first letter.

In her letter, Yali told of her love for the book and went on to tell about her own life—adopted from an orphanage in Mexico and raised with an older brother born in France, by French American parents in Vermont.

Imagine Yali's joy when a nicely typed full page answer arrived! Yoko wrote that although she had received many letters from readers of all ages, never had she opened a letter with 67 hand drawn hearts around it!

Thus began a passionate correspondence between the 54 year old Japanese author and the 9 year old American child. Finally, after an exchange of more than a half dozen letters, Yali invited Yoko to come visit her family and her school.

And come she did, with her American ex-serviceman husband, for a well planned 2 day visit to the warm hearth of Yali's farmhouse and family. From the minute Yoko and Yali laid eyes on each other the chemistry was obvious.

"We're sisters," beamed Yoko, spreading her arms to Yali, Despite their age difference, Yoko and Yali, both tan skinned with jet black hair, seemed physically well matched.

My sister marveled at the immediacy and strength of the bond between the two of them, as they sat down in front of the doll house and began to talk. Later, as they lay together on the "friend's room" bed, Yoko held Yali spellbound with stories about her life.

The next day Yali took Yoko to her 5 room elementary school to talk with each of the class groups. Yoko mesmerized her kindergarten through 8th grade audiences by telling and acting out parts of her amazing childhood adventures. The children were enthralled with how Yoko's heroic teenage sister Ko led her mother and her in their escape from Korea, and how at the end of the war they struggled for survival in war ravaged Japan.

When it finally was time to say goodbye to Yali's family, Yali asked Yoko what her next story would be about. Yoko responded that it is about her life in America with her brave sister, Ko, who is now in a wheelchair, but that Yali's story is also one that should someday be told.

When I think about this intense relationship between a 9 year old reader in Vermont and a 54 year old writer from Japan, I ponder what Donald Graves and Lucy Calkins have called "the reading-writing connection." I find myself wondering about some rather significant—if unanswerable—questions: What will the effect of this book and this relationship be on Yali as a reader? As a writer? As a human being?

For example, how did it happen that Yali was invited by the Brattleboro children's librarian to spend 3 summer days helping her to sort and file books? What motivation caused Yali to be found last week at 11:30 p.m. in bed with her light still on, writing "privately" in her notebook? What makes Yali the kind of reader who, when she finds a book she likes, reads with such intensity that she cannot be torn away? Finally, what feelings about people from very different cultures will Yali carry with her through the years from her Mexican beginnings and rural Vermont childhood?

Naturally, when Yali told me about Yoko Kawashima Watkins's visit to Vermont and about her passion for Yoko's book, I ordered *So Far from the Bamboo Grove* from my bookstore. Though it is listed as a story, for 10–14 year olds, I, like Yali, couldn't put it down and have enjoyed sharing it with my own adult children, my octogenarian parents, and my friends. And so the gift of a good book spreads like a pebble making ripples in a pond. Who can tell how deep the pebble will sink or how wide the circles will spread?

Source: Anne S. Watt, "A Book and a Friendship to Cherish," in *Reading Teacher*, Vol. 42, No. 9, May 1989, pp. 712–13.

SOURCES

Eckert, Carter, "A Matter of Context," in *Boston Globe*, December 18, 2006, p. A15.

"Censorship Dateline: Schools," in *Newsletter on Intellectual Freedom*, January 1, 1007, Vol. 56, No. 1, p. 12.

Speyer, Glenda, "Book Banning Would Deprive Pupils," in *Boston Globe*, November 19, 2006, p. 7.

Watkins, Yoko Kawashima, *So Far from the Bamboo Grove*, Beech Tree, 1994.

Watt, Anne S., "A Book and a Friendship to Cherish," in *Reading Teacher*, May 1989, Vol. 42, No. 9, pp. 712–13.

FURTHER READING

Addiss, Stephen, Gerald Groemer, and J. Thomas Rimer, eds., *Traditional Japanese Arts and Culture: An Illustrated Sourcebook*, University of Hawaii Press, 2006.

    Many of the traditional arts, including the tea ceremony and ikibana (flower arranging) that are mentioned in Watkins's novel, are discussed and illustrated in this comprehensive collection.

Nahm, Andrew C., *A Panorama of 5000 Years: Korean History*, 2nd revised edition, Hollym International, 1990.

    This book covers the history of Korea from ancient times to the present.

O'Neill, William L., *World War II: A Student Companion*, Oxford University Press, 1999.

    Reviewers found this text to be a very concise, informative, and readable history of World War II. This book contains anything from one paragraph to several pages of information on some of the most important incidents in this war.

Schirokauer, Conrad, David Lurie, and Suzanne Gay, *A Brief History of Japanese Civilization*, Wadsworth Publishing, 2nd student edition, 2005.

    This volume covers the religion, arts, and culture of Japan, as well as its social, political, and economic history.

Sweetgrass

JAN HUDSON

1984

Although Jan Hudson's *Sweetgrass* (1984) is an historical fiction, based on events that took place during the winter of 1837–1838, it is a novel that has contemporary themes. Part love story, part coming-of-age story, and part intergenerational conflict story, Hudson's novel continues in the long tradition of historical fiction aimed at juvenile audiences. Recounting the story of a young girl's struggle for autonomy in a traditional culture that is itself in transition, *Sweetgrass* is a novel notable, too, for its careful attention to the details of daily life of First Nations women.

AUTHOR BIOGRAPHY

Janis (Jan) Mary Hudson was born on April 27, 1954, in Calgary, Alberta, Canada. Her parents, Laurence and Mary Wiedrick, moved north to Edmonton soon after Jan's birth, so her father could assume the position of head of library services for the Edmonton Public School Board; he would later become a professor of School Librarianship at the University of Alberta. Hudson attended school in Edmonton, before returning to the University of Calgary where she completed her Bachelor of Arts degree in English in 1978. She headed north again and completed a law degree at the University of Alberta in 1984.

Curiously, it was during one of her father's professional sabbaticals that Hudson's writing

career began in earnest. Moving with the family to Eugene, Oregon, for a short period when she was in eleventh grade gave Hudson the opportunity to meet Allan Woods, an English and drama teacher who recognized her talent for writing. He encouraged her to enter her work in local and state competitions, which she did. Although she was recognized only as one of two runners up in a competition organized by the National Council of Teachers of English (NCTE), Hudson had her first real taste of the writing life, which she was determined to return to as often as possible in the coming years.

During her law studies, Hudson found the inspiration to spark her first major project. Taking a course in First Nations treaties in Western Canada, she encountered several discussions of the historical period that would later provide the setting for *Sweetgrass*. Having decided to write the story from the perspective of a young girl, Hudson spent more than a year researching the period in which the novel is set. Even the names of the characters, with the exception of Sweetgrass, were chosen from documents that deal with Blackfoot stories.

When she finished the manuscript in 1979, Hudson discovered that American publishers had no interest in the book. Two years later she tried another strategy to get the story noticed, entering *Sweetgrass* in the inaugural Alberta Writing for Young People competition, where it placed second. While she continued to approach Canadian publishers who might be interested in the novel, Hudson was approached by Allan Shute, one of the competition judges who was also the publisher of Edmonton's small Tree Frog Press.

Sweetgrass was finally published in 1984 by Tree Frog and was promptly recognized with two of Canada's most significant awards for juvenile literature: the Canada Council's Children's Literature Prize and the Canadian Library Association's Book of the Year Award. Released in the United States in 1989, the American edition was well received, too. The American Library Association recognized it with a Best Book for Young Adults citation, and it received the Parent's Choice Award for Children's Books.

Jan Hudson died in Edmonton on April 22, 1990, from sudden respiratory failure associated with viral pneumonia. That same year her second and last novel, *Dawn Rider*, was published.

PLOT SUMMARY

Set mostly in southern Alberta but on occasion in northern Montana and based on events that occurred during the winter of 1837–1838, *Sweetgrass* opens with a struggle between fifteen-year-old Sweetgrass and her father, the respected but stubborn Shabby Bull. The central point of their conflict, as Sweetgrass explains to her closest friend Pretty Girl, hinges on Shabby Bull's belief that his daughter is too young to take on the responsibilities that come with marriage. Sweetgrass wants to marry her childhood friend Eagle Sun but is fearful that her parents will arrange a marriage with an older, wealthier man. Her greatest fear, as she confesses to Pretty Girl, is that she will be matched with "some older man with ten wives already." As the novel opens the girls spend time discussing the restrictions that weigh upon their lives and how their generation of young women have so many more limits to their autonomy than previous generations of Blackfoot women have had.

When the warriors return from a horse raid, the marriage question is complicated even more as the girls recognize that Pretty Girl's boyfriend, Shy Bear, is unable to match skills with the older warriors and, therefore, will never be able to compete with them in the marketplace for the young girl's hand in marriage. The tensions build as a Sun Dance gathering approaches, which will bring all branches of the Blackfoot nation together and provide the perfect opportunity for marriages to be arranged. As the extended family gathers for the Sun Dance, Sweetgrass reconnects with various other women, including her aunt Robe Woman and her supportive and strong-willed paternal grandmother She Fought Them Woman. Her grandmother is a balancing figure in the novel, a woman who remembers the traditions of the past but also recognizes that times are changing and attitudes will have to follow.

With the appearance of her grandmother, Sweetgrass finds support for her debates with her father. But intelligent and wise She Fought Them Woman enters into a series of conversations with Sweetgrass during which the younger woman is asked to think more about her demands for autonomy and come to understand her dreams in the context of Blackfoot history and future. Similar conversations accumulate as Sweetgrass spends time with various other members of her family, including Favourite Child. Sweetgrass observes during this time, too, the arrangement that is made for marrying Pretty Girl to Five Killer and how her younger friend deals with her disappointment.

The conversations are interrupted when the Blackfoot band comes under attack by Assiniboin warriors. Following the lead of her grandmother, Sweetgrass helps her family survive the attack by hiding in the grass that surrounds the settlement. Although no one is killed, the experience proves to be one of the first tests that the maturing Sweetgrass faces.

As the Sun Dance unfolds and conversations between the women of the band continue, the novel describes the women's daily routines and domestic rituals (gathering berries, for instance). Sweetgrass remembers her childhood experiences at previous gatherings while she looks forward to her life as a young woman. The Sun Dance also offers her a chance to listen to the stories of Blackfoot glories, of great raids and past victories in battle. Although she is bored by much of what she hears, Sweetgrass does come to understand more fully the cultural heritage of which she is part.

Pushing her father for more freedom to make decisions (about marriage, most obviously) about her own life, Sweetgrass is offered a test by her father that he believes will prove if she is strong enough physically and emotionally to become a wife. The task is a daunting one: to single-handedly prepare thirty buffalo hides in a single winter season. As winter draws near, the family is threatened with starvation, a condition that means that Shabby Bull is forced to head out to a nearby camp in an attempt to find food. As her Almost-Mother grows sicker and weaker, Sweetgrass is forced to step into the role of decision maker and primary caregiver, during which she exhibits both maturity and ingenuity that proves her status as a woman in the new generation of Blackfoot.

Sweetgrass's position is made even more dramatic when Almost-Mother is stricken with smallpox. The young woman must find food and water for her family while others (including Pretty Girl, She Fought Them Woman, and Dog Leg) succumb to the disease as the winter unfolds. To protect her family she throws out her father's traditional robes, which are infected with the deadly virus. It is a decision that in usual circumstances would be seen as disrespectful but

during the winter of the epidemic proves her strength and ingenuity. As her father is proud to announce upon his return, Sweetgrass has past the most dramatic tests of all and there is little doubt that she is now a woman who can balance her desire for autonomy with a respect for Blackfoot tradition. Despite her bright future, Sweetgrass is willing always to acknowledge the strength of those who came before her: "More than half my people were blackened and gone," she remembers at novel's end. "In some big camps everyone had died, some of them starving to death when no men had the strength to hunt. Others died because no one had nursed them. Some had hurled themselves into icy lakes and rivers to cool their fevers. ... And there were those many young warriors who, in their agony and their fear, had followed their brothers under the waters." In the end, Sweetgrass is recognized as a warrior woman who will make her own decisions about marriage and family.

CHARACTERS

Bent-over-Woman
An older woman whom Sweetgrass knows as her almost-mother, Bent-over-Woman dies during the winter epidemic during which Sweetgrass proves herself a woman.

Cuts Both Ways
Sweetgrass's uncle, Cuts Both Ways is the husband of Robe Woman and father of Favourite Child and Dog Leg.

Dog Leg
Dog Leg is Sweetgrass's young male cousin and brother of Favourite Child. Dog Leg and Otter show what young men face by contrast to the young women.

Eagle Sun
Sweetgrass's childhood sweetheart and the man she wants to marry, Eagle Sun is a brave raider, a fine hunter of buffalo, and generally respected by the elders. He is a fine physical and spiritual representative of the Blackfoot heritage and a key marker of the path of the future: "His skin was tanned red-brown, the deep red-brown that is the colour of buffalo-calf fur in the autumn. Slim with rope-tight muscles, he rode his horse bareback." Following the Sun Dance, he heads

north to trade at Fort Edmonton, the English trading post.

Favourite Child
Favourite Child is Sweetgrass's cousin and the daughter of Robe Woman. She is the *minipoka*, or the favorite child, of a powerful and respected family and is used to getting whatever she wants whenever she wants it.

Five Killer
Five Killer is a "tall and well-bodied" horse raider.

Otter
Otter is Sweetgrass's twelve-year-old stepbrother, whom she calls her almost-brother.

Pretty Girl
Pretty Girl is Sweetgrass's best friend and confidante, who, at thirteen, awaits information about the man whom her parents have selected to be her husband. Whereas her friend Sweetgrass is a romantic in her views on love and marriage, Pretty Girl is a realist, willing to accept the traditions of her people and her place in the arranged marriage. She recognizes, for instance, that because her family is *kimataps* (from a poor background) she will be married to the man willing to pay the highest price, which excludes her boyfriend Shy Bear who has not had time to collect the number of horses that it might take to buy Pretty Girl in marriage.

Robe Woman
Robe Woman is Sweetgrass's aunt and Shabby Bull's sister. She visits the band as they prepare for an important Sun Dance gathering.

Shabby Bull
Shabby Bull is the father of Sweetgrass and is a respected elder of the Blackfoot tribe. Despite his daughter's love for her childhood friend Eagle Sun, he does not believe that she is old enough to accept the responsibilities of marriage.

She Fought Them Woman
She Fought Them Woman is Sweetgrass's paternal grandmother and one of the strongest influences in the young girl's life. She is a strong figure of transition; she preserves memories of Blackfoot traditions while at the same time she recognizes that times are changing. Because the grandmother is a powerful advocate for Sweetgrass, her grand-

daughter believes She Fought Them Woman is "one person who cares" about the struggles that she is facing.

Shy Bear
Shy Bear is the boy whom Pretty Girl wants to marry. He has not yet accumulated enough wealth (measured in the number of horses that he owns) to compete with the older men whom Pretty Girl's parents are considering as a marriage match for their daughter. In an attempt to gain status within the band, he goes on a number of horse raids aimed at nearby Crow tribes. He is shot with a musket ball during the Assiniboin attack.

Sweetgrass
Sweetgrass is the fifteen-year-old protagonist of the novel. Watching as her friend, Pretty Girl awaits details of a marriage being arranged by her parents, Sweetgrass becomes increasingly concerned that her father will ignore her desire for a marriage based on love rather than one based on more practical concerns. She dreads the idea that she may be married to an older man who already has many wives. She is a romantic character in this regard, juxtaposed in the novel with the more pragmatic Shabby Bull and the more realistic Pretty Girl.

In order to prove to her father that she is strong enough to marry, Sweetgrass agrees to take on a test that he designs for her: to single-handedly prepare thirty buffalo hides during one winter season. An even greater test occurs when she suddenly finds herself caring for her family members when they are threatened by starvation and an epidemic of smallpox.

THEMES

Child-Parent or Intergenerational Conflict
Sweetgrass is a fifteen-year-old Blackfoot girl who resists the pressures brought to bear upon the new generation of women in her band. The tensions come to a head when she enters into a debate with her father over her marriage partner. She is in love with her childhood friend, Eagle Sun, but her parents seem to have other plans for her that involve a wealthier man and a dowry of many horses.

TOPICS FOR FURTHER STUDY

- One of the earliest publishers considering *Sweetgrass* for publication wanted Hudson to delete the character of Pretty Girl from the novel. Hudson refused, believing that she was crucial to the development of the story. Write a letter to an imaginary publisher in which you either support the decision to keep Pretty Girl in the story or support the idea that the character can be cut with little damage to the novel.

- Names take on special importance in Blackfoot culture, as they do in all cultures. Research the history of the name of a character or characters in *Sweetgrass* and write a report in which you discuss its historical and symbolic meanings.

- Throughout *Sweetgrass* Hudson uses such terms as almost-mother and almost-brother to refer to relationships that readers would call stepmother and stepbrother. Think about familiar terms that your culture uses today that might be reconfigured in this way and compile a list in which you bring together the familiar and the reconstructed labels for certain relationships.

- In the early stages of writing *Sweetgrass*, Hudson originally structured the story as told from the perspective of an adolescent male Blackfoot rather than an adolescent female. Rewrite one chapter of the novel, shifting the perspective from that of Sweetgrass to that of an imagined male counterpart. What changes would you have to make to the telling of the story and why?

What Sweetgrass sees is that her life has become restricted in significant ways by changes brought about through sustained contact with white culture. Through her conversations with her paternal grandmother, She Fought Them Woman, Sweetgrass recognizes that her autonomy (the ability to make decisions for herself) is quite limited when compared with the relative freedoms of an earlier generation

of women. Unwilling to accept this fate, she is determined to "make [her] life be what [she] wanted." Pushing her elders for greater freedoms, Sweetgrass finds herself responding to a test designed by her father, who sees the challenge as a traditional rite of passage. Should she succeed in preparing thirty buffalo skins during one winter season, Sweetgrass will prove herself worthy of greater autonomy. Should she fail to do so, she will reinforce her elder's concerns about her physical and intellectual maturity.

A much more dramatic test unfolds, though, when Sweetgrass must find a way to stay safe *and* keep her family safe following a raid from another tribe, during a period of winter starvation, and while coping with a smallpox epidemic. The terms of her earlier conflict with her father are pushed aside as Sweetgrass works to save her family, which she accomplishes using the same skills that her father had set out to test: self-reliance, ingenuity, and courage. Tellingly, and in a twist that teaches a lesson to a generation of elders that had overlooked the changing conditions of the world around them, Sweetgrass succeeds by breaking a number of the tribal rules that had restricted all women in the tribe for many years. In the end, Sweetgrass overcomes the conflict with her elders in ways that will serve to redefine the traditional belief that a "good Blackfoot girl is always obedient, quiet, hardworking, and . . . never says what she feels."

Coming of Age

Sweetgrass continues in the long tradition of juvenile literature that explores a young person's development from youthful innocence to a more mature and more knowledgeable understanding of the world. Such novels are often called coming-of-age stories or, to use the German term, *bildungsroman*. Traditionally, the subject of these novels is a balanced development of the protagonist's mind and character, often involving passage through a life-altering crisis that might be spiritual, intellectual, or emotional. Such classic novels as Charlotte Brontë's *Jane Eyre* (1847) and Charles Dickens's *David Copperfield* (1850) and *Great Expectations* (1861) are excellent examples.

For Sweetgrass, coming of age is a complicated and culturally specific exercise that takes on a traditional three-part structure: her debate with her father over the conditions of her marriage, the formal test that he develops for her, and the struggles she faces as she takes on the responsibilities of caring for a family stricken with smallpox. Read symbolically, each of these stages in Sweetgrass's development marks the acquisition of skills that she will need later in life to ensure not only her own future prosperity but in many ways the continuance of a Blackfoot band entering into its own transitional phase. She learns, through her conflict with her father, how to negotiate using her intelligence and words in order to take control of her life. She learns the limits of her physical strength and the extent of her autonomy as she sets out to complete the test set out by her father. Finally, all of these skills come together when Sweetgrass is forced to care for her family as the potentially fatal infection sweeps through the band.

STYLE

Narrative Point of View
Told with a first-person narrator, *Sweetgrass* hinges on the personality and perspective of a single subjective position, in this case that of the fifteen-year-old protagonist Sweetgrass. Referring to herself consistently as *I*, she provides the attitude and perspective that shape the novel and the reader's perception of events as they unfold. In this sense, readers see the world through her eyes, both in moments of good judgment and in those when she is unthinking or overly emotional. As Sweetgrass matures and begins to see the world differently, so, too, can readers begin to understand better the pressures that she feels and the struggles that she endures.

Dialogue
One of the strengths of Hudson's writing is her use of dialogue (conversation between two or more characters) as a strategy for illuminating both the complexities of Blackfoot culture and the emotional landscape of her characters, especially the women of the novel. Throughout the novel, conversations highlight the immediacy of the historical setting, most notably through Hudson's attention to speech rhythms and word choice. Talking with Favourite Child, for instance, Sweetgrass makes this observation, speaking in a rhythmic, almost poetic prose: "Eagle Sun says his mother wants to pick berries first, in the valleys, before they hunt for buffalo. But his father has promised to follow our bands later. So Eagle Sun says he will see you again before the moon has grown and faded."

Having two or more voices speaking at once in the story also allows for multiple conflicts to appear, reinforcing one of the novel's primary themes, child-parent conflict. Statements can be made and challenged, untruths told and challenged, and messages misunderstood, all of which adds to the dramatic tension of the story. Sweetgrass's conversations with her father, Shabby Bull, and her grandmother, She Fought Them Woman, are excellent examples of such moments, allowing for the similarities and differences between the generations to be articulated by representatives of each group.

HISTORICAL CONTEXT

Blackfoot History
The common name Blackfoot is technically the name of a subtribe of the Blackfoot Confederacy, which includes the Piegan (*Aamsskaapipiikanii*), the Kainai (Blood), and the Siksika (Blackfoot). Historically, Blackfoot territory was relatively large, extending from what later became Edmonton, Alberta, in the north to Yellowstone River, Montana, in the south, and from the Canadian Rockies to the eastern boundary of the Saskatchewan River, near what later became Regina, Saskatchewan. Primarily nomadic buffalo hunters and warriors, the Blackfoot were considered part of the British colonies and were not usually involved in the negotiation or signing of American trading agreements or treaties. During the period in which Hudson's novel is set, the Blackfoot leader was usually recognized to be Gros Blanc, who was succeeded around the mid-nineteenth century by the tripartite leadership of Old Swan, Old Sun, and Three Suns.

The basic political unit of the Blackfoot was the band, which varied from between ten and thirty lodges and usually were populated by between 80 and 240 people. Each band consisted of a respected elder who served as leader, though members of the tribe were free to migrate from band to band, which was often the case. Tribal gatherings took place in the summer, during which a dozen or so orders or societies would meet to discuss future plans and to celebrate past glories.

The traditional nomadic life continued well into the nineteenth century, at which point the imminent extinction of the great bison herds and growing pressure of white people for the Blackfoot to settle on reserves put an end to Blackfoot culture as it had been known. In the United States, white people initially assigned land to the Blackfoot under the Fort Laramie Treaty (1851) and later relocated them under the Sweetgrass Hills Treaty of 1887. In Canada, the Blackfoot settled on reserves in southern Alberta following their signing of Treaty 7.

Buffalo Hunting

The plot of Hudson's *Sweetgrass* hinges on a test that Shabby Bull designs to assess his daughter's strength, namely to prepare thirty buffalo hides during one winter. It is a test that underscores the centrality of the North American bison (colloquially known as buffalo) to the culture of such tribes as the Blackfoot, as well as hinting at the pressures put on traditional hunting cultures by the near extinction of the great herds by the end of the nineteenth century.

With excellent meat and a superior hide, the buffalo was an essential component of tribal life, providing food, leather, sinew for bows, grease, dried dung that could be used for fire fuel, and even a traditional form of glue that was rendered by boiling the hooves. In 1800, it appeared as though the buffalo would flourish indefinitely, with huge herds grazing on the prairies. Estimates suggest that at the turn of that century there were between fifty and sixty million buffalo moving across the North American prairies.

As the nineteenth century progressed, however, the white people increasingly destroyed buffalo habitat and buffalo populations. Supported and often paid by the railway companies that saw buffalo herds as an expensive nuisance, hunters descended on the massive herds slaughtering countless animals. Professional white hunters often killed hundreds of animals in a single day, and many boasted of killing thousands in their careers. The hunt reached its height in the 1870s when the commercialization of the hunt peaked, with several hundred hunting outfits estimated to have taken thousands of the remaining buffalo in a single day. By the mid 1880s, the North American buffalo, which had once numbered in the tens of millions, was close to extinction, marking an end to the great herds and to an ancient way of life for such nomadic tribes as the Blackfoot.

Smallpox and First Nations History

Smallpox, a highly contagious viral infection, was one of the first and most potent diseases introduced into the New World by European settlers. Arriving in North America sometime early in the seventeenth century with white people, it spread quickly through eastern native settlements, wiping out entire populations of indigenous peoples on its course westward. The disease remained a perpetual threat through the eighteenth and early nineteenth centuries, with epidemics appearing repeatedly.

As Hudson's novel suggests, Blackfoot history is riddled with the horrors of smallpox. The Blackfoot suffered great losses in 1780–1781, in 1837–1838, in 1845, in 1857–1858, and again in 1869. (During these years, white people repeatedly infected native populations; a particularly severe measles epidemic occurred in 1864, which caused devastating losses to the tribe.)

CRITICAL OVERVIEW

In one positive review of Hudson's *Sweetgrass*, Yvonne Frey declares the work a "masterpiece," summing it up as "an historical, a native American, a survival, and a coming-of-age novel set in the 19th-Century western Canadian prairies." A "welcome addition to fictional works on the American Indian because of its point of view and . . . its rich detail of Indian life," it is a book, Frey concludes, that "will invite re-reading." One of the reasons for this enthusiastic response is what Frey sees as the "message" of the novel: "maturity is not measured by one's physical growth alone but by the manner in which one faces both the emergencies of life and the ordinary and practical chores of everyday living." Perhaps it is this explicit message that leads Alleen Pace Nilsen and Ken Donelson to state that *Sweetgrass* is "more like a children's book" than a novel aimed at juvenile audiences.

Surveying recent award-winning juvenile novels for the *English Journal*, Terry C. Ley calls this novel "an unusual story [that] is powerfully told in the lyrical voice of the young Blackfoot maiden." Although concerns might arise from Hudson's decision as a white person to adopt the voice of a girl from an indigenous culture, opening her to charges of cultural appropriation or disrespect, Ley actually sees the decision as one of the novel's strengths. "This technique," he argues, "provides an intimate look at the daily life among North American Indians during the early 1800s." Despite the fact that "the setting is historical," he concludes, "contemporary young readers will relate to the themes of parent-child conflict and coming of age as Sweetgrass is cruelly tested."

CRITICISM

Klay Dyer

Dyer holds a Ph.D. in English literature and has published extensively on fiction, poetry, film, and television. He is also a freelance university teacher, writer, and educational consultant. In the following essay, he discusses Hudson's Sweetgrass *in terms of the long tradition of social history stories for juvenile readers.*

Although Jan Hudson's *Sweetgrass* is often described in terms of its relationship to traditional coming-of-age novels or adventure stories, it is also a novel that fits into the broadly defined genre of stories that focus on social history. Building generally on the theme of wilderness adventures in a historical setting, historical survival novels like *Sweetgrass* are representative of a particular shift in Canadian juvenile fiction that began in the 1970s. Earlier examples of such stories usually blended freely imagined characters and events with more factual accounts of familiar events in North American history. Alternatively, these early works used the past as a backdrop for more familiar tales of adventure, family, or pioneer life, mysteries, or even animal stories.

For the new generation of writers of juvenile fiction, though, the challenge has been to develop strategies that bring new dimensions to this traditional pattern. Faced with increasingly sophisticated readers whose taste in historical stories is more informed and more critical than previous generations, these writers sought strategies that might bring new dimensions to the already established genre of historical fiction. Turning away from overly elaborate plots and heavily romanticized stories that had little or no connection to contemporary concerns, they wrote novels that could reflect current ideas about youth and issues associated with the maturation.

The result broadened the established genre of historical novel to include elements of social realism (representations of the common and the everyday), mysticism (elements having to do with a divine spirit), and psychological portrayal of protagonists experiencing a life-changing rite

WHAT DO I READ NEXT?

- Although Hudson was often approached with requests to write a sequel to *Sweetgrass*, she never did so. She did, however, write a second novel, *Dawn Rider* (1990), which picks up Blackfoot history in the mid-eighteenth century. Focusing on another female protagonist, Kit Fox, this novel explores the changes that come to traditional culture in the years following the appearance of the first horse in Kit Fox's tribe.

- Suzanne Fisher Staples's *Shabanu: Daughter of the Wind* (1989), a Newbery Honor Book, is often compared with *Sweetgrass* because of its focus on the attitudes of another culture (in this case, Pakistan) toward marriage arrangements for daughters.

- Readers interested in the stories and myths of the Blackfoot people will enjoy Percy Bullchild's *The Sun Came Down: The History of the World as My Blackfoot Elders Told It* (1985) and Sharon Oakley's *Black Plume's Weasel People: Native American Stories as Told by Blackfoot Nation Elders* (2006).

- For the slightly older reader, Hugh A. Dempsey's *The Vengeful Wife and Other Blackfoot Stories* (2006) is an eclectic collection of Blackfoot Indian stories.

of passage. Whereas traditional historical stories often represented the wilderness as a place of threat or challenge, for instance, the newer generation of writers portrayed it as an external parallel to the internal struggles of adolescence. The wilderness was also seen as a haven or place of respite where tests could be faced, usually with a more emotional or spiritual focus than a physical one. As the process and politics of growing were understood differently with the unfolding of the twentieth century, so, too, did the stories written about children and young adults.

With its combination of detailed social history, traditional survival story, and psychological maturation tale, *Sweetgrass* is clearly part of

RESISTING CONVENTIONAL RESTRICTIONS ON HER AUTONOMY, SWEETGRASS GRADUALLY COMES TO SEE HER LIFE AS SHAPED BY CHANGES CAUSED BY TECHNOLOGICAL CHANGE (IN THE FORM OF MUSKETS), ECONOMIC PRESSURES (THE PRESENCE OF THE TRADING POST), AND BY INCREASING CONTACT WITH EUROPEAN SETTLERS (THE SMALLPOX EPIDEMIC THAT TAKES THE LIVES OF MANY OF HER EXTENDED FAMILY)."

this next generation of writing. The realities of social history provide the foundation for Hudson's novel. Resisting conventional restrictions on her autonomy, Sweetgrass gradually comes to see her life as shaped by changes caused by technological change (in the form of muskets), economic pressures (the presence of the trading post), and by increasing contact with European settlers (the smallpox epidemic that takes the lives of many of her extended family). Heightening this frustration is Sweetgrass's sense that her own grandmother, the respected She Fought Them Woman, enjoyed relatively more freedom during her adolescence and young adulthood. Once a "famous warrior," She Fought Them Woman has a honorable past whose story "still was told" by the new generation of women. Yet Sweetgrass wonders "what did it have to do with [her]."

Confused and frustrated by her situation, Sweetgrass searches for ways to challenge traditional expectations and to take responsibility for her own decisions. Like the reader of the novel, she discovers that living in the past (that is, living within a traditional structure) depends in large part on her ability to make that past relevant to her own present and to revitalize traditions so that they allow her the freedom to move forward with her own life. It is a tough negotiation that she enters into, and one that allows her to interpret the past alone or with the help of elders (notably her grandmother and her father, the respected Shabby Bull). Alternatively, she can attempt to ignore the past, to recognize in it a set of rules and assumptions that are no longer pertinent to her sense of her own future. She

hopes, in this sense, to move beyond the bounds of the past, to "find the signs, the power to control [her] own days" and to "make [her] life be what [she] wanted." It is a journey, as she comes to understands, that must be undertaken as much with respect and wisdom as with tenacity and will power.

Between the competing pulls of past and future, and tradition and autonomy, Sweetgrass struggles to find a psychological and emotional position upon which to make a firm stand. Avoiding the path of disobedience or even open rebellion, which would allow her to obtain her goal of marrying Eagle Sun, she finds herself forced to prove her mettle initially through conversations with her grandmother. In these moments, past and present fuse, as the two women remember stories and rituals en route to rewriting them, renegotiating them within the terms and conditions of a new generation. The dual nature of their discussions is important, allowing Sweetgrass to become steeped in the lore and traditions of her Blackfoot ancestry while at the same time moving forward to establish herself as a model for the next generation of Blackfoot women.

Covering a single year, *Sweetgrass* presents a richly drawn world that reflects both the historical cycle of the prairie seasons and the spare, seemingly tireless cycle of women's struggle with domestic routine and patriarchal assumptions. Pushing historical fiction forward, just as Sweetgrass strives to push her own life and own story toward a dreamed of freedom, Hudson does not adjust or alter the attitudes of the day. Historical verisimilitude is maintained as Hudson describes both the protagonist's psychology and the women's routines and chores. The emotional ebb and flow of Sweetgrass's life parallel the ebb and flow of the Blackfoot people. Her struggles with her father are reflected in the conflicts with the attacking Assiniboin, and her growing sense of a lack of control is captured in the hopelessness associated with the smallpox epidemic that sweeps through the band. As Sweetgrass struggles, so too does the community in which she lives.

Sweetgrass, then, is both an historical story, drawing as it does on the actual events of the winter of 1837–1838, and a history of a psychological rite of passage. It is a novel that blends a respectful observance of the past with a vivid exploration of a more personal history. As

Sweetgrass states in the final sentence of the novel, the future holds much promise: "Strong with the dignity of a full-grown woman, I lifted my burden and went forward from the scorched land, into the years ahead."

Source: Klay Dyer, Critical Essay on *Sweetgrass*, in *Novels for Students*, Gale, Cengage Learning, 2009.

Laura Pryor

Pryor has a B.A. from the University of Michigan and over twenty years experience in professional and creative writing with special interest in fiction. In the following essay, she compares and contrasts the title character of Sweetgrass *with the main character of Jane Austen's* Pride and Prejudice, Elizabeth Bennet.*

At first thought, it would seem that a teenage Native American girl living a hard life on the Canadian western plains in 1837 would have little in common with a genteel young Englishwoman of 1813. However, the title character of Jan Hudson's *Sweetgrass* and Elizabeth Bennet, the heroine of Jane Austen's *Pride and Prejudice*, do share some of the same frustrations and face some of the same barriers, because both are women living in societies steeped in ritual and tradition.

Everyday life for Sweetgrass is often harsh, filled with hours of manual labor, and, in the winter, even survival cannot be taken for granted. At just fifteen, Sweetgrass tells the reader that next year, at sixteen, she "will probably be the oldest unmarried girl among all the Bloods." With the perpetuation of the tribe at stake, the Blackfoot girls do not have the luxury of a long childhood but are expected to marry and begin bearing children as soon as they are physically capable. In contrast, Elizabeth lives in relative comfort; though her family is not considered wealthy, they are far from poor, and Elizabeth's mother is quick to point out to a dinner guest that they employ a cook and that "her daughters had nothing to do in the kitchen." This idleness, a point of pride for Mrs. Bennet, would be a source of shame for Sweetgrass, who is expected to work hard to help ensure the family's survival.

Though their everyday life is drastically different, both Sweetgrass and Elizabeth are preoccupied with the search for a husband. In both the Blackfoot tribe and nineteenth-century English society, a woman of a certain age without a husband is an object of both pity and derision.

> SWEETGRASS AND ELIZABETH BENNET ARE ADMIRABLE BECAUSE THEY FIND A WAY TO CHART THEIR OWN COURSE AND ACHIEVE THEIR GOALS WHILE STILL WORKING WITHIN THE CONFINES OF THEIR OWN SOCIETY. "

When Sweetgrass asks her grandmother if she will soon be married, her grandmother tells her to be patient, but Sweetgrass replies, "But what is a woman without a husband?" Elizabeth is less impatient to be engaged, but Mrs. Bennet is eager to marry her daughters off. Mr. Bennet's estate has been entailed away from his daughters, because he has no male heir, and so the quality of life for the Bennet sisters in the future is determined solely on their husbands' financial resources (or lack thereof). Wealth and status play an equally important role in finding a husband for Blackfoot girls; Sweetgrass's best friend, Pretty-Girl, comes from a poor family, so her father gives her hand in marriage to Five-Killer, an older, wealthier man who can give more horses in exchange for her than Shy-Bear, the young man whom Pretty-Girl loves. Sweetgrass has higher hopes because her father was a great warrior and as such has greater status than Pretty-Girl's father. Still, Sweetgrass fears that her father will not let her marry her love, Eagle Sun, and that she, too, may end up with an older husband. The young Blackfoot bride is treated as a commodity to be purchased. Sweetgrass tells her cousin Favorite-Child that in her grandmother's day, "the price for a wife was lower."

Though Elizabeth and her sisters have more say in their choice of a mate, they cannot help but be aware of the importance of choosing carefully. Just as financial considerations force Sweetgrass's friend Pretty-Girl to marry someone she would rather not, Elizabeth's good friend Charlotte Lucas accepts the proposal of Elizabeth's cousin, Mr. Collins, "a conceited, pompous, narrow-minded, silly man," in order to secure a comfortable home for herself. Because she is plain and comes from a large family, she does not have Elizabeth's greater expectations for a marriage and thinks along more practical lines. In both Elizabeth's and Sweetgrass's worlds, love is not considered sufficient reason for marriage, but rather a bonus for those fortunate enough to fall in love with someone who is already a suitable candidate. Love and happiness are secondary considerations to comfort, freedom from want, and in the case of the Blackfoot tribe, survival. As Pretty-Girl tells Sweetgrass, "Nobody gets married to be happy." Elizabeth Bennet, in insisting on marrying for love, is unusually independent for her era and milieu. In fact, when Elizabeth refuses the odious Mr. Collins's offer of marriage, he is incredulous, not because he fancies himself so handsome or charming, but because, as he puts it, "it is by no means certain that another offer of marriage may ever be made you. Your portion is so unhappily small that it will in all likelihood undo the effects of your loveliness and amiable qualifications."

This lack of control over the future results in frustration and anxiety for both characters. Sweetgrass thinks to herself, "The only things that happened, it seemed, were things I could not touch or change." More than once, Sweetgrass wishes she were a man: "A warrior can move with dignity against his fears. But there was nothing I could do." Elizabeth relieves this frustration through her outspoken, independent nature. When Lady Catherine de Bourgh, a woman most of the characters treat with the utmost deference due to her status, demands to know if Elizabeth plans to marry her nephew, Mr. Darcy, Elizabeth replies defiantly, "I am only resolved to act in that manner, which will, in my own opinion, constitute my happiness, without reference to *you*, or to any person so wholly unconnected with me." Sweetgrass is similarly determined to direct the course of her own life, regardless of others' wishes: "I would find the signs, the power to control my own days. I would make my life be what I wanted."

Both cultures rely heavily on ritual and custom, which further restricts the young women's behavior. Sweetgrass often refers to these rules, as though she is trying to convince herself she should follow them, though she would rather not. "A good Blackfoot girl is always obedient, quiet, hard-working, and she never says what she feels"; "Wanting is not right for a young woman"; and "Staring is not proper for a young woman." Elizabeth's mother laments pitifully when Mr. Bennet refuses to introduce himself to Mr. Bingley, their new neighbor, because according to custom, this means that the rest of the family cannot then be properly introduced to

him either, and she is hoping that Mr. Bingley may fall in love with one of her daughters.

Though Sweetgrass and Elizabeth's behavior is restricted by the mores of their respective society, it is interesting to note that the role a woman plays in the Blackfoot society commands a great deal of respect, and it is acknowledged that their contribution is critical to the survival of the tribe. Sweetgrass's grandmother, speaking of the men in the tribe, says, "Their lives without our lives are worth less than our lives without theirs. . . . We Blackfoot women must expect our men to die at any moment, and we must be strong to do our part." Later, after the smallpox epidemic decimates the tribe, Sweetgrass notes that many young warriors committed suicide when afflicted with the disease: "They found death the easier trail, the one for which they had trained." The men have been brought up to face the threat of a quick death in battle, but the women have been conditioned for endurance and survival. Women in the middle class world of Elizabeth are encouraged to be ornamental; they are bred to be polite and pleasant companions. To a Blackfoot warrior, a wife is a necessity, key to his comfort and survival, whereas men like Mr. Bingley and Mr. Darcy, with the means to hire servants, could remain bachelors and live comfortably as such.

Both Sweetgrass and Elizabeth begin their stories with simplistic worldviews that mature as a result of the trials they experience. Elizabeth, quick-witted and observant, trusts her first impressions of Mr. Darcy and Mr. Wickham and hastily makes black-and-white judgments concerning their characters. Through a series of revelations, she learns that while Mr. Darcy is certainly not without fault, he is not deserving of her early wholesale condemnation and that Mr. Wickham is likewise not deserving of her quick praise. Her error in judgment is fully revealed when Wickham elopes with Elizabeth's younger sister, though he has no real intention of marrying her. Elizabeth comes away from these events with a more realistic view of people in general and the knowledge that a man's entire character cannot be fully known from just a few encounters. Sweetgrass, likewise, has simple views that have been handed to her from her tribe, views that she defends at first, even when faced with contrary evidence. Sweetgrass believes, for example, that a girl's marriage is a joyous occasion and that every girl should be excited and thrilled to leave her parents and live with her husband. When her friend Pretty-Girl laments tearfully that she will be Five-Killer's slavewife and do all the hardest work, Sweetgrass thinks, "Tears are the wrong way to greet the marriage that every Blackfoot girl longs for. What could I say to make her act the right way?" When Sweetgrass is left alone to care for her stricken mother and brother during the smallpox epidemic, she learns that strength and wisdom lie not in blind adherence to rules but in knowing when to choose a different path. By feeding her family fish—a food strictly forbidden by Blackfoot beliefs—Sweetgrass keeps her family alive through the bitter winter and epidemic. The rules she has been given are now tempered by her own hard-won wisdom: "Maybe someday the river demons would come for me. Who knows, but I doubted it."

The likelihood that women are indeed the weaker sex seems to decrease given the amount of work there is to be done. In Austen's privileged middle-class sphere, women were more likely to be viewed as delicate creatures with fragile constitutions. However, in the Blackfoot tribe, the men were likely to be gone for long periods hunting, and women were expected to shoulder the rest of the work involved in ensuring the tribe's survival. Sweetgrass's grandmother tells her daughter-in-law, "Be strong and mighty like a true Blackfoot." It is unlikely that "strong and mighty" would be used to describe a woman of Austen's world.

Sweetgrass and Elizabeth Bennet are admirable because they find a way to chart their own course and achieve their goals while still working within the confines of their own society. Elizabeth does not flaunt convention like her sister Lydia, who brings disgrace to the family, but she still maintains her independence and individuality. Sweetgrass's resourcefulness and unwavering belief in her own strength, brings her through an ordeal that kills many others. In the end, each gets her man, but more importantly, each gains a greater knowledge of herself in the process.

Source: Laura Pryor, Critical Essay on *Sweetgrass*, in *Novels for Students*, Gale, Cengage Learning, 2009.

Bryan Aubrey

Aubrey holds a Ph.D. in English. In the following essay, he discusses the ways in which Sweetgrass *accurately portrays the customs, practices, and beliefs of the nineteenth-century Blackfoot.*

> IN ADDITION TO PRESENTING IN HER NOVEL SOME OF THE COMMON CUSTOMS AND PRACTICES OF BLACKFOOT SOCIETY IN THE NINETEENTH CENTURY, HUDSON UNOBTRUSIVELY MANAGES TO CONVEY THE DISTINCTIVE NATIVE AMERICAN VIEW OF THE WORLD, IN WHICH EVERYTHING IN NATURE IS A LIVING ENTITY IMBUED WITH CONSCIOUSNESS."

One of the many merits of Jan Hudson's *Sweetgrass* is that it succeeds in telling a story that is solidly rooted in a remote time and an unfamiliar culture and yet is also fully alive to twenty-first century American sensibilities. Fifteen-year-old Sweetgrass is a heroine whom young English-speaking readers can quickly take to their hearts. She is like many an American teenager, in love for the first time, squabbling with her younger brother, fed up with being treated as a child by her father, and resenting what she sees as the limited role ascribed to her simply because she happened to have been born a female: "A good Blackfoot girl is always obedient, quiet, hard-working, and she never says what she feels," she says, heavy with regret. Like a proto-feminist, Sweetgrass is determined to rewrite the social contract that determines the conditions of her life. Desiring to go beyond the traditions of her tribe and live her life on her terms, she resolves, "I would find the signs, the power to control my own days. I would make my life be what I wanted." She feels the strength of a warrior in herself.

It might seem at first blush that these are unlikely thoughts for a young Blackfoot girl in the 1830s to have and that they are attributed to her only because the author needs to bridge the gap between the time and culture in which the story is set and the need of a modern young female reader, accustomed to seeing powerful female role models on television and in movies, to identify with the heroine of the tale. But closer examination of the historical records suggests that Sweetgrass's desire to break out of the traditional gender role in her tribe was not unheard of among Blackfoot women of the period. As Hugh

A. Dempsey explains in the introduction to his book, *The Vengeful Wife and Other Blackfoot Stories*, the place of women was not quite as fixed as one might have supposed. He points out that although it was customary for young girls to spend their days learning their appointed tasks of collecting firewood and water, tanning hides, and cooking meals, "occasionally, some girls broke out of that mold to become warriors and were ultimately accepted in their chosen roles." He gives historical examples of such women, who were called *awau-katsik-saki*, ("warrior woman") including a woman from the Blood tribe named Running Eagle. Running Eagle swore revenge when her husband was killed by Crows. She went to war and showed great bravery, killing an enemy and capturing many horses. Men began to follow her, and she organized her own raiding parties. Another warrior woman was named Trim Woman, who was also accepted and honored by the men of her tribe. Dempsey quotes a Blood elder who recalled, "That kind of woman is always respected and everyone depends on them. . . . They are admired for their bravery. They are lucky on raids so the men respect them."

Hudson lists Dempsey's book in her extensive bibliography, and the information about the warrior women was no doubt the inspiration for the character of Sweetgrass's grandmother, who in her time had been a famed warrior known as She-Fought-Them-Woman: "She had ridden like the wind, stolen horses, and counted coup on the dead." The story of her deeds is still told. Not surprisingly, it is Grandmother who becomes Sweetgrass's role model. She sees the warrior courage and strength that the old woman still exudes and longs to emulate it. Indeed, it is Grandmother who predicts that Sweetgrass will become a warrior, and she also shows her the way. During the raid mounted by the Assiniboin, Grandmother stands firm in her resolve, telling her frightened daughter, Sweetgrass's Almost-Mother, to "Stand and save your children. Be strong and mighty like a true Blackfoot." Young Sweetgrass, listening, draws courage from Grandmother's example.

Although there is no corresponding example in *Sweetgrass*, in which all the men (with the possible exception of Shy-Bear) are very much men, Dempsey also points out that just as a few Blackfoot women adopted masculine roles, some males opted out of their prescribed warrior role, wore dresses and helped the women in their daily tasks. Others dressed as women but were still warriors. There is a specific term in the Blackfoot language, *a'yai-kik-ahsi*, to describe a man who "acts like a woman." (This does not refer to homosexuality.) Dempsey tells the story of a man named Four Bears, who wore women's clothes and believed he had been given holy powers by the sun. Four Bears was a warrior who apparently had great success in horse raids, partly due to the fact that if the enemy saw him they took no notice of him because he was dressed as a woman.

As the example of Grandmother the warrior shows, *Sweetgrass* is a well-researched novel, and the result is an authentic story that seems genuinely to capture the flavor of Blackfoot life in those long-gone times, before the existence of Indian reservations, when relations between Native Americans and white men were still tolerable (as is shown by the trips the Blackfoot in the story make south to the American trading stations at Fort McKenzie and Fort Union, and north to the English Hudson's Bay Company at Fort Edmonton).

One central element in Blackfoot life at the time, as will be well apparent from *Sweetgrass*, was war. In the 1830s, when the story is set, the Blackfoot tribes were at war with the Crows and had been for generations. A regular part of the warfare was the horse raids; in fact, the desire to obtain horses appears to have been the principal inducement to go to war. Sweetgrass must have witnessed many times the return of the young warriors of her tribe with their stolen horses, just as she reports in chapter 2, when the "victorious young men of our band and Five-Killer's band walked their new horses back and forth with smug dignity." According to Dempsey, the young men would plan the raids in the spring and would travel on foot for hundreds of miles to the enemy camp. During the night they would creep up on the best horses, which were tied to the owners' tipis or otherwise secured nearby. Cutting the bonds that tied the horses, the raiders would then lead them out of the camp and ride back home. Dempsey reports that if the raids went wrong, the consequences might be fatal:

> But if the snapping of a twig, the growling of a dog, or any other noise, awoke the owner, then the results might be different. Gunfire, screams of rage, and defiant war cries might echo through the still night as the raiders rushed for the safety of darkness. If they were lucky, they escaped. If not, their scalps adorned the lodges of their adversaries.

Ownership of horses was thus a vital part of Blackfoot life and became a criterion of wealth. Some Blackfoot in the early nineteenth century owned thirty or forty horses, according to John C. Ewers in his book, *The Blackfoot: Raiders on the Northwestern Plains*. By the 1860s, wealthy Blackfoot owned fifty to a hundred horses. Poor families, however, would own only one or two horses, which provided them with a much lower standard of living than others in their tribe. Horses were essential for moving camp, which the Blackfoot did frequently during spring, summer, and fall. A horse could move four times the load that a dog could manage and carry it twice as far in a day. The average family of eight (two men, three women, and three children) needed ten horses to move camp efficiently.

Horses were also important in marriage bargaining, as *Sweetgrass* makes clear. The more horses a warrior could acquire, the greater would be his chances of finding a desirable wife, since the horses could be offered as gifts (payment, in effect) to the girl's father. This is why in the novel, Sweetgrass's friend Pretty-Girl never has a chance of marrying her sweetheart, Shy-Bear. He is not much of a warrior and can only come home from the horse raid with pack-horses rather than riding horses, unlike the formidable Five-Killer, whom Pretty-Girl does not find attractive because he is much older than she. But Pretty-Girl is powerless to prevent the match being made. In a contest between a girl's desires for a love-match and a father's desire and need for horses, there could be only one outcome.

Sweetgrass also provides historically accurate insight into other aspects of marriage practices among the Blackfoot. Polygamy was common, according to Ewers, "because it was a practical means of caring for the excess of women created by heavy war losses." To possess several wives was a sign of social status, and more than half the men had at least two wives. In the novel, Sweetgrass's father has three wives, all sisters. This too was common, since it was thought that sisters would be less likely to be jealous of each other. A man who married the eldest sister might later expect the younger sisters to be offered to him as additional wives. Girls were usually married by the time they reached their mid-teens, although some became wives when they were younger than twelve. Sweetgrass, then, at the age of fifteen, has every reason to believe that she is ready for marriage.

Arranged marriages were the most common, but it was also known for couples to make a free choice of each other out of love. Sweetgrass tells her cousin Favorite-Child that her father and deceased mother chose each other of their own free will. Therefore, it was not unreasonable (or historically inaccurate) for Sweetgrass to hope that she would be able to marry the young warrior of her choice, Eagle-Sun. As reported by Kenneth E. Kidd in *Blackfoot Ethnography*, some Blackfoot couples, desiring each other but meeting opposition from their families, would even take some horses and elope together. Needless to say, this did not go down well with the girl's father and was regarded as theft. The man had to find a way to conciliate the father before he could return to his tribe.

In addition to presenting in her novel some of the common customs and practices of Blackfoot society in the nineteenth century, Hudson unobtrusively manages to convey the distinctive Native American view of the world, in which everything in nature is a living entity imbued with consciousness. There is no split in this view between the human world and what Western thought regards as the inanimate world. Consciousness pervades everything. Nature spirits are everywhere and they interact with humans. As Betty Bastien explains in *Blackfoot Ways of Knowing: The Worldview of the "Siksikaitsitapi"*:

> The land, animals, and spirits are not separate but an integral part of the *Siksikaitsitapi* world. [*Siksikaitsitapi* refers to all Blackfoot-speaking tribes.] They too are the source of science and knowledge. This same relationship exists with the elements, earth, wind, water, and rock—all are within the consciousness of the universe . . . and make up the circle of life.

This sense possessed by the Blackfoot that everything is alive and interconnected is frequently conveyed in *Sweetgrass*. "The earth is crying with joy!" exclaims Sweetgrass as she and Favorite-Child thrash around in the river one morning, sending water flying upward. In other words, the earth too possesses consciousness; it is not inanimate; it throbs with joy. In Western thought this is known as the pathetic fallacy, the attribution of human emotions to natural objects or things. To the Blackfoot, however, it is simply the way things are. This way of experiencing the world can be sensed again at the Sun Dance, when "Chief Mountain, *Ninastako*, looked down from on high" at the camp site, a description that strongly suggests that the mountain itself is a living being.

It is not surprising, then, to discover that Sweetgrass's world is full of spirits. When she looks into the river and sees a fish, for example, she identifies it as "one of the mysterious water people, one of the river spirits." Her brother Otter has a spirit helper who tells him he will become a man soon. The Blackfoot believed that the spirits present everywhere could be enlisted to help them, if approached in the correct manner. The spirits had power to bestow gifts. Horses, for example, were considered to be gifts from thunder, the water spirits, and the morning star. The greatest of the spirits, in the Blackfoot worldview, was the sun. Heroes, says Sweetgrass, get their power "from their offerings to Sun." What should be noted here is the capitalization of Sun and the omission of the definite article, the presence of which tends to objectify the sun as a thing, whereas referring to it simply as Sun evokes it as a living being. "Who but Sun would give them [the heroes] victory?" Sweetgrass continues. In this view, humans can ask the sun for what they want. "A Sun Dance Woman is a great woman who has asked a big thing from the sun, and Sun has made it true," says Sweetgrass. She remembers a story about how, after Grandmother lost four babies, she promised that she would cut off part of her next child's finger as a gift to Sun if Sun would let the baby live. (This explains why Sweetgrass's father has a short left-middle finger.) Favorite-Child expects to give many gifts to Sun when she is married. She must then be alert to how Sun might reward her. According to Kidd, "it was seldom that the Sun answered prayer directly. More often it was a much inferior creature that appeared to a visionary as a helper. Usually it was some bird or animal."

Such is the world inhabited by Sweetgrass in this finely crafted novel, written in crystal-clear prose with a poet's sensitivity to language. In showing how Sweetgrass matures from powerless young girl, gossiping about possible husbands with her friend Pretty-Girl, to a young woman whose courage, steadfastness, and ingenuity save her almost-mother and brother from certain death from smallpox, Hudson gently educates her young readers about a culture and a way of seeing the world that is far removed from the beliefs, habits, and preoccupations of mainstream America in the early twenty-first century.

Source: Bryan Aubrey, Critical Essay on *Sweetgrass*, in *Novels for Students*, Gale, Cengage Learning, 2009.

SOURCES

Austen, Jane, *Pride and Prejudice*, Borders Classics, 2006, pp. 55, 90, 112, 290.

Bastien, Betty, *Blackfoot Ways of Knowing: The Worldview of the "Siksikaitsitapi,"* University of Calgary Press, 2004, p. 82.

Dempsey, Hugh A., *The Vengeful Wife and Other Blackfoot Stories*, pp. ix–x, 29, 48, 57, 59.

Ewers, John C., *The Blackfoot: Raiders on the Northwestern Plains*, University of Oklahoma Press, 1958, p. 99.

Frey, Yvonne A., Review of *Sweetgrass*, in *School Library Journal*, April 1989, p. 102.

Hudson, Jan, *Sweetgrass*, Penguin Putnam, 1984.

———, *Sweetgrass*, Philomel Books, 1989.

———, *Sweetgrass*, Tree Frog Press, 1984.

Kidd, Kenneth E., *Blackfoot Ethnography*, Archeological Survey of Alberta, Manuscript Series, No. 8, 1937, p. 175.

Ley, Terry C., "Paperback Books for the Teenage Reader: Writing Awards Winners Demonstrate How to Bake Rainbow Poems," in *English Journal*, Vol. 80, No. 6, October 1991, p. 95.

Nilsen, Aleen Pace, and Ken Donelson, "Books for the Teenage Reader: Honor Listing Update, 1989: Some New Kids on the Block," in *English Journal*, Vol. 79, No. 8, December 1990, p. 79.

FURTHER READING

Bollet, Alfred J., *Plagues and Poxes: The Impact of Human History on Epidemic Disease*, Demos Medical Publishing, 2004.

This engaging series of essays explores the changing disease patterns in history and some of the key events and people involved in them. Tracing the details of major outbreaks of disease, including smallpox, Bollet shows how, in many cases, the spread of these diseases is supported inadvertently by human actions, including warfare, commercial travel, social adaptations, and dietary modifications.

Francis, Daniel, *The Imaginary Indian: The Image of the Indian in Canadian Culture*, Arsenal Pulp Press, 1992.

This fascinating, revealing history of the stereotypical Indian image shows how it came to be mythologized by popular Canadian culture after 1850. From the paintings and photographs of the nineteenth century to the Mounted Police sagas and the spectacle of Buffalo Bill's Wild West Show through the performances of Pauline Johnson, Grey Owl, and Buffalo Long Lance, the Indian image alternated from friend to foe and from Noble Savage to blood thirsty warrior. This is not a book about First Nations peoples, but it is a compelling story of the images and ideas that have been forced upon them.

New, W. H., ed., *Encyclopedia of Literature in Canada*, University of Toronto Press, 2002.

Generally an invaluable reference companion to the literatures of Canada, this book brings together leading scholars to look at literature in Canada from a variety of perspectives. These entries discuss authors and their work, related literary and social issues, professional institutions that play a role in the lives of Canadian writers, and the major historical and cultural events that have shaped Canada. Essays by Adrienne Kertzer on children's literature in English and Lally Grauer on First Nations in literature provide detailed and accessible contexts for discussion.

Vanderhaeghe, Guy, *The Englishman's Boy*, McClelland and Stewart, 2005.

For the more mature reader, this award-winning novel links Hollywood in the 1920s with one of the bloodiest, most brutal events of the nineteenth-century Canadian West: the Cypress Hills Massacre. A historian by training and an evocative storyteller by trade, Vanderhaeghe tells a story about power, greed, and the pull of the frontier dreams.

The Waves

VIRGINIA WOOLF

1931

Virginia Woolf established herself as one of the most important writers of the twentieth century before her 1941 death by suicide. Although her early life was marked by tragedy and she struggled with bouts of debilitating depression, Woolf persevered and wrote prolifically. She was also one of the founders of the Bloomsbury group, an intellectual gathering of some of the top minds of the day.

After the publication of several novels, essays, and short stories, she began writing the books for which she is most famous. *Mrs. Dalloway* (1925), *To the Lighthouse* (1927), and *Orlando* (1928) all received positive critical reviews and were also commercial successes. Thus, as she worked on a book she tentatively called *The Moths*, Woolf was at the height of her form. This new novel was to be a sort of autobiography, highly experimental, and abstract in form. Woolf envisioned a novel without a plot, but a novel that would reveal the rich interior lives of its six characters. When this strange, mystical novel was published in 1931, it was titled *The Waves*. For Woolf scholars and the general reader, *The Waves* is an endlessly fascinating book, one that leads to many interpretations. In its exploration of selfhood, identity, and death, *The Waves* remains Woolf's modernist masterpiece. A 2006 edition of *The Waves*, edited by Mark Hussey and introduced and annotated by Molly Hite, is available from Harcourt.

Virginia Woolf (AP Images)

AUTHOR BIOGRAPHY

Virginia Woolf was born Adeline Virginia Stephen on January 25, 1882, in London, to Sir Leslie Stephen and Julia Jackson Duckworth Stephen. Her father was an eminent Victorian critic, writer, and essayist who founded the *Dictionary of National Biography*. His first marriage was to Minny Thackeray, the daughter of the famous novelist, William Makepeace Thackeray. When Minny died in 1875, she left Stephen with a daughter, Laura, who was insane. Julia Jackson Duckworth was a widow when she married Stephen, and she brought into the marriage three children, George, Gerald, and Stella. Together, the couple had an additional four children, Vanessa, Adrian, Thoby, and Virginia.

The family was highly literary and some of the best minds of the day were frequent visitors at the Stephen home. Woolf's godfather, for example, was the American poet James Russell Lowell, who was also the American ambassador in London. Although she never was able to attend university like her brothers, Woolf had the access of her father's library and she read extensively. While there were many advantages for the young woman in her father's home, there was also the disturbing reality of sexual abuse. Both Woolf and her sister Vanessa were troubled by the unwanted advances of their older half-brothers, George and Gerald. A number of biographers credit this early abuse with causing or exacerbating Woolf's recurring bouts of depression.

In 1895, Julia Stephen died. This tragic event led to Woolf's first mental collapse. Moreover, in 1897, Stella Duckworth, who had become a second mother to Woolf, also died. Seven years later, in 1904, her father died, triggering yet another breakdown for Woolf. By 1905, however, Woolf was well enough to live with her remaining family in the Bloomsbury section of London. Friends of her brother Thoby frequented the house for intellectual discussion, and ultimately became known as the Bloomsbury group. Thoby's death in 1906 was another deep tragedy for Woolf; her depiction of Percival in *The Waves* and Percival's death are based on her brother's death.

In 1912, the author married Leonard Woolf. He was supportive of her writing, and together they founded the Hogarth Press in 1917, a publishing endeavor that printed some of the most important texts of their day, including the 1922 edition of T. S. Eliot's *The Waste Land*. During the 1920s, Woolf published a series of novels and essays that contributed to her stature as an important writer. Most notable among these was *Mrs. Dalloway* (1925) and *To the Lighthouse* (1927). The latter book contained many autobiographical details, based on Woolf's childhood experiences with her family during their summers in Cornwall, England, near the sea. Although she cycled between periods when she was emotionally ill and periods when she felt well, she continued to write. Around 1929, Woolf began work on the novel that would become *The Waves* (1931). *The Waves* achieved surprising commercial success, given its abstract and mystical format.

In the decade following the publication of *The Waves*, Woolf published another novel, *The Years*, and drafted an eighth novel, *Between the Acts*, as well as several important nonfiction essays and books. In 1941, increasingly fearful of war and aware that she was slipping into yet another period of depression, Woolf drowned herself in the River Ouse.

Although her life was one filled with tragedy and struggle, Woolf maintained an active intellectual life, filled with devoted friends. Her work remains some of the most important of the twentieth century.

PLOT SUMMARY

The Waves is by all accounts a difficult book for readers, particularly since the plot structure one expects to find in a novel is nearly absent. Prose poems set in italic font separate the nine chapters. Each of the prose poems describes a seascape, with waves breaking on the shore, and each is set at a different time of day, from very early morning until night. Following the prose poems are chapters in which the six characters, Bernard, Louis, Neville, Jinny, Susan, and Rhoda, speak in monologues that reveal their inner thoughts and life experiences. The novel traces these characters from infancy to maturity, with the introductory prose poems symbolically signaling the stages of the characters' lives.

Chapter 1

The first prose poem in the book describes waves crashing on shore in the pre-dawn hours. Woolf sets the chapter at a school for young children. Each of the characters awakens into consciousness. Although their language is highly stylized and not that of young children at all, their perceptions reflect their maturity level. That is, they seem to be fully in the present, observing what is immediately before them, the way a child would. Each character perceives the world differently, although there is little to distinguish one voice from the other. The children each describe their experiences during lessons, and from this the reader can begin to discern their individual personalities and talents. Rhoda's experience with her mathematics lesson is excruciating: " Now Miss Hudson ... has shut the book. Now the terror is beginning. ... I cannot write. I see only figures. The others are handing in their answers, one by one. Now it is my turn. But I have no answer. The others are allowed to go. They slam the door. ... I am left alone to find an answer."

There is also a significant sensory detail in their perceptions. For example, Bernard describes the experience of being bathed by their nurse: " Mrs. Constable, girt in a bath-towel, takes her lemon-colored sponge and soaks it in water; it turns chocolate brown; it drips; and, holding it high above me, shivering beneath her, she squeezes it. Water pours down the runnel of my spine. Bright arrows of sensation shoot on either side. ... Now hot towels envelop me, and their roughness, as I rub my back, makes my blood purr."

MEDIA ADAPTATIONS

- An audiobook of *The Waves*, narrated by Frances Jeater, was produced by Naxos Audiobooks in 2005.

Chapter 2

The children are older in the second section of the book. The boys have gone to one boarding school and the girls to another. The headmaster, Dr. Crane, figures prominently in the boys' experience. Bernard, although he loves "tremendous and sonorous words" understands that Dr. Crane's words are not always true. Louis, on the other hand, loves Dr. Crane, while Neville hates him. In this section, the boy Percival is also introduced, and he becomes friends with each of the speaking characters, although he never speaks himself. It becomes clear that Neville is in love with Percival. In addition, the boys' personalities and ambitions begin to take form. In particular, Bernard continues to be the storyteller, and he speaks often of the novels he will write in the future. Neville seems destined for a life as an academic, while Louis continues to feel inferior to the other boys due to his Australian accent and his father's work as a banker.

The girls are also at a boarding school, although they have very different experiences from the boys. Susan is unhappy being away from her home in the country, and the reader can begin to associate Susan with the natural world. Jinny, on the other hand, loves the city and looks forward to the social life she will have as an adult. Rhoda, still dreamy and odd, demonstrates what will become a recurring theme for her, the insubstantiality of life and the fragmentation of her own identity: "I came to the puddle. I could not cross it. Identity failed me. We are nothing, I said, and fell."

Chapter 3

In this chapter, Bernard and Neville are at university and remain close friends. Percival is also at the same college, and the three see each other frequently. Neville is in love with Percival. Bernard identifies closely with the poet Lord Byron; and this leads to significant reflection on identity. Bernard considers how his relationships with the other characters have formed his personality and psyche. Louis, although he was the best student of the three male characters, has not been able to continue his education for financial reasons and finds himself working as a clerk in a shipping firm, although he continues to have literary ambitions. Susan has returned to her father's home and becomes ever more deeply identified with nature. Jinny and Rhoda live in London, but with very different attitudes toward their lives: Jinny loves the social whirl of parties and the bustling activity of a major city, while Rhoda lives in fear and terror much of the time. Increasingly, Rhoda feels herself to be disappearing.

Chapter 4

The characters have reached young adulthood. Percival has taken a job with the colonial government in India and is preparing to leave. Consequently, the characters have planned a farewell dinner for him. This is the first time that all six characters have been together since their early schooling, and they have some difficulty reconnecting. Ultimately, however, they feel themselves to be deeply connected:

> "Now once more," said Louis, "As we are about to part ... the circle in our blood, broken so often, so sharply, for we are so different, closes in a ring. Something is made."

In spite of this sense of communion, the members of the group part. Neville, closing the chapter, speaks of his agony over the departure of Percival.

Chapter 5

Only three voices speak in this middle chapter of the novel. Neville, who closed the last chapter in pain, opens the fifth chapter in even greater distress: "He is dead. . . . He fell. His horse tripped." Neville is, of course, speaking of Percival, dead in far off India. He cannot seem to square that life goes on without Percival in it. Bernard, on the other hand, is torn between joy and sorrow. He has just become a father, and although he mourns Percival, he also rejoices in the birth of his son. Rhoda, in her grief, imagines how each of the others will react to the news. For herself, Percival's death demonstrates once more that life is futile and meaningless. Rhoda seems lost in her own loneliness.

Chapter 6

This chapter opens some years after Percival's death with Louis's affirmation of himself: "I have signed my name ... already twenty times. I, and again I, and again I." He has risen to a position of great importance in his company and seems to enjoy both the prestige and the power. At the same time, he finds himself drawn to the darkness of public houses and taverns when the day is done. In addition, readers learn that he and Rhoda, the two outsiders, have become lovers. Susan has married and lives on a farm with her husband and children. Susan, who once loved nothing more than walking in the fields, now finds her life shrunk to the inside of her house and to the responsibility of caring for her children: "Yet sometimes I am sick of natural happiness, and fruit growing, and children scattering the house with oars, guns, skulls, books won for prizes." Jinny has not settled down, and continues to move from lover to lover, as does Neville. For Neville, however, sexual relationships are a hollow echo of his first pure love for the now-dead Percival.

Chapter 7

All the characters, now in midlife, reflect on their own aging and the passing of time. It is as if the cold wind of mortality has begun to blow around them. This reflection comes to Bernard while traveling in Rome and seeing ancient ruins. He has begun to understand that stories do not substitute for reality, and that language has no way to fully re-create the reality it represents. Susan finds herself filled with conflicting emotions: deep contentment for all that she has produced and nurtured on her farm and regret for the lives she did not live elsewhere. Jinny senses herself aging, a particularly frightening reflection for a beautiful woman who has spent her time with various lovers. Neville, too, finds himself aging, with younger lovers moving through his life. Louis continues his fractured existence of success at his work, attempts at writing literature, and excursions into the seamy streets of London. Rhoda has left him; always in search of solitude, she travels to Spain. Overlooking the distant sea from a cliff, there is a moment when the reader wonders if Rhoda will throw herself over the edge. Yet she withdraws: "Putting my foot to the ground, I step gingerly and press my hand against the hard door of a Spanish inn."

Chapter 8
The friends meet once again for dinner, reminiscent of their meeting many years earlier to bid Percival farewell. This meeting, however, is not a light-hearted affair of young friends, but rather the gathering of aging people who know that their time is coming to a close. Bernard comments on both their closeness and their isolation: "Marriage, death, travel, friendship ... town, and country; children and all that; a many-sided substance cut out of this dark; a many-faceted flower. Let us stop for a moment; let us behold what we have made. Let it blaze against the yew trees. One life. There. It is over. Gone out." There is a sense that not only will the characters themselves come to an end, but the "thing" that they made, their friendship, is also quickly drawing to a close.

Chapter 9
In the final chapter, only one voice speaks: Bernard has the task of summing up everything. The reader learns that Rhoda has killed herself, and learns about the fate of the other characters. Most of all, Bernard contemplates the role of language in the creation of reality, and understands the futility of words. "My book, stuffed with phrases, has dropped to the floor. It lies under the table to be swept up by the charwoman. ... What is the phrase for the moon? And the phrase for love? By what name are we to call death? I do not know. ... I need a howl; a cry. ... I have done with phrases." In spite of his sense of isolation, in spite of his understanding of the unremitting passage of time, he vows at end to continue to fight: "Against you I will fling myself, unvanquished and unyielding, O Death!"

CHARACTERS

Bernard
Bernard is one of the male narrators. Although early on he shares the stage nearly equally with the other characters, by the end of the book, it is Bernard's voice that holds the story together. When the children are small, he creates for them an imaginary world where they play together. As they grow older, he continues to narrate the facts of all their lives. Early in the

book, it becomes apparent that Bernard is fascinated by language. He keeps a notebook by his side at all times in which to note interesting words and phrases. By doing so, however, he also demonstrates the way that words can distance a person from reality. That is, by continually considering how a scene will play out in written form, the writer never fully experiences the event as it happens. Bernard, perhaps more than any of the other characters, questions the nature of selfhood. As a younger man, he imagines himself like the Romantic poets Byron and Shelley. As he grows older, he wonders if all the other characters are a part of himself, that together they are whole, but apart, merely facets of a human being. "And now I ask, 'Who am I?' I have been talking of Bernard, Neville, Jinny, Susan, Rhoda and Louis. Am I all of them? Am I one and distinct? I do not know."

Bernard is also the most important character in the novel because he so often echoes Woolf's own preoccupation with language and the power of story. As time passes in the novel, Bernard becomes increasingly concerned over the ability of language to adequately describe lived experience. Although he has been the story teller and narrator throughout the novel, by the last pages, he says that he is "done with phrases." Molly Hite, in an introductory essay to *The Waves*, asserts that the character of Bernard draws both on Woolf, and on the critic and editor Desmond MacCarthy, one of Woolf's close friends. MacCarthy, although brilliant, never completed a novel, but often spoke of the novels he would write someday.

Jinny
Jinny is one of the female narrators. She is a beautiful, sensual girl and woman. Early in the book, Jinny sees Louis lying under a bush. Fearing he is dead, she kisses him. This kiss resonates throughout the book, having a different effect on each of the characters. Jinny is fully in her body and does not enter into the kind of metaphysical reflection that dominates the monologues of many of the other characters. Like a graceful animal, Jinny is not self-conscious about her own body nor does she sense any dichotomy between body and soul. Rather, Jinny sees the world on a physical plane, and she interacts with the other characters on the physical plane. As she matures, she becomes sexually promiscuous, asserting her own strength and power through her ability to attract men. This

is not a negative statement, however; Woolf presents Jinny as a woman who experiences the world directly, without the complications of language and thought. She is unashamed of her body, even as she senses that she is growing older. She is not concerned with creating something permanent that will last into the next generation but rather with the sensual experience of the present. Woolf does not seem to judge Jinny harshly, and there are critics such as Hite who argue that Jinny is a stand-in for Woolf, whose nickname as a young girl was Ginny.

Louis

Louis is one of the male narrators. Early on, the reader becomes aware that Louis understands himself to be an outsider. He is from Australia and so his accent does not match that of his wealthy English peers. In addition, his father is a banker who has made his own money, not inherited it. For these reasons, Louis does not feel himself to be the social equal of the other characters. Louis does not go to college with his friends due to financial constraints and instead becomes a clerk in a shipping firm, where his attention to detail and his fine work move him up the ladder of success. At the same time, he is devoted to poetry. Paradoxically, he also finds himself attracted to working class bars and greasy restaurants. Most critics commenting on *The Waves*, including Hite, recognize the Anglo-American poet T. S. Eliot in Louis's characterization. As an American, Eliot was also an outsider in elite English intellectual circles, and he worked successfully at a bank and later at Faber and Faber Publishing. He was a close friend of Woolf and her husband, and he published his poetry through their Hogarth Press. Indeed, Louis's journeys through dark, dingy streets is reminiscent of the wandering of Eliot's alter ego, J. Alfred Prufrock, in Eliot's first important poem, "The Love Song of J. Alfred Prufrock." In this poem, and in his later masterpiece, *The Wasteland*, Eliot experiments with mixing the language of the streets with the elevated language of the classics, just as Louis attempts to do in his own poetry.

Neville

Neville is the third male narrator. He is a fussy, tidy child and man caught up in the ideal beauty of the masculine form. It becomes apparent early in the book that he is homosexual. He is not good at sports, but instead centers his life around art. His desire for order motivates him to subdue the chaos of life through careful application of artistic ideals. He falls deeply in love with Percival while still at school, a love that he continues throughout college. This relationship, however, does not appear to be mutual nor consummated. Of all the characters in the novel, Neville is the most successful as a writer, and he becomes well known for his poetry. He lives the life of an academic, on the faculty of a major university. The death of Percival in India devastates him; and he spends the rest of his life engaging in short affairs with young men who come in and out of his life. Indeed, his entire life seems to shrink to the room in which he lives, with his books, waiting for the next lover to arrive. Like Jinny, he does not look to future generations for meaning. Unlike Jinny, he sees in artistic creation the possibility of perfection and immortality.

Percival

Percival is a young man who attends the same school as the male narrators. Among the characters, he alone does not speak. Rather, he is spoken about by the others. They portray him as a beautiful young man, a fine athlete and a good friend. In one way or another, all of the other characters love him, most notably Neville, who never fully recovers from his death. Woolf draws the name Percival from the Arthurian legend. In many redactions of the legend, Percival is the Grail knight who heals the Fisher King and dies a virgin after achieving the Grail. Woolf is perhaps being ironic with her choice of name for the young man who goes to India on an imperialistic quest and dies in the process. This seems particularly likely as Percival does not achieve a heroic death at all, but rather an accidental one through a fall from a horse. Although Percival does not speak in the novel, his presence and later his absence are central to the work.

Rhoda

Rhoda is the second female narrator. Like Louis, she is an outsider. However, it is not the situation of her birth that makes her an outsider, but rather her own emotional and mental state. As a child, Rhoda does not achieve excellence in her studies and appears to be miserable most of the time she is at school. She does not have a firm hold on her own identity and often seems lost in her private thoughts. Unlike Jinny, she hates living in London because of the masses of humanity. She searches for solitude, and at times finds it within her own mind. She engages in a brief affair with Louis, also an outsider, in a vain attempt at intimacy. However, she breaks off with him because she cannot stand human contact. If Jinny lives wholly in her body, then Rhoda is her opposite, living entirely within the realm of her own mind. Bernard relates in the last chapter of the book that Rhoda commits suicide, although he does not expand on the statement. Certainly, in Chapter 7, there is a strong element of foreshadowing as she stands upon a cliff in Spain and looks out over the ocean waves far below. Given Woolf's choice of drowning for her own suicide several years after the publication of *The Waves*, it is certainly possible that she had a death by drowning in mind for Rhoda's suicide.

Susan

Susan is the third female narrator. Susan is a country girl who loves nature. When she goes away to school, she is miserably homesick and longs for the fresh sights and scents of the outdoors. As an adult, Susan chooses a life that includes marriage and children. She wishes to procreate, connecting herself to the vast circle of life that plays itself out so apparently in a place such as a farm. Among the narrators, she is the nurturer. She seeks meaning in life through growing plants, animals, and children. And yet, by the end of the novel, although Susan has chosen her own life, she seems regretful about what she has missed. She envies Jinny's freedom even while she sees Jinny's life as devoid of meaning. Many critics suggest that Susan is loosely based on Woolf's sister, Vanessa Bell.

THEMES

The Self and Others

In *The Waves*, Virginia Woolf returns to a subject she addresses in several of her earlier books, the relationship of the self to others. Put another way, through *The Waves* she explores both individual and group identity, attempting to determine if the individual exists independently or if the individual is actually the sum total of his or her interactions with others. That this is a thorny topic is evidenced by the number of critics who argue that the six characters are not individuals at all, but rather are just six facets of the same

TOPICS FOR FURTHER STUDY

- Research the French philosopher Henri Bergson and his notions of time. What differences does Bergson see between clock time and psychological time? How do these ideas influence the narrative of *The Waves*? Write an essay on the topic.

- Give a multimedia presentation on the Bloomsbury group after writing short biographies of each member and finding images that illustrate each person's contribution to the intellectual milieu. How do the ideas of the Bloomsbury group find their way into *The Waves*?

- Virginia Woolf claimed that *The Waves* is an autobiographical book. Read a biography of Woolf and determine what elements from Woolf's life are recognizable in *The Waves*. Write a report on your findings.

- Research the life and work of poet T. S. Eliot, studying in particular his first major poem, "The Love Song of J. Alfred Prufrock." Write an essay in which you compare and contrast the character of Louis from *The Waves* and Prufrock from Eliot's poem.

- During the early years of the twentieth century, art, music, and literature became increasingly abstract. Give a multimedia presentation with representative modern abstract art, music, and literature contrasted with Victorian art, music, and literature. What are the major changes? Why have such changes taken place?

personality. Woolf, in writing what she called an autobiography, might have been trying to dramatize the different elements of her own individual personality by inventing the six voices to represent different parts of her own selfhood.

As her treatment of selfhood illustrates, throughout *The Waves* Woolf rejects either/or logic, embracing instead the modernist (and postmodernist) rejection of such a limited way of looking at reality. While she inherited a Western philosophical system built around a logic that holds that two contradictory statements cannot both be true, Woolf nevertheless demonstrates throughout *The Waves* that two contradictory positions can be held simultaneously. Therefore, Woolf's answer to the question "Are the characters in *The Waves* individual identities, or are they part of some larger whole?" might very well be simply, "Yes."

David Trotter argues in *The Cambridge Companion to Modernism* that "the notably disjunctive *The Waves* sets in parallel series the reflections of six characters, in such a way as to suggest the permeability or friability of selfhood. ... it is striking that while [Bernard] does speak of the dissipation or streaming away of identity, he also speaks of its accumulation, accretion, acceleration, augmentation and sedimentation." For Woolf, selfhood as a concept is both fluid and dynamic, sometimes solidly bounded and at others times flowing freely among others. Her characters, therefore, exist as both individuals and group, as single identities and unified society. While these may seem mutually exclusive positions, Woolf's treatment of the theme suggests that both positions are equally true.

Permanence and Impermanence

Another important theme in *The Waves* is that of permanence and impermanence. Throughout the novel, the characters struggle with the changes wrought by time. They move from childhood, to adolescence, to adulthood, aware that they are moving inexorably toward their own deaths. Each character deals with this knowledge in his or her own way. Susan and Bernard, for example, are both parents; although their individual identities will eventually be erased, they have created children who will take a part of their parents into the future. Rhoda, on the other hand, chooses to acknowledge her own mutability very early, and her response is to negate her own individuality through suicide. Jinny's attitude is one of carpe diem; because she knows she will eventually die, she chooses to grab all the life she can, one day at a time. Louis finds himself torn between success as a businessman and his attraction for the dark side of human existence. He, and Neville, for that matter, both believe that art is the only permanence a human being can achieve. Regardless of how each character deals with the knowledge of

his or her mortality, their passage through time demonstrates the mutability of human existence.

Woolf's choice to front each chapter with a poetic interlude describing the breaking of waves on a seashore ironically emphasizes the smallness of human efforts against the great forces of implacable, impersonal nature. The waves were breaking against the shore before the characters awaken to their lives, and will break against the shore after their deaths, without thought, without consciousness. On a larger scale, however, the waves themselves demonstrate that permanence and impermanence are not mutually exclusive. As each wave move towards shore, its height, weight, appearance, and dissolution are unique to it; no other wave will ever be exactly like another. The wave itself is impermanent, its existence ended as it crashes on the shore. At the same time, the waves are constantly reconstituting themselves out of the permanence of the ocean. They are simultaneously short-lived and immortal.

STYLE

Experimental Point of View

Point of view is the vantage point from which a narrative is told. First person point of view uses a character in the novel who tells everything from his or her perspective, and refers to himself or herself as "I." Third person point of view is of two kinds: in a third person limited point of view, the narrator can only reveal what he or she experiences and observes, while in a third person omniscient point of view, the narrator is all knowing and can reveal the thoughts of any characters at any time.

Woolf experiments with point of view in *The Waves*. While technically the novel is in third person point of view, signaled by the use of "he said" and "she said," the third person narrator has no other participation in the text. Rather, Woolf allows each of her characters to function as a serial first person narrator. The same events are narrated from the perspective of each character, offering a six-sided description of the event. This choice tampers with traditional literary structures such as setting, chronology, and characterization. The reader sees events and characters through six sets of eyes, creating ambiguity and uncertainty. In many ways, this literary experimentation mirrors experimentation in the visual arts where artists such as Pablo Picasso attempted to show a scene from multiple perspectives at one time.

Allusion

An allusion is an indirect reference in a text to a person, character, or event from another literary text, popular culture, or history. For example, when a character in a movie says: "We're not in Kansas anymore, Toto," the character is alluding to the classic American film, *The Wizard of Oz*. A writer who chooses to use allusions assumes that his or her readers will have the necessary background and knowledge to both recognize and understand the allusion.

Woolf was an extraordinarily well-read person; consequently, her work is packed with allusions that many readers will miss on a first or even second read. Her characters in *The Waves*, for example, often quote the Romantic poets Percy Shelley, John Keats, and Lord Byron. One allusion that is fairly obvious is her choice of names for the young man Percival. Students of the legend of King Arthur will recognize the name Percival as one of Arthur's knights. Although the stories of Percival differ from one redaction to the next, there is a core group of stories that identify Percival as the knight who travels through the wasteland, heals the Fisher King, and finds the holy grail.

Woolf's use of the name Percival for the character who goes off to India as a member of the colonial government is ironic, and an indictment of the imperialist project. Percival believes that he is going on a quest, a quest of the magnitude of the search for the holy grail. In actuality, he is going to India as a member of a ruling class to impose the will of the British on indigenous people. This quest, Woolf seems to imply, is neither innocent or moral. Moreover, Percival does not die bravely in battle or in doing good deeds; he merely falls off his horse. Her use of the name suggests that heroism belongs to another age.

Stream of Consciousness

Stream of consciousness is a narrative technique that presents the thoughts and sensory impressions of a character in a flow that mimics the inner workings of the human mind. Just as the mind moves from one thought to the next, often by association rather than by rational, step-by-step logic, a novel written in stream of consciousness will move from one impression to the next with very little guidance for the reader. Perhaps

the most famous stream of consciousness novel is James Joyce's *Ulysses*, although Woolf's *To the Lighthouse* and *Mrs. Dalloway* make extensive use of the technique as well. In *The Waves*, Woolf further experiments with the technique by offering six characters who speak in internal monologues, one after another. Unlike dialogue in a traditional novel, the inner monologues follow the internal workings of each mind. The free associations, sensory impressions, and jumbled chronology of each character's stream of consciousness give to *The Waves* a dreamy, fragmented and abstract quality, much different from the popular realist fiction of the day.

HISTORICAL CONTEXT

Europe between the Wars

By the time World War I ended in 1918, the combatant nations, including England, France, and their Allies against Germany, Austria and their allies, had fought for four bitter years across the face of Europe. A whole generation of young men were wounded or killed in this horrible conflagration and in the influenza epidemic that raged during 1918. In all, there were forty million casualties. In addition, the face of Europe was entirely changed with the dissolution of the Austro-Hungarian and Ottoman empires and the creation of nations such as Czechoslovakia.

The terms of the Treaty of Versailles that finally brought peace to Europe were deeply punitive to the Germans; there are many scholars who argue that the seeds for World War II were planted at Versailles. Germany was stripped of its colonies and was forced to pay heavy war damages to the Allied nations. As a result, Germany entered a period of rampant inflation and severe economic turmoil.

In 1929, the crash of the American stock market sent shudders throughout the world. Europe, as well as the United States, entered a dark period of extreme economic depression. This climate led to the rise of fascist powers in both Germany and Italy, and increasingly led to a surge of nationalism in virtually every European state.

Modernism

At the beginning of the twentieth century, the Western world experienced dramatic and tumultuous

COMPARE & CONTRAST

- **1930s:** Modern writers such as T. S. Eliot, Virginia Woolf, and James Joyce make a decisive break from the realistic fiction of the Victorian era.

  Today: Postmodern writers such as Thomas Pynchon, Don DeLillo, and Umberto Eco continue to experiment with literary form and subject matter.

- **1930s:** Although World War I ended in 1918, the rise of fascism in Germany and Italy moves Europe inexorably toward another World War.

  Today: Nuclear weapons deter participation in multinational wars, although many individual nations continue to fight against terrorism.

- **1930s:** The work of Sigmund Freud is becoming known throughout the United States and England, although there is no effective diagnosis or treatment for depression of the kind Woolf suffered.

  Today: Advancements in the diagnosis of mental illness lead to medical definitions for conditions such as depression, bipolar disorder, schizophrenia, and social anxiety disorder. Effective medical treatments for these illnesses are developed.

- **1930s:** Although feminists such as Virginia Woolf argue for the complete equality of men and women, few women work outside of the home, and virtually none are in political leadership positions.

  Today: Women work in all professions and serve in high-ranking political positions in both England and the United States. Nevertheless, they still do not hold an entirely equal footing in the professional realm.

---

change. In virtually every field of endeavor, new ideas were being promulgated. Art and literature had already begun to change radically before World War I; however, the rate of change accelerated dramatically in the aftermath of the war. The damage to both the geographic and psychological landscape of Europe was unprecedented; the violence and death precipitated by the war led to a sense of loss, disillusionment, and fragmentation.

For members of the artistic community, the world seemed to have changed overnight. Ideas about time, physics, and psychology led intellectuals to see a world they once thought of as solid and governed by stable natural law as a fragmented wasteland. Some writers, such as T. S. Eliot, believed that art had the potential to reconstitute reality. Others, such as Samuel Beckett, came to see the world as essentially absurd.

In addition, the work of Carl Jung and Sigmund Freud offered writers new ways to think about human identity. Before Freud, the human mind was considered a unified repository of the person's identity. Freud, however, demonstrated that the human mind operated at both the conscious and subconscious level. Consequently, writers could use this knowledge to build sophisticated and complicated characters. Furthermore, modernist writers, artists, dancers, musicians, and architects looked to art to repair the rupture in reality caused by rampant change and burgeoning technology.

CRITICAL OVERVIEW

The Waves is undoubtedly Virginia Woolf's most experimental and abstract book. From the time of its first publication, it has puzzled and fascinated readers and critics alike. Leonard Woolf believed that it was his wife's finest work, although he expressed some reservations about

---

Godrevy Lighthouse, Cornwall, U.K. *(© Vince Bevan / Alamy)*

how many readers would actually persevere in the reading of it, as Molly Hite reports in her introductory essay to *The Waves*. Indeed, reviewers have disagreed widely as to the literary merit of the novel. As Christine Froula summarizes in her book *Virginia Woolf and the Bloomsbury Avant-Garde: War, Civilization, Modernity*:

> Formally the most original, ambitious, and adventurous of Woolf's books, *The Waves* has been widely acclaimed a "masterpiece" ... on the one hand; avoided, dismissed, judged an "aesthetic failure," a mere "warehouse," of materials and ideas, on the other.

Although the book originally sold quite well, its popularity declined through the 1940s and 1950s. Indeed, James Naremore's critique, in his book *The World without A Self: Virginia Woolf and the Novel*, is somewhat typical of the mid-century, masculine critical response to *The Waves*. Naremore recognizes the brilliance of the novel though he is not certain what to make of it. He asserts: "Certain passages in *The Waves* are extraordinarily beautiful; with the possible exception of the last chapter, however,

the prose is rather stifling in effect—the reader almost drowns in the language."

In the latter part of the twentieth century, a new interest in the novel emerged. Susan Rubinow Gorsky, for example, writing in her 1978 book *Virginia Woolf* states: "Virginia Woolf's analysis of human feelings and relationships in *The Waves* is unusually fine, her sensitive understanding of man's attempts to find a way out of his loneliness and his confusion is superb." In more recent years, critics have found a wide variety of ways to read *The Waves*. In her article in *Criticism*, for example, Lisa Marie Lucenti considers *The Waves* in terms of individual identity and the way that identity falters when confronted with the nothingness of death. Likewise, Froula discusses identity and autobiography in *The Waves*, stating:

> Loosed from objectivist notions of a singular, discrete individual, Woolf's self-portraiture abandons conventional ideas of resemblance between image and object (the subject as bounded identifiable entity; a recognizable body; its observable doings) to explore a more expansive and abstract concept of being.

Elicia Clements, on the other hand, in an article in the journal *Narrative*, suggests that music becomes increasingly important to Woolf in her writing. She argues: "From *The Waves* (1931) onward ... Woolf deliberately attempts to reconstitute novelistic methods by looking to the 'classical' tradition of music as a potential model."

Given that Woolf was writing during the birth of modern psychology, and given that she was an early feminist, her work has also been reviewed through the lenses of psychoanalysis and feminist critique. Indeed, because *The Waves* is such a mysterious and oddly constructed novel, and because it refuses to stay within generic boundaries, it is likely that critics and scholars will continue to find the work worth additional discussion.

CRITICISM

Diane Andrews Henningfeld

Henningfeld is a professor of English who writes widely for educational publishers. In the following essay, she argues that The Waves *rewards readers*

WHAT DO I READ NEXT?

- In her novel *Mrs. Dalloway* (1925), Woolf uses stream of consciousness to track one day in the life of Clarissa Dalloway and Septimus Smith, a shell-shocked veteran of World War I. The book is a precursor to the style and techniques used in *The Waves*.

- In *A Room of One's Own* (1929), Woolf considers the challenges women face in attempting to forge a career in literature.

- T. S. Eliot's epic poem *The Waste Land* (1922) is a prime example of modernist writing. It was first published by Virginia and Leonard Woolf at the Hogarth Press.

- *Inside Modernism: Relativity Theory, Cubism, Narrative* (1999), by Thomas Vargish and Delo E. Mook, is an interdisciplinary account of modernism that includes insights from physics, art, and literature, including the discussion of work by Virginia Woolf.

---

with a deeper and richer sense of what it means to be human.

Molly Hite, in an introductory essay to *The Waves*, writes that Leonard Woolf judged the novel to be his wife's best book. However, Leonard also added that he thought "the first 100 pages extremely difficult" and that it would be "doubtful how far any common reader" would follow. Later critics also found great value in the book, as well as great difficulty. As Mitchell A. Leaska asserts in his book *The Novels of Virginia Woolf: From Beginning to End*, "what *The Waves* means as a whole is a question of considerable difficulty." This sentiment is echoed by readers and critics alike.

Nonetheless, it is the very difficulty of the book that opens it to interpretation using a critical approach called reader response. While reader response critics use many different approaches in their analyses of literature, one

> FOR WOOLF, THE ONLY WAY TO ADEQUATELY REPRESENT THE HUMAN EXPERIENCE IN THE TWENTIETH CENTURY IS TO FIRST DISMANTLE THE CONVENTIONAL STRUCTURES AND THEMES OF TRADITIONAL LITERATURE."

---

tactic of the school is to examine the process of reading a given text. Reader response critics ask two important questions: first, what is the experience of the reader as he or she approaches this text; and second, how do readers and writers work collaboratively to produce meaning in a text?

The experience of reading *The Waves* can be disorienting and at times frustrating. Many readers will find themselves floundering, unsure of what they are reading or why. Considering what causes reader distress in the novel is the first step in understanding Woolf's project, and by extension, the novel itself.

Readers generally bring a whole tool kit of strategies with them when they begin reading a novel. They have developed these skills through practice and instruction. Anyone who has taken a high school literature class, for example, has probably learned about the various elements of a novel. Whether readers are aware of it or not, they use this learning to help them make sense of a text. Indeed, both instruction and experience will build for a reader what is known as a horizon of expectation. That is, experienced, educated readers bring to any given novel expectations and assumptions about what a novel is and is not. This is at the heart of the difficulty readers encounter with *The Waves*. As Hite remarks: "What is difficult about *The Waves* is its violation of certain narrative assumptions that are so ingrained we may not realize they *are* assumptions."

What are these assumptions? First, readers expect that a novel will be longer than a poem or a short story. Next, novels are written in prose, not poetry. In addition, novels will have a setting that defines time and place. Novels also have interacting characters who generally speak in dialogue. Most important for many readers, novels have plot. Readers learn to recognize such other features as point of view, conflict, rising action, falling action, climax, crisis, and denouement. More sophisticated readers will look for symbols, flashbacks, conflict, themes, and foreshadowing, among other details. Above all, readers know that novels are fiction, not fact; yet at the same time, they agree to enter the fictional world and regard it as real in order to participate in the events the writer provides.

Although novels vary greatly in how these assorted structural features are manifested, most readers can discern many of these features. Moreover, most readers *expect* to find these features. For example, someone who reads many murder mysteries will expect to find in such a text a setting; a protagonist whose job it is to solve the murder; an antagonist who has committed the murder; and a plot that provides suspense, conflict, danger, and eventually, resolution. By the end of a murder mystery, the protagonist has solved the crime. Readers work along with the protagonist to uncover clues and to analyze the crime. In a well-written mystery novel, readers will reach the same conclusion as the protagonist at about the same time. When the novel fails to follow these conventions and the protagonist demonstrates himself or herself to be particularly dense, for example, readers lose patience. Their horizons of expectation have not been met.

Thus, because Virginia Woolf, in writing *The Waves*, notoriously violates nearly every readerly expectation, the reader is not always sure what it is that he or she is reading nor is the reader sure how to read the book. In the case of Woolf, however, it is not because she is an unskilled writer who unwittingly violates generic conventions. Rather, she is a highly skilled author who breaks with convention in order to revitalize a genre she thinks has grown old and stale.

Woolf, and members of her generation, experienced radical shifts in their understanding of reality due to upheavals in science, art, music, mathematics, and psychology taking place in the early twentieth century. World War I also undermined many conventional ideas about morality and violence. As a modernist and a member of the Bloomsbury group, Woolf was intensely aware of the rapid change in perspective that the new physics and new technology manifested. Albert Einstein, for example, demonstrated that even time is not a stable function, and other physicists, theorizing at the quantum level, proved that solid objects only appear solid. Susan Dick, in her essay in *The Cambridge Companion to Virginia Woolf*, argues that what makes *The Waves* "so difficult to write and makes it so demanding to read is this radical shift of perspectives."

Looking at the features of *The Waves* individually will help clarify this concept. First, although readers are able to intuit that in the first chapter the children are at some sort of school, Woolf does not supply any specific geographic or temporal setting. When the boys and girls go off to their separate schools, she again does not specify either place or time. The characters seem to move in an eternal present. Indeed, the only setting that corresponds to the "real" world is London. As a result, the characters seem to reside in something like a dream space and time, where events and memories blur together poetically. Readers are unable to fix coordinates for the characters in either time or space.

Further, readers encounter the six speaking voices of Bernard, Neville, Louis, Jinny, Susan, and Rhoda. In a traditional novel, readers learn about individual characters through what they say, what others say about them, and by what the narrator says or implies. In the case of *The Waves*, there is no authorial or narrative voice that exists outside of the characters' monologues.

Likewise, the traditional novel will have a variety of major and minor characters. In *The Waves*, all six voices assume equal stature; one is not privileged over any of the others, or at least not until the final chapter when Bernard alone speaks. In addition, the voices are nearly indistinguishable one from another. Although the characters come from different backgrounds and are of both genders, their language is the same. They speak a highly educated, highly poetic language, all in the present tense. As Dick asserts: "The six speakers are not conventional characters. ... They live in ordinary reality ... but the point of view from which they perceive life and the 'purebred prose' they speak make even the most mundane activity seem latent with a larger significance ... their features and their clothing are rarely described."

Because the characters use the same vocabulary, register, and sentence structure, readers are unable to distinguish one from another based on these. Instead, readers must attend to the specific detail in each of their statements to learn about Rhoda's preoccupation with solitude or Louis's sense of inferiority, for example.

In addition, the characters have a strange relationship with each other. Although they never engage in dialogue, they appear to communicate with each other. Their odd form of communication creates a community that is at once unified yet separate. Susan Rubinow Gorsky asserts in her book *Virginia Woolf* that "for all their strange unity and unusual communication, the characters are individuals too, and a tension between unity and separation is constantly maintained." Thus, the soliloquies of the individual characters become not only a structural device, but a thematic device as well, demonstrating the push and pull between individual and group identity. Mitchell Leaska in *The Novels of Virginia Woolf: From Beginning to End*, for example, argues that

> *The Waves* suggests, first, that every human being is a distinct living unit while being simultaneously a part of every other unit of human life; that is, one is distinct from others because of the identity one has created for oneself by conscious or unconscious choices in life— choices determined by each individual's scale of values; and at the same time, one is a part of those people who have shared emotions and experiences in life.

Readers also encounter difficulty in trying to discern a plot in *The Waves*. Plot, however, is what Woolf wanted to avoid in her experimental novel. Gorsky cites a letter Woolf wrote to her friend and critic Lytton Strachey in which she stated baldly: "Plots don't matter." For Woolf and other modernists, the complexity and uncertainty of the modern world precluded traditional understandings of life or of plots. In life, events which previously might have been fraught with significance become merely a series of random happenings in the new world. Consequently, traditional plot movement with rising and falling action, hinging on particular actions or events, seemed no longer applicable to the modern novel. Thus, in *The Waves*, what is important is not what happens, but rather the interior meditations of the characters that reveal their feelings, their relationships, and their struggle for meaning in an often absurd world.

Again, as a modernist, Woolf felt deeply the fragmentation of contemporary life. The grand narratives of church and nationalism no longer held life together for the moderns, and they found themselves trying to use literature as a way to provide meaning and unity in the new reality. The push-and-pull of individual identity with group belonging substitutes for plot and provides the impetus for further reading.

Lisa Marie Lucenti summarizes the situation in *Criticism*. She writes: "Structurally, the 'voices' of this text have none of the traditional novelistic supports to sustain them—no descriptive setting, plot, or characterization beyond what they themselves say." Nevertheless, although Woolf takes away most of the familiar landmarks readers use to guide them through a novel, she extends her hand in collaboration to the intrepid reader trying to find meaning in *The Waves*.

Woolf does so in the poetic interludes that separate chapters. In her lovely descriptions of the breaking waves, she provides a symbolic pointer to the passage of time. In the first section, the sun has not yet risen. In the pre-dawn hours, the waves beat upon the shore. The children awaken to life in the early morning hours of their own existence. In each interlude, the sun grows higher in the sky and the characters become older. By the end of the novel, only Bernard remains to tell the story, and the sun slips below the horizon. This structure allows the reader to track outside events within the interior monologues and provide for themselves a kind of chronology for the story.

In addition, the periodic reference to the waves underscores Woolf's juxtaposition of the transience of life with the eternal pounding of water on shore. Bernard asks: "What has permanence?" Hite identifies this as one of the "one of the central questions of this novel and one of the ways in which the oceanic imagery is most effective." She further references a 1929 entry in Woolf's diary in which the writer asked: "Now is life very solid or very shifting? I am haunted by the two contradictions. This has gone on for ever, will last for ever; goes down to the bottom of the world—this moment I stand on. Also it is transitory, flying, diaphanous. I shall pass like a cloud on the waves."

Rhoda, with her need for solitude and her vanishing sense of self, seems to be the least permanent of any of the characters. It is Rhoda, however, who most desires communion with the permanent. While standing over a cliff in Spain, she seems ready to be joined with the great nothingness of nonexistence: "The cliffs vanish. Rippling small, rippling grey, innumerable waves spread beneath us. I touch nothing. I see nothing. We may sink and settle on the waves. ... Everything falls in a tremendous shower, dissolving me." At the last moment she turns away from nature, choosing instead the humanly constructed (and therefore impermanent) "hard door of a Spanish inn." Her later suicide suggests that she finally reaches a different decision.

Bernard, likewise, wavers. On the last page of the book, while seeming to come to an understanding of "the eternal renewal, the incessant rise and fall and fall and rise again," he suddenly veers away from abyss. He does not choose Rhoda's path. Rather than welcoming the nothingness of eternity, he vows to fight death: "Against you I will fling myself, unvanquished and unyielding, O Death!"

For Woolf, the only way to adequately represent the human experience in the twentieth century is to first dismantle the conventional structures and themes of traditional literature. For Woolf, these conventions can no longer address the disorientation, alienation, or fragmentation of contemporary life. Likewise, readers must abandon their preconceived assumptions about literature (and about life, for that matter) to enter into the world of *The Waves*. Such a task, while at times difficult, will result in a new understanding of both literature, and the human condition.

Source: Diane Andrews Henningfeld, Critical Essay on *The Waves*, in *Novels for Students*, Gale, Cengage Learning, 2009.

Herbert Marder

In the following excerpt, Marder connects the characters in The Waves *to biographical details from Woolf's life.*

... Like other modernist works, *The Waves* follows a model of spatial or organic form in a sense described more than a hundred years earlier by Schopenhauer. In his preface to *The World as Will and Representation* he declared that his book presents the elaboration of a single idea, a work in which all the parts are interdependent as in an organism, every part supporting the whole, and supported by it, so that though one encounters them in succession, they echo the unity of a living creature. Such works, he adds,

> WE ARE ARE PART OF ONE ANOTHER, VIRGINIA WOOLF BELIEVED, OUR SELVES OVERLAP, AND *THE WAVES* PORTRAYS SIX PARTS OF VIRGINIA, PARTLY DRAWN FROM HER FRIENDS, THOSE INTIMATE OTHERS CLOSEST TO HER, WHERE THEY CONVERGED AND THEIR SELVES MERGED WITH HERS."

should be read with the understanding that the end is already implicit in the beginning, forming "a connexion in which no part is first and no part is last ... and even the smallest point cannot be fully understood until the whole has been first understood." Similarly, in its presentation of a single cosmic day in which the whole cycle of human life unfolds, *The Waves* places its characters against an ever-present, timeless reality.

The central idea grew out of Virginia's meditations on her brother Thoby's death, which had happened in 1906, when she was twenty-four. It had been a shockingly senseless death— a vigorous young man in the bloom of health, killed by typhoid fever, which the doctors failed to diagnose till it was too late. He had shown great promise. His friends had expected that he would be one of the leaders of his generation. He drank contaminated water while touring Greece, grew ill and died. A quarter of a century later Virginia returned to that event, seeking to come to terms with its apparent arbitrariness. It was part of an inexorable cycle, the "many mothers, like one wave succeeding another," she wrote in her first draft of *The Waves*, "wave after wave, endlessly sinking and falling." She observed the cycle through the eyes of six friends, all of whom had been shaken by the early death of Percival (her idealized image of Thoby). The novel implicitly asks how one can or should live in a world in which such things happen.

The six characters explain their experiences and themselves, beginning in childhood and bringing the life stories up to late middle age, when a spokesman for them all offers a summing up of their collective wisdom. The friends have known each other intimately since childhood, and sometimes feel that they are parts of one another, forming a single complex organism—as if the separate soliloquies in which they tell the novel's events all compose a larger collective consciousness. Framing the nine groups of soliloquies, each standing for a different stage of life, from childhood to the eve of death, Woolf placed italicized interludes that describe the play of light over a seaside landscape at nine moments during a single day, from an hour before the sun rises to after it sets.

The Waves is still less conventional in its form than this summary suggests. The alternating soliloquies that compose the novel are only secondarily about external events. Woolf's emphasis is on the elemental beings of the characters, or what she called on the original manuscript's title page "the life of anybody ... life in general." The speakers anticipate the elusive or unknowable narrators of postmodern fiction since Samuel Beckett. Although there is a chronological order, these characters are outside time, speaking, even in childhood, with fully adult voices. Percival, the hero who dies, is associated with absence and negation, the void that is always there at the center and is too painful to be looked at directly. All memories imply this unspeakable thing and the speakers must make room, allow for this fact without allowing it to eclipse daily life.

We are are part of one another, Virginia Woolf believed, our selves overlap, and *The Waves* portrays six parts of Virginia, partly drawn from her friends, those intimate others closest to her, where they converged and their selves merged with hers. The novel was "autobiography" in this sense—a calling forth of her selves. Of all the complementary roles, Rhoda's was the most inward, mysterious and detached from mundane events, the image of a poetic visionary looking beyond society, which appalls her, toward ethereal pools "on the other side of the world ... where the swallow dips her wings." The others were more attached to outer things, implicated in worldly affairs. Jinny was related to Leslie Stephen's "poor little Ginny," a lovename for Virginia. She was the girl child responding to a formidable father, and later the young woman entranced by her body's dance of desirability. Susan represented a domestic self whom Virginia identified with her sister, Vanessa—calm earthiness, enfolding close-held passions—a body leaning on a gate in sunlight, the weight in her side foretelling the children she

would bear. The three women form a three-sided figure, each face looking in a different direction—Jinny within her billowing dress aware of her sexuality; Rhoda, longing to be faceless and bodiless; Susan absorbed in the routines of kitchen, farmyard, and nursery.

The male characters form a complementary triad. Louis derived many of his traits from her husband Leonard's austere and sensitive character. He was the thin-skinned outsider, surviving among strangers, seeking justice and haunted by deep racial memories—an innocent who felt shocked by his own sensuality, as by a blow on the nape of the neck. Neville was related to the homosexual Lytton Strachey, famous for his scathing wit—fastidious and lewd, part scholar and part sensualist. Finally, Bernard was the chronicler, a male story-telling self that Virginia Woolf the novelist associated with the literary tradition, a supple companion whose voice echoed the voices of Bloomsbury writers like Desmond MacCarthy and E.M. Forster. The male figures can be paired with members of the female triad: Bernard and Susan are absorbed in the natural world; Neville and Jinny are impelled by sensuality; and Louis and Rhoda pursue transcendental visions.

Taken together, the two three-sided figures describe a state of wholeness, "a six-sided flower," as Bernard calls it, "made of six lives." In their hexagram Virginia imagined "the complete human being whom we have failed to be, but at the same time, cannot forget."

The defensive quality of the Woolfs' marriage, their outsiders' alliance against the rest of the world, provides an important motif in *The Waves*. The novel describes their fictional counterparts, Rhoda and Louis, as "conspirators" who never can think and feel like other people, though they do their best to mask their singularities. Louis's severely critical attitude, his rational and businesslike manner, conceals his awareness of not fitting into English society and also his contempt for those who mindlessly conform. He is the son of a banker in Brisbane, his Australian accent corresponding to Leonard's Jewishness, which Virginia had once, at the beginning of their courtship, thought might come between them. "You seem so foreign," she had told him. Her account of Louis in *The Waves* stresses his racial memory, his insistence, even as a boy, that he has already lived many thousands of years and heard "rumors of wars

[and] seen women carrying red pitchers to the banks of the Nile." All this, that his roots go down deep, and into such darkness, he conceals behind his methodical, businesslike exterior.

Rhoda's singularity, on the other hand, is immediately apparent. Ordinary existence shocks and disorients her. Although she performs the expected social rituals, meets her friends and frequents drawing rooms, she is always turning toward the window with eyes fixed on something beyond the visible horizon.

The novel's two "conspirators" know the violence lurking near the surface of daily life and are attracted and repelled by it, feeling, like the heroine of *Mrs. Dalloway*, that it is "very, very dangerous to live even one day." Their speeches invoke elemental forces. Plain, uneventful days open into chaos for them; habit and routine conceal something monstrous. "I see wild birds," says Louis, "and impulses wilder than the wildest birds strike from my wild heart ... I hear always the sullen thud of the waves; and the chained beast stamps on the beach. It stamps and stamps." Rhoda's inner language, the tale she tells herself, reflects a similar sense of wild, uncontrollable energy, some monstrous form of life that "emerges heaving its dark crest from the sea. It is to this we are attached; it is to this we are bound, as bodies to wild horses." Louis and Rhoda's language, their vision of wildness and a rough beast from the sea, echoes the tone of the Romantic poets, from Shelley worshiping the west wind to Yeats declaring that great writers own "nothing but their blind stupefied hearts."

The Waves, in accord with the Romantic tradition, shows that artworks enable one to live in a world where Percival's death has happened. This knowledge is elaborated by Rhoda in an episode that progresses from Swiftian rage to aesthetic release. Having learned that Percival died after being thrown by his horse in India, she goes out walking along crowded Oxford Street, where she finds that "the human face is hideous" and that roaring motorcars "hunt us to death like bloodhounds." This knowledge of destructiveness is a "gift," she reflects, a shock of extreme reality. After a while Rhoda turns aside and buys a ticket for an afternoon concert. In the concert hall she merges with the sleek crowd, who have gorged themselves on beef and pudding enough to sustain them for a week and now "cluster like maggots," seeking to appease a

different hunger, swarming "on the back of something that will carry us on." The music begins. She hears it differently than ever before. Percival's death is the gift, enabling her to delve beneath mere semblances, to feel, while the music lasts, the permanence and clarity of pure forms and know their geometric rigor. "There is a square; there is an oblong. The players take the square and place it upon the oblong. They place it very accurately; they make a perfect dwelling-place. Very little is left outside. The structure is now visible; what is inchoate is here stated; we are not so various or so mean; we have made oblongs and stood them upon squares. This is our triumph; this is our consolation." Rhoda leaves the concert hall and throws a bunch of violets into the Thames as an "offering" to her dead friend, a romantic gesture, inspired by Shelley's poem "The Question," that invokes the consolation of art.

These scenes suggest a basic premise governing the novel's form. Its soliloquies do not render the characters' speech or even thought but represent neo-Romantic artworks, formal and stylized compositions, like Rhoda's "perfect dwelling-place." The selves of the speakers are conceived as artistic creations in their own right, each one a summing up, a fusion of indispensable elements. *The Waves* is a complaint against indifferent nature, as represented by the italicized progress of the primal day, an appeal for an aesthetically ordered world. Like the Romantic poetry it echoes, the novel encloses intensely personal feelings within patterned forms.

Destructive impulses can be temporarily checked, as Rhoda found in her lament for Percival. But the novel's interludes reflect the inevitable cycle of growth and decay, the putrefaction that follows all blossoming. From a panoramic view of the seashore, the narrator brings us down to ground level, observing oozing matter from rotten fruit and yellow excretions exuded by slugs. The corruption is coupled with glimpses of beauty. "The gold-eyed birds darting in between the leaves observed that purulence, that wetness, quizzically. Now and then they plunged the tips of their beaks savagely into the sticky mixture." The mood of formal elegance and romantic desolation climaxes with Rhoda's suicide, an event seen only indirectly, and tersely, almost casually, reported by Bernard. He ponders her extreme loneliness and constant search for "some pillar in the desert, to find which she had gone; she had killed herself." That is all, except for an equally terse suggestion that she had stepped in front of an oncoming vehicle in the street. Bernard's self-identification with Rhoda and his implicit approval of her act admit no special emphasis or explanation.

Virginia presented her idea of the composite self most fully in a long monologue spoken by Bernard at the novel's end. Shaping his memories into a complete artwork, he becomes a medium through whom all the other voices speak. In his summing up he is no longer certain whether he is a man or woman, poet or businessman. He has charted all the stages of despair, absorbed all the nihilism that flowed from Percival's death. He has lived through Rhoda's suicide and that too has entered the composite self. He cannot separate himself from his friends—living and dead. "Am I all of them? Am I one and distinct? I do not know... There is no division between me and them... Here on my brow is the blow I got when Percival fell... I see far away, quivering like a gold thread, the pillar Rhoda saw, and feel the rush of the wind of her flight when she leapt." Bernard resists the extremes of cynicism and nostalgia, returning us, in the heightened language of his final soliloquy, to the ordered space where players place an oblong upon a square. He strikes a final romantic pose, makes a last ironically self-conscious gesture—that of the solitary horseman riding out to defy death, the lance-bearing champion (Percival's double) who does all he can, knowing it is not enough, but constructing out of inevitable defeat some shelter, some accommodation in the "perfect dwelling-place" of art...

Source: Herbert Marder, "Lady Rosebery's Party," in *The Measure of Life: Virginia Woolf's Last Years*, Cornell University Press, 2000, pp. 43–62.

Julie Vandivere

In the following essay, Vandivere links grammatical constructions in The Waves *to issues of gender and social class.*

While scholars have for some time pointed out Woolf's concern with subject construction and the construction of the world, they have not analyzed how this interest appears on grammatical, rhetorical, syntactic, and figural levels. Accordingly, I want to explore *The Waves*, where, I suggest, Woolf's investigation of subject construction manifests itself primarily in linguistic

> THIS PASSAGE RELIES ON GRAMMATICAL STRUCTURES TO REVEAL THE FLUX BETWEEN THE ABSTRACT AND THE CONCRETE IN THE PROCESS OF SELF-DEFINITION. THE FIRST LINES THAT FOLLOW LOUIS'S CLAIM ABOUT KNOWING THE WORLD INCLUDE SUSAN'S COMPARISON OF WORDS TO STONES, A SIMILE THAT GIVES LOUIS'S WORDS ADDITIONAL WEIGHT AND SUBSTANCE."

terms, leading her to use constructs of language in such a way as to critique traditional assumptions about unified selves and patriarchal systems.

This concern with the relation between the grammatical and the ontological emerges most clearly when Louis claims, "'I know my cases and my genders; I could know everything in the world if I wished.'" Louis's optative assertion that knowing cases and genders would enable him to know the world materializes in several registers, most significantly through puns on the words "gender" as both sex and grammatical classification, and "case" as both "circumstance" and grammatical category. Since "gender" carries this dual implication, Louis is in part claiming that if he can make sexual distinctions, he can know the world.

Epistemological composition based on gender dichotomies is that of traditional society; patriarchy is built upon the ability to distinguish between male and female. Yet, as Woolf makes clear with her second pun, that on "case" as "circumstance" or "situation," gender is not the sole marker of social position. By linking "gender" to "case," Louis's statement suggests that gender distinctions are inseparable from the "case" in which they appear, and, consequently, that knowledge of gender must also be accompanied by knowledge of the circumstance within which that gender functions: class, education, social status.

Louis's claim to knowing genders and cases statement also suggests a more subtle and interesting reading of the link between the world's grammar and its construction. It may be taken to imply that neither the world nor language is a priori: that reality does not mimic grammar, nor grammar, reality. Such a relation is symbiotic. In making grammatical systems, one makes the world, and in making the world, one makes grammar.

Following Louis's avowal, we find an even more directly metalinguistic scene, as Woolf goes on to speculate about relationships between language and existence:

> "Those are white words," said Susan, "like stones one picks up by the seashore."
>
> "They flick their tails right and left as I speak them," said Bernard. "They wag their tails; they flick their tails; they move through the air in flocks, now this way, now that way, moving all together, now dividing, now coming together."
>
> "Those are yellow words, those are fiery words," said Jinny. "I should like a fiery dress, a yellow dress, a fulvous dress to wear in the evening."
>
> "Each tense," said Neville, "means differently. There is an order in this world, upon whose verge I step. For this is only a beginning."

This passage relies on grammatical structures to reveal the flux between the abstract and the concrete in the process of self-definition. The first lines that follow Louis's claim about knowing the world include Susan's comparison of words to stones, a simile that gives Louis's words additional weight and substance. Susan's analogy implies that words are material things that can mark reality, and, more, that they are especially solid and weighty objects—are stones—that each is, in fact, a petrus, a rock, an object upon which patriarchy and its religious systems are ultimately rounded.

However, the image of words as quintessentially concrete objects, as stones, gives way quickly to one of words as fluid, animate, mutable things which "flick their tails." Thus, Susan's analogy is not followed by a reinforcement of the concreteness of words, a move that would substantiate Louis's claim for the ordering power of words and strengthen his argument for a concrete reality. Instead, the discussion of words moves in free association to Bernard's comparison of words to capricious flying beings. No longer stones upon which to construct the world, the words now take on life as they metamorphose into some not-quite-identifiable beings who demonstrate in movement, ascension, even ethereality, the words' impossibility, their unpredictability, their groundlessness, their

refusal to establish the concrete that Louis is trying to claim. The next line moves even more hopelessly away from the concrete, as words are described in even less solid terms—as "yellow" and "fiery." Words ultimately, then, become shimmering substances of color and heat, elements that could not be more poorly suited to serve as the building blocks of self or reality.

The grammar of the passage replicates the instability of these "words," as Woolf couches each assessment of language (as either concrete or abstract) in language that demonstrates its claim. For instance, in the structure of her verbs, Woolf plays with implications of the indicative and subjunctive moods. The indicative, of course, refers to the concrete, empirical world of definition and fact, the subjunctive, to the abstract, the speculative, the non-objective. The parallels between grammatical moods and Woolf's construction of reality are straightforward. The indicative signals the myth of the concrete world wherein one can theoretically construct a sense of self, while the subjunctive signals a refusal of this myth, and acknowledges that the sense of self is rootless, grounded only in relations and transient images.

If the indicative points to the concrete and the subjunctive to its refusal, Louis's indicative declaration that "I know my cases and genders" asserts first that there is an indicative world, and second, that this world values the ability to distinguish between classes and genders. But Louis's next proclamation, "'I could know everything in the world if I wished,'" does not assert itself with the same empirical power. Had the statement been "I can know everything in the world," its grammar would have been consistent with the indicative case of the first half of the sentence and would then simultaneously posit the feasibility of Louis's second claim and augment the feasibility of his first. However, the phrase reads "I could know," thus pushing the possibility of knowing into the subjunctive optative: a mood of the wistful, the speculative, the noumenal. In the contiguity of these two sentences ("'I know my cases and my genders; I could know everything in the world if I wished'"), Louis speculates on the possibility of constructing a factual, objective world of the indicative from his position in the non-factual, the non-objective world of the subjunctive. The linguistic structure points to a contradiction inherent in Louis's assertion; the claim that one can construct a reality in the concrete can only ever be made from the hypothetical register of the abstract.

Throughout *The Waves*, the sorts of grammatical and figural complexities that I have been exploring are a primary manifestation of the text's recurrent doubts about the stability of any linguistic or ontological assertion. Neville's statement that "'There is an order in this world, upon whose verge I step,'" points to the impossibility of grounding in either the concrete or the abstract, the indicative or the subjunctive, the male or the female, and undermines any assumption that one may make such distinctions. A forging of the world and of selves within it rests on the thetic contradiction of living, we might say, enslaved by the ideal of the indicative, but perpetually drifting into the flight of the subjunctive. Ultimately, Woolf's language in *The Waves* suggests that there is no choice but to live straddling the aporia between inevitably opposing constructions embodied within grammatical ambiguities.

Source: Julie Vandivere, "Woolf's *The Waves*," in *Explicator*, Vol. 53, No. 1, Fall 1994, 3 pp.

Dorothy Brewster

In the following excerpt, Brewster analyzes each of the six characters in The Waves.

... Consider the Six as aspects of a multiple personality: Jinny, Susan, and Rhoda; Bernard, Neville, and Louis. Jinny lives in the body, with the body's imagination; she is at home in the ballroom, treading naturally on thick carpets, sliding easily over smooth polished floors, responding to radiance like a fern unfurling its curled leaves, riding like a gull on the wave, "dealing her looks adroitly here and there," with no time to sort out all the impressions she has gathered. But as she grows older she becomes more curious about the people she sees in the crowded rooms: "The door goes on opening. The room fills and fills with knowledge, anguish, many kinds of ambition, much indifference, some despair ... The common fund of experience is very deep ... In one way or another we make this day, this Friday, some by going to the Law Courts; others to the City; others to the nursery; others by marching and forming fours ... The activity is endless. And tomorrow it begins again ... Some will never come into this room again. One may die tonight. Another will beget a child. From us every sort of building, policy, venture, picture, poem, child, factory, will spring. Life comes; life goes; we

> WHAT IS IT LIKE, WHEN SOMEONE LOVED IS SUDDENLY GONE? EACH OF THE FRIENDS EXPERIENCES THIS LOSS DIFFERENTLY AND IS NEVER QUITE THE SAME AGAIN."

make life." Active herself, it is human activity that excites her occasional wonder.

Rhoda, who appears to move in the same social circles as Jinny, is alien and lost in the crowd. When a door opens, "the tiger leaps" an image for her constant fear of the person, the experience, coming to her. She escapes; imagery of marble columns and pools on the other side of the world suggests her dream life; she is mistress of nothing but her dreams, as, when a child, she rocked her ships of rose petals in a basin of water and was mistress of her fleet. She is always seeking something she can touch, and "so draw myself across the enormous gulf into my body safely," else "I shall be blown down the eternal corridors for ever." She wonders about the knowledge Jinny has when she dances, and about the assurance Susan has, when, stooping quietly beneath the lamplight, she draws the white cotton through the eye of the needle. "They say, Yes; they say, No ... But I doubt; I tremble; I see the wild thorntree shake its shadow in the desert."

Susan knows exactly what she is and what she wants. She is rooted, not blown about. She is homesick in her girls' school and later among the snows and pines of Switzerland for the country vicarage, and she is happy, after her marriage, on the farm. She likes the stare of shepherds and of gypsy women beside a cart in the ditch, and before her marriage, she knows that her lover will come, and "to his one word I shall answer my one word. What has formed in me I shall give him. I shall have children; I shall have maids in aprons; men with pitchforks; a kitchen where they bring the ailing lambs to warm in baskets, where the hams hang and the onions glisten. I shall be like my mother, silent in a blue apron, locking up the cupboards." Yet Susan is not placid. Her emotions are simple but violent; she can hate as well as love, as, when a child, she hated Jinny whom she saw kissing Louis.

Louis is the youngest and weakest among the children; the one left behind when the others troop off to breakfast; the one who has a curious sense of identity with those roots in the garden that go into the depths of the earth; down there, his eyes are the lidless eyes of a stone figure in a desert by the Nile. (It is scarcely necessary to say that no child could have put these strange intuitions into words.) Later it is the dark backward of time that fascinates his imagination: the history and the traditions of the human race. It is Louis among the boys at school who is aware that the stone flags in the chapel are worn by the feet of six hundred years, and who is grateful for the safeguards of tradition, because he has wild impulses—hears the sullen thud of the waves and the "chained beast" stamping on the beach. (That, at least, is one's guess at the meaning of the stamping beast.) Louis in maturity is of those who through the centuries have been the seekers and the builders of civilization; as he grows older, his sense of the continuity of human experience and of himself as part of it grows stronger; he watches "the eternal procession of women going with their attaché cases down the Strand as they went once with pitchers to the Nile." Louis and Rhoda both feel their separateness. They become lovers for a while. Bernard thinks of them as the "authentics," who exist most completely in solitude.

Louis, the best scholar of the three, does not go on to the university, being destined to retrieve in the City the failure of his father. But Bernard, both at the university and in later years, often thinks what a malevolent but searching light Louis would have thrown upon the university, and upon his own poses as a Byronic or a Tolstoyan young man. He often feels Louis's eye upon them all, "adding us up like insignificant items in some grand total . . . And one day, taking a fine pen and dipping it in red ink, the addition will be complete; our total will be known; but it will not be enough." Bernard, the phrasemaker, curious about other people, always making up stories about them, needs an audience—himself, if no other is present. He is plagued, or blest, with that double consciousness of the artist, who both sees and feels and thinks and at the same time watches himself seeing and feeling and thinking; who in the very act of taking part watches himself taking part.

Neville, unlike Louis who seeks to reduce chaos to order, sees an order already existing in the world—to be discovered, not imposed. He is a precise scholar. At Cambridge he is in love with life, and with the beauty of young men especially; and he is close to Bernard at this stage, both of them seeking an identity—who among these selves am I? They try to read each other. Neville sees through Bernard's poses and Bernard is aware of the rent in his defenses made by Neville's "astonishing fine rapier." Neville will always slip into cushioned firelit rooms, with many books and one friend. He sees himself becoming a don and going with schoolmasters to Greece and lecturing on the ruins of the Parthenon; and with a flash of repugnance—or of insight—"it would be better," he thinks, "to breed horses and live in one of those red villas than to run in and out of the skulls of Sophocles and Euripides like a maggot." (He remains a scholar, but does not—though his story is a little vague here—become a don.)

All these Six, different yet complementary, look to their friend Perceval [sic, et al.], feel his fascination, and love him in their individual ways. What he is comes to us only through them. He dies young, joining Rachel and Jacob in the company of those whose promise is unfulfilled and who leave behind them the question— what did the world lose when they died? Perceval had grace of body, the courage that goes with it, unself-consciousness; he possessed the irresistible attraction that one who seems at ease with life has for those who are plagued by doubt and inner conflict.

The moment in *The Waves* when Inner and Outer fuse, creating harmony and radiance, rounding the globe, comes with the farewell dinner to Perceval on the eve of his departure for India. They have all gone different ways after their shared school and university years, but they are still only on the threshold of life. When they meet and wait for Perceval, and after he comes, fragments of their childhood experiences keep slipping into their reveries, almost as if it were a group mind remembering. The monologues are here close to dialogue—yet not spoken. "From these close-furled balls of string we draw now every filament (said Louis) remembering, when we meet." They have come together to make one thing—not enduring, for what endures?—but seen by many eyes simultaneously. Yet each of the Six asserts himself; their self-realization is at its youthful peak. The roar of London around them isolates them—as Louis perceives: "Motorcars, vans, omnibuses pass and repass continuously. All are merged in one turning wheel of single sound. All separate sounds—wheels, bells, the cries of drunkards, of merry-makers—are churned into one sound, steel blue, circular. Then a siren hoots. At that shores slip away, chimneys flatten themselves, the ship makes for the open sea."

"But India lies outside," thinks Neville. And Bernard imagines Perceval's life in India. The others see different visions, but their thoughts are focused on Perceval, and on their own promise as well. They experience the youthful sense of infinite time and open choice before them. It is Susan who perceives that something irrevocable has happened; the little heaps of sugar, the peelings of fruit, the plush rims of the looking-glasses in the restaurant, look strange, as if she had not seen them before; everything is fixed—"a circle has been cast on the waters; a chain is imposed. We shall never flow freely again." Let us hold this moment, thinks Jinny, "love, hatred, by whatever name we call it, this globe whose walls are made of Perceval, of youth and beauty, and something so deep sunk within us that we shall perhaps never make this moment out of one man again." Bernard sees them as creators, who have made "something that will join the innumerable congregations of past time. We too, as we put on our hats and push open the door, stride not into chaos, but into a world that our own force can subjugate and make part of the illumined and everlasting road."

Perceval is thrown from his horse in India and killed.

What is it like, when someone loved is suddenly gone? Each of the friends experiences this loss differently and is never quite the same again. Bernard hears of Perceval's death on the same day that his son is born. "Such is the complexity of things that as I descend the staircase I do not know which is sorrow, which is joy ... I need silence, and to be alone and to go out, and to save one hour to consider what has happened to my world, what death has done to my world." So he goes out into the streets and looks at the details of a world Perceval no longer sees. He feels the rhythm, the throb, but for the moment he is outside the machine of living. He thinks of what the world has lost in Perceval, who was "borne on by a natural sense of the fitting, was indeed a great master of the art of living so that he seems to have lived long, and to have spread calm around him, indifference one might almost say, certainly to his own advancement, save that he also had great compassion." He goes into the National Gallery,

seeking some answer from the paintings, but "the perpetual solicitation of the eye" weighs upon him. "Arrows of sensation strike from my spine, but without order." Something lies just beyond his grasp; perhaps in some moment of revelation after a long lifetime he may lay hands upon it. "Ideas break a thousand times for once that they globe themselves entire." Although bodies soon look ordinary again, what is behind them differs—the perspective. Bernard begins to want life around him again, and wishes to remember Perceval with someone Perceval was at ease with and liked "(not Susan whom he loved, but Jinny rather)."

Rhoda, after hearing that Perceval has been killed, goes to a concert, and, more successful than Bernard, finds consolation in a perception of order beneath all the sensations: "There is a square; there is an oblong. The players take the square and place it upon the oblong. They place it very accurately ... Very little is left outside; the structure is now visible." But this perception of meaning will never, for Rhoda, be enough to release her from her dream of escape.

The reunion with Perceval at the dinner marks the high tide, the hot sunshine, of the progress through the day, through life. His death forces reflection, readjustment, reassessment. To cover the declining day, two sections follow, preceding the Hampton Court reunion and the final summing-up by Bernard. The essential personality of each becomes more strongly marked as the choices before them narrow. Here is Louis: "My shoulder is to the wheel; I roll the dark before me, spreading commerce where there was chaos in the far parts of the world ... If I press on, I shall inherit a chair and a rug; a place in Surrey with glasshouses, and some rare conifer, melon or flowering tree which other merchants will envy. Yet I still keep my attic room ... There I watch the rain glisten on the tiles till they shine like a policeman's waterproof; there I see the broken windows in poor people's houses; the lean cats; some slattern squinting in a cracked looking-glass as she arranges her face for the street corner; there Rhoda sometimes comes. For we are lovers." Susan is completely absorbed in her children and her household: "Whether it is summer, whether it is winter, I no longer know by the moor grass, and the heath flower; only by the steam on the window-pane, or the frost on the window-pane." There will be more children, "more baskets in the kitchen and hams ripening;

and onions glistening; and more beds of lettuce and potatoes." But she sometimes wishes the weight of the sleeping house would lift from her shoulders, sometimes hears broken voices and laughter, and Jinny's voice as the door opens, calling "Come!" Neville lives over some of the past as he sits waiting, in front of the fire, for the one friend he must have—in spite of the meetings, the partings, that finally destroy us. There must be someone so in tune with oneself that one can point at something for the other to look at and share without talking: "to follow the dark paths of the mind and enter the past, to visit books, to brush aside their branches and break off some fruit." With all his seeking after perfection, he is not disinterested; there is always the color of some personal emotion staining the page; it is someone's voice speaking the poem—Perceval's or another's. "There is no end to the folly of the human heart—seek another, find another, you." Bernard is not of those who find satisfaction in one person; the private room bores him: "My being only glitters when all its facets are exposed to many people." He knows at the onset of middle age that he has outlived many desires, but not the desire for the ultimate answers. "Let a man get up and say, 'Behold, this is the truth,' and instantly I perceive a sandy cat filching a piece of fish in the background. Look, you have forgotten the cat, I say."

A dinner at Hampton Court brings the six middle-aged men and women together again, to remember Perceval, to wonder what each has made of life. Each is measured against the others, each wishes to impress one of the others. They all share the realization that choice is no longer possible. "Before, when we met in a restaurant with Perceval, all simmered and shook; we could have been anything. We have chosen now, or sometimes it seems the choice was made for us—a pair of tongs pinched us between the shoulders." Susan compares herself with Neville; her body had been used daily, like a tool by a good workman, all over; "seen through your pale and yielding flesh, even apples and bunches of fruit must have a filmed look, as if they stood under glass." Bernard, knowing that he, with sons and daughters, is wedged into his place in the puzzle, yet cherishes the illusion that it is only his body that is fixed; his mind is more capable than when he was young of disinterested thought: "I throw my mind out in the air as a man throws seeds in great fan-lights, falling through the purple sunset." The dinner is steeped in the atmosphere of

subconscious thought, never rising to the surface to become close to spoken dialogue as it did during the earlier dinner.

After they have dined well—for they do dine—"the sharp tooth of egotism" is blunted, anxiety for the moment is at rest, life is stayed here and now, and in the silence they seem to pass beyond life. But they are soon back on shore. They go out into the darkening gardens, where lovers in the shadow of the trees are scarcely to be distinguished from the ghosts of the past—King William on his horse; court ladies sweeping the turf with their silks and satins. A disembodied mood is upon them. They pair off, Rhoda and Louis, Bernard and Susan, Neville and Jinny, and disappear along the great avenues, among the trees, in the twilight and then the moonlight. It is all a dissolving dream. And it comes with something of a shock when we join Bernard and Susan, pacing the terrace by the river, and come back to life in general—watching the lights coming on in the bedrooms of small shopkeepers on the other side of the river, and imagining with Bernard the stories of the lives of all these people, who are going to sleep, thinking perhaps of their Sunday dinner (the rabbit in its hutch in the garden), or of the chance of winning the football competition. We are back to the knock, knock of one event following another, of the must of life—must go, must catch the train, must walk to the station; and we leave Bernard clasping the return half of his ticket to Waterloo—that, at least, life had taught him to hold on to.

To compare the two dinners as "moments," this seems to be a moment *manqué*. And this impression is strengthened by Bernard's recollection of it years later. He sees them all under the seduction of the wine, ceasing to measure themselves against each other, feeling around them "the huge blackness of what is outside us, of what we are not. The wind, the rush of wheels became the roar of time ... We were extinguished for a moment, went out like sparks in burnt paper and the blackness roared. Past time, past history we went." Then they become again six people at a table and rise and walk together down the avenue. Bernard sees them, against the gateway, against some cedar tree, burning there triumphant in their own identity. Then as a wave breaks, they burst asunder, surrender, draw apart, "consumed in the darkness of the trees." This is not the perfect globe. The globe of

Bernard's imagining has walls of thinnest air, and, pressed, will burst.

In the final section Bernard, a rather heavy elderly man, gray at the temples, sits in a restaurant with a chance companion, for, like the Ancient Mariner, he must have an audience for his tale. "In the beginning, there was the nursery, windows opening on a garden, and beyond that the sea . . . " We already know the story, from six different viewpoints. Now we have it subtly modified from the one viewpoint, with the different lights and shadows and meanings that advancing years and altered perspectives have brought to the storyteller. "On the outskirts of every agony sits some observant fellow who points." Bernard is not that observant fellow, but he is one who looks where the finger points—"beyond and outside our own predicament; to that which is symbolic, and thus perhaps permanent, if there is any permanence in our sleeping, eating, breathing, so animal, so spiritual and tumultuous lives." We learn to order life, to fill up the little compartments of our engagement book, but always deep below this orderly progress, even when we arrive punctually at the appointed time, there is "a rushing stream of broken dreams, nursery rhymes, street cries, half-finished sentences and sights . . . that rise and sink even as we hand a lady down to dinner." The pageant of existence has never ceased to fascinate Bernard; he seems to himself to have lived many lives: "I do not altogether know who I am—Jinny, Susan, Neville . . . I do not always know if I am man or woman . . . so strange is the contact of one with another." There are moments of ebb tide, when no fin "breaks the waste of this immeasurable sea"; moments when everything is drained of color, of life, when the earth dies, withers. "How then does light return to the world after the eclipse of the sun? Miraculously . . . The earth absorbs color like a sponge drinking water." The chance companion leaves, and the elderly Bernard must take himself off and catch some last train. There is the usual street, there is a stir of dawn. "Dawn is some sort of whitening of the sky; some sort of renewal . . . The stars draw back and are extinguished. The bars deepen themselves between the waves." And in the elderly man, too, the wave rises, a new desire, a new determination to meet the advancing enemy. And who could that be now, but Death? . . .

Source: Dorothy Brewster, "Fiction: Shaping the Globe," in *Virginia Woolf*, New York University Press, 1962, pp. 79–161.

SOURCES

Clements, Elicia, "Transforming Musical Sounds into Words: Narrative Method in Virginia Woolf's *The Waves*," in *Narrative*, Vol. 13, No. 2, May 2005, pp. 160–82.

Dick, Susan, "Literary Realism in *Mrs. Dalloway, To the Lighthouse, Orlando* and *The Waves*," in *The Cambridge Companion to Virginia Woolf*, edited by Sue Roe and Susan Sellers, Cambridge University Press, 2000, pp. 50–71.

Froula, Christine, *Virginia Woolf and the Bloomsbury Avant-Garde: War, Civilization, Modernity*, Columbia University Press, 2005, pp. 4–5, 175–77, 201–205.

Gorsky, Susan Rubinow, *Virginia Woolf*, Twayne's English Authors Series 243, Twayne Publishers, 1978, pp. 20–22; 110–19.

Hite, Molly, Introduction, in *The Waves*, by Virginia Woolf, Harcourt, 2006, pp. xxxv–lxvii.

Jouve, Nicole Ward, "Virginia Woolf and Psychoanalysis," in *The Cambridge Companion to Virginia Woolf*, edited by Sue Roe and Susan Sellers, Cambridge University Press, 2000, p. 257.

Leaska, Mitchell A., "*The Waves*, 1931," in *The Novels of Virginia Woolf: From Beginning to End*, John Jay Press, 1977, pp. 159–89.

Lucenti, Lisa Marie, "Virginia Woolf's *The Waves*: To Defer That 'Appalling Moment,'" in *Criticism*, Vol. 40, No. 1, Winter 1998, pp. 75–97.

Naremore, James, *The World without a Self: Virginia Woolf and the Novel*, Yale University Press, 1973, pp. 151–89.

Trotter, David, "The Modernist Novel," in *The Cambridge Companion to Modernism*, edited by Michael Levenson, Cambridge University Press, 1999, pp. 94–95.

Vandivere, Julie, "Waves and Fragments: Linguistic Construction as Subject Formation in Virginia Woolf," in *Twentieth Century Literature*, Vol. 42, No. 2, Summer 1996, p. 221.

Woolf, Virginia, *The Waves*, annotated and with an introduction by Molly Hite, edited by Mark Hussey, Harcourt, 2006.

FURTHER READING

Childs, Peter, *Modernism*, Routledge, 2000.
    The Modernist movement radically changed how people viewed literature and culture. This

book provides a comprehensive introduction to the movement.

Goldman, Jane, ed., *Virginia Woolf: To the Lighthouse, The Waves*, Columbia Critical Guides, Columbia University Press, 1998.
> This book offers a history of the critical reception of both *To the Lighthouse* and *The Waves*. Goldman presents the criticism as it relates to three theoretical positions: postmodernism, modernism, and feminism.

Kolocotroni, Vassiliki, Jane Goldman, and Olga Taxidou, eds., *Modernism: An Anthology of Sources and Documents*, University of Chicago Press, 1999.

The editors of this book have pulled together excerpts from the essential literary, historical, political, and philosophical texts of the modernist era.

Lee, Hermione, *Virginia Woolf*, Alfred A. Knopf, 1997.
> Lee provides the definitive biography of Virginia Woolf in this well-written and carefully researched volume.

Marder, Herbert, *The Measure of Life: Virginia Woolf's Last Years*, Cornell University Press, 2001.
> Marder's biography tells the story of Woolf's final ten years of life, beginning with her composition of *The Waves* and ending with her suicide in 1941.

White Noise

DON DELILLO

1985

Published in 1985, Don DeLillo's *White Noise* is designed to critique the society it reflects, the United States during the 1980s. The novel focuses especially on how the representation of things has become more real than things in and of themselves. DeLillo's technique, derived in large measure from film rather than literature, depends upon non-sequential jumps from scene to scene. This is an attempt to create the hyper-awareness of a world that has become oblivious to criticism via its mind-numbing familiarity—a familiarity achieved particularly through the omnipresence of uniform information that is repetitively generated by an all-pervasive mass media. DeLillo's means of representing reality is not through the exploration of character or environment but through caricature.

DeLillo's style is frequently called postmodern. Postmodern writing often offers a critique of its own content, and it presents the familiar in jarring, hyperbolic ways in order to question the accepted nature of meaning and reality. A satirist of contemporary reality, DeLillo presents the story as a caricature of itself rather than as a realistic representation. Because of this, the book has attracted much critical applause, and has remained popular with readers. While the book critiques 1980s America, it has remained relevant over the following decades. Indeed, a 1999 paperback edition of *White Noise* is still in print.

AUTHOR BIOGRAPHY

Don DeLillo was born to Italian immigrants on November 20, 1936, in the Bronx borough of New York City. His father was an auditor at the Metropolitan Life Insurance Company. Although DeLillo abandoned his family's Roman Catholic beliefs by the end of adolescence, he retained affection for its rituals and disciplines. DeLillo was a lackluster student in high school. And he only began to read seriously around the age of eighteen when he had a summer job as a park attendant. DeLillo majored half-heartedly in Communications Arts at Fordham University, but spent most of his time in the bohemian world of Manhattan in the late 1950s and early 1960s. He went to jazz clubs and art-house cinemas instead of studying.

After graduating from college in 1958, DeLillo became a copywriter for a major advertising agency. He quit after five years. While working on his first novel, *Americana* (1971), he earned money writing feature articles for national magazines. Through the 1970s, DeLillo wrote six more novels, none of which received a lot of critical attention. In 1975, DeLillo married Barbara Bennett, an investment banker who switched careers to become a landscape designer. In the last years of the 1970s, DeLillo lived in Greece, where he wrote *The Names*, which was published in 1982. In 1985, *White Noise* was published. The novel won the National Book Award and established his reputation as a serious mainstream American novelist. The following year, DeLillo's first play, *The Day Room*, an exploration of anxiety about death, was produced. In 1988, DeLillo's novel *Libra*, concerning the assassination of John Kennedy, was published. *Mao II*, his 1991 novel about art and terrorism, received the PEN/Faulkner award in 1992. In 1999, DeLillo was awarded the Jerusalem Prize, and his play *Valparaiso* was produced. The play *Love-Lies-Bleeding* was produced in 2005. His third play, *The Word for Snow*, saw its first production in 2006.

DeLillo's 1997 novel, *Underworld*, was judged in a 2006 *New York Times* survey to be among the best American novels of the preceding twenty-five years. DeLillo's work, like *White Noise*, continues to reflect the contemporary world. DeLillo tried his hand at writing for film with the screenplay for *Game 6* in 2005. In 2007, DeLillo published *Falling Man*, a book centered on the destruction of the World Trade Center in 2001. He has continued to write and live near New York City.

PLOT SUMMARY

Part I: Waves and Radiation

CHAPTER 1

Jack Gladney, Hitler studies specialist, watches station wagons bring students back to college. He offers a catalogue of the students' possessions—essentially luxury toys like televisions, stereos, personal computers, and miniature refrigerators—as they are removed from the parents' vehicles. Gladney also describes the self-satisfied, somewhat ironic complacency of the parents. The scene prepares the reader for the novel's exploration of vacuous consumerism.

CHAPTER 2

Jack's wife, Babette, teaches an adult education course in posture and reads to a blind man, Mr. Treadwell, from supermarket tabloids. Four of their children from previous marriages live with them—Denise, Heinrich, Steffie, and Wilder. Jack's older daughter, Bee, does not live with them.

It is lunchtime in the Gladney kitchen. Everyone prepares his or her own lunch, but the family eats together.

CHAPTER 3

On campus, Jack wears a sleeveless black academic robe and dark glasses. He and Murray Siskind visit "THE MOST PHOTOGRAPHED BARN IN AMERICA." The barn stands as an emblem for one of the major themes of the novel, that image supersedes substance and that celebrity is a function not of achievement but of the hype that can be developed around something.

CHAPTER 4

Jack sees Babette at the high school track running up and down steps in her sweat suit. They watch their daughters run. Driving home, Jack says his daughter, Bee, wants to visit. That evening, they eat take-out Chinese food and watch television. Afterwards, Jack reads Hitler. In bed, he tells Babette his first department chair advised him to change his first name in order to be "taken seriously." Jack confesses he feels inauthentic. Each expresses the wish to die before the other.

CHAPTER 5

At breakfast, Babette reads everyone's horoscope aloud. That night, in bed, Jack thinks about death. The next morning, the family shops at the supermarket and run into Murray. He praises Babette's hair. Jack drives Murray home.

CHAPTER 6

Jack talks with Heinrich about whether reality can be described and if anything can be known. Commenting on the plot to kill Hitler to his Advanced Nazism class, Jack says the nature of plots is to tend toward death.

CHAPTER 7

Babette returns from posture class. She and Jack check on the children and go to bed. They discuss what sort of pornography he would like her to read aloud. They mock the language of pornographic literature. They decide on trashy magazines. Jack goes to get some from Heinrich, who is in his room doing a physics experiment as Wilder watches. Heinrich tells Jack to look downstairs. Jack finds old photo albums. He and Babette look through them; each wonders "Who will die first?"

CHAPTER 8

Jack does not speak German and decides to learn it for an upcoming Hitler conference. Howard Dunlop, a reclusive boarder in Murray's rooming house, is his teacher. After the lesson, Jack invites Murray home for dinner. Murray watches as Denise compacts the garbage; Heinrich talks on the telephone about incest and neutrinos; Babette looks for Wilder; Steffie reports that on the radio someone said to boil water for safety. Jack thinks about the mystery of their family connection.

CHAPTER 9

Because a toxic substance is found in the children's school, the building is closed. Denise, Steffie, Wilder, Babette, and Jack see Murray at the supermarket. He thanks Babette for dinner. Steffie tells Jack that Denise believes Babette is secretly taking medication. Murray tells Babette about the Tibetan idea of death. Babette notices that Wilder is not in the shopping cart. Murray spots him in another woman's cart. Murray invites the family to dinner. In the parking lot, they hear that one of the men examining the school building and wearing a protective but possibly toxic "Mylex" suit "collapsed and died."

CHAPTER 10

Jack observes how students sprawl in the library. At home, Denise warns Babette that the gum she chews causes cancer in lab animals. Steffie talks on the phone. Neighbors call, wanting to drop by. Steffie makes excuses. Jack and Heinrich talk about the prisoner with whom Heinrich plays chess by correspondence, about how many people he killed, how he killed, and whether will or brain chemistry caused his action.

CHAPTER 11

Jack wakes in the night terrified of death. In the morning, Steffie makes burnt toast. Jack, Steffie, and Babette discuss age and Steffie's mother, who works part time for the Central Intelligence Agency (CIA). Steffie takes a computerized marketing survey phone call. In the evening Jack and Babette have dinner in Murray's room and talk about the importance of television. Walking home, Jack and Babette discuss her forgetfulness. Jack asks if she is on medication. She denies it.

CHAPTER 12

Jack attends a German class. Denise's father, Howard Pardee, is in the kitchen. Denise expresses anxiety about his checkered work history. Bob takes the older kids to dinner. Jack drives Babette to Mr. Treadwell's. Jack waits in the car with Wilder. The Treadwells are missing. Jack, Babette, and Wilder join Bob and the kids in the restaurant. The next morning the river is dragged.

CHAPTER 13

Heinrich goes to the river to watch. Treadwell and his sister are found dazed in an abandoned cookie store in a mall.

CHAPTER 14

The family watch a sunset from the window in Steffie's room. Heinrich distrusts its splendor. Jack studies German. Denise and Jack discuss their plot to discover if Babette is taking medication. Steffie joins them. Heinrich says there are pictures of a plane crash on television. The girls go to watch. That evening, a Friday ritual, the family gathers in front of the television, eat takeout Chinese food, and watch disaster reports.

Monday morning Murray is waiting in Jack's office. He fears another faculty member will be appointed the Elvis Presley specialist. Jack offers to support his appointment by dropping in on his class. The chairman of the department, Alphone

Stompanato, bullies the department members at lunch, challenging them with pop culture trivia questions.

CHAPTER 15
Jack co-teaches Murray's class providing an observation about Hitler for every remark Murray makes about Elvis Presley.

CHAPTER 16
Wilder begins to cry in the afternoon and cries non-stop into the night. Babette takes him to the doctor to no effect. Jack drives her to her posture class and waits in the car with Wilder on his lap, listening attentively to his crying. As Jack drives Babette home, Wilder stops.

CHAPTER 17
Jack drives the family to a mall. Denise asks Babette what she knows about Dylar. Babette diverts the conversation to other subjects. At the hardware store, Jack meets a colleague who says he does not look as frightening off campus as he does in his academic robe and dark glasses. Jack becomes animated by shopping. He tells the children to select Christmas presents. They eat in the food court and listen while "a band played live Muzak." At home, Jack notices Steffie mouths the words of the characters on television as she watches.

CHAPTER 18
Jack drives to the airport to meet Bee; he notices the blandness of his town. He sees Tweedy Browner, Bee's mother, there. Bee's flight has not yet arrived. They discuss their failed marriage and her present, unfulfilling marriage. Passengers arrive whose plane lost power and dropped four miles, but the motors returned and the pilot landed safely. Bee arrives.

CHAPTER 19
Bee makes the family self-conscious. After Jack drives her to the airport at the conclusion of her visit, he stops at a cemetery and senses the dead as a presence in his life.

CHAPTER 20
Reading obituaries, Jack thinks about his own death and fantasizes about Attila the Hun's death, picturing the scene as it might be presented in a Hollywood epic. Jack and Babette talk about who will die first. Babette leaves for her class. Murray visits, talks to the children about popular culture, and watches television

with them. Jack makes coffee; Heinrich and Jack talk about the wasteful motions people go through performing daily routines. Jack brings Murray coffee. Babette is on television; her class is being broadcast. Everyone is excited except Wilder, who sits in front of the set afterwards and cries softly as Murray observes him and takes notes.

Part II: The Airborne Toxic Event
CHAPTER 21
Unlike the other chapters of the novel, all quite brief, the account of the evacuation is presented in one long chapter, appropriately representing a kind of relentless disruption of routines that comes to feel, itself, like a routine event. Indeed, this chapter comprises the entirety of the novel's second section. A train carrying a toxic chemical derailed and spilled it into the atmosphere. With radio reports in the background, the family tries to follow their normal routine until a passing sound truck orders all houses evacuated. In a traffic jam, they listen to radio reports that deadly Nyodene D. has been released. They follow radio directions to a designated shelter. Men wearing special suits and their dogs patrol the area. The children wonder about the toxic effects on dogs and consider the differences between mammals and vermin. Jack sees Babette swallow something and suspects Dylar. She says it is a Life Saver. Jack fills the tank at an untended gas pump, possibly exposing himself to Nyodene D.

At the shelter, Heinrich explains Nyodene D. Jehovah's Witnesses proselytize. A computer technician tells Jack that, although it is too soon for certainty, he may be endangered by exposure to the gas.

Wilder, Denise, and Steffie sleep. Heinrich makes notes on maps. Jack listens as Babette reads tabloid stories to Mr. Treadwell and other blind people. Heinrich points out to Jack how little he knows about the technology that runs his life. Outside, Jack sees Murray negotiating with some prostitutes for a session. Jack and Murray talk about the toxic spill, the evacuation, about Jack's exposure, and about death. Jack wants to be able to stop thinking about himself. In the morning, everyone is moved from this shelter to another shelter, where they remain for nine days before going home. A man carrying a small television set complains about the lack of media coverage. He says he feels like he has seen Jack before. Déja vu is reportedly a symptom of exposure to the gas. He says Jack looks "Haunted, ashen, lost."

Part III: Dylarama

CHAPTER 22

Murray becomes the Elvis Presley specialist after his rival drowns. Jack drives Babette to class; they stop to watch the sunset. Sunsets are lengthy and spectacular since the chemical spill. Jack is aroused by Babette's leg warmers. She has been asked to teach a course on eating and drinking. He is melancholy about the death within him because of his exposure to Nyodene D. He does not tell Babette about it, fearing how upset she would be to know his death will precede hers.

CHAPTER 23

Jack continues German lessons. The town is patrolled by men in Mylex suits with German shepherds. At dinner, the family discuss the degree of danger and whether the government is withholding disturbing findings. Heinrich says the danger from toxic spills is inconsequential compared to the danger of radiation from radios, TVs, microwaves, radar, and power lines.

CHAPTER 24

Jack discovers a bottle of Dylar taped to the underside of a radiator cover. He telephones Babette's doctor. He has not prescribed Dylar, has never heard of it. Jack decides to take a tablet to school and ask a colleague in the chemistry department to analyze it. Heinrich chins in his closet and tells Jack about his friend, Orest Mercator, who gave him the bar and is preparing to sit in a cage with poisonous snakes, hoping to set a record. He is tempting death, Jack observes, when most people seek to avoid it.

CHAPTER 25

Jack gives a Dylar tablet to Winnie Richards to analyze. He asks Babette about Dylar. Babette denies knowing what Jack is talking about and says she feels like going to bed with him. The next day, Richards says she can explain how the time release polymer case containing the medication functions but cannot say what Dylar is.

CHAPTER 26

In bed, Jack shuts the radio as Babette listens to a woman recount a disturbing experience; Jack tells Babette he found the Dylar, and asks her what it is. Because of her great fear of dying, she contacted a man, after reading an advertisement in a tabloid, hoping to be given an experimental drug that could block the receptors in her brain that cause the fear of death. In order to get the medication, Babette had sexual relations with him. Jack is less upset about the sexual infidelity than about her fear of death. She had been his protection against his fear. Babette says the medication did not work. When Jack searches for the Dylar underneath the radiator cover in the bathroom, it is missing.

CHAPTER 27

Jack's repeated medical exams show no sign of illness. Driving to the supermarket, Jack turns into a street where a simulated catastrophe is being rehearsed. Steffie plays a victim. Heinrich is a "street captain." Orest Mercator is with him. Jack asks why he is in a hurry to die. Orest asks how many pounds Jack can bench press and mentions his own desire to punch someone in the face to know what it feels like. In the kitchen at home, Babette feeds Wilder. Jack asks where the Dylar is; she tells him not to take any; it does not work. He says it is not behind the radiator. She says she has not taken it. Denise refuses to say if she has removed the bottle. Jack wonders if Dylar might stifle his fear of death.

CHAPTER 28

Wilder sits on a stool by the stove watching water boil. Jack and Steffie discuss her trip to Mexico to visit her mother. In the college cafeteria, American Popular Culture department members argue about movies, boast about daredevil stunts they have performed, and describe the pleasure of imagining their own death. Jack and Murray walk around campus; Murray says he thinks car crashes in American movies represent a "spirit of innocence and fun."

CHAPTER 29

Jack and Babette, in the supermarket, discuss his health and their death anxiety. Jack continues his German lessons. Harold Dunlop shows him *The Egyptian Book of the Dead*. When Denise is not home, Jack searches through her things for Dylar. He begins "throwing things away." On television, he sees a dead body carried out of a backyard grave. A few nights later Heinrich watches an update of the story. A mass grave is not found. Jack "tried not to feel disappointed."

CHAPTER 30

Waking in the night with the dread of death, Jack insists Babette say who the man who gave her Dylar is and how to find him. She refuses, saying Dylar is ineffective and she no longer sees that man. On a campus hilltop, Jack and Winnie Richards watch the sunset. Jack tells her that Dylar suppresses fear of death. She thinks "it's a mistake to lose one's sense of death, even one's fear of death."

CHAPTER 31

Jack pays a cable TV bill. The family eats fast food in the car. They discuss astronauts, the temperature of outer space, and UFOs. Babette tells Jack she wants to die before him and she wants "Wilder to stay the way he is forever."

CHAPTER 32

Murray says Harold Dunlop "looks like a man who finds dead bodies erotic." Jack and Heinrich watch an insane asylum burn down until the fire releases a toxic smell; everyone disperses. Jack and Heinrich drink warm milk. Jack stays up thinking of the man who gave Babette Dylar.

CHAPTER 33

Jack mistakes Babette's father, sitting in the garden, for death. He stays for a few days and gives Jack a loaded gun. Jack searches Denise's room for Dylar. She wakes and says she put it in the garbage compactor.

CHAPTER 34

Jack searches for Dylar in the garbage. He goes for a medical exam. The doctor sends him for more tests.

CHAPTER 35

Babette listens to talk radio, plagued by fear of death. Being with Wilder comforts her because he does not talk. Babette goes running; Denise insists she wear sunscreen. Jack takes Heinrich and Orest to dinner. They discuss Orest's training, being bitten by snakes, and death. Steffie, about to visit her mother, is nervous her mother will not send her back. Jack assures her she will and that he would travel to Mexico to get her. There is a simulation of an evacuation for a noxious smell. A few days later, a real noxious odor settles on the town for a few hours. No one does anything. The smell disappears.

CHAPTER 36

Heinrich's mother wants Heinrich to visit her at her ashram. She tells Jack her swami says it is the "Age of Darkness," the "last age." After the Hitler conference, Jack goes for medical tests. They are inconclusive. Walking the streets at night, Jack imagines a family phone call between a teenager who likes bagging groceries in a supermarket and his grandparents.

CHAPTER 37

Jack tells Murray death does not give life meaning, only makes it incomplete. Murray says religious or scientific systems designed to negate death are comforting even if bogus. He suggests Jack submerge himself in studying Hitler, hide from death in Hitler's immensity, and promote his identity through the fame scholarship can bring. Murray says there are only killers and diers, and asks Jack which he is. Jack throws more things away and thinks about how he can say good-bye to himself.

CHAPTER 38

Jack tells Babette that Murray advised him to repress his fear of death. She says repression causes neurotic symptoms and is unnatural. He says it is natural for human beings to repress their nature: that distinguishes them from animals. He thinks of the man who gave her Dylar. The next day, Jack begins to carry the loaded gun. Jack learns from Heinrich that Orest sat in a hotel room with three non-poisonous snakes and was bitten and has now gone "into complete seclusion." Jack goes to his office to look at final exams. Winnie Richards tells him of an article in a psychology magazine about Willie Mink, the man whose ad Babette answered. Mink is in a motel in the German section of the city. Babette is going out running and needs the car to drive to the stadium. Jack steals his neighbor's car and goes searching for the motel.

CHAPTER 39

Jack confronts Mink. After a conversation about malaise, death, and Dylar, Jack shoots him. He places the gun in Mink's hand, thinking he is dead; Mink fires and wounds Jack in the wrist. Bloody, Jack drags Mink to the car and takes him to an emergency room. Jack talks with a nun about the need people have for nuns to believe in God and Heaven *for* them. The nun says she does not believe but her "dedication is [not] a pretense," her "pretense [to believe] is a dedication." The doctor tells Jack that Mink will not die. Jack drives home.

CHAPTER 40

Wilder rides his tricycle across a busy highway safely and tumbles into a muddy, shallow creek. A stranger stops his car, goes down the embankment and rescues him. Jack, Babette, and Wilder drive to the overpass and watch the sunset. The pollution detectors in their Mylar suits continue to patrol the city. Jack decides not to continue medical tests. In the supermarket, the merchandise has been rearranged and the shoppers are confused. Jack describes the scanners, the colorful packaging, and the tabloids, which have, Jack says, "everything we need that is not food or love."

CHARACTERS

Babette

Babette, Jack's fifth wife, runs to keep her weight down after she stops smoking, reads tabloids to old Mr. Treadwell, who is blind, and teaches an adult education class in posture. She also listens habitually to Talk Radio. Like Jack, she is afraid of dying. Although apparently personal, her fear is also symbolically symptomatic of the gnawing sense of vacuousness that is widespread, although often unacknowledged, in the novel. She answers an ad in one of the tabloids she reads to Mr. Treadwell that is soliciting participants for an experiment taking a medication, Dylar, designed to banish the fear of death. Her husband, Jack, wants to think of Babette as a solid, comforting, cheerful prop for him, but she is haunted by the same malaise, a destabilizing fear of dying, as he is.

Bee

Bee is Jack's daughter who does not live with him. When she visits, the others feel self-conscious because of the way she watches everything.

Dana Breedlove

Dana Breedlove is one of Jack's former wives and works part time for the CIA.

Tweedy Browner

Tweedy Browner is one of Jack's former wives, his daughter Bee's mother. She is married to a CIA type operative who often lives in jungles.

Sundar Chakravarty

He is Jack's doctor. Jack and Babette admire him for what they consider to be a beautiful use of English when he speaks.

Dimitrios Cotsakis

Cotsakis worked as a bodyguard for rock groups. He teaches at the college and is Murray's chief rival for the position of Elvis Presley specialist, until Cotsakis drowns.

Denise

Babette's daughter Denise is a feisty, rather bossy pre-teen. She has a habit of reading about medications, badgers Babette about her health, and tells Jack she suspects Babette of surreptitiously taking medication.

Vernon Dickey

Vernon Dickey is Babette's father. Despite his age, he nevertheless considers himself a ladies' man. A gun enthusiast, he gives Jack a pistol, which Jack takes to Mink's motel room. As with most of the characters in the novel, Dickey defines himself by the image he projects. Aging though he is, he tries to maintain an image of wild youthfulness.

Howard Dunlop

Dunlop is Jack's German teacher. He is a withdrawn man who lives in the same rooming house as Murray, who says that Dunlop looks like a necrophiliac.

Tommy Roy Foster

Heinrich plays chess by mail with Foster, who does not appear in the book in person. He is in jail for a series of murders.

Heinrich Gerhardt Gladney

Heinrich is Jack's fourteen-year-old son. He is intellectually combative and argues against the authority of sensory data or the certainty of knowledge. Although he seems to know a great deal, most of what he knows comes in the form of factoids. Often his knowledge is confused, as when he conflates the playwright Tennessee Williams with the singer Tennessee Ernie. He is beginning to lose his hair.

Jack Gladney

Jack, the narrator of the story, is the Hitler Studies specialist at the College-on-the-Hill. He has been married five times and has four children. He is anxious that he lacks authority and has attempted to fashion an imposing image. To that end, he has changed his first name Jack to J.A.K., and he always wears dark glasses on campus. His academic interest in Hitler is devoid of any sense of the horror of Nazi history or of any awareness of its violation of humanity. Jack's expert knowledge of Hitler merely inflates his own self-image and gives him an aura of importance. His abiding fear of dying is intensified after his exposure to the toxic chemical Nyodene D.

Nicholas Grappa

Grappa is one of the members of the American Events department at the university.

Elliot Lasher

Lasher is one of the members of the American Events department at the university.

Eric Massingale

Massingale is a former microchip salesman now teaching in the computer science department. When Jack runs into him at the hardware megastore, Massingale says that Jack does not seem as imposing outside the academic context as he does at school.

Orest Mercator

Orest Mercator is Heinrich's friend, a nineteen-year-old high school senior who is in training to sit in a cage with poisonous snakes, hoping to set a world record. Ultimately, he sits in a hotel room with three non-poisonous snakes and, after being bitten, disappears. Heinrich idolizes him at first but, after his failure, regards him with disdain. Mercator is a weak reflection of Jack. In himself, he is nothing. As Jack takes on a persona because of his association with Hitler, so Orest hopes to take on importance through his association with dangerous snakes.

Willie Mink

Mink appears at the end of the novel under his own name. Earlier, Jack and Babette refer to him as Mr. Gray. He is the inventor of Dylar, the medication supposed to effect relief from fear of death. Babette answers his ad in a tabloid and carries on a sexual relationship with him in order to obtain the medication. When Jack finally encounters him, Mink is holed up in a motel room watching television and scarfing down Dylar. After Jack shoots him and, thinking he

is dead, plants the gun in his hand to make it look like suicide, Mink shoots Jack in the wrist. Mink represents the banality and futility of the attempt to evade death.

Bob Pardee

Babette's ex-husband, he is Denise's father and appears briefly, practicing his golf swing and taking the kids to dinner.

Winnie Richards

Winnie Richards is a neurochemist at the college with a reputation for brilliance and evasiveness. She runs wherever she goes in order not to be seen. Jack gives her a Dylar capsule to analyze, but she cannot identify its contents. She advises Jack that awareness of death is important and ought not to be avoided. Unlike most of the characters in the novel, she is not concerned with her image. In fact, she wishes to avoid being seen.

Janet Savory

Janet Savory is one of Jack's former wives and is Heinrich's mother. She had been a foreign currency analyst but abandoned that career, entered an ashram, and changed her name to Mother Devi.

Murray Jay Siskind

Murray is a New York Jewish intellectual and a visiting lecturer in the American Events department at the university. His specialty is Elvis Presley. He lives in a rooming house, fantasizes about late night liaisons with a dominatrix, and studies children, transvestites, and popular culture in order to get a sense of the American experience. Jack confides his fear of death to Murray. Murray is interested in the influence of images on culture, but not with his own image. He observes, rather than projects, images.

Steffie

Jack's pre-teen daughter, Steffie, who is younger than Denise, is moved by the calamities she sees on television and participates in emergency drill simulations.

Alphonse Stompanato

Stompanato is the chair of the American Events department at the college. He puts down his colleagues and has the general demeanor of a thug. He has the same name as the movie actress Lana Turner's underworld boyfriend, Johnny

Stompanato; Johnny Stompanato was stabbed to death by Turner's daughter when he attacked Turner.

Adele T.

Mentioned briefly, she is a psychic whom the police employ to find missing people and things. She always finds something, but it is always something other than what the police were immediately seeking.

Gladys Treadwell

She is the sister of the old blind man to whom Babette reads. Jack reads her obituary along with several others as he thinks about his own death.

Mr. Treadwell

Mr. Treadwell is a blind man. Babette reads to him from supermarket tabloids. He and his sister get lost in an abandoned cookie store in a mall and are thought to be dead before they are found.

Wilder

Babette's two year old son, Wilder, speaks little and seems to have a deeper understanding of being alive than the rest of his family. He watches water boil, cries for almost seven hours one day, crosses a dangerous highway on his tricycle without injury. Wilder is a comfort to Babette just by his existence, particularly, she says, because he does not yet talk. Wilder is the one who shows Jack death in the form of Babette's father waiting for him in the garden.

THEMES

The Blandness of Vicarious Experience

Experience in *White Noise* is, in large measure, bland, vicarious, and determined by the mass media, that is by those who simulate reality for popular consumption. The Gladney family's main sources of stimulation are watching television, listening to the radio, and going to the supermarket and the mall, where they listen to live Muzak, that is, to a live performance of music designed to sound canned. Steffie mouths the words the actors speak as she watches them on television. Reality is filtered through tabloids. Disasters are simulated and, when a real disaster occurs, it has the look of a movie. Even Jack's

TOPICS FOR FURTHER STUDY

- Jack and Heinrich discuss whether our actions are the results of our free will or of our brain chemistry and genetics. Write a research paper detailing the state of contemporary thought among biologists, psychologists, and philosophers regarding the forces that determine human actions.

- If you can, get a copy of the films *Weekend*, *Pierrot Le Fou*, or *Alphaville*, by Jean-Luc Godard, on DVD or video. Prepare a presentation for your class showing some stylistic and thematic similarities between one of these films and *White Noise*.

- A toxic disaster is at the center of *White Noise*. Compile a list of actual environmental disasters that have occurred since 1980 and discuss their social, ecological, and industrial effects, as well as the effect they have had on individuals. What is the progress or lack of progress in dealing with these disasters?

- Construct a questionnaire about death and anxiety about death. Using your questionnaire, interview people of varying ages and report your findings in an essay.

plot to kill Willie Mink is set up like a parody of a B movie. Only Wilder, whose name suggests an uncivilized state, and who is preverbal, seems to be in touch with authentic experience whether it is crying from the depth of his soul as an existential act, or weeping in front of the television, or facing the danger of a crowded highway.

Death, Fear of Death, and Attraction to Death

Death, a pervasive theme throughout the novel, is first introduced in Jack and Babette's conversation about who will die first. Later, both confess their terrible fear of death after Denise discovers Babette's Dylar pills and Jack finally learns that Dylar is supposed to suppress the fear of death. The toxic event brings death into the foreground of the town's landscape and to the foreground of Jack's consciousness until it becomes his obsession. The near crash of an airplane, preceding the chemical spill, is a harbinger of that disaster. Heinrich's friend Orest attempts to expose himself to death as he prepares to sit in a cage with poisonous snakes. Lecturing to his class and discussing the plot to kill Hitler, Jack asserts that "all plots tend to move deathward," a hypothesis which, whether valid or not, forecasts the momentum and direction of the plot of *White Noise*. Echoing the closing words of James Joyce's story "The Dead," the last words of *White Noise* are "and the dead."

Free Will versus Determinism

Inside the context of a society in which people's attitudes and behaviors are shaped and propelled by mass media, the age-old conflict between free will and determinism (the belief that human behavior is not a result of an individual's will, but of superior, unseen forces outside of the individual's control, whether divine, social, or chemical), takes on renewed importance. The problem is the subject of a conversation between Jack and Heinrich as they discuss the serial killer Tommy Roy Foster.

Consumerism

As a kind of white or background noise, *White Noise* presents a continual flow of allusions to consumer products and brand names, indicators of the pervasive environment surrounding Americans in the latter part of the twentieth century. People themselves, Jack and his academic colleagues, for example, are also presented as competing, marketable products. Consumption, in the novel, becomes a means of vicarious experience. The characters in the novel are defined by the cultural markers they ingest rather than by something essential about themselves.

The Constant Presence of Catastrophe

The possibility of catastrophe is juxtaposed throughout the novel with the habitual blandness of daily life. Airplane crashes, toxic spills, a memory of Nazi atrocities, and a murder plot all take place against a background of dull routines and vicarious, media stimulation. Daily life seems to be a continuous effort to evade mortality and repress awareness of death. Through catastrophe, the repressed is ever present.

Repressed Violence

Although overt violence enters into the plot with Jack's assault on Willie Mink, violence in *White Noise* is usually of a repressed sort. Alphonse Stompanato bullies the members of his department, the television reports a backyard gravesite, Vernon Dickey is obsessed by guns, Murray glamorizes car crashes, and both the shadow of Nazism and industrial disaster hover over the lives of the characters in the novel.

STYLE

Cinematic Construction

Narrative in *White Noise* often imitates cinematic form, rather than literary form. Juxtaposition of elements often replaces expository presentation. As family members gather, for example, their activities may be punctuated with snippets of phrases coming from the radio or television playing in the background, just the way music fades in and out of the scenes in a film. Often, transitions between scenes in the novel are lacking and are instead replaced by cuts (a jarring move from one thing to the next). This is a common device in movies. In addition, many scenes in the novel have a filmic feel. The long evacuation chapter is reminiscent of such scenes in disaster movies.

Satire

DeLillo is a satirist targeting the inauthenticity of life as lived in contemporary society. His technique is to highlight events so common that they often are accepted without thought and to present truly uncommon and frightening events, like the toxic spill, as routine. He salts the narrative with random, free-standing words, product names, and phrases from television and radio, as if they were floating in the air, as if they were themselves escaped toxic particles. In addition, DeLillo actually composes the sorts of items that actually do appear in supermarket tabloids, stretching the genre only slightly. These intrusive bits are not explained. They are not presented as ideas about contemporary reality. They are presented without connectives so that they actually impose themselves on the narrative as pieces of reality.

Power Station beside the Rhine River *(Lars Baron / Getty Images)*

Random and Trivial Details

Punctuating the narration throughout the novel, becoming part of the narration, is a presentation of the landscape of daily life, snatches of phrases from the radio or the television, descriptions of the washer or dryer spinning or tumbling the laundry, descriptions of traffic jams, of computer terminals or of printouts, or even of the detritus left in garbage compactors. There are also continuously intruding trivial details. When Jack and Murray, for example, are leaving Murray's rooming house in chapter 8, Murray stops to tell the landlord about a leaking faucet.

HISTORICAL CONTEXT

Hitler

Adolph Hitler, 1889–1945, leader of Germany's National Socialist German Workers Party (the Nazi Party), became chancellor of Germany in 1933. The following year, he consolidated his power through terror and by murdering his opponents. In 1938, Hitler annexed Austria and the Sudetenland in Czechoslovakia. With the German invasion of Poland in 1939, World War II and Hitler's quest for world domination, began in earnest. Emblematic of the evil of the Hitler regime were the concentration camps and death camps established for the incarceration and extermination of people abhorrent to the Nazis. More than ten million people—Gypsies, Communists, homosexuals, and Jews—were tortured and exterminated by the Germans in these camps.

The Reagan Years

Ronald Reagan was inaugurated in January, 1981, as president of the United States and was re-elected in 1984. The years of his presidency are reflected in *White Noise*. The Reagan years were characterized in general by a feel-good consumerism of the sort DeLillo depicts along with a media infiltration of consciousness that allowed appearance to become more compelling than reality. Reagan, for example, told a story about how a brave pilot behaved during World

COMPARE
&
CONTRAST

- **1980s:** Although they publicly proclaim that the United States will never make a deal with Iran to supply arms for hostages, President Ronald Reagan and his administration do the exact opposite. This fact is not overtly reported by mass media.

  Today: In 2002, President George W. Bush and his administration mistakenly claim that Iraq has weapons of mass destruction and is connected to the 2001 bombing of the World Trade Center. The strategy allows them to begin the Iraq War in 2003. In 2007, they claim that the Iranian government is secretly in the process of developing nuclear weapons. While the former is not overtly reported by the mass media until well after the Iraq War has begun, the latter is indeed reported by the mass media.

- **1980s:** Environmental disasters like the toxic gas leak in Bhopal, India, the nuclear meltdown in Chernobyl, Ukraine, and the dioxin contamination in Times Beach, Missouri, are shocking examples of the dangers of the careless handling of complex industrial technology.

  Today: Increased environmental safety standards and legislation reduce the occurrence of large-scale environmental disasters such as those that occurred in the 1980s. Nevertheless, small-scale industrial pollution may be contributing to climate change, the effects of which will eventually lead to environmental disaster.

- **1980s:** The power of the mass media, and especially of television, is widespread. It affects the political, cultural, and commercial behavior of the majority of the population.

  Today: The decentralization of media through advances in technology (such as the Internet) does not diminish the power and influence of the major media companies. In many instances, it only strengthens it by providing more outlets for standardized content. At the same time, the Internet does present an opportunity to communicate alternative points of view.

War II when, in fact, he was recalling the plot of the 1944 film *A Wing and a Prayer*.

Talk Radio

Since its inception, there have been people who spoke over the radio. Talk Radio, however, usually refers to a specific genre. Talk Radio of the kind that Babette habitually listens to involves a regular host who takes calls from listeners about a number of subjects, although most often about politics and cultural issues, or psychological and interpersonal issues. This format became dominant in the 1980s and has continued to grow until many radio programs adhere to it.

Industrial Accidents

On December 3, 1984, a Union Carbide pesticide plant located in the Indian city of Bhopal released forty tons of methyl isocyanate gas when a holding tank overheated and exploded in the wee hours of the morning. Over 2,500 people were killed and more than 100,000 people's health was affected. On April 26, 1986, at 1:23 a.m., a nuclear reactor at the Chernobyl Nuclear power plant in Ukraine, then part of the Soviet Union, exploded. The explosion sent highly radioactive material into the atmosphere in a plume like the one DeLillo describes in his novel. More than 330,000 people in the immediate area of the Chernobyl plant were evacuated; this disaster had an immediate death toll of 56, with nearly 10,000 believed to have died due to radiation exposure. The toxic radioactive material was spread by wind over the Soviet Union, Eastern, Northern, and Western

A shopping cart in a supermarket (© *Jim Zuckerman* / *Alamy*)

Europe, and possibly as far as eastern North America. This was not the first nuclear accident in the world. On March 28, 1979, at about 4:00 a.m., a meltdown occurred at the Three Mile Island Unit 2 nuclear power plant near Middletown, Pennsylvania. While there were several operator errors that exacerbated the accident, the core meltdown did not breach the containment building's walls. Some radioactive gases were believed to have escaped, however no deaths have been linked to this incident with certainty. A different, but no less compelling, disaster occurred on March 24, 1989, around midnight, when the oil tanker *Exxon Valdez* struck a reef in Prince William Sound. The tanker spilled nearly eleven million gallons of crude oil into the sea in Alaska that was home to salmon, seals, great white sharks, otters, and sea birds. The remoteness of the spill's location severely hampered the cleanup effort. These are but a few of the disasters that have marked and continue to mark the course of recent industrial and social history.

CRITICAL OVERVIEW

White Noise is DeLillo's eighth novel, and it won the 1985 National Book Award. It is considered to be the novel that brought DeLillo's work into the mainstream of contemporary American literature. Indeed, David Cowart reports in *Don DeLillo: The Physics of Language* that "*White Noise* has generated more critical attention than any other DeLillo novel." In the introduction to *New Essays on White Noise*, Frank Lentricchia observes that DeLillo is a novelist of ideas whose novels "are montages of tones, styles, and voices that have the effect of yoking together terror and wild humor." Lentricchia also comments on DeLillo's portrayal of "the essential tone of contemporary America." DeLillo's characters are, he argues, "expressions of—and responses to—specific historical processes." Michael Valdez Moses, also writing in *New Essays on White Noise*, argues that "*White Noise* is DeLillo's exploration of an America in which technology has become not merely a pervasive and mortal threat to each of its citizens, but also ... a deeply ingrained mode of existing and

WHAT DO I READ NEXT?

- Produced in 1986 (a year after the publication of *White Noise*), DeLillo's first play, *The Day Room*, is also an exploration of anxiety about death.

- Allen Ginsberg's "A Supermarket in California" (1955) is a phantasmagorical re-creation of a supermarket. The poem establishes the supermarket as a symbolic representation of America.

- Daniel Jonah Goldhagen's *Hitler's Willing Executioners* (1996) is a grim account of the role that the ordinary citizens of Germany played in the extermination of European Jewry.

- Paul Goodman's epic novel *The Empire City* (1959) explores American society and the values that guided or conflicted with it during the twenty-year period in which the novel was written.

- Norman Mailer's *An American Dream* (1965) is a portrait of America as it is idealized and is also a portrait of what Mailer saw as its raw corrupt actuality.

- Leo Tolstoy's 1886 novella *The Death of Ivan Ilych* explores the terror of death, the strain of enduring that terror, and the meaning of death in the construction of the meaning of life.

- Albert Camus's *The Plague* (1947) concerns the outbreak of a plague in an Algerian city and contemplates the problems of living in a world that is essentially irrational and stripped of meaning.

way of thinking that is the characteristic feature of the republic." Mark Osteen, in *American Magic and Dread: Don DeLillo's Dialogue with Culture*, states that "the characters of *White Noise* try to counteract dread by mouthing chants and litanies, practicing pseudo-religious rituals, crafting narratives that deflect or purge their fear, [and] performing violent or death-defying actions."

CRITICISM

Neil Heims

Heims is a writer and teacher living in Paris. In the following essay, Heims discusses the importance of style as content in White Noise.

White Noise is narrated by Jack Gladney, the college professor and specialist in Hitler studies, who explores what it is like to be alive in a world where life is devitalized and where being alive means becoming a consumable image. As he and his family are inside a mall, eating, "a band played live Muzak." Muzak is, by definition, recorded music of an essentially bland and seemingly unassuming nature that is piped into public spaces, usually shopping centers or elevators. Its general purpose is twofold, to sooth customers and, by enhancing the shopping environment, to stimulate them to buy things, even things they had never thought they wanted. The idea of live Muzak is an oxymoron, a yoking of contradictory terms. Nevertheless, it is clear that by refurbishing and updating the perennial insight that life imitates art, DeLillo is establishing a purposeful symbol.

Within the phrase "live Muzak" one of the novel's governing patterns of construction can be found. The live performance is a simulation. It is something real pretending to be something artificial, consequently conferring more authenticity to the artificial than it actually has. The actual, in fact, is in decline throughout *White Noise*. The actual is undermined by the media, the home of the ersatz (fake), and it is threatened by an increasing number of catastrophes that make actual experience less desirable than simulations. Actual experience, unmediated by style, is fraught with anxiety and difficulty. Style indicates a denial of anxiety and difficulty. It is an end run around death.

Indeed, Jack wonders why Babette's students, mostly senior citizens, want to improve their posture. He concludes that "we seem to believe it is possible to ward off death by following rules of good grooming." But, as with Jack and Babette, the fact of death is inescapable. It lodges deep within their psyches when it is forced out of their surrounding world. Of himself, Jack says: "I am the false character that follows the name around." He is the simulation of the person he tries to project, the person he would like to be rather than the one he is, or at least the person whom he would like others to think he is.

> RATHER THAN HOLDING A MIRROR UP TO NATURE (AS MOST WRITERS DO), IN *WHITE NOISE*, DELILLO HOLDS A MIRROR UP TO A MIRROR AND THEREBY MIRRORS THE MIRROR OF A CULTURE THAT HAS USURPED THE POWER AND THE AUTHORITY OF NATURE."

Jack represents a person whose reality is the result of his style, not of his content. His persona is a matter of his mastery of surface presentation rather than the expression of something deep-seated, the representation of a real personality. The paradox is, however, that style becomes content; persona becomes personality. Yet, as in Jack's case, the inadequacy of image when substance is essential creates a gnawing sense of insecurity, general inadequacy, and inauthenticity that express themselves symptomatically through his fear of death. Moreover, the deception achieved by style may be insufficient. When Jack runs into a colleague at a hardware megastore, his colleague comments that without his academic robe and dark glasses, "you look so harmless. ... A big, harmless, aging, indistinct sort of guy." Although Jack denies taking offense at his colleague's observation, he immediately pays for the "rope and hurr[ies] out the door." Jack then states that "the encounter put me in the mood to shop." This is odd, unless one realizes that shopping is a way of fortifying the power of style and of merging one's own individuality with, and surrendering it to, a received social image.

Jack notes "my family gloried in the event. I was one of them, shopping, at last." Of the effect of shopping, Jack says that "the more money I spent, the less important it seemed. I was bigger than these sums. ... These sums ... came back to me in the form of existential credit." A sense of sufficiency, of actually existing as oneself, is achieved through the sense of existing as the mirror image of oneself, the image that one wishes to see, the image achieved through conforming to the images that consumer culture projects.

What defines *White Noise* as a novel, as well as Jack's character and those of the others in the book, is its style rather than its content. The story in the book is, after all, simple, almost a contrivance of clichés rather than a story. The subject matter, too, is conventional, the sort of warning against consumerism, technology, alienation, and the loss of abiding values that can be seen in the works of such varying social critics as Vance Packard, Norman Mailer, C. Wright Mills, Neil Postman, or Paul Goodman.

In *White Noise*, a blended upper-middle class American family finds its daily routines shaken by the occurrence of the kind of industrial disaster that has become all too common over the last half century. The characters are familiar, if not stereotypical. To the degree that they become recognizable as individuals to readers, they do so because of DeLillo's skill in evoking stereotypes, that is, in creating convincingly familiar caricatures. The narrator and protagonist is an apparently comfortable college professor actually beset by anxiety about his lack of an imposing persona and a gnawing fear of death. He hides these anxieties under his style. His wife is a faculty wife who spends her days doing volunteer work, jogging, trying to eat well and not resume smoking, and tangentially tending to her family. She, too, is hiding a secret terror of death.

Fourteen-year-old Heinrich is a conventional nerd, a balding intellectual who doubts the possibility of the certainty of perception, yet he is a repository of factoids and is endlessly curious about the world around him. Denise and Steffie are regulation sitcom daughters. Denise is tart and bossy, but at heart she is worried about both her parents. She worries about whether Babette is secretly taking medication or exposing herself to carcinogens. Denise is concerned about her father, Bob Pardee, and his ability to hold a job and earn his living. Steffie is tender-hearted but also fearful. The baby, Wilder, embodies the magical life force often attributed to preverbal infancy. Meanwhile, Jack's academic colleagues are caricatures of neurotic, one-upping, self-aggrandizing professionals. Their trivial competitions in identifying pop phenomena at lunch reveal their grave, unacknowledged personal insecurities; their boasts about the death-defying stunts they have performed indicate their own repressed anxiety about death. They tempt the thing they fear and gain strength from eluding it at the last minute.

The action of the novel begins as a reflection of suburban life, segues into the kind of scenario found in disaster movies, and ends with a sort of film noir cat-and-mouse encounter between Jack and a man with the suggestive name of Willie Mink, who represents the forces of sex and death. The dialogue is a collage of common, even clichéd speech. The themes of death, insecurity, social malaise, and alienation—important in themselves—are, nevertheless, common, and are referred to rather than considered. They appear like Woody Allen's quirky one-liners, hooks, rather than thoughtful analyses. They constitute the decor of the novel rather than its subject.

The social environment evoked by the novel is derived from the televised representation of the world rather than from the world as it is experienced by individuals. Rather than holding a mirror up to nature (as most writers do), in *White Noise*, DeLillo holds a mirror up to a mirror and thereby mirrors the mirror of a culture that has usurped the power and the authority of nature. The triumph of style over content, of image over reality, of imitation over spontaneity and authenticity, of simulacra over nature, in effect, cripples or limits the range and power of the senses and, consequently, the capacity for experience and action.

The only authentic experience in the novel, the horror of Hitler's catastrophic battle against everything human and humane, exists merely in the background. The unspeakable horror is presented as a shadow, something Jack can approach only within an academic frame, as trivialized tidbits of gossip. He uses Nazism in order to exploit it for his own aggrandizement; it is something he never experiences in its terribleness. In a world where image trumps reality, equations between Hitler and Elvis Presley can be offered without embarrassment. Nor does the horror of the Holocaust ever enter into the world of the novel.

DeLillo, it seems, quite consciously borrowed the style of *White Noise* from the movies, particularly from the cinema of the great New Wave filmmaker Jean-Luc Godard. Eschewing sequence and linearity in his films, Godard introduced a technique of disjunction that allowed him to juxtapose sequences and images that go against a sequential narrative flow. Similarly, in *White Noise*, DeLillo harnesses disparate elements that exist in a disjunctive, coexistent, but alienated relationship with each other. The jumble of modern life that results from an overload

> JACK GLADNEY, THEN, IS BOTH 'TIMELESSLY' SEARCHING FOR UNIFICATION AND ARBITRARILY FRAGMENTED."

of information is reflected in *White Noise*. By this means, the novel offers a critique not only of information but of the information age itself, not by any expository argument but simply by an overwhelming accumulation of details. Radio and television sound bites are transcribed, cable TV bills reproduced, supermarket tabloid stories recounted, supermarket products described; the accidents of contemporary reality that tend to render everything absurd are represented.

Source: Neil Heims, Critical Essay on *White Noise*, in *Novels for Students*, Gale, Cengage Learning, 2009.

Lou F. Caton

In the following essay, Caton explores the elements of romanticism and postmodernism that can be found in White Noise.

A critical exploration of romanticism in Don DeLillo's eighth novel *White Noise* may initially seem misguided or odd. And yet, some of the values and topics commonly associated with popular notions of romanticism, like sympathy, unity, authenticity, and an interest in the "unknown," do emerge in this supposedly postmodern novel. They emerge not from overarching themes but rather from the common thoughts and desires associated with the novel's viewpoint character, Jack Gladney. By judging such characterization as romantic, that is, supportive of these broad transhistorical values, I find a deeply qualified postmodernism within *White Noise*.

Granted, in spite of these observations, a first response to DeLillo's fiction is probably not romantic; after all, his novels frequently show contemporary society struggling with a nostalgic palimpsest of old-fashion values that have been layered over by the textual, semiotic materialism of marketing, commodification, and computer codes. Cited as quintessentially postmodern, DeLillo reportedly writes a novel of simulacra with an endless regress of mediation. John Frow portrays DeLillo's curiosity here about simulation and iteration as "a world of primary representations which neither precede nor follow the real but are themselves real..." Bruce Bawer has gone so far as to claim that DeLillo merely presents "one discouraging battery after another of pointless, pretentious rhetoric. [DeLillo] does not develop ideas so much as juggle jargon." Paul Cantor directly calls sections of *White Noise* "self-reflexive" and "mediated;" a bit later, he claims *White Noise* transforms the "autonomous self" into the "inauthentic self."

Clearly such declarations portray DeLillo as uninterested in old-fashion romantic notions like a mysterious unknown or authenticity and sympathy. However, this sentiment centers itself on DeLillo's cultural critiques, his novel's "messages," while disregarding the possibility of any romantic human nature in his characters. For instance, John Kucich quickly looks past the psychology of DeLillo's male characters by stating only that they "persist" in the outdated belief that "oppositional stances can be differentiated and justified." Kucich, in other words, sees DeLillo's characters naively embracing the tired belief that cultural difference can be adjudicated, that a truth-system of correspondences can still order the arbitrary nature of reality. Such views by these characters must be devalued, according to Kucich, because DeLillo's larger postmodern message denies the possibility of truth statements; the supposed central idea of *White Noise* is that a romantic, nostalgic character like Jack Gladney is only deceiving himself. The novel forecloses on a character's romantic desires as it erects a technological society where metaphysical truth is replaced by the materialistic codes of media and capitalism. The hard truth for DeLillo, Kucich and others seem to say, is that Gladney's romantic belief in a unified, shared definition of cultural truth no longer exists.

What such an argument misses, though, is that DeLillo's romantic characterizations turn what might otherwise be thought of as an already clearly developed ideological position into a complex problem. Kucich is certainly right in stating that Gladney does believe in the unfashionable notion of an orderly universe; however, such a belief operates in healthy opposition to the postmodern anxiety within *White Noise*. Gladney's romantic assumptions regarding family unity and sympathy must be analyzed on their own merits; such views are

more than mere foils for the novel's worries about mediation and representation.

In effect, I am contesting Frank Lentricchia's observation that DeLillo is a political writer who "stands in harsh judgment against American fiction of the last couple of decades, that soft humanist underbelly of American literature..." This "humanist" tradition that DeLillo supposedly critiques is, among other things, a tradition that invokes transhistorical notions of consciousness (thus, romantic as well as humanist notions are being maligned here). According to Lentricchia, DeLillo's mind is made up; he advocates a contemporary political position which dismantles the mystified rhetoric of universals and timeless values about human nature:

> But the deep action of this kind of fiction [the non-DeLillo, old-fashion, transhistorical kind] is culturally and historically rootless, an expression of the possibilities of "human nature," here, now, forever, as ever. This is realism maybe in the old philosophical sense of the word, when they affirmed that only the universals are real.

Lentricchia presents DeLillo as already convinced, the problem of the romantic (i.e. transhistorical beliefs) and the postmodern having already been resolved; DeLillo becomes a cultural worker writing within a skeptical, antinomian tradition that prevents "readers from gliding off into the comfortable sentiment that the real problems of the human race have always been about what they are today."

Lentricchia is wrong here; DeLillo's novels *question* rather than *endorse* this historicist stance. The transhistorical perspective entangles the historical; their supposed separate spheres, I intend to demonstrate, rely on rather than compete against each other. Jack Gladney the naive sentimentalist, foil of the postmodernist (who still insists on universals, human nature, and the mythology of a human nature), recognizes but mourns the emergence of a constructed political postmodern culture (which rejects any universal subjectivity and sees all knowledge as interested and ideological). In appreciation of this conflict, DeLillo maintains a romantic uncertainty throughout *White Noise*.

Each of the following three scenes presents evidence for this uncertain romanticism composing the character of Jack Gladney. On the one hand, he is a traditionally unified character: a romantic who questions society but all along deeply values his personal relations and family.

He is a communal person who desires to tell a simple story about a man trying to understand the eternal human questions of life. His is, as DeLillo describes him, "a reasonable and inquiring voice—the voice of a man who seeks genuinely to understand some timeless human riddle."

Colliding with that, however, is his other growing awareness: that the world is turning him into a post-industrial, computer generated individual, someone who is slowly gaining a "non-authentic self" which is socially constructed, essentially valueless, and enveloped by an unstable matrix of material goods. This becomes clear to him when the SIMUVAC attendant reminds Jack that he is only "the sum total of [his] data. No man escapes that."

Jack Gladney, then, is both "timelessly" searching for unification and arbitrarily fragmented. This double-self, a self both materially *constructed* by a fragmented, commercial community and one authentically trying *to construct* a unified community, reflects the movement of the introductory scene. The novel's first paragraph uses the possessions of a college student to enact this clash of values about identity formation.

DeLillo's vision of cars as a stream of machines slowly weaving through a pastoral landscape implies that these students are products of an assembly-line culture. The opening procession of station wagons doubles as a mechanical pilgrimage or industrial wagon train. Similar to a metallic snake sliding and easing itself into the center of the university, the focus here is on the mechanical residue from the industrial age. Indeed, even the students appear to be machine-like as they "spring" out of their vehicles. Moreover, these students and parents seem not to stand in opposition to their possessions but, instead, to be themselves erected by these very same objects. Accenting their hard opacity, DeLillo refuses to give these students emotional and personal details; instead they are defined by the things that surround them. A college student seems, in this scene at least, to be a constructed product, not a transcendent being: "The stereo sets, radios, personal computers; small refrigerators and table ranges; the cartons of phonograph records and cassettes; the hairdryers and styling irons . . ."

And on and on. Eighteen lines of clothing, sporting equipment, electronics, grooming aids, and junk food, from nondescript "books" to specific "Kabooms" and "Mystic mints," the student becomes another commodity built from commodities. Even the parents seem propped up by this commercial world. They have "conscientious suntans" and "well-made faces."

However, these families do not simply add up to the products of an empty consumerism. DeLillo complicates the social constructivism of this scene with romantic, community matters; he sees the current obsession with materialism as ironically satisfying a deeper, spiritual urge. DeLillo completes the scene by brashly joining this consumerism with a unity provided by spiritual mad communal rhetoric: "The conscientious suntans. The well-made faces and wry looks. They feel a sense of renewal, of communal recognition . . . they are a collection of the likeminded and the spiritually akin, a people, a nation."

DeLillo here folds into the scene a dimension of spiritual identity. Our transcendent sense of who we are, the romantic desire to experience ourselves as part of a greater whole, strives for identity within the dynamics of capitalism. Even though the earlier emphasis on machinery would appear to devalue spiritual issues, DeLillo's combined use of religious and communal terms at the end of the scene reinstates these more metaphysical concerns. Instead of reading this mixture of social construction and spirituality as an ironic comment on the inferior position of religion in a postmodern world, one should interpret the scene as emphasizing the undying force of spiritual and communal urgings, whether fashionably inferior or not.

As things and students spill out, parents feel both renewed in a supersensible manner and materially affirmed; on the one hand, the virtuous and almost sacred gestalt of children and parents separating translates itself into the terms of material goods. Parents and students objectify this exalted moment. The parents are commodified by financial interests. DeLillo claims "something about them suggesting massive insurance coverage." Their money and things blend with all the other station wagons until they "earn" a sense of spiritual collectivism. And yet, on the other hand, students and parents do not uniquely accept this elite position of "buying" a college education; they also experience it as a celebratory, communal moment. The gathering of the wagons becomes almost a religious ceremony: "more than formal liturgies or laws." The upper-middle class has cashed in their material possessions for a taste of something which might have been denied them without the money to buy it: community and spirituality. The romantic desire for community may exist only ironically, only in this tainted capitalistic and privileged fashion; however, it still exists, resisting commodification and vying for its own legitimacy.

In the same manner of sensing spiritual desires among material possessions, DeLillo presents his viewpoint character, Jack Gladney, as being both essentially authentic and culturally constructed. Jack's narrative role as the story-teller infuses his cultural observations with a personal authority that makes it impossible to separate society's ills from Jack's personality. That is, DeLillo recognizes the influence of a psychological, unified ego, but simply sends it to the edges of the narrative; in its place a constructed, commodified lead character stalks center stage.

Jack Gladney speaks of himself only at the end of this first scene. His voice, seemingly of a single consciousness, feels subordinate, inferior to the grand reporting of the materiality of common things which preceded it. Indeed, even the description of the town takes precedence over any desire to humanize the ego of the only interior voice of the novel. In fact, the town itself is de-personalized, divested of any particular character; this dreary city called Blacksmith is home to a narrating voice as flat and common as the city itself.

Nothing seems very remarkable in Blacksmith. What details DeLillo gives are the details of sameness, of any small, college town: "There are houses in town...There are Greek revival and Gothic churches. There is an insane asylum with an elongated portico, ornamented dormers and a steeply pitched roof... There is an expressway ..." Not only does the town seem boring and sleepy but the method of using "there is" and "there are" is equally gloomy and uninspired. And yet such arid prose belies a deeper issue.

DeLillo counters this deadness with a brief, almost hidden recognition of the possibility of a mysterious, spiritual unknown. As the expressway traffic speeds by, it develops into "a remote and steady murmur around our sleep, as of dead souls babbling at the edge of a dream." Here the dead are mythically revived, muttering and rippling at the edge of consciousness. Their voices belong to past story-tellers who have refused to

be silenced. They represent an imaginary oversoul that resists this culture's particular ideology. The reference to souls and dreams babbling suggests an unknowable world of rivers and voices that refuses to be reified by the marketplace ethics of station wagons and stereos. The socially constructed world of commodification meets the myth of an universal consciousness that will not die.

This is the introductory conflict between matter and spirit embodied in the character of Jack Gladney. The immediate introduction of this viewpoint character is not metaphysical, philosophical, or even psychological but occupational: he is the chairman of Hitler studies. DeLillo offers a practical, materialistic definition of this narrator: he is what he produces; we are what our jobs say we are. However, like before, this recognition of material reality does not stand alone. DeLillo undercuts it with a closing sentimental, one might say "romantic," paragraph regarding lost dogs and cats. The concluding image in Jack Gladney's introduction arises in the crude, primitive vision of innocent youth. As the mechanized police in their "boxlike vehicles" prowl the streets, children cry for the intimacy of domestic animals: "On telephone poles all over town there are homemade signs concerning lost dogs and cats sometimes in the handwriting of a child."

DeLillo ends this first scene with one of the many romantic collisions that erupt throughout the novel. In this particular configuration the question is as follows: how can the desire to live in an innocent world persevere while at the same moment we experience ourselves as isolated, socially constructed, economic units? DeLillo retains this question, along with others, in order to inject a romantic mystery into *White Noise*.

A version of this same conflict reappears a few pages later when Jack and Murray visit the most photographed barn in America. Jack accompanies Murray as a student to a teacher. They approach the barn after seeing several signs declaring this barn to be "THE MOST PHOTOGRAPHED." Only the teacher talks; Jack listens silently to Murray's explanation as to why no one sees the "real" barn. For Murray, the commercial interests of marketing have replaced any natural, original, or unique qualities that the barn may have had: "Once you've seen the signs about the barn," Murray instructs, "it becomes impossible to see the barn." Speaking like a McLuhan disciple, Murray claims that one can never see the barn; one can only experience it as a consumer. Its marketplace representation as a commodity overrides any hopes of seeing the original, unaffected, unadulterated "barn." Murray's declaration that perception is predicated on economic forces links the viewer to that collective consciousness of consumerism. As with the students and parents in the previous scene above, forms of mass-marketing construct how we experience the world. And yet this selling and buying motif continually collides with Jack's spiritual desires.

In the post-Christian era, we religiously embrace whatever image popular culture devises for us; in this case, DeLillo's characters see themselves as consumers. They are financially essential, not only targeted but coveted by business strategists. Our objectified, exchange-value lives are sacred in the world of commerce. And that world of profit-and-loss commodification becomes the world from which they define themselves, according to Murray. It is one's information-age identity. Murray glories in this obscene recognition of a capitalistic spirituality:

> "Being here is a kind of spiritual surrender. We see only what the others see. The thousands who were here in the past, those who will come in the future. We've agreed to be part of a collective perception. This literally colors our vision. A religious experience in a way, like all tourism."

Business and tourist interests merge into a spiritual and collective recognition of consumerism: "We're not here to capture an image, we're here to maintain one. Every photograph reinforces the aura. Can you feel it. Jack? An accumulation of nameless energies."

Murray's "nameless energies" are the combined forces of spiritual desire and advertizing [sic] expertise. The barn represents a new-age mix of spirituality, media, and cultural constructions. Murray accelerates his pitch until his voice becomes that of a postmodern preacher; he basks in his realization that the contemporary consciousness has been manipulated and formed by advertising executives. We are what advertisements have made us: "'We can't get outside the aura,' Murray exclaims gleefully. 'We're part of the aura. We're here, we're now.' He seemed immensely pleased by this."

The economic representation has itself *become* the object. In fact, the conventional ontological object, the barn as a romantic object, dissolves. Jack is left only with perception. Frank Lentricchia contends that this scene presents a "strange new world where the object of perception is perception itself. What they view is the view of the thing." The experience of a correspondence between an object and its mental image has been altered; a single representative activity has faded into a fascination for an endless egress of images that forever occlude the original object.

Murray's upbeat mood regarding these disclosures underscores by contrast Jack's silence. Rather than jubilation, Jack registers caution and a death-like voicelessness. After all, this play involving the real versus the simulation also implies a loss, a kind of moral fall. For Murray, the primacy of simulation brilliantly bankrupts any urge to locate an original, romantic object. For Jack, however, the moment is less celebratory. His reticence implies a resistance to this contemporary account of a world empty of stable realities and non-commodified experiences. Jack's behavior later in the novel will confirm that, for him, the commodification of culture's self-referring systems of codes and arbitrary signifiers has not replaced or destroyed the spiritual myths of community and authenticity. Indeed, it is Jack's recognition of the potential, divine loss involved with Murray's analysis that propels the narrative toward these romantic themes.

Finally, I want to use my last scene to highlight how the romantic and communal base of Jack's personality challenges any totalized vision of a postmodern relativistic universe. In this third scene, DeLillo moves to his largest question: How can one communicate in a radically indeterminate world? Jack's exchange with his son Heinrich demonstrates the emotional cost around such a crucial contemporary dilemma.

Jack begins this scene in the role of an empiricist. The world can be known and trusted, he seems to say; it is not fundamentally a theoretical construct but, instead, a knowable and physical environment displaying somewhat predictable natural laws. He enters into a confrontation with his son in an effort to answer a simple question: Is it or is it not raining? The replies lead to a comic, and sometimes absurd, interchange while Jack drives Heinrich to school:

"It's raining now," I said.

"The radio said tonight..."

"Look at the windshield," I said. "Is that rain or isn't it?"

"I'm only telling you what they said."

"Just because it's on the radio doesn't mean we have to suspend belief in the evidence of our senses."

Heinrich's responses are deeply skeptical and distrustful; his answer to the question depends not on what he can see or assume but on the meteorologist speaking through the radio, an expert who clearly claims that it will rain later, not now. Thus, Heinrich defers his answer to Jack's question as to whether or not it is raining at that exact moment: "I would[n]'t want to have to say," he demurely replies.

Heinrich's non-answer frustrates Jack. His desire to gain assent from his son in regards to this banal but ingenuous question represents a common fatherly effort to meet with a son in conversation. For Jack, the question has little to do with rain but more to do with his romantic desire to join with his son in an appreciation of an intimate and shared physical event. Heinrich, instead, plays the mixed role of relativist, materialist, and cynical skeptic. He views the question not as a social, communal event but as a request for exact information, for verifiable data. Jack, however, pushes him to informally affirm the rain in order to achieve a simple, everyday, familial union; he wants confirmation of their common ground. Why not meet through the faith in our universal human situation, our shared physical senses, Jack seems to ask. Heinrich answers as a doubtful contemporary critic, not a son: "Our senses? Our senses are wrong a lot more often than they're right. This has been proved in the laboratory."

The dialogue continues in this vein; Heinrich meets each of Jack's desires for affirmation and community with the well-known skepticism and undecidability of the postmodern theorist. In the age of deconstruction, all we can know is our inability to know. Even the common social bonding implied in a father and son conversation about the weather has been subverted into an academic debate about the principle of uncertainty:

"You're so sure that's rain. How do you know it's not sulfuric acid from factories across the river? How do you know it's not fallout from a war in China? You want an answer here and now. Can you prove, here and now, that this stuff is rain? How do I know that what you call rain is really rain? What is rain anyway?"

Heinrich denies Jack the romantic bond of community between a father and son. This great theme of romance, the dialectic of love and union between a father and a son, becomes a nostalgic, outdated, dream for a naive world that no longer exists. And yet Jack's hunger to experience this common ground never dies in *White Noise*; in fact, it only gains authority as the novel progresses to its tragi-comical ending.

Source: Lou F. Caton, "Romanticism and the Postmodern Novel: Three Scenes from Don DeLillo's *White Noise*," in *English Language Notes*, Vol. 25, No. 1, September 1997, pp. 38–48.

SOURCES

Cowart, David, "Timor Mortis Conturbat Me," in *Don DeLillo: The Physics of Language*, University of Georgia Press, 2002, pp. 71–91.

DeLillo, Don, *White Noise*, Penguin, 1999.

Lentricchia, Frank, Introduction, in *New Essays on White Noise*, edited by Frank Lentricchia, Cambridge University Press, 1991, pp. 1–14.

Moses, Michael Valdez, "Lust Removed from Nature," in *New Essays on White Noise*, edited by Frank Lentricchia, Cambridge University Press, 1991, pp. 63–86.

Osteen, Mark, "The American Book of the Dead: Channeling *White Noise*," in *American Magic and Dread: Don DeLillo's Dialogue with Culture*, University of Pennsylvania Press, 2000, pp. 165–91.

FURTHER READING

Dewey, Joseph, *Beyond Grief and Nothing: A Reading of Don DeLillo*, University of South Carolina Press, 2006.
In this book, Dewey traces the development of the themes of retreat, recovery, and resurrection in DeLillo's fiction.

Lentricchia, Frank, ed., *Introducing Don DeLillo*, Duke University Press, 1994.
Lentricchia offers a collection of essays surveying DeLillo's themes and style. The volume also includes an interview with DeLillo.

McLuhan, Marshall, *The Mechanical Bride: Folklore of Industrial Man*, Vanguard Press, 1951.
The Mechanical Bride is a collection of observations on the popular culture of the United States during the first half of the twentieth

century, with particular attention paid to the language and imagery of advertisements.

————, *Understanding Media: The Extensions of Man*, McGraw Hill, 1964.

In this book, McLuhan explores the power of media, such as radio, television, and the telephone, to involve their users and to influence them psychically.

Glossary of Literary Terms

A

Abstract: As an adjective applied to writing or literary works, abstract refers to words or phrases that name things not knowable through the five senses.

Aestheticism: A literary and artistic movement of the nineteenth century. Followers of the movement believed that art should not be mixed with social, political, or moral teaching. The statement "art for art's sake" is a good summary of aestheticism. The movement had its roots in France, but it gained widespread importance in England in the last half of the nineteenth century, where it helped change the Victorian practice of including moral lessons in literature.

Allegory: A narrative technique in which characters representing things or abstract ideas are used to convey a message or teach a lesson. Allegory is typically used to teach moral, ethical, or religious lessons but is sometimes used for satiric or political purposes.

Allusion: A reference to a familiar literary or historical person or event, used to make an idea more easily understood.

Analogy: A comparison of two things made to explain something unfamiliar through its similarities to something familiar, or to prove one point based on the acceptedness of another. Similes and metaphors are types of analogies.

Antagonist: The major character in a narrative or drama who works against the hero or protagonist.

Anthropomorphism: The presentation of animals or objects in human shape or with human characteristics. The term is derived from the Greek word for "human form."

Anti-hero: A central character in a work of literature who lacks traditional heroic qualities such as courage, physical prowess, and fortitude. Anti-heroes typically distrust conventional values and are unable to commit themselves to any ideals. They generally feel helpless in a world over which they have no control. Anti-heroes usually accept, and often celebrate, their positions as social outcasts.

Apprenticeship Novel: See *Bildungsroman*

Archetype: The word archetype is commonly used to describe an original pattern or model from which all other things of the same kind are made. This term was introduced to literary criticism from the psychology of Carl Jung. It expresses Jung's theory that behind every person's "unconscious," or repressed memories of the past, lies the "collective unconscious" of the human race: memories of the countless typical experiences of our ancestors. These memories are said to prompt illogical associations that trigger powerful emotions in the reader. Often, the emotional process is primitive, even primordial. Archetypes are the literary images that grow out of the "collective unconscious." They appear in literature as incidents and plots that repeat basic patterns of life. They may also appear as stereotyped characters.

Avant-garde: French term meaning "vanguard." It is used in literary criticism to describe new writing that rejects traditional approaches to literature in favor of innovations in style or content.

B

Beat Movement: A period featuring a group of American poets and novelists of the 1950s and 1960s—including Jack Kerouac, Allen Ginsberg, Gregory Corso, William S. Burroughs, and Lawrence Ferlinghetti—who rejected established social and literary values. Using such techniques as stream of consciousness writing and jazz-influenced free verse and focusing on unusual or abnormal states of mind—generated by religious ecstasy or the use of drugs—the Beat writers aimed to create works that were unconventional in both form and subject matter.

Bildungsroman: A German word meaning "novel of development." The *bildungsroman* is a study of the maturation of a youthful character, typically brought about through a series of social or sexual encounters that lead to self-awareness. *Bildungsroman* is used interchangeably with *erziehungsroman*, a novel of initiation and education. When a *bildungsroman* is concerned with the development of an artist (as in James Joyce's *A Portrait of the Artist as a Young Man*), it is often termed a *kunstlerroman*.

Black Aesthetic Movement: A period of artistic and literary development among African Americans in the 1960s and early 1970s. This was the first major African-American artistic movement since the Harlem Renaissance and was closely paralleled by the civil rights and black power movements. The black aesthetic writers attempted to produce works of art that would be meaningful to the black masses. Key figures in black aesthetics included one of its founders, poet and playwright Amiri Baraka, formerly known as LeRoi Jones; poet and essayist Haki R. Madhubuti, formerly Don L. Lee; poet and playwright Sonia Sanchez; and dramatist Ed Bullins.

Black Humor: Writing that places grotesque elements side by side with humorous ones in an attempt to shock the reader, forcing him or her to laugh at the horrifying reality of a disordered world.

Burlesque: Any literary work that uses exaggeration to make its subject appear ridiculous, either by treating a trivial subject with profound seriousness or by treating a dignified subject frivolously. The word "burlesque" may also be used as an adjective, as in "burlesque show," to mean "striptease act."

C

Character: Broadly speaking, a person in a literary work. The actions of characters are what constitute the plot of a story, novel, or poem. There are numerous types of characters, ranging from simple, stereotypical figures to intricate, multifaceted ones. In the techniques of anthropomorphism and personification, animals—and even places or things—can assume aspects of character. "Characterization" is the process by which an author creates vivid, believable characters in a work of art. This may be done in a variety of ways, including (1) direct description of the character by the narrator; (2) the direct presentation of the speech, thoughts, or actions of the character; and (3) the responses of other characters to the character. The term "character" also refers to a form originated by the ancient Greek writer Theophrastus that later became popular in the seventeenth and eighteenth centuries. It is a short essay or sketch of a person who prominently displays a specific attribute or quality, such as miserliness or ambition.

Climax: The turning point in a narrative, the moment when the conflict is at its most intense. Typically, the structure of stories, novels, and plays is one of rising action, in which tension builds to the climax, followed by falling action, in which tension lessens as the story moves to its conclusion.

Colloquialism: A word, phrase, or form of pronunciation that is acceptable in casual conversation but not in formal, written communication. It is considered more acceptable than slang.

Coming of Age Novel: See *Bildungsroman*

Concrete: Concrete is the opposite of abstract, and refers to a thing that actually exists or a description that allows the reader to experience an object or concept with the senses.

Connotation: The impression that a word gives beyond its defined meaning. Connotations may be universally understood or may be significant only to a certain group.

Convention: Any widely accepted literary device, style, or form.

D

Denotation: The definition of a word, apart from the impressions or feelings it creates (connotations) in the reader.

Denouement: A French word meaning "the unknotting." In literary criticism, it denotes the resolution of conflict in fiction or drama. The *denouement* follows the climax and provides an outcome to the primary plot situation as well as an explanation of secondary plot complications. The *denouement* often involves a character's recognition of his or her state of mind or moral condition.

Description: Descriptive writing is intended to allow a reader to picture the scene or setting in which the action of a story takes place. The form this description takes often evokes an intended emotional response—a dark, spooky graveyard will evoke fear, and a peaceful, sunny meadow will evoke calmness.

Dialogue: In its widest sense, dialogue is simply conversation between people in a literary work; in its most restricted sense, it refers specifically to the speech of characters in a drama. As a specific literary genre, a "dialogue" is a composition in which characters debate an issue or idea.

Diction: The selection and arrangement of words in a literary work. Either or both may vary depending on the desired effect. There are four general types of diction: "formal," used in scholarly or lofty writing; "informal," used in relaxed but educated conversation; "colloquial," used in everyday speech; and "slang," containing newly coined words and other terms not accepted in formal usage.

Didactic: A term used to describe works of literature that aim to teach some moral, religious, political, or practical lesson. Although didactic elements are often found in artistically pleasing works, the term "didactic" usually refers to literature in which the message is more important than the form. The term may also be used to criticize a work that the critic finds "overly didactic," that is, heavy-handed in its delivery of a lesson.

Doppelganger: A literary technique by which a character is duplicated (usually in the form of an alter ego, though sometimes as a ghostly counterpart) or divided into two distinct, usually opposite personalities. The use of this character device is widespread in nineteenth- and twentieth-century literature, and indicates a growing awareness among authors that the "self" is really a composite of many "selves."

Double Entendre: A corruption of a French phrase meaning "double meaning." The term is used to indicate a word or phrase that is deliberately ambiguous, especially when one of the meanings is risqué or improper.

Dramatic Irony: Occurs when the audience of a play or the reader of a work of literature knows something that a character in the work itself does not know. The irony is in the contrast between the intended meaning of the statements or actions of a character and the additional information understood by the audience.

Dystopia: An imaginary place in a work of fiction where the characters lead dehumanized, fearful lives.

E

Edwardian: Describes cultural conventions identified with the period of the reign of Edward VII of England (1901-1910). Writers of the Edwardian Age typically displayed a strong reaction against the propriety and conservatism of the Victorian Age. Their work often exhibits distrust of authority in religion, politics, and art and expresses strong doubts about the soundness of conventional values.

Empathy: A sense of shared experience, including emotional and physical feelings, with someone or something other than oneself. Empathy is often used to describe the response of a reader to a literary character.

Enlightenment, The: An eighteenth-century philosophical movement. It began in France but had a wide impact throughout Europe and America. Thinkers of the Enlightenment valued reason and believed that both the individual and society could achieve a state of perfection. Corresponding to this essentially humanist vision was a resistance to religious authority.

Epigram: A saying that makes the speaker's point quickly and concisely. Often used to preface a novel.

Epilogue: A concluding statement or section of a literary work. In dramas, particularly those of the seventeenth and eighteenth centuries, the epilogue is a closing speech, often in verse, delivered by an actor at the end of a play and spoken directly to the audience.

Epiphany: A sudden revelation of truth inspired by a seemingly trivial incident.

Episode: An incident that forms part of a story and is significantly related to it. Episodes may be either self-contained narratives or events that depend on a larger context for their sense and importance.

Epistolary Novel: A novel in the form of letters. The form was particularly popular in the eighteenth century.

Epithet: A word or phrase, often disparaging or abusive, that expresses a character trait of someone or something.

Existentialism: A predominantly twentieth-century philosophy concerned with the nature and perception of human existence. There are two major strains of existentialist thought: atheistic and Christian. Followers of atheistic existentialism believe that the individual is alone in a godless universe and that the basic human condition is one of suffering and loneliness. Nevertheless, because there are no fixed values, individuals can create their own characters—indeed, they can shape themselves—through the exercise of free will. The atheistic strain culminates in and is popularly associated with the works of Jean-Paul Sartre. The Christian existentialists, on the other hand, believe that only in God may people find freedom from life's anguish. The two strains hold certain beliefs in common: that existence cannot be fully understood or described through empirical effort; that anguish is a universal element of life; that individuals must bear responsibility for their actions; and that there is no common standard of behavior or perception for religious and ethical matters.

Expatriates: See *Expatriatism*

Expatriatism: The practice of leaving one's country to live for an extended period in another country.

Exposition: Writing intended to explain the nature of an idea, thing, or theme. Expository writing is often combined with description, narration, or argument. In dramatic writing, the exposition is the introductory material which presents the characters, setting, and tone of the play.

Expressionism: An indistinct literary term, originally used to describe an early twentieth-century school of German painting. The term applies to almost any mode of unconventional, highly subjective writing that distorts reality in some way.

F

Fable: A prose or verse narrative intended to convey a moral. Animals or inanimate objects with human characteristics often serve as characters in fables.

Falling Action: See *Denouement*

Fantasy: A literary form related to mythology and folklore. Fantasy literature is typically set in non-existent realms and features supernatural beings.

Farce: A type of comedy characterized by broad humor, outlandish incidents, and often vulgar subject matter.

Femme fatale: A French phrase with the literal translation "fatal woman." A *femme fatale* is a sensuous, alluring woman who often leads men into danger or trouble.

Fiction: Any story that is the product of imagination rather than a documentation of fact. characters and events in such narratives may be based in real life but their ultimate form and configuration is a creation of the author.

Figurative Language: A technique in writing in which the author temporarily interrupts the order, construction, or meaning of the writing for a particular effect. This interruption takes the form of one or more figures of speech such as hyperbole, irony, or simile. Figurative language is the opposite of literal language, in which every word is truthful, accurate, and free of exaggeration or embellishment.

Figures of Speech: Writing that differs from customary conventions for construction, meaning, order, or significance for the purpose of a special meaning or effect. There are two major types of figures of speech: rhetorical figures, which do not make changes in the meaning of the words, and tropes, which do.

Fin de siecle: A French term meaning "end of the century." The term is used to denote the last decade of the nineteenth century, a transition period when writers and other artists abandoned old conventions and looked for new techniques and objectives.

First Person: See *Point of View*

Flashback: A device used in literature to present action that occurred before the beginning of the story. Flashbacks are often introduced as the dreams or recollections of one or more characters.

Foil: A character in a work of literature whose physical or psychological qualities contrast strongly with, and therefore highlight, the corresponding qualities of another character.

Folklore: Traditions and myths preserved in a culture or group of people. Typically, these are passed on by word of mouth in various forms—such as legends, songs, and proverbs—or preserved in customs and ceremonies. This term was first used by W. J. Thoms in 1846.

Folktale: A story originating in oral tradition. Folktales fall into a variety of categories, including legends, ghost stories, fairy tales, fables, and anecdotes based on historical figures and events.

Foreshadowing: A device used in literature to create expectation or to set up an explanation of later developments.

Form: The pattern or construction of a work which identifies its genre and distinguishes it from other genres.

G

Genre: A category of literary work. In critical theory, genre may refer to both the content of a given work—tragedy, comedy, pastoral—and to its form, such as poetry, novel, or drama.

Gilded Age: A period in American history during the 1870s characterized by political corruption and materialism. A number of important novels of social and political criticism were written during this time.

Gothicism: In literary criticism, works characterized by a taste for the medieval or morbidly attractive. A gothic novel prominently features elements of horror, the supernatural, gloom, and violence: clanking chains, terror, charnel houses, ghosts, medieval castles, and mysteriously slamming doors. The term "gothic novel" is also applied to novels that lack elements of the traditional Gothic setting but that create a similar atmosphere of terror or dread.

Grotesque: In literary criticism, the subject matter of a work or a style of expression characterized by exaggeration, deformity, freakishness, and disorder. The grotesque often includes an element of comic absurdity.

H

Harlem Renaissance: The Harlem Renaissance of the 1920s is generally considered the first significant movement of black writers and artists in the United States. During this period, new and established black writers published more fiction and poetry than ever before, the first influential black literary journals were established, and black authors and artists received their first widespread recognition and serious critical appraisal. Among the major writers associated with this period are Claude McKay, Jean Toomer, Countee Cullen, Langston Hughes, Arna Bontemps, Nella Larsen, and Zora Neale Hurston.

Hero/Heroine: The principal sympathetic character (male or female) in a literary work. Heroes and heroines typically exhibit admirable traits: idealism, courage, and integrity, for example.

Holocaust Literature: Literature influenced by or written about the Holocaust of World War II. Such literature includes true stories of survival in concentration camps, escape, and life after the war, as well as fictional works and poetry.

Humanism: A philosophy that places faith in the dignity of humankind and rejects the medieval perception of the individual as a weak, fallen creature. "Humanists" typically believe in the perfectibility of human nature and view reason and education as the means to that end.

Hyperbole: In literary criticism, deliberate exaggeration used to achieve an effect.

I

Idiom: A word construction or verbal expression closely associated with a given language.

Image: A concrete representation of an object or sensory experience. Typically, such a representation helps evoke the feelings associated with the object or experience itself. Images are either "literal" or "figurative." Literal images are especially concrete and involve little or no extension of the obvious meaning of the words used to express them. Figurative images do not follow the literal meaning of the words exactly. Images in literature are usually visual, but the term "image" can also refer to the representation of any sensory experience.

Imagery: The array of images in a literary work. Also, figurative language.

In medias res: A Latin term meaning "in the middle of things." It refers to the technique of beginning a story at its midpoint and then using various flashback devices to reveal previous action.

Interior Monologue: A narrative technique in which characters' thoughts are revealed in a way that appears to be uncontrolled by the author. The interior monologue typically aims to reveal the inner self of a character. It portrays emotional experiences as they occur at both a conscious and unconscious level. images are often used to represent sensations or emotions.

Irony: In literary criticism, the effect of language in which the intended meaning is the opposite of what is stated.

J

Jargon: Language that is used or understood only by a select group of people. Jargon may refer to terminology used in a certain profession, such as computer jargon, or it may refer to any nonsensical language that is not understood by most people.

L

Leitmotiv: See *Motif*

Literal Language: An author uses literal language when he or she writes without exaggerating or embellishing the subject matter and without any tools of figurative language.

Lost Generation: A term first used by Gertrude Stein to describe the post-World War I generation of American writers: men and women haunted by a sense of betrayal and emptiness brought about by the destructiveness of the war.

M

Mannerism: Exaggerated, artificial adherence to a literary manner or style. Also, a popular style of the visual arts of late sixteenth-century Europe that was marked by elongation of the human form and by intentional spatial distortion. Literary works that are self-consciously high-toned and artistic are often said to be "mannered."

Metaphor: A figure of speech that expresses an idea through the image of another object. Metaphors suggest the essence of the first object by identifying it with certain qualities of the second object.

Modernism: Modern literary practices. Also, the principles of a literary school that lasted from roughly the beginning of the twentieth century until the end of World War II. Modernism is defined by its rejection of the literary conventions of the nineteenth century and by its opposition to conventional morality, taste, traditions, and economic values.

Mood: The prevailing emotions of a work or of the author in his or her creation of the work. The mood of a work is not always what might be expected based on its subject matter.

Motif: A theme, character type, image, metaphor, or other verbal element that recurs throughout a single work of literature or occurs in a number of different works over a period of time.

Myth: An anonymous tale emerging from the traditional beliefs of a culture or social unit. Myths use supernatural explanations for natural phenomena. They may also explain cosmic issues like creation and death. Collections of myths, known as mythologies, are common to all cultures and nations, but the best-known myths belong to the Norse, Roman, and Greek mythologies.

N

Narration: The telling of a series of events, real or invented. A narration may be either a simple narrative, in which the events are recounted chronologically, or a narrative with a plot, in which the account is given in a style reflecting the author's artistic concept of the story.

Narration is sometimes used as a synonym for "storyline."

Narrative: A verse or prose accounting of an event or sequence of events, real or invented. The term is also used as an adjective in the sense "method of narration." For example, in literary criticism, the expression "narrative technique" usually refers to the way the author structures and presents his or her story.

Narrator: The teller of a story. The narrator may be the author or a character in the story through whom the author speaks.

Naturalism: A literary movement of the late nineteenth and early twentieth centuries. The movement's major theorist, French novelist Emile Zola, envisioned a type of fiction that would examine human life with the objectivity of scientific inquiry. The Naturalists typically viewed human beings as either the products of "biological determinism," ruled by hereditary instincts and engaged in an endless struggle for survival, or as the products of "socioeconomic determinism," ruled by social and economic forces beyond their control. In their works, the Naturalists generally ignored the highest levels of society and focused on degradation: poverty, alcoholism, prostitution, insanity, and disease.

Noble Savage: The idea that primitive man is noble and good but becomes evil and corrupted as he becomes civilized. The concept of the noble savage originated in the Renaissance period but is more closely identified with such later writers as Jean-Jacques Rousseau and Aphra Behn.

Novel: A long fictional narrative written in prose, which developed from the novella and other early forms of narrative. A novel is usually organized under a plot or theme with a focus on character development and action.

Novel of Ideas: A novel in which the examination of intellectual issues and concepts takes precedence over characterization or a traditional storyline.

Novel of Manners: A novel that examines the customs and mores of a cultural group.

Novella: An Italian term meaning "story." This term has been especially used to describe fourteenth-century Italian tales, but it also refers to modern short novels.

O

Objective Correlative: An outward set of objects, a situation, or a chain of events corresponding to an inward experience and evoking this experience in the reader. The term frequently appears in modern criticism in discussions of authors' intended effects on the emotional responses of readers.

Objectivity: A quality in writing characterized by the absence of the author's opinion or feeling about the subject matter. Objectivity is an important factor in criticism.

Oedipus Complex: A son's amorous obsession with his mother. The phrase is derived from the story of the ancient Theban hero Oedipus, who unknowingly killed his father and married his mother.

Omniscience: See *Point of View*

Onomatopoeia: The use of words whose sounds express or suggest their meaning. In its simplest sense, onomatopoeia may be represented by words that mimic the sounds they denote such as "hiss" or "meow." At a more subtle level, the pattern and rhythm of sounds and rhymes of a line or poem may be onomatopoeic.

Oxymoron: A phrase combining two contradictory terms. Oxymorons may be intentional or unintentional.

P

Parable: A story intended to teach a moral lesson or answer an ethical question.

Paradox: A statement that appears illogical or contradictory at first, but may actually point to an underlying truth.

Parallelism: A method of comparison of two ideas in which each is developed in the same grammatical structure.

Parody: In literary criticism, this term refers to an imitation of a serious literary work or the signature style of a particular author in a ridiculous manner. A typical parody adopts the style of the original and applies it to an inappropriate subject for humorous effect. Parody is a form of satire and could be considered the literary equivalent of a caricature or cartoon.

Pastoral: A term derived from the Latin word "pastor," meaning shepherd. A pastoral is a literary composition on a rural theme. The conventions of the pastoral were originated by the third-century Greek poet Theocritus, who wrote about the experiences, love affairs, and pastimes of Sicilian shepherds. In a pastoral, characters and language of a courtly nature are often placed in a simple setting. The term pastoral is also used to classify dramas, elegies, and lyrics that exhibit the use of country settings and shepherd characters.

Pen Name: See *Pseudonym*

Persona: A Latin term meaning "mask." *Personae* are the characters in a fictional work of literature. The *persona* generally functions as a mask through which the author tells a story in a voice other than his or her own. A *persona* is usually either a character in a story who acts as a narrator or an "implied author," a voice created by the author to act as the narrator for himself or herself.

Personification: A figure of speech that gives human qualities to abstract ideas, animals, and inanimate objects.

Picaresque Novel: Episodic fiction depicting the adventures of a roguish central character ("picaro" is Spanish for "rogue"). The picaresque hero is commonly a low-born but clever individual who wanders into and out of various affairs of love, danger, and farcical intrigue. These involvements may take place at all social levels and typically present a humorous and wide-ranging satire of a given society.

Plagiarism: Claiming another person's written material as one's own. Plagiarism can take the form of direct, word-for- word copying or the theft of the substance or idea of the work.

Plot: In literary criticism, this term refers to the pattern of events in a narrative or drama. In its simplest sense, the plot guides the author in composing the work and helps the reader follow the work. Typically, plots exhibit causality and unity and have a beginning, a middle, and an end. Sometimes, however, a plot may consist of a series of disconnected events, in which case it is known as an "episodic plot."

Poetic Justice: An outcome in a literary work, not necessarily a poem, in which the good are rewarded and the evil are punished, especially in ways that particularly fit their virtues or crimes.

Poetic License: Distortions of fact and literary convention made by a writer—not always a poet—for the sake of the effect gained. Poetic license is closely related to the concept of "artistic freedom."

Poetics: This term has two closely related meanings. It denotes (1) an aesthetic theory in literary criticism about the essence of poetry or (2) rules prescribing the proper methods, content, style, or diction of poetry. The term poetics may also refer to theories about literature in general, not just poetry.

Point of View: The narrative perspective from which a literary work is presented to the reader. There are four traditional points of view. The "third person omniscient" gives the reader a "godlike" perspective, unrestricted by time or place, from which to see actions and look into the minds of characters. This allows the author to comment openly on characters and events in the work. The "third person" point of view presents the events of the story from outside of any single character's perception, much like the omniscient point of view, but the reader must understand the action as it takes place and without any special insight into characters' minds or motivations. The "first person" or "personal" point of view relates events as they are perceived by a single character. The main character "tells" the story and may offer opinions about the action and characters which differ from those of the author. Much less common than omniscient, third person, and first person is the "second person" point of view, wherein the author tells the story as if it is happening to the reader.

Polemic: A work in which the author takes a stand on a controversial subject, such as abortion or religion. Such works are often extremely argumentative or provocative.

Pornography: Writing intended to provoke feelings of lust in the reader. Such works are often condemned by critics and teachers, but those which can be shown to have literary value are viewed less harshly.

Post-Aesthetic Movement: An artistic response made by African Americans to the black aesthetic movement of the 1960s and early '70s. Writers since that time have adopted a somewhat different tone in their work, with less emphasis placed on the disparity between black and white in the United States. In the words of post-aesthetic authors such as Toni Morrison, John Edgar Wideman, and Kristin Hunter, African Americans are portrayed as looking inward for answers to their own questions, rather than always looking to the outside world.

Postmodernism: Writing from the 1960s forward characterized by experimentation and continuing to apply some of the fundamentals of modernism, which included existentialism and alienation. Postmodernists have gone a step further in the rejection of tradition begun with the modernists by also rejecting traditional forms, preferring the anti-novel over the novel and the anti-hero over the hero.

Primitivism: The belief that primitive peoples were nobler and less flawed than civilized peoples because they had not been subjected to the tainting influence of society.

Prologue: An introductory section of a literary work. It often contains information establishing the situation of the characters or presents information about the setting, time period, or action. In drama, the prologue is spoken by a chorus or by one of the principal characters.

Prose: A literary medium that attempts to mirror the language of everyday speech. It is distinguished from poetry by its use of unmetered, unrhymed language consisting of logically related sentences. Prose is usually grouped into paragraphs that form a cohesive whole such as an essay or a novel.

Prosopopoeia: See *Personification*

Protagonist: The central character of a story who serves as a focus for its themes and incidents and as the principal rationale for its development. The protagonist is sometimes referred to in discussions of modern literature as the hero or anti-hero.

Protest Fiction: Protest fiction has as its primary purpose the protesting of some social injustice, such as racism or discrimination.

Proverb: A brief, sage saying that expresses a truth about life in a striking manner.

Pseudonym: A name assumed by a writer, most often intended to prevent his or her identification as the author of a work. Two or more authors may work together under one pseudonym, or an author may use a different name for each genre he or she publishes in.

Some publishing companies maintain "house pseudonyms," under which any number of authors may write installations in a series. Some authors also choose a pseudonym over their real names the way an actor may use a stage name.

Pun: A play on words that have similar sounds but different meanings.

R

Realism: A nineteenth-century European literary movement that sought to portray familiar characters, situations, and settings in a realistic manner. This was done primarily by using an objective narrative point of view and through the buildup of accurate detail. The standard for success of any realistic work depends on how faithfully it transfers common experience into fictional forms. The realistic method may be altered or extended, as in stream of consciousness writing, to record highly subjective experience.

Repartee: Conversation featuring snappy retorts and witticisms.

Resolution: The portion of a story following the climax, in which the conflict is resolved.

Rhetoric: In literary criticism, this term denotes the art of ethical persuasion. In its strictest sense, rhetoric adheres to various principles developed since classical times for arranging facts and ideas in a clear, persuasive, appealing manner. The term is also used to refer to effective prose in general and theories of or methods for composing effective prose.

Rhetorical Question: A question intended to provoke thought, but not an expressed answer, in the reader. It is most commonly used in oratory and other persuasive genres.

Rising Action: The part of a drama where the plot becomes increasingly complicated. Rising action leads up to the climax, or turning point, of a drama.

Roman à clef: A French phrase meaning "novel with a key." It refers to a narrative in which real persons are portrayed under fictitious names.

Romance: A broad term, usually denoting a narrative with exotic, exaggerated, often idealized characters, scenes, and themes.

Romanticism: This term has two widely accepted meanings. In historical criticism, it refers to a European intellectual and artistic movement of the late eighteenth and early nineteenth centuries that sought greater freedom of personal expression than that allowed by the strict rules of literary form and logic of the eighteenth-century neoclassicists. The Romantics preferred emotional and imaginative expression to rational analysis. They considered the individual to be at the center of all experience and so placed him or her at the center of their art. The Romantics believed that the creative imagination reveals nobler truths—unique feelings and attitudes—than those that could be discovered by logic or by scientific examination. Both the natural world and the state of childhood were important sources for revelations of "eternal truths." "Romanticism" is also used as a general term to refer to a type of sensibility found in all periods of literary history and usually considered to be in opposition to the principles of classicism. In this sense, Romanticism signifies any work or philosophy in which the exotic or dreamlike figure strongly, or that is devoted to individualistic expression, self-analysis, or a pursuit of a higher realm of knowledge than can be discovered by human reason.

Romantics: See *Romanticism*

S

Satire: A work that uses ridicule, humor, and wit to criticize and provoke change in human nature and institutions. There are two major types of satire: "formal" or "direct" satire speaks directly to the reader or to a character in the work; "indirect" satire relies upon the ridiculous behavior of its characters to make its point. Formal satire is further divided into two manners: the "Horatian," which ridicules gently, and the "Juvenalian," which derides its subjects harshly and bitterly.

Science Fiction: A type of narrative about or based upon real or imagined scientific theories and technology. Science fiction is often peopled with alien creatures and set on other planets or in different dimensions.

Second Person: See *Point of View*

Setting: The time, place, and culture in which the action of a narrative takes place. The elements of setting may include geographic location, characters' physical and mental environments, prevailing cultural attitudes, or the historical time in which the action takes place.

Simile: A comparison, usually using "like" or "as", of two essentially dissimilar things, as in "coffee as cold as ice" or "He sounded like a broken record."

Slang: A type of informal verbal communication that is generally unacceptable for formal writing. Slang words and phrases are often colorful exaggerations used to emphasize the speaker's point; they may also be shortened versions of an often-used word or phrase.

Slave Narrative: Autobiographical accounts of American slave life as told by escaped slaves. These works first appeared during the abolition movement of the 1830s through the 1850s.

Socialist Realism: The Socialist Realism school of literary theory was proposed by Maxim Gorky and established as a dogma by the first Soviet Congress of Writers. It demanded adherence to a communist worldview in works of literature. Its doctrines required an objective viewpoint comprehensible to the working classes and themes of social struggle featuring strong proletarian heroes.

Stereotype: A stereotype was originally the name for a duplication made during the printing process; this led to its modern definition as a person or thing that is (or is assumed to be) the same as all others of its type.

Stream of Consciousness: A narrative technique for rendering the inward experience of a character. This technique is designed to give the impression of an ever-changing series of thoughts, emotions, images, and memories in the spontaneous and seemingly illogical order that they occur in life.

Structure: The form taken by a piece of literature. The structure may be made obvious for ease of understanding, as in nonfiction works, or may obscured for artistic purposes, as in some poetry or seemingly "unstructured" prose.

Sturm und Drang: A German term meaning "storm and stress." It refers to a German literary movement of the 1770s and 1780s that reacted against the order and rationalism of the enlightenment, focusing instead on the intense experience of extraordinary individuals.

Style: A writer's distinctive manner of arranging words to suit his or her ideas and purpose in writing. The unique imprint of the author's personality upon his or her writing, style is the product of an author's way of arranging ideas and his or her use of diction, different sentence structures, rhythm, figures of speech, rhetorical principles, and other elements of composition.

Subjectivity: Writing that expresses the author's personal feelings about his subject, and which may or may not include factual information about the subject.

Subplot: A secondary story in a narrative. A subplot may serve as a motivating or complicating force for the main plot of the work, or it may provide emphasis for, or relief from, the main plot.

Surrealism: A term introduced to criticism by Guillaume Apollinaire and later adopted by Andre Breton. It refers to a French literary and artistic movement founded in the 1920s. The Surrealists sought to express unconscious thoughts and feelings in their works. The best-known technique used for achieving this aim was automatic writing—transcriptions of spontaneous outpourings from the unconscious. The Surrealists proposed to unify the contrary levels of conscious and unconscious, dream and reality, objectivity and subjectivity into a new level of "super-realism."

Suspense: A literary device in which the author maintains the audience's attention through the buildup of events, the outcome of which will soon be revealed.

Symbol: Something that suggests or stands for something else without losing its original identity. In literature, symbols combine their literal meaning with the suggestion of an abstract concept. Literary symbols are of two types: those that carry complex associations of meaning no matter what their contexts, and those that derive their suggestive meaning from their functions in specific literary works.

Symbolism: This term has two widely accepted meanings. In historical criticism, it denotes an early modernist literary movement initiated in France during the nineteenth century that reacted against the prevailing standards of realism. Writers in this movement aimed to evoke, indirectly and symbolically, an order of being beyond the material world of the five senses. Poetic expression of personal emotion figured strongly in the movement, typically by means of a private set of symbols uniquely identifiable with the individual poet. The principal aim of the Symbolists was to express in words the highly complex feelings that grew out of everyday contact with the world. In a broader sense, the term "symbolism" refers to the use of one object to represent another.

T

Tall Tale: A humorous tale told in a straightforward, credible tone but relating absolutely impossible events or feats of the characters. Such tales were commonly told of frontier adventures during the settlement of the west in the United States.

Theme: The main point of a work of literature. The term is used interchangeably with thesis.

Thesis: A thesis is both an essay and the point argued in the essay. Thesis novels and thesis plays share the quality of containing a thesis which is supported through the action of the story.

Third Person: See *Point of View*

Tone: The author's attitude toward his or her audience may be deduced from the tone of the work. A formal tone may create distance or convey politeness, while an informal tone may encourage a friendly, intimate, or intrusive feeling in the reader. The author's attitude toward his or her subject matter may also be deduced from the tone of the words he or she uses in discussing it.

Transcendentalism: An American philosophical and religious movement, based in New England from around 1835 until the Civil War. Transcendentalism was a form of American romanticism that had its roots abroad in the works of Thomas Carlyle, Samuel Coleridge, and Johann Wolfgang von Goethe. The Transcendentalists stressed the importance of intuition and subjective experience in communication with God. They rejected religious dogma and texts in favor of mysticism and scientific naturalism. They pursued truths that lie beyond the "colorless" realms perceived by reason and the senses and were active social reformers in public education, women's rights, and the abolition of slavery.

U

Urban Realism: A branch of realist writing that attempts to accurately reflect the often harsh facts of modern urban existence.

Utopia: A fictional perfect place, such as "paradise" or "heaven."

V

Verisimilitude: Literally, the appearance of truth. In literary criticism, the term refers to aspects of a work of literature that seem true to the reader.

Victorian: Refers broadly to the reign of Queen Victoria of England (1837-1901) and to anything with qualities typical of that era. For example, the qualities of smug narrowmindedness, bourgeois materialism, faith in social progress, and priggish morality are often considered Victorian. This stereotype is contradicted by such dramatic intellectual developments as the theories of Charles Darwin, Karl Marx, and Sigmund Freud (which stirred strong debates in England) and the critical attitudes of serious Victorian writers like Charles Dickens and George Eliot. In literature, the Victorian Period was the great age of the English novel, and the latter part of the era saw the rise of movements such as decadence and symbolism.

W

Weltanschauung: A German term referring to a person's worldview or philosophy.

Weltschmerz: A German term meaning "world pain." It describes a sense of anguish about the nature of existence, usually associated with a melancholy, pessimistic attitude.

Z

Zeitgeist: A German term meaning "spirit of the time." It refers to the moral and intellectual trends of a given era.

Cumulative Author/Title Index

Cumulative Nationality/Ethnicity Index

Subject/Theme Index

Subject/Theme Index